THE MARKET POWER
OF TECHNOLOGY

THE MARKET POWER OF TECHNOLOGY

Understanding the Second Gilded Age

MORDECAI KURZ

Columbia University Press
New York

Columbia University Press
Publishers Since 1893
New York   Chichester, West Sussex
cup.columbia.edu

Library of Congress Cataloging-in-Publication Data

Names: Kurz, Mordecai, author.
Title: The Market power of technology : understanding the second gilded age
    / Mordecai Kurz.
Description: New York : Columbia University Press, [2022] | Includes
    bibliographical references and index.
Identifiers: LCCN 2022006546 (print) | LCCN 2022006547 (ebook) | ISBN
    9780231206532 (paperback) | ISBN 9780231206525 (hardback) | ISBN
    9780231556521 (ebook)
Subjects: LCSH: Technological innovations–Economic aspects–United States.
    | Monopolies–United States. | Corporate power–United States. |
    Capitalism–United States. | Wealth–United States.
Classification: LCC HC110.T4 K87 2022 (print) | LCC HC110.T4 (ebook) |
    DDC 338/.0640973–dc23/eng/20220623
LC record available at https://lccn.loc.gov/2022006546
LC ebook record available at https://lccn.loc.gov/2022006547

Cover design: Elliott S. Cairns

To Linda

CONTENTS

PREFACE

Inequality and its social and political consequences are among the central problems of our time, and these have attracted a substantial amount of research in the past two decades. Although I have always had a keen interest in income and wealth inequality, and much of my early work on economic growth was motivated by income distribution problems, it was only in 2012 that I decided to return to the subject and devote my full time to it. By 2015, many of the ideas developed in this book took shape and I wrote about some of them in a Stanford working paper that was later circulated under the title "On the Formation of Capital and Wealth." Talking to colleagues about these ideas revealed the intense but diverse opinions about the subject and how to approach it. When discussing it over lunch with Ken Arrow, he told me that Bob Solow was also very interested in the subject, and I sought his advice as well. He was gracious in giving me detailed comments on my draft, but he advised me not to sit on the work for too long. I did not take his advice because the problems involved cannot be resolved in a single paper, utilizing a cleverly designed model to address all the relevant issues adequately. The problem has several dimensions, and its solution requires the tools of theory, empirical analysis, and policy analysis, and this can only be accomplished in a book. By 2016–2017, it became clear that I was working on such a project.

The book is composed of three parts. The first consists of chapters 1–4, in which I make my case by developing the basic theory (chap. 1), examining its macroeconomic implications (chap. 2), and measuring the degree of market power from 1889 to 2017 (chaps. 3–4). A detailed review of the relevant, some opposed, literature is presented only at the end of chapter 4, after I make my own case. The second part of the book consists of the three applications, which are covered in chapter 5 (on diffusion of innovations), chapter 6 (on asset prices), and chapter 7 (on research and development [R&D] and technological competition). The third part, chapters 8–10, discusses the policy implications.

The reader may benefit from my explanation of the key turning points in my own thinking during the six years of research. Ever since my graduate studies at Yale, the quest for a better understanding of the process of economic growth has been an important part of my research. Much of the work on economic growth in the postwar period was conducted under the assumption of perfect competition. Paul Romer was among those who demonstrated that one cannot study economic growth and technological innovations within the framework of a competitive model of an economy. This observation led him to concentrate on the effects of R&D and intentional inventions on the rate of growth, but my conclusion was different. It led me to the first, central theme of this book: once technological inventions are introduced, firms with different technological knowledge have different market positions and the vision of small, equal-opportunity, firms is not applicable. Technological market power becomes the dominant feature of the market.

With that insight, I proceeded to explore how durable such market power is, and I discovered an almost unanimous view among scholars: that a monopolist is considered a formidable incumbent whose replacement occurs only very rarely. But then, over time, successive innovations plant new seeds of added technological market power. In most cases, later innovations are designed to enable the expansions and consolidations of market power gained from earlier innovations. Thus, in a capitalist market economy, successive innovations and technology acquisitions by leading firms result in the consolidation of technological market power in the hands of a few large firms, in decreasing relative shares of labor and capital in value added, in rising income and wealth inequality, and in the emergence of a plutocracy. These conclusions are supported by the simple fact that today's biggest and most powerful firms derive their extraordinary profit margins—often exceeding 50%—and their high degree of market power from the accumulation of proprietary technologies that they either develop on their own or acquire. My conclusion, that market power is a durable feature of a technologically growing economy, leads one to the inference that a free-market economy contains a fundamental dynamic force that eliminates competition and threatens the foundations of democracy. It also leads to the observation that capital and wealth are two different concepts, and the difference between them can be very large. I call this difference monopoly wealth, which, in equilibrium, is the present value of expected monopoly profits derived from a firm's proprietary technology. Many scholars ignore this distinction and estimate the size of the capital stock by using firms' stock prices, leading them to erroneous conclusions. The ideas outlined here are the foundations of the theory developed in chapter 1.

These conclusions lead to a sharp perspective that raises many questions, and in this book, I try to answer as many of them as possible. One of the more essential questions arises with respect to the nature and timing of the mechanism described in the previous paragraph. Firms do die and new firms are born, so it is natural to ask, When does the process of building market power begin and when does it end? What are the exact features of technological competition that give rise to the emergence of the large superstar firm? I address these questions mostly in chapters 1 and 7. The answer is tied to the concept of general-purpose technology (GPT), developed by Bresnahan and Trajtenberg (1995), which describes major technologies that change the way we live, such as the steam engine or electricity. These are not innovations designed to challenge a specific incumbent firm. Instead, they reflect changes in the state of human knowledge and become platforms for creating major innovations that transform all sectors of the economy. Such innovations are rare, occurring maybe once in a century. A new GPT opens up a new era in which real technological competition begins. Existing firms have an opportunity to reinvent themselves, adapt to the new GPT, and prosper. Many do, but some fail and die. Young firms are born and join the competition as well. I then show in chapter 7 that, in the absence of strong public policy, technological competition has only one or a very few winners, and therefore it explains the emergence of the superstar firms. Technological competition is fundamentally different from regular competition and the two should not be confused. One mechanism that characterizes technological competition is its incorporation of the success-breeds-success process, explained in detail in chapter 7.

In seeking to explain, in chapter 4, the U.S. economic record since the 1980s, my theory proposes this performance is the consequence of the dynamics of a free-market economy outlined above. In the absence of public policy, it leads to the emergence of a few dominant firms and results in extreme inequality of income and wealth. This is what took place in the First Gilded Age, at the turn of the twentieth century, and it has taken place again since the 1980s, which is why I define this period as the Second Gilded Age. These two periods in American history are similar in two essential ways. In both periods, economic growth was propelled by a rapid rate of innovations created by the GPTs of the time, combined with passive, laissez-faire public policy that allowed the mechanism of growing market power to operate without restraint. Government policy permitted the rising market power of firms, revoked old regulations and avoided issuing new ones, kept tax rates low, and tolerated the sharp rise in inequality.

It is hard to assess the level of industrial concentration and inequality that could result, in the long run, from the dynamics of rising market power in an unregulated free-market economy. Theoretical considerations show that even under ideal conditions of free entry into R&D, patent expiration, and obsolescence, the dynamic process under technological competition results in an extreme degree of industrial concentration. Empirical evidence from the two Gilded Ages, which is presented in chapter 2, confirms these findings and suggests that this degree is so extreme that it causes deep social division that weakens the institutions of democracy. Consequently, aggressive economic policy to restrain the rise of market power is the only force available to prevent the expansion of such market power and to attain a superior economic allocation and a more egalitarian income and wealth distribution.

Because rising market power results from innovations and private ownership of technology, both active policy to promote high productivity and Supreme Court decisions have exempted it from antitrust considerations. This fact shows that the legal foundations of the Sherman Antitrust Act are not suitable for addressing the problems created by technological market power, and my policy proposals in chapters 8–10 center on creating a new legal basis for a sustained public action to contain technological market power but preserve the incentive to innovate.

Primarily focusing on current research, this book has for its first audience professional economists; students in economics and related social sciences; and professionals concerned with public policy in areas related to antitrust, patent law, taxation, and inequality. In some chapters (particularly chapters 2 and 7), I use standard mathematical and quantitative techniques to study the problems involved because their rigorous examination is difficult without mathematical and statistical tools. Such chapters require familiarity with more advanced tools of economics.

But because income and wealth inequality is a highly charged social problem with strong ideological and political ramifications, it attracts a much wider audience. In addition, the policy proposals in chapters 8–10 are relevant to the general public and to those in public service who are interested or engaged in policymaking. Some policy-oriented readers may want to focus more on policy and less on theory, undergraduate students can include some nontechnical chapters in advanced seminars, and educated readers may be drawn to the work as well. For this reason, I have adopted a more relaxed writing style than is common in formal economic publications. In addition, to assist all readers, the introduction offers a plain English, nontechnical statement of the central arguments and conclusions of the book. The introduction offers only a brief description of my policy proposals because the policy proposals in chapters 8–10 are already virtually nontechnical. In addition, I provide on page xvii a guide called "Suggested Nontechnical Reading of the Book" for nontechnical readers on how to navigate through the book and focus only on the nontechnical parts. To enable readers to replicate all my quantitative results, I will make available all data and computer codes used in the research on my personal website at http://web.stanford.edu/~mordecai/.

The work required for the completion of this project could not have been done without the help of many people to whom I am deeply indebted. Since the beginning of my work on this project in 2015, a scholar who supported me with encouraging suggestions has passed away and my tribute to him is mixed with deep sorrow. Richard Sutch departed in 2019, but before that he was my main guide through the complex pre-1929 national accounting data of Kendrick, Kuznets, and Goldsmith. Without his help I would not have been able to carry out the pre-1929 study.

Since August 2019, my gifted research assistant Nathan Lazarus was the main source of help that made this project possible, particularly the computational parts. I benefitted from his extraordinary talent that enabled him to learn advanced topics of economic theory quickly and acquire the technical skills needed for this project. I also benefitted from his excellent editorial skills that contributed to the quality of the exposition. I am thankful to Ken Judd, whose advice on computational methods was vital and who helped Nathan acquire the skills needed for this project. Maurizio Motolese was generous in hosting Nathan for two weeks in Milan, giving him an accelerated course in computational economics. I also thank Maurizio for constructive suggestions on parts of the final manuscript. My colleague Gavin Wright has been very generous with his time since the very beginning of this project. He commented on various parts of the manuscript, and offered much needed advice on many different issues. As I have noted, Bob Solow read some parts of the manuscript and offered valuable advice. Martin Carnoy has encouraged me throughout the project, read several parts of the manuscript, and offered detailed comments. He also helped by contacting other scholars who helped resolve several specialized questions. Michael Reich provided invaluable assistance in navigating through the modern literature of labor economics and labor policy. Carsten Nielsen provided extensive suggestions that improved the final version of the introductory chapter. Reiko Aoki taught me all that I know about Japanese laws regarding fair negotiations. William B. Gould IV and Robin Feldman were very helpful in offering legal perspective on some of the policy proposals in chapter 9. H. Woody Brock was very helpful in my preparation of the proposal submitted to potential publishers. I also wish to express my thanks for their gracious help to Nathan Balkie, Avner Greif, Alexander Field, Hiroyuki Nakata, Paul Rodes, and Ken Snowden.

Several friends and associates provided specialized assistance to the research effort. A group of noneconomist friends agreed to read sections of the Introduction, offering a sample of the public's response to the nontechnical material. For that I thank Bruce Bienenstock, Adi Gamon, Jonathan Krass, and Richard Parry. This project required a broad understanding of the inner workings of Silicon Valley, and my friend Adi Gamon was my constant guide on all issues related to the way the valley works. I benefitted specially from his technical knowledge and experience with Silicon Valley financing. I thank Zina Shapiro for providing valuable help with Graduate School of Business (GSB) data files in general and Wharton Research Data Services (WRDS) Compustat in particular. I am also thankful to the University of Wisconsin for being able to use the computational resources of the Center for High Throughput Computing (CHTC) at the University of Wisconsin at Madison. Cambridge Proofreading and Editing LLC provided excellent editing services for the manuscript, and the technical assistance of Yiming He was very crucial in preparing the final manuscript. I also thank my editor, Christian P. Winting, for help in the publication process.

Finally, my most devoted and loving assistant was my wife Linda C. Kurz. During the years of this project, she read and commented on most parts of the manuscript and was very attentive to all public developments that had some implications to the book. I dedicate this work to her.

Mordecai Kurz
Stanford, California

SUGGESTED NONTECHNICAL READING OF THE BOOK

As I say in the preface, a rigorous examination of the problems related to inequality is difficult without advanced mathematical and statistical tools. Yet most of the conclusions of those examinations and what they say about public policy are relatively simple and can be expressed in nontechnical terms. With that in mind, the introductory chapter offers a nontechnical exposition of the main arguments and conclusions of the book. Virtually everything said in that chapter is repeated in more detail in later chapters. In addition to the introduction, there is a nontechnical path through the various chapters that can be used by nontechnical readers, particularly if their interest is focused on the policy implications of my study. This path is as follows:

Introduction: the entire introduction

Chapter 1: sections 1.1-1.5 excluding subsection 1.5.5

Chapter 4: sections 4.3 to 4.4 on the history of U.S. market power and section 4.6 on alternative views

Chapter 6: sections 6.1 to 6.3

Chapters 8–10: nontechnical policy discussion, excluding the appendix to chapter 10

THE MARKET POWER
OF TECHNOLOGY

has entered a Second Gilded Age; many contemporary economic and political indicators are similar to those of the First Gilded Age.

The policy experience from the 1930s to the 1980s provides valuable knowledge about the efficacy of equitable economic policies. Significant research conducted in recent years has also revealed much more about the economic and social consequences of the rising inequality seen since the 1980s. Nevertheless, the big questions remain unanswered: How does a market economy generate rising inequality? What causes changes in income and wealth distributions? Does capitalism under democracy inevitably lead to an equitable society, as claimed by Kuznets? It is clear that if we want to craft an efficient policy to counter rising inequality, we must first understand its causes. Only then can we ask what the choices are and what risks we face in adopting any particular policy. These are the questions I endeavor to answer in this book. I develop a theory of the cause of changes in inequality and examine its implications in light of the history of income and wealth inequality since 1889.

This introduction explains that economic inequality, both personal and functional, is driven primarily by changes in the technological market power of firms that arises from their ownership of proprietary technology. Control of technology is translated into market power over goods and services that enable firms to charge prices well in excess of their cost and extract high excess profits from the market. Their monopoly power over privately owned technology is thus very valuable. The profits end up in the hands of a relatively small circle of owners of companies and their managers.

But that explanation is not complete. If rising inequality is a consequence of rising market power, then why does market power rise or fall? I argue that the dynamics of market power can be explained by two forces:

1. Innovations give their creators a competitive advantage and therefore market power. This market power can be increased by firms using a long list of available strategies for consolidation and expansion. These strategies include building layers of patents around the initial innovation that prevent the entry of competitors and acquiring competitors' technology in order to develop or suppress it because it may be a potential threat.
2. Public policy determines how much of their income innovators and business owners pay in taxes. Legal considerations fix the level of protection granted innovators with patent and trade secret laws. Antitrust policy determines which innovators are permitted to consolidate their power by buying out competitors or using other strategies for expanding such power.

These two forces need to be considered in conjunction with each other. They can complement or oppose each other, and their interaction is what drives the rise or fall in market power. Active policy that employs high income taxation and aggressive antitrust policy can keep market power at bay. But when public policy is passive in regulating market power, innovators are able to drive out competitors and turn a small initial competitive advantage into a sprawling monopoly. It is during times of significant technological upheaval and rapid rate of innovations that powerful technology firms can take advantage of passive policies to increase their market power.

I offer an economic analysis of market power that explains

1. how to measure technological market power;
2. the distinction between capital as an input to production and monopoly wealth, which is the wealth created by market power;
3. the impact of rising market power on functional and personal inequality;
4. why rising market power lowers investments, consumption, and gross national product (GNP) and slows down the growth rate of an economy;
5. why high market power slows down the rate at which new innovations are used and enjoyed by the general public, further slowing down economic growth; and
6. how high market power can rise in an unregulated economy, increasing inequality, deepening social discord, and weakening the foundations of democratic institutions.

This introduction also presents an analysis of the historical evolution of market power in the United States, linking it to technological and political changes. It shows that, in addition to all its benefits, the IT revolution created a wave of rising market power that was supported by the passive, laissez-faire policy put in place by the Reagan administration in the 1980s. This introduction explains why inequality has risen since the 1980s and why the United States has entered a Second Gilded Age. Rising inequality shifted the balance of power in society and resulted in a sharp decline of the middle class. I therefore argue that, unrestrained by policy, rising market power threatens the foundation of democratic institutions.

I then briefly outline a wide-ranging set of proposals for new policy to rein in market power, compensate losers of technological changes, and, in general, address the negative side effects of these changes, particularly inequality. This policy must avoid obstructing the innovative processes of capitalism, which constitute a core source of general economic progress.

0.1   Capitalism Perpetually Plants New Seeds of Legal Market Power

To introduce the ideas developed in this book, I begin with illustrative examples of young firms at the start of their economic and technological journey (see

TABLE O.1   A sample of ten initial public offerings*

Firm	Year founded	Products or activity	Net worth	Market value	Intangibles and goodwill
Slack Technologies†	2009	Work collaboration platform	749.8	21,255.4	61.7
NGM Biopharmaceutical	2007	Biotechnology and health products	−119.2	922.6	0
Uber Technologies	2009	Ridesharing technology platform	10,333.0	73,266.0	235.0
Beyond Meat Inc.	2009	Plant-based food technology	78.9	8,825.3	0
Chewy Inc.	2010	Online pet food platform	−358.0	13,125.0	9.6
Pinterest Inc.	2010	Visual discovery and advertising	−634.0	18,522.8	0
CrowdStrike Holdings, Inc.	2011	Digital security technology	−485.2	12,853.0	8.7
Fastly, Inc.	2011	Specialized cloud technology	89.9	227.4	1.0
Zoom Video Communication	2012	Video collaboration technology	167.4	27,559.0	0
TCR2 Therapeutics Inc.	2015	Biotechnology and health	192.7	355.3	0
		Totals	10,015.4	176,912.1	316.0

*Issued in the first half of 2019, values on June 12, 2019, in millions of dollars.
† Data for Slack Technologies is for the closing price on June 20, 2019.
Source: Standard & Poor's (S&P).

table 0.1). Each firm has a relatively straightforward financial story that masks a technically complex and distinct history. Since these firms are young, they have only a few assets and products and are thus easy to understand. They often have just one major piece of proprietary technology and are managed, in many cases, by the technological innovators who created it. I examine such firms to gain insight into how innovations affect the process of wealth creation and to clarify the role of innovation in a modern capitalist economy. Examining these firms is a jumping-off point for considering most of the problems discussed in this book.

Early in 2019, the U.S. market for the sale of newly issued securities (that is, common stocks, preferred stocks, and the like) was particularly active. As a result, a long list of young firms completed their first sale of stock to the public—their initial public offering (IPO). Table 0.1 records the information for a random sample of ten firms, from among those that went public in the first half of 2019. Net worth is the value of assets owned by the firm, net of liabilities. If a firm were broken up and its assets sold for the values recorded on its balance sheet, the value left after paying off all debts is the net worth. The market value in Table 0.1 is the market valuation of the firm. I thus compare the net worth of the firm (which is the sum of its net assets) with its market value as a whole entity. Table 0.1 shows that the firms considered are all less than twelve years old. Therefore, one can conclude that in less than twelve years, $10.0 billion of capital invested in those firms by stockholders turned into $176.9 billion of actual market value, a wealth creation that introduced a few new members into the exclusive club of the world's billionaires. This process of wealth creation is common to all successful young technology firms, and it is useful to understand more of its characteristics.

Economists have long recognized that the market value of a firm is rarely equal to the sum of the values of its component assets. Higher market value is often explained by the fact that a firm has the added value of being a "going concern" or having expended "organizational costs." Such value reflects the fact that, even if one owned all of the machines in a factory, it would be costly to hire workers, establish relationships with suppliers, and incorporate a firm. Going-concern value also includes the value of special advantages a firm may have, such as superior management, unique resources at its disposal, and its location.[1] Few of these considerations apply to the young firms in table 0.1. They are mostly applicable to mature firms, often those with many divisions and complex asset structures. These young firms have created billions of dollars in new wealth, but not because they have unique management practices that no one else has or particularly valuable relationships with suppliers. It is thus vital to understand how that wealth creation happens by tracing the events associated with the firms' origins.

0.1.1   Innovations Are the Source of Legal Market Power

A typical firm in the age of technology begins with an idea developed by innovators. Then it conducts some research or experiments, funded by seed capital investment, to advance the idea to a proof-of-concept stage. Steps to establish

---

[1] There are, of course, also opposite cases when the market value falls short of the combined values of the firm's components and breaking up the firm enhances stockholders' value. The classical cases for that are the breakup of Standard Oil in 1911 and of AT&T in 1984. In both cases, the sum of the values of the parts turned out to be far greater than the original value of each firm before the breakup.

ownership through legal protection of the technology, like patent application, incorporation, and acquisition by the founders of the initial stock at nominal values, are all routine. The next stage, production and marketing, usually requires financing by a first-round sale of securities to a venture capital group or private investors. Additional rounds of financing are needed as the firm reaches production goals. But as the value of the new technology becomes clear, financing is done at progressively higher prices of the firm's securities. The public sale of securities, at prices based on valuations like those in table 0.1, is the final stage of this journey.

For the firms in table 0.1, the difference between their market value and their net worth is the present value of future profits they are expected to earn. But where do these profits come from? Since the firms own superior proprietary technologies, they each, technically speaking, have a monopoly power over some technology. I will shortly explain why they can translate this technological monopoly power into economic power in markets for goods and services. With this power, they can extract from the market excess profits above and beyond the normal return on investment. The market capitalizes such future excess profits, translating this market power into private wealth. For the firms in table 0.1, the $166.9 billion difference between their market value and their net worth is the market value of the private ownership of the technology. If somebody were to buy the technologies of these young firms, the market would value this private ownership at $166.9 billion.

But why does the market place any value on technology? Engineers think of technology as the tools used by humans to control the natural world. Economists, however, think of technology in much broader terms. It is the totality of human knowledge used to produce goods and services. That includes knowledge used to create buildings, equipment, software, goods, and services but also knowledge about human communication and managerial methods of control. By this definition, technology is just a form of knowledge. Patenting a technology requires full disclosure of all new knowledge for which the patent was issued and therefore, like algebra, geography, or physics, the patented knowledge is known to the public. But unlike algebra, geography, or physics, some patents are extremely valuable. The crucial difference is that while no one owns algebra, geography, or physics, each patented technology is privately owned and anyone who wants to buy or use that technology must pay the owner for its transfer or use. Ownership of technology allows an owner to prevent others from using the underlying knowledge! This provides a valuable economic power to these young firms—the power to prevent others from using the technology.

To explain how this power is translated into wealth, consider that the firm's monopoly power over the technology gives it many possible advantages over other firms. This power may allow the firm to produce and offer for sale new superior products or services. It may also take the form of enabling the firm or others to produce existing products or services at a lower cost than is possible under the current technology. Whatever form that advantage takes, the firm obtains the power to set prices higher than its costs and, because it is a technological monopolist, no competitor will force its prices down. The ability to control the price creates excess abnormal profits and wealth.

It is obvious that technology is useless without a strategy to implement it and exploit the advantages it offers. This means that behind every firm in table 0.1 there is a strategy it has adopted in using the technology to create products or services offered to the market. Given a limited experience, two firms with the same technology may end up with different market valuations. This means that the values in table 0.1 also reflect each firm's strategy of using its technology. A sale of the firm would usually require that management, who have been executing the firms' strategies, assist in the transition. These market values therefore change as firms gain more experience in executing their business plan.

Examination of the proprietary technologies of the firms in table 0.1 reveals the diverse forms of market power gained by their innovations. Some challenge producers in a market segment who employ an old technology (for example, Uber bringing IT to taxi hailing and TCR Therapeutics bringing patented immunotherapy to the cancer-treatment market). A second category creates a new market or at least expands an existing one beyond recognition: Pinterest's competitors are probably magazines, and Zoom's competitors are likely video and telephone services, but these novel technologies have attracted users who were not magazine readers or businesses that never met by telephone before Zoom. A third category includes innovations that complement and enhance the capabilities of other technologies owned by well-established firms that have power in some market segment (for example, Fastly, Inc.). Such complementarity makes these young firms natural acquisition targets for established firms.

I stated that these firms would earn excess profits because of their private ownership of technologies. The term "excess profits" has a very precise economic meaning and is an important one in this book. "Excess profits" refers to profits beyond the cost of labor and capital. To take a simple example, suppose that Marvel hires someone to write a new comic book about one of its superheroes. The writer will be paid a wage, and there will be some costs associated with printing the books. But Marvel will likely make significant profits after accounting for those costs. Why is this? Because Marvel has a copyright on the likeness of the popular superhero and can therefore charge a higher price. It is thus necessary to divide income into three categories: wages paid to labor (the writer's time), capital costs (the cost of the printing machines, which includes depreciation of the machines and normal market interest on the machines' value), and profits. Economists often divide income into labor and capital, lumping profits with capital income, and this practice omits important information about profits and market power.

The value added of the firm, which is the value of sales minus the cost of all material purchases from other firms, is the real value of the output of the firm. Its costs of production are the combined costs of labor and capital. This includes buildings, software, and equipment (including depreciation) as well as the cost of market interest on the value of fixed assets. Firms that own proprietary technologies can then charge prices for their products that far exceed their cost. This leaves a large surplus value earned as a consequence of their monopoly power over the technology they own and the products it produces. Some economists call this "factorless output" because of its ambiguous relation to standard inputs-output relations. But it is clear who receives the missing value of output: it is paid to those who own the technology.[2] The income created by a firm or an economy is then divided into three compensations: labor compensation, capital compensation, and profits brought about by market power or monopoly profits.[3] This division is an important concept that is central to this book and will be discussed in detail later. It also creates some accounting challenges discussed later in this chapter and assessed in more detail in chapter 3.

Technological market power is then transformed into the ability of a firm to influence the price of the products or services it sells or the production cost of its products or services. It may take different forms: monopoly, oligopoly of several firms, monopolistic competition of many firms, or monopsony power over its suppliers. A firm with market power benefits from the barriers to entry faced by its potential competitors. These barriers allow the firm to raise its price above the incremental cost to produce an extra unit of output or to lower the price

---

[2] Ownership of corporate technology is distributed among many market participants, and it is not entirely easy to identify them. Briefly stated, the distinction between capital compensation and profits is centered on the intent of investors. Investors such as retirees, pension funds, or insurance companies seek low-risk income and invest in highly diversified portfolios of corporate bonds, utility stocks, preferred stock, or limited partnerships. Return on capital is then the compensation for a low-risk use of this resource over time arising from complete market diversification. Profits of a firm arise from its unique monopoly power over technology and result from activities associated with firms' actions such as its pricing strategy, innovations, and acquisition of competing firms. Stockholders who had acquired their shares without investing capital (innovators, owners of acquired technologies, management) benefit from the profits of the firm. Regular common-stock owners receive capital compensation as well as their share of the profits, but they take all the risks associated with the success or failure of the firm.

[3] This terminology is different from that used in standard accounting practice that divides income into two parts: labor income and capital income. In addition, the commonly used accounting term of *corporate profits* blurs the distinction between normal income of capital and those profits that are attributable to market power. In this book the term *profits, without exception*, refers to profits that are attributable to market power. In contexts where one needs to avoid thinking of these as "corporate profits," I may use the term *monopoly profits* as a substitute for the equivalent but longer term *profits attributable to market power*.

it pays suppliers, thus lowering its cost relative to competitors. There are also criminal ways for a firm to create market power, such as conspiring with rivals to limit output or bribing public officials to obtain an advantage. Such criminal strategies are not the subject of this book.

A government-granted monopoly, like a patent, gives the owner the legal right to prevent others from using the proprietary technology. It is a barrier to entry that is created and actively protected by law and strongly supported by public policy that aims to encourage innovation. One may observe that possession of technological monopoly power by any one firm in a competitive economy grants that firm a high degree of power that has negative economic and political consequences. Therefore, the act of granting legal monopoly power by means of patents or other similar instruments has long been controversial.[4] I later explain that the current antitrust policy has the clear aim of eliminating all forms of market power to restore perfect competition, and this is in conflict with patent law. Correspondingly, the conflict between competition and innovation is the reason why public policy proposals made in this book are more complex and more subtle than prevailing antitrust policy.

As noted, market power enables a firm to obtain profits that exceed normal[5] competitive market returns on investments. The capitalized value of future profits I call "monopoly wealth." These future profits will be the income of the stockholders who own the firm, so the stock prices of more profitable firms are higher. Monopoly wealth that takes the form of high stock price is then based on expected future flow of profits. For the firms in table 0.1, these expected profits have, within a very short time, generated $166.9 billion of monopoly wealth. Although the term *monopoly wealth* is imprecise because such wealth can arise from any form of market power, it is simpler than referring to the longer expression of "wealth created by the market power of firms."

The real problem arising from the nexus between capitalism and technology is, however, much deeper. The idea of free and competitive markets presumes a society in which all economic players have equal opportunities, each is small relative to the market, and no firm has the ability to "restrain trade." This could have been a realistic model of a progressive society before the Industrial Revolution. Once a successful innovation appears, the presumed symmetry among firms disappears because the innovator has a more favorable position, known as

---

[4]Since any market power impairs the resource allocation of a market economy, proposals have been made for other forms of compensation to innovators, such as prizes, public honors, and others. Although the subject remains controversial, no practical alternative that substitutes for patents in every field has emerged. For an opposite view see Boldrin and Levine (2013).

[5]The concept of a "normal" rate of return on capital plays an important role in some chapters of this book. Think of it as the long-run rate of return that one can expect from well-diversified investments for a given level of risk. For medium-risk investments, it can be approximated by the Moody's Seasoned Baa Corporate Bond rate or the average rate of return on a diversified portfolio of utilities and preferred stocks.

the first-mover advantage. This advantage exists even without the legal protection of a patent because it is supported by the use of other methods of creating market power. An innovator's firm has more experience and a better organization marketing the new product than do competing firms. As a result, the firm could acquire a good reputation for selling the product. Such a firm can raise barriers to entry by keeping secret all knowledge about its new technology and successfully keeping it away from competitors. It can then use many strategies, which I detail in chapter 1, to protect its ownership of the technology. Some such strategies are applauded: barriers to entry built on patents or copyrights and trade secrets, considered as rewards for innovation, without which "the goose would cease to lay the golden eggs." As a result, the motive to innovate is a primary driver of firms in a modern capitalist economy. The perfectly competitive model of a large number of small firms without any market power is thus not an adequate description of a growing economy in which technology is a crucial engine of rising productivity.

Market power resulting from technological advances is then an unavoidable feature of the modern capitalist economy. Technological advances arise from a combination of the human search for knowledge and a mobilized entrepreneurial motive to innovate. Consequently, modern capitalism is a perpetual seeding ground for new monopoly power. This creates a permanent conflict between liberal democracy's preference for growth and its preference for equal opportunity and competition. Our society has chosen to promote economic growth by permitting the formation of initial legal market power and allowing innovators to gain monopoly power. The successful companies in table 0.1 are the beneficiaries of that choice. But such a choice has consequences, and the policy proposals made in this book address the challenges posed by the resulting market power.

The standard argument in support of legal market power is that it is temporary and a small price to pay for the great benefits of progress. It is further supported by the assumption that the market will restrict the duration of such power because technological competition will bring down monopoly power by promoting superior alternate technologies. In chapter 1, I demonstrate that once introduced, market power granted to innovators becomes entrenched and "creative destruction" does not offer an effective mechanism to eliminate market power; such power is durable even when the legal protection of any particular innovation is temporary.

0.1.2   Technological Competition and the Durability of Market Power

As explained, every successful innovation creates new market power for its owner. Firms often choose not to take out a patent since that requires public disclosure of their knowledge. They prefer to protect their private knowledge by keeping it secret and by relying on laws enacted in most states that prohibit the theft of trade secrets while permitting imitation through reverse engineering. The crucial point is that an innovator has the initial first-mover advantage regardless of whether the ownership of the innovation is protected by a patent.

Over time, firms with an initial advantage consolidate and expand their market power with many strategies that vary depending on the technology at their disposal. They build layers of related innovations (known as patent pyramids) or perform ongoing updates. These constitute defensive moats around their initial innovations that are difficult for competitors to breach. In addition, such firms accumulate substantial wealth from their excess profits. Therefore, they have the financial ability to defend their market power against potential entrants. The most powerful strategy is to acquire challengers or purchase their patents for the purposes of developing or suppressing competing technologies. Strong incumbents often impede the growth of competitors by taking actions that make it difficult for them to obtain support services such as suppliers of talented workers. In most cases, innovating challengers prefer to profit by selling out rather than engage in a battle against a well-established rival with superior financial ability. A first mover gains other natural advantages like reputation, customer loyalty, and accumulated private information about customers and suppliers. They are also able to set technological standards that customers recognize, choose the best business location, establish banking relations, and obtain all legally required permits.

Chapter 1 contains a detailed review of research on the diverse strategies that firms use to translate the first-mover advantage created by innovation into durable market power. In that chapter, I also review the industrial organization literature on the problem of entry deterrence by firms with market power, who use diverse strategies to deter the entry of potential competitors. Most studies conclude that such firms are typically able to deter the entry of rivals.

To see the durability of market power, it is helpful to compare the young firms in table 0.1 with older firms. Table 0.2 documents market values and monopoly wealth of a sample of more mature technology firms. The conclusion one can draw from this table is that even twenty-five to forty-five years after their initial innovations, these firms have monopoly wealth as a proportion of their market value, which is just like the very young firms. Many of these firms leveraged market power to expand both in their primary market as well as in related markets, and that is the source of much of their wealth. The durability of market power can then be seen from the ratios of monopoly wealth to market value; it is 83.3 percent for the older firms and 94.5 percent for the young ones, suggesting that market power does not fade away.

The natural question is: Why can't technological competition erode market power over time? The question is examined in chapters 1 and 7, where I explain

TABLE 0.2 Monopoly wealth of more mature firms*

Firm	Year founded	Net worth at market value[†] (1)	Market value (2)	Intangibles and goodwill at market value (3)	Monopoly wealth = (2) − (1) + (3)	Monopoly wealth as a percentage of market value
Alphabet (Google)	1998	275.1	754.2	22.6	501.7	66.5
Microsoft	1975	142.3	1,015.4	56.5	929.6	91.6
Facebook	2004	129.7	517.6	22.0	409.9	79.2
Netflix	1997	8.5	148.5	23.7	163.7	110.2
Apple	1976	158.7	886.8	0	728.1	82.1
Adobe	1982	14.8	133.8	14.4	133.4	99.7
Salesforce	1999	24.6	116.4	17.2	109.0	93.6
Totals		753.7	3,572.7	156.4	2,975.0	83.3

*Values on June 12, 2019, in $ billions.
[†] Balance sheet data is reported at historical values and taken from the nearest quarterly report. I converted these to market values by using the ratio of asset valuation of nonfinancial business at market prices to asset valuation at historical prices, as reported by the Federal Reserve and BEA Z1 publication for 2019, table B.103, comparing values on lines 3–6 with values on lines 48–51.

that technological competition is fundamentally different from regular competition. In the case of standard competition, new entrants can bring down any firm that earns excess return derived from pricing above marginal cost. They can do so by simply hiring capital and labor and selling at a slightly lower price until profits fall to zero. This only requires the entrant to have enough resources, either on hand or by taking a loan, to hire the needed capital and labor and produce the product or service. As a result, regular competition has many small winners who can coexist in a competitive equilibrium.

Technological competition has the simple property that it has only one or two technological winners who innovate the best technology. There are thus, at the outset, only one or two leaders with, perhaps, a few weaker firms surviving at low profitability. To bring down a technological monopolist, the entrant must innovate a superior technology. This is very difficult, given the need to come up with new and superior ideas while the incumbent firm engages in many strategies to undermine competitors. Once the winner or few winners consolidates and then expands the initial market power, it earns substantial excess profits. This gives the firm (or firms) a financial advantage. As stressed earlier, potential entrants mostly prefer to be acquired by the strong incumbent rather than enter into a costly battle with a well-financed adversary. In fact, there is substantial evidence that small potential competitors often plan, even at the start-up stage, to be acquired by the leading firm if successful rather than confront it. Such a business plan positions these competitors as research labs for the dominant firms. In some sectors, like pharmaceuticals, this has now openly taken the form of the major firms' replacing much of their own research efforts with joint ventures with small start-ups. Such ventures have specific research agendas that, if successful, often lead to the dominant firms' acquiring their smaller partners. All of these technological-competition strategies result in only one or very few survivors in each market segment. Because technological competition is the form of competition that has dominated the economic scene in recent decades, it is not surprising that a few superstar dominant firms have emerged as winners.

But firms do die, and new ones are born. In chapter 1, I explain that understanding technological competition requires distinguishing between innovations within a technological paradigm and revolutionary innovations, like the steam engine, electricity, or the internet, that change the paradigm. These innovations do not arise from a challenge of one firm by another and are not weapons to bring down any particular incumbent. Rather, these general-purpose technologies (GPTs) represent fundamental changes in the human state of knowledge (see Bresnahan and Trajtenberg, 1995). They act as platforms for innovating technologies implied by the GPT in all sectors of the economy. A GPT dominates for decades or even for more than a century, and such innovations occur only infrequently. When a new technological paradigm emerges, widespread technological competition develops. Existing firms who use the old technologies can compete, reinvent themselves, and survive. But some older firms do not adapt, and they die. In this period of turmoil new firms are born that become leaders in the new technology, and these firms experience the durability of market power discussed here. A second class of firms whose market power follows the pattern of durability discussed here consists of all new firms that use the new GPT to innovate applications that change diverse sectors of the economy. Such applications are all innovations within the new prevailing GPT. Even if a superior competitor emerges at any stage and an incumbent firm with a technological monopoly is displaced by a challenger's innovation, the winner is simply a new monopolist. Whether the incumbent is the one who reorganized and adapted to the new technology or the challenger is the one who took over the market, the result is that during long periods of rapid technical advance, consumers and suppliers face a sequence of reorganized and sometimes new firms with market power. Over time, all that may change is the identity of the firms exerting market power. In sum, technological competition is marked by very few leaders and possibly some laggards. It never resembles the model of perfect competition with its many atomistic firms.

0.2   Capital and Monopoly Wealth

I have already introduced the new and important concept of monopoly wealth. Because it plays a central role in this book, it is important to discuss how it differs from the conventional concept of capital.

0.2.1   Accounting of Monopoly Wealth: How Most Intangible Assets Are Created

Time will bring about different experiences for the young firms in table 0.1. Some may grow and develop markets for their products or services and, over time, consolidate their own power in those markets. Others will be acquired by larger and more established firms that have developed their economic moat to prevent competitors from entering. For the firms that are not acquired, monopoly wealth will remain a value that can be deduced from their stock price. But for the acquired firms, their monopoly wealth will be recorded on the balance sheets of the acquiring firms. Following this accounting procedure helps explain the concept and composition of monopoly wealth. As an example, I follow a young firm that was acquired in 2019, when the firms in table 0.1 went public. The acquiring firm, Salesforce.com Inc., is a leader in the market for business software, in which it has some market power. In June 2019, it offered to buy Tableau Software (Tableau), an interactive data visualization software company, for $15.3 billion to be paid for entirely by issuing additional common stock in Salesforce.

Tables 0.3a and 0.3b trace the accounting consequences of this transaction. Because no cash was involved in the transaction, the assets and liabilities of Tableau are simply added to the balance sheet of Salesforce. But the accountants correctly believe it would be illogical for Salesforce to pay $15.3 billion and receive assets with net worth of only $1.019 billion, thus recording a loss of $14.281 billion. We know that this $14.281 billion discrepancy is the capitalized

TABLE 0.3a **Balance sheet of Tableau Software***

Assets		Liabilities	
Tangible assets	1,794.3	Short- and long-term debt	820.7
Intangible assets and goodwill	45.4	Net worth	1,019.0
Total assets	1,839.7	Total liabilities and net worth	1,839.7

*In millions of dollars.
Source: Standard & Poor's (S&P).

TABLE 0.3b   Change in the balance sheet of Salesforce after the merger*

Assets		Liabilities	
Tangible assets	+1,794.3	Short- and long-term debt	+820.7
Intangible assets and goodwill	+14,326.4	Net worth	+15,300.0
Total assets	+16,120.7	Total liabilities and net worth	+16,120.7

*In millions of dollars.

expected monopoly profits of Tableau, and the accounting practice is to add it to the balance sheet of Salesforce as an intangible asset.

The practice of accountants is to call the difference between market value and acquired asset values goodwill or, as in the example, intangible assets. The monopoly wealth of the acquired firm becomes an intangible asset owned by the acquiring firm! In fact, about 60 percent of all intangible assets on the balance sheet of the corporate sector in the United States is the monopoly wealth of acquired firms. Intangible assets also include the value of a firm's investment in purchased patents and other intellectual property rights, including proprietary designs and software. Chapter 3 is devoted to evaluating this accounting practice. It shows that all intangible assets are just different forms of monopoly wealth. This implies that the $45.4 million of intangibles that were on Tableau Software's balance sheet must then be added to the $14.281 billion of monopoly wealth computed earlier following the acquisition. This is a total of $14.326 billion of monopoly wealth added to the Saleforce balance sheet. Furthermore, when computing the monopoly wealth of firms in table 0.1, one should add the $316.0 million of intangible assets owned by the ten firms to the difference between their market value and net worth of $166,896.7 million. Their monopoly wealth was thus actually $167,212.7 million.

0.2.2   Capital and Wealth Are Different Concepts with Different Values

The study, in chapter 6, of the stock market and asset prices leads to two key conclusions that generalize the observations made about tables 0.1 and 0.2. In that chapter, I study leverage and monopoly wealth in the corporate sector of the United States from 1959 to 2019. I show that the ratio (monopoly wealth)/(market value of the firms) was close to 0 in 1985 and rose to about 75 percent in 2019 (see figure 0.1). This means that 75 percent of the value of all stocks of publicly traded companies in 2019 was composed of monopoly wealth. This is compatible with results for the selected firms in table 0.2, where this ratio is 83.3 percent. In chapter 6, I also show that nonfinancial corporations

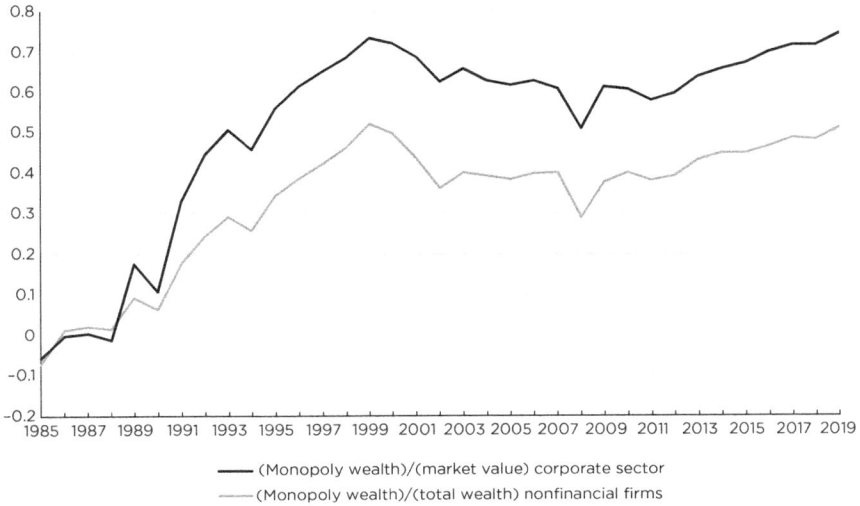

Figure 0.1 Monopoly wealth as a fraction of market value and as a fraction of total wealth, 1985–2019

have trended toward financing their fixed capital investment with debt. The debt/capital ratio had risen from 25 percent in 1950 to 71 percent in 2019. Today, capital invested in U.S. corporations is mostly financed by bondholders, while stockholders own and trade mostly monopoly wealth. The distinction between the concepts of capital and wealth is then very important for understanding the developments in this book.

The textbook model of capital formation was essentially developed in Adam Smith's *The Wealth of Nations* and was refined in the work of neoclassical economists that led to the seminal work of Fisher (1930) and Solow (1956). The model's description of the growth of capital as the outcome of hard work and slow savings over the life cycle is a good description of the allocation problem of the household. However, this model does not describe adequately how the wealth of nations is actually created. Standard measures of capital exclude some items on the balance sheet of the firm (for example, financial assets). Once allowance is made for these, the market value of a firm's tangible assets is a good approximation of the value of capital it employs as an input in its production process. The total tangible assets of the firms in table 0.1 was $28.5 billion (not shown in the table). However, the total wealth created by these ten firms was $195.4 billion, consisting of $176.9 billion owned by stockholders plus $18.5 billion owned by debt holders. The difference between total wealth and the value of capital is the monopoly wealth of $167.2 billion. In short, total wealth is the sum of total capital, built up by savings and deferred consumption, plus monopoly wealth. I show in chapter 6 that in 2019, monopoly wealth was a very large component of total wealth. For all nonfinancial firms, I estimate that this proportion was about 51 percent, which demonstrates that capital and wealth are two different asset concepts that measure two different economic quantities.

In more general terms, capital is an input to production, consisting of all fixed assets, such as structures and equipment, used to produce other goods and services, and the value of capital is then the value of all such inputs. Wealth is the total net market value of assets owned by individuals and firms in the economy. Total wealth has, therefore, two components:

$$\text{Value of Capital} + \text{Monopoly Wealth} = \text{Total Wealth}.$$

As long as the profit share of income is not zero, total wealth is larger than total capital. The difference between the values of capital and wealth explains the speed at which wealth was created by firms during the IT revolution. Capital grows at a slow pace as a result of the economy's saving a fraction of its annual output. By contrast, monopoly wealth is created by the market's valuation of new ideas and their related innovation waves. Wealth created by cumulated savings exhibits lower fluctuations than wealth created by innovations. The latter rises rapidly with rapid rates of innovations and stock prices and falls sharply when that rate slows.

My discussion has focused on technology-based monopoly wealth, but I stress that monopoly wealth is also created by firms owning brand names and through illegal collusion. I treat brand names that are supported by trademarks in the same way I treat patents, and I have already noted that, in this book, I do not address the problem of market power created by illegal means. But it is useful to understand that technological monopoly wealth is also different in substance from monopoly wealth created by collusion and other illegal methods to restrain free trade. Both forms of monopoly wealth capitalize income earned because of market power. However, in the case of technology-based market power, it is created by a privately owned technological knowledge, and it is the market value of the future income stream earned by the firm that owns that technology. That income stream is typically a reflection of increased productivity as a result of the improved technology. Collusion, by contrast, does not increase productivity. Market power from collusion leads to the creation of monopoly wealth that is a measure only of the ability of those who violate the law to extract income from the rest of society.

This last distinction raises a question. If technology-based monopoly wealth is the present value of the contribution of technology to the value of output, then is monopoly wealth also the correct social valuation of the technology? If this is the case, why view technological monopoly power as a social problem? This is a crucial question because my main policy proposal in chapter 9 aims to restrain market power and prevent it from rising above the level determined by patent law. The evidence presented in chapter 4 shows that actual market power is far greater than that.

The question of why monopoly wealth is an incorrect social valuation of the technology and why it distorts wealth distribution among individuals has a simple answer. The stream of profits whose capitalized value is monopoly wealth is not determined in competitive markets. The pricing of commodities and services sold in these markets is distorted by market power, causing prices to exceed marginal production cost. This is socially undesirable because it compels the economy to allocate scarce resources inefficiently. In addition, the stream of income contains a large component of value that would, in a competitive economy, belong to consumers but is extracted by the owners of the technology. Although monopoly wealth has some association with a technology's social benefit, the actual value of this wealth depends upon the ability of the technology's owner to extract profits from the market. This ability is derived from the owner's monopoly power, not from the technology's true contribution to society.

0.3   Market Power Has Significant Economic and Social Side Effects

Economics textbooks explain that excessive power of any firm in its market distorts the allocation of resources in that market and leads to the waste of social resources. But when such power extends to many firms over the entire economy, it has other economic and political consequences. These negative effects motivate my proposed policies in chapters 8–10 to restrain market power.

0.3.1   Rising Market Power Is the Main Cause of Rising Income and Wealth Inequality

One of the central arguments of this book is that market power is a major cause of inequality. Market power affects the functional distribution of income, which is the distribution of income among the three components noted earlier: labor, capital, and profits. Next, I explain how rising inequality among these three components is the cause of rising personal inequality, which is inequality among individual members of society. Some of my points are deduced from technically complex formal arguments, and some are just common sense.

I start with the effect of market power on income and wealth inequality. During periods of rapid innovation, relatively few innovator-entrepreneurs work with a small group of capital owners to promote and develop their enterprises. As the number and size of these new and more dynamic firms grow, the average rate of market power rises. This has several consequences. Innovations certainly bring about more economic growth, but, as I explain in detail in chapter 1, the rise of market power suppresses the share of total income going to labor and capital. To understand why this is the case, consider monopoly power. To generate excess profits, a firm with rising monopoly power will raise the prices of the goods it controls and thereby lower demand and restrict output. The amount by which a monopolist restricts output is often around 50 percent of the output that would have been produced under perfect competition. But when rising monopoly power restricts output, it also lowers the demand for labor and the demand for capital (structures, equipment, and the like). This leads to a fall in the quantity of labor and capital used, and in the prices of labor and capital (wages and the interest rate, respectively), lowering their income and their share in GNP. The consequence of rising market power is then a rising share of profits and declining shares of capital and labor.

Second, in addition to its impact on relative shares, rising market power also increases income and wealth inequality among individuals. This occurs because, as noted, rising market power cuts the share of income going to labor and capital and raises profits and monopoly wealth. Virtually all profits and capital gains of these rapidly growing firms are owned by a very small group of people, innovators, and early investors. As the firms grow over time, some members of the general public may invest in these innovative firms at much higher prices than those paid by early investors and share in the rising profits and monopoly wealth generated by them. Nevertheless, since the ownership of common stock is highly concentrated among the very wealthy, the growth of these firms results in more income and wealth flowing to a small group of people, leading to increased income and wealth inequality. The worldwide increase, over the last two decades, in the number of billionaires who made their capital gains from new innovations is a simple index that supports these conclusions.

Third, monopoly profits are less equitably distributed than either returns to labor or capital. Capital income is earned by broadly diverse individuals, and that includes stockholders. But it is also earned by bondholders like retirees who seek income with small risk or people who buy life insurance. By contrast, profits are earned by a small population segment that accepts the high risk associated with the profit making of young and rapidly growing firms. This includes the risk of activities such as innovations, mergers and acquisitions, and strategic pricing. It means that a very small segment of the population earns the increased, albeit riskier, profits. To indicate the size of this effect, consider the period since the 1980s. Figure 0.2 shows that in the early 1980s, profits were as low as 6 percent of the total income produced by U.S. corporations. Since then, the share of

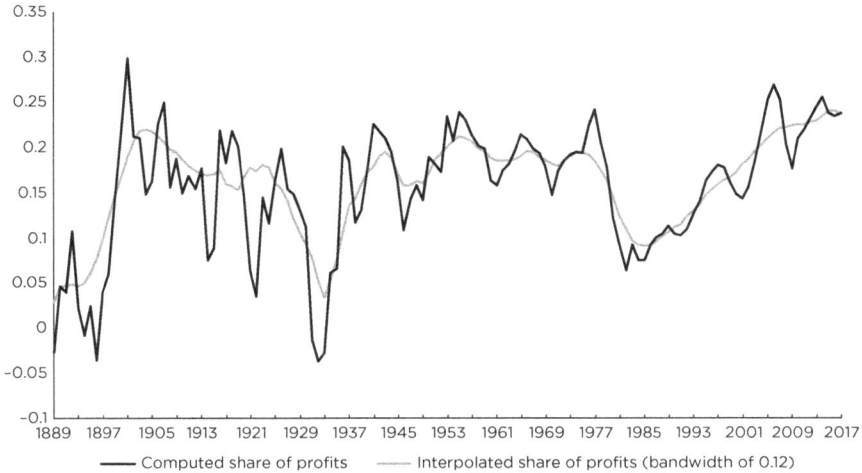

Figure 0.2   Rising and falling share of profits, 1889–2017

profits has steadily risen, reaching 24 percent in 2017. This means that during the 1982–2017 period, the combined shares of labor compensation[6] and return on capital declined by 18 percentage points. The outcome is an increased income and wealth inequality among owners of wealth.

Fourth, over the last thirty years, the level of labor and capital income has increased as a result of general economic growth. But by progressively lowering the level of labor and capital income below their prior trajectory, rising market power has served as a headwind, slowing gains in the living standards of workers, retirees, and other bondholders. Indeed, while automation and globalization are always cast as the villains in explanations of the plight of American workers, rising market power has been the more significant factor.

0.3.2   Rising Market Power Lowers the Level of Economic Activity and Chokes Off Innovation

As explained in section 0.3.1, rising market power lowers the incentives of firms to produce and invest. When market power expands throughout the economy, it has several negative effects on the economic aggregates of investment, capital, output, and consumption.

---

[6]Wages or wage income always includes all compensation to labor. It is a bit easier to use the term "wage" since it is shorter than "compensation to labor," but all wage data in this book are data on total compensation to labor.

First, it causes firms to restrict output and charge higher prices, or, for monopsony firms, to restrict their purchases of inputs and pay lower prices for them. If customers buy less than previously because prices are higher than they otherwise would be, or if suppliers supply less than before, the firm's required capacity is smaller and therefore the firm reduces its investment. This explains how rising market power causes a fall in private investment. This is hardly radical thinking: the simple models introduced in elementary economics courses confirm that higher monopoly power leads to lower capacity and a lower rate of private investment.

Second, I show in chapter 2 that, because a high degree of market power in the economy lowers the rate of investment and decreases productive capacity, it permanently lowers the level of wages; consumption; and, of course, gross domestic product (GDP). This means that at any moment of time, the level of output, consumption, and capital stock is lower than in the same economy absent the active market power of firms.

Third, as to the growth rate of the economy, there are two key factors that need to be considered. One is the growing evidence that, at times, firms with high market power protect their market position by buying their competitors or their technologies to suppress innovations that might threaten their market position. Such actions result in a lower innovation rate and lower aggregate growth rate for the economy. Second, market power can temporarily lower the interest rate and the growth rate. The decline in the growth rate and interest rate over the last thirty years has been the subject of a great deal of research. I argue that these declines are, in part, a consequence of the rise in market power. In chapter 2, I lay out the theoretical mechanism by which this occurs (see section 8), and it is confirmed empirically by the work of Gutiérrez and Philippon (2016). The temporary declines in growth and interest rates are a consequence of rising rather than high market power. An economy with high market power will have less capital and lower output in the long run. As market power rises, output falls, and the capital stock shrinks to adjust. Output falling results in a temporary, but medium-term, lower growth rate and the shrinking of capital stock means that investment dries up, which leads to a lower interest rate. Thus, rising market power since the 1980s is one of the causes of the U.S. economy's low rate of growth.

Fourth, in chapter 5, I explore the effect of high market power on the rate at which new innovations diffuse through the economy. I examine the innovation of electricity and conduct a case study of the effect of the market power of General Electric (GE) and Westinghouse, because of their ownership of key electric technology, on the speed at which electrification progressed from 1888 to 1929. I find that, although electrification of the urban United States was mostly completed by 1929, it was sharply slowed down by the market power of the GE–Westinghouse monopoly. These firms kept prices of electric equipment high by using a patent-sharing agreement signed in 1896 that covered the basic patents of electricity production and distribution. I estimate that the resulting high prices of electricity slowed the electrification of the United States by about twelve to fifteen years.

In short, rising technological market power has important negative effects on aggregate economic performance. In a technologically advancing economy without a strong policy to contain it, market power becomes a permanent and insidious force with deeply harmful economic and social effects. Rising market power increases inequality; results in inefficient allocation of resources; and lowers the levels of output, consumption, and investment. It slows the growth of the economy and of the diffusion of new technologies, and prevents workers and savers from enjoying the benefits of rising productivity. I will also explain that it alters the delicate balance of power in society in favor of the rich and, by awarding their voices more weight, weakens the foundations of democratic institutions.

0.3.3   Why Democracy Can Fail: The Political Impact of Rising Market Power

The IT revolution and the rise of market power since the 1980s did not lead only to a rise in inequality. They also caused a deterioration in the labor market (see Case and Deaton, 2020; Pfeffer, 2018) and a sustained decline of the middle class. This decline has been amplified significantly by the differential effect of IT on labor skills.

It is well understood that electricity and the combustion engine, the leading GPTs of the twentieth century, were very beneficial to low-skilled workers. They created jobs that can be performed by workers without advanced education and that could be learned relatively quickly through experience on the production lines. The only requirement of these jobs was an ability to follow precise instructions in performing high-precision tasks. Consequently, they gave rise to high-productivity blue-collar workers who earned enough to join the middle class. The computer had a different effect.

IT-based automation is effective in replacing jobs requiring precise repetitive execution. Therefore, the IT automation created machines that replaced those same workers that prospered under the prior GPTs, contributing to the decline of the middle class. But IT has also had an effect on high-skilled workers, and this dual effect is known as the *job polarization effect* (for key references see Autor et al., 2003; Levy and Murnane, 2004; Acemoglu and Autor, 2011; Autor and Dorn, 2013; Autor, 2014; see Frey, 2019 for a complete survey). This research shows that IT-based automation has increased the productivity of high skilled workers with college education because the computer and internet technologies complement those jobs rather than displace them. In addition, IT has created many new high-skilled jobs, such as computer programmers and technical support specialists. As to the former low-education, high-skills tasks that were replaced by IT, workers who would have qualified for these jobs in the past have gradually migrated to rising number of low-skilled jobs requiring low education.

In sum, job polarization has resulted in the rising number of jobs in either high-skilled, high-paying jobs whose productivity was increased by advances in IT, or in a sharply rising number of low-skilled service jobs. Many of the jobs in the middle section of the skill distribution were eliminated by the advancing technology and contributed to the decline of the middle class.

The middle class has been defined in many ways. If measured by income alone, then in 1971 the proportion of Americans with income in the middle class was 61 percent, and that fell to 49.9 percent in 2015 (see Luhby, 2015). But the middle-class lifestyle, that includes access to healthcare, good education for children, some vacations, and retirement funding, has eroded not only from the loss of those good jobs but also because the prices of these services have risen much faster than nominal wages.

The consequence of these changes has been a growing division between the rich and poor, and a very large fraction of Americans who are poor with little prospect of returning to the middle class. The emergence of this chasm separating rich and poor has reduced social solidarity. When the American dream was alive, those at the bottom of the income distribution did not feel as far from those at the top. High mobility meant there were opportunities to move between economic classes. The sense of lost opportunities has created a large class of Americans who are angry and feel betrayed by the institutions of democracy. This sense of betrayal can be exploited by an authoritarian demagogue who offers simplistic answers that replace the already declining trust in the opinions of experts who are dismissed as elites. The distinction between truth and falsehood disappears, and scientific facts become mere opinions of untrusted professionals.

The willingness to adopt conspiracy theories originates from the fact that, in the age of science and technology, people without advanced education do not have the scientific knowledge to assess the veracity of any expert opinion. Under such conditions, the stability of democratic institutions depends on people's trust in technical experts and political leaders. Without such universal trust, democratic institutions are distinctly weakened. But trust is based on the premise that democratic policy is designed to help all citizens, not to benefit narrow interest groups while abandoning others. As I discuss below and more fully in chapter 10, our growth and innovation policy has been conducted without compensating those negatively affected. This has led to a loss of trust and disillusion with democracy itself among those who have lost as a result of these policy choices.

A more difficult problem arises when one asks why the U.S. political system has allowed policy changes that benefited the rich at the expense of the poor. And what is the impact of the declining middle class on the lost trust in democratic institutions?

The constitutional scholar Ganesh Sitaraman (2017) explains that, apart from slavery, the United States was an egalitarian society at birth, and this is how the framers of the Constitution expected it to remain. They thus designed a constitution without legal provisions to resolve conflicts between rich and poor, such as giving the rich representation in an upper house with some rights and the poor a representation in a lower house with their own set of balancing rights. Sitaraman makes a persuasive case that in the absence of a mechanism for an economic balance of power, democratic institutions in the United States rely for their stability on a strong middle class that has the incentive to find compromises between the interests of the rich and poor. A strong middle class prevents extreme or narrow interests from prevailing. Sitaraman asserts that, because the middle class has drastically declined in size, in the absence of public policy to restrain the rise of market power, American democracy is in peril.

In chapter 10 and section 0.6 below, I make the case that, if democracy is to survive, a new economic policy must restore some egalitarian character to American society. This policy should empower workers and create permanent institutions that restore the middle class. Despite this need, in today's political arena one often hears the claim that government is not the solution; it is the problem! In contrast with this claim, the fact is that, without effective government policy to contain market power, capitalism's perpetual creation of market power results in the transfer of income; wealth; and, consequently, political power to the very rich. Such concentration of power undermines democracy as moneyed interests manage, and often corrupt, public institutions.

Paradoxically, as I noted earlier, the United States experienced in the First Gilded Age, late in the nineteenth century, the same dynamics of growing inequality, a widening gap between the very rich and the very poor, and popular movements for reform. The form of government in Western Europe during the nineteenth century and in the United States at the end of that century can justifiably be labeled plutocracy. Piketty (2014) offers a vivid picture of nineteenth century inequality when wealth and class were required for progress in life and nominally democratic governments were controlled by the wealthy. During the First Gilded Age, the power of democratic institutions in the United States was shrinking: J. P. Morgan was more powerful than the president of the United States.

Progressive reformers in the late nineteenth century attempted to bring about change but met with limited success. The government cracked down violently on union organizers and ignored the cries of farmers and miners. Real change came in 1901 when the assassination of President McKinley resulted in the progressive

Theodore Roosevelt becoming president. The change of administration in 1901, strikingly visible in figure 0.2 below, meant that public policy became an active force against rising market power. The Progressive Era ushered in many drastic reforms. These were then strengthened as part of the New Deal programs of Franklin Roosevelt. A more egalitarian society emerged from the New Deal era, leading to the 1936–1973 Golden Age of the American experiment.

0.4   Market Power Is Determined by Technology and Economic Policy

0.4.1   The Dynamics of Market Power in the United States, 1889 to the Present

Until now, I have mostly considered the effect of rising market power because this has been the trend since the 1980s. Chapter 4 examines the evolution of market power in the United States from 1889 to 2017, and the record shows that such power has risen and fallen over the course of U.S. history. In figure 0.2, I present a summary of the time pattern of the rising and falling share of income going to profits, which is one index of market power. These shares are measured as fractions of the gross value added of the corporate sector in the United States,[7] as follows:

- In 1889 the share of profits was −2.6 percent, and it rose until 1901, when it reached 29.9 percent.
- From 29.9 percent in 1901, the share of profits declined until 1932, when it reached −3.7 percent.
- From −3.7 percent in 1931, the share of profits rose until 1953, when it reached 23.5 percent.
- From 23.5 percent in 1953, the share of profits declined until 1985, when it reached 7.6 percent.
- From 7.6 percent in 1985, the share of profits rose until 2017, when it reached 23.8 percent.

The record reveals three periods of rising market power, 1889–1901, 1931–1953, and 1985–2017, and two periods of declining market power, 1901–1931 and 1953–1985. Much has been written about the change in income and wealth inequality since 1982, and economists have developed creative theories

---

[7]The corporate sector is where market power is exercised. For this reason, all relative shares discussed here are of the gross value added of this sector.

to explain it. Authors such as Acemoglu and Restrepo (2020), Autor et al. (2020), Bessen (2020), Karabarbounis and Neiman (2014), and Piketty and Zucman (2014) combine careful empirical work with a desire to explain this increase in inequality. I discuss these studies in chapters 4 and 6 and observe that most of the theories need to be generalized in order to explain trends in the data before the 1970s. Since there have been periods of rising and falling relative shares of profits, I offer a single theory to explain the full record of rising and falling market power. This theory is one of the main contributions of the book.

Briefly, the theory states that the dynamic of market power is determined primarily by two opposing forces. The first is technology's impact on the economy. Capitalist economies perpetually create new market power that originates in innovative new technologies. Left unchecked, firms with initial market power have the means to consolidate and expand that power to levels incompatible with a free, competitive market economy. The second, potentially opposing force is public policy to restrain market power, aided by a degree of technological obsolescence. The rate at which market power is created is so high that without a restraining public policy, it will rise to levels that threaten the foundations of democracy. Public policy could eliminate almost all market power if the government were willing to regulate prices or if it chose not to enforce private property rights. These would be unwise directions to take, and I instead advocate for a public policy that allows innovators to gain initial market power but prevents them from further consolidating that power. Whatever public policy is chosen, that policy, as I underscore throughout the book, is entirely consequential in determining the dynamics of market power. In setting the rules regarding whether firms may merge, what tax rates are applicable to their profits, and what conditions they must provide their workers, policy sets the terms by which firms compete in the market. Unfortunately, as I have already noted, we have reached the Second Gilded Age. Our policy since the 1980s has promoted the growth of market power, and the policy tools at our disposal are outmoded and unsuitable for addressing the problem of technology-based market power. This theoretical view was first developed in my earlier papers (see Kurz, 2016, 2017, 2018a, 2018b), Those papers explain the rising market power and income inequality since the 1980s. I now offer a brief review of the history of U.S. market power from 1889 to 2017 through the lens of my theory's specified role of policy and technology:

1. 1889–1901: Most discussions of the First Gilded Age focus on the market power of the trusts resulting from waves of mergers and acquisitions at the time. The more important fact is that it was an extraordinary period of innovation, led by inventions in electricity and the combustion engine. Innovations that led to many of today's conveniences of life were actually made at the turn of the twentieth century. Consequently, market power rose rapidly and was further augmented by a

wave of mergers and acquisitions, and, equally important, no active policy or regulatory institutions existed to constrain this rising trend. All that changed in 1901.

2. 1901–1932: The assassination of President McKinley resulted in Theodore Roosevelt, a leader of the Progressive movement, ascending to the presidency. Roosevelt and his reformist allies had a vision of a substantially more active regulatory state. They created long-lasting institutions such as the Food and Drug Administration (1906), the Federal Trade Commission (1914), the Federal Reserve (1913), and the Clayton Antitrust Act (1914) that reinforced the Sherman Antitrust Act by restricting mergers, and settled the constitutionality of the federal income tax (1913). Progressive policy also supported the rising power of labor unions, in contrast with previous administrations that intervened to help in breaking strikes. Although innovations in electricity and combustion engine continued to give rise to new firms with market power, the effect of the stricter regulatory regime was stronger. The share of profits declined, and labor's share rose.

3. 1931–1953: The rise of market power during the Great Depression and World War II is surprising but has two explanations. First, Field (2006) shows that, as the technologies of electricity and combustion engine were maturing, productivity growth between 1929 and 1941 was the highest of any comparable period in the twentieth century, causing a rapid creation of new market power. Second, the Great Depression allowed only the larger and stronger firms to survive (see Hunter, 1982). To prevent deflation, policy also encouraged businesses to cooperate in raising prices. During World War II, the country needed business to mobilize for the war effort, leaving only little space to restrict or regulate business activity. As a result, in the 1930s and during the war, antitrust policy was lax and laws for regulating business were only partially enforced. After the war, there was also a massive transfer to private hands of technology that was developed in wartime with public funding, contributing to a postwar productivity boom. This informal alliance between the nation's military and the defense industry was later criticized by President Eisenhower as becoming the military-industrial complex. The outcome of a high innovation rate and lax policy from 1932 to 1953, which deprioritized regulation and the containment of market power, led to a rapid rise in the share of profits.[8]

4. 1953–1985: The decline in market power during this period is as expected. Although the rate of innovations remained elevated in the 1950s and 1960s,

---

[8]However, the rise of the share of profits to the estimated value of 23.5 percent in 1953 is, most likely, too high because it is deduced in chapter 4 with a methodology that relies upon the assumption that market interest rates reflect the cost of capital. Interest rates were regulated during World War II and, although the March 1951 Accord between the Federal Reserve and the Treasury freed the markets from control, the adjustment was slow and financial repression resulted in interest rates that were, up to 1959, far too low. Consequently, my estimated profit shares are too high and the true profit shares from 1952 to 1959 were probably lower by about 3–5 percentage points.

it slowed down substantially during the 1970s. On the policy front, antitrust enforcement was pursued with vigor, and the legal machinery of the New Deal enabled substantial regulation of business. In addition, during this period, labor unions were very strong. Corporate income taxes were very high, and top individual tax rates were essentially confiscatory. As a result, market power and the share of profits declined.

5. 1985–2021: Two major changes worked in the *same* direction. The IT revolution ended the technological stagnation of the 1970s. It transformed many sectors with a widespread impact, not unlike that of the prior two GPTs. At the same time, policy drastically loosened regulations on key sectors, declined to take antitrust actions, and slashed corporate and individual tax rates. With both forces benefiting business, innovators gained market power, and the permissive policy enabled them to expand that power. The result has been a steep rise in market power, as seen in figure 0.2. This period is examined in greater detail in the next section.

0.4.2   Some Policy Factors May Have Asymmetric Impact

Has changing market power been the only force changing the share of labor since 1889? The theory in chapters 1 and 2 shows that, in response to changes in market power, the relative shares of capital and of labor in income would change in the same proportion. This is true for the period from 1889 to 1932 but not so after 1932. In measuring labor share, I exclude corporate officers' compensation from labor income. In chapter 4, I explain this by arguing that, in a technological age, corporate officers, like innovators, are essential firm partners whose main task is to preserve the firm's technological dominance and are compensated under profit-sharing rules. Under this accounting, the time pattern of labor share of total corporate income is summed up as follows:

- In 1889, labor share was 71.3 percent, and it fell until 1901, when it reached 50.8 percent.
- From 50.8 percent in 1901, labor share rose until 1932, when it reached 60.5 percent.
- From 60.5 percent in 1932, labor share remained roughly constant until 1970, when it was 59.7 percent.
- From 59.7 percent in 1970, labor share declined until 2017, when it reached 52.4 percent.

The difference between the time paths of the relative share of labor and the relative share of capital between 1932 and 1985 is summarized in the following:

1. The share of capital declined from 1931 to 1953, while the share of labor fluctuated, but remained in the same range.

2. The share of capital rose from 1953 to 1985, while the share of labor remained in the same range until 1970 and began to decline after 1970.

Several implications of this time patterns of labor share are analyzed in chapter 4 and reveal an important difference in the responses of labor income and capital income to changes in market power.

Fluctuating market power benefits or inflicts damage on both labor and capital. The question, however, is, on which of the two is the effect of changes in market power stronger? For example, market power rose sharply from 1985 to 2017, and the question is, Who suffered more? Was it workers whose labor share declined, or retirees, pension funds, and the like, whose share of capital declined? I show in chapter 4 that between 1889 and the 1930s, the proportional effect on the two was approximately the same. Since the 1930s, the effect of market power on capital has been stronger than its effect on labor. Rising market power lowers capital share proportionally more than it lowers the share of labor, while falling market power benefits capital proportionally more than it benefits labor. This means that after 1935, labor appears relatively more shielded than capital against the impact of rising or falling market power. In the recent period from 1985 to 2017, the share of capital in the corporate sector's value added declined by 46 percent, while the share of labor declined by only 5.1 percent!

This result suggests that economic and political forces have stabilized the share of labor relative to capital and kept the personal distribution of corporate income more equitable than would have been warranted by market power. Our society may have already recognized the tendency of capitalism toward inequality of unregulated markets and created institutions to partly protect labor, by tools such as the social safety net, public education, and minimum wages. Alternatively, it is possible political considerations have, since the 1930s, discouraged firms from using their full market power to maximize profits by employing much harsher labor practices to increase profits at the expense of workers. Can we imagine the political consequences of a 46 percent decline of labor share from 1985 to 2017, rather than the relatively smaller amount it actually fell?

0.5   The Rise in Market Power and the Failure of Policy Since the 1980s

0.5.1   The Second Gilded Age: IT and Laissez-Faire Policy Has Caused Rising Inequality Since 1985

The evidence for rising inequality and falling relative labor share since 1985 is decisive. However, the cause of these changes is yet to be agreed upon by economists. Diverse explanations have been proposed. I review these in chapter 4 but briefly summarize some of them here.

Karabarbounis and Neiman (2014) and Acemoglu and Restrepo (2020) argue that capital goods or "robots" have replaced workers because of falling relative marginal cost of capital goods, leading to a decline in wages at the bottom of the income distribution. Piketty (2014) proposes that the decline in wages is the result of an erosion of proworker policies like the minimum wage and unions. Bessen (2016) argues that regulations are to blame because big firms are better able to navigate, and in some cases manipulate, the federal regulations created in recent years. Bessen (2020) proposes that IT increased corporate profits and therefore inequality. IT made it easier for large firms to organize and coordinate while not being much help to small firms. De Loecker et al. (2020) give a similar explanation for rising market power, arguing that new technology has increased the fixed cost of starting a business and lowered the costs of expanding and operating at scale. Farhi and Gourio (2018) suggest the rise in profits was caused by the rise in business equity risk premiums. Van Reenen (2018) and Autor et al. (2020) argue firms vary in their productivity and the rise of markup is a reflection of the higher productivity of the larger firms. As competition caused by globalization intensified, the weaker, low-productivity firms defaulted, and their customers migrated to the bigger and more efficient superstar firms.

In contrast, as explained earlier, my theory suggests that the rise in market power since 1985 was driven mostly by the two forces of technology and public policy complementing each other, both pushing market power upward. Specific to the last forty years, on the technology side, IT is a GPT that began to develop in the 1970s and has affected almost all sectors of the economy. For example, banks are clearly not in the computer industry; their business is financial services. But computers and the internet have transformed banking, enabling banks to develop proprietary software technologies that resulted in the consolidation of banks and added monopoly wealth in banking. Because every major firm uses proprietary technology and sells its own trademarked goods and services, the transformation to the digital age offers all firms an opportunity to bolster their market power.

Apart from the general tendency of innovations to plant new seeds of market power, IT has unique features that bolster that power. The IT revolution caused a sharp increase in speed and a decrease in the costs of processing, storing, transmitting, and sharing information. These factors have contributed to increased market power by raising the barriers to entry of competitors for the following reasons:

1. The computer and the internet have increased management's control over larger organizations at lower costs; IT has thus sharply expanded the range of corporate increasing returns to scale.

2. Users place greater value on information platforms if they have more users. If a start-up tries to compete with Facebook, it will find that no one wants to use a social network that is not used by their friends and family. A start-up trying to compete with Amazon will find that suppliers will not respond to offers because the start-up does not have enough customers and that customers will show little interest because the start-up does not have enough suppliers. Firms in the digital age are often platforms for interaction of customers and suppliers, and such interdependence causes network externalities that lower marginal cost, making entry of competitors difficult.

3. IT allows firms to collect a vast amount of private information about customers and suppliers, and that information is unavailable to new entrants. IT also enables firms to use sophisticated targeting algorithms to increase customer loyalty.

These unique properties have meant that, as IT has been adopted, firms have grown larger and fewer in number. This has resulted in rising market concentration driven by the nature of the technology. IT has thus compounded the growing market power created by the underlying process of innovative firms improving their technologies, introducing new and more desired products, acquiring potential competitors, and consolidating their market positions.

The second force driving market power is public policy, which in the 1980s shifted drastically away from policies limiting market power toward those that enabled further consolidation of market power. President Ronald Reagan's goal was to eliminate, as much as possible, the regulatory structure and policies of the New Deal. He limited the power of unions and initiated wide-ranging policies known as supply-side policies. The central objective of these policies was to increase the incentives of individuals and business firms to invest and innovate, and eliminate government policies that restrain such incentives.

A central instrument of Reagan's approach was the Tax Reform Act of 1986. It cut the top marginal tax rate, which had been 70 percent when Reagan took office, to 28 percent in 1988, and cut the corporate tax rate from 46 percent to 34 percent. When signing the act, President Reagan denounced the prior tax system as "un-American" and, reflecting on its egalitarian goals, claimed that its "steeply progressive nature struck at the heart of the economic life of the individual." The administration also eliminated a wide range of business regulations and reinterpreted antitrust policy to allow a sharp rise in mergers and acquisitions, and hence in business concentration. Government-permitted mergers have led to the consolidation of important sectors such as airlines, banking, communication, chemicals, drugs, and high-tech. Virtually no regulations have been enacted to curtail the growing market power of big technology firms that have been acquiring competing firms at will. No regulations or restrictions exist today in areas of vital public interest, such as the use of private information, disclosure of search criteria by internet giants, and liability for false information posted on social media platforms. In short, no policy has been employed to counterbalance the sharp effect of technology in generating rising market power. The United States essentially returned in the 1980s to a free-market ideology and to the laissez-faire economic policy that prevailed during the First Gilded Age, prior to the efforts of the early twentieth-century reform movement.

The impact of the combined forces of technology and public policy is shown in figures 0.1 and 0.2. As noted earlier, the share of profits in the corporate sector rose from 7.6 percent in 1985 to 24 percent in 2017, causing a sharp rise in inequality. Piketty and Saez (2003) show that personal income inequality today is close to those levels in the First Gilded Age, and in figure 0.2 I show the share of profits in 2019 is not too far from the share of profits in 1900.

The policy environment since the 1980s is also similar to that of the First Gilded Age in the role of money in politics. Ample historical evidence shows that before 1901, big money ran U.S. politics. Since the 1980s, the amount of money spent to influence policy has risen sharply, aided by supportive decisions of the Supreme Court. It should thus not be surprising that by enacting similar economic policies, the United States reached in the Second Gilded Age an economic and social outcome similar to that of the First Gilded Age.

The central role of public policy in the rise of market power since the 1980s has been documented by several authors, who provide valuable empirical evidence supporting the theory advanced in this book. Grullon et al. (2019) argue that the rise in concentration is an outcome of the weak enforcement of antitrust laws and increasing technological barriers to entry. Gutiérrez and Philippon (2016) show that declining investment over the last thirty years has been caused by increased limits on entry, increased concentration, and lower competition. Gutiérrez and Philippon (2017b) offer more evidence of the effect of lower competition on investment and propose alternative methods to measure the decline in competition. Gutiérrez and Philippon (2018) document a higher level of competition in Europe compared with the United States, where concentration is higher. Their argument points to lobbying and other forms of influence peddling as the causes of increased market power in the United States. The same theme is developed in more detail in Philippon (2019) and in Gutiérrez and Philippon (2019), where the authors provide further evidence that policy allowed the increased concentration.

0.5.2   Current Antitrust Policy Tools Are Unsuitable for Stabilizing Market Power

An examination of current antitrust legislation shows that current U.S. antitrust laws and regulations are not suitable for addressing the problem of legal technological market power. The design of current antitrust laws is based on the principle that free trade needs to prevail, and any restraint of trade must be eliminated. The law presumes that any market power is not legal because it was acquired by human acts, such as collusion or mergers, that aim to restrain trade. Current policy then exempts regulated public utilities but aims to remove all other market power entirely in order to restore the natural order of perfect competition. But at the same time, patent law grants monopoly power to owners of new innovations. This explains why most attempts by the Justice Department to use antitrust laws to address technological market power have failed in court. When policy did curtail market power, it relied upon other tools, discussed earlier in section 0.4.

To clarify why current tools have failed, I review the example of the Justice Department's efforts to prosecute General Electric for its light bulb monopoly under antitrust laws. The failure of this effort buried any hope of enforcing antitrust laws against technological monopolists. It is a tale of two legal principles and practices in conflict with each other.

The case began in 1909 when GE received a patent on the use of tungsten as a filament. By 1911, its laboratory was able to develop a practical way to manufacture a light bulb with this tungsten filament. This discovery gave GE a superior product. However, even before the tungsten discovery, the production of light bulbs was a manual operation. It required skilled glassblowing labor to make the glass casing, called the glass bulb, and to attach the mounts and bases to the glass by hand. This removed the advantage of scale and enabled small producers to stay in the market and compete with the larger suppliers, GE and Westinghouse. But the small firms also realized early that to compete, they had to share the fixed cost of research, finance, and marketing. To solve this problem, many of them created in 1901 a jointly managed firm called the National Lamp Company. Each small firm operated its own production plant, but they pooled their funds to pay for the research and engineering work of the National Lamp Company. Because they lacked the capital needed for setting up the engineering laboratory, GE granted the producers and the National Lamp Company licenses for many of its patents and technologies. It also invested in the National Lamp Company enough capital to make GE the majority owner of the corporation without being active in its daily work. This ownership was not public information.

In 1911, the Justice Department brought an antitrust suit that charged that GE and the National Lamp Company were not competing. They argued that the National Lamp Company was nothing but an instrument for price fixing and that they, together with Westinghouse, were fixing market shares and thus engaged in the restraint of trade. The suit also charged that the pyramiding of patents on improvements in the filament was creating a monopoly after the expiration of the initial 1880 patent on the incandescent lamp owned by GE. Therefore, GE and the National Lamp Company were using false patents. GE's defense was simple but surprising: they agreed that the key factual claims were correct, but that because GE had a patent, all these actions were legal. This defense was novel and led the Justice Department to reconsider. It agreed to settle with GE on the condition that GE would acquire the National Lamp Company and incorporate it into its own bulb division. This may have ended the collusion, because a firm cannot collude with its own subdivision, but it only strengthened GE's market power!

The second part of this failed campaign against technological market power is an antitrust suit brought by the Justice Department against GE and Westinghouse for colluding by agreeing to a patent-sharing agreement. In 1896, GE and Westinghouse agreed to pool their patents instead of competing with one another over a number of different electric technologies. After GE received the patent for the tungsten filament bulb and, based on the patent-sharing agreement, it licensed Westinghouse to manufacture and sell incandescent light bulbs with a tungsten filament. Under the agreement, GE fixed the price and determined their market shares. The Justice Department alleged this was collusion to fix prices, a clear violation of antitrust laws. The case made its way to the Supreme Court. In its 1926 landmark ruling, the court stated GE granted only production rights to Westinghouse and, as a patentee, GE was entitled to all monopoly profits that can be gained from the sale of bulbs, even if this resulted from fixing prices with Westinghouse. The ruling did not cover all possible patent-sharing agreements or, more generally, all patent pools, which are patent-sharing agreements among many parties.[9]

The government's failure to restrict GE's monopoly power resulted from the fact that patent laws and antitrust laws are in conflict with each other, just as the conception of a competitive economy conflicts with the award of market power as compensation for innovations. For the remainder of the twentieth century, the Justice Department made repeated attempts to bring suits for antitrust violations against legal patent owners, in patent pools or individually. The typical strategy was to claim either that the pool violated the law or that, for many different reasons, the patent rights should be revoked by the courts to allow an antitrust case to proceed. These suits mostly failed, and this strategy does not apply to the vast majority of patent holders who are law-abiding economic actors with legal market power. There is no way to revoke their patents and, for this reason, the strategy employed did not address the real problem. My first policy proposal is to extend current antitrust law to cover technological market power, and I discuss the steps to achieve this in section 0.6.1.

---

[9] Policy regarding patent pools has changed several times, and additional court rulings, at different levels have been made about them. The effects of such pools on incentives to innovate and on the degree of competition have been extensively debated. For a recent article on the problem, see Lampe and Moser (2016).

0.5.3   The Problem of Compensation

Perhaps the most basic idea economists teach is that opening an economy to free trade makes everybody better off. But if not stated correctly, this statement is false. One cannot gloss over the fact that within each country, free trade results in some people losing, like workers whose jobs go overseas, while others gain, like consumers who get access to cheap imports. A free-trade policy makes everybody better off only if those who gain from the policy compensate the losers. In many cases, public compensation is the actual practice. When the government builds a road, it compensates landowners whose property is expropriated. When an oil company is granted the rights for a pipeline, it assumes the legal obligation to compensate all harmed by the project.

In the age of technology workers develop industry-specific skills. The elimination of an industry causes a sharp decline in the demand for some technical skills. Such a change causes the devaluation of some human capital that develops from a lifetime of accumulated experience. The problem is more acute if the displaced workers are older; restarting one's professional career late in life is difficult, expensive, and often painful. When these results emerge on a large scale, it becomes a massive catastrophe for many innocent citizens.

The problem of compensation is of importance when applied to policy concerning innovation. It is an efficient public policy to pay compensation to workers whose jobs were eliminated and whose wages were depressed by innovations and by the rising market power of innovators. A compensation policy can be financed by taxing products of innovations that result in displaced workers or of equipment used for such displacement. Most in business reject this principle, although, if economic conditions are favorable, they often pay some compensation for eliminating their own long-term jobs. Stressing their vital contribution to economic growth, they insist that in a capitalist economy they have the natural right to innovate anything profitable and that society should protect all intellectual property rights resulting from their innovations. Some even insist "competition is for losers" (see Thiel, 2014, p. 1) and champion their own monopoly power. Recently some corporate leaders have expressed openness to policies that hold corporations responsible for their effects on society. The fact is, however, that a policy of free innovations with no compensation has amounted to a policy that allowed innovators to accumulate vast wealth at the expense of the middle class and the unskilled workers of America. The economic and political consequences of this fact have become unacceptable to many.

In contemplating a new policy, it is clear that precise compensation that takes into account both the exact cost and the exact benefits each individual worker receives from innovations is not practical. Instead, I propose expanding the social safety net to provide better social insurance that enables those displaced access to healthcare, basic necessities, and education for their children. A more specific and permanent compensation policy should increase the mobility of children of displaced workers from the bottom of the income distribution back into the middle class. This will also stabilize the middle class and strengthen democracy. To that end, I propose in section 0.6 the creation of a permanent national fund for equity and democracy. In addition, the government needs to develop policies that create good-quality jobs for dislocated workers.

The future of robotics and artificial intelligence raises the deeper question of whether policy can create incentives for cooperation between machines and humans. How could policy alter the incentives of innovators to create technologies that, rather than displace labor, complement labor and increase its productivity?

0.5.4   A Policy to Restrain the Superstar Firms Increases Social Welfare

The most widely used argument against regulating the big high-tech superstar firms has been based on the idea that imposing restrictions on them amounts to punishing the most productive for being the most productive. Instead of regulating them, it is claimed, free entry and competition will weaken their market power. This reasoning has not only been at the foundations of the Chicago school's legal opposition to antitrust (e.g., Friedman, 1999; Posner, 2014), but it has also been commonly used in the industrial organization literature and in the evaluation of market power by some in the mainline literature (e.g., Autor et al., 2020; Bessen, 2020; Van Reenen, 2018). A typical reasoning proposes that these firms do not prevent free entry. Moreover, because they are more productive, they sell their output for lower prices, causing their less productive competitors to default and depart from the market. This causes a migration of their customers to the superstar firms and results in increased industrial concentration. Instead of antitrust, policy should be based on the idea that competition will bring down the market power of those highly productive firms. Because this line of reasoning is used so often, it is important to address it directly.

I have already explained that technological competition is different from regular competition because it requires the winner to invent something that is new and superior to what is available at the start of competition. Moreover, as explained in chapter 1, when engaged in technological competition, firms take many defensive actions to impede the growth of their competitors, making it so much harder for a new entrant to challenge an incumbent firm with market power. The effect of policy is more complex and is taken up in chapter 7, where I build a formal model of technological competition with free entry in which winners are indeed the most productive. To endow technological discoveries with more realism, competition among firms is based on the model of success breeds success, in which successful discoveries improve the probability of future success, while failure to discover leads nowhere. In addition, success of the leading firms lowers the probability of future success of the lagging firms, thus impeding their future success and future growth.

Using mathematical simulations, I show that, while in regular competition all have equal opportunities and many small firms survive simultaneously, in technological competition an early sequence of successful events endows those few leaders, who have such a realization, with an advantage of higher success probability than their competitors. Such advantage typically builds up to a point that it becomes overwhelming, leaving all lagging firms or any new entrants with negligible probability of ever gaining significant market share. Technological competition thus results in one or very few winners taking it all. This model of technological competition is then a dynamic theory of the formation of superstar firms in the absence of policy to prevent it.

Once I introduce an explicit public policy that prevents any firm from acquiring more than a designated proportion of technological and economic market share, the conclusion changes dramatically. Such a policy increases the number of surviving firms, reduces industrial concentration and *increases social welfare*! Society at large is made better off because average productivity increases, product prices are lower, and there are more products to choose from in the market. Society is made better off by preventing the superstar firms, who are indeed the most productive, from increasing in size and exercising increased market power that comes with being superstar firms.

0.6   Policy Proposals to Contain Market Power and Reverse Inequality

In chapters 8–10, I outline the various components of a new policy framework to contain market power. These chapters are not technical, and the policy-oriented reader may consult them for the detailed motivation for each proposal. Here I briefly highlight some of these proposals.

0.6.1   Antitrust and Patent Policy

My central proposal is to expand the Sherman antitrust regime and include an explicit goal of preventing market power from exceeding the level granted by patent law. I propose outlawing and aggressively cracking down on strategies firms use to consolidate market power. The goal of this policy is not to prevent a firm from gaining market power by innovating but to prevent it from consolidating and expanding such power, and turning it into a permanent economic force. To this end, I propose banning firms with more than $500 million in revenue from acquiring their technological competitors. Evidence reveals that some firms acquire other firms with competing technologies or their patents in order to suppress them (see Cunningham et al., 2021). There is also evidence that too many patents are issued. To address these issues, I propose significant changes to patent law:

- There should exist two types of patents, primary and secondary. I propose primary patents be awarded a twenty-year life, but secondary patents should only have a life of ten years.
- The number of patents issued should be reduced by raising the degree of novelty required for a patent.

0.6.2   Improve Functioning of the Labor Market

Substantial evidence has surfaced in recent years on the deterioration of working conditions, particularly for the 60 percent of U.S. workers without a college degree. The data indicate these workers are experiencing increased rates of alcoholism, drug abuse, obesity, family breakdown, and chronic disease. Krueger (2017) and others document employment practices that disempower lower-ranking workers, making their jobs unstable or lower paying. These practices include unnecessary noncompete clauses, wage fixing by employers, and widespread use of contract labor. This rise in contracting deprives workers of the benefits of stable employment, better working conditions, and an environment where a worker can develop human capital. To restore vitality to the labor market, I propose a long list of reforms that aim to improve working conditions and the functioning of labor markets.

0.6.3   Taxation

To attain a more egalitarian income and wealth distribution, I join many others who propose that the top marginal personal income tax rate should be over 50 percent, and perhaps as high as 70 percent (see Diamond and Saez, 2011; Piketty et al., 2014). My focus is mainly on taxation of corporate profits and monopoly wealth that arise from market power. The main concern with such a tax is that it could cause a decline in the rate of innovation. I study the effect of profits taxation on the incentive to innovate and conclude that a tax of up to 50 percent of monopoly profits will not have a significant effect on the rate of innovations. I thus propose to tax these profits at 50 percent. This is not a 50 percent tax on accounting corporate profits. Monopoly profits are computed by subtracting the cost of capital owned by the firm from the standard reported accounting corporate profits. I do not support a permanent wealth taxation but support such a short-term tax for the purpose of financing a national fund for equity and democracy, discussed next.

0.6.4   National Fund for Equity and Democracy

The motivation for the fund is the need for a permanent institution tasked with the redistribution of profits to those at the bottom of the income distributions to increase mobility, restore the middle class, and enable a partial compensation of those who are displaced by innovations. I briefly outline my proposal.

I have explained that we need to remedy the current no-compensation policy and that such a need is permanent. Therefore we need to create a permanent institution to address the problem with a long-term horizon, free of annual budgetary considerations. To that end I propose creating a permanent fund to increase the flow, back into the middle class, of the children of workers in the bottom 50 percent of the income distribution. It will be financed by taxes on the gains from technology. The fund does not aim to alter the employment status of those in the bottom 50 percent. Rather, it aims to give their children opportunities equal to those available to the children of the wealthy, or at least to close that opportunity gap. The fund will own 10 percent of the corporate sector market value, to be held in trust by the general public for the benefit of the children of those in the bottom of the income distribution. The annual expenditures of the fund will be dedicated to upgrading all levels of education and health, aiming to equip them with the human capital to return to the middle class.

0.6.5   The Urgent Need for Public Investment in Basic Research

Substantial evidence shows that public investment in basic research has played a vital role in the development of modern technology. These studies also show that, to promote growth, public policy must invest in long-term basic research. National Science Foundation data show that in the early 1970s, federal support of basic research amounted to more than 1.2 percent of GDP. That fraction had declined to about 0.7 percent in 2020. With the growing importance of science and technology in the economy, cutting spending on basic research is shortsighted. Raising the public contribution to basic research back to 1.3–1.4% of GDP would be a boon for economic growth.

0.7   A Final Thought

In September 1970, Milton Friedman (1970) published an article extolling the virtues of profit maximization by firms. He rejected the idea of business having social responsibility as a form of socialism and argued their only duty was to their shareholders. In the context of the Cold War and the contrast between free-market capitalism and Soviet-style economic planning, this argument carried the day. But ignoring the Soviet alternative and examining American capitalism on its own, it is obvious that without any public policy to regulate business, Friedman would agree that included in profit-maximizing activities are dumping toxic waste in rivers or building a five-story condo in Yosemite Valley. In the context of this book, merging with competitors to expand technological market power or acquiring competitors or their technology to suppress it is also profit-maximizing behavior, and these are actually widespread practices today.

Friedman (1970) did not explain to his readers that he was also opposed to antitrust laws on the highly questionable grounds that competition would remove all market power. He also opposed any redistributive taxation to compensate those whose income declined as a result of rising market power. Moreover, in *Capitalism and Freedom*, Friedman (1962) argues that political freedom is impossible without free-market capitalism and that a capitalist market economy performs at its best level only if it is free from government regulations and public interference. That is, government is not the solution; it is the problem! Again, in the context of a comparison with the Soviet planned economy, this appeared to be a compelling vision, and it had a profound impact around the world. But in the context of economic thought, it is obvious that society has complex needs, and the private sector can solve only some of our problems. To explore an example, I note first that economics textbooks provide wide accounts of markets that fail to generate socially desirable outcomes when firms maximize profits. The failure of the private retirement insurance system resulted in the elderly being the group suffering the deepest poverty early in the twentieth century, yet Friedman did not view businesses as responsible for contributing to their workers' retirement security. He went further and opposed even Social Security, whose greatest achievement has been the elimination of poverty among the elderly. Friedman and his supporters were successful in persuading the country to make the drastic policy changes of the 1980s. We know today the dire consequences of that choice.

Effective economic policy is needed to attain many public goals such as maintaining the economy's infrastructure, combating climate change, or controlling the technological monopoly power of corporations. The best social outcome is one resulting from profit maximization by private firms, as sought by Friedman, but constrained by the boundaries set by society. These boundaries incentivize the private sector to improve social welfare. In addition, direct action by the public sector is needed to carry out those socially desirable tasks that a profit-motivated private sector is neither able nor designed to perform. This requires recognition of the different roles played by the private and the public sectors, free of business using its economic power and armies of lobbyists to undermine the implementation of the democratic will. In contrast with Friedman's (1962) belief that democratic freedom is impossible without free-market capitalism, I find that democratic freedom is impossible without the collective action of public policy to prevent capitalism from weakening the foundations of democracy.

CHAPTER 1

THE NEXUS OF MARKET POWER, TECHNOLOGY, AND PUBLIC POLICY

1.1 Technology and Competition

In his address to the annual meeting of the American Economic Association in 1954, Simon Kuznets declared that capitalism under democracy led to an equitable equilibrium, where democratic institutions and policy contain the expansion of profits and enable labor to benefit from rising productivity (see Kuznets, 1955). This optimistic view echoes an earlier statement by Keynes (1939) that the constancy of relative shares was a "bit of a miracle." This miracle was, unfortunately, short-lived. The economic record since the 1970s shows that relative shares are not constant and that the distribution of income and wealth is not only far from egalitarian but is actually on a steep trajectory toward increased inequality.

Recent research on the changing income distribution since the 1970s has proceeded on two interrelated tracks: the study of the functional distribution of income and the study of personal inequality of income and wealth. In relation to the first track, the Bureau of Labor Statistics reports reveal that, since the 1970s, wages have risen slower than labor productivity, and labor's relative share has fallen. There are some persistent disagreements about measurement, such as the best price index for computing real wages, how to treat income of the self-employed, or how to treat wages paid to management. There is, however, general agreement about the declining labor share. On the other track, the seminal works of Piketty and Saez (2003) and Piketty (2014), based on Internal Revenue Service income data, revealed changing patterns of personal distribution of income and wealth over the preceding century. Their work shows that the degree of inequality in the United States has risen sharply since the late 1970s. This has held true to a point that all measures of inequality in 2019 are at levels close to those at the end of the nineteenth century, during the First Gilded Age. The United States, as well as the United Kingdom, Canada, and Australia, have been marching back to a time of massive inequality, marking this era as the Second Gilded Age.

Why have wages risen slowly and inequality risen rapidly, and what is the connection between these two clearly related phenomena? Why did inequality rise so dramatically in the late nineteenth century during the First Gilded Age, and why is the level of inequality today close to the levels at that time? Why, as Kuznets and Keynes observed, was labor share relatively stable in the mid-twentieth century, and what transformed the egalitarian conditions of that time into the spiraling inequality seen since the late 1970s? These questions are clearly connected, and to consider them in this way requires a single explanatory theory. This is what I endeavor to do in this book. To support my theory, I explore the history of market power in the United States from 1889 to 2017 and show the essential role that market power plays in answering these interrelated questions.

This first chapter outlines the theory that frames the rest of the book. It explains that changing market power is the cause of all changes in both functional and personal distribution of income. Market power itself is determined as an equilibrium of the two forces of technology and economic policy. But for market power to become such a central force, there must exist a primary economic mechanism by which it is generated. I thus start with a simple but basic observation.

Perfect competition requires that all firms have equal profit opportunities and make zero profits above cost. If the price of a product is above marginal cost, a firm in a perfectly competitive economy can hire capital and labor, expand output, and make profits by selling the product at a slightly lower price. There is no response available to the incumbent firm other than to expand its own output and cut its price. The implication is that, in equilibrium, no firm has any advantage and the price equals marginal cost. The ability to innovate and alter the technology changes all this. An innovating firm quickly gains an advantage over all other firms. Its innovation is effectively a valuable piece of knowledge that can be used to earn extra profits above capital costs. Such extra profit reflects the fact that an innovation gives an innovator some market power relative to other firms. To compete with such an incumbent innovator, a firm must do much more than just hire capital and labor. It must also invent something superior, which is often very difficult, and then it must face the response of the stronger incumbent who may enhance the initial innovation or deploy an arsenal of other strategies. Technological competition is very different from standard atomistic competition and should be studied on its own terms. This explains why one of the central themes of this book is that innovations enable firms to acquire market power from their control over technological knowledge not available to competitors.

This fact has, since the Industrial Revolution, led capitalism to pursue technology as a tool of excess profits. Despite the consequences of this pursuit, it is a near-universal view that the costs of the initial monopoly power gained by innovating firms are a small price to pay for the dramatic gains in productivity and economic growth brought about by technology innovations. The policy challenge underlying much of this book arises from the conflict between innovation's vital role in driving up economic growth and the negative consequences of the increased market power gained by innovative firms.

The problem is that the initial market power gained by innovation is only the beginning. Modern firms use diverse strategies to exploit this initial advantage, making market power a durable feature of an economy in the age of technology. A strong policy is needed to restrain the consolidation of such market power and limit its expansion if free-market capitalism is to be compatible with democracy. Many questions arise concerning the process of expanding and consolidating market power. Why is technological competition not sufficient to constrain the growth of market power? Given that innovation has, for a very long time, shaped human history, what is the origin of the nexus between market power and technology? In this chapter, I address these questions and explore the mechanism behind the growth of market power.

This part is covered in sections 1.2 through 1.5. The second part of the chapter provides a preliminary investigation of the consequences of market power; this is covered in sections 1.6 through 1.8. It is preliminary in the sense that, although most of the book is devoted to a study of these effects, this chapter develops the general methodological principles underlying the remainder of the book.

1.2 The Impact of Technology on Competition

Technical change is a central component of the engine driving economic progress. A growing economy is propelled forward by population growth, capital accumulation, and technological change. In the long run, however, it is technology that is the main force raising living standards. Technical change is also the essence of entrepreneurial development in a modern capitalist economy. Without such changes, most managerial functions of the firm become routine and subject to simple decision rules. Major changes in technology are driven by scientific discoveries and basic research, most of which takes place away from the business environment. The translation of that research and discovery into business applications is done by firms through their research and development

(R&D) that commercializes these discoveries. It is the private sector that transforms inventions into profit-oriented enterprises, and the knowledge produced through such innovation is privately owned. Businesses are motivated to protect their ownership of such knowledge from competing entities.

The protection of newly created knowledge takes two forms. First, an innovative firm gains experience and an organizational structure that is adapted to the knowledge it has created. It holds both trade secrets and a superior market position, and these provide initial protection against the use of that knowledge by others. Second, our laws and institutions protect intellectual property rights to incentivize future innovation. Such legal protection comes in the form of a patent or copyright that grants the innovative firm initial monopoly power over the knowledge created as compensation for the effort and risk taken in its development. This arrangement constitutes a bargain between society and innovators: in exchange for an initial temporary monopoly, innovators publicly disclose all technical details of their innovations. The term "monopoly power" is, for many, suggestive of a firm's engagement in illegal acts because there have been periods in history when such power primarily resulted from collusion, intimidation, corruption, and other illegal acts. Such illegal monopoly power is not the subject of this book. Rather, its focus is on market power created by technological superiority, which is legal and in fact actively encouraged by public policy. To distinguish these forms of power, I will thus often refer to the power with which I am concerned as "technological market power."

Technological market power is translated by its owner to an advantage in some market for products or services, and it takes many forms. The technology may be used to produce a novel product; it may enable some firm to cut its cost of production or to take advantage of suppliers who provide specialized goods or services used to produce a desired product. In all such situations, a technological market power is translated into an ability to affect the price of some good or service and that enables the firm to earn extra profits. That is, an ability to have some control over pricing of goods or services is the market power used by a firm to extract monopoly profits from the market. The standard economic terminology of rents has, in the past, related these profits to the pricing of land and does not adequately describe the nature of such profits.

There is a related point on terminology. As noted, innovations result in diverse forms of market power. They may lead to monopoly, to an oligopoly where several firms control a market, to monopolistic competition with many producers having power over their own market segments, or to a monopsony where a single buyer has power over its suppliers. I am not concerned with the specific forms of firms' market power but with the fact that each firm has a proprietary technology with which it can exercise market power in some market segment. The term "technological market power" is thus used as a general reference to any of these diverse forms.

I use the term "initial" market power since innovation is only the first stage in a long and complex process. An innovator is the winner of a technological race in which experience and knowledge are gained and an organizational structure formed. This provides an initial first-mover advantage. Being granted a patent or other legal protection of private intellectual property boosts market power but is not essential to its formation. The advantage of first mover enables the formation of market power even without the legal protection of patents and intellectual property rights. Many firms do not seek this legal protection and choose to rely instead on industrial secrecy. In the case of patents, firms prefer not to disclose to competitors the knowledge inherent in the patent application process because such knowledge is valuable in creating future innovations that may supersede those patented. More generally, they prefer to keep secret as much of their technological know-how as possible. In addition to relying on state laws that protect against the theft of corporate secrets, firms deploy various security measures to protect their secrets.

I will later explain that a firm with an initial market power derived from innovation will use a variety of techniques to entrench the power it gained in its market segment and expand into other market segments. Consequently, a wave of new innovations will, after a period of entrenchment and expansion, raise the average market power of firms in the economy. This is an articulation of the first part of the theory advanced in this book, that technology is the main driving force of market power in a capitalist market economy.

The impact of technology on market structure varies over time because of the way innovation waves are realized. To understand these technological waves, it is useful to distinguish between small changes within a given technological paradigm and revolutionary technologies that change everything. The latter is what Bresnahan and Trajtenberg (1995) call general-purpose technologies (GPTs), which are innovations of fundamental importance like the steam engine, electricity, or the internet. The feature that distinguishes a GPT is that it serves as a founding technology or platform for further technological innovation. The technologies built on a GPT transform all sectors of the economy. GPTs reflect fundamental changes in the state of human knowledge. They originate in basic research; reflect scientific advancement; and occur very infrequently, once in a generation or even once in a century. A GPT is not the consequence of an invention by a specific entering firm who challenges a specific incumbent firm. Instead, a GPT applies broadly to virtually all sectors of the economy and changes the way society functions. Such massive innovations give rise to extensive technological competition in various markets, with the winners gaining initial market power. I show in this chapter that such initial market power provides a firm with the profit and economic advantage that enable it to consolidate and expand that market power as the GPT-related innovations spread through the economy.

The idea that patents and other legal intellectual property protections imply the existence of technological monopoly power has been well recognized by economists. Nevertheless, most have not been concerned with this problem. They have argued that such power is temporary because patent protection is temporary, that it will be contained by technological competition and by "creative destruction" of new entrants. In addition, it is generally believed that the magnitude of the costs of monopoly power is small relative to the social benefits of rising productivity and economic growth. I question these notions. The central argument developed in this book is that increases in technological market power are not temporary, that technological competition will not remove this power, and the costs of its growth and consolidation are very high. Moreover, instead of thinking of monopoly power as a necessary temporary price of promoting innovation, my theory proposes the converse: that innovations are the cause of the growth of durable market power. Therefore, in an economy undergoing technological change, market power is a permanent feature. Its level fluctuates but is nonetheless a permanent and insidious force with harmful economic and social effects. Market power results in rising income and wealth inequality and in economic power being concentrated in the hands of a few. Unchecked, this force erodes the foundation of democracy and, with time, a democracy takes on the features of plutocracy or even oligarchy. In chapter 4, I present empirical evidence that twice in U.S. history such dynamic forces produced extreme results. Although innovations will continue to generate initial market power, a strong policy to limit and restrain the consolidation of this power is necessary for free-market capitalism to be compatible with democracy.

The fact that increased innovation causes increased market power and less competition creates a stark choice: an economy can have perfect competition, or it can have private knowledge, but it cannot have both. Market power that results from private ownership of knowledge sets up a conflict between competitive institutions and innovation. Therefore, economic growth that results from technical progress cannot be correctly described by a model of a competitive economy. This conclusion conflicts with the vast literature on economic growth, developed in the post–World War II era. This literature was based on models in which economic growth was caused by technological progress and markets were perfectly competitive. But results based on perfect competition with technical change are internally inconsistent. Consequently, the "stylized facts" of Kaldor (1961) do not hold, and standard neoclassical competitive growth models (e.g., Uzawa, 1961 or Diamond, 1965), based on the Solow (1956) or Swan (1956) models, do not describe the behavior of a realistic economy. If monopoly power fluctuates over time, the standard neoclassical result of constant relative shares in an economy with neutral technical change does not hold. This is the case even when a Cobb-Douglas production function is used. There are many applications of competitive neoclassical growth theory that must be revised when monopoly power is present. These include Solow's (1957) measure of total factor productivity and some of the policy implications developed in Arrow and Kurz (1970).

The nexus between technology and market power, together with the need for a revision of growth theory, has been widely anticipated in the literature for a very long time. Arrow (1962), like Schumpeter (1934), stresses that monopoly patent protection is required to allow innovators to appropriate the benefits of their innovations. Arrow (1962) actually assumes patents secure monopoly power forever. Grossman and Stiglitz (1980) demonstrate that a competitive equilibrium cannot exist where private firms undertake the costly production of information. That is, for an economy to produce costly information, producers must have monopoly power. All work in industrial organization on innovation and R&D assumes that innovators have monopoly power (see, for example, Tirole, 1988, chapter 10). Yet these theoretical developments had little impact on the mainstream economic growth literature of the 1950–1980 era. A possible explanation for this is the ingrained belief in the unimportance of legally protected market power because it was seen as temporary. Even when market power was explicitly introduced by Romer (1990) in the endogenous growth theory, or by the Schumpeterian version of the growth process (Aghion and Howitt, 1992; Barro and Sala-I-Martin, 1992), it was combined with a particular form of technological competition that permits innovators free entry and assume it to be a mechanism that restrains the growth of technological monopoly power and maintains it at a low level, close to zero.

The main task in this first chapter is to show that initial market power, unrestrained by policy, leads to the consolidation of that power and that this process of consolidation makes market power a durable feature of an economy with technological growth. To that end, I will explore the nature of technological competition and show how it is different from competition, as it is typically understood. I note first that the nexus between technology and market power is relatively new. Inventiveness has existed in all of human history, while technological market power is a creation of the modern capitalist economy. It must be the case then that financial compensation is not the only motive for innovation. Indeed, the idea of financially compensating creators of knowledge through granting them legally protected monopoly power over their creations is relatively recent. I start by tracing the history of this idea.

1.3   Capitalism and the Quest for Market Power

How long has technology served as an active channel for profit-maximizing entrepreneurs in their quest for excess returns with some protected market power? Human inventions have transformed civilizations, but older innovations did not emerge from well-developed capitalist market economies. For example, it is now well known that as late as the seventeenth or early eighteenth century, Imperial China was technologically ahead of the West (Lin, 1995; Liu and Liu, 2007). This raises the question of what the motives of Chinese innovators were. Needham (1965, p. 17) reports that most large-scale Chinese inventions were created in imperial workshops. Some innovations were made by high officials who benefited, as a result of their innovation, in their bureaucratic careers, but these were isolated cases. Needham (1965, p. 32) documents that most inventions credited to officials were most likely the work of artisans in their employ. For these artisans, there was little in the way of upward mobility. Needham stresses that the aristocracy took little pride in technological inventions. Astronomy and mathematics were considered much more prestigious pursuits. High administrators who spearheaded technological projects were rewarded as capable administrators, but there is no evidence of significant rewards to lower-ranking innovators.

A deeper fact drives Needham's observations. The prevailing view in Imperial China was that all knowledge they had, as passed to them by their ancestors, was all there was to know. Innovations were nothing but rediscoveries of facts that were known to their ancestors but had been forgotten. This means that innovations were accidental events, not results of a cumulative intentional knowledge creation (see Mokyr, 2018). In addition, all useful innovations were expropriated for the benefit of the sovereign; therefore, even accidental innovations were not expected to be a source of added returns. Under such conditions, innovators could typically not expect to gain even from accidental discoveries. Therefore, from a commercial perspective, one could not build a business expecting to benefit from innovations. Whatever privately owned commercial interests existed in ancient times, no evidence exists to establish any nexus between business and technology. But even without these incentives, a significant number of innovations occurred, reflecting the natural force of human curiosity.

Similar ideas about human knowledge also prevailed in the West. This worldview implies that there is no point in trying to develop a theory of natural phenomena or conduct controlled experiments because there is no knowledge to be learned and nature is far too complex for humans to replicate it in a controlled environment. Even Newton, early in the eighteenth century, did not believe his discoveries were new. He thought all were known to the ancient Greeks but had been subsequently lost (see Iliffe, 1995, pp. 165–168; Mokyr, 2018, p. 101).

Profit-maximizing businesspeople did, of course, search for opportunities to earn excess profits, but, given the prevailing worldview, technology or innovations were of limited interest. There are, however, exceptions. Around 1493, Johannes Gutenberg, a goldsmith, invented the movable-type printing press, independently of its invention in China. In the West, this was a new invention, and if Gutenberg could have prevented others from copying it, he would have made a great deal of money. But, naturally, he could not. Seeking ways to profit from his invention, he came up with the idea of printing an ornate illustrated Bible that would be sufficiently unique to create a differentiated product. The printing press would allow him to produce his version much more cheaply than a hand-written Bible that requires the work of a scribe. Even this did not yield a profit because, according to Hessels (1911), Gutenberg borrowed capital to finance the project and ended up in a dispute with the lenders. He lost the case in court and, following default, had to transfer ownership of his printing shop to the lenders, who continued to print books under their own label.

Gutenberg's failure to profit from his invention illustrates the need, under capitalism, for some protection of an innovator's intellectual property rights. The need for profitability is obviously the ultimate reason for introducing patent protection. However, the printing press is an isolated example for the time; in-novations by private individuals were rare in the fifteenth century. Other major innovations during that century were in shipbuilding, but these were made with the support of various sovereigns.

In the absence of intellectual property protections, there were two other routes open to an active business who sought excess returns at that time. First, the business could find a local lord or petition the sovereign who could grant it a legal right to charge a toll, collect a tax, or extract a natural resource, with the proceeds being shared with the lord or sovereign. Second, it could explore routes to distant lands in Asia or Africa and build a network of personal rela-tionships along each route. Naturally, these arrangements would involve a great deal of secrecy, and the entire enterprise would be very risky. The first approach amounted to gaining a legal monopoly over a resource, and one can easily find such legal monopolies in the twenty-first century as well. The second approach entails creating a monopoly over a newly established trade route, protected as a valuable trade secret. Competitors could not easily replicate it because it re-quired privately developed information, trading connections and security ar-rangements en route, and a reputation for reliable trading. Military support of the city or state was helpful as well. These barriers to entry are how Italy's city-states accumulated much of the wealth that made them Europe's commercial and cultural centers (see Greif, 2006).

In parallel with the Italian development of trading routes in the Mediter-ranean and over the Arabian desert to southern Asia, world explorations ex-panded in the fifteenth and sixteenth centuries, led by Spanish and Portuguese explorers often financed and supported by the monarchs. The Spanish efforts concentrated on what was known as the New World, mostly in search of gold and silver. The Portuguese established the first European trade routes to African destinations. Their ultimate goal, however, was to develop ocean routes for spice trading with India that avoided the risks of going to South Asia through the Arabian Peninsula. Vasco da Gama reached India in 1498, following a century of exploratory voyages by the Portuguese off the coast of Africa. This enabled the Portuguese to establish a European monopoly on the spice routes to India, and in later years, on routes to destinations in south and east Asia, from where they could import to Europe other valuable commodities. For about a century, until challenged by Dutch, English, and French traders, Portugal maintained naval supremacy and a monopoly on the route around the Cape of Good Hope. The point relevant to the discussion here is that this exploration was motivated by a desire to establish a monopoly on trade. It resulted, in the centuries that followed, in the award of royal charters to establish trading companies with exclusive monopoly power over trade, production, mineral extraction, and sometimes even the deployment of military force.

The British crown uses royal charters to authorize diverse activities such as the establishment of universities or public corporations, and many historically issued charters remain in existence today. Examples include the University of Cambridge, the Bank of England, and the British Broadcasting Corporation. However, what is relevant here is the considerable number of joint-stock companies awarded monopoly power over territories and trade routes around the world through charters issued by various European sovereigns.[1] The charter for each company typically granted it the rights to a specific territory claimed by the sovereign, including legal title to assets, a monopoly on trade or production, and governmental and military jurisdiction in that territory.

A royal charter granted in Britain took the form of "letters patent," which means an open letter, implying its availability for public inspection. The word *patent* comes from the Latin word *patere*, which means "to lay open." Letters patent were issued by the crown from as early as medieval times to confer diverse rights and privileges. Most monopoly powers granted by the crown were based on a profit-sharing arrangement, which proved a boon to the crown's finances. In 1624, Parliament, guarding its revenue-raising powers, passed the Statute of Monopolies, which invalidated many letters patent and curtailed the crown's power to grant monopoly powers. However, the statute did permit the continued issuing of letters patent for inventors, and these grant monopoly rights for a fixed duration. This is the origin of the British patent system.

The emergence of a formal patent system in the seventeenth century is not accidental. Its development is part of the Age of Enlightenment, when views about the effect of humankind on the natural environment shifted radically, and business attitudes to technology were transformed. Mokyr (2018) considers Francis Bacon (1561–1626) and Isaac Newton (1642–1727) to be the leading "cultural entrepreneurs" who helped usher in the Age of Enlightenment. The hallmark of the age is the change in the role of science and technology in shaping human life and of the understanding of humankind's ability to control nature. Although it

---

[1] The English East India Company is well known; what is less known is that there were actually seven East India Companies established by the different European countries.

took another century for the Industrial Revolution to get underway, the Age of Enlightenment was a time when businesses saw the possibility of alternatives to natural resource concessions and geographic discoveries as paths to excess returns. It pointed to technology as the primary source of new opportunities for market power, excess returns, and economic growth, and this understanding cemented the nexus between capitalism and technology. At the same time, a new legal structure, patent law, emerged to motivate innovators and provide business with the incentive to take risks and invest the effort and capital required to exploit technological opportunities.

Questions about the nature and scope of patent protection have long been debated and remain somewhat unresolved (see, for example, Johns, 2009; Boldrin and Levine, 2013). In essence, sovereigns have historically granted legal monopoly power to align the interests of private business owners with their own. The fact that the resultant market power conflicts with free competition and equal opportunity has led to calls for alternate forms of compensation for innovation, such as prizes or other forms of public recognition; these alternatives have rarely been tried in the business world. Indeed, most businesspeople see the pursuit of monopoly power as a noble goal and would oppose the government granting less of it (see, for example, Thiel, 2014).

In *The Wealth of Nations*, Smith (1776) expresses his opposition to monopolies but does not recognize the central role in economic growth played by technology and technological monopolies. He formulates the now-standard competitive model of a local firm that optimally allocates capital and labor and says that an owner of capital "endeavours to employ his capital as near home as he can, and consequently as much as he can in the support of domestic industry" (p. 421). In contrast with the efficiency of competition, monopolies are the "enemies of good management" (p. 147), "they derange the natural distribution of the stock of society" (p. 596) and "are supported by unjust and cruel laws" (p. 612). Yet he insists that

> when a company of merchants undertake, at their own risk and expense, to establish a new trade with some remote and barbarous nation, it may not be unreasonable to incorporate them into a joint stock company, and to grant them, in case of their success, a monopoly of the trade for a certain number of years.... A temporary monopoly of this kind may be vindicated upon the same principle upon which a like monopoly of a new machine is granted to its inventor, and that of a new book to its author.

Writing in 1776, Adam Smith failed to recognize that the most important force that builds the wealth of nations is technological progress and that specialization and thrift play only a supporting role. Therefore, his small-government, laissez-faire economy that lacks a strong policy to stabilize market power generated by technology is in fact inconsistent with pure competition. In writing *The Wealth of Nations*, Smith could not anticipate that over the next 150 years, the wealth of Great Britain would rise mostly from profits generated by two types of monopoly power: monopolies of British companies granted the exclusive right to operate in various parts of the British empire, and monopolies created by the innovators at the forefront of the Industrial Revolution.[2]

1.4   The Durability of Technological Market Power

1.4.1   First-Mover Advantage Versus Consolidated Market Power

I turn now to trace the path of market power, born first out of an initial innovation. It can grow or shrink as a consequence of strategic decisions made by the innovative firm. However, a technological race may be won by one or a few firms. Evidence in the United States suggests that market power is often shared in duopolies or oligopolies, in which firms use different proprietary technologies, produce differentiated products, and have dominant market power in their own market segments. In assessing the durability of market power, I will repeatedly refer to the initial innovator or to the firm with initial market power, but these statements should be understood as applying to each innovating firm that, after winning a technological race, is a dominant player in its own market segment.

The first-mover advantages of an innovator manifest in a variety of ways and have long-term consequences. As noted earlier, a first mover is the first to gain experience in producing and selling a new product and service. Because experience typically lowers cost as firms learn by doing, a first mover usually has the advantage of a lower cost. A new product or service requires potential users to know about it, learn how to use it, and be able to incorporate it into their normal life. A first mover therefore has the opportunity to set the standards for the industry, educate users, and develop a reputation for reliability, even if subsequently developed products are superior. The typewriter QWERTY keyboard layout, video home system (VHS), and the disk-operating system (DOS) are

---

[2]The conventional wisdom has been that innovators during the Industrial Revolution were poorly remunerated because intellectual property rights were not sufficiently enforced at that time. I have explained that property rights are only one piece of the puzzle that helps the innovator acquire the advantage of the first mover. Equally important is the consolidation stage, when legal protection is less important and other factors play a more important role. Many contemporary innovators forego legal protection altogether and rely on trade secrets, asymmetric information, and reputation to establish the first-mover advantage. It is thus not surprising that Bottomley (2019) uses modern research methods to demonstrate that the conventional view of the Industrial Revolution is false and, as would be predicted by this argument, innovators in the Industrial Revolution were well compensated.

well-known examples where the first movers set the technical standards and prospered because of their initial advantage, despite the fact that their products were inferior. The first-mover monopolist also has the advantage of being able to establish political connections to secure needed permits for operations and banking and capital market relations that would not be equally available to a later potential entrant. These same advantages can accrue to first movers with superior technology who rely only upon industrial secrecy, ownership of private information, experience, or reputation to establish their market position. This explains why, in many cases, foregoing the legal monopoly power of patents is optimal for the consolidation of future market power.

Without strategies to consolidate market power by erecting barriers to entry, the first-mover advantage would fade away. Patents have a limited duration, and trade secrets can be revealed. The reality, however, is that once an initial monopoly is established, firms use a wide array of strategies to build economic and technological moats that block potential entrants. Below, I outline the most common strategies firms employ:

1. *A patent strategy.* A firm can engage in preemptive research that builds upon the initial innovation by constructing a multilayered system of patents, sometimes called a patent pyramid. These subsequent patents reflect marginal improvements on components of the initial patent, creating a mixture of old and updated patents. When the old patent expires, the confusing morass of marginal patents can prevent competitors from entering the market, effectively extending the initial patent's effectiveness (see Gilbert and Newbery, 1982). For example, General Electric owned the Edison patent for the incandescent lamp, issued in 1880, but it continued in its efforts to improve the design. Over time virtually every part of the lamp was patented: the lamp's glass, the casing into which the glass is placed, the material from which the casing was made, and the filament used for illumination. New patents for improved filaments were issued well into the 1920s. Such a pattern of issuing a sequence of updated, sometimes marginally improved versions of the same product is a routine business practice. To prevent competition, some firms patent even inferior alternatives to their invention. DuPont did this with nylon, patenting 200 similar synthetic fibers it had no plans to use in its products but in doing so prevented other firms from entering.

2. *Acquire potentially competing firms or their technologies.* Technology firms often make such acquisitions and subsequently either develop the acquired technologies or suppress them. Innovation suppression is intended to prevent the obsolescence of a firm's profitable product or service and to allow time for it to upgrade its product line. Large technology firms own a vast number of patents acquired from potential competitors. Although many are being developed further, many others are simply shelved (see Gilbert and Newbery, 1982, who explore the motive for shelving, and Cunningham et al., 2021 for empirical evidence). If a patent

for a competing technology is offered for sale, a monopoly firm has a stronger motive to bid up the price of the patent than a potential competitive new entrant because it has more to lose (its present monopoly profits). This is known as the efficiency effect of deterring entry (see Gilbert and Newbery, 1982; Tirole, 1988, p. 393). There is a substantial information asymmetry in the act of technological acquisition. A firm with a technological monopoly has more knowledge of the technology and can better assess the value of a potentially competing technology. It is thus able to acquire that technology in its infancy, before others recognize its value. In addition, with financial asymmetry, the incumbent monopoly firm has the resources needed to acquire the new technology. A (typically young) innovator faces a choice between selling the technology for a price that will make him wealthy overnight, and entering into risky economic battle with a strong and well-financed adversary. It is not surprising that most choose to sell their innovation.

3. *Suppress innovations by intimidating and destroying potential competitors.* A strategy routinely used by leading firms to deter potential entrants is to launch a campaign of intimidation and economic pressure against suppliers and to use various other tactics that suppress innovation. An example of the extent of such strategies was revealed in the investigation of Microsoft by the European Commission (2009) and in the record of the trial in the U.S. case.[3] The failure of Netscape was the result of a campaign against it by Microsoft. However, it is also widely acknowledged that the most important impact of the lengthy antitrust suit against Microsoft was the suspension of its campaign against potential competitors. The result was an opening up of the market that permitted the resurgence of innovations that enabled Google, Apple, Amazon, and Facebook to take their own turn at rapid growth. These companies have, in turn, become the forces that routinely pursue the same strategies once used by Microsoft to suppress competition. Another example that recently came to light in congressional hearings is Facebook's threat to use its "Facebook Camera" application against Instagram, which it subsequently acquired. This experience provides the basis for the policy studied in chapter 7.

4. *Scale and network externalities.* If there are increasing returns to scale over a wide range of output, the incumbent has an advantage. To reduce cost to the level of the incumbent, an entrant has to grow to a similar size. If they fail to grow rapidly at the outset, their higher costs will result in losses (see Schmalensee, 1981). Network externalities arise when the value of a product or service increases with the size of the user base. These externalities are, in a sense, the flip side of returns to scale: the value per unit increases with the quantity sold rather than costs per unit falling. Network externalities can operate within a market; for example, people prefer the same social network their friends use, and credit card customers

---

[3] See *United States v. Microsoft Corp.* (2001).

prefer a card that is accepted by most merchants. But they can also operate between markets. For a more popular car, there are more dealers to service it, and a computer with a larger user base will have more software available at a lower cost. Modern technology offers many of these advantages to the established monopoly firm, making it harder for a competitor to enter the market.

5. *Create an ecosystem of dependence.* By creating new products, services, or technologies that can function only when linked to the initial technology, a firm with market power broadens its reach beyond the initial innovation. Linking many technologies in this manner creates a corporate ecosystem of products and services, expanding market power far beyond the initial innovations. For a potential competitor, this makes entry much more difficult. This technique is well recognized in antitrust law, where it is called tying and bundling, but restrictions on the practice have proved difficult to enforce. The most celebrated legal challenge was the successful suit brought by the Justice Department against Microsoft for bundling their internet browser with their Windows operating system. Microsoft was forced to settle, but the lawsuit failed to deter similar behavior.

6. *Reputation for quality.* If a firm introduces a new high-quality product or service, it sets a technological standard to which customers adjust, giving it a major advantage. A good reputation gives the firm a natural priority that arises from the inherent uncertainty about the quality of new competing entrants. This reputational difference between the incumbent firm and potential new entrants can become a crucial part of a monopoly strategy when the service provided is important (for example, if it is related to health), and the cost to the customer in case of bad service is very high.

7. *Loyalty programs and volume discounting.* An incumbent firm can offer customers rewards for purchasing its products that accumulate over time, functionally lowering the price of future purchases. These rewards allow the incumbent firm to undercut future rivals on the basis of price. A similar mechanism is volume discounts, which were at issue in the *Advanced Micro Devices (AMD) v. Intel* (2007) antitrust suit. Intel set a high price on its initial processors but offered companies a discount if they purchased all their processors from Intel and none from AMD. This meant that if at some point in time buyers decreased their orders of Intel processors and raised those of AMD processors, at the time of the switch they would lose the Intel discount. Consequently, the effective marginal cost of the AMD processors would be far too high to justify the switch.

8. *Location.* The physical location of a new firm can offer a big advantage (see Prescott and Visscher, 1977). A good location could entail proximity to customers, suppliers, or government offices, enabling the firm to establish advantageous early relationships that are hard to replicate.

9. *Asymmetric information.* In a broad sense, asymmetry of information is the general condition required for maintaining market power because it means that an innovator can prevent others from using their innovation. Apart from private

technological knowledge, firms' private information about their customers and suppliers has always been an important component of a marketing strategy. In the age of information technology (IT), this knowledge has become an even more important tool to deter entry. Firms with initial market power acquire private information about customers and suppliers, and these assets function as barriers to entry. Private data are also vital for use by artificial intelligence, and monopoly control of such data will be a powerful force in consolidating future market power in this arena.

10. *Dynamic game reasoning for the durability of an incumbent monopoly firm.* The study of how innovators consolidate market power in the markets for their innovations is a special case of a widely studied phenomenon—how incumbents in monopolistic markets generally work to deter firms from entering their market. Starting with the pioneering work of Bain (1956), the industrial organization literature has examined characteristics of barriers to competition that limit entry into a market dominated by an incumbent monopoly firm, even when that incumbent lacks the defensive weapon of a propriety technology. Bain's question was motivated by the frequently made observation that no entry takes place in markets where the existing firms have market power and earn abnormal profits. The research in which this observation is made shows that, using its monopoly profits, an incumbent can deter entry by means of various strategies. Their common nature is explained by a Stackelberg-type reasoning (see Tirole, 1988, p. 315), by which an incumbent can make a commitment to take action that reduces the total profits of the industry if the challenger enters. This lowers the potential profits such an entrant could expect to make. This efficiency effect is an incentive for the incumbent to preemptively commit to taking such action, and for the challenger not to enter. Some of this research utilizes technical, game-theoretic reasoning that is not central to the discussion here (see Tirole, 1988 chap. 8; Shy, 1995, chap. 8 and references there). To illustrate, I mention three examples of commitments that an incumbent can make before entry:

(a) Build, and maintain over time, an irreversibly higher capacity that would lead to negative profits for both firms if entry takes place.
(b) Price lower in order to signal to a potential entrant, who is assumed to be uncertain about the demand elasticity of the incumbent, that the firm's profitability is low.
(c) Sign long-term contracts with buyers, depriving a potential entrant of large market segments.

A consensus has thus emerged in the literature that a firm with market power can mostly deter entry even without the powerful moat of proprietary technology. The incumbent's already solid position becomes even more compelling when it has the additional advantage of a proprietary technology. This evidence supports my conclusion that the initial monopoly power awarded to innovators is not temporary. It is likely to last a very long time.

1.4.2   Technological Competition and Schumpeter's Creative Destruction

I explained in section 1.1 that technological competition is very different from regular textbook competition. After being the winner of a technological race, the evidence presented in section 1.4.1 shows the incumbent firm is most likely to maintain its market power and remain the dominant firm even if confronted by potential new entrants. This reasoning is further supported by the reasoning presented in chapter 7, where I offer a mathematical model of success breeding success that amplifies the power of an initial advantage of the incumbent firm. The model is based on the observation that, in the production of new knowledge, scientific success opens the door to further success, whereas scientific failure often leads either to a dead end or to a lower probability of future success.

The endogenous-growth literature introduces technological competition in a manner that is analogous to standard competition. It typically assumes an entrant can simply hire labor, borrow capital, and start a firm that produces a new product that is a substitute for the product of the incumbent firms (see, for example, Grossman and Helpman, 1991). This formulation does not permit the natural head-on competition between two alternative products and does not allow the incumbent to employ strategies to deter entry, as discussed in section 1.4.1. Consequently, these models, typically formulated under conditions of full certainty, ignore the real difficulty faced by an innovator, which is the need to take on the risk of innovating a product that is not only a substitute but is actually superior to the incumbent product. Those who use the Dixit–Stiglitz model and assume an innovator starts a new firm with a new product make the extreme assumption that an innovator knows how to create a new product that is *required* for consumption because in that model variety of products is strictly desired.

The theoretical and empirical evidence that technological monopolists for the most part succeed in defending against innovative entrants negates Schumpeter's (1934) "creative destruction" process by which an innovation leads to the displacement of an incumbent firm. Schumpeter's emphasis on the importance of technical change and on the centrality of technological competition has been accepted by present-day economic thinking. But creative destruction is hardly a well-formulated process. Schumpeter offers little in the way of clarification on how such a process works and expresses only the vague long-term evolutionary idea that there is a natural, long-term cycle in any market.[4] Schumpeter's chapters 6–7 contain a broad attack on standard competitive theory and promote the idea of the monopoly firm having greater vigor and stronger incentive to innovate than the weak competitive firm. But Schumpeter's vigorous incumbent monopolists seem to keel over at surprising speed. If the incumbent has such financial strength, economic vigor, and incentive to innovate on its own, why would an upstart innovator choose to engage in technological war against it? In the rare cases of successful innovations, the innovators could do better by offering their innovations for sale, and as explained earlier, the incumbent monopolist is then motivated to overbid for the innovations to prevent entry. In short, given Schumpeter's own construction, the scenario of an upstart innovator going to war against a well-entrenched monopolist and winning is implausible. In fact, the evidence suggests that most innovations are made by incumbents (see Garcia-Macia et al., 2019).

This book's view of the relation between monopoly power and innovations is the converse of the Schumpeterian view. Schumpeter (1934) and many contemporary scholars view monopoly power as temporary and necessary to promote innovations. My view is that innovation is the *cause* of rising monopoly power. Market power initially gained through innovation and supported by law is then expanded. In the absence of strong public policy to constrain it, market power grows far stronger and becomes much more widespread than that afforded by the initial legal protection granted innovators. Simply put, according to Schumpeter, monopolies create innovations, while my view is that innovations create and expand monopolies.

1.4.3   Technological Reinvention

Given the substantial empirical evidence that firms with market power resulting from innovations can defend their market positions, it may be helpful to

---

[4] A large modern literature has emerged in recent years that offers new interpretations of Schumpeter's views. See, for example, Acemoglu et al. (2018); Aghion and Howitt (1992); Aghion et al. (2014); Klette and Kortum (2004); and Lentz and Mortensen (2008). The literature offers a rich formulation of endogenous growth theory with an active R&D sector. The concept of creative destruction is sometimes formulated using a vintage model where later vintages dominate earlier ones. By assuming production is linear in labor, earlier vintages are "destroyed" because all workers move to the new vintage. But, as in the Solow (1960) vintage model, had production in these "neo-Schumpeterian" models allowed substitution of capital and labor, older vintage technologies, embodied in already built capital, would not be destroyed but rather employed with different proportions of capital and labor. The evidence supports Solow's (1957) model of obsolescence instead of destruction. In some later work (e.g., Garcia-Macia et al., 2019) all "destruction" and "creation" is defined in terms of jobs not technology, but then the problem of identifying the exact cause of job change is far more demanding because it may result from change in consumer taste, price on global markets, and the like.

consider the very long life of dominant technological firms like AT&T, DuPont, Johnson & Johnson, Procter & Gamble, General Electric, Gillette, Microsoft, and many others. Such examination shows that the process by which dominant firms lose their technological edge and are replaced by new firms with new technologies is very slow, measured in decades or even centuries. In contrast to the hypothetical innovating firm that challenges the incumbent monopolist burdened by an aging technology, strong and technologically savvy monopolists continuously reinvent themselves. They perpetually search for improved products and technology, either developed by internal R&D or bought on the open market. Technology leaders are uniquely well suited to understand a newly developed technology. When a new, potentially competing innovation appears, in most cases, the incumbent firm either acquires the new technology or purchases the innovating firm before the market realizes the new technology's value. For example, Google acquired YouTube in 2006 for $1.65 billion. Today, in 2021, YouTube is worth $175 billion. Similarly, Facebook purchased Instagram for $1 billion in 2012 and WhatsApp for $19 billion in 2014, and both are worth more than $100 billion today.

The fact is that strong firms are rarely destroyed by a new entrant. In chapter 5, I detail a case where an incumbent firm and an entrant ultimately cooperate. General Electric owned the original 1880 Edison patent on the incandescent lamp but used the inferior direct current (DC) technology. Westinghouse, by contrast, acquired in 1888, from Nikola Tesla the rights to the superior technology of alternating current (AC) patented in 1886–1887, which gave the company a major advantage over General Electric. After a protracted AC versus DC legal battle, Westinghouse did not destroy General Electric. Instead, the parties arrived at a patent-sharing agreement in 1896. Together they acted as a monopoly, producing the same products and partitioning markets to avoid direct competition. The agreement was later upheld by the Supreme Court decision *U.S. v. General Electric Co.* (1926) as a legally protected use of intellectual property rights.

But leading firms do fail. Detailed analysis of the decline of dominant firms such as Sears, Kmart, Xerox, Polaroid, Enron, or WorldCom points to either bad management[5] or an inability to reinvent themselves as a reason for their decline. Such failures may reflect organizational weakness or a core technology that relies on an old GPT that has reached its limit, depriving the incumbent of the possibility of technologically reinventing itself. A lack of innovation results in the decline of market power in any industry. One also finds that drastic new innovations occur in response to a demand that exceeds the limits of the

---

[5] Because the present discussion is about the potential technological challenge of a new innovator to an incumbent monopolist, the case of bad management is not applicable. In such a case, new entrants would be attracted into the industry, and most likely succeed in taking over, even without a superior technology.

current technology. Steam power was invented because the industrial revolution could not proceed without an effective power source to generate motion. The automobile and airplane were not created to destroy the railroads; it was the expansion of the population over the continent that created demands that the railroads could not meet.

Christensen (1997), who coined the term "disruptive innovations" in his influential book on business practices, studies the dilemma facing an incumbent firm. On the one hand, the firm needs to serve its customers who demand the firm's current products. On the other hand, it must also defend its market dominance against an entrant that makes an innovative product that is not, at that point, desired by the incumbent's customers. In the early development stage, a new product has only a small niche market of low value, but ignoring it puts the firm in great danger. Ignoring the product opens the door to the entry of a new innovator that can establish dominance over the new niche market and that can quickly transform it into dominance in the whole market. These ideas have inspired a generation of young entrepreneurs, but a careful reading of Christensen's book shows it also contains a long list of suggestions to incumbent firms on how to avoid such errors. Judging by the vast number of patents owned and the large number of young firms acquired each year by leading firms, incumbents are very aware of these defensive strategies.[6]

1.4.4   Death and Renewal

If durable market power is established, how long does it last? If market power starts with an innovation and grows from there, how is that starting time determined and how is that power renewed? After all, beyond Johnson & Johnson and Procter & Gamble, the economy has also seen the creation of Apple, Microsoft, Amazon, and Netflix.

Firms are born and die every day, divisions of existing firms are eliminated, and new divisions are created frequently. Every new area of innovations is associated with the formation of many small firms who are often the source of the new innovative ideas but seldom grow to maturity. Almost all of these firms either fail or are merged into established incumbents with market power. It is then vital to keep in mind the distinction between innovations within the paradigm

---

[6] The academic world offers another demonstration of both the durability of market power and the assumption of most economists that it has an insignificant impact. Most business school curricula have extensive permanent programs on "strategy" that is to be employed in a wide range of business activities such as financing, mergers and acquisitions, R&D, or marketing. This permanent education of MBA students reflects the schools' belief in its permanent usefulness. Yet at the same time economics departments offer many courses that teach students the opposite perspective, that market power is temporary and insignificant.

of a GPT and innovation of a *new technological paradigm* or a new GPT. Some GPTs, like electricity or IT, change everything and ultimately transform the entire economy. Others, like the discovery of DNA and genetic sequencing, change completely only a segment of the economy.

Many innovators within a well-established GPT offer improvements in the existing technology or products, but the firms they create, or their innovations, are acquired by the large established firms. Naturally, these innovations do not lead to the growth of long-run firms as described in section 1.4.1. Although it is difficult to measure an innovator's intent, it appears that a very large fraction of Silicon Valley start-ups intends, *at the outset*, to be acquired by leading technology firms. Such small firms, operating within a paradigm, thus act as research labs for the large established firms with market power. This is almost a universal phenomenon in the biotechnology industry.

Ambitious innovators with new ideas always seek opportunities to challenge incumbent firms within a well-established new GPT. As I have explained, well-established incumbents are most likely to overcome such direct challenges. But the early developments of a newly established GPT create new niches of markets or products that, as Christensen (1997) has warned, firms may ignore at their peril. These create temporary opportunities that could be exploited by creative innovators who could start a business that will then develop along the path of initial market power and consolidation described in section 1.4.1. For example, although the hospitality industry has adapted to the digital age, Airbnb was able to introduce the superior technology of the internet to enter a market niche that was ignored by that industry. One may suggest the firm introduced a new product, but a more accurate description is that it introduced a new technology to produce the same product or service but broaden it to a market niche that was not served well before. So my first answer to the question of when this process begins is that it starts every time innovators use a new GPT to open up a niche market or product ignored by existing firms.

The most intense technological competition arises when the technological paradigm itself is changed, and a new GPT is invented. This leads to the eruption of economy-wide technological competition in which winners begin the long journey to consolidate market power described in section 1.4.1. Every existing incumbent firm can enter the competition, adapt to the change, reinvent itself, and prosper. Some do so, extending their life. But such adjustment is difficult. Many weak firms that cannot reinvent themselves die, and this is the end of the process described in section 1.4.1. This is also the time when new firms have the highest probability of winning and beginning the process described in section 1.4.1.It is thus not surprising that sectors that are most vulnerable to a paradigm change are the weak, fragmented, inefficient, and less profitable industries.

Empirical evidence for the process of death and renewal described here is offered in chapter 6, where I study the age distribution of firms with the most market power and profits. I show that in 2019, firms with the most market power and profits consisted of two groups. Either they were young, IT-related firms that were founded after the 1970s (often containing merged older firms), which is the decade when the IT revolution was initiated, or they were American legacy firms, older than 100 years at that time, that reinvented themselves, adapted to the digital age, and were winners of the technological competition in their market segment.

Leading weak firms that fail are supplanted by newly created firms that build up their market power as described earlier. They are not exact replacements for those that disappeared because they use different technologies and often offer new products. But the distinction between new products and improvements of existing products is merely semantic.

If we identify products by defining a finite list of specific human needs and identifying products by the needs they satisfy, then an airplane, like a horse, is just another means of transportation. After all, a finite number can be very large! This means that, once change of ownership is accounted for, a model with a finite number of products produced by a finite number of firms with market power is a good approximation[7] for an economy with changing technology. There is no need to introduce new firms and new products.

Regardless of what path innovations take and the precise manner in which firms decline and are replaced, over time consumers and resource suppliers face a sequence of firms with varying market power. For some purposes, the death and rebirth process is of direct interest, but for more aggregate purposes it is useful to model the economy as consisting of a finite number of infinitely lived firms with fluctuating market power, just as it is common to describe the economy as consisting of a finite number of infinitely lived households. As a result, in much of what I do in this book, I assume an economy with a fixed number of permanent firms with market power. This can be interpreted as a model of "sectors" or "dynasties" where the knowledge and technology that each firm creates is merged into the surviving firms. The wealth each creates is thus invested in the next generation of innovators. My focus is largely on allocation and distribution rather than on the death and birth process of any one particular firm.

1.5   Stabilizing Market Power: The Centrality of Public Policy

I have argued that public policy is the key tool society has for restraining market power. Without an active policy, market power expands and causes income and

---

[7] After all, this is also the manner in which general equilibrium theory treats uncertainty and time, both of which are correctly described by continuous variables but are very often approximated by a finite number of commodities and prices.

wealth inequality to grow. Expansion of this power entails the transfer, to a top social group, of income, wealth, and consequently political power, thus allowing a small class of individuals to receive a rising proportion of total income and wealth. An increased concentration of wealth and market power weakens the foundations of free markets and, as a result, a small-government laissez-faire economy becomes, in the long run, dysfunctional. I now turn to discuss the lessons from the experience of past policies and to a general assessment of the role of public policy in the dynamics of market power.

1.5.1   History's Natural Experiments with Policy Efficacy

It is hard to predict the extent to which market power can expand and inequality grow without the restraint of policy. Evidence is available from two periods, 1870 to 1901 and 1981 to the present day, when almost no policies were in place to restrain technological market power. These periods provide natural experiments for assessing the dynamics of market power. They offer insight into the possible degree of market power expansion and the potential impact such expansion can have on economic growth, income distribution, and the functioning of democratic institutions. In chapter 4, I study the evolution of market power in the United States from 1889 to 2017 and identify these two periods when market power grew to extreme heights. In chapter 2, I compare data from these two periods with that from periods when active policy was used to restrain market power. This comparison allows a statistical estimate of the impact of policy on restraining market power. Because of the importance of this baseline evidence, it is useful to briefly review these two periods.

During the nineteenth century, there was no active policy to restrain the rise of market power. Western Europe was essentially ruled by a plutocracy. At that time, the idea that government should regulate the economy for the benefit of the general public was just working its way into the mainstream. A similar picture emerged in the United States in the late nineteenth century, during the First Gilded Age. Although no precise data are available on personal inequality in 1901, Piketty and Saez (2003) report a very high level of inequality in 1913. My study of functional inequality in chapter 4 shows that the rising profitability of firms resulted from a wide array of innovations related to the inventions of electricity and the combustion engine. Consequently, during the First Gilded Age, the degree of market power soared, and the share of profits in total gross value added of the private sector reached an extreme level of 31 percent in 1901. From 1889 to 1901, the labor share in gross value added of the private sector declined from 78 percent to 58 percent.

Beginning in the 1980s, during the Reagan administration, the share of profits once again began to grow. Firms with expanding market power, arising from

IT innovations, benefited from the growing efforts of policymakers to lower tax rates, curtail business regulations, and limit antitrust activity. Gutiérrez and Philippon (2017b, 2018) and Philippon (2019) document the rising business influence on public policy. Government-permitted mergers enabled the consolidation of vital sectors. These included airlines, banking, and much of the technology sector in which the large firms had been acquiring young firms with novel and potentially competitive technologies. New antitrust case law, supported by ideas coming out of the Chicago School of Economics, found most market to be "contestable" and left little room for antitrust enforcement, contributing to rising legal market power. Virtually no regulations have been enacted to restrain the growing market power of big technology firms. Furthermore, no restrictions have been placed on activities of vital public interest, such as the use of private information, false information on social networks, and corporate restrictions of consumer choice created by technologically linking a firm's various products. Consequently, since the 1980s, the level of market power and inequality have risen sharply enough to warrant calling this period the Second Gilded Age. I show in chapter 4 that from 1982 to 2019, the share of profits in value added of the corporate sector rose from 6 percent to a very high level of 24 percent. At the same time, labor share in income created in the corporate sector, excluding corporate officers' compensation, fell from 57 percent to 52 percent. Measures of inequality today are similar to those that prevailed at the height of the First Gilded Age.

The comparison between the two periods offers more insight. In both periods, the economy experienced major technological advances, and, as explained earlier in this chapter, such strong waves of innovations inevitably lead to rising tides of market power. While technology propelled market power upward in both periods, public policies during these two periods went in different directions. Whereas public policy after the 1980s accommodated the rise of market power, economic policy in the First Gilded Age took, in 1901, a sharp turn against that power.

Led by President Theodore Roosevelt, the reform movement established a determined policy program to restrain the power of business, which included the famed trust-busting campaign. The origins of the movement can be traced to the failure of late-nineteenth-century U.S. institutions that used laissez-faire policy and ignored the growing social problems. Some were long-standing issues the movement sought to reform, such as voting rights for women, a deficient educational system, and popular election of senators. But, the core problem was the rising market power of business and consequently the rising inequality that was associated with the impoverished conditions of most Americans. The issues debated were all related to the economic poverty of the majority. This manifested in problems such as the need for income tax revenue, farmers failing in the face of confiscatory monopoly pricing of railroads, poor health without information on available medicines, poor quality of food with no public knowledge of the contents of canned products, unhealthy and often dangerous working conditions with no public safety regulations, and financial instability with no control on the conduct of financial institutions.

The early period of reform led to the creation of basic institutions such as the Federal Trade Commission, the Food and Drug Administration, the Federal Reserve System, and the constitutionality of a federal income tax. After being interrupted during the 1920s, this broad policy reform effort was strengthened by the New Deal legislation. With variations in the intensity of enforcement occasioned by the Great Depression and World War II, this reformist policy remained in force until the 1980s. The policy was not an unqualified success. I show in chapter 4 that during the period from the mid-1930s to the mid-1950s, market power was actually high. However, public policy efforts were largely successful in attaining the goals of the movement for a reformed and more egalitarian society. It is, as Keynes (1939) could have put it, something of a miracle that public policy stabilized the relative share of labor and attained some degree of egalitarian income distribution for the half century from around 1930 to around 1980. This relative stability also explains the optimistic address of Kuznets (1955).

1.5.2   Key Lessons of the Equitable Policy of 1930–1980

The theoretical framework in section 1.4 regarding the durability of market power offers the first lesson: the current antitrust policy is the wrong tool to attack the problem of technological market power. The Sherman Antitrust Act of 1890, which is the foundation of current U.S. antitrust law, as well as the subsequent legislation that strengthened it, was explicitly designed to codify American and English common law doctrine that aims to prevent the restraints of trade. The current antitrust regime is then premised on the idea that, apart from some special cases like natural monopolies (e.g., utilities), free competition is the natural order and all market power is acquired by illegal means. Therefore, the aim of policy in this area is to destroy all market power in order to restore competition.

Technological market power does not fit into this framework because it is mostly legal. Intellectual property rights are promoted by policy, and Supreme Court decisions have given the policy of protecting these rights precedence over antitrust law. But these two policy goals are in conflict because they set the two objectives of increased productivity and free competition in opposition. This conflict is resolved by a public desire to promote productivity and growth, leading current policy to pronounce technological market power as legal and sidestepping the assumption in the current antitrust regime that all market power is illegitimate.

The conflict between promoting innovations and current antitrust also leads to a more subtle lesson. Promotion of innovations does not mean society supports the consolidation of market power resulting from waves of innovations. That is, any effective policy must distinguish between the limited duration of market power acquired by an initial innovation and the growth of market power through other means. These include patent pyramids, mergers and technology acquisitions, suppression of new innovations, and other strategies discussed earlier in section 1.4.1. Such concerns point to the need for the current antitrust policy to be supplemented by a new policy approach that aims not to eradicate technological market power but to contain it by ensuring its short duration. The courts have already played some role in restraining technological power after the 1950s, when they began to apply the antitrust regime against monopoly power acquired through patents. It was done by revoking or limiting the scope of patents, forcing the patent office to raise its standards. Some courts also denied patentees exclusive use when that use resulted in rising market power and imposed compulsory licensing requirements. In some cases, judges limited the scope of patents just on the grounds of their owners gaining excessive market power (see, for example Markham, 1962, p. 602–607).

A second lesson can be drawn from an examination of the reasons why the egalitarian policies to address inequality were successful. In general, this egalitarian distribution resulted primarily from safety-net redistribution programs and a very high top-income marginal tax policy that practically set an upper limit on the actual, post-tax income of any citizen in the United States. The policy was formulated by President Franklin Roosevelt in 1936 and its application led Congress to raise the top marginal tax rate to 79 percent. Roosevelt exceeded that in 1942, proposing a maximum income of $25,000 (about $416,000 in 2021 dollars) and a top marginal rate of 100 percent. Congress set the top marginal tax at 94 percent on income above $200,000, and the corporate tax rate at 52 percent. This policy was reaffirmed in peacetime by later administrations. With such a high marginal tax rate, there is no point earning higher income because it would be virtually taxed away. This tax policy was gradually weakened, first in 1964 when the top rate was lowered to 77 percent, and then by various deductions and exclusions from personal income tax so that, although the top marginal rate remained at 70 percent until 1981, the effective tax rate declined over time.

At least as important as high top-income tax rates in restraining market power was a 52 percent corporate income tax. Corporate taxes are vital for a progressive income tax policy. Many wealthy individuals do not have large current income but instead own assets in the form of common stocks of firms that pay small or no dividends. A 52 percent corporate tax rate is then, in effect, a tax on high-income individuals who, without the tax, receive their income in the form of capital gains on their stock portfolios. A high corporate tax rate lowers asset prices, reduces capital gains, and thus effectively lowers wealth inequality.

A high corporate tax rate is central to the dynamics of market power. Given that firms are highly leveraged today (see chapter 6 for details), and both labor cost, interest, and depreciation are deductible for income tax purposes, a corporate tax is mostly a tax on profits enabled by market power. This contrasts with the common view that corporate income tax is a tax on capital and therefore the tax rate should be low to avoid taxation of savings (see Judd, 1985; Chamley, 1986). A high corporate tax rate lowers the firm's stock price and reduces total after-tax profits enabled by market power. Lower profits limit the ability of the firm to acquire potential competitors or to purchase the technology of potential entrants. This is so because large-scale acquisitions are typically paid for, whether in full or in part, with common stock. In addition, heavy corporate taxation deprives the firm of valuable cash flow and forces it to finance acquisitions with borrowed capital or by the sale of additional equities. Such rising cost of capital reduces the incentive to engage in risky transactions. A high corporate tax rate therefore limits the ability and incentive of firms to increase their market power through the acquisition of competitors or their technologies.

Tax revenues were redistributed directly to the public in a progressive way through a variety of government transfer programs. These transfer programs began with the New Deal, but the safety net was greatly expanded by the War on Poverty, initiated in the 1960s, and by the expansion of Social Security and Medicare. I use the term "direct redistribution" because such policy initiatives either made direct payments to individuals who qualified according to some criteria (for example, family welfare payments), or they supported programs that benefited particular population segments (for example, financial support based on affirmative action). Many of these programs excluded some population segments that did not qualify. Note, however, that the unique feature of Social Security and Medicare is that they are universal in the sense that they define qualification by objective criteria, such as age, that apply to all members of society. This universality has significantly contributed to the popularity and longevity of these programs.

The final lesson is related to labor. As early as 1901, unions sought to use political power as a vehicle to improve the balance of power in the labor market. These efforts were supported by various laws enacted under the New Deal and in the post–World War II era. Unions' ability to improve labor share is exemplified by the 1950 Treaty of Detroit, a five-year contract between the United Auto Workers and General Motors that was extended to cover all automobile workers. The agreement granted the firms freedom from the production and marketing disruptions of annual strikes. In return, the union gained health, unemployment, and pension benefits; extended vacation time; and cost-of-living wage adjustments for workers. In broader terms, the contract altered the burden of risks. The firms reduced the risk of current profits but ended up taking on the risk of workers' welfare and change in relative prices of the promised benefits. In the long run, this additional risk, particularly the burden of health and pension benefits, turned out to be very costly. The contract was replicated in many industries and became a model for labor-management agreements. I later assess the ability of union power to alter the relative share of labor.

1.5.3   Why Did the United States Make a Sharp Turn to the Right in the 1980s?

I now seek to explain the sharp rightward policy shift in the 1980s. It is this regime that my policy proposals in chapters 8–10 are designed to supplant. It is therefore important to understand the origins of the 1980s policy regime and how it ended the preceding policy regime.

The Great Depression shattered the social standing of business, which was held responsible for the devastation wrought in that period. This standing improved during World War II, when business made a vital contribution to winning the war. This recovery continued in the period following the war, and there was a growing view that the prosperity of the nation was closely linked to corporate prosperity. Rising productivity and improved economic conditions at that time were partly the result of the advances in business technology and innovations. These innovations created new consumer goods and increased business demand for technical skills. Public sentiment in support of business was reflected by General Motors' CEO Charles Wilson. In hearings for his nomination to be Secretary of Defense, he famously stated that "what was good for our country was good for General Motors, and vice versa." The stature of business was further enhanced during the Cold War when new technologies were mobilized to support U.S. policy at home and abroad.

The postwar boom led to rising income and wealth at all income levels, including at the top. As in all periods of time, the rich always seek to justify their position at the top. In the First Gilded Age, the rich adopted and popularized the ideology of eugenics, a doctrine that applied natural selection to intelligence, suggesting that they were genetically superior to others. In the postwar period, this ideology took the more politically correct form of heterogeneity in ability and was rooted in the belief that the rich are innately more productive. If the rich are entitled to their gains, then the high tax rates they pay are unjustified and should be avoided if possible. This sentiment gave rise to the tax avoidance industry (see Saez and Zucman, 2019b, chap. 3–4) and to growing political pressure for tax exemptions of some expenses. Libertarian ideology expanded the political agenda to include deregulation, spending cuts, reduced scrutiny of mergers and acquisitions, and other items that became components of the policy changes of the 1980s. However, no such change could take place without the formation of a new majority coalition that would support these views and then change the policy.

The changes made during the Reagan administration were the culmination of a long process of coalition building. An example of the growing mobilization of business and the wealthy is the 1971 memorandum by future Supreme Court justice Lewis Powell to a member of the U.S. Chamber of Commerce, entitled "Attack on American Free Enterprise System." Powell begins by explaining that the free-enterprise system itself is under attack from various sources. He then calls for business to mobilize on all fronts for aggressive collaborative action to preserve the free-market economy and counter the growing domestic and foreign opposition to the American way. Leading firms and other business organizations began to engage in joint actions against several relatively modest labor law reforms under consideration by Congress at that time. The broader aim of these efforts was to change the balance of political power. The defeat, in 1978, of the Labor Law Reform Act was a sign that political and business forces were coming together in a new coalition that was to change the course of the country. From a political perspective, I see the success of this coalition as driven by three central factors: the unpopularity of direct redistribution, the rising power of labor, and racial bias and religious sentiments harnessed by the rising conservative movement.

The first factor in the successful formation of the new coalition was dissatisfaction with targeted redistribution programs. I have already noted that the relatively egalitarian distribution from 1930 to 1980 was achieved, in part, by a direct redistribution funded by heavy taxation of high incomes. This approach was criticized for having undesirable incentive effects (for example, in relation to work effort) and for creating a culture of dependency. It led those excluded from public benefits to perceive discrimination (for example, affirmative action in college admission) and was criticized for being wasteful, inefficient, and perhaps corrupt. The targeted redistribution policies were attacked by leading scholars such as Robert Nozick, Milton Friedman, Ludwig von Mises, and Friedrich Hayek, who painted these as humanmade, arbitrary, or politically motivated choices. They championed a free competitive economy as an objective, natural, efficient, and fair mechanism of compensating those deemed worthy and punishing those who they saw as refusing to accept responsibility for their own private actions. By the 1980s, growing segments of U.S. society had become sympathetic to this point of view.

The second factor was the relative gains of labor between 1930 and 1970. I explain in chapter 4 that from about 1940 to the 1970s, relative to capital, labor share exceeded its expected level given the degree of corporate market power. This disparity peaked in the late 1950s, when the greatest gains were made by the labor movement, reflected in the Treaty of Detroit. These gains were also partly the result of legislation advanced by the reform movement, like the National

Labor Relations Act. Opponents of the labor movement often pointed to the relative strength of labor as a cause of the hyperinflation of the 1970s. At the behest of business, political forces were building to counter labor's perceived strength. They were bolstered by the public's favorable view of business in the post–World War II era and by the 1970s realization that U.S. business was facing serious challenges of rising oil prices and growing competition from Japan and Germany.

The unpopularity of direct redistribution and labor power alone could not change the direction of policy. Those opposed to redistribution and to the labor movement were insufficient in number to constitute a majority. The third component of the 1980s policy turn, racism and conservative religious belief, was decisive in boosting the political strength of the coalition that sought the change. The Civil Rights Act of 1964 was one of the greatest achievements of the liberal movement, but its passage provoked the racist sentiment that caused the Southern states to turn right. Racist feelings were also behind much of the opposition to public redistribution more generally because benefits were often perceived as going to the "wrong" people. Religious beliefs added a combustible element to politics, in particular around the issue of abortion. These additional forces, which trigger personal identities that often supersede economic interests, were sufficient to consolidate the new majority coalition led by the Republican Party.

The academic debate about antitrust policy suffers from similar ideological dynamics. The turn to the right in U.S. politics resulted in diverse economic models being used to justify the change in policy. For example, the model of contestable markets provided a broad conceptual justification for disregarding well-entrenched market power and exempting industries like airlines, communication, and banking from antitrust scrutiny. More generally, leading scholars on the right oppose antitrust policy based on the heterogeneity hypothesis. It insists that firms with market power are just the highly productive firms that have an advantage over their weak and inefficient competitors. On this view, antitrust policy punishes the most efficient firms for being the most efficient. Because there is free entry into research and all firms can engage in R&D, competition will do the job of antitrust policy by rewarding new and more efficient firms that will then remove those currently holding market power.

This last claim applies to regular competition, which, as I noted earlier, is distinct from technological competition. I evaluate, in detail, the heterogeneity argument in chapter 8. In addition, when assessing technological competition in chapter 7, I show that most of those with market power attain it by pure luck. Under such conditions, restraining the market power of those at the top will actually give smaller firms an opportunity to grow and increase their productivity. Restraining market power is then shown to be a welfare-improving policy.

In short, the 1980s policy turn to the right resulted from the convergence of diverse forces of political expediency and pure ideology. The important lessons from it are the resulting negative economic, social, and political consequences that are a central part of the background of this book.

1.5.4   The Policy Goal: Speed Up the Dissipation Rate of Initial Market Power Resulting from Innovations

There is a profound difference between the laissez-faire policy regime that has prevailed since the 1980s and the egalitarian, active policy regime that preceded it. They represent different visions of society, with different values and different institutions. The differences have manifested in deep social divisions that have emerged around the world since the 1980s and stand in contrast to the more cohesive societies of the 1930s to 1970s era. Yet, from the perspective of the dynamics of market power described in section 1.4.1, the difference is relatively simple and boils down to the rate at which the initial market power resulting from innovations actually dissipates.

Both policies promote innovation and economic growth, and both accept the price it imposes in the form of an initial market power supported either by law or market forces, offering an advantage to innovators. But the two differ sharply on how to treat the consolidation and expansion of market power over time. They thus diverge on the level of accumulated market power a policy should permit. I have already noted (see more details in chapter 8) that supporters of a laissez-faire policy have opposed antitrust policy, insisting that market forces are sufficient to contain market power. So what are those market forces?

Market power does indeed wane because of the finite life of trade secrets and intellectual property rights. However, I have demonstrated earlier that innovative firms can take many different actions to slow this decline and instead use diverse strategies to consolidate and expand market power. These responses explain why technological competition cannot eliminate market power and why, even in the paradigm-shifting case of a new GPT, such innovation may reduce or terminate the power of firms using the old GPT but does not eliminate market power as such. Innovation can merely result in the market power of some old firms being replaced by the power of leading new firms that introduce the GPT. Finally, demand shocks and business cycles can cause market power to fall temporarily. In the long run, however, they strengthen the leading firms because the less profitable firms suffer more from demand shocks. In short, absent active policy to contain market power, technology enables market power to expand at a high rate.

In contrast, active policy prevents the expansion of the initial market power by guiding all such initial power to dissipate at the rate designed by patent law.

This is done by prohibiting the use of many strategies used to expand market power outlined in section 1.4.1. Because this level has been chosen by society, one presumes it is the socially optimal rate of dissipation, reflecting the trade-off between the incentive to innovate and the cost of market power.

The difference between the two policies is then distinguished by the *speed at which the initial market power afforded innovations is made to decline*. An active policy approach dictates a high speed of dissipation, preventing market power and inequality from growing to unacceptable levels. A laissez-faire, free-market policy allows only a slow speed of dissipation, and consequently the rate of innovation causes market power and inequality to rise to their highest feasible levels.

1.5.5   The Medium-Run Impact of Policy Shifts

Associated with the two policy intervals discussed in section 1.5.1 are two major policy shifts that took place, one in the early 1900s and a second in the 1980s. To explain the impact of such policy shifts, note the case made in section 1.5.4 that the key difference between the two policies is the speed at which they require market power to dissipate. When policy dictates a high speed of dissipation, market power cannot grow to very high levels, but when policy allows a slow speed of dissipation, the rate of innovation results in rising market power to much higher levels. I will then show that each such shift has, on its own, a large, temporary, but important impact on economic performance, with potentially long-lasting effects that depend upon the difference between the two policies. I illustrate the reason for this with a simplified version of the model used in chapter 2.

To quantify the impact of different dissipation speeds, I denote by $\mathcal{P}_t > 1$ an index of market power and by ζ_t an index of productive technology's deviation from the steady-state value of 1. The combined effect of policy and technology is then expressed by the change of $\mathcal{P}_t$, which I describe with the simplified equation

$$\mathcal{P}_{t+1} = g \mathcal{P}_t^{\lambda_{\mathcal{P}}} \zeta_{t+1}^{\lambda_{\zeta}} e^{\varepsilon_{t+1}}.$$

The parameter g measures the constant effect of the trend in technology's productivity growth on market power, while ζ_{t+1} reflects the effect of technology shocks. When ζ_{t+1} is above 1, market power rises, and when it is below 1, market power declines. The effect of policy is then to change the speed at which $\mathcal{P}_t$ adjusts over time, expressed by the parameter $\lambda_{\mathcal{P}}$. When only two policies are used, as described above, a laissez-faire policy is described by the high value $\lambda_{\mathcal{P}} = \lambda_{\mathcal{P}}^{H}$, causing higher persistence or *low dissipation* of market power. The active, more egalitarian policy is defined by the low value $\lambda_{\mathcal{P}} = \lambda_{\mathcal{P}}^{L}$, causing low persistence or *high dissipation* of market power. The term ϵ is a random one with mean 0. The full dynamics of market power is then described by

$$\mathcal{P}_{t+1} = \begin{cases} g\mathcal{P}_t^{\lambda_{\mathcal{P}}^H} \zeta_{t+1}^{\lambda_{\zeta}} e^{\epsilon_{t+1}} & \text{when policy is laissez-faire,} \\ g\mathcal{P}_t^{\lambda_{\mathcal{P}}^L} \zeta_{t+1}^{\lambda_{\zeta}} e^{\epsilon_{t+1}} & \text{when policy is active.} \end{cases}$$

Under each policy regime, the economy has its own steady state defined by the policy parameter remaining constant permanently. But each policy regime lasts for a long time, measured in decades, and if each is dynamically stable, in the long run the complete system fluctuates between its two steady states. The two steady states are defined by

$$\mathcal{P}^\star = \begin{cases} g^{\frac{1}{1-\lambda_{\mathcal{P}}^H}} & \text{when policy is laissez-faire,} \\ g^{\frac{1}{1-\lambda_{\mathcal{P}}^L}} & \text{when policy is active.} \end{cases}$$

These two steady states can be very far apart. For example, suppose $g = 1.014$, indicating an annual productivity growth of 1.4 percent and $\lambda_{\mathcal{P}}^H = 0.95$ while $\lambda_{\mathcal{P}}^L = 0.80$. These imply the values $\mathcal{P}^{\star H} = 1.32$ and $\mathcal{P}^{\star L} = 1.07$. A good measure of the market power of a monopolist is its markup, the percentage by which a monopolist's price is higher than the marginal cost. Given this, the steady-state markup under the laissez-faire policy regime is 32 percent, whereas under the active policy regime, it is only 7 percent.

Anticipating results discussed later in this chapter and proved precisely in chapter 2, it is important to keep in mind that monopoly firms curtail outputs as they raise their prices and profits. Consequently, the effect of high market power is to reduce demand for capital input, curtail the rate of investment, and thus lower the steady-state level of the capital stock.[8] Therefore, it results in lower steady-state equilibrium levels of output, investment and consumption. Because the laissez-faire policy results in higher market power, the implied steady-state level of the capital/output ratio is low, and this is associated with lower steady-state levels of output, consumption, and investment. The converse occurs under the active policy regime that reduces market power: higher capital/output ratio and the higher steady-state equilibrium level of all economic aggregates.

Now consider a time when policy changes, and suppose the change is from an active to a passive policy. When the change is made, the capital stock inherited from the previous regime is high because active policy was implemented to control market power. The new laissez-faire policy allows market power to rise,

---

[8] All economic aggregates discussed here are normalized by the level of technological advance. This means that if K is the level of the capital employed, then the steady-state value discussed in the text is of the variable $k = K/A$, where A is the rate of labor-saving technological change. The same is true for output, consumption, and investment.

and under this regime, the equilibrium steady-state value of the capital stock and the capital/output ratio are low. This means that the mere shift in policy regime unleashes a dynamic adjustment from a high capital/output ratio to a low capital/output ratio. This adjustment is slow because it entails a gradual decline of the capital/output ratio and of all other economic aggregates affected by a change in capital stock. This includes the growth rate of the economy and the levels of consumption, investment, and employment. The opposite is true if the policy shift is from a laissez-faire policy to an active policy: the mere shift in policy causes a powerful transition from a steady state with a low capital/output ratio to a steady state with a high capital/output ratio.

Simulations carried out in chapter 2 for realistic parameters show that such transitions can take as many as twenty to forty years, and because they are only consequences of changes in steady-state values, they do not alter the economy's asymptotic growth rates. They do, however, cause temporary, medium-run changes in the realized growth rates of economic aggregates.

Suppose we shift to a new laissez-faire policy at some date. An economist who takes measurements each quarter will observe a long transition period in which the capital/output ratio declines and the economy experiences lower than potential growth rates of capital, output, investment, and consumption. Lasting a period of twenty to thirty years, this could easily be interpreted as a form of secular stagnation when in fact it is merely an adjustment forced upon the economy by the change in policy regime.

This last conclusion is surprising and contradicts the claims of those who advocated the shift, in the 1970s, to a free-market, laissez-faire policy regime. Those advocates claimed the new policy would increase incentives to work, invest, and innovate, and therefore they forecasted an immediate rapid economic expansion. This did not happen. Instead, the mere shift from the earlier active policy regime to the new laissez-faire policy triggered a transition lasting about forty years. During these years, the growth rate of the economy was actually lower than trend growth. However, the theory presented here shows that it could have been predicted to be lower than potential because of the adjustment in the level of all economic aggregates to lower steady-state values.

1.6   Capital, Wealth, and the Actors in an Economy with Market Power

1.6.1   Capital and Wealth Are Different Concepts

In an economy with technological market power, gross value added of any entity is divided into three functional income categories: compensation to labor, gross compensation to capital employed, and profits resulting from market power.[9] Each of these is determined by its role in the entity's activities and the risk associated with those activities. In section 1.6.2, I identify those who receive these flows. Here, I focus on the fact that in the case of capital income and profits, the market capitalizes the future flows of each of them in order to arrive at today's asset prices. The value of these assets equals the market's assessment of the present values of all their future income flows.

In the case of capital income, the present value of its future flow equals the market value of the capital goods employed in production today. As for profits, one defines the asset value to be the capitalized value of its future flow of profits, and I call this present value *monopoly wealth*. This last term is a bit narrow because profits or rent may arise from other forms of market power like duopoly, oligopoly, monopsony, or monopolistic competition, but it is simple enough to convey the desired idea.[10] Because monopoly wealth is the *market value of future profits, and profits are the results of human knowledge that is privately owned*, it is useful to think of aggregate monopoly wealth as the market value of technological knowledge that is privately owned, much of which is protected by intellectual property rights. Such valuation obviously depends upon the market power of firms who own that knowledge and how they translate this market power into profits. Recognizing the centrality of intellectual property rights to monopoly wealth shows the crucial role of public policy and of the force of the law in creating and maintaining that wealth.

There is a long tradition in economics of distributing income into two categories, capital and labor. In that tradition, both normal returns to capital as well as excess returns from monopoly power are counted as returns to an entity, which, for the moment, I call Kapital. This misses a very important distinction between the value of capital input used in production and monopoly wealth because this assumption implies that the value of Kapital is the present value of the sum of capital income plus profits. But then the value of Kapital equals the sum of the value of capital goods used in production and monopoly wealth. Because my treatment deviates from this tradition, it is important to explain the difference between capital used in production and monopoly wealth, and why the value of Kapital is not the same as the value of capital employed in production.

The concept of capital I use is the standard aggregate, consisting of all assets used as fixed factors of production. These include inventories, structures, and various types of equipment. The production function is then of the form

---

[9]The term "profits" or "monopoly profits" used in this book is, *with no exception*, the part of value added that is extracted by market power in the form of rent. In the case of technological market power, it is then the compensation to those who own the technology. When discussing the commonly used term of "profits," I explicitly refer to accounting corporate profits.

[10]I could use the term "capitalized value of market power" but this is a bit long. "Monopoly wealth" is shorter and conveys the correct message.

$F_t(K_t, L_t)$, where the two factors are lists of different types of capital assets and different types of labor. Capital includes real assets, but it does not include "intangible assets" since, as I argue in detail in chapter 3, these are just specific forms of monopoly wealth that found their way into the balance sheets of corporations. Technology affects the production function through the functional form of F, changing the productivity of the inputs and not through its capital input designated by K_t.

In contrast to capital, wealth is the total value of all assets, so Kapital is equal to total wealth. Total wealth equals capital plus monopoly wealth, and because monopoly wealth exists only in an economy with market power, capital and wealth are equivalent when the economy is purely competitive. As long as there are innovations and market power in the economy, total wealth is larger than total capital. My study of asset prices in chapter 6 shows that the ratio of monopoly wealth to total wealth in the U.S. corporate sector has grown dramatically in recent years, reaching 51 percent in 2019. Profits of U.S. corporations have similarly risen, reaching about 24 percent of corporate value added in that year. Consequently, monopoly wealth created by the sector has grown dramatically since 1985. In addition, U.S. corporations are heavily leveraged so that most of their capital stock can be thought of as being owned by bondholders who have lent their capital to the corporate sector. It is not unreasonable to conjecture that, within the next decade, virtually 100 percent of the capital employed by U.S. corporations will be financed by debt and therefore bondholders will be the owners of all capital used by the corporate sector. To clarify the implication of the rise in leverage, consider the two simple[11] identities noted:

Wealth Created by U.S. Corporations = Monopoly Wealth + Capital   (1.1a)

Wealth Created by U.S. Corporations = Value of Stocks
                                    + Value of Corporate Debt.   (1.1b)

If total capital equals total corporate debt, then the value of all stocks is equal to the total monopoly wealth created by the U.S. corporate sector. At present, the United States has not reached quite that degree of leverage: 71 percent of capital was financed by debt in 2019 and 75 percent of all trades of corporate shares were trades of monopoly wealth.

The share of monopoly wealth in total wealth rises when the rate of innovation rises and falls rapidly when the rate of innovations falls. This explains the high volatility of monopoly wealth, which responds strongly to changes in the rate of innovation, productivity, public policy, and market sentiment. The capital stock grows at a pace determined by the savings and depreciation rates; therefore it exhibits lower fluctuations than total wealth.

---

[11] Since this is a conceptual argument, I keep matters simple and ignore, for the sake of this discussion, all open economy considerations and focus only on a rudimentary domestic economy.

Many researchers fail to distinguish between capital and monopoly wealth. Instead they add the two to obtain Kapital, which is a measure of wealth, and identify it with capital. This procedure leads to wrong conclusions about recorded economic trends. To see why, I denote output by Y and assume neutral technological change. I can then write, for example,

$$Y_t = F\left(K_t, A_t L_t\right) \Rightarrow \frac{Y_t}{K_t} = F\left(1, \frac{A_t L_t}{K_t}\right).$$

In steady state, it is a standard result that the output/capital ratio converges to a constant:

$$y^\star = F\left(k^\star, 1\right) \quad \text{where} \quad y_t = \frac{Y_t}{A_t L_t}, \quad k_t = \frac{K_t}{A_t L_t} \tag{1.2a}$$

$$\frac{k^\star}{y^\star} = \frac{s}{g + n + \delta}, \quad g = \frac{\dot{A}_t}{A_t}, \quad n = \frac{\dot{L}_t}{L_t}, \quad \dot{K}_t = I_t - \delta K_t \quad \text{where} \quad \dot{X} \equiv \frac{dX}{dt}. \tag{1.2b}$$

These results remain true in economies with market power. But as I show in proposition 2.3, if market power rises over time, the capital/output ratio *declines* if all variables that correspond to (1.2a)–(1.2b) are computed for K standing for capital, not wealth. In contrast, during the same time, the wealth/output ratio rises. That is, the long-term responses of the capital/output ratio and the wealth/output ratio to changes in market power exhibit movements in opposite directions: if one rises, the other declines. This means that if one equates wealth with capital, one would deduce the wrong empirical result about long-run trends of the economy.

Many books and articles derive equations like (1.2a)–(1.2b) but estimate the capital stock from values of corporate stock prices. This is an error because it leads to estimates of wealth instead of capital. I return to this question in chapter 6, where I discuss the dynamics of the capital/output ratio.

1.6.2   The Economic Actors: Who Are the Recipients of the Three Relative Shares?

The division of gross value added of a firm into three distributional components requires an explanation of who the recipients of these shares are, the markets in which they trade, and the risk they bear. Labor income is paid to the workers of the firm. Capital income is paid to the bondholders who lend capital to the firm and to the stockholders who receive the income of the capital the firm owns. Profits are received by the stockholders who own the firm. The difficulty in distinguishing capital from profits is clear: a dividend to stockholders may contain both capital income and profits.

First, however, I want to dwell on an issue that causes difficulty in distinguishing labor income from profits. In a technological age, enhancing and preserving a firm's market position is the most challenging job management faces, far exceeding the challenge of managing the firm's production. It requires decisions about pricing and marketing strategies, patenting, mergers and acquisitions, purchasing and licensing technologies, R&D efforts, and other strategies listed in section 1.4.1. This requires management to be well versed in the firm's technology and its potential. Consequently, their compensation consists mostly of a performance bonus and of the exercise of stock grants and options (see Moylan, 2008; Elsby et al., 2013). Indeed, rising management income from the exercise of stock options has slowed down the decline of the Bureau of Labor Statistics published labor share and explains the rise of payroll labor share during the dot-com years between 1998 and 2002 (see Elsby et al., 2013). Because management compensation is mostly dependent on performance, managers function more as partners of the firm than as employees. I have thus decided to treat officers' compensation as profit share rather than as wages. I will, however, provide adequate information to enable the reader to adjust all empirical results to include officers' compensations in labor income.

The distinction between return to equity capital and profits is crucial but more subtle. It hinges on the role of capital as distinct from the role of market power. Labor and capital are factors that the firm can rent in the open market and are substitutable for equivalent factors employed by other firms under similar combinations of risk and return. Profits are a payoff for the firm's unique market power, proprietary technology, and management, and sometimes I refer to them as monopoly profits. They are therefore compensation for the activities related to innovating, exploiting current market power, and enhancing future technology and market power. The recipients of profits assume all risks that result from these activities. Although profits are the result of market power, recipients of profits do not form a homogeneous class of economic agents.

Owners of capital, on the other hand, rent their capital to the firm and are promised that they will receive back the undepreciated part of their capital but not its price. They assume the risk of the marginal return on their capital when that return equals the stochastic marginal productivity of the capital stock in the economy. Because capital owners can fully diversify and reduce risk down to the aggregate level, the productivity risk they actually take equals the risk to aggregate productivity in the economy, and the rental they receive is the same from all firms that rent capital. Capital return is then the rate paid to investors whose risk preference leads them to desire only the normal return on their capital holdings without attempting to earn monopoly profits from the strategic behavior of any specific firm. These are individuals like retirees, wealthy risk-averse capital owners, pension funds, and insurance companies that seek capital income flows with fully diversified portfolios.

With this specified investment goal, such individuals typically invest in bonds or other debt instruments, but they may also purchase preferred stocks, utility stocks, real estate investment trusts, and limited partnerships. It also follows from the defined goal that bondholders are major owners of capital, but they are promised full return of their capital and take contractually less risk than other capital owners (because they have priority over collateral). Therefore, their return is slightly smaller than the required return to diversified equity capital.

Because the wealth created by any firm consists of the capital it owns and the monopoly wealth it created, there are two identities that need to be kept in mind:

$$\text{Capital Income} + \text{Profits} - \text{Officers' compensation}$$
$$= \text{Total return on the firm's wealth}$$

and

$$\text{Profits} - \text{Officers' compensation}$$
$$= \text{Return on monopoly wealth owned by stockholders.}$$

It follows from these identities that the pool of capital income and profits is distributed to three recipients: stockholders, bondholders, and managers. Bondholders' income is part of the imputed capital income. Managers are compensated out of the firm's profits. Stockholders are the largest recipients of profits, but they are a hybrid group. They receive both capital income and profits because they must own both capital and monopoly wealth (both of which are included in the price of the stock) to take part in the firm's technology and strategic risks. Their capital income is compensation for their capital investment, and their share of the profits is a consequence of their proportional ownership of monopoly wealth. Because bondholders receive less than the return on fully diversified equity capital, stockholders receive the extra return and take the extra risk of leverage.

1.7   The Functional Distribution of Income Under Market Power

1.7.1   A General Formulation

The effects of market power on the functional distribution of income can be deduced from a very general model. The textbook model, which goes back to Robinson (1933), is formulated here to provide a foundation for more specialized models used in other chapters.

I study an economic environment with a finite number of firms, each using a proprietary technology and producing a differentiated product. The firm is a monopolist in its own market, but its product may, in part, be substitutable with the products of other firms. No two commodities produced by different firms are identical. There may be one dominant monopolist, or the market might consist of several dominant firms with oligopoly power resulting from their ownership of partially substitutable products. The market equilibrium is assumed to be a Nash equilibrium so that each firm takes the price of its competitors as given.

Because I focus on the optimal behavior of such a monopoly firm, the notation will suppress all information about the other firms. I thus assume the firm faces a demand function $D(P_t, Z_t)$ for its own product with price P, and all other market conditions Z. The firm has a constant returns to scale production $Y_t = F(K_t, A_t L_t)$, where K is capital, L is labor, and A is labor-augmenting technology. Both capital and labor trade on competitive open markets at wage rate W and capital rental rate R, and the firm hires whatever quantity of these factors it desires. Factor costs are entirely variable because the time scale of the analysis is one year, which is sufficiently long for the firm to adjust its inputs freely. The timing of economic events is simple: first, all uncertainty with respect to productivity is resolved. Then firms hire their resources, paying wages and the capital rental rate to households, and production takes place under known input prices.

Denote by λ_t the Lagrange multiplier on the condition that equates supply with demand, and the optimizing problem of the firm is

$$\text{Max}_{P_t, L_t, K_t} \left[P_t Y_t - W_t L_t - R_t K_t \right] + \lambda_t \left[Y_t - F\left(K_t, A_t L_t\right) \right] , Y_t = D\left(P_t, Z_t\right).$$
(1.3)

The monopoly first-order conditions of the profit maximization are then

$$D + P_t \frac{\partial D}{\partial P_t} = \lambda_t \frac{\partial D}{\partial P_t}$$
(1.3a)

$$W_t = \lambda_t F_L$$
(1.3b)

$$R_t = \lambda_t F_K$$
(1.3c)

Condition (1.3a) implies that

$$D + P_t \frac{\partial D}{\partial P_t} = \lambda_t \frac{\partial D}{\partial P_t} \Rightarrow \lambda_t = P_t \frac{(\theta_t - 1)}{\theta_t} \text{ where I define } \theta_t = -\frac{P_t}{D} \frac{\partial D}{\partial P_t}, \theta_t > 1.$$

Therefore, I conclude that

$$\frac{W_t}{F_L} = \frac{\theta_t - 1}{\theta_t} P_t \quad , \quad \frac{R_t}{F_K} = \frac{\theta_t - 1}{\theta_t} P_t.$$
(1.3d)

This is the familiar *marginal cost = marginal revenue* condition, where the left side, the ratio of an input's market price to its marginal productivity, is the marginal cost, and λ_t is the marginal revenue. The term $\mathcal{P}_t = \theta_t/(\theta_t - 1)$ is called a markup, the factor by which a firm can price above cost. One can write (1.3d) in the form

$$\frac{W_t}{F_L}\frac{\theta_t}{\theta_t - 1} = P_t \quad , \quad \frac{R_t}{F_K}\frac{\theta_t}{\theta_t - 1} = P_t.$$

The markup term is an index of market power. It quantifies the degree to which a firm is able to price its product above marginal cost, which will be greater for a strong monopolist than for a small firm with multiple competitors. When the term "market power" is used in this book, it refers to this ability to charge a markup over marginal cost. Because the markup is a function of the elasticity of demand θ_t, market power is a consequence of the desirability and the differentiated nature of the firm's product.

To focus on income distribution, I multiply each equation by its input and divide by $P_t Y_t$ to write them in the equivalent form of

$$\frac{L_t W_t}{P_t Y_t} = \frac{\theta_t - 1}{\theta_t}\left(\frac{F_L L_t}{Y_t}\right), \quad \frac{R_t K_t}{Y_t} = \frac{\theta_t - 1}{\theta_t}\left(\frac{F_K K_t}{Y_t}\right).$$

Next, I introduce the notation for the elasticities of output with respect to the two factors, which sum to 1 by the assumption of constant returns to scale:

$$1 - \alpha_t = \frac{F_L L_t}{Y_t} \quad , \quad \alpha_t = \frac{F_K K_t}{Y_t}.$$

The distribution of income created by the monopoly firm is then

$$\text{Relative share of labor} \quad \frac{W_t L_t}{P_t Y_t} = \left(1 - \alpha_t\right)\frac{\theta_t - 1}{\theta_t}$$

$$\text{Relative share of capital} \quad \frac{R_t K_t}{P_t Y_t} = \alpha_t\frac{\theta_t - 1}{\theta_t} \qquad (1.4)$$

$$\text{Relative share of monopoly}^{12}\text{profits} = \frac{1}{\theta_t}.$$

The conditions in (1.4) show that fluctuating monopoly power alters the functional distribution of income. They reveal that a rise in such power depresses labor as well as capital income. Most studies assume that the capital

---

[12] Monopoly profits are often called "rents" in the economic literature. I use the term "profits" to identify all current gains from market power. Note that some of the gains are not from a monopoly but rather from a monopsony, where an analogous accounting is carried out for a firm that is a large buyer with a power to lower the prices paid to its suppliers. This analysis can be found in the next section.

elasticity of output α_t in (1.4) is constant because numerous econometric studies, going back to Cobb and Douglas (1928), have demonstrated that this is approximately the case for the aggregate economy. All fluctuations in monopoly power cause fluctuations in relative shares, implying that the standard neoclassical growth theory prediction of constant relative shares does not hold when market power fluctuates.

1.7.2   The Partial Equilibrium Effect of Monopoly Power on Output Is Large

Although models of monopoly or monopolistic competition are used extensively in the fields of industrial organization and new-Keynesian macroeconomics, economists often assume such power is not significant and its effect on the quantity produced in the economy is not large. To examine if this is indeed the case, I present a simple procedure by which to assess the order of magnitude of the effect of monopolies on output.

For given prices (W_t, R_t), and given that firms have enough time to adjust the inputs, it follows from (1.3d) that the marginal cost of additional output is

$$\frac{W_t}{F_L} = \frac{R_t}{F_K}$$

and does not vary with output. This is equal to the competitive price P_t^c, so that

$$\frac{P_t^c}{P_t} = \frac{\theta_t - 1}{\theta_t}. \tag{1.5}$$

$D_t(P_t^c, Z_t)$ is the output level the firm would have produced under competitive conditions. Therefore, the ratio of the competitive to the monopoly output is

$$\frac{D_t\left(P_t^c, Z_t\right)}{D_t\left(P_t, Z_t\right)}.$$

To assess the order of magnitude of this expression, I present two options. The first maintains the generality of the demand function and uses a log linear approximation to estimate it. The second assumes a well-recognized and commonly used form for the demand function. I briefly explore both under the assumption that one knows or can estimate θ_t.

1. *Approximation.* I log-linearize around the monopoly solution because, by assumption, I know θ_t at that solution and can approximate the function at that value. Hence:

$$D_t\left(P_t^c, Z_t\right) = D_t\left(P_t, Z_t\right) + \frac{dD_t}{dP_t}\left(P_t^c - P_t\right).$$

Therefore:

$$\frac{D_t\left(P_t^c, Z_t\right) - D_t\left(P_t, Z_t\right)}{D_t\left(P_t, Z_t\right)} = -\theta_t\left(\frac{P_t^c}{P_t} - 1\right)$$

but by (1.5) I have that

$$\frac{D_t\left(P_t^c, Z_t\right)}{D_t\left(P_t, Z_t\right)} = -\theta_t\left(\frac{\theta_t - 1}{\theta_t} - 1\right) + 1 = 2 \tag{1.6a}$$

which is the well-known result for a linear demand function. This suggests that monopoly output is *approximately half* the output that would be produced by a competitive firm, *independent* of θ_t. The fact that the result does not depend upon the elasticity is not surprising because the log linear approximation disregards the curvature of the demand function.

2. *Constant elasticity demand function* $D_t(P_t, Z_t) = G_t P_t^{-\theta_t} Z_t^{\Psi}$. This demand function has been extensively used in all branches of economics. It then follows that

$$\frac{D_t\left(P_t^c, Z_t\right)}{D_t\left(P_t, Z_t\right)} = \left[\frac{P_t^c}{P_t}\right]^{-\theta_t} = \left[\frac{\theta_t - 1}{\theta_t}\right]^{-\theta_t}. \tag{1.6b}$$

If θ_t is equal to 4, which is the value I estimate for the U.S. economy in 2019 in the empirical work of chapter 4, the value (1.6b) takes is 3.05, implying that monopoly output *is about 1/3* of the competitive output, a very large reduction.

The estimates above are not mysterious or surprising. All studies of monopoly behavior find similarly large proportions, and the monopoly solution for a linear demand function is a standard example found in all textbooks. The effect of market power in a general equilibrium context will be studied later, in chapter 2.

1.7.3 Invariance of Relative Shares Under Free Factor Prices and Elasticity of Substitution Between Capital and Labor That Is Equal to 1

Equations (1.4) help understand the durability of the neoclassical belief in constant relative shares. To explain it, consider the effect of a change in the relative price of labor and capital. The effect depends upon the elasticity of substitution between capital and labor. If this elasticity is equal to 1, then any change in their relative price will not change the shares of labor and capital in income created because the rise in the price will be offset by a decline in quantity.[13] I will refer to this as the invariance theorem. Virtually all empirical studies find that, although

---

[13] Here is a proof. Let $L/K = x$, $W/R = y$, then the ratio of marginal products in (1.3b)–(1.3c) is written as $y = g(x)$, and relative shares are $S = g(x)x$. The elasticity of substitution is defined by $e_s = -dx/dy = -g(x)/(g'(x)x)$, and the reaction of relative shares to changed relative prices is equal to $dS/dy = ((g'(x)x + g(x))(dx/dy) = x(1 - 1/e_s) = 0$ if $e_s = 1$.

there are variations in this elasticity across sectors, for the aggregate production function the elasticity of substitution is close to 1, implying no effect of relative prices on relative shares. Most studies also find that the elasticities of output with respect to factor inputs have not changed either over time.

The invariance theorem has far-reaching implications because many things may change the prices of labor or capital. To be precise, the theorem asserts that if a competitive firm with elasticity of factor substitution equal to 1 and constant factor elasticities of output maximizes profits, and can freely select inputs of labor and capital, then no change in factor prices can alter the relative share of factors. The proof follows from equations (1.4).

This question has recently surfaced in the work of Karabarbounis and Neiman (2014). These authors find that, in their data, this elasticity is close to 1.25, which, they argue, opens the door to explaining the decline in labor share by the increase in the relative price of labor to capital goods since World War II, particularly because of the sharp decline in IT equipment prices. Unfortunately, estimating the elasticity of substitution in aggregate data presents many challenges, and the result of Karabarbounis and Neiman (2014) is in conflict with evidence of virtually all other studies of this parameter (see Lawrence, 2015; Oberfield and Raval, 2021; and Rognlie, 2015 and references therein).

Even if the elasticity of substitution between capital and labor is different from 1, a change in the relative price of factors would explain only changes in the distribution of income between capital and labor; *it cannot explain the rise in the share of profits*. By (1.4), the share of profits depends only on the degree of market power. The same reasoning applies to the possibility that the input elasticities change over time; such change can alter the relative shares of capital and labor but not the share of profits. A change in market power will, however, change the distribution of factor shares, as seen in (1.4), where an increase in the markup depresses the share of both capital and labor and raises the share of profits. Because market power and the markup change over time, relative shares are not constant even if output elasticities are constant.

But now consider other changes in the labor market that do not violate any conditions of the theorem. More specifically, consider (1) unions raising wages, (2) globalization reducing wages by migrating business abroad or (3) automation reducing demand for labor and lowering wages. In all cases, the changes affect wages and employment, but they do not change equations (1.4). Therefore, the firm's factor income shares remain the same. Because changes in the market power of firms do change factor shares, the invariance theorem points out that any explanation of changes in factor shares need to recognize the centrality of the impact of market power. The theorem is also useful for understanding the role of labor unions. If their aim is to change the distribution of income, they cannot achieve it just by bargaining for higher wages (as I argue in detail later). They must instead use other strategies that can alter the distribution.

1.7.4   Imperfections in the Labor Market

I note first some implications of rising market power. It follows from (1.4) that

$$\frac{\text{Labor share}}{\text{Capital share}} = \frac{W_t L_t}{R_t K_t} = \frac{1 - \alpha_t}{\alpha_t}. \tag{1.7}$$

This ratio is independent of θ_t because market power in product markets exerts equal pressure on labor and capital shares. This is a testable result, and it is studied empirically in chapter 4. In addition, empirical evidence reveals the elasticity α_t is either a constant or it changes very little. So, under the assumption of perfectly competitive factor markets, the ratio of the relative share of labor to the relative share of capital should be approximately constant.

Labor market imperfections take two forms. First, a monopsony firm has an effect on the prices it pays its suppliers. More specific to the labor market, such imperfection arises in markets with substantial search and matching frictions that narrow workers' alternative employment options. Second, the opposite case arises when unions have some control over labor markets and become monopolists in the supply of workers to the firm. The wage may be set arbitrarily by the union or chosen through negotiations between the firm and the union. Nevertheless, the firm can freely choose employment, given the wage, so the invariance theorem holds.

Starting with monopsony, the recent literature on the deteriorating conditions in the U.S. labor market (see Krueger, 2017) has stressed the role of monopsony behavior of firms. To formulate this hypothesis, I modify (1.3) to study the case where the firm has the power to set wages in addition to its ability to select the price. The firm faces a labor supply function $L_t(W_t, Z_t)$, where W is the wage and Z is other market conditions and its problem is

$$\text{Max}_{P_t, w_t, K_t} \left[P_t Y_t - W_t L_t \left(W_t, Z_t \right) - R_t K_t \right] + \lambda_t \left[Y_t - F \left(K_t, A_t L_t \right) \right], \tag{1.8}$$

$$Y_t = D \left(P_t, Z_t \right).$$

The first-order conditions of the firm's profit maximization are then

$$D + P_t \frac{\partial D}{\partial P_t} = \lambda_t \frac{\partial D}{\partial P_t} \tag{1.8a}$$

$$L + W_t \frac{\partial L}{\partial W_t} = \lambda_t F_L \frac{\partial L}{\partial W_t} \tag{1.8b}$$

$$R_t = \lambda_t F_K. \tag{1.8c}$$

I first write (1.8a)–(1.8b) in the form

$$P_t \left(1 + \frac{P_t}{D}\frac{\partial D}{\partial P_t}\right) = \lambda_t \frac{\partial D}{\partial P_t}\frac{P_t}{D}$$

$$W_t \left(1 + \frac{W_t}{L}\frac{\partial L}{\partial W_t}\right) = \lambda_t F_L \frac{\partial L}{\partial W_t}\frac{W_t}{L}.$$

I add the definition of

$$\varepsilon_t^{\,s} = \frac{W_t}{L}\frac{\partial L}{\partial W_t}$$

and proceed as in (1.3d)

$$P_t \left(\theta_t - 1\right) = \lambda_t \theta_t$$

$$W_t L_t \left(1 + \varepsilon_t^{\,s}\right) = \lambda_t \left(F_L L_t\right)\varepsilon_t^{\,s}$$

$$R_t K_t = \lambda_t \left(F_K K_t\right).$$

Even if the labor supply function is backward bending, a monopsonist will never select an allocation on that segment so that the ratio of the two relative shares is

$$\frac{W_t L_t}{R_t K_t} = \frac{1 - \alpha_t}{\alpha_t}\left(\frac{\varepsilon_t^{\,s}}{1 + \varepsilon_t^{\,s}}\right) \quad , \quad \left(\frac{\varepsilon_t^{\,s}}{1 + \varepsilon_t^{\,s}}\right) < 1. \tag{1.9}$$

In (1.9), the relative share of labor is lowered by *two factors*: the monopoly power of the firm in the product market and the further effect of monopsony power in the labor market. Given an estimate of $(1 - \alpha_t)/\alpha_t$, the added effect of monopsony power can be computed as the deviation of the ratio of relative shares from $(1 - \alpha_t)/\alpha_t$.

Are there factors in the labor market that can have the opposite effect on $(W_t L_t)/(R_t K_t)$? My earlier discussion of the balance of power in the labor market contrasted monopsony power of a firm with a possible monopoly power of labor in a labor market. To find out how a monopoly power of unions alters the distribution of income, I note that such power allows the union to choose a point on the firm's labor demand function, which is defined by the condition

$$\frac{W_t}{P_t} = \frac{\theta_t - 1}{\theta_t} F_L \left(\frac{A_t L_t}{K_t}\right) \Rightarrow L_t = F_L^{-1}\left(\frac{W_t}{P_t}\frac{\theta_t}{\theta_t - 1}\right)\frac{K_t}{A_t}. \tag{1.10}$$

Because a union represents the workers, it maximizes household utility by choosing employment and the real wage, subject to (1.10). This selection of an optimal mix does not alter any of the firm's optimal conditions in (1.4) because the firm still selects its inputs in an open market where the prices are taken as given. Because the elasticity of substitution between labor and capital is close to 1, the invariance theorem applies, and this optimization *will not alter the distribution of income, although it would alter the level of income.*

To change the distribution of income, a union must either concentrate its efforts on sectors where the elasticity of substitution is different from 1 or use its economic and political power to limit the ability of the firm to carry out the optimization that leads to (1.4). It is therefore not surprising that union negotiations are rarely focused only on wages. Their demands often aim to gain benefits that are not functions of hours or wage rates, such as working conditions, commitments to lump-sum contributions to the union's health and pension funds, or individual health and pension plans, that shift future risk onto the employer; bargain for bonus payments which are forms of profit sharing; or to alter hiring and firing policies. Many of these affect aggregate compensation, not wages, and therefore can alter relative shares.

More generally, some evidence suggests firms cannot carry out the assumed optimization. Unions may prevent the firm from optimizing by shaping public policy. Since early in the twentieth century, unions used political action to promote their cause. Consequently, New Deal labor legislation created regulations that can restrict the firm's ability to take profit-maximizing actions that unions oppose. In addition, many researchers stress the evidence for wage rigidity and noncompetitive wage setting.[14] If the government is supportive of union activities, a union has an implicit threat to punish the firms. In response, firms may take some unprofitable actions such as not laying off workers in a recession or paying above-market wages to avoid retaliatory political actions by unions. Nonunion firms would have an incentive to pay higher wages to convince their workers not to join a union. The fact that wages do not fall in recessions also implies that the ratio $(W_t L_t)/(R_t K_t)$ exhibits procyclical fluctuations. These diverse actions do cause deviations from the equilibrium conditions in (1.4) in favor of labor and may result in

$$\frac{W_t L_t}{R_t K_t} > \frac{1 - \alpha_t}{\alpha_t}.$$

There is also substantial evidence that wages paid by highly profitable firms are higher than wages paid *for the same jobs* by low-profitability firms, which suggests that firms do not simply pay wages proportional to the marginal productivity of the worker. For example, consider the wages of janitors. In 2019, the

---

[14]This is a very large literature that is not essential to my treatment here. For references, see the work included in the Mankiw and Romer (1991) edited volume and references there. The volume contains various research works on wage rigidity and the efficiency theory of wages.

average salaries of janitors in different locations were:

United States	$22,000
California	$26,400
Silicon Valley	$31,000
Apple	$33,000.

Such differences suggest that more profitable firms voluntarily transfer some monopoly profits to employees, perhaps aiming to increase workers' morale and loyalty.[15] Also, Kline et al. (2019) show that some firms share with their workers the benefits of profitable news for the firm. These facts are also consistent with the evidence for wage stickiness.

I then define an aggregate measure of the balance of power in the labor market. Values of the ratio $(W_t L_t)/(R_t K_t)$ that are less than $(1 - \alpha_t)/\alpha_t$ reflect monopsony pressures in the labor market, while values above $(1 - \alpha_t)/\alpha_t$ reflect diverse factors that tip the balance *in favor of labor relative to capital*. I then write the final condition in the form

$$\frac{W_t L_t}{R_t K_t} = \frac{1 - \alpha_t}{\alpha_t} \left(1 + \Upsilon_t\right) \quad , \quad \Upsilon_t > 0 \quad \text{or} \quad \Upsilon_t < 0. \quad (1.11)$$

Equation (1.11) measures the effect of other factors that may influence relative shares by changing the ratio between labor and capital shares. As I argued above, α is approximately constant over time, so I interpret changes in the ratio between labor and capital shares as changes in forces other than market power in product markets. The $\Upsilon_t < 0$ measures monopsony in the labor market, while $\Upsilon_t > 0$ reflects other forces discussed earlier that award labor an outcome superior relative to the return to capital, while both compensations are changed by market power.

1.8   Personal Inequality and Other Harmful Effects of Market Power

I now turn to the effect of market power on personal income and wealth inequality. Changes in the functional distribution of income have a direct effect on the personal distribution of income, and this relation is reinforced by the fact that monopoly profits accrue to a very narrow group in society. I also explain why the speed at which monopoly wealth is created and destroyed is important for understanding the dynamics of wealth inequality.

---

[15]This reasoning has been proposed by the efficiency theory of wages, but the janitors' example suggests that they may not be applied equally by all firms. See Solow (1979), Akerlof (1982), and Bewley (1999).

1.8.1   Market Power Is the Central Cause of Income Inequality

Given the fact that market power changes the functional distribution of income, I now show that most changes in personal income distribution are directly traceable to changes in the functional distribution of income. Personal income before redistribution is derived from labor and from diverse assets. Therefore, the personal distribution of income is determined by labor income and by the personal distribution of asset holdings. But income from any asset is determined by the functional distribution of income at the firm that the asset represents. To illustrate these relations, I examine the effect of market power on the components of personal income. For example, if market power rises, the profit share rises and the shares of labor and capital fall. These imply that:

1. The income of workers in the bottom 90 percent of the income distribution declines because they receive only wage income.
2. One major portion of capital income is earned by retirees and other people who receive income from diversified portfolios. A second major portion is earned by wealthy individuals. The income of both groups declines. Knowledge of the proportion of capital ownership of each of the groups can be used to determine the exact effect of falling capital income on each group.
3. Rising profits are received by corporate managers and by owners of common stocks. But then there is an exact relationship that determines the share of stockholders in gross value added of the corporate sector, which I denote by S_E. Now, let ℓ_k be mean leverage in the corporate sector and let s_π be the share of profits, s_k be the share of capital, and s_m be the share of management. These definitions imply that $S_E = s_\pi + (1 - \ell_k)s_k - s_m$. A rise in market power increases s_π and s_m but decreases s_k, while ℓ_k is not directly affected.

The above reasoning can be used to calculate the effect of rising market power on each income group in the population. For example, suppose a nonmanagerial income group of individuals owns X percent of total common stock in the economy. What is the proportion of total profits resulting from market power that the group receives? The answer is $X \cdot (s_\pi - s_m)$.

To further illustrate this approach, consider the effect of the dramatic rise in market power sine the 1980s, demonstrated in chapter 4. The decline of labor share is well documented, but then how has the rise of market power affected the relative share of, say, the bottom 90 percent of individuals in the distribution of personal wealth? To assess this, one can use data on this group's ownership of stocks and bonds and their debts.

Consider first the ownership of equity in young firms. The majority of shares is held in most firms by a small group consisting of the innovator, management team, venture capital investors, and angel investors. Among these, the innovator is typically the largest owner of the firm's shares. This extreme concentration implies that successful new ventures result in heavily concentrated financial gains, making innovative firms major drivers of a rising share of profits.

Older firms have wider public ownership that benefits from growth in their market power. Nevertheless, these owners are still largely drawn from the ranks of the wealthy. The fraction of all outstanding equity shares owned by those in the bottom 90 percent of the wealth distribution changes over time, but, using data from 2016 as an example, Wolff (2017) reports that fraction to be 16 percent.[16] Based on that fact, I now ask: What is the proportion of total monopoly profits that was received in 2016 by people in the bottom 90 percent of the wealth distribution?

In chapter 4, I estimate that, in 2016, the share of monopoly profits in corporate gross value added was 23.5 percent. The share received by officers was 5.1 percent, and none of it accrued to the bottom 90 percent. Subtracting the share of officers shows that the share of profits that accrued to stockholders was then 18.4 percent, which is 78 percent of all monopoly profits. Finally, because individuals at the bottom 90 percent of the wealth distribution owned 16 percent of that wealth, they actually received 12.48 percent of the total monopoly profits of the corporate sector. In other words, 88 percent of all profits attributable to market power in 2016 were received by individuals in the top 10 percent of the wealth distribution.

The striking disparity between the top 10 percent receiving 88 percent of profits and the bottom 90 percent receiving only 12 percent should leave no doubt as to the effect of rising share of profits on inequality. The sharp rise of market power since the 1980s increased both profits and monopoly wealth dramatically, and individuals in the top 10 percent of the wealth distribution gained almost all of it.

An important qualification about the distribution of labor income is in order. Personal inequality of labor income among workers is strongly determined by the skill distribution, which is unrelated to the functional distribution of income. I will briefly address this question later in section 1.8.4.

1.8.2   The Speed of Wealth Accumulation and Intergenerational Transfer

There are two important characteristics of the process of wealth accumulation that result from rising market power. They are the speed of accumulation and the mechanism by which the implied intergenerational transfer of wealth takes place. Since the 1970s, when the IT revolution got underway, the institution

---

[16] This measure includes direct ownership of various forms of stock and indirect ownership through mutual funds, trusts, individual retirement accounts (IRAs), Keogh plans, 401(k) plans and other retirement accounts.

of venture capital and general financing of innovations has been developed to the point that, in a relatively short period, an innovator with a successful idea can turn it into major personal wealth. A modest part of the windfall is shared with venture capitalists and investment bankers, but very little is shared with the public. In Silicon Valley, they call a new innovation a unicorn if its market value reaches $1 billion and urge companies to cross that threshold with ever-greater speed. It is thus not surprising that in a time when investors measure their success in billions of dollars, since the 1970s, thousands of entrepreneurs around the world have become billionaires overnight. The outcome is then the increased speed of business development and wealth creation, a conclusion supported by other studies (see, for example, Greenwood and Jovanovic, 1999). In chapter 6, I show that monopoly wealth owned by stockholders was virtually zero in 1982 but, as IT innovations developed, it rose dramatically. This wealth reached $25 trillion in 2019, which was 75 percent of the total value of the stock market. This $25 trillion is the extra wealth of stockholders, which is the result of rising market power above and beyond the wealth attained via normal savings and added capital assets such as buildings, factories, and equipment.

The speed of wealth accumulation due to market power conflicts with Piketty's (2014) explanation of rising income and wealth inequality taking place through a slow intergenerational process where the rate of return on wealth held by dynastic families exceeds the growth rate of the economy and causes wealth inequality to rise.[17] The process of accumulation described in this book shows

---

[17] Piketty proposes to explain this gradual process with a relation between the interest rate and the growth rate, but this relation does not explain what he proposes to explain. To see this, denote the interest rate by r and the growth rate of the economy's output by g. Piketty's main hypothesis, that $r > g$ has caused increased inequality, is entirely flawed in two ways. First, the condition $r > g$ is the well-known efficiency requirement that the capital stock not exceed the Golden Rule stock. Piketty's effort to show it is empirically satisfied is a nice victory for neoclassical growth theory. Second, r is the net rate of return on capital and g is the growth rate of output, and these are two different quantities and their relationship has no implications. The growth of capital depends upon the savings rate s and upon the depreciation rate d, not upon the income of the wealthy. Therefore, the interest rate tells us nothing about the growth rate of capital. For example, if capital owners do not save anything, their capital will decline at the rate d, regardless of the interest rate. If they save and reinvest a fraction s of their gross capital income, then the growth rate of their capital stock will be $(s(r + d) - d)$. Why should this have any relation to g? If the wealthy execute an optimal intertemporal saving plan, the long-term growth rate of their capital stock will be g. If they give away part of their wealth to charity or place part of their wealth in foundations designed to attain some social goals, family wealth will grow slower than g. Ignoring optimal savings, arithmetically speaking it is possible technology enables the wealthy's capital stock to grow faster than the growth rate of the economy, in which case $s(r + d) - d > g$. But then how much would they need to save out of gross capital income? Consider realistic numbers like $g = 2.5$ percent, $d = 5.0$ percent, $r = 4$ percent; then $s > (2.5 + 5)/(4 + 5) = 0.83$. A different savings program could call for the wealthy to plow back all depreciation and, in addition, a fraction s^* of net capital income (i.e., rK). In that case, the required added net saving amounts to $s^* > (2.5)/4 = 0.625$.

that wealth creation since the 1970s had a drastic effect on the process of intergenerational transfer of wealth. It was caused by the *rapid rise* of individual wealth of younger innovators and entrepreneurs, enabled by information-based innovations, together with the *rapid decline* of wealth created in older industries such as railroads, automobiles, steel, or chemicals, much of it owned by older stockholders. These facts call into question standard views of wealth dynamics, which appear motivated by simplistic intergenerational models of wealth accumulation, where assets are transferred slowly from generation to generation. The data reveal a volatile process of monopoly wealth creation, together with a precipitous decline of older industries, as the U.S. economy becomes a service-dominated economy.

1.8.3   Other Harmful Side Effects of Market Power

I now turn to the significant economic and social side effects that, apart from increasing income and wealth inequality, make a high degree of market power a high price to pay for the social benefits of innovations. In addition, I show in chapter 9 that a high degree of permanent market power is not needed to preserve the rate of innovation. Much more detail about these negative effects is provided in later chapters when these issues come up again. Here, I limit my comments to a short list of these effects:

1. *Static inefficiency.* This effect is the standard textbook inefficiency in the use of economic resources. The usual remedy for such distortions is the use of the tax system to counter them, but when market power is widespread and at a high level, such a remedy is not feasible.
2. *Dynamic inefficiency.* The slowdown of U.S. growth is linked to lower rates of private investment. A key reason for the slower investment rate is the rising market power of corporations, which causes firms to restrict output and lower demand for labor and capital inputs. In chapter 2, I study a growth model with market power. I show that, apart from lowering the rate of investment, a rise in market power permanently lowers the level of wages, consumption, and gross domestic product (GDP).
3. *Slowing down the rate of innovations.* In protecting their market power, firms routinely acquire potential competitors or their technologies and shelve part of them. In suppressing this knowledge, firms with market power prevent new ideas from being developed, effectively retarding economic growth. Substantial evidence also points to leading firms impeding innovation and the growth of smaller competitors. Such practices were the main cause of the Justice Department taking legal action against Microsoft, but it has been difficult to address the problem under existing laws.

4. *Slowing down the diffusion of innovations.* The slow rate at which new innovations diffuse through the economy is a well-documented fact. In chapter 5, I demonstrate that a high rate of market power is the main cause of slow diffusion of innovations resulting from the high price the innovating firm charges for its own products.

Apart from the direct effect of market power on inequality, there are specific side effects of inequality that call for public scrutiny. I review two of these here, although the growing body of research on inequality is likely to bring to the surface new evidence.

5. *Deteriorating health in the U.S. workplace.* The rising market power of corporations and the declining power of unions altered the balance of power in the labor market and resulted in a deterioration of the quality of the American workplace. Pfeffer (2018) documents the deterioration in working conditions, particularly for those earning low wages. He reports on how pressure to overperform without rest, without paid vacation or adequate medical care, combined with stagnating wages, causes deteriorating health, alcoholism, and drug addiction. Case and Deaton (2020) document a trend of decreased life expectancy of middle-aged white American workers.

6. *Tilted social balance of power.* Rising inequality, the result of rising market power, alters the delicate balance of power in society in favor of the rich, awarding their voices more weight than others. This enables the rich to have a greater impact on policy. Because policy is the only significant force that can restrain the growth of market power and regulate its behavior, if the rising power of the rich enables them to prevent policy from restraining market power, then market power could spiral out of control. This would delegitimize democratic institutions and render the American political system a plutocracy.

In sum, in a technologically advancing economy, market power may fluctuate over time, but if unrestrained by policy, it becomes a permanent and insidious force with deeply harmful economic and social effects. Rising market power results in an inefficient allocation of resources, but, beyond that, together with skill-biased technical change (see section 1.8.4) it has also caused rising inequality and a decline of the middle class. This decline has removed an important stabilizing force of democracy because the middle class is the balancing group with the weight and incentive to force society's extreme elements to compromise (see Sitaraman, 2017). It means that rising market power weakens the foundations of democratic institutions, as happened in nineteenth-century Europe and the United States in the First Gilded Age. Developments since the 1980s reflect the same dynamics in the Second Gilded Age.

1.8.4   The Vital Impact of Skill-Biased Technical Change on the Weakening of the Middle Class

Because the market premium paid skilled workers has a strong effect on personal income distribution, to explain changes in this distribution, the attention of scholars was naturally directed to the study of the effect of capital accumulation and innovations on this premium. It was motivated by a desire to explain why advances in modern technology have often been perceived as resulting in capital replacing repetitive jobs performed by unskilled labor. Griliches (1969) was the first to formulate the problem as a study of capital-skill complementarity, proposing that the elasticity of substitution between capital equipment and unskilled labor is higher than that between capital equipment and skilled labor. It implies that the accumulation of capital increases the marginal product of skilled labor but decreases the marginal product of unskilled labor. This causes the growth of capital to replace unskilled labor and raise the wage of skilled labor, increasing the skill premium. This turned out to be the case (see Krusell et al., 2000). However, many labor economists consider the rise of the premium to be a result of a skill biased *technical change*, and I take it up next, in relation to the job polarization phenomenon.[18]

Electricity and the combustion engine, the two leading GPTs of the twentieth century, were very beneficial to workers who lacked a college education. They created jobs and tasks that could be performed by workers without advanced education and that could be learned relatively quickly through experience on the production lines. These jobs tended to be repetitive and required dexterity and discipline of workers who were able to perform according to clear rules. Consequently, these technologies gave rise to a class of blue-collar workers whose productivity rose sharply so that they earned enough to join the middle class. This contributed to the expansion of the middle class in the twentieth century. Computer technology and more generally, IT automation, has been effective in replacing exactly these same blue-collar workers with lower levels of education who benefited from the prior technologies earlier in the twentieth century. But the job polarization effect requires the assessment of the effects of capital-skill complementarity on the job prospect of highly skilled workers as well (for key references see Autor et al., 2003; Levy and Murnane, 2004; Acemoglu and Autor,

---

[18]The rise in the skill premium is an uncontested empirical observation, but labor economists disagree about the factors that contribute to the change. Griliches (1969) and Krusell et al. (2000) attribute the cause to the capital accumulation process itself, given a production function that allows the capital-skill complementarity. Other scholars (see Goldin and Katz, 1998, 2010 and the references in the next paragraph) attribute the rise in the premium to technical change that altered the parameters of a given production function, causing an increase of the elasticity of substitution between capital equipment and unskilled labor relative to the elasticity of substitution between capital equipment and skilled labor.

2011; Autor and Dorn, 2013; Autor, 2014; see Frey, 2019 for a complete survey and additional references).

Extensive research on job polarization has thus demonstrated that, apart from lowering the demand for blue-collar workers with lower levels of educaion, IT-based automation has increased the productivity of educated workers, holding highly skilled jobs, mostly in the service sector. The computer and internet complemented those jobs rather than displacing them. IT has also created new highly skilled jobs required for its implementation and operations, such as computer programmers, support specialists, web developers and systems analysts. This conforms to the common observation that professional workers have benefited from advances in IT.

This dual effect on the composition of skills has contributed significantly to the decline of the middle class because the blue-collar workers replaced by IT-based automation were well paid, increasing the skill premium. As to the workers with lower levels of education who would have qualified in the past for the high-paying blue-collar jobs, they have gradually migrated to the rising class of low-skilled and low-paid workers.

In short, the job polarization effect has caused a shift to a U-shaped skill employment distribution. It created a wide gap in employment opportunities, contributing to the decline of the middle class.

CHAPTER 2

ECONOMIC GROWTH UNDER THE EFFECT
OF MARKET POWER

his chapter expands the scope of the analysis to explore the effect
of market power on standard neoclassical growth theory. I seek to
quantify the macroeconomic impact of fluctuating market power
and to clarify the mechanism proposed in chapter 1, in which technological innovations cause rising market power. I formulate a dynamic model that preserves the basic elements of neoclassical growth theory but allows for varying
market power, formulated as an endogenous state variable. I focus on studying
general theoretical effects of changing market power on the dynamics of growth
rather than engaging in precise calibrations, but I follow existing empirical estimates where they are available.

I use the Dixit-Stiglitz model of demand in which firms have pricing power.
This is a standard model used by others to address diverse problems. For example, Hornstein (1993) and Chatterjee and Cooper (1993) use it (with increasing
returns) to assess the propagation of productivity shocks. Karabarbounis and
Neiman (2014) use it to explain the decline of labor share due to capital/labor
substitution motivated by the decline in the relative price of capital to labor.
Barkai (2020) uses a similar model to deduce the markup and aggregate profits.

In section 1.7, I showed that income and wealth inequality can be studied
without a complete general equilibrium model (see also Solow, 1960). Here, I
study other aggregate implications of changing market power, and for that, one
needs a dynamic general equilibrium treatment.[1] To avoid too high a level of

---

[1] The model formulation in this chapter is the same as the one developed in Kurz (2016) and
further discussed in Kurz (2018a). See also Eggertsson et al. (2018).

abstraction, I work with the *simplest* possible assumptions, but the results remain valid even under more general conditions. The model has M firms each producing a distinct product. The products are differentiated by the firms' proprietary technologies. There is no free entry,[2] but if M is large and all M goods are substitutes, it becomes a model of monopolistic competition.

In much of this book, I use models with identical consumers (or, equivalently, a representative consumer) and a finite number of firms producing differentiated products. Here I assume that there is a single consumption good that is created by a composition of M different intermediate goods. I consider only symmetric general equilibria out of a desire for simplicity.

2.1   A General Equilibrium Model of Growth

A large number of identical consumer-households with utility over consumption and labor optimize dynamically over time with a utility function

$$U_t = \sum_{\tau=t}^{\infty} \beta^{(\tau-t)} u(C_\tau, L_\tau). \tag{2.1}$$

Consumption follows a Dixit and Stiglitz (1977) framework but with only M firms producing intermediate products. Because innovations generate new firms with new technology who may replace old firms, one may think of the firms as dynasties where the name may change over time. As noted earlier, the firms that produce differentiated intermediate goods have proprietary technologies. These goods are used by households to produce final consumption or investment goods, which are CES composites of the intermediate goods:

$$Y_t = C_t + I_t = \Omega \left[\sum_{j=1}^{M} \vartheta_{jt} (Y_{it})^{\frac{\theta_t-1}{\theta_t}} \right]^{\frac{\theta_t}{\theta_t-1}}. \tag{2.2}$$

Y_{it} is the amount of intermediate good i, measured in units of that good, used in producing output Y_t, consumption C_t, and investment I_t, which are *all measured in units of consumption goods*. The variable θ_t is the elasticity of substitution, with $\theta_t = \infty$ being the case of perfect competition, but I consider only $\infty > \theta_t > 1$ that permits profit maximization. Fluctuations of θ over time are of central interest because they reflect endogenous changes in average market power in the economy.

---

[2] As explained in chapter 1, if entry is possible but difficult due to barriers to entry, a successful challenge of a new entrant may just replace one firm with market power with a new firm with market power, maintaining the same number of firms. One may thus interpret the current model as allowing the introduction of new firms, not by adding new products but by successful replacements of firms already in the model.

I introduce the index ϑ_{jt} in the CES aggregator to express differences in quality and efficacy of intermediate goods, which may change over time. In chapter 7, I briefly discuss the idea of allowing this variable to be an endogenous one. Here, I incorporate ϑ_{jt} in (2.2) so that the basic model formulation need not be repeated later. However, in the simulations in this chapter, I will set ϑ_{jt} to be a constant. Each intermediate good is produced by a firm that has monopoly right to produce that commodity, and I have explained in chapter 1 my view that the model with fixed number of commodities and with changing quality and/or productivity is very general.

It is important to clarify my assumptions about capital ownership. I study long-term processes, and the unit of time in the analysis is a year. With such a long time horizon, I can assume that capital and labor are freely mobile, hired in free markets, and paid the competitive wage rate and rental rates (W_t, R_t). Hence, the treatments of capital and labor are symmetric, and households own[3] the capital they rent to firms. Aggregate capital is given by $K_{t+1} = (1 - \delta)K_t + I_t$ (δ being the depreciation rate), and aggregate labor available is exogenous and fixed at the level of 1. In profit calculations, firms take the market costs of capital and labor as given and maximize profits at any date by choosing the quantity of those inputs to hire from households. The key assumption made is that consumers, households, or capital owners do not form coalitions to break the pricing power of firms. Firms' ownership shares are traded in open markets, and profits are distributed to stockholders as dividends only after capital and labor are paid their incomes according to the market prices at which they are hired.

To derive demand functions, I first address the issue of measurement units. As in Dixit and Stiglitz (1977), it is common to use labor as a numéraire. Because I integrate the model with a neoclassical production structure, I prefer to use consumption as a reference. I therefore first introduce an abstract unit of account with which to write the budget constraints. Values in consumption units are then deduced from prices relative to the price of the consumption good.

Because the utility function is increasing in consumption, one can derive the implied demand functions for intermediate goods with prices P_{jt} from the following consumer optimization:

$$\text{Maximize } Y_t = \left[\sum_{j=1}^{M} \vartheta_{jt}(Y_{jt})^{\frac{\theta_t-1}{\theta_t}} \right]^{\frac{\theta_t}{\theta_t-1}} \quad \text{subject to the cost of } P_t Y_t = \sum_{j=1}^{M} P_{jt} Y_{jt}.$$

$$(2.3)$$

---

[3]This assumption is made for simplicity because, as I shortly explain, it implies the firm needs to solve only a static optimization problem, while the households do all dynamic optimizations and take the risk of the actual return on capital they receive, which is determined one period after they make the saving decision. If the firm owns the capital, it must also perform a dynamic optimization.

The implied demand functions depend upon expenditures $P_t Y_t$. The first-order conditions are

$$P_{jt}\lambda_t = Y_t^{\frac{1}{\theta_t}}\vartheta_{jt}(Y_{jt})^{-\frac{1}{\theta_t}} \Rightarrow \left(\frac{\vartheta_{it}P_{jt}}{\vartheta_{jt}P_{it}}\right)^{-\theta_t} = \left(\frac{Y_{jt}}{Y_{it}}\right),$$

which implies

$$P_{jt}Y_{jt} = Y_{it}\left(\frac{P_{it}}{\vartheta_{it}}\right)^{\theta_t}\left(\frac{P_{jt}}{\vartheta_{jt}}\right)^{1-\theta_t}\vartheta_{jt} \quad \text{all i and j.} \qquad (2.4)$$

Add up the last expression, using the right-hand side of (2.3)

$$P_t Y_t = \sum_{j=1}^{M} P_{jt}Y_{jt} = Y_{it}\left(\frac{P_{it}}{\vartheta_{it}}\right)^{\theta_t}\sum_{j=1}^{M}\left(\frac{P_{jt}}{\vartheta_{jt}}\right)^{1-\theta_t}\vartheta_{jt},$$

which implies

$$Y_{it} = \frac{(P_{it}/\vartheta_{it})^{-\theta_t}}{\sum_{j=1}^{M}\vartheta_{jt}(P_{jt}/\vartheta_{jt})^{1-\theta_t}}P_t Y_t.$$

Define the price

$$P_t = \left[\sum_{j=1}^{M}\vartheta_{jt}\left(\frac{P_{jt}}{\vartheta_{jt}}\right)^{1-\theta_t}\right]^{\frac{1}{1-\theta_t}} \qquad (2.5)$$

and the demand functions, with $C_t + I_t = Y_t$

$$Y_{jt}^{C} = \frac{(P_{jt}/\vartheta_{jt})^{-\theta_t}}{(P_t)^{-\theta_t}}C_t, \quad Y_{jt}^{I} = \frac{(P_{jt}/\vartheta_{jt})^{-\theta_t}}{(P_t)^{-\theta_t}}I_t, \quad Y_{jt} = \frac{(P_{jt}/\vartheta_{jt})^{-\theta_t}}{(P_t)^{-\theta_t}}Y_t. \qquad (2.6)$$

This amounts to assuming that capital is measured in units of consumption and a unit of capital is exchanged for a unit of investment at the rate of 1-to-1; hence the consumption-savings decision does not change the relative price of consumption and capital goods.

The price P_t is the cost of a unit of consumption or investment at the optimal mix of intermediate goods (see Brakman and Heijdra, 2001, chap. 1). Although (2.5) depends upon individual P_{jt}, if M is large and all firms are the same, the effect of P_{jt} on P_t is negligible, and in this chapter, I assume firms don't take into account their effect on P_t. When discussing market concentration in chapter 7, I study models in which M is relatively small, so the firms are large and the effect of P_{jt} on P_t is significant. In that case, firms will take into account their effect on P_t.

So far, I used only the right-hand side of (2.3). To define gross national product (GNP) in consumption units, I add

$$\sum_{j=1}^{M}\left(\frac{P_{jt}}{P_t}\right)Y_{jt} = \sum_{j=1}^{M}\vartheta_{jt}\left(\frac{P_{jt}}{\vartheta_{jt}}\right)^{1-\theta_t}\left(\frac{1}{P_t}\right)^{1-\theta_t}Y_t.$$

Plugging in the production functions of intermediate goods discussed below, I have

$$Y_t = \sum_{j=1}^{M} \left(\frac{P_{jt}}{P_t} \right) Y_{jt} = \sum_{j=1}^{M} \left(\frac{P_{jt}}{P_t} \right) \zeta_t \Omega \Psi_{jt} (K_{jt})^\alpha (A_t L_{jt})^{(1-\alpha)}.$$

To evaluate λ_t, multiply (2.4) by Y_{jt} and sum to deduce

$$Y_t P_t \lambda_t = \sum_{j=1}^{M} Y_{jt} P_{jt} \lambda_t = Y_t^{\frac{1}{\theta_t}} \sum_{j=1}^{M} \vartheta_{jt} (Y_{jt})^{\frac{\theta_t-1}{\theta_t}} = Y_t^{\frac{1}{\theta_t}} Y_t^{\frac{\theta_t-1}{\theta_t}} \Rightarrow \lambda_t = \frac{1}{P_t}.$$

2.2   Optimization by the Producers of Intermediate Goods

Each intermediate producer j has a production function of the form

$$Y_{jt} = \zeta_t \Omega \Psi_{jt} (K_{jt})^\alpha (A_t L_{jt})^{(1-\alpha)}$$

where Ψ_{jt} is firm-specific productivity, which will be used in chapter 7. In this chapter, I work with symmetric equilibria where $\Psi_{jt} = 1$. The variable ζ_t is a Markov process of productivity shocks, and $A_t = g_0 g^t$ is a common deterministic productivity factor growing at a constant rate g. The parameter Ω is introduced to adjust the units of intermediate goods so that the steady-state relative price of intermediate goods to consumption is 1.

The date t profit function is

$$\Pi_t^j = P_{jt} Y_{jt} - P_t W_t L_{jt} - P_t R_t K_{jt},$$

where factor costs (W_t, R_t) are in units of consumption. Producers of intermediate goods maximize profits by setting their own prices and choosing the quantities of labor and capital they employ at each date:

$$\text{Max}_{P_{jt} N_{jt}, K_{jt}} [P_{jt} Y_{jt} - P_t W_t L_{jt} - P_t R_t K_{jt} + \lambda_{jt} [\zeta_t \Omega \Psi_{jt} K_{jt}^\alpha (A_t L_{jt})^{1-\alpha} - Y_{jt}]]$$

$$Y_{jt} = \left(\frac{P_{jt}}{\vartheta_{jt} P_t} \right)^{-\theta_t} Y_t.$$

$$(2.7a)$$

The first-order conditions are then

$$(\theta - 1) \left(\frac{P_{jt}}{\vartheta_{jt} P_t} \right)^{-\theta_t} Y_t = \lambda_{jt} \theta_t \left(\frac{P_{jt}}{\vartheta_{jt} P_t} \right)^{-\theta_t} Y_t P_{jt}^{-1} \Rightarrow \lambda_{jt} = P_{jt} \frac{(\theta_t - 1)}{\theta_t} \quad \text{all } j$$

$$(2.7b)$$

$$W_t = \frac{P_{jt}}{P_t} \frac{(\theta_t - 1)}{\theta_t} (1 - \alpha) \Omega \Psi_{jt} [\zeta_t A_t^{1-\alpha}] (K_{jt})^{\alpha} (L_{jt})^{-\alpha} = \frac{P_{jt}}{P_t} \frac{(\theta_t - 1)}{\theta_t} \frac{\partial Y_{jt}}{\partial L_{jt}}.$$

(2.7c)

$$R_t = \frac{P_{jt}}{P_t} \frac{(\theta_t - 1)}{\theta_t} \alpha \Omega \Psi_{jt} \left[\zeta_t A_t^{1-\alpha}\right] (K_{jt})^{\alpha-1} (L_{jt})^{1-\alpha} = \frac{P_{jt}}{P_t} \frac{(\theta_t - 1)}{\theta_t} \frac{\partial Y_{jt}}{\partial K_{jt}}.$$

(2.7d)

Variations in the quality parameters ϑ_{jt} do not affect (2.7c)–(2.7d). Because all income distribution results depend upon (2.7c)–(2.7d), these distributions are invariant to heterogeneity in ϑ_{jt}. Based on section 1.7, one could have expected this conclusion because (1.4) was developed for general demand functions. Thus, by (2.7c)–(2.7d) and by the definition of output, it follows that

$$Y_t = \frac{\theta_t}{\theta_t - 1} \left[R_t \sum_{j=1}^{M} K_{jt} + W_t \sum_{j=1}^{M} L_{jt} \right] = \frac{\theta_t}{\theta_t - 1} [R_t K_t + W_t L_t],$$

which implies that the functional distribution of income is:

$$\text{Labor income} \quad W_t L_t = (1 - \alpha) \frac{\theta_t - 1}{\theta_t} Y_t$$

$$\text{Capital rental income} \quad R_t K_t = \alpha \frac{\theta_t - 1}{\theta_t} Y_t \qquad (2.8)$$

$$\text{Monopoly profits} \quad = \frac{1}{\theta_t} Y_t.$$

Equation (2.8) is the same as (1.4). The share of profits due to market power is $1/\theta_t$.

A similar functional distribution of income takes place at the level of each firm, so that the profits of firm j are then defined by

$$\text{Monopoly profits of firm } j = \Pi_{jt} = \frac{Y_{jt} P_{jt}}{\theta_t}.$$

2.3 Aggregation and the Key Role of Relative Prices in Measured Productivity

I now proceed to the aggregation of this economy. To that end, I start with the following proposition, taking advantage of the symmetry of the producers:

Proposition 2.1. *In equilibrium:*

1. Relative prices satisfy $\frac{P_{jt}}{P_t}\psi_{jt} = \varphi_t$ for all j where

$$\varphi_t = \left[\sum_{j=1}^{M} \vartheta_{jt}^{\theta_t} \Psi_{jt}^{\theta_t-1} \right]^{\frac{1}{\theta_t-1}}. \tag{2.9a}$$

2. Equilibrium quantities act in accordance with an aggregate production function and

$$Y_t = \varphi_t \zeta_t \Omega (K_t)^{\alpha} (A_t L_t)^{(1-\alpha)}. \tag{2.9b}$$

Proof.   1. (2.7c)–(2.7d) imply

$$\frac{W_t}{R_t} = \frac{(1-\alpha)}{\alpha} \left(\frac{K_{jt}}{L_{jt}} \right) \qquad \text{for all } j;$$

hence (K_{jt}/L_{jt}) is independent of j. By (2.7c),

$$\frac{P_{jt}}{P_t} \Psi_{jt} = \frac{W_t}{\left(\frac{\theta_t-1}{\theta_t} \right) (1-\alpha) \Omega \zeta_t A_t^{1-\alpha} (K_{jt}/L_{jt})^{\alpha}} = \varphi_t \text{ is also independent of } j.$$

Insert this result into (2.5) to deduce

$$P_t = \left[\sum_{j=1}^{M} \vartheta_{jt}^{\theta_t} \left(\frac{P_t \varphi_t}{\Psi_{jt}} \right)^{1-\theta_t} \right]^{\frac{1}{1-\theta_t}} \Rightarrow \varphi_t = \left[\sum_{j=1}^{M} \vartheta_{jt}^{\theta_t} \Psi_{jt}^{\theta_t-1} \right]^{\frac{1}{\theta_t-1}}.$$

2. By the definition of output and using part (1) above,

$$Y_t = \varphi_t \sum_{j=1}^{M} \zeta_t \Omega (K_{jt})^{\alpha} (A_t L_{jt})^{(1-\alpha)}.$$

Because K_{jt}/L_{jt} are the same for all firms,

$$\sum_{j=1}^{M} \varphi_t \zeta_t \Omega (K_{jt})^{\alpha} (A_t L_{jt})^{(1-\alpha)} = \varphi_t \zeta_t \Omega \left(\frac{K_{jt}}{A_t L_{jt}} \right)^{\alpha} \sum_{j=1}^{M} A_t L_{jt}$$

$$= \varphi_t \zeta_t \Omega \left(\frac{K_{jt}}{A_t L_{jt}} \right)^{\alpha-1} \sum_{j=1}^{M} K_{jt}$$

$$\text{with } K_t = \sum_{j=1}^{M} K_{jt}, L_t = \sum_{j=1}^{M} L_{jt}.$$

These imply that

$$\frac{K_t}{L_t} = \frac{K_{jt}}{L_j} \quad \text{for all } j$$

and

$$Y_t = \varphi_t \zeta_t \Omega K_t^{\alpha} (A_t L_t)^{1-\alpha}.$$

$\square$

Proposition 2.1 makes a clear point. In equilibrium, the value of the output of intermediate goods produced by firm j, *in units of consumption goods*, is defined by the expression

$$\left(\frac{P_{jt}}{P_t} \Psi_{jt} \right) \zeta_t \Omega (K_{jt})^{\alpha} (A_t L_{jt})^{(1-\alpha)} = \varphi_t \zeta_t \Omega (K_{jt})^{\alpha} (A_t L_{jt})^{(1-\alpha)}. \qquad (2.10)$$

Therefore, the proposition shows that, adjusting for the factor Ψ_{jt}, the relative price of an intermediate good to the price of the consumption good is the same for all intermediate goods. In addition, (2.9a) also shows that any change in the quality of intermediate good j shows up as a change in the relative price of intermediate goods to consumption good.

If firm j's ϑ_{jt} increases, then for a large economy where the firm takes the price P_t as given, it follows from (2.6) that the demand for its own product will increase as well because its product has a higher relative weight in consumption. But then it follows from (2.9a) that this will also change the prices of intermediate goods relative to consumption, which causes a higher aggregate exchange rate with consumption, measured by the change of a single term ϑ_{jt} in φ_t. Because the value of profits, in units of the consumption good, of any firm k is

$$\frac{\Pi_{kt}}{P_t} = \varphi_t \frac{Y_{kt}}{\Psi_{kt}} - W_t L_{kt} - R_t K_{kt},$$

the profits of all firms rise because of this decrease in the price of consumption goods relative to the price of intermediate good j.

If, on the other hand, for a given level of inputs, the quality of *all* intermediate goods rises by the same proportion ξ, it follows from (2.9a) that the new relative price $(\hat{P}_{jt}/\hat{P}_t)$ becomes

$$\frac{\hat{P}_{jt}}{\hat{P}_t} = \xi^{\frac{\theta_t}{\theta_t - 1}} \left[\sum_{i=1}^{M} \Psi_{jt}^{\theta_t - 1} \vartheta_{it}^{\theta_t} \right]^{\frac{1}{\theta_t - 1}} = \xi^{\frac{\theta_t}{\theta_t - 1}} \varphi_t.$$

Equation (2.6) implies that the demand for all intermediate goods will decline by a proportion $\xi^{-\theta_t}$ but the relative prices of consumption to intermediate goods will fall by the proportion $\xi^{-\theta_t/(\theta_t - 1)}$.

Analogous conclusions are drawn about measured productivity. Changes in observed productivity in units of the consumption good, $\varphi_t(\zeta_t A_t^{1-\alpha})$, can be decomposed into changes in φ_t, the component of relative prices, and $\zeta_t A_t^{1-\alpha}$, the effect of technological improvements. Although these are partial equilibrium results, they suggest an important observation. Because improvements in the quality of intermediate goods lead to changes in the prices of such goods relative to the price of consumption, errors in price indexes used to measure real changes in intermediate goods cause errors in measured productivity. That is, measured productivity is sensitive to the price indexes of the inputs. This theoretical result confirms conclusions drawn by Griliches (1987, 1994), Gordon (1990), and Foster et al. (2008) about the impact of relative prices on measured productivity.

In the symmetric equilibrium studied next, $\vartheta_{it} = \vartheta$, $\Psi_{jt} = 1$, and, because

$$\varphi_t = \vartheta^{\frac{\theta_t}{\theta_t-1}} M^{\frac{1}{\theta_t-1}}, \text{ if } \vartheta_i = \vartheta = \frac{1}{M} \text{ then } \varphi_t = \frac{1}{M}.$$

Here I do not study the effect of changing quality or firm specific productivity. I assume for the rest of this chapter that $\vartheta_i = \vartheta = 1/M$ and $\Omega = M$. By (2.7c)–(2.7d), this implies that for each producer j the adjusted price ratio is $(P_{jt}\Omega\Psi_j)/P_t = 1$. Therefore, after aggregation,

$$W_t = \frac{(\theta_t - 1)}{\theta_t}(1 - \alpha)(\zeta_t A_t)(K_t)^\alpha (A_t L_t)^{-\alpha} \tag{2.11a}$$

$$R_t = \frac{(\theta_t - 1)}{\theta_t}\alpha\zeta_t(K_t)^{\alpha-1}(A_t L_t)^{1-\alpha} \tag{2.11b}$$

$$Y_t = \zeta_t K_t^\alpha (A_t L_t)^{1-\alpha}. \tag{2.11c}$$

These are the first-order conditions linking factor prices to the input allocation of the production sector in equilibrium. Because all production functions are the same, the model becomes one of a fully symmetric industrial structure.

2.4   Optimal Household Behavior

I have assumed that capital is owned by households and they rent it to the firms. Their saving decision is based on the expected rental rate of capital, which is realized in the next period, when the demand for capital by firms is formulated. Because I assume that the relative price of capital in terms of consumption is 1, the rental rate is endogenously determined by productivity that, in equilibrium, equals the interest rate plus depreciation. Total profits of the intermediate goods firms are paid as dividends to the owners of their shares. The distinction between rental on capital employed and profits of the firm implies that the market value of the firm is exactly equal to the market value of the stream of its profits due to market power.[4]

My main interest here is in the response of the economy to changing market power. Following the theory described in chapter 1, I define the dynamic link between market power and the dynamics of productivity. This links market power to the rate of innovations. I treat productivity as exogenous and hold quality constant.

The representative household carries out the following dynamic optimization:

$$\text{Max}_{(C,I,L)} \sum_{\tau=0}^{\infty} \beta^\tau \left[\frac{1}{1-\sigma} C_\tau^{1-\sigma} \left(1 - \frac{\mathcal{H}}{1+\eta} L_\tau^{1+\eta} \right) \right]. \tag{2.12a}$$

In the simulations of the next section, I also explore the effect of the alternative utility function

$$\text{Max}_{(C,I,L)} \sum_{\tau=0}^{\infty} \beta^\tau \left[\log C_\tau - \frac{\mathcal{H}}{1+\eta} L_\tau^{1+\eta} \right].$$

The household maximizes utility subject to the budget constraint

$$C_t + K_{t+1} + P_t{}^s S_t = W_t L_t + K_t (R_t + (1-\delta)) + S_{t-1} \left(P_t^s + \Pi_t \right), \quad R_t = r_t + \delta. \tag{2.12b}$$

S is the number of shares; L is the fraction of time worked; P^s is the stock price; and R is the rental rate, which is the sum of interest plus depreciation δ. The parameter $\mathcal{H}$ pins down the steady-state value of L at 0.3, reflecting the estimate[5] that the fraction of time of a year spent at work is 30 percent. I specify the standard form of capital accumulation and technological change:

$$K_{t+1} = (1-\delta)K_t + I_t \tag{2.12c}$$

$$\log(\zeta_{t+1}) = \lambda_\zeta \log(\zeta_t) + \varepsilon_{t+1}^\zeta, \quad \varepsilon_{t+1}^\zeta \sim N\left(0, \sigma_\zeta^2\right), \text{ i.i.d.} \tag{2.12d}$$

The dynamics of market power are formulated in terms of the markup notation

$$\mathcal{P}_t = \frac{\theta_t}{\theta_t - 1}$$

---

[4] This is clearly an unrealistic financial structure because most firms own some capital. This structure is, however, very useful for a distinction between capital and wealth in the analysis below.

[5] There does not appear to be a consensus in the literature on the value of this parameter. King and Rebelo (1999) estimate it to be 0.2, but this value is on the low side. Variations of this parameter have no effect on the main results reported here.

and follow the theory developed in chapter 1 that technology and policy are the two forces that determine $\mathcal{P}_t$. Because no obvious aggregate indexes express these two factors, I specify the following Markov process to incorporate them:

$$\mathcal{P}_{t+1} = g\mathcal{P}_t^{\lambda_{\mathcal{P}}} \left[\zeta_{t+1}^{\mu_{\zeta}} \zeta_t^{(\mu_{\zeta})^2} \zeta_{t-1}^{(\mu_{\zeta})^3} \zeta_{t-2}^{(\mu_{\zeta})^4} \zeta_{t-3}^{(\mu_{\zeta})^5} \right] e^{\varepsilon_{t+1}^{\mathcal{P}}}$$

$$\varepsilon_{t+1}^{\mathcal{P}} \sim N(0, \sigma_{\mathcal{P}}^2), \varepsilon_{t+1}^{\mathcal{P}} \text{ i.i.d., independent of } \varepsilon_{t+1}^{\zeta}.$$

(2.12e)

I offer the following interpretation:

1. *Technology* has two effects. First, the constant g—the trend growth of productivity—is the factor that introduces constant new market power. Second, the term $\zeta_{t+1}^{\mu_{\zeta}} \zeta_t^{(\mu_{\zeta})^2} \zeta_{t-1}^{(\mu_{\zeta})^3} \zeta_{t-2}^{(\mu_{\zeta})^4} \zeta_{t-3}^{(\mu_{\zeta})^5}$ is the cumulative effect due to fluctuations of new innovations on market power, with geometric declining weights on past innovations. This term has one parameter μ_{ζ} that approximates, with a finite sequence of five years, a distributed lag model as in Koyck (1954). This therefore requires a nonlinear estimation procedure.

2. *Policy* and technological obsolescence are not represented by any specific variable because containing market power is too complex a process to be summarized by any one index. Instead, it is represented by the key parameter $0 < \lambda_{\mathcal{P}} < 1$, which determines the rate at which current market power decays. Policy clearly aims to promote innovations that are also the source of initial market power. As explained in chapter 1, the main impact of policy comes into play after the innovation is made. If $\lambda_{\mathcal{P}}$ is close to 1, market power can consolidate and expand faster, while if $\lambda_{\mathcal{P}}$ is lower, market power dissipates more rapidly. That means that, at each period, the economic policy chosen by society is expressed by selecting a value of $\lambda_{\mathcal{P}}$. A more aggressive policy in containing market power leads to a smaller $\lambda_{\mathcal{P}}$. This procedure expresses my basic approach to the problem of policy formation. *Its main task is to promote as high an innovation rate as possible but ensure that market power decays rapidly, preventing it from consolidating into a large and permanent negative force.* In empirically estimating $\lambda_{\mathcal{P}}$, it takes only two values, describing either aggressive or inactive laissez-faire policies.

   Combining the two forces of technology and policy, in steady state we have

$$\zeta^{\star} = 1, \quad \mathcal{P}^{\star} = g^{\frac{1}{1-\lambda_{\mathcal{P}}}} > 1.$$

(2.13)

In the long run, technology is represented by the growth rate g and policy by the parameter $\lambda_{\mathcal{P}}$. In an economy without technological change, $\zeta^{\star} = g = 1$. This stagnant economy converges to the competitive equilibrium where $\mathcal{P}^{\star} = 1$ because there are no sources for new market power.

2.5 Equilibrium with Market Power

2.5.1 Equilibrium Conditions

I combine the first-order conditions of the household with the pricing equations of each of the intermediate goods producers after aggregation. The equilibrium conditions are then written in units of consumption as follows:

$$(C_t)^{-\sigma}\left(1 - \frac{\mathcal{H}}{1+\eta}L_t^{1+\eta}\right)$$

$$= \beta \mathbf{E}_t\left[(C_{t+1})^{-\sigma}\left(1 - \frac{\mathcal{H}}{1+\eta}L_{t+1}^{1+\eta}\right)(R_{t+1} + (1-\delta))\right]$$

$$(C_t)^{-\sigma}\left(1 - \frac{\mathcal{H}}{1+\eta}L_t^{1+\eta}\right)$$

$$= \beta \mathbf{E}_t\left[(C_{t+1})^{-\sigma}\left(1 - \frac{\mathcal{H}}{1+\eta}L_{t+1}^{1+\eta}\right)\left(\frac{P_{t+1}^s + \Pi_{t+1}}{P_t^s}\right)\right]$$

$$\frac{\mathcal{H}}{1-\sigma}L_t^{\eta} = \left(1 - \frac{\mathcal{H}}{1+\eta}L_t^{1+\eta}\right)\frac{W_t}{C_t}$$

$$W_t = \frac{1}{\mathcal{P}_t}(1-\alpha)\zeta_t g^t (K_t)^{\alpha}(g^t L_t)^{-\alpha}$$

$$R_t = \frac{1}{\mathcal{P}_t}\alpha\zeta_t(K_t)^{\alpha-1}(g^t L_t)^{1-\alpha}$$

$$C_t + (K_{t+1} - K_t(1-\delta)) = Y_t = W_t L_t + K_t R_t + \Pi_t \quad \text{(which assumed } S_t = 1\text{)},$$

$$Y_t = \zeta_t K_t^{\alpha}(A_t L_t)^{1-\alpha}.$$

$$(2.14)$$

To study these conditions, I write the aggregate production function in the standard form of

$$Y_t = \zeta_t(K_t)^{\alpha}(A_t L_t)^{(1-\alpha)} = \zeta_t A_t\left(\frac{K_t}{A_t}\right)^{\alpha}(L_t)^{1-\alpha} = \zeta_t A_t\left(k_t\right)^{\alpha}(L_t)^{1-\alpha},$$

$$k_t = \left(\frac{K_t}{A_t}\right),$$

and the conditions in (2.14) can now be scaled by the growth rate. Define first

$$c_t = \left(\frac{C_t}{A_t}\right), w_t = \left(\frac{W_t}{A_t}\right), y_t = \left(\frac{Y_t}{A_t}\right), p_t^s = \left(\frac{P_s}{A_t}\right), g = \left(\frac{A_{t+1}}{A_t}\right),$$

$$y_t = \zeta_t k_t^{\alpha} L_t^{1-\alpha}.$$

Keeping in mind that $\Pi_t = \frac{1}{\theta_t} Y_t = \frac{\mathcal{P}_t - 1}{\mathcal{P}_t} Y_t$, the conditions are reduced to

$$c_t + g k_{t+1} = \zeta_t k_t^\alpha L_t^{1-\alpha} + k_t(1 - \delta) \tag{2.15a}$$

$$1 - \frac{\mathcal{H}}{1+\eta} L_t^{1+\eta} = \beta \mathbf{E}_t \left[\left(g \frac{c_{t+1}}{c_t} \right)^{-\sigma} \left(1 - \frac{\mathcal{H}}{1+\eta} L_{t+1}^{1+\eta} \right) (R_{t+1} + (1 - \delta)) \right] \tag{2.15b}$$

$$1 - \frac{\mathcal{H}}{1+\eta} L_t^{1+\eta} = \beta \mathbf{E}_t \left[\left(g \frac{c_{t+1}}{c_t} \right)^{-\sigma} \left(1 - \frac{\mathcal{H}}{1+\eta} L_{t+1}^{1+\eta} \right) \right.$$
$$\left. g \left(\frac{p_{t+1}^s + \frac{\mathcal{P}_{t+1}-1}{\mathcal{P}_{t+1}} \zeta_t k_{t+1}^\alpha L_{t+1}^{1-\alpha}}{p_t^s} \right) \right] \tag{2.15c}$$

$$\frac{\mathcal{H}}{1+\sigma} L_t^\eta = \left(1 - \frac{\mathcal{H}}{1+\eta} L_t^{1+\eta} \right) \frac{w_t}{c_t} \tag{2.15d}$$

$$w_t = \frac{1}{\mathcal{P}_t} (1-\alpha) \zeta_t k_t^\alpha L_t^{-a} \tag{2.15e}$$

$$R_t = \frac{1}{\mathcal{P}_t} \alpha \zeta_t k_t^{\alpha-1} L_t^{1-\alpha}. \tag{2.15f}$$

Because aggregate labor supply is constant at the level of 1, the asymptotic growth factor of the economy is g and that growth rate is independent of $\mathcal{P}_t$.

2.5.2   Steady-State Response to Rising Market Power

I begin to analyze this model by treating market power $\mathcal{P}$ as an exogenous parameter that alters the steady state of the economy. I will call it a $\mathcal{P}$-steady state. These steady-state comparisons are helpful for understanding the dynamic model, in which $\mathcal{P}$ is linked to the level of productivity. I will later compute impulse response functions at various points in the space to determine if steady-state comparisons provide sufficient information about the effect of market power.

The $\mathcal{P}$-steady state at $\mathcal{P} = \mathcal{P}^\star$ is expressed by the following set of equations:

$$c^\star + g k^\star = (k^\star)^\alpha (L^\star)^{1-\alpha} - k^\star(1 - \delta) \tag{2.16a}$$

$$1 = \beta g^{(-\sigma)} [R^\star + (1 - \delta)] \tag{2.16b}$$

$$p^{s\star} = \beta g^{(1-\sigma)} \left[p^{s\star} + \frac{1}{\theta} (k^\star)^\alpha (L^\star)^{1-\alpha} \right] \tag{2.16c}$$

$$\frac{\mathcal{H}}{1+\sigma}(L^\star)^\eta = \left(1 - \frac{\mathcal{H}}{1+\eta}(L^\star)^{1+\eta}\right)\frac{w^\star}{c^\star} \tag{2.16d}$$

$$w^\star = \frac{1}{\mathcal{P}}(1-\alpha)(k^\star)^\alpha(L^\star)^{-\alpha} \tag{2.16e}$$

$$R^\star = \frac{1}{\mathcal{P}}\alpha(k^\star)^{\alpha-1}(L^\star)^{1-\alpha}. \tag{2.16f}$$

This is a system of six equations in the six unknowns $k^\star, c^\star, p^{s\star}, L^\star, w^\star$, and $R^\star$, all functions of $\mathcal{P}$. Because I want to study analytically the way the steady state responds to changes in $\mathcal{P}$, it is convenient to transform it once more by defining

$$\tilde{k}_t = \left(\frac{K_t}{A_tL_t}\right), \tilde{c}_t = \left(\frac{C_t}{A_tL_t}\right), \tilde{w}_t = \left(\frac{W_t}{A_tL_t}\right), \tilde{y}_t = \left(\frac{Y_t}{A_tL_t}\right),$$
$$\tilde{p}_t^s = \left(\frac{P_s}{A_tL_t}\right), g = \left(\frac{A_{t+1}}{A_t}\right). \tag{2.17}$$

This transformation could have been used at the outset, instead of (2.14), but this would have complicated the dynamics of the resulting system because $\tilde{k}_{t+1}$ is a random variable from the perspective of date t, while k_{t+1} is not. Using (2.17), I can rewrite the $\mathcal{P}$-steady-state equations as

$$\tilde{c}^\star + g\tilde{k}^\star = (\tilde{k}^\star)^\alpha - \tilde{k}^\star(1-\delta) \tag{2.18a}$$

$$1 = \beta g^{-\sigma}[R^\star + (1-\delta)] \tag{2.18b}$$

$$\tilde{p}^{s\star} = \beta g^{(1-\sigma)}\left[\tilde{p}^{s\star} + \frac{1}{\theta}(\tilde{k}^\star)^\alpha\right] \tag{2.18c}$$

$$\frac{\mathcal{H}}{1+\sigma}(L^\star)^\eta = \left(1 - \frac{\mathcal{H}}{1+\eta}(L^\star)^{1+\eta}\right)\frac{\tilde{w}^\star}{\tilde{c}^\star} \tag{2.18d}$$

$$\tilde{w}^\star = \frac{1}{\mathcal{P}}(1-\alpha)(\tilde{k}^\star)^\alpha \tag{2.18e}$$

$$R^\star = \frac{1}{\mathcal{P}}\alpha(\tilde{k}^\star)^{\alpha-1}. \tag{2.18f}$$

The first important point to note about this formulation of the $\mathcal{P}$-steady state is the following.

Proposition 2.2. *The steady-state growth rate and the interest rate are independent of the degree of market power.*

Proof. The growth rate of the system is a constant, g. The interest rate, $r^\star$, is given by $R^\star = r^\star + \delta$, so it follows from (2.18b) that the steady-state interest rate is also independent of $\mathcal{P}$. $\square$

Because there are long periods of rising or falling market power, one is interested in the response of the economy to a sequence of rising or falling rates of market power. The effect of such a sequence is a lower or higher capital stock. I will thus show that investment is the main force that drives changes in the economy's aggregates in response to rising monopoly power.

Proposition 2.3. *The variable $\tilde{k}^*$ is monotonically falling in $\mathcal{P}$, hence a $\mathcal{P}$-steady state with higher market power has a lower level of capital. In addition, by changing the steady state, a rise in market power has the following permanent effects: (1)* **lower** *output level, (2)* **lower** *consumption level, (3)* **lower** *level of investment, (4)* **lower** *wage rate, (5)* **lower** *labor participation L^*, (6)* **lower** *capital/output ratio, (7)* **lower** *investment/output ratio but (8) a* **higher** *ratio of wealth to capital, and (9)* **higher** *wealth/output ratio.*

Proof. I will first show that $\tilde{k}^*$, $\tilde{c}^*$, $\tilde{p}^{s*}$, $\tilde{w}^*$, $\tilde{R}^*$, and L^* fall with $\mathcal{P}$. Then I show that these imply that k^*, c^*, p^{s*}, w^*, R^*, and L^* fall as well. I thus start by noting that because, in (2.18b), the rental R^* does not change with $\mathcal{P}$, it requires $\frac{1}{\mathcal{P}}\alpha(\tilde{k}^*)^{\alpha-1} = \text{constant}$. Differentiation of this expression implies

$$\alpha(\alpha-1)(\tilde{k}^*)^{(\alpha-2)}\frac{1}{\mathcal{P}}\frac{d\tilde{k}^*}{d\mathcal{P}} - \alpha(\tilde{k}^*)^{\alpha-1}\frac{1}{\mathcal{P}^2} = 0;$$

therefore

$$\frac{d\tilde{k}^*}{d\mathcal{P}} = \frac{1}{(\alpha-1)}\tilde{k}^*\left(\frac{1}{\mathcal{P}}\right) < 0.$$

This proves the first statement that as $\mathcal{P}$ increases, $\tilde{k}^*$ declines.

1. $\tilde{y}^* = (\tilde{k}^*)^\alpha$, which is monotonically falling with a decline in $\tilde{k}^*$.
2. Net investment equals $\tilde{k}^*[g - (1-\delta)]$ and is also monotonically falling with a decline in $\tilde{k}^*$.
3. By (2.18a), $\tilde{c}^* = (\tilde{k}^*)^\alpha - (\tilde{k}^*)[g-(1-\delta)]$, which monotonically falls with a decline of $\tilde{k}^*$ because $\alpha(\tilde{k}^*)^{\alpha-1} > [g - (1-\delta)]$. This decline results from the fact that for any optimal investment, $\tilde{k}^*$ is *lower* than the Golden Rule level, defined by $\alpha(\tilde{k}^*)^{\alpha-1} = [g-(1-\delta)]$.
4. To see why the wage rate declines, rewrite (2.12e) as

$$\tilde{w}^* = \left[\frac{1}{\mathcal{P}}\alpha(\tilde{k}^*)^{\alpha-1}\right]\frac{(1-\alpha)}{\alpha}\tilde{k}^*.$$

By proposition 2.2, $[\frac{1}{\mathcal{P}}\alpha(\tilde{k}^*)^{\alpha-1}]$ is a positive constant independent of $\mathcal{P}$; therefore

$$\frac{d\tilde{w}^*}{d\mathcal{P}} = \left[\frac{1}{\mathcal{P}}\alpha(\tilde{k}^*)^{\alpha-1}\right]\frac{1-\alpha}{\alpha}\frac{d\tilde{k}^*}{d\mathcal{P}} < 0.$$

5. To prove that L^* falls with $\mathcal{P}$, rewrite (2.18d) in the form

$$V(\mathcal{P}) = \frac{\frac{\mathcal{H}}{1+\sigma}(L^*)^\eta}{\left(1 - \frac{\mathcal{H}}{1+\eta}(L^*)^{1+\eta}\right)} = \frac{\tilde{w}^*}{\tilde{c}^*}.$$

Differentiating the left-hand side, I find that

$$\frac{\frac{dV(\mathcal{P})}{d\mathcal{P}}}{\frac{dL^*}{d\mathcal{P}}} = \frac{\eta\frac{\mathcal{H}}{1+\sigma}(L^*)^{\eta-1}\left(1 - \frac{\mathcal{H}}{1+\eta}(L^*)^{1+\eta}\right) + \frac{\mathcal{H}}{1+\sigma}(L^*)^\eta\mathcal{H}(L^*)^\eta}{\left(1 - \frac{\mathcal{H}}{1+\eta}(L^*)^{1+\eta}\right)^2} > 0. \quad (2.19)$$

On the other hand,

$$\frac{d\left(\frac{\tilde{w}^*}{\tilde{c}^*}\right)}{d\mathcal{P}} = \frac{1}{\tilde{c}^*}\frac{d\tilde{w}^*}{d\mathcal{P}} - \left(\frac{\tilde{w}^*}{(\tilde{c}^*)^2}\right)\frac{d\tilde{c}^*}{d\mathcal{P}}. \quad (2.20)$$

Now use (2.18a) and (2.18e) to deduce

$$\frac{1}{\tilde{c}^*}\frac{d\tilde{w}^*}{d\mathcal{P}} - \left(\frac{\tilde{w}^*}{(\tilde{c}^*)^2}\right)\frac{d\tilde{c}^*}{d\mathcal{P}}$$

$$= -\frac{1}{\tilde{c}^*}\left(\frac{1}{\mathcal{P}^2}\right)(1-\alpha)\tilde{k}^{*\alpha}$$

$$+ \left[\frac{1}{\tilde{c}^*}\frac{1}{\mathcal{P}}(1-\alpha)\alpha\tilde{k}^{*\alpha-1} - \frac{\tilde{w}^*}{(\tilde{c}^*)^2}\left(\alpha\tilde{k}^{*(\alpha-1)} - (g-(1-\delta))\right)\right]\frac{d\tilde{k}^*}{d\mathcal{P}}$$

But then detailed computations lead to the conclusion

$$\frac{1}{\tilde{c}^*}\frac{d\tilde{w}^*}{d\mathcal{P}} - \left(\frac{\tilde{w}^*}{(\tilde{c}^*)^2}\right)\frac{d\tilde{c}^*}{d\mathcal{P}} = -\frac{\tilde{w}^*}{(\tilde{c}^*)^2\mathcal{P}}(\tilde{k}^*)^\alpha < 0.$$

Using this last inequality with (2.19) and (2.20) leads to the implication that

$$\frac{dL^*}{d\mathcal{P}} < 0. \quad (2.21)$$

6. This capital/output ratio is $\frac{\tilde{k}^*}{(\tilde{k}^*)^\alpha} = (\tilde{k}^*)^{1-\alpha}$; therefore one concludes that

$$\frac{d(\tilde{k}^*)^{1-\alpha}}{d\mathcal{P}} = (1-\alpha)(\tilde{k}^*)^{-\alpha}\frac{d(\tilde{k}^*)}{d\mathcal{P}} < 0.$$

7. The investment/output ratio is $\frac{\tilde{k}^*[g-(1-\delta)]}{(\tilde{k}^*)^\alpha} = (\tilde{k}^*)^{(1-\alpha)}[g-(1-\delta)]$; therefore

$$\frac{d[(\tilde{k}^*)^{(1-\alpha)}(g-(1-\delta))]}{d\mathcal{P}} = (1-\alpha)(\tilde{k}^*)^{-\alpha}\frac{d(\tilde{k}^*)}{d\mathcal{P}}[g-(1-\delta)] > 0.$$

8. Wealth is $(\tilde{p}^{s*} + \tilde{k}^*)$, which is the sum of capital and stock price. For brevity, I use the notation

$$\hat{z} = \frac{\beta g^{(1-\sigma)}}{1 - \beta g^{(1-\sigma)}}.$$

By (2.15c), the value of the stock is

$$\tilde{p}^{s\star} = \hat{z}(\tilde{k}^{\star})^{\alpha} \frac{\mathcal{P}-1}{\mathcal{P}}; \tag{2.22}$$

hence, wealth/capital ratio is

$$\frac{\tilde{p}^{s\star} + \tilde{k}^{\star}}{\tilde{k}^{\star}} = \frac{\hat{z}(\tilde{k}^{\star})^{\alpha} \frac{\mathcal{P}-1}{\mathcal{P}} + \tilde{k}^{\star}}{\tilde{k}^{\star}} = \hat{z}(\tilde{k}^{\star})^{\alpha-1} \frac{\mathcal{P}-1}{\mathcal{P}} + 1$$

and thus

$$\frac{d[(\tilde{p}^{s\star} + \tilde{k}^{\star})/\tilde{k}^{\star}]}{d\mathcal{P}} = \hat{z}\left[\frac{\mathcal{P}-1}{\mathcal{P}}(\tilde{k}^{\star})^{\alpha-2}\frac{\tilde{k}^{\star}}{\mathcal{P}} + \frac{1}{\mathcal{P}^2}(\tilde{k}^{\star})^{(\alpha-1)}\right] = z(\tilde{k}^{\star})^{(\alpha-1)}\frac{1}{\mathcal{P}} > 0.$$

9. By (2.22), the wealth/output ratio is

$$\frac{\tilde{p}^{s\star} + \tilde{k}^{\star}}{(\tilde{k}^{\star})^{\alpha}} = \frac{\hat{z}(\tilde{k}^{\star})^{\alpha}\frac{\mathcal{P}-1}{\mathcal{P}} + \tilde{k}^{\star}}{(\tilde{k}^{\star})^{\alpha}} = \hat{z}\frac{\mathcal{P}-1}{\mathcal{P}} + (\tilde{k}^{\star})^{1-\alpha}.$$

Therefore,

$$\frac{d[(\tilde{p}^{s\star} + \tilde{k}^{\star})/(\tilde{k}^{\star})^{\alpha}]}{d\mathcal{P}} = \hat{z}\frac{1}{\mathcal{P}^2} + (1-\alpha)(\tilde{k}^{\star})^{1-\alpha}\frac{d\tilde{k}^{\star}}{d\mathcal{P}}.$$

Using earlier results and the definition of $\hat{z}$, I conclude that

$$\frac{d[(\tilde{p}^{s\star} + \tilde{k}^{\star})/(\tilde{k}^{\star})^{\alpha}]}{d\mathcal{P}} = \frac{\beta g^{(1-\sigma)}}{\mathcal{P}^2}\left[\frac{1}{1 - \beta g^{(1-\sigma)}} - \frac{1}{1 - \beta g^{(1-\sigma)}(1-\delta)}\right] > 0.$$

This completes the proof that $\tilde{k}^{\star}$, $\tilde{c}^{\star}$, $\tilde{p}^{s\star}$, $\tilde{w}^{\star}$, $\tilde{R}^{\star}$, and $L^{\star}$ falls with $\mathcal{P}$. To prove that this implies that all of $k^{\star}$, $c^{\star}$, $p^{s\star}$, $w^{\star}$, $R^{\star}$, and $L^{\star}$ also decline with $\mathcal{P}$, observe that the following facts apply to each one of these variables, which I denote generically by the letter X:

$$\tilde{X}^{\star} = \frac{X^{\star}}{L^{\star}}, \quad \frac{dL^{\star}}{d\mathcal{P}} < 0, \quad \frac{d\tilde{X}^{\star}}{d\mathcal{P}} < 0.$$

Differentiating with respect to $\mathcal{P}$ leads to

$$\frac{d\tilde{X}^{\star}}{d\mathcal{P}} = \left(\frac{1}{L^{\star}}\right)\frac{dX^{\star}}{d\mathcal{P}} - \left(\frac{X^{\star}}{L^{\star 2}}\right)\frac{dL^{\star}}{d\mathcal{P}} \quad \Rightarrow \quad \frac{dX^{\star}}{d\mathcal{P}} = L^{\star}\frac{d(\tilde{X}^{\star})}{d\mathcal{P}} + \left(\frac{X^{\star}}{L^{\star}}\right)\frac{dL^{\star}}{d\mathcal{P}} < 0.$$

The capital/output ratio and the wealth/output ratio are not altered by the division by $L^{\star}$. Therefore, the proofs of (8) and (9) are sufficient.

The effect of rising market power on stock prices is more subtle. By (2.22), increased market power increases the share of monopoly profits in output, *but it also lowers output!* There is therefore a threshold level above which increases in market power actually lower stock prices.   □

Proposition 2.4. *A rising market power increases the steady-state level of the stock price if $\mathcal{P} - 1 < (1 - \alpha)/\alpha$.*

Proof. Differentiation of (2.22) results in the condition

$$
\frac{dp^{s\star}}{d\mathcal{P}} = \hat{z} \left[\frac{\mathcal{P} - 1}{\mathcal{P}} \alpha (k^\star)^{\alpha-1} \left(\frac{1}{\alpha - 1} \frac{k^\star}{\mathcal{P}} \right) + (k^\star)^\alpha \frac{1}{\mathcal{P}^2} \right]
$$
$$
= \hat{z}(k^\star)^\alpha \frac{1}{\mathcal{P}^2} \left[(\mathcal{P} - 1) \frac{\alpha}{\alpha - 1} + 1 \right].
$$

Therefore,

$$
\frac{dp^{s\star}}{d\mathcal{P}} > 0 \quad \text{if} \quad (\mathcal{P} - 1) < \frac{1 - \alpha}{\alpha}.
$$

$\square$

For $\alpha = 0.32$, the condition above requires $\mathcal{P} < 3.125$, which translates to requiring the share of profits to be less than 68 percent. In chapter 4, I show that this share fluctuates between 0 percent and 30 percent. Hence, for all relevant parameter values, rising monopoly power causes the steady-state stock price to rise.

The *opposing* predictions of the theory with respect to the effect of market power on the capital/output ratio, as opposed to its effect on wealth/output ratio, explains a common error made by scholars who study the capital/output ratio over long horizons. The source of the error is the data used for estimating the capital stock. Use of capital data deduced from real investments can lead to opposite conclusions than those derived from analysis that uses estimated capital deduced from the aggregate stock market value of the firms employing that capital. This last method ends up studying the wealth/output ratio rather than the capital/output ratio. I demonstrate an example of such an error in the study of asset pricing in section 6.3.

Steady-state analysis offers only a partial description of the effect of market power on the economy. Because the economy is not in steady state most of the time, I devote the rest of this chapter to study the effect of market power on the dynamic evolution of the economy, carried out with computer simulations.

2.6   Estimating Parameters by Identifying Periods with Different Policies to Contain Market Power

The values of most parameters are specified based on well-known econometric estimates. The key model parameters are then $\alpha = 0.32$, $\beta = 0.98$, $\sigma = 0.9$, $\delta = 0.08$, $\eta = 2.0$, $\mathcal{H} = 31.1$ in the case of additive utility in (2.12a) and $\eta = 2.09$ and

$\mathcal{H} = 3.0725$ in the case of multiplicative utility, where $\mathcal{H}$ and η are chosen so that the Frisch elasticity equals 0.50 and steady-state participation rate is $L = 0.30$. I set the growth factor to $g = 1.014$. This is a difficult choice because estimates of recent productivity trends reveal a decline in the rate of productivity growth compared to the earlier part of the twentieth century. Some insist on secular stagnation and a decline of the trend based on a relatively small number of recent observations, but such an inference is questionable.

The dynamic parameters are λ_ζ, σ_ζ, $\lambda_\mathcal{P}$, μ_ζ, and $\sigma_\mathcal{P}$, and one difficulty in identifying them is the data used to estimate them. The annual data used for $\mathcal{P}$ are those I develop in chapter 4. Data on ζ_t requires a choice of a source for total factor productivity (TFP), a controversial topic in the economic literature. The objections to the use of TFP are well known. Nevertheless, because it is needed only for estimating the model parameters, I used mostly the Bank of France data developed by Bergeaud et al. (2016) by virtue of the fact that it covers the years from 1890 to 2019. The variable ζ_t was computed as the deviation from a trend of the estimated cumulative productivity. To increase the reliability of the estimated values of $(\lambda_\zeta, \sigma_\zeta)$, I also consulted the Federal Reserve Bank of San Francisco data from 1947 to 2019. The main difference between the two sources is the significant adjustment for capacity utilization used in the San Francisco data, based on Basu et al. (2006). Data without adjustment for capacity utilization are similar to the Bank of France data, while data with that adjustment are significantly different.

The estimated equations with annual data are then

$$\log(\zeta_{t+1}) = \lambda_\zeta \log(\zeta_t) + \varepsilon_{t+1}^\zeta \tag{2.23a}$$

$$\log \mathcal{P}_{t+1} = \log(g) + \lambda_\mathcal{P} \log \mathcal{P}_t + \mu_\zeta \log \zeta_{t+1} + \mu_\zeta^2 \log \zeta_t$$
$$+ \mu_\zeta^3 \zeta_{t-1} + \mu_\zeta^4 \log \zeta_{t-2} + \mu_\zeta^5 \log \zeta_{t-3} + \varepsilon_{t+1}^\mathcal{P}, \mathcal{P}_t \geq 1. \tag{2.23b}$$

The key parameter $\lambda_\mathcal{P}$ is a summary of the intensity of policy to contain market power. Changes in policy are then defined as *exogenous and unexpected* changes in the parameter $\lambda_\mathcal{P}$. Because every policy is a complex collection of laws and regulations, to assess the impact of any policy, one needs to translate it into this summary parameter. I now explain how I get a coarse representation of policy regimes in $\lambda_\mathcal{P}$.

I will show in chapter 4 that in the years from 1889 to 1901 and from 1985 to 2017, no effective policy was employed to contain market power in the United States, and it is appropriate to view these as periods when the policy used was an inactive, laissez-faire economic policy. In contrast, from 1901 to 1985, the prevailing policy aimed to attain a reasonable degree of egalitarian income distribution, albeit with variations in policy formulation and enforcement. Progressive reformers enacted important legal changes after 1901 and most were enforced, but these changes were introduced slowly due to the strong resistance to them.

A formal egalitarian policy was firmly adopted with the New Deal, and it remained in effect up to the 1970s, after which it was weakened by various factors discussed in chapter 4. These two policy shifts create a natural experiment for estimating the inactive, laissez-faire policy parameter $\lambda_\mathcal{P}^H$ that was in effect during the eras of 1889–1901 and 1985–2017, and an active-policy parameter $\lambda_\mathcal{P}^L$ that was operative during the egalitarian era of 1902–1984. The difference of parameter values is expected because the policy changes in 1901 and in 1985 were *sharp regime shifts*. In short, equation (2.23b) will be estimated with dummy variables for these two periods.

Table 2.1 presents estimates of the parameters λ_ζ and σ_ζ, and of the trend in productivity growth, g. There is no evidence λ_ζ has changed materially, and my choice is $\lambda_\zeta = 0.92$. The different data sources lead to different estimates of σ_ζ. It has declined since early in the twentieth century, but it is not clear the decline is permanent. A choice of $\sigma_\zeta = 0.017$ is a compromise. Finally, as noted earlier, it is too early to determine that secular stagnation renders the decline in trend growth permanent. Thinking about the future, my choice for the three parameters is then

$$\lambda_\zeta = 0.92, \sigma_\zeta = 0.017, g = 1.014. \tag{2.24}$$

Turning to $\lambda_\mathcal{P}$, μ_ζ, and $\sigma_\mathcal{P}$, table 2.2 presents parameter estimates. I use only the Bank of France data because it is essential to include the years from 1889

TABLE 2.1 Estimates of λ_ζ, σ_ζ and of trend productivity g

Data source and years covered	λ_ζ	σ_ζ	Trend g
Bank of France data			
1890–2019	0.9601	0.0357	1.0183
	(0.0284)		(0.00027)
1947–2019	0.8750	0.0137	1.0132
	(0.0390)		(0.00024)
1985–2019	0.9625	0.0075	1.0121
	(0.0676)		(0.00036)
San Francisco Fed (without utilization adjustment)			
1947–2019	0.9072	0.0169	1.0115
	(0.0377)		(0.00031)
1985–2019	0.8665	0.0118	1.0094
	(0.0950)		(0.00047)
San Francisco Fed (with utilization adjustment)			
1947–2019	0.9245	0.0140	1.0111
	(0.0304)		(0.00030)
1985–2019	0.8983	0.0130	1.0093
	(0.0810)		(0.00037)

TABLE 2.2 Estimated Parameters of Equation (2.23b)

Year Covered	Constant	λ_P^H	λ_P^L	μ_ζ	H Pres party	L Pres party	H Max tax	L Max tax	Pat/pop	Output/Man-hour	$\sigma_{\mathcal{P}}$	R^2
All years: 1894–2017												
	1.0450	0.8777	0.7123	0.0859							0.0428	0.763
	(0.0101)	(0.0591)	(0.0570)	(0.0345)								
	1.0549	1.0554	0.6552	0.0942	-0.0178	0.0076	-0.1101	-0.0026			0.0412	0.780
	(0.0125)	(0.0850)	(0.0599)	(0.0411)	(0.0133)	(0.0106)	(0.0495)	(0.0191)				
	1.0366	0.9587	0.6274	0.1315	-0.0227	0.0094	-0.1134	-0.0078	0.0703		0.0408	0.784
	(0.0168)	(0.1062)	(0.0628)	(0.0463)	(0.0136)	(0.0107)	(0.0493)	(0.0195)	(0.0473)			
	1.0177	1.0011	0.7447	0.0654	-0.0127	0.0029	-0.0851	-0.0054	0.0305	0.6749	0.0349	0.842
	(0.0147)	(0.0914)	(0.0570)	(0.0473)	(0.0118)	(0.0092)	(0.0426)	(0.0168)	(0.0410)	(0.1051)		
Excluding 1932–1953												
	1.0371	0.9180	0.7399	0.0962							0.0411	0.773
	(0.0113)	(0.0651)	(0.0609)	(0.0372)								
	1.0537	1.0711	0.6861	0.1198	-0.0169	0.0079	-0.1103	-0.0159			0.0393	0.792
	(0.0127)	(0.0847)	(0.0717)	(0.0486)	(0.0128)	(0.0117)	(0.0478)	(0.0230)				
	1.0348	0.9702	0.6594	0.1613	-0.0221	0.0085	-0.1145	-0.0239	0.0745		0.0388	0.798
	(0.0170)	(0.1052)	(0.0729)	(0.0523)	(0.0132)	(0.0116)	(0.0475)	(0.0236)	(0.0478)			
	1.0075	1.0158	0.8210	0.1276	-0.0108	0.0036	-0.0821	-0.0362	0.0458	0.7443	0.0319	0.864
	(0.0146)	(0.0871)	(0.0649)	(0.0469)	(0.0110)	(0.0096)	(0.0396)	(0.0196)	(0.0397)	(0.1119)		
Postwar 1946–2017												
	1.0151	1.0145	0.8118	0.1343							0.0265	0.868
	(0.0116)	(0.0788)	(0.0682)	(0.0678)								
	1.0064	1.0323	0.7228	0.1381	0.0063	-0.0050	0.0050	0.0367			0.0261	0.872
	(0.0242)	(0.0901)	(0.1085)	(0.0757)	(0.0108)	(0.0089)	(0.0706)	(0.0379)				
	0.9864	0.9096	0.6419	0.1981	0.0029	-0.0036	0.0136	0.0385	0.0786		0.0251	0.881
	(0.0251)	(0.1017)	(0.1129)	(0.0723)	(0.0106)	(0.0087)	(0.0684)	(0.0368)	(0.0362)			
	0.9820	0.9314	0.7015	0.1478	0.0043	-0.0035	0.0101	0.0363	0.0556	0.5010	0.0236	0.896
	(0.0238)	(0.0965)	(0.1092)	(0.0786)	(0.0100)	(0.0082)	(0.0648)	(0.0348)	(0.0351)	(0.1747)		

to 1901. In addition to the variables in (2.23b), I experiment with other variables that could represent technology or policy. On the side of technology, Pat/Pop is the number of patents granted in that year per million people, and Output/Man is the growth in output per man-hour, an alternate measure of productivity. On the policy side, Pres Party is a dummy variable taking the value 1 for Democratic presidents and 0 for Republican presidents. Max Tax is the top marginal income tax rate in the year. The effect of policy is measured by the shift between parameters $\lambda_\mathcal{P}^H$ for periods of passive policy and $\lambda_\mathcal{P}^L$ for periods of active policy.

The results in table 2.2 are consistent with the theoretical paradigm that market power is an equilibrium outcome of the forces of technology and policy. Apart from the main parameters, there are two other statistically significant explanatory variables of market power, and both are consistent with the theory. One is the patents/population ratio: rising market power is positively associated with more inventive activity. The second is the *negative* effect of the maximal tax rate, where higher tax rates are associated with lower market power. This variable is correlated with the two policy regime variables because taxes were low during the periods of passive policy and high during periods of active policy. This correlation affects the estimates of $\lambda_\mathcal{P}^H$ and $\lambda_\mathcal{P}^L$. Output per man-hour is obviously highly correlated with TFP, but it is less valuable because it doesn't correspond to ζ in the model.

Considering first the estimated values of $(\lambda_\mathcal{P}^H, \lambda_\mathcal{P}^L)$, it is reasonable to conclude that $0.90 < \lambda_\mathcal{P}^H < 1$ and $0.72 < \lambda_\mathcal{P}^L < 0.82$. Turning to μ_ζ, this parameter has an impact on the convergence properties of the model; therefore it is best to consider only long-term series for higher reliability, which leads to a choice of $\mu_\zeta = 0.086$. As to $\sigma_\mathcal{P}$, table 2.2 shows that, similar to σ_ζ, it has declined, but this may not be permanent. My final selection is then $\lambda_\mathcal{P}^H = 0.95$, $\lambda_\mathcal{P}^L = 0.80$, $\sigma_\mathcal{P} = 0.03$, $\mu_\zeta = 0.086$.

The theory underlying model (2.23b) postulates the growth rate of productivity to be a constant force that propels market power up. The estimated average growth rate of productivity for the postwar period reported in table 2.1 is 1.32 percent and, as indicated earlier, I set the constant for the simulations in the next section at 1.4 percent.

Because the aim is to highlight key features of the theory, I will comment on the sensitivity of the results to parameter values. This is particularly important with respect to $\lambda_\mathcal{P}^H$, $\lambda_\mathcal{P}^L$, $\sigma_\mathcal{P}$, and μ_ζ, the parameters of the transition equation of $\mathcal{P}$, which are new to the literature. As to the difference between the two utility functions, with respect to the effects of market power and productivity on the equilibrium, surprisingly, the two utility functions lead to virtually identical conclusions, with minor differences because the additive utility in (2.12a) is logarithmic while the elasticity of intertemporal substitution for the multiplicative utility in (2.12a) is 0.90. *All results reported here are for the multiplicative utility.* Finally, the theoretical experiments that follow are computed with perturbation methods using fourth-order approximation to ensure high accuracy. The constraint $\mathcal{P} > 1$ was enforced with a Chen-Mangasarian (1996) smoothing function.

2.7   The Effect of Market Power in a Fixed Policy Regime

To understand the effect of market power, it is important to focus on long-run tendencies. I report results of simulating sixty years or more because market power changes slowly. The autoregressive parameter that reflects policy has an obvious effect on the speed of convergence, but the role of technology is equally important: more innovations entail a more rapid rise in $\mathcal{P}_t$. Consequently, technology affects the rate at which market power grows or falls through *runs* in productivity. A *productivity run* is a sequence of values of ζ_t whose deviations from the mean 1 have the *same* sign. During a run of $\zeta_t > 1$, the path of productivity is above trend, so the economy experiences a higher rate of innovations and therefore rising market power. The opposite occurs during a run of $\zeta_t < 1$. Because ζ_t is a highly persistent Markov process, runs occur frequently and the duration of such runs guides the changes of market power: the longer the run, the greater the deviation in $\mathcal{P}_t$ from its steady-state value.

2.7.1   Impulse Response Functions

1. *The effect of rising productivity can be negated by the secondary effect of increased market power.* The functions in figures 2.1a and 2.1b are impulse response functions to one standard deviation shocks to either ζ_t or $\mathcal{P}_t$. In Figure 2.1a, the top panel is the response of $\mathcal{P}_t$ to these shocks. The solid line is the response to a shock to $\mathcal{P}_t$, and it shows that active policy suppresses the effect much faster than inactive policy. The dashed line is the response of market power to a positive ζ_t shock, and under either policy regime, the secondary effect of a productivity increase is *to raise market power*. The process is slow and can take as much as fifteen years to peak. The gradual rise in market power occurs because a positive impulse to ζ_t leaves ζ_t above its steady-state value for many periods, which, by equation (2.12e), leads to continuous upward pressure on $\mathcal{P}_t$. Note that this secondary effect is more pronounced under a regime of an inactive policy because it allows market power to expand. Under this inactive policy, the value at the peak is larger and the effect on market power lasts longer. In the inactive policy regime, twenty to forty years after an increase in productivity, capital is actually below its long-run steady-state value. This implies that, with time, the secondary effect

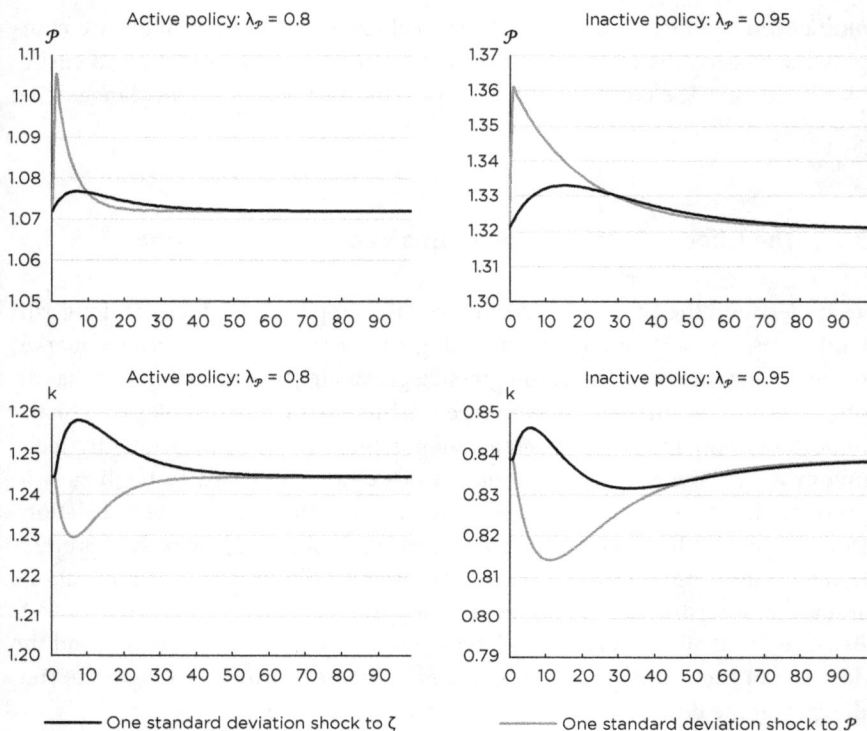

Figure 2.1a Impulse response functions of $\mathcal{P}$ and k

of productivity on market power becomes the dominant component. The direct effect of the productivity shock dissipates in the medium run, and the main consequence is its effect on market power. Finally, because these impulse responses are computed starting from steady state, the two scales are different, showing that the steady state of $\mathcal{P}$ is higher and the steady-state capital stock is lower under an inactive policy regime.

The secondary effect of productivity on market power explains the impact of a productivity shock on capital in the bottom panel of figure 2.1a. Under either policy, a positive productivity shock initially increases the capital stock, and a positive market power shock lowers it. But consider the difference between the two policies. Under an active policy, the secondary effect does not cause capital to decline too far: it rises first and then converges back to steady state. Under an inactive policy, capital rises initially, but then it falls due to the secondary effect that raises market power. Over time, the secondary effect dominates the dynamics of capital. This shows that in the long run, the movement of capital is affected significantly by changes of market power initiated by productivity shocks. The policy regimes also differ in the time it takes to return to steady state. An active policy

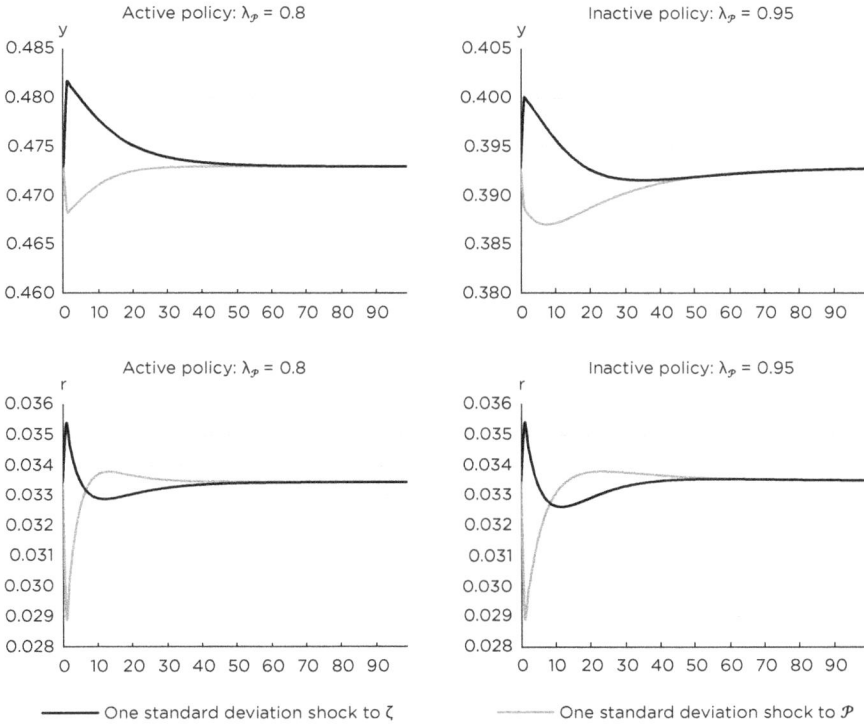

Figure 2.1b   Impulse response function of y and r

restrains the expansion of market power and accelerates the return to steady state, while under an inactive policy, market power expands enough to force a reduction in capital before the return to steady state.

The dynamics of capital are mirrored by all the aggregates that are functions of capital. These dynamics show that policy prevents market power from consolidating, growing, and becoming a large permanent component of the economy by increasing the rate at which it dissipates and shortening the duration of market power formed by each innovation.

2. *Rising market power causes output and the interest rate to decline.* This result was demonstrated for capital in figure 2.1a and is now seen in figure 2.1b, which shows impulse response functions of output and interest rate to positive shocks of ζ_t and $\mathcal{P}_t$. The top panel presents the response of output. It is similar to the response of capital, and the same is true for other variables: consumption, investment, wage rate, and labor participation. All of these aggregates decline in response to higher market power, similar to the steady-state analysis in proposition 2.3. As for a productivity shock, its primary effect is to increase output, investment, consumption, wage rate, and labor input, but it has the secondary effect of increased market

power, which lowers them before steady state is restored. In all cases, active policy prevents the secondary effect from becoming dominant, while inactive policy allows the secondary effect to take hold. Note that a secondary effect remains operative under either policy; the issue is only its size. This fact is demonstrated, in the bottom panel, by the response of the interest rate. This rate's response to a shock to $\mathcal{P}_t$ is subtle under either policy regime: it first declines, then rises, and only then declines back to steady state. In response to a productivity shock, the secondary effect is operative under both policy regimes: the interest rate first rises, then falls, and only then rises back to steady state. This complexity will be further explored later, when I study the simulated dynamics of the interest rate away from steady state.

As to sensitivity to parameters, the difference between the two policy regimes is driven by the two parameters $\lambda_\mathcal{P}^H = 0.95$ and $\lambda_\mathcal{P}^L = 0.80$, but the qualitative results are the same for all parameters in the empirically relevant ranges of $0.90 < \lambda_\mathcal{P}^H < 1$ and $0.72 < \lambda_\mathcal{P}^L < 0.82$ discussed in section 2.5.1.

2.7.2   Simulations: High Market Power Lowers the Equilibrium Level of All Aggregates

Figure 2.2 reports the dynamics of market power together with equilibrium capital for sixty years, computed under the two alternative policy regimes with the same values of ζ_t and $\epsilon_t^\mathcal{P}$, each starting from the steady state implied by that policy. The central difference between the effect of the policies is the level of

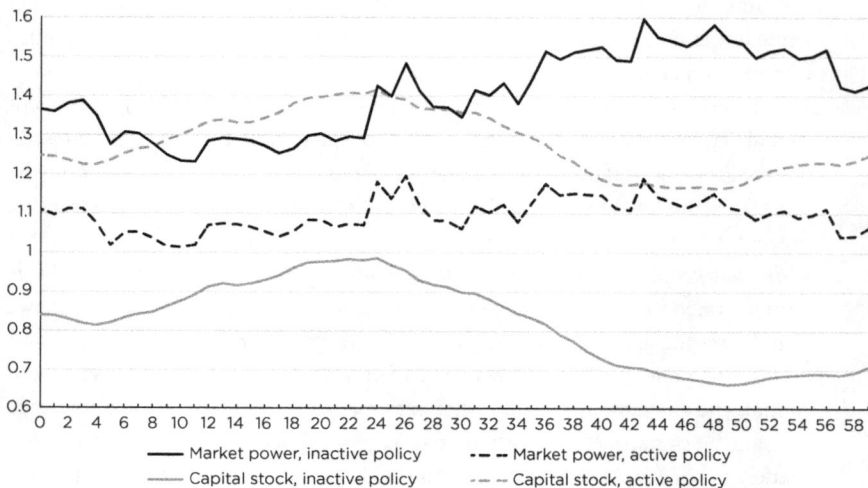

Figure 2.2 Market power and capital under the two policies

the variables. As to the effect of market power, the figure reveals several important results:

1. *Market power changes slowly over decades.* It is driven by shocks to $\mathcal{P}$ together with productivity runs that reflect abnormal innovative activity. In the figure, market power under either policy remains within a narrow range in the early years but, fueled by a run of productivity, it begins to rise after period 23. In general, it changes in response to cumulative effects of the two opposing forces of productivity and depreciation. Although ζ_t exerts upward pressure on capital, increased market power causes capital to decline under either policy. This observation completes the discussion started with the impulse response function: rising market power lowers the level of all the economic aggregates *at any equilibrium in the space* and under either policy.

2. *Changes in policy regime are unexpected changes in structure that alter the steady state.* The steady state of $\mathcal{P}$ is 1.072 under the active policy and 1.321 under the laissez-faire, inactive policy, and these alter the level of the variables. Figure 2.2 shows that active policy causes a higher equilibrium value of capital, and other simulations show that the same holds with respect to all other aggregates.

3. *An inactive policy lowers the equilibrium value of capital and enables $\mathcal{P}$ to rise and fluctuate around 1.321.* It is expressed in the figure by a higher level of market power and lower level of the capital stock under the inactive policy regime. Being more volatile, it sometimes reaches the level of 1.6, which has large consequences. On the other hand, an active policy prevents market power from rising above 1.2, reducing both the level of market power and its volatility.

4. *What is the limit to inequality under a lax, laissez-faire policy regime?* To appreciate the extreme nature of the results in figure 2.2, note that a markup of 1.6 implies a 37.5 percent share of profits in corporate value added. If capital share cannot fall below 10 percent, and because taxes on production take about 9 percent, a markup of 1.6 implies a 43.5 percent labor share. The model cannot speak to the limit on inequality that is sustainable in a democratic society, but the level of inequality implied by a 43.5 percent labor share and 37.5 percent share of monopoly profits is not likely to be tolerated by a democracy. If one postulates that the degree of inequality tolerated by society would restrict the share of profits to be less than 30 percent, then $\mathcal{P} = 1.6$ is not a politically feasible outcome. The important fact is, however, that the model *predicts* that a libertarian, laissez-faire policy regime that does not limit the expansion of market power is highly likely to bring about levels of inequality that are incompatible with democracy. Any such policy regime will therefore face a reform movement that will fight inequality of income and wealth and seek to overturn that policy. Some democratic societies already have constitutions that enable such challenges to an existing regime. Throughout history, most constitutions of democratic societies have built institutions that made it possible to restrain the power of the rich and prevent

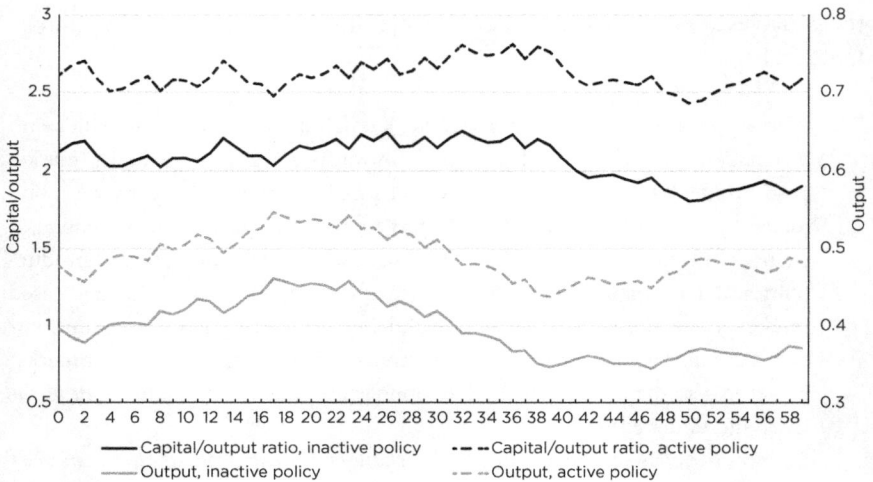

Figure 2.3   Output and capital/output under the two policies

inequality from reaching those critical levels, but this is not the case with the U.S. Constitution.

5. *Rising market power depresses output and capital/output ratio.* Figure 2.3 traces the association of changing market power with output[6] and with the capital/output ratio under the two policy regimes. It exhibits the values of output and the capital/output ratio implied by the same values of $\mathcal{P}_t$ and ζ_t used to construct figure 2.2. Output follows a similar pattern as capital in figure 2.2, and, with some delay, the capital/output ratio also declines with a rise in market power. However, the speed at which endogenous variables respond to rising or falling market power is important. In the case at hand, in response to the sharp rise in market power after year 31, capital declines at a higher rate than the rate of decline of output, causing the capital/output ratio to decline as well. In addition, the steady-state level of the capital/output ratio is lower under the inactive policy regime. This result provides a hint regarding the effect of a switch in the policy regime: it causes the capital/output ratio to transition gradually between the high and low levels implied by the two policies.

2.7.3   The Interest Rate Declines in Repsonse to the Sustained Rise of Market Power

The effect of market power on the interest rate is complex. By (2.18b), the steady-state interest rate equals $(g^{-\sigma}/\beta - 1)$, and this implies that, under either policy,

---

[6]All equilibrium aggregates are normalized variables that result from division by trend growth; therefore only *percentage differences* in their value has unambiguous meaning.

the interest rate continues to fluctuate near the same steady state. Therefore, changes of policy have an ambiguous effect on the dynamics of the interest rate. To understand the effect of market power on the interest rate, note that the interest rate must satisfy

$$r_t = \frac{1}{\mathcal{P}_t} \alpha \zeta_t \left(\frac{k_t}{L_t} \right)^{\alpha-1} - \delta. \tag{2.25}$$

To explore comparisons across steady states, note that in any steady state $\zeta_t = 1$. Therefore, a change in $\mathcal{P}^\star$ must be matched exactly by a change in $(k^\star/L^\star)^{\alpha-1}$. As to changes close to steady state, the impulse response functions in figure 2.1b show that market power lowers the interest rate initially, explained by (2.25) as being caused by an increased $\mathcal{P}_t$ accompanied by a decline of L_t. The subsequent sharp *overshooting* of the interest rate is caused by the increase, at $t + 1$, of k_{t+1} in response to the rise of market power, followed by convergence to steady state. The size of such responses are determined by the proximity to the steady state. Impulse response functions with starting points away from steady state (not exhibited here) have the same pattern as those in Figure 2.1b but with varying sizes of responses depending upon the point in space.

In actual simulations, all variables change, and the interest rate is also affected by the time path of productivity, which is a central variable affecting market power as well as capital productivity. But, as Figure 2.1b shows, a rise of $\mathcal{P}$ has a primary effect of causing the interest rate to decline as the return to capital is marked down, while the secondary and subsequent decline of (k_{t+1}/L_{t+1}) causes it to rise back. Therefore, the movement of the interest rate depends upon the relative strength of these two forces. Because the k/L response is secondary, during sustained periods of rising market power the primary markdown effect will dominate the secondary effect of the declining future values of (k_t/L_t), causing the interest rate to decline. Only when the rise of $\mathcal{P}$ slows down will the interest rate begin to rise back to its steady-state value.

To see this mechanism in a simulation, figure 2.4 records an equilibrium sequence of these variables. At the early time period, a rapid decline of $\mathcal{P}$, together with k/L remaining within a narrow range, cause the interest rate to rise. The rise of $\mathcal{P}$ after date 17 causes k/L to fall, but, with $\mathcal{P}$ exhibiting a sustained rise, the markdown effect dominates, causing the interest rate to decline. From date 37 to date 60, the interest rate rises back to its steady-state level because both k/L as well as $\mathcal{P}$ exhibit downward movement.

The United States has experienced a sustained decline of interest rates since the high rates of the 1980s, and drastically low interest rates since about 2000. I will demonstrate in chapter 4 that market power rose sharply from the 1980s to 2019, and, although the capital/output ratio has also declined during these

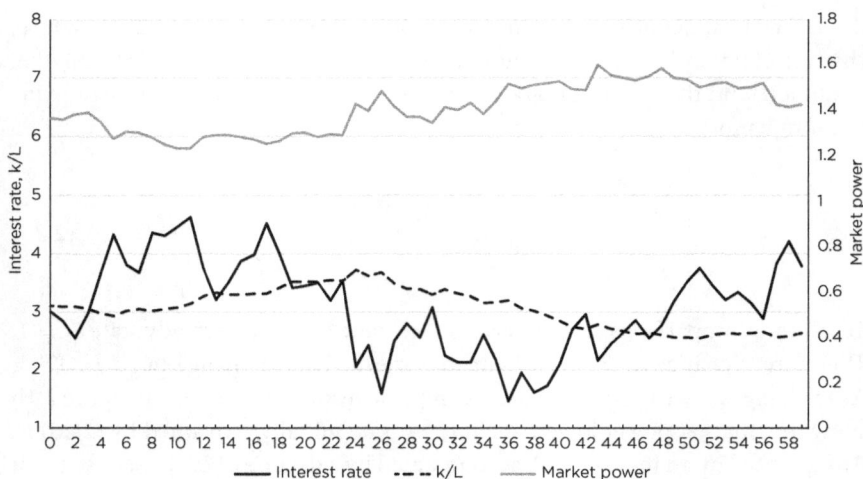

Figure 2.4 Market policy and interest rate—inactive policy

forty years, the sustained nature of rising market power provides a partial explanation for the declining interest rates. The theory presented here does not take into account an additional important factor, *also caused by the rise of market power*, which provides a powerful added force that contributes to keeping the interest rate low. That is the change in income distribution. By its construction, the model of this chapter ignores the different propensities to save of the rich and the poor. One of the main effects of rising market power is rising income inequality. That means more income moving into the hands of the rich, who have a very high propensity to save, and less income going to the poor, who have a low propensity to save. Such a shift in income distribution increases the supply of savings in the economy, which exerts sustained pressure for lower interest rates. These assertions are confirmed empirically by Mian et al. (2021), who show that it may explain a large portion of the decline in interest rates. This component of the effect of rising market power is not accounted for by the reported simulations because the underlying model does not consider the effects of income distribution, but it is a vital factor with long-term consequences.

Analysis of the data reported in figure 2.4 offers a hint about the main difference between the effect of the two policy regimes on the dynamics of the interest rate. The laissez-faire policy regime results in higher volatility of the interest rate. Under active policy, the interest rate fluctuates mostly between 2 percent and 4 percent, while under the laissez-faire policy regime, it ranges from 0.2 percent to 5.2 percent.

2.8   The Far-Reaching Effect of Market Power Resulting from Changes in the Policy Regime

2.8.1   Asymmetric Impact of Changes in Policy Regimes on the Level of Equilibrium Variables

Many different factors bring about radical change in economic policy. But the *mere change of policy*, between the two policy regimes under discussion, has far-reaching effects on economic performance because it alters the steady-state levels of equilibrium variables. To understand why this matters, note that discussions of economic growth are often focused on equilibrium growth rates, not on equilibrium *levels* of economic variables. Yet policies that alter the levels of growing variables have a significant impact on the trajectory of growth and hence on the effective growth rates of an economy during the transition periods from one policy regime to the other.

To set the stage for discussing these issues, figure 2.5 presents a simulated sequence of 200 years of equilibrium values of capital, output, and market power, with policy regimes that change unexpectedly every fifty years. At time 0, the starting values of the state variables are randomly chosen from the ergodic set of values that the endogenous variables take under the inactive policy. However, the starting policy at time 0 is a *newly* active policy, initiating a transition from an equilibrium with steady state under the laissez-faire policy to a steady state under the active policy. The inactive policy is restored unexpectedly in period 51. The active policy is then restored in period 101, and the inactive policy is finally restored in period 151. Each change of policy initiates a transition from

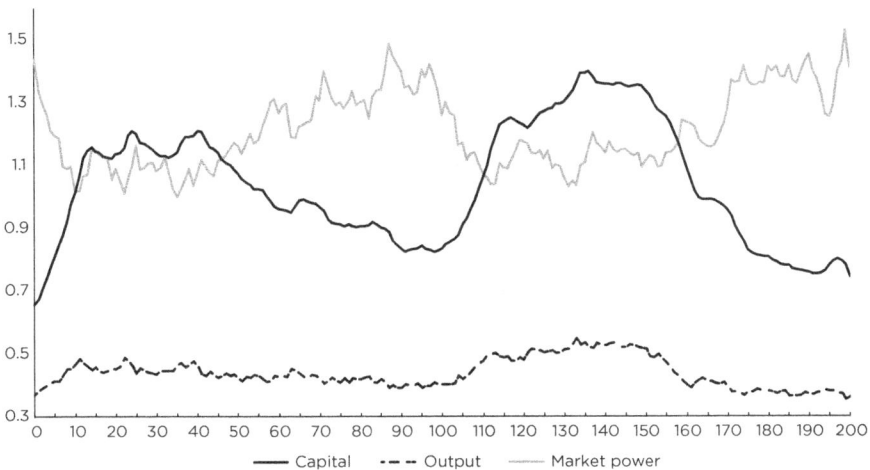

Figure 2.5 Asymmetric effects of changing policy regimes

one equilibrium to the next; therefore, figure 2.5 describes the simulated history of the economy under a random sequence of ζ_t, ϵ_t^ζ, and $\epsilon_t^\mathcal{P}$, but under four policy regimes. The multiplicity of shocks imply that the timing of policy change is not the only factor that affects the dynamic evolution of the variables in the figure.

A change in policy amounts to an unexpected change in the dynamic structure of the economy. Under the laissez-faire, inactive policy, the steady-state value of market power is $\mathcal{P}^* = 1.32$, while under the active policy, $\mathcal{P}^* = 1.07$. Consequently, under the inactive policy, k^*, y^*, and c^* take low values, while under the active policy, these aggregates take high values. The implication is that a change in policy changes the steady state and the entire trajectory of economic aggregates. At the end of an era of active policy, the aggregates take values that are close to the high steady-state values (because $\mathcal{P}^*$ is low). Therefore, the policy change causes the aggregates to begin a long *decline* to a new lower steady-state level. During such a transition, the economy experiences a growth rate lower than its normal trend. After the end of an era of inactive policy, the aggregates begin a long period of abnormally high growth rates in transition toward higher steady-state values. The first question is then how long the transition takes between those two different steady states. The results in figure 2.5 reveal that these periods are surprisingly long! In a random simulation of 1,000 years, the average length of the economic booms caused by the introduction of an active policy was 21.2 years, while, apart from some fluctuations in the initial phase, the decline of the aggregates caused by turning to the inactive policy lasted, in most cases, the entire fifty years.

Apart from the fact that the transition periods that follow a change in policy are very long, figure 2.5 also exhibits asymmetry in the speed of economic response to the introduction of a new policy between the active policy at dates 1 and 101, and the inactive policy at dates 51 and 151. The active policy causes a sharp decline of market power; a rapid rise in the levels, relative to trend, of capital, income, consumption, investment, and wages; and a sharp decline in profits and in income and wealth inequality. The restoration of a laissez-faire, inactive policy leads to a slow rise in market power, associated with a slow decline, relative to trend, of all economic aggregates and a rise in income and wealth inequality. The asymmetry is a consequence of the fact that an active policy regime causes market power to dissipate rapidly when $\lambda_\mathcal{P}^L = 0.80$, while a restoration of an inactive policy regime entails $\lambda_\mathcal{P}^H = 0.95$, which allows market power to become gradually entrenched. The inactive policy results in high persistence of economic aggregates and a slow rise of market power.

An increased level of a variable, relative to trend, can significantly alter the observed growth rate of that variable for a long time and may lead to confusion about the underlying trend. As an example, the underlying trend growth in the model is 1.4 percent, but in figure 2.5, the detrended variable y grows in the first twelve years by 30.7 percent and declines from date 51 to date 91 by 7.6 percent. The effective growth rate of output Y is then 3.7 percent in the first twelve years and 1.2 percent in the forty years from date 51 to date 91. More dramatic are the changes from date 101 to date 200. The active policy introduced at date 101 causes an initial boom of output that lasts thirteen years, with an average growth rate of 3.13 percent. On the other hand, restoration of the inactive policy at date 151 results in a random steep decline of y over the next sixteen years and an actual average output growth rate of -0.5 percent. An econometrician studying quarterly data on economic growth could easily declare the first thirteen years a golden age of growth and the sixteen years after date 151 a secular stagnation. The underlying trend is actually the same in both cases.

2.8.2   Implications for Policy Analysis and a Prediction

The unique nature of the argument in section 2.8.1 is that these significant changes in effective growth rates, often over long periods, are not caused by changes in productivity but by changes in policy. Radical policy changes occur infrequently, and in chapter 4 I show that in the twentieth century it happened only twice: in 1901 and in the 1980s. The 1901 change took some years to take hold, while the change in the 1980s took relatively less time to affect the economy.

The analysis leads to an important implication for the measured growth rates of the economy following a change in policy. These growth rates are affected by the convergence toward a new steady state of the economy, more specifically:

1. When a change is made from an active policy to an inactive policy, the trajectories of economic aggregates are altered, resulting in *slower realized economic growth relative to potential trend*.
2. When a change is made from an inactive policy to an active policy, there is *more rapid realized economic growth relative to potential trend*.

These implications of the theory provide a partial explanation of U.S. economic performance since the 1980s. One of the repeated arguments of those who supported the shift to a laissez-faire policy in the 1970s and 1980s was that the new policy would increase private incentives to work, invest, and innovate. They forecasted a substantial boom in investment and a higher growth rate of the economy. None of that materialized, and the implication of the theory presented here is *exactly the opposite*: such a change in policy would trigger a long period of adjustment marked by a *decline* in the rate of investment relative to potential trend and a lower growth rate of the economy relative to trend. This reasoning helps explain the decline of the rate of investment and economic growth from

1986 to 2020. It also questions the validity of the interpretation of the recent low growth rates as foreshadowing a prolonged period of secular stagnation.

The theory also proposes that the restoration of a strong active policy to contain market power and reduce inequality would have an important secondary effect: it would cause a higher observed growth rates, relative to trend, of output and all other economic aggregates. It would also lead to higher wages, a higher capital/output ratio, and a higher interest rate. This economic boom, relative to trend growth, would last about twenty to thirty years but would not be permanent. The level of output would be higher, but the growth rate would gradually converge to its potential trend. This trend is determined by the growth of scientific knowledge, which is affected by the degree of society's support of basic research. I take up this important topic of the trend growth rate in chapter 7.

It is also important to add that many features of either policy regime are not reflected in these analytical results. An example is the effect of firms with stronger market power lowering the aggregate growth rate by either reducing their rate of innovations to avoid cannibalizing their own markets or by using other strategies to suppress technologies of potential competitors and impede the growth of their productivity. In chapter 7, I consider policies that intervene in this competition among firms.

2.9   A Comment on Differential Risk Between Capital Return and Profits

I have stressed in chapter 1 the difference in riskiness between the return on capital and profits, yet the model of this chapter has ignored this distinction. It is instructive to note that in an economy where risk is expressed by diverse uncertain states of the world, trading of risk is made by trading state-contingent claims. In such an economy, capital and monopoly wealth would just be defined as two different securities, and the difference in their riskiness would be identified by the difference in their state-contingent payoffs. This easy solution is not available in the incomplete markets model used in this chapter, where the return on both capital and monopoly wealth are subject to the same exogenous shocks. The distinction in chapter 1 should be interpreted as requiring capital income to be subjected only to the aggregate exogenous ζ_t shock, while profits are subject to shocks to ζ_t as well as other shocks resulting from innovations, acquisitions, strategic pricing, and the competitive environment, all represented in the model by shocks to $\mathcal{P}_t$. To model these differential risks, it is necessary to think of an equilibrium of the incomplete market economy as a rolling process that takes place in two separate stages within the same date. In the first stage, ζ_t is revealed, after which labor and capital are hired and their incomes determined. In the second stage, all shocks resulting from strategic decisions of firms are revealed and then values of output, profits, and consumption are set. The household's commitment to the level of capital in period $t - 1$ and the firm's commitment to input levels in the first stage reflect the frictions that are the source of the incomplete nature of the market involved.

To further explain how such a rolling equilibrium functions, note that the household's investment level is chosen at date $t - 1$, which makes k_t a known state variable at the start of date t. Consequently, in the first stage of date t, the household makes only its labor supply decision, while the firm makes its capital and labor input decisions given the wage rate and the rental rate, both of which are then determined in stage 1. That is, factor quantities and prices are determined given the expected value of all strategic variables associated with market power, all of which are not revealed in stage 1. This means that the equilibrium conditions at stage 1 are the conditions in (2.14) where all strategic variables related to the evolution of market power are formulated as expected values. In that stage, $\hat{K}_{t+1}$, $\hat{L}_t$, $\hat{W}_t$, and $\hat{R}_t$ are determined and, because K_t is a given state variable, labor income and capital income are also determined. The firm is then committed to employment of $(K_t, \hat{L}_t)$ at specified compensations. In the second stage, the shock to market power is revealed and a revised equilibrium is established. At this point factor prices and quantities, based as they were on expected values of market power, are inefficient relative to the new resulting equilibrium values. This creates a degree of misallocation. In stage 2, when $\mathcal{P}_t$ is known, the household makes its consumption-savings decision of K_{t+1}, given that its income is defined by the known quantities $\hat{L}_t$, $\hat{W}_t$, and $\hat{R}_t$, supplemented by the newly determined profits and output.

In such an equilibrium, profits are more risky than capital because they are subject to the risk of all strategic decisions. However, in my experiments with diverse strategic decisions, including heterogeneous firm productivity as in (2.7a)–(2.7d), the results about all the economic aggregates reported earlier in this chapter remain the same. Because the two-stage equilibrium is far more complex, I have chosen to report the simpler equilibrium and ignore the risk differential. The code for computing this equilibrium is available in the Online Appendix available on my website at http://web.stanford.edu/~mordecai/.

CHAPTER 3

MONOPOLY WEALTH AND INTANGIBLE CAPITAL

During the nineteenth and early twentieth centuries, the common view of intangible assets, typically goodwill, was that these were not real assets and did not merit being reported by a firm on its balance sheet. Consequently, the standard accounting practice at the time was to consider reporting the value of intangible assets as optional. It was for a firm's board of directors to decide how much information to provide its stockholders. Times have certainly changed. In the last forty years, the proportion of intangible assets on the balance sheet of firms has risen around the world, to the point that corporate decisions about investing in these assets are treated as being as important as those concerning tangible assets (see Haskel and Westlake, 2017). Nevertheless, the treatment of intangibles has remained one of the most controversial subjects in contemporary accounting practice. For economists, identifying the economic function of intangible assets at the firm level and their appropriate category in the accounting of the aggregate economy has remained equally problematic.

The U.S. Bureau of Economic Analysis (BEA) used to treat research and development (R&D) expenses as the cost of intermediate inputs used in the production of other products. As a result, it did not include them directly in gross domestic product (GDP). This policy was changed in 2013 when the BEA recognized such cost as investments in fixed assets, specifically intangible assets. It now classifies R&D expenses as a component of gross fixed investments, called intellectual property products. The increase in measured investment, resulting from this accounting change, increased measured GDP. Given an appropriate depreciation rate, standard perpetual inventory methods are used to compute the implied stock value that R&D investment generates over time, which results in a stock of intangible assets. But the BEA stock, measured in this manner, does not correspond to the stock of intangible assets on the balance sheets of firms.

Two examples will highlight the disparity between these measures. The first is a patent purchased by a firm. It appears on the firm's balance sheet as an investment in an intangible asset but is not included in the BEA's definition of R&D investment. The second is an R&D spending of $1 billion on a failed drug. BEA treats this $1 billion as an investment in intellectual property products. The firm, however, retains nothing of that value on its books because it would write off the entire expenditure. As a result, the expenditure is recorded as part of aggregate investment, but there is no intangible asset on the books of the private sector that reflects that investment.

The BEA explains the logic underlying this second example by drawing an analogy with investments in tangible assets. Such investments may be very successful, or they may fail, but the strategy adopted by the BEA has been not to evaluate their success in constructing its measure of tangible capital. The BEA explains that competition among projects will bring the net excess profit down to zero. This argument does not apply to inventions and technological discoveries for two reasons. First, the distribution of final outcomes has a very fat tail. To see how fat it is, note that virtually no R&D investments were made in the original technological ideas that led to the creation of firms like Amazon, Facebook, Netflix, or Google. Their market value and intangible wealth today bear no relation to the original R&D cost of their technologies. Second, my argument in chapters 1 and 7 demonstrates that technological competition is different from standard competition. Technological competition results in one or few winners and does not reduce to zero the excess profits earned from innovations. The BEA practice is based on the assumption of a perfectly competitive equilibrium among innovators, but these two arguments show that aggregate R&D expenditures may bear only a limited relation to the aggregate increase in asset values resulting from innovations over any time interval.

The problem of identifying the economic nature of intangible assets is an important one. It goes to the heart of a key implication of my theory: capital employed is different from wealth, the difference being monopoly wealth, defined and discussed in chapter 1. Identifying the economic nature of these assets affects my empirical work in chapter 4 because I need to define the capital stock in order to compute the capital share in value added. My solution is to exclude intangible assets from the definition of capital. Some scholars estimate capital employed by deducing it from the market value of corporate securities, assuming implicitly that intangible assets are included in the definition of capital (see, for example, Piketty and Zucman, 2014). It is well known that there is a difference between the market value of many firms and their net worth, even if valued at market prices. This difference is reduced by the inclusion of intangible assets in the firm's capital, and some scholars have noted that such a practice resolves a number of puzzles in financial economics (see Lev, 2001; Hulten and Hao, 2008). There is no doubt that intangibles help to explain part of the difference between the market value of a firm and the value of its tangible assets. But this does not imply that they should be labeled as capital assets. Intangibles are not like capital inputs because a firm can replicate them at no cost—they are nonrivalrous. By contrast, capital, the input to production, has a strictly positive marginal cost. Instead, I show in this chapter that the value of all intangibles is part of monopoly wealth. I begin, in the next section, by reviewing the wide-ranging views found in the literature about the nature of intangible assets.

3.1   Value of Intangible Assets: Diverse Perspectives

Many studies treat intangibles as regular capital assets by deducing the capital stock from the market value of securities with no adjustment for intangibles. Most aggregate databases like the BEA or the World KLEMS Initiative include intangibles in their definition of capital (see Jäger, 2017; Jorgenson et al., 2019), and the authors justify this by the perspective of national income accounts.

To see that this procedure has important consequences, consider the constant returns to scale production function $Y = F(K, AL)$. Growth theory allows a prediction of how the ratio of K/Y evolves over time and how it depends on parameter values, but any empirical test of that prediction depends upon the data used to measure Y and K. Studies such as Piketty and Zucman (2014) and Karabarbounis and Neiman (2014) include intangibles in the definition of K and make the important claim that the capital/output ratio has risen since the 1980s. Based on this observation, they then formulate several questionable hypotheses to explain it. When fixed capital is correctly measured and excludes intangibles, and as I show in chapter 6, the K/Y ratio has actually *declined* rather than increased in that time period and this is also the exact key prediction of my theory, developed in chapter 2 (see proposition 2.3).

Some studies in financial economics also treat intangibles as tangible capital. Peters and Taylor (2017) study the behavior of investment using Tobin's q model. They treat intangible assets as a different type of the firm's required capital input and assume the firm can freely buy and sell intangible assets on open markets. The authors show that, with intangible assets added, regressions of investment on q produce higher R^2 values and lower implied adjustment costs at both the firm and aggregate levels. They conclude that if intangibles are included, there is a match between the data and Tobin's q theory, according to which investment should flow to firms with a market value that exceeds the replacement value of their assets.

The textbook explanation of why market value differs from net worth is often focused on the fixed cost required in a firm's creation and on the fact that such costs do not leave behind a distinct asset on the firm's balance sheet. These fixed organizational costs must be borne by an entrant and function as a barrier to entry. Consequently, all firms charge a markup over their marginal costs to cover these fixed costs. Under monopolistic competition, the equilibrium number of products is determined by such fixed costs (see, for example, De Loecker et al., 2020). Recent work on organizational capital places more weight on how the firm develops and on its current organization and management, but these are explained in different ways by different authors. Lev and Radhakrishnan (2009) offer the standard description of organizational capital. They see it as "unique systems and processes employed in the investment, production, and sales activities of the enterprise, along with the incentives and compensation systems governing its human resources." They propose that organizational capital is a firm-specific resource that is not on the firm's balance sheet and that yields abnormal returns. This organizational capital is then a proprietary form of private knowledge, analogous to any propriety technology. Eisfeldt and Papanikolaou (2013) see organizational capital as an outgrowth of the special, firm-specific match between the firm and its key talent, where the benefits to stockholders depend upon the outside options available to the organization's key talent. Others see it in a different light, but in any of the models that include organizational capital, the crucial feature of such an asset is that it is a firm-specific proprietary asset, unavailable to a potential entrant and thus a barrier to entry.

Conceptualizing organizational capital as an intangible asset is analogous to the idea behind the valuation of goodwill. In the nineteenth century, the accounting concept of goodwill was developed to reflect the effort made by an entrepreneur to build his personal reputation, thereby creating value for the firm beyond its tangible assets. In the early days of accounting, when the courts rejected the treatment of intangibles as a form of capital, goodwill was often used as an example of an intangible asset that is unique to the firm.

Some models that include the element of organizational capital and intangible assets propose to explain the rise of markup since the 1980s by using an explanation based on firm heterogeneity discussed in chapters 1 and 7. These theories explain the superior performance of some firms not by their having market power but because they privately own superior technology or have a superior, firm-specific organization that results in their being better at using technology than their competitors. I offer a different line of reasoning in chapters 7 and 8. Firms with proprietary technology and proprietary knowledge may be more or less productive than others, but it is just a simple empirical fact that their having market power is the consequence of their private ownership of propriety technology and knowledge.

Taking the accounting approach to the problem, some studies in financial economics examine the role of intangibles in explaining the difference between the value of the firm and its net worth. Hulten and Hao (2008) study this difference by using the Compustat data files. They use an expansive definition of intangible capital that far exceeds the value of intangible assets on corporate books and encompasses most of monopoly wealth as I have defined it (see chapter 6 for my estimates of monopoly wealth for publicly traded firms). They then show that these defined intangible assets, not on corporate balance sheets, narrow the gap between the market value of firms and their net worth.

Hall's (2001) is the first rigorous work that assesses the difference between the market value of corporate assets and the reproduction cost of recorded capital. He uses a perfect competition model with adjustment costs to infer the capital stocks of firms from their market prices and concludes that recorded capital is too small. Hall argues that the data suggest U.S. corporations own large amounts of intangible capital not recorded on their books or in government statistics.

Hansen et al. (2009) accept Hall's (2001) evidence and propose the possibility that the discrepancy in market valuation may be because intangible capital has a larger macroeconomic and undiversifiable risk exposure than does tangible capital. Looking at the problem from an alternate perspective, Hulten and Hao (2008) study 617 R&D-intensive firms and find that conventional book value explains only 31 percent of the market capitalization of these firms in 2006, confirming Hall's (2001) conclusion. McGrattan and Prescott (2005) study the aggregate market value of the U.S. corporate sector but, contrary to Hall (2001), claim the value accords with competitive theory and that the fluctuations in value are explained by changes in tax law.

Many other researchers have, in empirical studies, treated the value of intangible assets recorded on corporate books as providing a causal explanation for other variables. They treat intangible assets as an index of the level of technological advancement of the firms that own them. This interpretation is a consequence of the view that intangible assets embody the results of R&D and innovation. Therefore, their market values reflect the level of a firm's technological success and, at the sectoral or aggregate levels, are a measure of the technological level of the sector or economy. Haskel and Westlake (2017) propose that the rise of intangibles in the last forty years reflects the move, under modern capitalism, away from investments in tangible capital assets and toward advanced technology embodied in intangible assets. McGrattan (2020) adds intangible investments as technological nonrivalrous goods to supplement observed fixed investments in an endogenous growth general equilibrium model and shows this improves the model's accuracy in explaining business-cycle behavior. Gutiérrez and Philippon (2016) seek to explain the decline in the rate of investment and ask if it can be caused by the substitution of investment in intangibles for fixed capital investment. In a cross-sectional study, they use data on the value of intangibles and other factors, including globalization, to explain empirically the decline in the rate of fixed investments at the industry level in the last thirty years. They find that the explanatory power of both intangibles and globalization is quantitatively limited.

This review identifies three concepts of the role of intangibles. The first views intangible assets as a distinct form of capital, and their value is taken to be a component of capital as a factor input. That measure has been used in empirical research to questionable effect.

The second view, originating in Hall (2001), establishes that competitive models cannot explain the gap between market value and the reproduction cost of capital employed, and something else, perhaps intangible assets, is needed to fill the gap. If so, competitive theory suggests that the role of intangibles cannot be understood in a purely competitive economy. The theory that I propose calls this gap monopoly wealth, of which intangible assets on the books of firms is one component. The level of monopoly wealth created by the corporate sector from 1959 to 2019 is then estimated in chapter 6.

The third point of view considers intangible assets as a proxy for the technological level of a firm, sector, or an economy. The market value of the intangibles owned by a firm is then taken as a measure of its technological advancement. This point of view is related to the endogenous growth literature, where the stock of technological knowledge is an important variable. Intangibles could be treated as either the output of the economy's investment in technology or the actual inputs to the process that generate the improved technology. A firm purchasing an intangible is then interpreted as investing in technology rather than in fixed capital.

In the next section, I argue that intangible assets are certainly not inputs to ordinary production and in fact operate very differently from capital. Therefore, their recorded aggregate value should not be counted as part of the capital stock. As to their value being an index of technology level, it is true that the market value of intangibles is a price or cost of the technology that the intangibles represent. But it is misleading to think of it as an index of firms' technological level because the intangibles on the books of any firm represent only a fraction of the total value of the firm's monopoly wealth.

3.2   The Value of Intangible Assets Is Part of Monopoly Wealth

From the point of view of a firm, the purchase of a building, a patent, or an entire competing firm are alternative investments that are evaluated with the same tools of standard cost-benefit analysis. Therefore, from the firm's perspective, there is little reason to distinguish among them. For this reason, I have already noted that some scholars view intangible assets as another form of capital goods, an intangible capital, analogous to structures and equipment, and, in this view, entering the production function in the same way.

The novel observation made by the endogenous growth literature is that not all business investments are made in capital (see, for example, Romer, 1990; Grossman and Helpman, 1991). In that literature, R&D expenditures generate new designs that increase the knowledge stock of the firm and the economy. This stock then determines the level of productivity and enters the production function through the productivity term, often labeled A_t. This led to the idea that the value of the intangible assets owned by the firm is associated with its technological level. It is then noteworthy that the idea that firms can invest in improving their productivity and not in their capital stock is vital for understanding the economy in a technological age. The literature on human capital also recognized, even earlier, that not all investments are made in fixed capital. Instead, some are made in labor (see, for example, Mincer, 1958; Becker, 1964).

The firm's point of view, that all investments can be analyzed as capital investments, is not the economic-theoretic point of view or the social perspective. When firm A buys firm B, the price paid may exceed the recorded net worth at market value on the books of firm B. The difference between these two values is recorded as goodwill on the books of the purchasing firm. Goodwill is actually the largest component of intangible assets on the balance sheets of U.S. corporations. As shown in chapter 1, the acquired goodwill is, in fact, the market value of the proprietary technological knowledge of the acquired firm. But then, in equilibrium, this market value is equal to the present value of the expected future excess profits of the acquiring firm, created by the market power it gains. But such added market power is a direct result of the acquired proprietary technology. This demonstrates that the resulting goodwill is simply part of monopoly wealth: the capitalized value of profits due to market power.

Most corporations are not purchased or sold, and most monopoly wealth is thus not traded in mergers or acquisitions. Therefore, given the way the values of goodwill are recorded, most monopoly wealth is not recorded on corporate balance sheets. In chapter 6, I show that in 2019, recorded intangibles on corporate balance sheets accounted for only 30 percent of monopoly wealth of the corporate sector. It means that the difference between the market value of all corporations and their aggregate net worth at market prices was about 70 percent of the monopoly wealth of the corporate sector. The value of monopoly wealth created by a firm is computed by adding the difference between market value and net worth to the total value of intangibles already on its books.

It is useful to explore why intangible assets on the balance sheet of a firm represent only a fraction of the firm's monopoly wealth. First, items like organizational capital or trade secrets are intangible assets that reflect firm-specific proprietary knowledge that gives rise to market power. Their contributions to monopoly wealth are unrecorded on the books of the firm but are reflected in the firm's stock price. Second, standard accounting practice leads a firm to record only expenditures on investments and R&D that are actually spent or lost. This procedure results in under-reporting of the true cumulative value of innovations on the balance sheets of firms. The innovation process has a positive expected value, but unsuccessful innovations are written off against current income, while the values of successful innovations end up reflected mostly in rising stock prices. Because innovation outcomes are distributed with a very thick tail, the most successful innovations have very high returns relative to cost. This means that the most successful innovations, those that generate market power, higher stock prices, and monopoly wealth, have a relatively small recorded intangible R&D investment. Third, over 60 percent of recorded intangible assets consist of goodwill created by mergers and acquisitions. But because a firm acquires another firm in order to strengthen its technology and its market power, this increased market position implies that the monopoly wealth of the combined firms exceeds the combined monopoly wealth of the separate firms. This added monopoly wealth is never recorded as an intangible asset on the books of the combined firm.

The reasoning I offer for classifying goodwill as a component of monopoly wealth is based on the fact that this value results from the firm's ownership of intellectual property, the valuation of which reflects its contribution to the firm's market power. This valuation mechanism is the same for all intangibles. In a perfectly competitive economy, knowledge is a nonrivalrous public good; it is valuable but not excludable because it is not owned by anyone. In an economy with private ownership of knowledge, firms acquire a monopoly over knowledge, which is the defining property of intangible assets. Because monopoly wealth is the market value of assets whose value is derived from market power, the value of any intangible is then part of monopoly wealth. I briefly examine three key intangible assets to illustrate the principle:

1. *Patents.* The market value of a patent reflects the desirability of the technology it covers. But now imagine that a patent owned by a firm unexpectedly expires. The firm now has the same technological knowledge but it no longer has the market power of the patent. Its revenue will fall not because its productive capacity declines but because it loses control of the price, which will be brought down by competition. The value of the patent reflects the firm's market power—the value of the firm's ability to prevent others from using the patented knowledge.
2. *Software.* Suppose a firm purchases software for its own unrestricted use at a price that reflects the software owner-developer's monopoly power. Now suppose that free copies of the software begin to circulate, either because the developer released

the software into the public domain or due to piracy. Does the firm's technological capacity decline? The answer is no, for the same reason as in the case of a patent. The firm's technological level depends on the knowledge embodied in the software, not on its price. The only change is in the pricing power and therefore in the market power of the firm that owns the intangible.

3. *Organizational capital and trade secrets.* As I noted in section 3.1, organizational capital is a firm-specific proprietary asset. It is unavailable to potential entrants and is therefore nonrivalrous and excludable, and is part of the monopoly wealth generated by the firm. This asset consists of knowledge about administrative procedures, methods of compensation, and other unique components of a firm's culture. Trade secrets are similarly part of this monopoly wealth because they comprise firm-specific knowledge that is not legally protected other than by state laws that specifically criminalize the theft of trade secrets. Suppose, however, that these secrets are uncovered by competitors who copy and make them public. Their value as a barrier to entry vanishes, and the profitability of the firm declines, but its technological level and productive capacity do not diminish. The only change is the decline in its market power.

By identifying all intangible assets as components of monopoly wealth, I suggest that all products of the R&D effort by the corporate sector are just different forms of monopoly wealth. This flows naturally from the fact that the motive for corporate R&D is either the defense of existing market power or the acquisition of new market power that enables the firm to earn a higher rate of return on its assets. My conclusion is that intangible assets are an important component of monopoly wealth, but they are not ordinary factor inputs like labor and capital.

As to technology's valuation, intangible assets derive their value from proprietary technology or other private information. However, their value, as recorded on the books of a corporation, does not constitute a good index of the level of advance of the technology employed by a firm because much of its technology is erected either on the foundations of general scientific knowledge or on proprietary knowledge that is owned by the firm but whose value is not found on its balance sheet.

This conclusion points to the theoretical difference between conceiving the value of an intangible as a measure of the value of a technology rather than of market power. It appears paradoxical that much of the current literature on intangible assets, outlined in section 3.1, utilizes models that assume competitive markets. The paradox arises because intangibles derive their value from private ownership of valuable information. This cannot occur in a competitive economy because such an economy prohibits the formation of monopoly power over innovations and private knowledge. When private knowledge is produced by R&D at marginal cost, the endogenous growth literature has attempted to resolve the paradox by assuming free entry into the production of knowledge through R&D.

Under perfect competition, firms earn zero profits, and models of endogenous growth seek to replicate this feature with respect to private information. To that end, in models like those of Grossman and Helpman (1991), where firms have private information and earn monopoly profits, ex ante expected profits are zero because the firms incur costs developing the proprietary technologies that earn those profits. This R&D market achieves an equilibrium when the costs of developing the proprietary technologies equal the monopoly profits derived from them. In these models, if the costs of developing the technologies are less than the profits generated, new firms can freely enter the R&D market and compete to innovate valuable technology. If the costs of development exceed the profits, existing firms will exit until profits rise to zero. This is how De Loecker et al. (2020) structure their model of rising market power with free entry. In such an equilibrium, the value of all intangibles becomes equal to their cost of production. This assumes success in the R&D market is only a function of expenditure. It also assumes that the incumbents do not have any advantage and cannot use any of the strategies listed in chapter 1 to defend their markets by building upon their existing knowledge and market position.

In chapters 7 and 8, I demonstrate that technological competition is drastically different from regular competition. Technological competition has one or few winners and results in winners having market power that can only be challenged with better innovations. The theory developed in chapter 1 shows such an environment will not result in perfect competition. Incumbents are more likely to survive and if not, winners will just be alternate monopolists. All winners have advantages that they use to consolidate their market power and make it durable. The R&D models of free entry and with zero profits do not describe the reality of technological competition.

If intangibles are not an input to production and their value is a poor index of technology, why do many authors such as Haskel and Westlake (2017) or McGrattan (2020) find them to be a useful explanatory variable in empirical work? There are two reasons. The first is related to the fact that the value of intangible assets is part of monopoly wealth. When the value of a firm's intangible assets equals its total monopoly wealth, such wealth is a good measure of the firm's market power. This value would certainly explain many phenomena, as proved in chapter 2. However, because the actual value of intangibles on a firm's books is only a fraction of its total monopoly wealth, that fraction is an imperfect proxy for the firm's market power and monopoly wealth. It is thus not surprising that the results are only partially satisfactory, although very useful in some cases. The second reason for the usefulness of intangibles as an explanatory variable is that this form of asset is most prevalent in industries in which there is a high rate of mergers and acquisitions. As mergers and acquisitions have risen over time, so too have intangibles on corporate books. Rising market concentration, in large part a result of mergers and acquisitions, is an important indicator of the dramatic rise in market power since the 1980s that is documented in chapter 4. Consequently, the growth in the total value of intangible assets on the books of firms is correlated with the rise in market power and with all phenomena associated with it.

I next turn to the possible impact of intangibles on the level of fixed investment. Firms may choose between investment in intangibles and investment in capital assets. This leads to the question of whether these two investments might be substitutes, and whether firms' investments in intangible assets displace tangible real investments, as suggested by some. The next section explores this question. The answer depends upon the nature of the technology that a firm can purchase. Therefore, I investigate the potential displacement of tangible capital by purchases of intangibles that take two forms: labor-saving and capital-saving innovations.

3.3   Can an Innovation or Purchased Intangible Cause a Decline in Tangible Investment?

It is sometimes argued that intangible assets offer higher returns, which causes a shift toward intangible assets and away from tangible capital, and this could explain the decline in tangible capital investments. This type of reasoning is the basis of Palley's (2019) interpretation of Keynes's theory of the liquidity trap, and Summers and Stansbury's (2019) version of the secular stagnation hypothesis. On its own, this explanation is not persuasive or complete because tangible and intangible assets are different objects, and if firms can rent these assets in competitive markets at two different rental rates, equalization of their return would be accomplished simply by an adjustment of their relative price. But Palley and Summers and Stansbury propose a mechanism, which they ascribe to Keynes, that a shock (demand or supply) could have a *differential* effect on the demand for these two assets, and therefore a price adjustment may be accompanied by a quantity adjustment that lowers the equilibrium level of investment in tangible assets. This is a more subtle equilibrium response of two different assets that results from differences in the economic functions of these two assets. The function performed by tangible capital, as an input in production, is clear, and therefore a formal analysis of this issue depends on the precise function of intangible assets. This is my first task.

I will formulate the problem first by clarifying the market structure and the role of intangible assets. Suppose a firm has a monopoly in the product market and it uses capital and labor to produce output with a production function of the form $Q_t = A_t F(K_t, L_t)$. I also consider the cases of labor or capital augmenting technical change. Suppose also that a small innovating firm develops

a technology[1] that improves the monopolist's productivity because it complements its existing technology. The invention can be used in other unrelated
markets where it can be sold for a price P^N, which is the price the monopolist
needs to pay to acquire the technology. Equivalently, suppose the monopolist
can carry out a proprietary R&D program, requiring knowledge unavailable to
competitors, and with an expense of P^N can become the owner of the technology. Suppose also that markets for capital and labor are competitive so that, by
(1.3d), the equilibrium conditions of the firm are

$$W_t = \frac{\theta_t - 1}{\theta_t} P_t^\star A_t F_L(K_t^\star, L_t^\star) \tag{3.1a}$$

$$R_t = \frac{\theta_t - 1}{\theta_t} P_t^\star A_t F_K(K_t^\star, L_t^\star) \tag{3.1b}$$

where θ_t is the demand elasticity and $(P_t^\star, K_t^\star, L_t^\star)$ are the solutions to the monopolist's optimization problem (output price, capital input, and labor input)
that entail monopoly profits of $\Pi_t^\star$. The key question left is the technological
impact of the intangible asset under consideration. Suppose it can increase the
productivity factor A_t in one of two possible ways: (1) increase A_t by a proportion $\wp$, or (2) increase A_t by an amount Δ. Under what conditions would the
monopoly firm purchase the intangible asset, and can such a purchase lower
the equilibrium level $K_t^\star$?

The two propositions in the mathematical appendix show that innovations,
or the purchase of intangibles, can cause a reduction in capital employed under a well-defined but *very narrow* set of conditions. These depend upon the
elasticity of substitution between capital and labor. If this elasticity is close to 1,
then such a reduction can occur only when the increase in the firm's productivity is large and the elasticity of its demand is small and restricted to a very
narrow interval. This is a rare event. Although there is substantial evidence that
the elasticity of substitution is close to 1, estimates that diverge from that tend
to place it higher than 1, in which case, for labor-augmenting innovations, the
result reported in (A3.7) proves that capital/labor ratio will actually *rise* rather
than decline. The opposite is true for capital augmenting innovations. In that
case, the result reported in (A3.8) shows that the capital/labor ratio declines if
the elasticity is greater than 1.

In sum, the combination of circumstances required for the purchase of an
intangible asset or an innovation to cause a decline in the rate of investment
in tangible capital suggests *it is a relatively rare event, and one cannot expect it*

---

[1] The event that triggers the change is not a demand shock, as considered by Keynes, but an
innovation, which is the subject of interest here. A formal assessment of the response to a
demand shock also requires a precise specification of the role played by the different assets.

to be the foundation of a general theory to explain any slowdown in investments. Of course, innovations can have many effects that are different from the cases considered here, and some firms may own technologies with elasticity of substitution far different from 1. The most likely candidates for such negative effects are capital-augmenting innovations made by firms with elasticity of substitution above 1. However, there is no compelling evidence for conditions that would lead innovations or the purchase of intangibles to cause a general reduction in economy-wide aggregate capital investment.

My exploration of the potential effect of investment in intangible assets does not provide insight into the possible mechanism by which demand shocks may lead to increased demand for intangible assets and therefore explain a sharp fall of investment in tangible assets, an effect conjectured by Keynes (1936). Palley's (2019) figure 6, which he uses as a tool for making his case, does not offer a sufficiently formal characterization. Scholars studying monetary policy may examine such cases with formal models that are suitable for the task. I avoid such examination here because it would divert attention to problems that are not central to this book.

Finally, it is instructive that the proofs in the appendix do not distinguish between an innovation and the purchase of an intangible asset because they have the same effect on the production function. Intangible assets are legal rights to privately owned technological knowledge, and their market value is determined in exactly the same way as the market value of any other privately owned intellectual property right is determined. They are both part of monopoly wealth.

Mathematical Appendix to Chapter 3

Proposition 3.1. *Assume for simplicity that the demand elasticity $\theta > 1$ and the market interest rate is constant. The monopolist will purchase the innovation, or, equivalently, develop it if*

$$\sum_{t=1}^{\infty} \left(\frac{1}{1+r}\right)^{t-1} \left[\theta_t \frac{\wp}{1+\wp} \Pi_t^\star + \left(\frac{1+\wp+\theta_t\wp}{1+\wp} \frac{\wp}{1+\wp}\right)(W_t L_t^\star + R_t K_t^\star)\right] > P^N.$$

$$(A3.1)$$

The adoption of the innovation will result in lower inputs of labor and capital if $1 < \theta < 1 + \wp$.

Proof. I drop the time index because it is not essential and the problem of the firm is the same in every period. First, the monopoly profits and sales, in units of consumption, are defined by the following two equations:

$$\Pi^* = \text{Max}_{P,L,K}[PQ - WL - RK + \lambda[AF(K,L) - Y]], \quad Q = D(P,Z)$$

$$S^* = P^*AF(K^*, L^*).$$

I first consider case (1) when the innovation or intangible increases A_t by a proportion $\wp$. I later adjust the results for case (2), where the effect is additive. The proof is developed in two steps.

Step 1: The monopolist purchases the technology but keeps output at the same level so that the price does not need to change. Then its profits, disregarding the purchase price, become

$$\hat{\Pi} = P^*(1 + \wp)AF\left(\frac{K^*}{1 + \wp}, \frac{L^*}{1 + \wp}\right) - \frac{1}{1 + \wp}(WL^* + RK^*).$$

Therefore,

$$\hat{\Pi} - \Pi^* = \frac{\wp}{1 + \wp}(WL^* + RK^*).$$

But by adopting the innovation, the optimal conditions (3.1a) and (3.1b) are replaced with new conditions:

$$W = \frac{\theta - 1}{\theta}P(1 + \wp)AF_L(K, L) \qquad (A3.2a)$$

$$R = \frac{\theta - 1}{\theta}P(1 + \rho)AF_K(K, L). \qquad (A3.2b)$$

Replacing A with $(1 + \wp)A$ causes an increased demand for capital and labor. Because W and R do not change, the ratio K/L, which depends only on the ratio W/R, remains the same as well. To optimize, the firm will raise the *scale* of operation, increasing capital, labor, and output in the same proportion, but the question is, By how much? Because the elasticity θ is constant, (A3.2a) and (A3.2b) imply that the price must decrease to $\tilde{P} = P^*/(1 + \wp)$.

Step 2: Given the lower price, the new output is

$$\tilde{Q} - Q^* = -\theta\left(\frac{Q^*}{P^*}\right)(\tilde{P} - P^*) = -\theta\left(\frac{Q^*}{P^*}\right)(-P^*)\frac{\wp}{1 + \wp}.$$

Therefore,

$$\tilde{Q} = Q^*\left(\frac{1 + \wp + \theta\wp}{1 + \wp}\right).$$

To generate this output, labor and capital must be raised by a factor of $(1 + \wp + \theta\wp)/(1 + \wp)$ so that the new profit level is

$$
\tilde{\Pi} = \frac{P^\star}{1 + \wp}(1 + \wp)AF\left(\frac{K^\star}{1 + \wp}, \frac{L^\star}{1 + \wp}\right)\left(1 + \frac{\theta\wp}{1 + \wp}\right)
$$

$$
- \frac{1}{1 + \wp}(WL^\star + RK^\star)\left(1 + \frac{\theta\wp}{1 + \wp}\right)
$$

$$
= Q^\star\left(1 + \frac{\theta\wp}{1 + \wp}\right) - \frac{1}{1 + \wp}(WL^\star + RK^\star)\left(1 + \frac{\theta\wp}{1 + \wp}\right)
$$

$$
= \left(\Pi^\star + \frac{\wp}{1 + \wp}(WL^\star + RK^\star)\right)\left(1 + \frac{\theta\wp}{1 + \wp}\right)
$$

$$
= \hat{\Pi}\left(1 + \frac{\theta\wp}{1 + \wp}\right) > \hat{\Pi} > \Pi^\star.
$$

Because $\tilde{\Pi} - \Pi^\star = \Pi^\star\left(\frac{\theta\wp}{1+\wp}\right) + \frac{\wp}{1+\wp}(WL^\star + RK^\star)\left(1 + \frac{\theta\wp}{1+\wp}\right)$, this equation proves condition (A3.1).

To assess the impact of the innovation on the demand for labor and capital, compare the quantity demanded before and after the innovation. The following then holds:

$$
\tilde{L} = L^\star\frac{1}{1 + \wp}\left(1 + \frac{\theta\wp}{1 + \wp}\right)
$$

$$
\tilde{K} = K^\star\frac{1}{1 + \wp}\left(1 + \frac{\theta\wp}{1 + \wp}\right).
$$

For the inputs to decline, it is necessary that

$$
\frac{1}{1 + \wp}\left(1 + \frac{\theta\wp}{1 + \wp}\right) < 1 \Rightarrow \frac{\theta\beta}{1 + \wp} < \wp. \tag{A3.3}
$$

For this inequality to hold, it is necessary that $1 < \theta < 1 + \wp$, which is a relatively narrow range.

The second case, where the innovation increases productivity by an additive amount Δ, is solved in the same way, with a simple change of variables:

$$
\bar{\wp} = \frac{\Delta}{A} \quad \Rightarrow \quad \Pi^\Delta = P^\star(1 + \bar{\wp})AF\left(\frac{K^\star}{1 + \bar{\wp}}, \frac{L^\star}{1 + \bar{\wp}}\right) - \frac{1}{1 + \bar{\wp}}(WL^\star + RK^\star).
$$

The entire argument is then repeated for $\bar{\wp}$, which is now a function of time.   □

What if technological change is not Hicks-neutral, as assumed in proposition 3.1? The production function then takes one of the following two forms:

$$Q_t = F(K_t, A_t L_t) \quad \text{or} \quad Q_t = F(A_t K_t, L_t).$$

The proof is symmetric and will apply to both cases; therefore, I consider the more common case of labor-augmenting technological improvements. The monopoly optimum in that case is then

$$W_t = \frac{\theta_t - 1}{\theta_t} P_t^\star A_t F_2(K_t^\star, A_t L_t^\star), \text{ where } F_j(X_1, X_2) = \frac{\partial F(X_1, X_2)}{\partial X_j} \quad j = 1, 2$$

(A3.4a)

$$R_t = \frac{\theta_t - 1}{\theta_t} P_t^\star F_1(K_t^\star, A_t L_t^\star).$$

(A3.4b)

Because the discussion applies to each date, I again simplify the exposition by omitting the time index. As before, an intangible asset is available for purchase at the price P^N, and it increases productivity from A to $A(1 + \wp)$. I then define the ratio

$$(1 + \tilde{\wp}) = \frac{F_1(K^\star, AL^\star)}{F_1(K^\star, A(1 + \wp)L^\star)} > 1 \text{ since } \wp > 0.$$

(A3.5)

Proposition 3.2. *Assume, for simplicity, the demand elasticity θ is constant, $\theta > 1$, and $F(K_t, A_t L_t)$ is concave with constant returns to scale. Suppose the gain from the innovation justifies the monopolist's purchasing the innovation. If the elasticity of substitution between labor and capital is 1, factor proportions will be unchanged, and the adoption of the innovation will result in lower inputs of labor and capital if $1 < \theta < 1 + \tilde{\wp}$. If the elasticity is greater than 1, the optimal capital/labor ratio will rise.*

Proof. By constant returns to scale, the optimum conditions are

$$W = \frac{\theta - 1}{\theta} PA(1 + \wp) F_2\left(\frac{K}{A(1 + \wp)L}\right) = \frac{\theta - 1}{\theta} PA(1 + \wp) F_2\left(\frac{X}{1 + \wp}\right)$$

$$X = \frac{K}{AL}$$

$$R = \frac{\theta - 1}{\theta} PF_1\left(\frac{K}{A(1 + \wp)L}\right) = \frac{\theta - 1}{\theta} PF_1\left(\frac{X}{1 + \wp}\right).$$

Equilibrium values before the purchase are (P^*, K^*, L^*, X^*). Define the two functions g and Ψ:

$$\frac{R}{W} = \frac{F_1\left(\frac{X}{1+\wp}\right)}{A(1+\wp)F_2\left(\frac{X}{1+\wp}\right)} \equiv \frac{1}{A(1+\wp)}g\left(\frac{X}{1+\wp}\right) \equiv \Psi(X, \wp). \qquad \text{(A3.6)}$$

It follows from the concavity of F that the function g is monotonically decreasing and that

$$\epsilon_S(X) = -\left(\frac{dX}{d(R/W)}\right)\left(\frac{R/W}{X}\right) = -\frac{g(X)}{g'(X)X}$$

$$= \text{ elasticity of substitution between capital and labor.}$$

Step 1: Examine the response of factor proportions to the technology purchase. Because factor prices are unchanged, it follows from (A3.6) that only X changes in response to change in $\wp$. Take first difference of (A3.6), evaluate at $(X^*, \wp = 0)$, and set to zero to find

$$\Psi_X(X - X^*) + \Psi_\wp(\wp) = 0 \quad \Rightarrow \quad (X - X^*) = -\frac{\Psi_\wp}{\Psi_X}\wp.$$

But then, from (A3.6):

$$\Psi_X = g'(X^*)\frac{1}{A(1+\wp)^2}$$

$$\Psi_\wp = -g(X^*)\frac{1}{A(1+\wp)^2} - g'(X^*)X^*\frac{1}{A(1+\wp)^3}.$$

Therefore, one concludes, from evaluating the derivatives at $(X^*, \wp = 0)$, that

$$(X - X^*) = -\frac{g(X^*) - g'(X^*)X^*}{g'(X^*)}\wp = (\epsilon_S(X^*) - 1)\wp. \qquad \text{(A3.7)}$$

If the elasticity of substitution is equal to 1, then there is no change in factor proportion, and this proves the first part of the proposition. For the capital/labor ratio to fall, the elasticity has to be less than 1. Conversely, if the elasticity is greater than 1, the ratio will rise.

Step 2: If factor proportions are unchanged, it follows from (A3.4b) that the new price $\tilde{P}$ must satisfy

$$\tilde{P}F_1\left(\frac{X^*}{1+\wp}\right) = P^*F_1(X^*) \quad \Rightarrow \quad \tilde{P} = P^*\frac{F_1(X^*)}{F_1\left(\frac{X^*}{1+\wp}\right)} = \frac{P^*}{1+\tilde{\wp}}.$$

Because, by assumption, $\wp$ is small, then so is $\tilde{\wp}$. The proof is concluded by repeating the argument of proposition 3.1 starting from step 2. $\square$

Corollary 3.1. *Under the same technical conditions as in proposition 3.2, if technological change is capital augmenting, then such innovation will cause a decline in the capital/labor ratio if the elasticity of substitution is higher than 1.*

Proof. In this case, (A3.7) is replaced by

$$(X - X^\star) = -\frac{g(X^\star) - g'(X^\star)X^\star}{g'(X^\star)}\wp = (1 - \epsilon_S(X^\star))\wp. \tag{A3.8}$$

$\square$

CHAPTER 4

DETERMINANTS OF MARKET POWER IN THE UNITED STATES, 1889–2017

4.1 Measuring Market Power

In previous chapters, I noted that the average degree of market power in the United States has risen since the 1980s, showing that income and wealth distribution are not constant. But measures of market power taken at any point in time or even over any short horizon are subject to random factors. These can obscure the real social and political forces at work. Instead, this study aims to identify the longer time spans of rising or falling market power and to assess the circumstances associated with these long-term changes. It is then an inductive exploration of the historical forces that best explain the causes of rising or falling market power. In this chapter, I study the evolution of market power over the period 1889–2017 and the associated historical developments in this era. When taking the longer view, one discovers that any period of rising or falling market power is long and can be measured in decades, reflecting political and social forces that change very slowly.

Studying the extended period of 1889–2017 adds an important perspective to the debate on the causes of changing income and wealth inequality. A long horizon compels us to focus on more durable factors that cause these changes rather than on temporary factors unique to a particular period of change. Contemporary studies have focused, for the most part, on the period since the 1980s, although some begin their examination in 1948. Data applicable to these more recent periods are abundant and more reliable than those from earlier eras. But for any hypothesis compatible with recent data to be accepted as a valid theory of income and wealth distribution, it must also offer insight into distributional changes in earlier periods. If a theory proposes to explain income and wealth distribution by relying on factors operative between 1985 and 2017 but not at any other time in economic history, it is, at best, a questionable explanation of changes in these distributions.

One of the central conclusions of this chapter is that the era of rising share of profits that began in the 1980s is one of three subperiods of rising share of profits within the longer span of 1889–2017. The first of these periods, during the First Gilded Age, runs from 1889 (or earlier) to 1901. The second began during the Great Depression and ended around 1953. Contemporary writers offer different explanations for the changes in the distribution of income and wealth since the 1980s, attributing them to factors such as the impact of robots, falling prices of capital goods relative to consumption goods, globalization, and rising intangible investments. The problem is that all of these factors were not present in the late nineteenth century and in the first half of the twentieth century. How then are we to apply these ideas to explain the earlier distributional changes?

There is a large literature on the measurement of market power. Estimates developed in this literature have been used extensively in the industrial organization and New Keynesian literatures. Much of this research covers recent short intervals and requires data unavailable for the full period studied here. Recent developments in measuring market power have converged on two alternative methods with broad applications. The first approach estimates directly the profits gained due to market power. It does so by computing the price markups of sectors or individual firms and then, given the share of labor, estimates the share of capital as a residual. The second method imputes capital rental to measure the share of capital directly and then, given the share of labor, estimates the share of profits as a residual.

The first method uses individual output and cost data and directly computes the marginal cost and marginal revenue of a firm or a sector. The methodology was initially developed by Hall (1988), and more recent research that uses it to estimate market power includes De Loecker et al. (2016, 2020) and Hall (2018). The estimates of De Loecker et al. (2016, 2020) appear too large (see on this issue Gutiérrez and Philippon, 2017a; Traina, 2018; Karabarbounis and Neiman, 2019). Hall (2018) shows that, when properly applied, his revised method results in a smaller, more accurate estimate of the recent rise in market power. This revised method is based on virtually no assumptions about the behavior of the firm. The data needed for its application are available only after the 1980s, which makes the method not feasible for the long-horizon application required here.

The second method was developed by Hall and Jorgenson (1967). It was first used by Barkai (2020) to estimate the capital share and then applied by Barkai and Benzell (2018) to estimate the capital share over the period 1946–2015. The method requires an estimate of a required capital rental rate, which is used to obtain a direct estimate of capital share. From labor and capital shares, one deduces profit share, which provides an estimate of the mean market power. A key component of capital rental is the applicable interest rate. Because long-term time series data on interest rates are available, this second method is the one I have adopted here. I introduce important new refinements to minimize the possible errors made in using this method.

To clarify some of these possible errors, we know from (1.3d) and (1.4) in chapter 1 that, in the case of certainty and because a monopoly firm equates marginal cost to marginal revenue, the relative share of profits equals $(1/\theta_t)$, where θ_t is the elasticity of demand for the firm's product. From this, one deduces the markup $\theta_t/(\theta_t - 1)$, which is a measure of market power. All changes in the relative share of profits are then interpreted as changes in market power. But in the realistic case of uncertainty, owners of capital assume some of the risk of the return on their investment and must make decisions based on their expected return. The imputed rental rate is based on expected returns, which, along with the computed relative share of profits, also fluctuate over time. Expected returns also contain errors resulting from the forecast errors of the agents. If forecast errors are uncorrelated with any other variables, they do not matter in the long run. This is not the case here, and these errors are thus a source of concern.

I will explain in the next section that the modeled forecasts are computed by projecting past data in a standard statistical manner. This may or may not reflect forecasts made during the period 1889–2017 by economic agents in real time, particularly in times of very major events, mostly associated with the Gold Standard, the two world wars, and the Great Depression. Unfortunately, in these cases, the model forecast errors are clearly not orthogonal to other economic variables, and these will thus be addressed as special cases. More generally, it is possible that unexpected changes in inflation or deflation, in macroeconomic conditions, or in economic policy may generate errors that cause imputed capital returns and the share of profits to fluctuate over time. When such changes are large, they lead to substantial fluctuations in relative shares that obscure the long-term trends of market power.

The overriding aim of this study is to deduce the long-term tendency of the relative shares, from which I deduce market power. For this reason, my general approach is to compute relative shares from the data as long as no direct evidence is available that brings their accuracy into question. Where compelling evidence is available about economic or political factors responsible for data distortions, I will take steps to adjust the data and explicitly inform the reader of such changes. All data adjustments are made with one aim in mind: minimizing the random, short-term fluctuations of relative shares that represent noise and that obscure the true measure of market power.

This chapter covers two distinct periods that intentionally overlap by five years: 1889–1929 and 1925–2017. Data files for the first period are based mostly on Kendrick (1961), Kuznets et al. (1946), and Goldsmith (1955), and cover the private, nonfarm, nonresidential economy. Data for the second part mostly come from the U.S. Bureau of Economic Analysis (BEA) and cover the private corporate sector, where most market power is exercised. That is, data files for the later period cover only the corporate sector, while data for the first period include the noncorporate part of the private economy. Online Data Appendices A and B provide detailed information on all data sources used, including all the entirely new data series that I built. Because their data sources and historical developments are very different, the measurement of relative shares is done separately for each of the two periods. The degree of data accuracy is clearly higher in the later period, after 1925. The sectoral difference is not big but cannot be ignored, and there is also an important difference in the treatment of labor income. In addition, differences in errors of observation and coverage require care to be taken in creating an integrated data file of relative shares for the years 1889–2017. In the methodological discussions of the next few sections, I use illustrations drawn mostly from the later period, for which most data are publicly available.

4.2 Construction of the Capital Rental Rate

4.2.1 The Methodology

To explain how the rental rate is computed, keep in mind the difference between the usual equity investor and the owners of capital. A regular equity investor is both an investor in capital and an investor in the monopoly wealth of the firm. However, strict capital owners do not participate in profits, capital gains, or risks associated with technological market power. As formulated in the model of chapter 1, such investors rent capital to the firm under a contract specifying that their risky return equals the competitive return on a fully diversified portfolio of investments that do not participate in the profits and risks of technological market power. That cost of capital is the same for all firms. Standard examples of securities in such a portfolio include bonds, utility stocks, preferred stocks, real estate investments, and limited partnerships. Bondholders do not fit exactly this financial grouping because they receive fewer benefits and assume less risk, but income received by bondholders is certainly included in the share of capital income.

A formal deduction of the rental rate required by investors for date t investment is carried out in Hall and Jorgenson (1967), Barkai (2020), and Barkai and Benzell (2018), but the conclusion is standard. Let R_t^k be the investor's required nominal rental rate, r_t the nominal interest rate, δ^k the depreciation rate, and P_t^k

the price of capital goods. Under full certainty, the required rate must cover interest and depreciation cost adjusted by capital gains or losses from the changed value of the undepreciated part of capital:

$$R_t^k = (r_t + \delta^k) - (1 - \delta^k)\left(\frac{P_t^k - P_{t-1}^k}{P_{t-1}^k}\right). \tag{4.1}$$

Under uncertainty, I introduce two changes. I add an appropriate risk premium ρ_t, and change in value is taken as an expected price change. The unit of time assumed in this book is a year—long enough for full adjustment of factor inputs. In that case price expectation is assumed to be based on $t - 1$ information, and the required rate is then

$$R_t^k = (r_t + \rho_t + \delta^k) - (1 - \delta^k)\pi_t^k, \quad \pi_t^k = E_{t-1}\left(\frac{P_t^k - P_{t-1}^k}{P_{t-1}^k}\right). \tag{4.2a}$$

For investment decisions made in real rather than nominal terms, one reformulates the problem by introducing a general inflation rate of

$$\pi_t = E_{t-1}\left(\frac{P_t - P_{t-1}}{P_{t-1}}\right).$$

The required real rate is then denoted by r_t^R and the rental function is

$$R_t^{Rk} = (r_t^R + \rho_t + \delta^k) - (1 - \delta^k)(\pi_t^k - \pi_t). \tag{4.2b}$$

The price forecasting model that I use is standard; the expected change of price is measured using a four-year moving average of past changes in that price. Consequently, the procedure used in the rest of this chapter is to estimate the required percentage rental rate by the expression

$$\hat{R}_t^k = [r_t + \rho_t + \delta^k] - (1 - \delta^k)\Delta_t^k,$$

$$\text{where } \Delta_t^k = \frac{1}{4}\left[\frac{P_{t-1}^k}{P_{t-2}^k} + \frac{P_{t-2}^k}{P_{t-3}^k} + \frac{P_{t-3}^k}{P_{t-4}^k} + \frac{P_{t-4}^k}{P_{t-5}^k}\right] - 1. \tag{4.2c}$$

There are three capital assets for which rental is computed: equipment, structures, and inventories. Implementing the outlined procedure requires price data for different asset classes. This is not a problem for equipment and structures. As for inventories, the temptation is to replace $\delta^k - (1 - \delta^k)\Delta_t^k$ with the ratio (inventory valuation adjustment [IVA])/ (inventory's value) because this would account for depreciation and capital gains or losses. The problem is that IVA is employed in national accounting to address the problem of inventory revaluation that is *unexpected* by the firm. If it is unexpected, what should be used to forecast it? To address the problem, I elected to replace $\delta^k - (1 - \delta^k)\Delta_t^k$ with the long-term average of (IVA)/(inventory's value). These rates are -1.68 percent in the period 1889–1929 and -2.38 percent in the period 1925–2017. The standard sign reversal for IVA means that the long-run inflation generates a positive gain in the rental function (4.2c) for inventories.

The outlined procedure is simple, but its implementation requires complex data refinements, and much can go wrong in the process of estimating equation (4.2c). This method of imputing capital rental is based on the idea that rational behavior by firms and investors, together with market equilibrium, reveals the rental required by owners of capital. The implication of computing capital income with this method and computing profits as a residual is that errors in computing capital income, or macroeconomic events that distort computed capital income, also cause errors in or distort the computed share of profits. I identify three areas in which these errors are systematic and data refinement is called for.

In the remainder of this section, I review the estimation procedure and then explain the three systematic errors that arise and the methods I use to solve them. There are some important differences between the data available for the earlier period 1889–1929 and the data used in the later period after 1929. Sections 4.3.1 and 4.3.2 review the data used, the estimation problems solved, and the actual estimates of relative shares for the period 1889–1929. In section 4.3.4, I explain the data used and the estimates made for the years 1929–2017.

4.2.2   The Risk Premium

I have noted that the required return to capital exceeds the return to bonds, the difference being a premium on the riskiness of capital payoff to its owners. To identify this premium we must engage in a somewhat hypothetical reasoning. I distinguish between the risk of a fully diversified portfolio taken by owners of capital and the risk taken by those receiving the profits of firms. Owners of capital do not, for example, share in risks associated with the firm's pricing strategies, competition for market power, merger and acquisition decisions, or innovations.

A constructive way to think of the diversified return to capital is to consider it as being approximated by the return on a diversified portfolio of good-quality utilities, real estate assets, and preferred stocks. The portfolio is vulnerable, however, to shocks of demand or aggregate productivity, requiring a premium in compensation. There is no consistent data source of such return for the entire period 1889–2017. The best approximation, with insufficient premium, for this desired yield is the Moody's Seasoned Baa Corporate Bond Yield[1] of nominal return on debt, including expected inflation and default risk. This will be my basic interest rate series that goes back to 1919. For the period prior to 1919, a suitable and comparable nominal interest rate is the Unadjusted Index of Yields of American Railroads. To this rate, I will add a premium for the components of risk not included in the bond rate.

The computed return on capital does not assume that all owners of capital will invest their capital in a perfectly diversified way. Some might choose to invest part of their capital in the common stock of a firm with highly advanced technology or in other assets. But the moment an owner of capital invests in other assets, the portfolio of that investor contains risk and return that are different from those of the fully diversified portfolio. With this in mind, I note that the actual rental rates will be computed for three specific asset categories: structures, equipment, and inventories. These have different depreciation rates and different relative prices. I thus treat the rental rate for each of the assets as consisting of two parts. The first is a general return on capital, which is the same for all assets and is reflected in the selected bond rate. The second part is each asset's specified own depreciation rate and expected change in its relative price.

It follows from these two components that there are two risks that need to be assessed when considering the required return on each asset. The first risk is that of fluctuations in aggregate capital productivity that have already been noted. The second is the risk of changes in the relative prices of the specific capital asset, which varies with the asset category. This risk is not negligible. As will become clear later, persistent movements in relative prices of asset, particularly strong fluctuations of real estate prices, have significant effects on computed asset returns. Therefore, the risk premium component of the rental on these assets need to be taken into account.

To assess the risk of capital productivity, ignore prices for the moment and set all equal to 1. It follows from equation (1.4) in chapter 1, that, in equilibrium without uncertainty, capital rent is

$$K_t R_t = \left(1 - \frac{1}{\theta_t}\right) \alpha_t Y_t \tag{4.3a}$$

where, in the certainty case $Y_t = F(K_t, g^t L_t)$, $g \geq 1$. Under uncertainty we have

$$Y_t = e^{\zeta_t} F(K_t, g^t L_t), \quad \zeta_t = \lambda_\zeta \zeta_{t-1} + \varepsilon_t^\zeta, \quad \varepsilon_t^\zeta \sim N(0, \sigma_\varepsilon^2) \text{ i.i.d.} \tag{4.3b}$$

---

[1] Moody's Seasoned Aaa Corporate Bond Yield is a close alternative. I have chosen the Baa rate because it is more responsive to inflation and deflation shocks. When such short-term shocks are not reflected in the nominal rate, they become a strong source of short-term volatility of measured return to capital, and this volatility often obscures the long-term changes in market power.

These equations do not reflect the timing of decisions and the specific risks borne by investors. At decision time, which is the start of period t (or the end of period $t-1$), all factor inputs are known, while risky production takes place only after the inputs are in place. Consequently, risk of capital productivity is restricted to the riskiness of output realization defined by e^{ς_t}, disregarding the risk of market power, expressed by taking θ_t as a fixed parameter. Taking ϵ_t^{ς} as reflecting the riskiness of capital productivity implies that the rental per unit of capital is

$$R_t = \left[\left(1-\frac{1}{\theta_t}\right)\alpha_t\left(\frac{e^{\lambda_\varsigma \varsigma_{t-1}}F(K_t, g^t L_t)}{K_t}\right)\right]e^{\epsilon_t^{\varsigma}} \tag{4.4}$$

where ϵ_t^{ς} is taken to be uncertain at decision time, and all terms in the square brackets are known. Because the added risk is proportional to the term in the brackets, the premium to the required return per unit of capital is proportional to this term. These are exactly the conditions encountered in the literature on the equity premium puzzle (Mehra and Prescott, 1985). Given that σ_ϵ is known to be 0.0072 at the quarterly frequency (see King and Rebelo, 1999, table 2), and because in all models I use a discount rate of 0.96–0.98 and a risk aversion coefficient $\sigma = 0.90$, the implied risk premium for the productivity risk of $e^{\epsilon_t^{\varsigma}}$ is negligible and can be ignored. In this context I take this result to mean that stockholders' risk in the market is dominated by risks related to the firm's strategy to advance, preserve, and consolidate its proprietary technology, market power, and profitability. This includes risks of technological competition, innovations, marketing, and pricing strategies. These risks are much larger than those of capital productivity.

Turning to the risk of change in relative price, I will avoid the construction of a structural model from which to deduce the premium. Instead, I will compute the premium according to its direct definition of being the cost paid by a risk-averse investor who wants to avoid the risk of price change. To explore this premium, consider the investment to be $(1-\delta^k)$, so that without a premium one would expect to receive back the amount

$$(1-\delta^k)\left(\frac{E_t P_{t+1}^k}{P_t^k}\right). \tag{4.5}$$

The risk arises because the amount actually received is as follows:

$$(1-\delta^k)\left(\frac{P_{t+1}^k}{P_t^k}\right) = (1-\delta^k)\left(\frac{E_t P_{t+1}^k}{P_t^k}\right) + (1-\delta^k)\left(\frac{P_{t+1}^k - E_t P_{t+1}^k}{P_t^k}\right)$$

$$= (1-\delta^k)\left(\frac{E_t P_{t+1}^k}{P_t^k}\right)\left(1 + \frac{P_{t+1}^k - E_t P_{t+1}^k}{E_t P_{t+1}^k}\right).$$

It then follows that the added risk premium is

$$\rho_p = (1 - \delta^k)\left(\frac{E_t P_{t+1}^k}{P_t^k}\right)\left(\frac{1}{2}\right)\sigma_p^2\sigma, \quad \sigma_p^2 = \text{Var}\left(\frac{P_{t+1}^k}{E_t P_{t+1}^k} - 1\right). \quad (4.6)$$

The data reveal that the values for σ_p^2 are different for the different capital goods. For the period 1925–2017, these variances are:

- equipment $\sigma_{peq}^2 = 0.01032,$
- structures $\sigma_{pst}^2 = 0.02118.$

For the period 1889–1929, the only available data are for the relative price of aggregate capital to consumption, and the variance of the implicit price of aggregate capital is $\sigma_{pA}^2 = 0.02307$. The depreciation rates are different for different asset categories, but because the aggregate δ^k is about 0.09 and $\sigma = 0.90$, the mean aggregate risk premium is about 0.9 percent before 1929. After 1929, data are available for the three asset categories, but the average premium is about 0.6 percent. For more details, see the Online Data Appendix. I now turn to the three problems noted earlier.

4.2.3   Problems When Market Interest Rates Are Not Determined in Free Markets

In a free capital market, the nominal rate responds to inflation or inflation expectations. That is, if r_t^R is the real interest rate, π_t is the inflation rate, and Δ_t is expected inflation, then the Fisher equation is expressed in two alternate ways: either by $r_t = r_t^R + \pi_t$ or by the requirement that $r_t = r_t^R + \Delta_t$ and that the condition $\Delta_t = \pi_t + \epsilon_t$ holds, where ϵ_t is pure noise, orthogonal to all date t information. Equation (4.2b) is then the rental rate applied when decisions are made in real terms, where the capital gain or loss component arises only because of the change in the relative prices of consumption and capital good k. Although small differences may occur in the timing of these two inflation rates, taking a four-year moving average of the two renders the last term in (4.2a) a small quantity in most years. When the Fisher equation fails to hold, equation (4.2a) can lead to implausible results. One such occasion occurred in the long period of financial repression during the period 1939–1951, when the interest rate was not determined in free markets and capital was essentially rationed.

To explore the 1939–1951 conditions, note that, although the Moody's Baa seasoned bond rate is the basic nominal rate I use to impute rent, an alternative

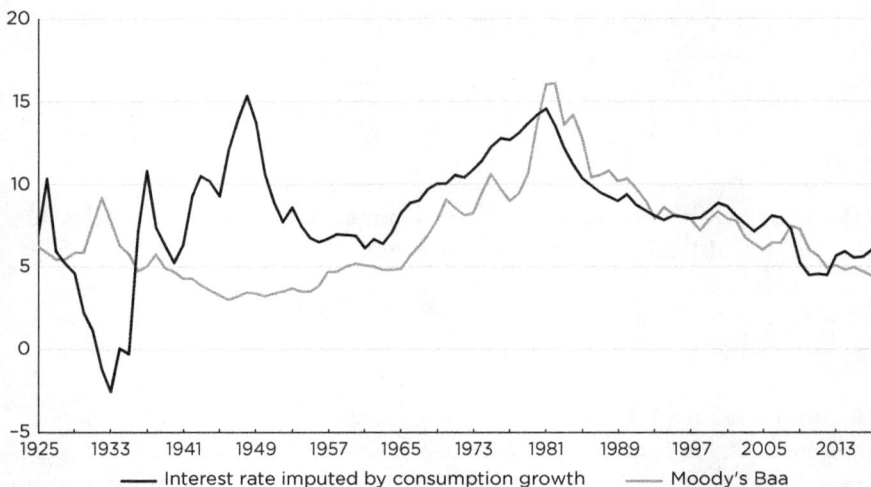

Figure 4.1 Comparison of interest rates, 1925–2017

measure of the interest rate is suggested by the standard Euler equation of bond pricing where U is the utility function

$$\frac{1}{1 + r_t} = \beta E_t \left(\frac{U_c(C_{t+1})}{U_c(C_t)} \right).$$

Here, the real interest rate is computed as an equilibrium rate implied by the growth rate of aggregate consumption. To derive this rate, I use a risk aversion coefficient of 0.90, approximate the expected value of $(C_{t+1}/C_t)^{-0.90}$ by a four-year moving average of $(C_{t+1}/C_t)^{-0.90}$, and use a discount rate of 0.98. I add to the imputed real interest rate a measure of the expected inflation, estimated by a four-year moving average of the change in the consumer price index (CPI). In figure 4.1, I compare these two interest rates. The rate implied by equilibrium consumption growth and Moody's Baa rate are very close after the 1950s, but they differ substantially before then.

The difference is due to two separate factors. One is associated with World War II, during which the two rates are sharply different. The second is associated with the Great Depression, during which the Moody's Baa rate is stable apart from a rise in the risk premium during the period 1931–1933. My computed implied rate is volatile, particularly during the years 1930–1934. This volatility results from two conflicting factors. One is the unexpected drastic fall in consumption growth, which causes the implied rate to decrease. The other is the sharp unexpected deflation of 1930–1933 (see table 4.1) that increases the implied rate. Because the implied rate actually declines sharply in figure 4.1, it follows that the dominant factor is the decline in the growth rate of consumption.

As part of the effort to finance World War II, starting in 1939, interest rates and bank reserves were fully controlled by the U.S. Treasury. That control continued beyond the war. Apart from price control, banks at that time were required to hold government bonds as reserves, and individual citizens were urged to purchase government bonds (first called war bonds and after Pearl Harbor renamed defense bonds). American private purchases of such bonds during the war totaled $185.7 billion, which financed 54 percent of the total U.S. cost of World War II. The practical consequence of this period of financial repression was that market interest rates were kept low, and capital was effectively rationed. These restrictions on the bond market remained in effect until the March 1951 Treasury-Federal Reserve Accord, designed to revive normal monetary policy under free debt markets.

But even after the Federal Reserve regained its independence, the Korean War forced continued effective coordination between the Fed and the Treasury (see Friedman and Schwartz, 1963, chapter 11). It took some years, perhaps up to 1959, to restore normal free-market operation of the bond market. Figure 4.1 shows the Moody's Baa rate, reflecting the debt-market repression during that era: the nominal rate implied by consumption growth is much higher than the then prevailing bond rate and a mortgage rate of an entirely subdued housing market. The sharp postwar burst of inflation in the years 1946–1948 following the elimination of war-era price control added a tax of about 30 percent on the value of all bond holdings. This last event is reflected in the inflation component of the implied nominal rate but not in Moody's rate.

This long period of financial repression associated with World War II has important implications for this study. From a purely accounting perspective, the low interest rates mean that owners of capital would be imputed too small a share of output, and the computed profit share would be much higher than the share computed if the capital market were free. Because the aim is to deduce market power and not just profit share, the elevated computed profit share due to financial repression would mean that a direct computation of market power would be strongly biased upward from 1939 to 1951 and perhaps for several years beyond. The rate implied by consumption growth offers an estimate of the interest rate that would have prevailed had markets been free. Using this rate leads to the computed profit share that would have been recorded had markets been free. This profit share corrects for the upward bias and is therefore a more accurate measure of market power.

To avoid the bias caused by the controlled interest rate during the period 1939–1951, I replace the Moody's Baa interest rate with the nominal rate implied by consumption growth[2] and refer to the combination of the Moody's Baa bond rate and the implied rate during the war as the war-adjusted Moody's Baa nominal interest rate. I will refer to the imputed capital rent as the capital rent with war-adjusted interest rates.

4.2.4   Unexpected Inflation and Deflation Events Related to World War I and the Great Depression

Large unexpected inflations and deflations occurred around World War I and the Great Depression. We know they were unexpected because nominal interest rates exhibited little response to bursts of very high rates of inflation or deflation. Table 4.1 reports those specific years in which such events occurred and in which the nominal interest rate did not respond, even approximately, in accordance with the Fisher equation.

World War I was the war that, politically speaking, was not supposed to happen, and it took twists and turns that were mostly unanticipated. The progression of the resulting inflation to over 100 percent from 1916 to 1920 surprised financial markets, as one must conclude from the course of the nominal interest rates at that time.

A more precise examination of the period from 1889 to 1933 is offered by the excellent studies of Barsky and De Long (1991), Perez and Siegler (2003), and others surveyed by Binder (2016). They suggest that under the gold standard, market participants did not fully understand the mechanisms of price level determination, inflation, or deflation, nor did they have the statistical tools to arrive correctly at the Fisher effect. In fact, their research demonstrates that the best model that describes expectation formation under the gold standard is one of static expectations by market participants, who expected the rates of price changes to equal the normal past average rates of price change. From 1889 to 1915, the annual rates of inflation fluctuated around 1 percent, falling in the early part and rising in the later part of the period. Therefore, forecasting inflation by the four-year moving average of past price changes, which is the approach I use, expresses well the forecasting model of the agents. Under this long-run conception, all sudden inflation and deflation events seen in table 4.1 were taken as unusual and temporary. As a result, none altered the long-established patterns of inflation expectations. Computing rental rates with the four-year

---

[2] A case can be made for adjusting the interest rate up to 1959 because the Korean War and its economic impact, together with subsequent institutional factors, slowed the adjustment of the Fed's implementation of its own monetary policy. With insufficient information about the rate of such delay, I use the implied rate instead of the market rate up to and including 1952, but one may question the reliability of the results for the period 1953–1959 (see figure 4.11) as possibly resulting in too high estimates of the share of profits from 1953 to 1959.

TABLE 4.1   Impact of unexpected changes in prices on nominal rates

Year	Percentage change of the CPI	Percentage change of the implicit price of equipment and structures	Nominal interest rate
1915	1.00	8.62	4.62
1916	7.92	18.37	4.49
1917	17.43	21.15	4.79
1918	17.97	15.10	5.23
1919	14.35	11.87	5.29
1920	15.94	−1.32	5.81
1921	−10.83	−12.98	5.57
1922	−6.54	−2.81	4.85
1930	−2.50	−2.62	5.90
1931	−8.80	−5.05	7.62
1932	−10.30	−6.27	9.20
1933	−5.10	−4.68	7.76

moving average of price changes that include the temporary bursts of inflation or deflation would then introduce into the rental rate fluctuations that are due only to price effects of my own model of expectation, not to changes in market power. The United States abandoned the gold standard in 1933.

To add some background to the data in table 4.1, I note that the act establishing the Federal Reserve System was passed by Congress in 1913. The Federal Reserve became operational in November 1914, and in its early years was dedicated mostly to preserving the gold standard (see Friedman and Schwartz, 1963, chapter 5; Crabbe, 1989). The United States entered the war in April 1917 and, to prevent a drain on its gold reserve, effectively[3] suspended the gold standard from September 1917 to June 1919. When free exports of gold were permitted again, there was a sustained drain of U.S. gold, and the Fed decided that urgent action was needed. Determined to restore the gold standard and attract gold back to the United States, it resorted to a tight monetary policy, raising the discount rate and causing the deflation and recession of 1920 to 1921. Initially, the Fed raised the discount rate by 1.25 percentage points in early 1920. It continued by raising the rate to 7 percent in June 1920 and keeping it at that level until May 1921. It appears that these policy changes surprised financial markets because the economy was plunged into an eighteenth-month recession and deflation, but long-term nominal interest rates were hardly changed.

---

[3] The United States maintained full convertibility of notes in circulation into gold, but President Woodrow Wilson issued a proclamation stipulating that exports of gold from the United States required a permit, and most applications for permits were denied.

To highlight the acute effect of large divergences of the nominal rate from the rate of inflation, consider the two examples of 1917 and 1932, and I start with 1917. Because the mean depreciation of equipment and structures was 4.99 percent, the capital "gain" induced by the 21.15 percent inflation would have been 20.09 percent. Assume, for the sake of discussion, an added risk premium of 1 percent. Then, under a no-forecast-error price forecast of 21.15 percent, the computed rental for equipment and structures would have been

$$(4.79 + 1.00 + 4.99) - (1 - 0.0499) \times (21.15) = -9.31 \text{ percent.}$$

Because the ratio of (equipment + structures)/(private, nonfarm, nonresidential output) was 1.81, the computed share of capital would have been −16.85 percent, and the share of profits would have been about 60 percent. An analogous computation for 1932 would have led to a rental rate of

$$(9.20 + 1.00 + 6.77) + (1 - 0.0677) \times 6.27 = 22.82 \text{ percent.}$$

With (equipment + structures)/(value added) = 2.94, the capital share would have been +67.09 percent, and the share of profits would have been less than 30 percent.

Neither result is reasonable. First, when the imputed rental rate is negative, owners of capital would not rent their capital at all. Second, it is implausible to suggest such capital rental rates would be required rates under the stipulated circumstances because, in the middle of the Great Depression, owners of capital did not expect to earn 22.82 percent on their capital investments.

In short, I compute the expected price change by projecting current price changes into the future. Therefore, when the market fails to forecast inflation, actual higher inflation does not raise the future nominal rate, but then my higher forecast of inflation creates a wrong imputed capital "gain" in (4.2a), which lowers the required rental rate in (4.2a). Similarly, when markets fail to forecast deflation, actual deeper deflation rates do not cause declines in the nominal rate, in contrast with my deeper deflation forecasts, errors that generate large imputed capital "losses" that raise the required rental in (4.2a). These extremely wrong estimates generate artificial fluctuations in the shares of capital and profits, when the implied imputed capital gains or losses have nothing to do with market power. They only obscure the true market power of firms.

As I noted earlier, forecasting inflation with the four-year moving average of past price changes works well for the years 1889–1914. An alternative hypothesis is needed for the years specified in table 4.1. For these, I adopt the model of Barsky and De Long (1991). It applies to unanticipated sharp bursts of inflation or deflation, as well as to the unanticipated change in the Federal Reserve policy that caused the 1920–1921 recession and deflation. The model proposes that in each of the years 1916–1922, the market persisted in forecasting the constant average rate of inflation that prevailed from 1900 to 1915, which was 1.21 percent for the CPI and 1.55 percent for equipment and structures. In addition, their model proposes that in the 1930–1933 period, the market continued to forecast the average change of price level for the years 1925–1929, which was approximately 0 percent. To assist the reader in assessing the impact of this procedure, I present later, in figure 4.4, the computed share of profits under the two inflation forecasts for 1916–1922: constant CPI change of 1.21 percent and capital goods price changes of 1.55 percent against a variable forecast equal to the four-year moving average of price changes.

Because nominal rates do not change in exact conformity with changes in inflation rates, some inflation forecasts that fail orthogonality may cause artificial fluctuations in computed relative shares. Below, when analyzing the long-term trend of rising or falling market power, it is useful to keep in mind this effect of inflation that accounts for some changes in computed relative shares.

4.2.5   Unexpected Major Decline of Output During the Great Depression, 1932–1934

Changes in the equilibrium capital/output ratios at the firm level have significant effects on relative shares. But if a unique event changes the capital/output ratio drastically, and if the event is caused by well-recognized factors out of the firm's control and unrelated to market power, then the event may justify an adjustment of the data. The decline of corporate output during the Great Depression, particularly from 1932 to 1934, is such a case. During those years, the sharp decline in output was associated with a steep decline in capacity utilization. Because imputed capital income is the product of imputed rent and capital employed, the decline awards income to capital that was either unemployed or drastically underutilized. This results in an upward bias of the estimated high capital share, and a negative share of profits, which is not feasible. I carry out data adjustments that address the problem, but the reader may prefer to disregard the results for these three years.

Turning first to capacity utilization, Bresnahan and Raff (1991) report that from 1929 to 1933, the number of operating automobile plants fell by one-third. But this does not account for the decline in output of plants that continued to operate. A sample of declines in sectoral outputs from 1929 to 1933 reported by Kendrick (1961, appendix) shows declines of 37 percent in manufacturing, 37 percent in mining, 33 percent in transportation, and 15 percent in public utilities and communication. At the same time, Kendrick estimates that the capital stock on the books of firms in the private domestic economy fell by only 2.4 percent (see table A-XV). Based on these facts, I adjust the actual rental received for 1932, 1933, and 1934 by assuming that in these years, capital owners received, on average, 70 percent of the imputed amount.

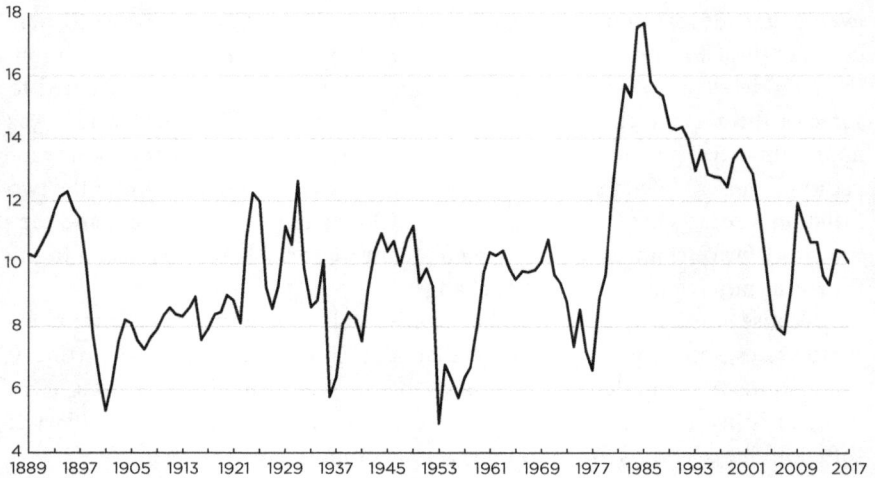

Figure 4.2   Mean nominal capital rental rate, 1889–2017

The adjustments made in the data are intended to prevent the inflation and deflation associated with World War I, the Great Depression, and the World War II market repression from biasing the estimated share of profit. In most cases, the adjustments prevent an upward bias. Because these changes affect only the imputed rent on capital, they alter only the allocation of income between the share of capital and the share of profits. They have absolutely no effect on labor income or on labor share. Figure 4.2 presents the fully adjusted weighted average nominal[4] capital rental rate with war-adjusted Moody's Baa bond rates, the 30 percent adjusted utilization rate for the years 1932–1934, and the adjusted capital gains due to bursts of inflation or deflation for the periods 1916–1921 and 1930–1933. The mean rental is computed as a weighted average of the rental rates on equipment, structures, and inventories.

4.2.6   Transitory Variations in the Capital Rental

My aim is to study the long-term changes in market power by estimating this power from the share of computed profits. Figure 4.2 shows that identifying the

---

[4]Relative shares in 1889–1929 are computed using real capital rental rates in accord with equations (4.2b) and (4.2c), whereas real rates are computed from known nominal rates by using Fisher's equation. I explain in the text that this leads to difficulties around World War I, which requires adjustment in inflation expectations. In figure 4.2, I transform these real rates to nominal rates, but then a corresponding computation is made by adjusting the expected change in prices of capital goods.

long-term trend is a problem because the rental rate fluctuates due to transitory factors. That is, the great noted events of the twentieth century generated transitory events that may obscure the long-term trend of market power. In particular, all major inflations or deflations are reflected in the computed shares, as are all sharp changes in real estate prices, because they generate capital gains or losses. To clarify the trends, I provide interpolated data for the estimated series of the three relative shares.

Recall that the share of profits is deduced from the primary data of capital share and labor share. Because the impact of transitory factors is recorded in the data for these two primary shares, I will report first the raw results and then the filtered results of these primary shares, thereby postponing the discussion of profits. Because I use different methods of estimation for each, I report these results separately for the periods 1889–1929 and 1925–2017.

4.3   Relative Shares of Labor and Capital: Raw Results Without Filtering

As explained in chapter 1, value added is divided into four shares: labor, capital, profits, and taxes on production and imports. The share of taxes rose from about 2 percent in 1889 to 8 percent in 2017, and I will not allocate the burden of these taxes. Hence, the three relative shares of labor, capital, and profits add up to less than 1. In addition, as explained in chapter 3, the concept of capital I use is the sum of the values of fixed equipment, structures, and inventories, but it excludes intangible assets. When relevant, I present results that reflect the inclusion of intangibles in total capital. In calculating compensation to employees, I assume that officers are partners of the corporation and that their compensation is part of profits. Officers' compensation is then excluded from labor income. This can be done for the years 1925–2017, but no such data exist in the period 1889–1929. The method used to impute officers' compensation in the first period will be discussed later.

Before commenting on the data used to study the private, domestic, nonfarm, nonresidential sector in the period 1889–1929, I note the obvious: data prior to 1929 are limited, and those that are available are less reliable than more recent data. While recognizing the inherent difficulty of studying the earlier period, I have already stressed the importance of comparing market power and inequality for the years 1985–2017, with the analogous dynamics of about 100 years earlier, for the period 1889–1914. Therefore, extending the period of observation as far back as possible can only help, even if the quality of the data is not as high as we wish.

Due to the complexity of the data required, I begin by briefly explaining the reasons for the choice of data files used in the study of the first time span, 1889–1929. I then provide a general description of the data sources used and explain how I constructed some of the data not available elsewhere. However, I leave the details and references to Online Appendix A, which includes all basic data files used.

4.3.1   Some Comments on Data Sources, 1889–1929

In constructing the data for the period 1889–1929, I was concerned about the need for comparability with the data for the second period, 1925–2017. From the theoretical perspective, the object of the analysis is the business sector of the economy, where market power is exercised. I have noted earlier that for the second period, 1925–2017, the best data are provided by the BEA for the corporate sector of the U.S. economy, but no data for such a sector exist before 1925. Consistent data files that come closest to being comparable are those covering the *private economy* since 1889 in Kendrick (1961). Kendrick's data files begin in 1889, and my end date of 1929 was selected to create a five-year overlap that permits some test of comparability. The aim was then to construct a data file for the domestic, private, nonfarm, nonresidential economy for the period 1889–1929. Although the data for such a sector did not exist and hence needed to be built up, the constructed sector is not entirely comparable with the corporate sector of the later period. This is because "firms" in the older sector include all noncorporate entities, and labor earnings in that sector include compensation of officers. The difference in corporate structure across time presents no real difficulty, but the issue of officers' compensation is significant and will be addressed later.

Given the stated objective, the Kendrick (1961) data files were taken as a foundation over which the final data files were erected. Unfortunately, most variables required some adjustment. The final data files are reported in Online Appendix A, together with the specific citation of the source used in constructing each file. There is, however, one point that needs to be clarified. All of Kendrick's data files are available in real 1929 prices, and no implicit price deflator is available for the value added of the domestic, private, nonfarm, nonresidential sector. This requires capital rental functions to be defined in real terms. This makes equation (4.2b) the applicable equation for constructing the equilibrium capital rental. This is different from the later study covering 1925 to 2017, which is conducted in nominal terms when accurate implicit prices of all goods in the model are available from the BEA for the period.

Figure 4.3 Labor share

4.3.2   Relative Share of Labor and Capital: The Private, Nonfarm, Nonresidential Sector, 1889–1929

Figure 4.3 reports the estimated labor share. The decline of labor share from 1889 to 1901 is dramatic. It reflects both the U.S. transformation, late in the nineteenth century, from agriculture to manufacturing, but also the growing market power of firms during the First Gilded Age. In addition, between 1889 and 1901, the population of the United States rose from 61.8 million to 77.6 million. It is possible the high proportion of low-skilled immigrants changed the composition of the labor force, contributing to the slow rate of wage increase and the sharp decline in labor share.

The year 1901 stands out as the year when the decline of the share of labor stops. Relative labor share rose from 58 percent in 1901 to 64 percent in 1929, but many transitory factors affected labor share between 1889 and 1929. The decline of this share was slowed by the depression of 1893–1897. It fell in the panic of 1907 but rose in the recession that followed. The share of labor then rose during the panic of 1914 in anticipation of World War I and then declined in the recessions of 1920–1921, 1923–1924, and 1926–1927. The panic of 1914 is particularly noteworthy because the total compensation of labor in 1913 was similar to that in 1914. However, the value added produced by the private sector fell sharply by 11.6 percent, causing a sharp rise in labor share. The most important takeaway from figure 4.3 is that labor share declined precipitously from 1889 to 1901 and then recovered and fluctuated around 64 percent up to 1929.

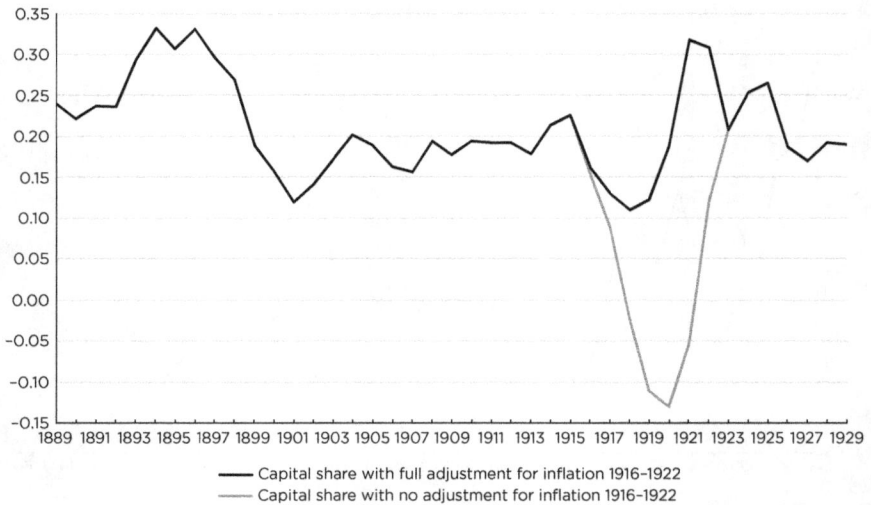

Figure 4.4 Capital share with and without adjusting expected inflation, 1916–1922

Turning to capital, figure 4.4 presents the estimated capital share from 1889 to 1929. Again, although entirely different sources are used, the year 1901 stands out: the share of capital declined sharply during the First Gilded Age from 1889 to 1901. The share of capital rose from 12 percent in 1901 to 19 percent in 1929, which is a significant increase. Also, as explained earlier, the share of capital is particularly affected by inflationary or deflationary events.

Consonant with the discussion in section 4.2.4, figure 4.4 reports the estimated share of capital for the period 1889–1929 under two forecasting assumptions for the sharp inflationary and deflationary period of 1915–1922. Without the adjustment for estimated expectations, there is a drastic fall in the share of capital simply because of the failure of the Fisher equation. In contrast, the constant expectation models of Barsky and De Long (1991) imply an estimated share of capital, which is consistent with the prewar pattern, and this is the assumption I have adopted.

It is noteworthy that during the 1889–1929 period, the dynamics seen in the share of capital are parallel to those of the share of labor: a sharp decline during the First Gilded Age, reaching a low point in 1901. Similarly, both relative shares recovered after 1901 and were higher in 1929 than they were in 1901. The more precise long-term pattern in these dynamics will be discussed after short-term fluctuations are filtered out. World War I and the rapid industrialization and electrification of the 1920s appear to have contributed to the rising shares of labor and capital.

As explained in Online Appendix A, the data used to compute labor share come from entirely different sources than those used to compute capital share.

Apart from an adjustment of value added to account for value added of owner-occupied housing, all data used to compute relative labor share come from published sources. The relative share of capital is imputed in accordance with the procedures outlined earlier in this chapter. Nevertheless, the year 1901 stands out in the data as reflecting an important turning point. The theory developed in chapter 1 explains that changes in relative shares result from change in the two forces of technology and policy, and therefore changes in the distribution of income can be very slow. Great innovations take time to take hold, and even policy changes can take time to affect the economy. Yet the two dates of 1901 and 1986 stand out. I will now consider the significance of 1901 from the perspective of the theory in chapter 1.

4.3.3   The Year 1901 from the Perspective of Technology and Public Policy

The turn of the last century saw a great transformation caused by the electric revolution and partly by the combustion engine (1884). A vast number of innovations altered all dimensions of life. A short list of the major innovations or discoveries in this era includes the telephone (1876), gramophone (1877), incandescent lamp (1879), the S-shaped toilet trap (1880), digital clock (1883), automobile (1886), electric fan (1887), alternating current induction motor (1888), movie camera (1891), electric toaster (1893), radio (1894), X-ray machine (1895), radioactivity (1896), automobile assembly line (1901), television (1906), Ford Model T (1908), and airplane (1909). Gordon (2017) argues that this period of innovation created and developed the technologies that drastically altered daily life in the century between 1870 and 1970. He goes on to argue that such a rate of innovations cannot be repeated, and therefore U.S. economic growth cannot continue unabated in the next century. In chapter 1, I presented the basic proposition that innovation plants the seeds of market power, and an increased rate of innovation accelerates the growth of that power. I also explain that such market power will be consolidated and will expand over time. This explains the rising share of profits up to 1901.

Because the high rate of innovation, particularly in applications of electricity and the combustion engine, proceeded well into the twentieth century, the economic pressure to increase market power continued unabated beyond the First Gilded Age. This raises the question of why there was a change in 1901, when market power began to decline. If innovations provide seeds for market power, why did such power fall between 1901 and 1931? The answer has already been given in chapter 1.

The ascension of Theodore Roosevelt to the presidency in 1901 was an accidental consequence of the McKinley assassination, and, to that extent, the peaking of market power of the First Gilded Age at that time was not a result of predictable economic forces but the outcome of a random turn in economic and political policy. However, the significance of Roosevelt's coming to power was not lost on the markets. The McKinley administration allowed a massive wave of mergers, while Theodore Roosevelt was known to advocate a strong antitrust policy. Baker et al. (2018) find that firms with greater vulnerability to antitrust enforcement saw abnormal declines in their returns in the immediate aftermath of McKinley's assassination. Roosevelt's Progressive policies were continued up to the 1920s by his successors, William Howard Taft and Woodrow Wilson.

The significance of the change in 1901 can only be understood in relation to the laissez-faire policy and ideology that prevailed before 1901. The idea of free enterprise without any government interference or regulation was taken to be the natural order of things, and to many legal minds, the true intent of the U.S. Constitution. For many, this view remains true even today. Within that political environment, major economic problems were building up as the industrialization of the United States progressed, and growing public needs were being ignored. Therefore, the change in policy by Roosevelt's administration had been sought by a generation of Progressive reformers since early in the 1880s, and signs that change was coming could be seen even before 1901. These signs include the adoption of the Sherman Antitrust Act (1890) and the Interstate Commerce Act (1887) that aimed to curb the collusive practices of the railroads, and the formation of the American Federation of Labor (AFL) (1886), which was the first national union to fight for higher wages and improved working conditions. Although unions played a minor role at this stage, their expansion reflected the coming Progressive age. The Labor Bill of Grievances (1906) was an indicator of the impact of the labor movement on wages and working conditions. The poor condition of food consumed at the turn of the century can be deduced from the fact that since 1879, nearly 100 bills had been introduced in Congress to regulate food and drugs, culminating in the passage of the Pure Food and Drug Act (1906) and the creation of the Food and Drug Administration (1906). These actions were propelled by the exposure of the meatpacking industry's appalling working conditions in Upton Sinclair's book *The Jungle* (1906).

With such background, the nature of the policy change, and consequent decline in market power after 1901 can be gleaned from the small sample of laws enacted and institutions created by the Progressive movement that were listed in chapter 1 (see section 1.5.1). Given the intensity of innovations and the consequential creation of new market power after 1901, the actual decline of market power shows that the constraining force of policy was stronger than the force of technology and innovations that built up market power. But policy enforcement fluctuates over time. In periods of major wars and major recessions, policies designed to restrain business are not as strictly enforced, and the public attitude tends to be more accommodating. Although after 1901 the policy of constraining market power dominated, its enforcement was weakened by Republican administrations after 1920.

4.3.4   Relative Shares of Labor and Capital: The Domestic Corporate Sector, 1925–2017

Study of relative shares after 1925 is different from that of the earlier period because more accurate data sources are available. As noted earlier, the economy under study is the corporate, nonresidential sector, and the main data sources for this are available at the BEA. Capital can be properly divided into its components, and implicit price indexes and rates of implied capital gains and losses can be constructed for each component. Details of all data construction are provided in Online Data Appendix B.

Starting with labor, figure 4.5 presents labor share both with and without officers' compensation for the years 1925–2017. Their trends differ mostly after 1970: excluding officers, labor share begins declining in the 1970s; if officers' compensation is included, the decline begins only in 2000. The figure shows labor share is rather volatile, and this is a further justification for the need to filter out short-term factors. The fall of labor share during the Great Depression is obvious, and its rise during World War II is a result of temporary labor shortages. The decline from 1946 to 1949 is the result of the high rate of post–World War II inflation that lowered real wages and resulted in a wave of strikes in 1945 and 1946. The strikes were finally stopped by the adoption of the Taft-Hartley Act

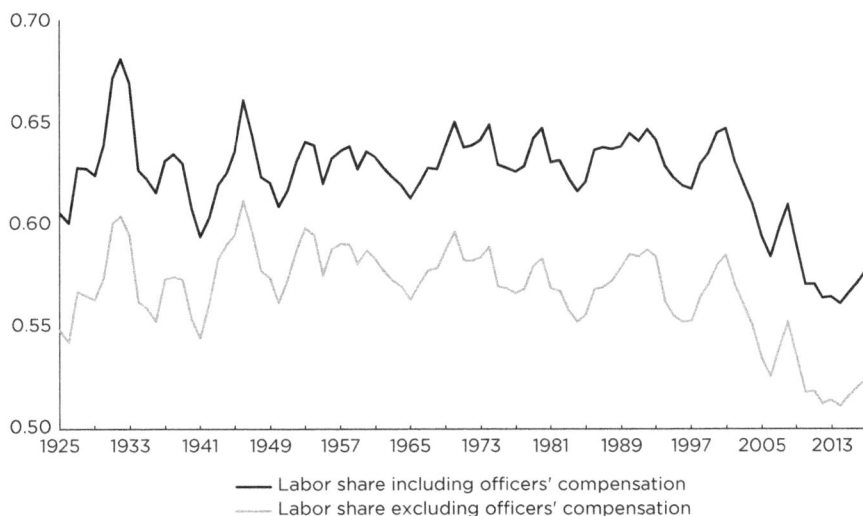

Figure 4.5   Labor share with and without officers' compensation

(1947) that prohibited various types of union strikes, defining them as "unfair labor practices." However, it is also evident that, on the whole, between 1932 and 1970, labor share fluctuates within a wide but stable range.

Turning to the share of capital, figure 4.6 presents the results for capital share for the years 1925–2017. Again, it provides a more nuanced view of the process than that obtained by looking only at the period after 1980 or even after 1945 (see Barkai, 2020; Barkai and Benzell, 2018). The figure reveals a clear pattern of decline from 1931 to about 1953, followed by a rise from 1953 to about 1984, and then another decline from then to 2017. However, the figure also reveals sharp fluctuations that are eliminated by smoothing the data in the next section.

In general, most short-term fluctuations of capital share are related to business cycles. But an important specific cause of short-term spikes in capital share are the booms and busts in real estate prices. Such price fluctuations are very sharp and are recorded as capital gains or losses in the structures component of the capital stock. They thus alter the realized share of capital. The sharp rise in capital share in 1931, an obvious reflection of the Great Depression, was amplified by an 18 percent decline in the price of structures in 1930–1931. Every real estate boom, relative to the CPI, causes a decline in the share of capital: it reduces the required rental rate because of short-term expected capital gains. This factor caused sharp spikes that lowered capital share in the years 1936, 1940–1941, 1951–1952, 1968–1976, and 2003–2006. All such movements cause variability in the share of profits that does not reflect changes in long-term market power.

Figure 4.6 also shows that capital share would have been sharply lower and the share of profits sharply higher had I not made the war interest rate and Great

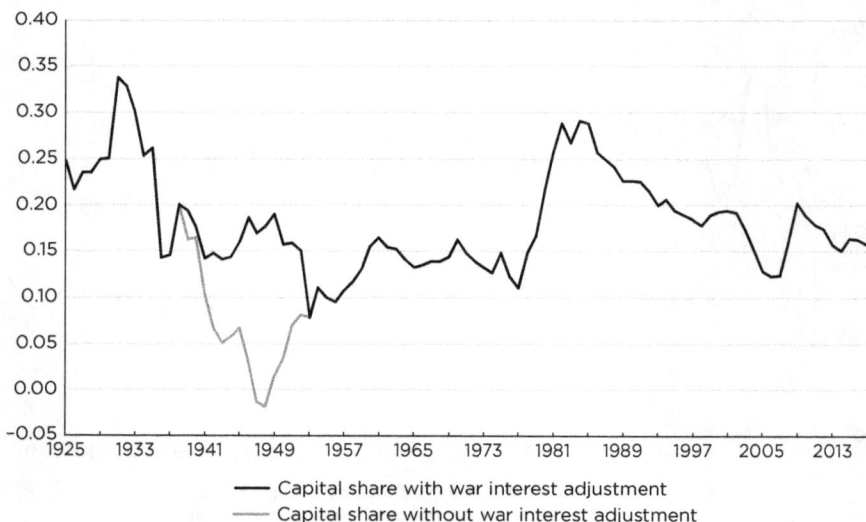

Figure 4.6 Capital share with and without interest rate war adjustment

Depression adjustments discussed in sections 4.2.3 and 4.2.5. These adjustments are intended to avoid biasing upward the estimated share of profits. The same reasoning could justifiably be used to argue that the share of capital is also too low in the years 1952–1959 because the adaptation of the Federal Reserve to free capital markets was too slow.

The pattern of capital share over time is similar to that of labor share, with two big differences. First, labor share remained essentially unchanged from 1931 to 1953, while capital share declined. Second, capital share began to rise after 1953 and continued to increase until 1984, while labor share remained unchanged until 1970 and began to decline thereafter. This lack of perfect correspondence between the evolution of the shares of labor and capital presents an analytical challenge. By equation (1.4), high market power shifts income from both capital and labor to profits, and one may therefore presume that high market power would result in a lower capital share and, simultaneously and in the same proportion, a lower labor share. This pattern does not hold in the approximate period of 1931–1984, which shows that, while market power in product markets drives both labor and capital shares, other factors play an important role, which I discuss later.

4.4   Trends of Relative Shares, 1889–2017

4.4.1   Integrating the Results of the Two Parts

How do the results in figures 4.5 and 4.6 compare with the results in figures 4.3 and 4.4 during the overlapping years of 1925–1929? Furthermore, how should the 1889–1929 files be integrated with those for the years 1925–2017? To explore this problem, tables 4.2a and 4.2b compare the relative shares estimated in the two parts for the overlapping years.

Table 4.2a shows the difference between the two parts of the study, 1889–1929 and 1925–2017. These differences arise for two reasons. First, in the first period, the only labor income available includes officers' compensation. For the second part, however, data are available to allow officers' compensation to be separated out of labor income. Second, the earlier part includes smaller business firms that are not public corporations, while the later part covers only the corporate sector. Table 4.2a shows that once officers' compensation is included in both parts, the difference due to the different populations is small: during the overlapping years, the mean labor share computed in the earlier part is 62.54 percent, and in the later part, 61.74 percent. This indicates that the series that need to be comparable, the 1889–1929 data and the 1929–2017 data with officers' compensation included in labor income, are reassuringly similar. For the purpose of integrating the two series, I will ensure that the mean values in this

TABLE 4.2a Comparison labor shares in the overlapping years*

Year	Study of 1889–1929	Study of 1925–2017	
	With officers' compensation	With officers' compensation	Without officers' compensation
1925	62.00	60.58	54.81
1926	60.80	60.12	54.25
1927	62.81	62.80	56.72
1928	63.56	62.77	56.53
1929	63.54	62.41	56.32
Mean	62.54	61.74	55.73

*Relative shares, percentages.

overlapping period are the same. To construct the integrated series with officers' compensation excluded from labor income, I subtract the gap of 6.81 percentage points uniformly from the labor share in the earlier period. To complete the integration, I turn to the shares of capital and profits, reported in table 4.2b.

Comparing the results for the overlapping years 1925–1929, the differences between the averages of the two parts of the study are:

Average difference in labor share	+6.81 percentage points
Average difference in capital share	−3.64 percentage points
Average difference in profit share	−1.80 percentage points
Average difference in share of taxes	−1.37 percentage points

TABLE 4.2b Comparison share of capital and profits in the overlapping years*

Year	Share of capital		Share of profits	
	Study of 1889–1929	Study of 1925–2017	Study of 1889–1929	Study of 1925–2017
1925	26.50	24.72	8.48	16.32
1926	18.64	21.74	17.64	19.92
1927	17.00	23.51	17.02	15.45
1928	19.15	23.55	13.51	14.85
1929	18.95	23.94	14.15	13.27
Mean	20.05	23.69	14.16	15.96

*Relative shares, percentages.

I adjust the data for the years 1889–1924 by *reducing* labor share uniformly by 6.81 percentage points and raising the other shares by these differences. This results in a unified set of data of relative shares for the period 1889–2017, which I report next.

4.4.2   Trends in Relative Labor and Capital Shares, 1889–2017: The Policy Miracle of 1931–1981

The long-term evolution of market power is reflected in the share of profits, but as noted, changes in market power may be obscured by short-term factors that affect the observed shares of labor and capital. To deduce a clear direction of market power, I first use smoothing to show the long-term trends of capital share and labor share. I then deduce from these trends the long-term trend in the share of profits.

I use locally estimated scatterplot smoothing (LOESS) with bandwidth of 0.12–0.16. Figure 4.7 reports the result for labor share, using the integrated data, from 1889 to 2017. The figure contains two smoothing estimates, with bandwidths of 0.12 and 0.16, respectively. The dramatic decline of labor share from 1889 to 1901 has already been noted, and the decline from 0.597 in 1970 to 0.524 in 2017 has been the subject of a vast literature. Taking the longer view, from 1889 to 2017, it is evident labor share has exhibited a long-term secular decline. The more subtle question is how to describe and explain the record from about 1901 to the 1970s.

One way of reading figure 4.7 is to conclude that, from 1901 to 1970, relative labor share remained constant, fluctuating within a fixed band of about 500 basis

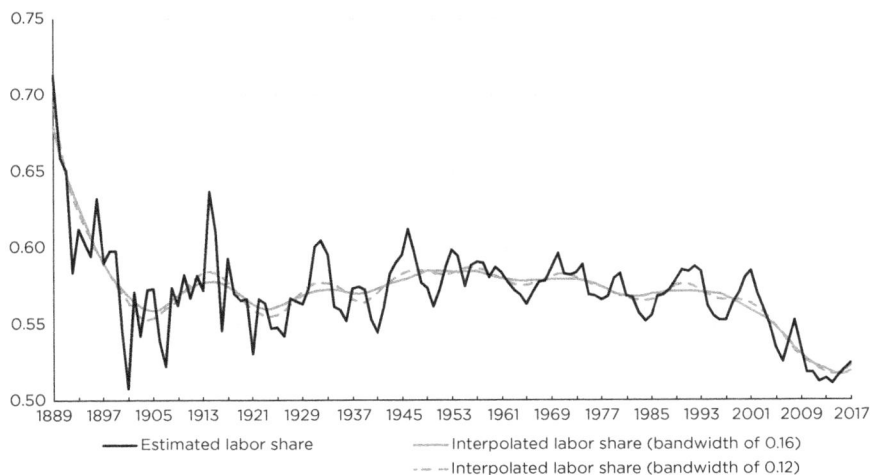

Figure 4.7 Labor share, 1889–2017

points. The caveat here is that such a band is very wide because a change of 5 percentage points in labor share constitutes a major change in income distribution. My interpretation of the record is different, and I divide my discussion into two parts. A direct statistical argument is presented here, but I offer an economic argument in section 4.5.

Keeping in mind that each percentage point of relative labor share has an important impact, there are two statistical facts to be noted. Labor share in 1901 was 0.508 and rose to 0.599 in 1953, which is a rise of 9.1 percentage points. Labor share was 0.584 in 1980 and declined to 0.524 in 2017, implying a total fall of 6.0 percentage points, which is universally viewed as a large decline. This highlights the fact that the rise of labor share from 1901 to 1953 is significant and deserves further examination. Recognizing that labor share took an extreme value in 1901, I return to figure 4.7 to suggest that, from 1901 to 1953, there was a slow and persistent rise in labor share, and this trend is obscured by known factors:

1. Labor share was artificially raised to a high level by the panic of 1914; private sector value added declined by 11.6 percent, while total labor compensation remained unchanged. This accidental rise in labor share was further amplified by World War I shortages.
2. Labor share declines sharply in the recessions of 1921–1922, 1923–1924, and 1926–1927 during a period when electrification was progressing and productivity rising.

These two temporary factors obscure the long-term rise in labor share, which can be expressed by comparing ten-year averages of labor shares at the start and end of the period. Average labor share over the ten-year period of 1901–1910 was 0.556, while average labor share over the ten-year period of 1944–1953 was 0.587, 3.1 percentage points higher. Such a difference between two ten-year averages of labor shares is significant.

The slow rise of the share of labor after 1901 was the result of the change in policy, starting in 1901, put in place by the Progressive movement. This policy resulted in a decline of market power and a corresponding rise in labor and capital shares. The 1920 elections returned the presidency to conservative hands, and the thrust of the Progressive policy was suspended but could not be reversed. After 1921, labor share continued to rise until 1931. I will also shortly show that market power continued to decline after 1920, and the share of capital continued to rise until 1931. Policy supporting labor was resumed during the Great Depression and continued until the 1970s.

Leaving aside the rise of labor share from 1901 to 1931, and the fact that labor share continued to rise until 1953, when it reached the temporary level of 59.9 percent, it is clear that during the forty years from 1931 to the 1970s,

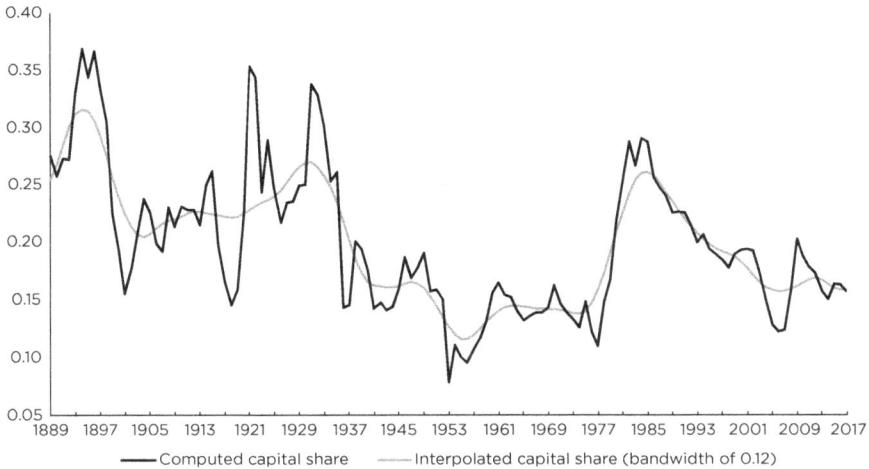

Figure 4.8 Capital share, 1889–2017

the share of labor was relatively stable. That is, apart from the volatility during the Great Depression and World War II, and in contrast with the changes in the shares of capital and profits, it remained within a steady range. This stability is contrasted by my own later demonstration that from 1932 to 1954, market power rose, and from 1954 to 1985, market power declined. This stability of labor share, despite the rising or falling of market power, is a sort of miracle. But it is not the miracle of a mysterious market mechanism; it is a miracle that demonstrates the crucial role of public policy.

Turning to capital share, figure 4.8 presents the raw results for 1889–2017 and the smoothed version with a bandwidth of 0.12. The figure shows that the trend of capital share can be summed up as follows:

- 1889 to about 1901 capital share falls
- 1901 to about 1930 capital share rises
- 1930 to about 1954 capital share falls
- 1954 to about 1985 capital share rises
- 1985 to 2017 capital share falls

There are two features of figure 4.8 that should be noted. The first is the fall of capital share in the two eras of 1889–1901 and 1985–2017. The size of the decline from top to bottom is about the same in the two periods, and it is only to be expected that the share of profits would also rise. The fact that capital share declined in the Second Gilded Age from 1985 to 2017 has been reported by others (see Barkai, 2020), but now I add the comparable period of the First Gilded Age, which is similar in many ways to the situation since 1985. The second noteworthy feature is the sharp decline in the share of capital from 1930 to 1954. This decline took place, in part during the period for which I imputed the nominal interest rate (1939–1951). As figure 4.2 shows, the decline of the share of capital cannot be due to my interest rate imputation. Rather, this decline is a robust result that would continue to hold for any reasonably imputed nominal interest rate. Its cause is the rise in market power from 1931 to 1954, and this is perhaps the most surprising conclusion of this empirical analysis. I turn now to the key topic of the share of profits in 1889–2017.

4.4.3   Historical Trends in Market Power, 1889–2017

Figure 4.9 reports both the actually computed share of profits and the share of profits deduced from the smoothed data of capital and labor shares. The long-term trends are as follows:

- 1889–1901 the share rose during the First Gilded Age
- 1901–1932 the share declined from 1901 to 1932
- 1932–1954 the share rose during the Great Depression, World War II, and the postwar period
- 1954–1985 the share declined after 1954, reaching its low point around 1985
- 1985–2017 the share has been rising since 1985

Note that the trend line in figure 4.9 accomplishes the goal of smoothing over all short-term inflationary effects, real estate price fluctuations, and most

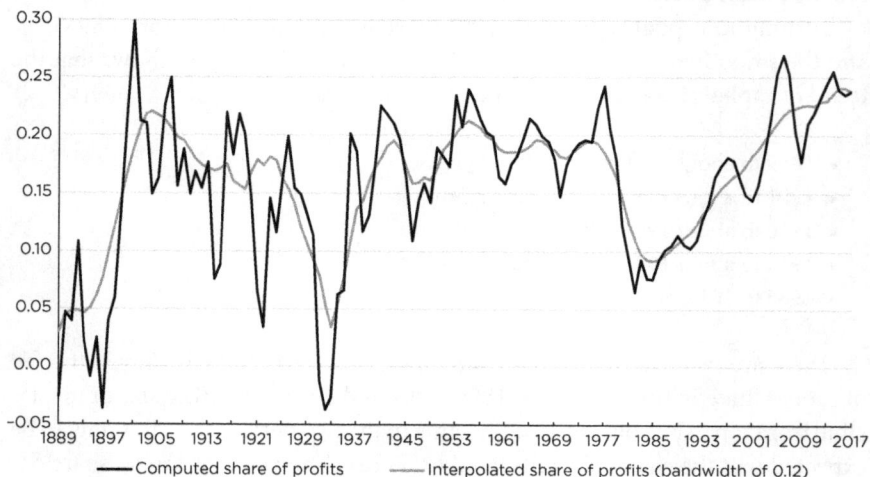

Figure 4.9 Rising and falling share of profits, 1889–2017

short-lived recessions. The smoothed share of profits comes as close as possible to describing the long-term level of market power, free of short-term factors. Before proceeding, I pause to consider a possible alternative reading of figure 4.9. One may conclude that the share of profits was constant from about 1902 to about 1976, except for a big shock caused by the Great Depression that sent the share to 0 in 1931 and 1932. This is not a sound economic argument for three reasons:

1. Although the decline in the share of profits began in 1901, the shock, which is the steep decline in this share, begins around 1923, significantly before the Great Depression.
2. The time span of the sharp decline and recovery is twenty years, from about 1923 to about 1943. In economic terms, this is too long to be considered a shock; it is a path of an endogenous variable.
3. The share of profits declined from about 30 percent in 1901 to about 13 percent in 1929, before any effect of the Great Depression comes into play. The recovery of the share of profits began in the middle of the depression, around 1932, due to factors that I study later. The Great Depression was far from over, but the share of profits was already rising!

My interpretation is that the decline in the share of profits after 1901, and the corresponding rise in the shares of labor and capital, were the results of the policies initiated by the Progressive movement. These policies were successful in restraining market power. The Republican administrations of the 1920s did not endorse the Progressive agenda. Nonetheless, the laws enacted, the regulatory agencies, and the administrative practices in place could not be changed. Although reform-minded principles guided policy during the Great Depression and in the postwar period, in assessing the evolution of market power between 1901 and 1955, the decisive fact is that the share of profits was 29.9 percent in 1901, went down to 13.3 percent in 1929 before the Great Depression, and went up back to 24.0 percent in 1955, and these differences are very significant.

The rise of market power after 1932 is a surprise. The fact that the Great Depression and World War II were actually catalysts for growing market power appear to be inconsistent with the view that public policy from 1930 to the 1970s was successful in establishing an egalitarian and democratic society. This follows from the incorrect presumption that public policies initiated during the Great Depression and World War II restrained market power, combined with the correct observation that labor share was, in fact, stabilized by several policy factors. These included the heavy taxation by the Roosevelt administration that explicitly aimed to suppress income inequality, the new transfer payments during the depression, and legislation that created an environment much more favorable to unions. This rise of market power is obscured by two developments that are difficult to predict by the theory developed in chapter 1. The theory predicts that a rise in market power would cause a decline of equal proportions in the relative shares of labor and capital. The fact is that labor share continued to rise, or perhaps remain stable, up to the 1970s while the share of capital continued to decline until 1954, as predicted by the theory. The divergent responses of labor and capital shares shows that public policy was more protective of labor than of capital from 1932 to the 1970s, and I return to discuss this fact further in section 4.5. A declining capital share is then consistent with the rising share of profits, but I will shortly show that the estimated share of profits during the period 1951–1959 is probably too high and the true share was, most likely, lower by about three or four percentage points.

A deeper study of the problem reveals two causes for the rising share of profits from 1932 to 1954. The first is technology. The general-purpose technologies (GPTs) of electricity and the combustion engine were maturing and were altering all sectors of the economy. Important discoveries were made in chemistry as well. Field (2006) shows that technological developments in manufacturing, combined with advances in transportation, public utilities, and distribution, fueled in part by investments in public infrastructure, resulted in productivity growth between 1929 and 1941 that was the highest of any comparable period in the twentieth century. This rapid rate of innovations caused a rapid creation of new market power. The second factor is the combined effect of the Great Depression and World War II. During the Great Depression, many weaker firms defaulted or were acquired by stronger firms. When conditions improved, the weaker firms did not recover, and the survivors were firms with better technology, superior marketing, and better financial conditions, and that enabled them to gain market power. Although relations between the president and business leaders were strained, cooperation between the government and business was needed to enhance the recovery policy. In fact, public policy aimed to prevent cutthroat competition. The National Industrial Recovery Act was explicitly designed to strengthen trade associations and to raise prices and wages in order to counter destructive deflationary pressures. There were enough laws on the books from the Progressive Era for the government to initiate a strong antitrust policy, but these laws were not enforced. The depression created conditions that made policy place greater weight on economic recovery. After long hesitation, some action was taken but not for long. In 1938, Thurman Arnold, the assistant attorney general in charge of the Antitrust Division in Roosevelt's Department of Justice, increased antitrust enforcement. But as World War II approached, the Roosevelt administration backed off and deemphasized all such antitrust enforcement for the openly stated purpose of allowing corporations to concentrate on efforts to win World War II. Under these conditions, very little antitrust policy was implemented, and the strong firms that survived the Great Depression were able to employ pricing strategies to enhance their profitability.

The above argument is consistent with the Brinkley (1996) account regarding the change of the New Deal's policy direction in the second Roosevelt administration, motivated by the more urgent need to end the depression. Brinkley (1996) argues that instead of aiming to alter the structure of the economy under capitalism (including strong enforcement of antitrust), policy makers chose regulations and public spending by an expanded fiscal policy and social safety net as the more effective methods to end the depression and restore full employment. This was actually the formal discovery of fiscal policy as a central tool of stabilization policy.

Turning to World War II, I note two facts. First, during the war, American business was mobilized to produce the vast amount of war-related materiel considered essential for victory. In wartime, the government and the public saw business as a vital ally that, rather than being restrained, must be given the freedom to carry out its task. Second, the government's war demand created shortages of essential goods, and instead of allowing prices to rise, wage and price controls were implemented along with a rationing system. Although some firms were convicted and fined for violating price controls or for engaging in price fixing, the number of convictions was relatively small. Because all price control methods are based on markups, a knowledge of these markups in relation to all goods and services requires knowledge of business practices and a massive accounting force. This was not feasible in wartime. Once wages were effectively restrained and labor unions prevented from striking, it is not difficult to see how businesspeople found ways to ensure high profitability.

The fact is that both World War I and World War II were very profitable for American business. World War II and the subsequent Cold War established a unique relation between the military and private business, as well as sustained high levels of military expenditure. One direct aspect of this is the increased concentration in sectors that contracted with the Defense Department. Military expenditures have also increased private market power through the transfer, to private firms, of major technologies developed with military funds. Some such transfers were the basis for the later development of Silicon Valley (see, for example, Nash, 1990; Mazzucato, 2015; Wright, 2020). Given these relations between business and the government, one can expect only limited implementation of policies to restrain business and curtail market power.

In short, although many formal measures of public restrictions on business, such as antitrust laws, tax rates, and enacted regulations, were at high levels during the Great Depression and World War II, the actual implemented policy was favorable to business. Market power was thus able to rise to very high levels. The true level is probably not as high as suggested in figure 4.9. I noted that an accord between the Fed and the Treasury was reached in March 1951, but as explained earlier, markets adjusted to it slowly. Because my imputed interest rate ends in 1952, the market interest rate used to compute profit share is probably too low. It is then most likely that the profit share estimates for the years 1952–1959 are a bit too high.

The change of effective policy in the 1950s was not prompted by a political movement demanding change. It simply resulted from a natural transition to a realistic implementation of the intended policy of the New Deal and laws already on the books. The share of profits peaked in 1954, but this date is not explained by any particular historical event. In 1952, Dwight D. Eisenhower was elected president. He was a moderate conservative who preserved most, and expanded some, of the New Deal's policies and agencies. He was particularly concerned by the growth of big business during World War II and the Cold War that followed. In his farewell address, he warned against the rising combined power of business and the military. He coined the term "military-industrial complex" to describe this combined power and argued that it must be restrained. Antitrust actions initiated by his administration were not drastic; they were sustained and deliberate. The changing policy environment of the 1950s is then recognized as a delayed response to the accumulated problems unresolved after the long twenty years of the Great Depression and World War II.

And the policy framework of the Roosevelt administration was indeed the foundation of policy in the 1950s. The Truman and Eisenhower administrations accepted and built upon the essentially confiscatory upper-income taxation rates of the Roosevelt administration. These had aimed to prevent individual income from rising above some upper limit. In 1952, the top marginal income tax was raised to 92 percent, and the corporate income tax was raised to 52 percent. In addition, there were sufficient laws and regulations already on the books from the Progressive Era and the New Deal to restrain market power. And in the early 1950s, the restraint of business power once again became a high-priority public policy objective. The concern with excessive corporate power was shared by the Democratic administrations of the 1960s. Antitrust policy activity was expanded throughout the period 1953–1970, and the power of unions' continued to rise well into the late 1960s.

I turn now to the years 1985–2017. As indicated in chapter 1, the changes of relative shares since 1985 result from the fact that the two forces that shape market power —technology and public policy—have pushed technological market power *in the same direction*. First, the innovation wave in information technology (IT) began to take hold. Here is a sample of events that mark the early phase of the IT revolution: Apple 1 was released in 1976; IBM's PC, using Microsoft's disk-operating system (DOS) as the operating system, was released in 1981; the military communication network, ARPANET, adopted the Transmission Control Protocol/Internet Protocol (TCP/IP) (which expedited development of the internet) in 1983; Microsoft went public in 1986; Celgene was founded in

1986; Gilead Sciences was founded in 1987; Marc Andreesen developed the first browser, Mosaic, in 1993 (its name was changed to Netscape Navigator in 1994).

Public policy, the second force shaping market power, turned decidedly against efforts to arrest market power, similarly to the passive policy in the First Gilded Age up to 1901. Passive policies were adopted in the 1980s that enabled consolidation of market power. President Ronald Reagan was elected in 1981 and took office with the clear aim of eliminating, as far as possible, the regulatory structure and policies of the New Deal. He took strong action to limit the power of unions, breaking the air traffic controllers' strike in 1981. His administration initiated supply-side policies that came to be known as Reaganomics. The central objective was to increase the incentives of individuals and business firms to work, invest, innovate, and reduce reliance on government. These ideas led to the elimination of a wide range of business regulations, the lowering of individual and corporate income tax rates, and the removal of many other significant components of the prior policy to restrain market power of business, such as the shift to a very tolerant policy toward mergers and acquisitions, which are essential tools for building market power. The consequence of the combined change in technology and policy was the same as seen in the First Gilded Age. It resulted in an increased profit share of value added in the corporate sector from 8 percent in 1985 to 24 percent in 2017.

The two Gilded Ages are similar in one more respect: the influence of money in politics. Ample historical evidence shows that before 1901, big money ran U.S. politics. The historian Mark W. Summers (1993) documents the vast political corruption of the era. It was a time when business leaders bribed politicians to ensure that the government did not interfere in their business, and they mostly got their way. Such corruption was so common that in 1868 New York state legalized political bribery. Since the 1980s, money's influence in politics has risen sharply, aided by supportive decisions of the Supreme Court (see Gutiérrez and Philippon, 2018; Philippon, 2019).

The rising influence of money, the rising market power, and the passive policy caused, in both ages, rising inequality and increased social strife that has threatened democratic norms. Increased social division is a direct consequence of the sharp rise in the income and wealth inequality at the expense of the low-skilled and less-educated workers. With the lack of protection from the forces of technology and markets, displaced workers tend to lose their trust in democracy. This points to the fact that the stability of democratic institutions requires a strong public policy that attains a balance between the two goals of an equitable distribution of income and wealth and a high rate of economic growth. In chapters 8–10, I outline the nature of the policy needed to meet that balance. From this perspective, a successful public policy is essential for capitalism to function in a democratic society. Without restraint on market power, capitalism unleashes forces that can turn free-market democracy into plutocracy.

The United States could, in the twenty-first century, be on the threshold of a policy change paralleling the Progressive Era of the nineteenth and twentieth centuries. Recent demands for the regulation of big tech companies, direct re-distribution, increased progressivity of the tax code, and wealth taxation are all analogous to demands made by the Progressive movement before 1901.

4.4.4   On the Share of Profits and Intangible Assets

I do not count the rewards of intangible assets as part of capital share for reasons explained in chapter 3.[5] Figure 4.10 shows how this choice affects the results presented here. The figure shows that excluding intangibles from capital does not change the time pattern of events since 1925 but only the magnitude of the recent rise in profits. The quantitative effect is small before the 1970s and becomes more pronounced with time. In 2017, the value of intangible assets is 14.9 percent of total corporate nonfinancial assets. It is thus not surprising that the computed share of profits falls from 24.5 percent to 17.6 percent in 2017 if intangibles are added to the capital stock.

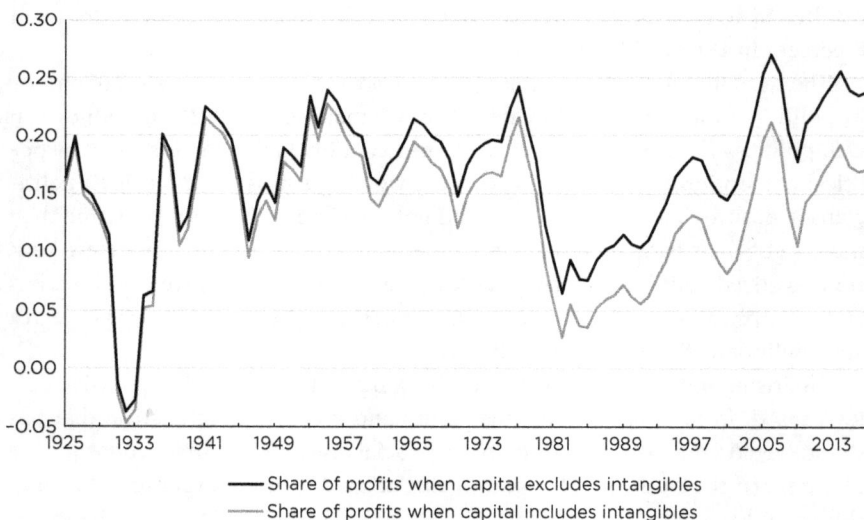

—— Share of profits when capital excludes intangibles
—— Share of profits when capital includes intangibles

Figure 4.10 Share of profits when capital includes or excludes intangibles

---

[5]In chapter 7, a case is made that research and development (R&D) expenses are the costs of developing future market power and consolidating existing power. This suggests that a fraction of current R&D cost should be considered the cost of maintaining market power and subtracted from the share of profits in value added. Because no data is available for such a decomposition and because my focus is on creating a consistent measure of market power, I chose to ignore this factor and compute the profit rate as a gross measure without subtracting the small cost of maintaining it.

Apart from the theoretical reasons given in chapter 3 to justify the exclusion of intangibles from capital, there is also an empirical reason to do so. Because of the exclusion of intangibles, my results on the share of profits can be compared with estimates of market power made by direct measures using production and marginal cost data. I noted earlier that the estimates of De Loecker et al. (2020) are viewed as too large and that Hall's (2018) estimates are more accurate. I also note there is a difference in coverage because I study only the U.S. corporate sector, while Hall studies sixty KLEMS industries for 1988–2015. Therefore, although the estimates may not be identical, they should be of the same order of magnitude. The following summary compares Hall's average estimated share of profits with mine, both including and excluding intangibles from capital:

	1988	2015
Average estimate of Hall (2018)	11.0 percent	28.0 percent
My estimate with intangibles excluded from capital	10.5 percent	23.9 percent
My estimate with intangibles included in capital	6.4 percent	17.6 percent

The inclusion of intangibles leads to results that are contradicted by conclusions derived with either method.

4.5   Rising Market Power Is the Cause of the Decline of Labor Share Since the 1980s

4.5.1   The Effect of Other Factors in the Labor Market

Figure 4.7 explains why, in addressing the American Economic Association in 1954, Simon Kuznets could adopt an optimistic view of relative shares under democracy in the United States. Focusing on U.S. data from 1929 to 1950,[6] and discounting fluctuations of labor share due to the Great Depression and World War II, he could argue that labor share was relatively stable and, by implication, the *combined* share of capital and profits was relatively stable as well. This conclusion was supported by the strong U.S. policy to eliminate excessive wealth and attain a higher degree of income equality than the United State had prior to the Great Depression. If one ignores the volatility due to the big shocks of the era, the estimated labor share was about the same in 1929 and 1955, and personal income inequality declined.

---

[6] Kuznets (1955) also offers comparisons of inequality in isolated years for three European countries. He cites a decrease in personal inequality in the United Kingdom by comparing 1880, 1913, 1929, and 1947; a rise in inequality in Prussia comparing 1875 with 1913; and no change in inequality in Saxony comparing 1880 and 1913. In all cases, skipping the changes between 1880 and 1913 is particularly misleading.

Because Kuznets (1955) did not study the relative shares of capital and profits, he did not know that, exactly at the time of his address, the market power of U.S. corporations was at the highest level since the First Gilded Age. After 1929, market power had risen at the expense of capital, not labor. This can be deduced from the fact that the time pattern of rising or falling market power does not correspond to the time pattern of rising and falling labor share in figure 4.7. The theoretical problems raised by this fact were assessed in chapter 1, section 1.4.3.

In chapter 1, I characterized the problem by noting that the conditions in (1.4) imply that the ratio of the shares of labor and capital should be relatively constant and satisfy

$$\frac{\text{Labor share}}{\text{Capital share}} = \frac{W_t L_t}{R_t K_t} = \frac{1 - \alpha}{\alpha}.$$

This implies that changes in market power alter labor share and capital share by the same proportion. Figures 4.7 and 4.8 show that this is not supported by the data, giving rise to the alternate formulation of the ratio in (1.9). Generalizing the model to allow for imperfect competition or imperfect adjustment in the labor market, the ratio becomes

$$\frac{W_t L_t}{R_t K_t} = \frac{1 - \alpha}{\alpha} \Upsilon_t.$$

The variable Υ_t reflects the balance of forces operating in the labor market that either shield it from the changing market power or aggravate the impact of such changes. The expression $\Upsilon_t < 1$ arises when firms have monopsony power in the labor market, and $\Upsilon_t > 1$ reflects forces that tip the balance in favor of labor.

Econometric estimates of the elasticity α are around 0.30–0.33 so that $(1 - \alpha)/\alpha \simeq 2.2$, but the qualitative results are the same for all α such that $2 \leq (1 - \alpha)/\alpha \leq 3$. Figure 4.11 reports the values of $(WL)/(RK)$, with a horizontal line indicating a constant level of 2.2.

Before discussing the results, I note that the steep rise of this ratio in the 1950s is one more transitory price effect. This time it is due to the Korean War, when prices rose sharply, but nominal interest rates did not adjust. At the same time, nominal wages adjusted almost immediately, resulting in the observed spike in the ratio. Another factor that contributes to this spike is the slow normalization in the Fed's monetary policy in 1953–1958, which I have noted earlier (see section 4.2.3 and footnote 2). These extreme values are temporary, and for the purpose at hand, they are disregarded.

The surprise in figure 4.11 is the response of the relative shares of capital and labor to changes in market power. The data reveal that during the early period of 1889–1937 and a short period around 1983, we have approximately $\Upsilon_t = 1$, otherwise $\Upsilon_t > 1$. It means there is no evidence of *widespread* monopsony power

Figure 4.11 Ratio of (labor share)/capital share

at work in the U.S. labor market, but it does not preclude scattered monopsony behavior in some market segments. The data also reveal that in most years after 1937, changes in market power had smaller impacts on labor share than they had on the shares of capital and profits. In the years from 1984 to 2017, market power rose, but the decline in the relative share of capital was much steeper than the decline in the relative share of labor. The phenomenon of shielded labor share, expressed in $\Upsilon_t > 1$, is very pronounced from 1936 to 1980. From the early 1920s until 1954, labor share rose slowly, and then it declined slowly after 1954. But in both segments, the shift was not in tandem with the relative share of capital's decline and subsequent rise. The data point to the fact that during those years, economic and political forces kept labor share relatively higher, and the personal distribution of income more equitable, than would have been warranted by the changing market power. In short, after 1936, labor appears relatively more shielded than capital from the impact of rising market power, but it also benefits less from declining market power. How can this be explained?

Several explanations are possible, and each has encountered criticism. As explained in chapter 1, one group of explanations focuses on wage rigidity, labor compensation in accord with the efficiency theory of wages to improve loyalty, and labor compensation in the form of profit sharing. The second explanation could be the political effect of unions, as argued by Piketty (2014). But then the explanation has to be the political power of unions to gain advantages that could alter labor share, for example, through profit-sharing arrangements or preventing firms from maximizing profits by ensuring workers are retained in recessions. As shown in chapter 1, by itself, wage fixing by unions would not have changed the relative share of labor. A third explanation could focus on the possible effect of skill-biased technical change[7] combined with the rapid rise in educational attainment in the United States up to the 1970s and its decline since then. Or, perhaps it was the golden age of national cohesion and idealism in the United States that led firms to share with their workers some of the rising American wealth from innovations. Some recent research supports this possibility (see Kline et al., 2019).

4.5.2   Rising Market Power Is the Decisive Factor Suppressing Wages and Labor Share from 1984 to 2017

For many scholars, the undisputed decline of labor share, particularly after the 1980s, is the most crucial problem to be explained in a study of the distribution of income and wealth. It has deep social and political ramifications and has been studied by many, including the authors discussed in section 4.6. The factors often mentioned as possible explanations for the decline of labor share are automation, globalization, and the decline of unions. The political power of unions has been weak since 1984, and all three factors thus must operate primarily through the market mechanism. That is, they can only alter market conditions that change the wage rate firms face. This is because unions may set wages but not employment; globalization suppresses wages by introducing a cheaper alternate supply of labor or by firms moving abroad who create an excess supply of domestic labor. In some sectors, automation lowers the wage at which labor is available to firms in the rest of the economy. But as explained in Chapter 1.4.3, because the elasticity of substitution between labor and capital is close to 1, in all three cases the firm continues to be free to select its demand for labor and *that freedom to adjust negates any effect of these three factors* on the relative share of labor.[8] This fact has been the basic theoretical explanation for the long-held belief that labor share is constant. I therefore question the validity of these three lines of explanation for the change in labor share. The presence of rapidly rising market power changes everything. As explained in chapter 1, rising market power applies constant pressure to suppress wages and lower the share of labor.

Examination of figures 4.8, 4.9, and 4.11 leads to the conclusion that labor share declined sharply in the two Gilded Ages of 1889–1901 and 1984–2017.

---

[7]See, for example, Krusell et al. (2000), Autor et al. (1998), Goldin and Katz (2010), and Card and DiNardo (2002). The effect of skill-bias technical change on inequality depends crucially on assumptions that indirectly amount to postulating that the elasticity of substitution between aggregate capital and aggregate labor is different from 1.

[8]The exception is recent models of robots that are assumed to replace labor directly. This replacement is made with the highly questionable assumption of not allowing any substitution between labor and capital by adjusting the capital/labor ratio.

During both periods, capital share also fell, and in both periods rising market power, propelled by technology and a passive policy, was the dominant cause of the decline in the shares of both labor and capital. On the other hand, during the intermediate period of 1901–1984, strong public policy restrained market power and established more egalitarian income and wealth distributions, but, as explained, policy during that period was more protective of labor than capital. But Figure 4.11 also shows that the forces that shielded labor share weakened somewhat after 1970: labor share declined from 0.60 in 1970 to 0.55 in 1984 while, *at the same time*, the share of profits declined and capital share rose sharply, because of the dramatic rise of interest rates.

Focusing next on the period from 1984 to 2017, I decompose the change in labor share into two components related to the two forces that changed that share in this period. The first is rising market power that suppressed wages and labor share. The opposing force is policy or other factor that shielded labor and was explained earlier in section 4.5.1. I isolate the path that labor share would have taken were it only affected by changes in market power. I do so by assuming that it would mirror the path of the capital share because, without the differential treatment of policy, rising market power should affect the two shares in equal proportion. The question is, then, how these two forces affected labor share since 1984.

I rewrite equilibrium relative shares (see 1.4) in the following alternate forms:

$$\text{Relative share of labor} \quad s_{w,t} = \frac{W_t L_t}{P_t Y_t} = (1 - \alpha)\frac{\theta_t - 1}{\theta_t}\Upsilon_t \qquad (4.7a)$$

$$\text{Relative share of capital } s_{k,t} = \frac{R_t K_t}{P_t Y_t} = \alpha\frac{\theta_t - 1}{\theta_t}. \qquad (4.7b)$$

I now isolate the effect of rising market power on labor share from the effect of other factors reflected in the term Υ_t. To do that, I express each component defining labor share in terms of the known shares of labor and capital. That is, from (4.7a), I have

$$\text{Proportional effect of market power} \ = \frac{\theta_t - 1}{\theta_t} = \frac{1}{\alpha}s_{k,t} \qquad (4.8a)$$

and from (4.7a)–(4.7b) I have

Proportional effect of labor market policy and imperfection

$$= \Upsilon_t = \frac{s_{w,t}}{s_{k,t}}\left(\frac{\alpha}{1 - \alpha}\right). \qquad (4.8b)$$

I assume that the elasticity α is equal to 0.32, and given the estimated values of the shares of labor and capital, figure 4.12 presents the two effects.

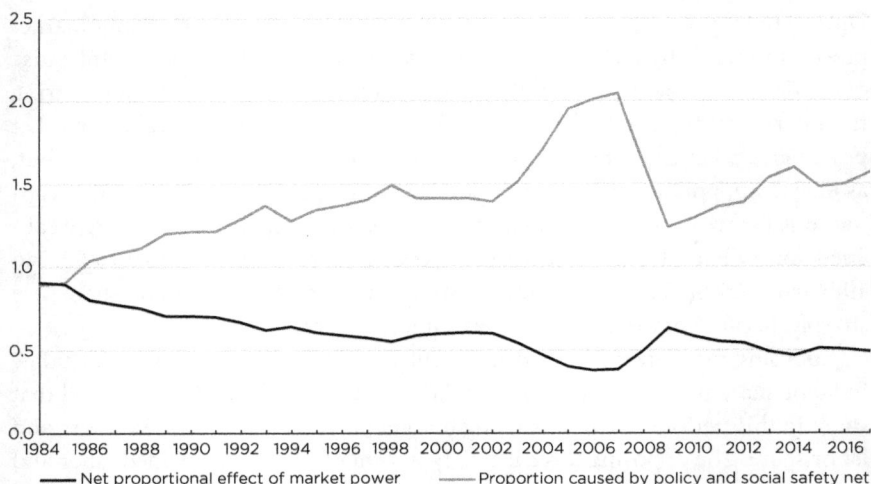

Figure 4.12   Decomposition of the factors causing a decrease in labor share, 1984–2017

It is then clear that rising market power has suppressed the share of labor, but public policy, wage rigidities, and other factors that supported labor prevented the share of labor from declining as much as it otherwise would have because of the rise in market power.

To illustrate the degree by which labor share could have decreased from the rise in market power, consider the comparison between the decline in labor share and the decline in the share of capital from 1984 to 2017:

	Labor	Capital	
Relative share in 1984	0.552	0.291	(4.9)
Relative share in 2017	0.524	0.157	
Percent decline from 1984 to 2017	5.08 percent	46.0 percent	

The sharp rise in market power since 1984 is well reflected in the sharp decline of the share of capital. However, the decline in labor share since the 1980s was not as sharp as would be expected from the 46 percent decline in the share of capital. The presence in the labor market of other mitigating factors is clear, but are they constant over time? Do they reflect permanent structural factors that prevail in all labor markets, or do they reflect changes in the labor market during the last century? I can answer these questions by comparing this period of labor market dynamics with those during the First Gilded Age.

First, recall that the rise of market power in the Second Gilded Age, from 1984 to 2017, is of the same order of magnitude as the rise in market power during the First Gilded Age. This is seen in the comparison of the profit share in those periods:

Share of Profits: 1889–1901	Share of Profits: 1984–2017
1889 : −0.026	1984 : 0.076
1901 : 0.299	2017 : 0.238

Second, consider now the comparison between the decline in labor share and the decline in the share of capital from 1889 to 1901:

	Labor	Capital	
Relative share in 1889	0.713	0.275	
Relative share in 1901	0.508	0.155	(4.10)
Percent decline from 1889 to 1901	28.8 percent	43.6 percent	

Comparing (4.9) with (4.10) shows that the decline in capital share was of the same order of magnitude during the two Gilded Ages, but the decline of labor share during the First Gilded Age was 5.7 times larger than during the period from 1984 to 2017. This strongly suggests that it was both society's view of labor and the institutions underlying the labor market that changed since the First Gilded Age. Recognizing that the United States was transformed at the end of the nineteenth century from an agriculture-based to a manufacturing-based economy, it remains true the data used here are for the *private, nonfarm, nonresidential sector*. This was not agricultural employment. It is hard to imagine the economic and political ramifications of a decline of labor share from 1984 to 2017 being as steep as the decline of capital share since 1984, or even as steep as that of 28.8 percent during the First Gilded Age. This suggests that although the United States has witnessed a dramatic rise in market power since 1982, the U.S. economy has not sustained the full economic and social consequences of that rise. The social safety net and the institutions of the New Deal have protected labor and the fabric of democracy, perhaps helped by innovating firms' sharing profits with employees.

4.6   Alternative Explanations of the Falling Labor Share and Rising Inequality Since the 1980s

The literature on the changing distribution of income and wealth since the 1980s is extensive, with scholars taking different approaches to the problem. Some address the falling share of labor directly, while others focus on the change in markup, profitability, and rising industrial concentration. These are clearly interrelated issues, but here I restrict my discussion to the work of other scholars in order to explain the trends of rising markup, the fall in labor share, and the rise in inequality since the 1980s. In considering their views, it is useful to keep in mind the question of how these explanations could apply to the two previous eras of rising market power, from 1889 to 1901 and from 1931 to 1953. Also relevant is how such explanations clarify the reasons for extended periods of *declining* market power.

Hall (1988) was the first to document that in some industries, marginal costs were well below price and notes that "the evidence against competition is reasonably convincing" (946). Some authors contribute to measuring the rise in markups but take it as an exogenous factor and do not address the question of why they have risen since the 1980s (see, for example, Barkai, 2020; Barkai and Benzell, 2018; Hall, 2018). The important contribution of De Loecker et al. (2020) is mainly in measuring the markup and documenting its rise over the period 1980–2016. In considering the implications of the rise in markups (see chapter 1), their formal model assumes fixed start-up cost. It is treated as a new factor in production, and they assume free entry and ex-ante expected zero profits. Such a model is then one of a zero-profit, monopolistically competitive economy, where the markup appears to be an equilibrium device to enable the firm to cover its fixed start-up cost. In this equilibrium, effective market power is not durable, and positive average profits are short-term deviations from long-run zero profits.

Farhi and Gourio (2018) focus on explaining the rising wedge in the last thirty years between the measured marginal product of capital and the risk-free rate. Their results place less weight on the rise in market power than I do. Instead, they place more weight on their estimated increase in risk premiums and on what they call "the rise in a significant increase in the unmeasured component of intangibles." They, like other authors, use the questionable method of including intangibles in their estimated capital stock. They correctly find the BEA estimated intangibles to be too small.[9] They then add the missing intangibles and find that returns to intangibles is a more important explanation for rising profits than rising market power. But as explained in chapter 3, intangibles are in fact a form of market power. The Farhi and Gourio (2018) result then occurs mechanically because, as seen in figure 4.10, if intangibles are included in the stock of capital, it shifts value added from profits to capital and reduces estimated market power.

Several authors recognize the rise in markups since the 1980s and provide valuable empirical evidence in support of various components of the theory advanced in this book. They describe rising market power by empirically showing that the markup is correlated with rising economic concentration and declining competition. Grullon et al. (2019) maintain that the rise in concentration is an outcome of weak enforcement of antitrust laws and increasing

---

[9] I explain in chapter 3 why intangibles should not be included in the capital stock, but I also make the same argument to suggest that the BEA estimated stock of intangible assets has limited value because it is far too small.

technological barriers to entry. Gutiérrez and Philippon (2016) show that declining investment over the last thirty years has been caused by increased limits on entry, increased concentration, and reduced competition. Gutiérrez and Philippon (2017a) offer more evidence on the effect on investment of lower competition and use alternative methods to measure the decline in competition. Gutiérrez and Philippon (2018) document a higher level of competitiveness in Europe than in the United State, which also has a correspondingly higher level of concentration. Their argument points to the causes of increased market power in the United States as being the lobbying and other political methods used by firms to advance their interests. The same theme is developed in detail by Philippon (2019). Gutiérrez and Philippon (2019) provide strong evidence for the decline in the incentive to enter profitable industries characterized by a large Tobin's q. Eggertsson et al. (2018) take the rising markup as an exogenous variable whose effect explains why neoclassical growth theory should be revised.

Other scholars recognize the rise in profit margins since the 1980s but reject the explanation of rising market power. For example, Bessen (2016) argues that rising profitability resulted from increased regulations and heavy investment in intangible assets. Bessen (2020) recognizes the rise in industry concentration since the 1980s and maintains that IT raised the productivity of the top firms relative to others, thereby causing the increased industry concentration and increased profit margins. This argument is one of firm heterogeneity, which is the foundation for many models in the industrial organization literature. I return to this topic in chapters 7 and 8.

Extensive research has documented the decline of labor share in many countries since the 1970s, and this decline has been accepted as an established fact. Some disagreement has persisted about the degree of decline because of some measurement issues. Recall that I exclude officers' compensation from labor share (see also Smith et al., 2019), but other issues have come up in the literature, such as the treatment of imputed wages of the self-employed (for example, Elsby et al., 2013; Gollin, 2002), the depreciation of capital (for example, Bridgman, 2018) and the role of housing (for example, Rognlie, 2015).

More extensive disagreement exists about the cause of the decline in relative labor share. Karabarbounis and Neiman (2014) explain it as the consequence of the sharp decline in the relative price of capital goods and wages, particularly the sharp fall in equipment prices of information and communication technologies. This conclusion requires the elasticity of substitution of capital for labor to exceed 1.[10] Acemoglu and Restrepo (2020) propose that the introduction

---

[10] This is a difficult parameter to estimate. Karabarbounis and Neiman (2014) provide some evidence for an elasticity around 1.25, but this result is in conflict with evidence of all other studies, such as Lawrence (2015), Oberfield and Raval (2021), Rognlie (2015), and others referenced in these articles.

of robots contributed to the decline in labor share. Elsby et al. (2013) stress the importance of trade and international outsourcing, especially with China. Piketty (2014) places great weight on labor market norms, unions, and a minimum wage. I have explained in chapter 1 that it is difficult to see how such wage-setting behavior affects the relative share of labor and suggest these may be interpreted as conditions that prevent the firm from optimizing its use of labor.

Koh et al. (2020) argue the decline in the national income and product accounts (NIPA)-computed relative share of labor after 1929 can be explained as a consequence of the accounting change where the BEA began to treat intellectual property products (IPPs) as investment rather than as consumption. The change in accounting increases value added and capital share, thereby lowering labor share in value added simply because relative shares add up to 1. This work leads to two comments. I have criticized the BEA for defining IPP as capital and show in chapter 3 that intangible assets should not be treated as capital. Nevertheless, it remains true that IPPs are long-lasting assets, and the BEA's past treatment of these assets as consumption was unjustified, while the treatment of these expenditures as an output of long-lasting assets is fully justified. This implies that the old accounting treatment obscured the true functional distribution of income, and the changed accounting treatment simply revealed the extent of the decline in labor share on the aggregate level. Second, the argument made by these authors does not apply to the procedure used in this book because I do not use the BEA-computed relative shares. I exclude intangibles from capital and estimate capital income by imputing required rent to the capital employed in the corporate sector. The main results of this book are often driven by the division between the share of capital and the share of profits, not by labor share. The decline in labor share makes a significant contribution to the rising share of profits only after 2000 (see figure 4.5).

Smith et al. (2019) identify the income sources of individuals in the top 1 percent who receive pass-through income from the ownership of S-corporations or partnerships. These are professionals like lawyers, physicians, or small business owners. The authors investigate whether their income should be classified as human capital income or as income of invested financial capital. Their answer is that it is mostly the high return to human capital and high skill. Their research aims mostly to contest Piketty's (2014) argument that human capital has a small impact on incomes of the top 1 percent. All results in this book are about the corporate sector, which covers only C-corporations. The Smith et al. research clarifies the roles played by physical capital and the human capital of skilled workers in S-corporations, which would be necessary to disentangle if one were to construct capital and labor shares for the entire economy.

Van Reenen (2018) acknowledges the increased markup but rejects it as proof of a rise in market power. Stressing heterogeneity in productivity, he sees the rising markup as an outcome of the rising size of the most productive firms and the default of less productive ones. In a recent study by the Brookings Institute and Chumir Foundation, Qureshi et al. (2019) review problems related to falling relative share of labor, slowing productivity, and rising inequality. Among other topics, they also review studies that use models with heterogeneous firms. Such reasoning has been used extensively in the industrial organization literature and more recently to address the effect of globalization (for example, Melitz, 2003). I next comment on these models briefly here, but because the heterogeneity theory is also the basis for the scientific and political opposition to antitrust policy, I postpone its detailed discussion to chapters 7 and 8.

An argument of heterogeneity is also used in the superstar firms model of Autor et al. (2020). The authors note that if the elasticity of demand falls with price, the transfer of output from firms who charge higher prices to those who charge lower prices increases firms' markup, implying they have rising market power. The model of Autor et al. assumes firms randomly draw their productivity levels, and the term "superstar" simply identifies the firm with the lowest cost. This random selection is made once for all firms and can never be changed by new innovations or by any firm upgrading its technology and productivity. It further assumes an exogenous rise of market toughness (that is, some level of competitiveness) because of globalization, which causes small, less efficient firms to default. Output then migrates to the lowest cost superstar firm that charges lower prices, increasing average markup. Autor et al. offer the interpretation that these winning firms do not seek market power; they just passively acquire the customers of the defaulting, unproductive firms. This is merely an interpretation of statistical regressions suggesting that the sales of big firms rose over time while those of smaller firms declined. The more drastic conclusion is that the successful big firms with market power are just those with superior productivity, and any antitrust action against them would simply be an act of punishing success. I explain in chapter 8 that this is the standard argument used by conservative economists who oppose antitrust laws on the grounds that they penalize success, and that, over time, competition will eliminate the market power of these superior and productive firms.

It is noteworthy that a growing number of research articles examine firm heterogeneity and test the specific question addressed by Autor et al. (2020), whether in industries with rising superstar firms, such firms do not exercise market power and gain market share just by being more productive than others. All offer results that contradict the interpretation of Autor et al. In studying the effect of concentration across industries, Andrews et al. (2016), Cette et al. (2016), and Égert (2016) show that higher concentration is associated with a decline in output growth rate, a lower rate of productivity, and slower diffusion of new technologies. Gutiérrez and Philippon (2016, 2017b) and Égert (2016) report a reduced incentive to invest and innovate. Comin and Mestieri (2014) document a reduction in the rate at which new technologies are adopted and new ideas diffused. These are all symptoms of markets that are dominated by market power. In chapter 7, I construct a theoretical model in which this heterogeneity emerges not exogenously but out of competing firms' quest for market power. I find that these superstar firms do emerge in an unregulated market but that society would be better off if their growth were checked.

CHAPTER 5

THE EFFECT OF MARKET POWER ON THE DIFFUSION OF INNOVATIONS

5.1 Background and Motivation

Rapid diffusion of innovations through the economy has a significant impact on economic growth and productivity. However, data suggest that the rate of diffusion of innovation is very slow. The aspects of diffusion that have mainly been discussed in the literature are in the domain of innovation "adoption," and the early, applied literature on technology diffusion is typically statistical in nature. The variable explored is the percentage of the population that adopts a technological innovation at a given time and the time pattern of this variable. The pioneering work, done by Griliches (1957) and Mansfield (1961, 1963), was followed by numerous studies that focused on specific innovations (e.g., Coleman et al., 1966; Davies, 1979; Gort and Klepper, 1982; Alm and Cox, 1996; and Skinner and Staiger, 2015). This research established the fact that the diffusion of innovations takes the form of a logistic function. The S-shape of this function implies adoption that is slow at early dates but accelerates with time and then slows again to converge to the long-run fraction of users in the population. Different innovations have been characterized by two distinct parameters of the logistic functions. The first regulates the adoption speed; the second defines the asymptotic fraction of users.

The logistic time pattern has prompted many different interpretations of the causes for this S-shaped delay in technology adoption. Two such proposed causes are as follows:

1. *Heterogeneity* arises when users have different adoption costs or derive different benefits from the innovation. Early adopters have the highest net benefits, and an S-shape is realized when the adoption cost falls, leading to more rapid and widespread integration of the innovation (e.g., Chari and Hopenhayn, 1991).
2. *Learning* is naturally necessary given the novelty of a new product or service (e.g., Griliches, 1957; Mansfield, 1961, 1963; Davies, 1979; and Levin et al., 1987). Potential adopters need to discover how useful an innovation is for their applications, but because learning requires time, adoption is slow at the start. The adoption time falls progressively as learning accelerates due to increased understanding and availability of learning resources. To substantiate this theory, Arthur (1989) and Banerjee (1992) offer a particular learning mechanism in which experiments by early potential adopters generate information about the desirability of a technology. Once a few users decide to adopt the technology, a cascade of information is generated, stimulating other potential users to adopt it as well. An interesting study describing this hypothesis is that of Geroski (2000).

Other than this early work, the literature on the causes and consequences of heterogeneous rates of technology diffusion within and across countries is extensive and beyond the scope of this chapter (see the excellent and extensive survey by Comin and Mestieri, 2014). My approach to the problem focuses on structural modeling of the slow diffusion. Comin and Hobijn (2010) and Comin and Mestieri (2018) formulate an endogenous adoption process in which, at any given time, a set of innovative technologies is available and to adopt one of them, a firm must invest some fixed cost. The cost incurred by the firm is higher for more recent, state-of-the-art technologies. The lag between the time of invention and its adoption is an endogenous variable defined as adoption delay. In equilibrium, when an economy is in the process of adopting a new technology, the output and capital employed are functions of this delay. *Relative to the theoretical steady state* of that same economy, the actual equilibrium paths of capital and output exhibit growth paths that are concave with respect to time, and the concavity reflects the delay. In essence, instead of being measured in terms of the percentage of users, diffusion is deduced in terms of an endogenous delay variable that causes a concave time path of growth relative to the steady-state path of that economy. The authors go on to study the diffusion of fifteen major technologies across 166 countries and find that the mean delay over all countries and all innovations is a staggering forty-five years.

The central idea of the research cited above is then to define technology diffusion in terms of a deviation of the equilibrium paths from the steady-state growth path of the economy. In principle, this is a plausible approach, although the specific definition of "deviation" used may be questioned because it is far from clear that any economy is ever in its deterministic steady state. In my study, diffusion is also defined as a *relative* concept.

The fact of slow diffusion of innovation is widely accepted, but the estimated time period of forty-five years reported in the previous studies is long enough for consumers and producers to acquire all available knowledge about an innovation and learn how it can be useful in their businesses or households. In other words, the delay is so long that the factors that slow down the rate of diffusion must be structural, not transitory, as noted earlier with respect to the logistic function, such as learning, that restrict demand. This also implies that the term "adoption" is somewhat misleading because its negation, "not adopting," places too much weight on factors that restrict demand and disregard other limiting factors. Important innovations that have changed people's lives and raised living standards were not adopted slowly due to the reluctance of potential users to adopt them. Instead, *structural economic factors* made it impossible for them to use the new innovation. I therefore avoid using the terms "adopt" and "adoption" in the rest of this chapter. The literature on technology diffusion offers a wide array of additional reasons for the low utilization of new technologies. Here I list a sample of common reasons offered:

1. The need to build social infrastructure to enable use of the new products (e.g., the rate of use of automobiles depends upon the rate at which new roads are constructed).
2. Friction in adapting to a new technology that requires new methods of production and different managerial approaches (e.g., a new factory requires new buildings, new machines, and new business management techniques).
3. Political and financial resistance to an innovation by owners of an existing technology that is threatened by diffusion of the competing technology.
4. Legal and political restrictions that reflect beliefs and culture (e.g., objections to the use of stem cells).

These factors vary across countries and innovations (for more details and references, see Comin and Mestieri, 2014). However, there are two economic factors that influence the rate of diffusion on which all writers agree: the price of the new technology and the effect of aggregate demand. *But price and demand are always considered exogenous* and in most cases are taken to be set under normal competitive conditions, where the price equals the marginal cost of production.

In this chapter, I propose that the price paid for products developed from new technologies should not be taken as exogenous, and especially should not be taken to reflect the competitive cost of production. I consider the price to be a variable set by the firm that owns the new technology, and I measure the effect that price has on the rate at which innovations diffuse. This firm gains initial monopoly power due to its ownership of the technology being introduced. However, as explained in chapter 1, this monopoly power is only the start. It provides the firm with the advantages of a first mover, which enables it to build an economic moat around the market and impede entry of competitors through strategies like layering related patents on top of the original one or purchasing competing innovations to either absorb or suppress them. In this way, an innovating firm can consolidate and broaden its position, thus retaining market power long after the monopoly power secured by the initial innovation begins to dissipate. These same dynamics are applicable to oligopolies.

Monopoly pricing of products that embody an innovation lowers the rate at which the innovation diffuses *relative to the rate at which the innovation would have diffused* had it been priced competitively. In essence, regardless of whether demand is restricted by transitory learning problems or by lack of information, a monopolist firm *has an economic incentive to slow down the diffusion rate* of an innovation by keeping the price high to maximize profits. This reduction in the diffusion rate comes in addition to the impact of all other factors discussed in the literature and noted earlier. The quantitative effect of such monopoly pricing may vary for different innovations and under different legal and political environments, but the monopoly price always exceeds the competitive price, while the monopoly output is always smaller.

To evaluate the effect of monopoly pricing on the diffusion rate, I adapt the theoretical tools developed in chapter 4. I use these tools to explore a case study and quantify the effect of market power on the diffusion rate. This theoretical development is carried out in the following section. The main application is my extensive case study of the effect of General Electric's (GE) monopoly power on the diffusion of electric power.

The case of electric power is of great interest on its own, and much has been written about it. Electricity is a general-purpose technology (GPT), a major innovation that serves as a foundation for innovations in all sectors of the economy. Some writers (e.g., David, 1989, 1990a, 1990b) have compared the diffusion of electricity in the United States with the way in which information technology, the contemporary GPT, has evolved and affected the economy.

5.2 How to Measure the Effect of Market Power on the Diffusion of an Innovation

Following the model used in chapter 1, I consider an industry in which one or a few firms have market power. There may be one dominant monopolist whose power is derived from ownership of a technology and the product supplied by it or several dominant firms with market power arising from their ownership of proprietary technologies and products that may be partly substitutable. The market equilibrium is assumed to be a Nash equilibrium so that each firm takes the price of its competitors as given.

5.2.1   The Monopoly Problem

Because I focus on the optimal behavior of a monopoly firm, my notation suppresses all information about other firms. As in chapter 2, I assume the firm faces a demand function $D(P_t, Z_t)$ for its own product with price P and all other market conditions Z, where Z encompasses the behavior of other firms and consumer tastes. The firm has a constant returns to scale production function $Y_t = F_t(K_t, L_t)$, where K is capital, L is labor, and F_t indicates the presence of productivity-enhancing technical change. Capital and labor are traded in competitive markets at wage rate W and capital rental rate R, and the firm hires their services. Both factors are variable because the time scale of the analysis is one year, which is long enough for the firm to adjust them freely. The timing of economic events is simple: first, uncertainty with respect to technology and other stochastic variables is resolved; then firms hire their resources, and production takes place under known prices of inputs. In chapter 1, it is shown that firm optimization leads to equilibrium pricing P, defined by

$$P_t = \frac{\theta_t}{\theta_t - 1} \frac{W_t}{F_L} = \frac{\theta_t}{\theta_t - 1} \frac{R_t}{F_K}, \quad \theta_t = -\frac{P_t}{D} \frac{\partial D}{\partial P_t}, \theta_t > 1. \tag{5.1}$$

Because the production function is characterized by constant returns to scale and both factors are variable, the marginal cost does not vary with output level and is equal to the competitive price P_t^c. Therefore,

$$\frac{P_t}{P_t^c} = \frac{\theta_t}{\theta_t - 1} = \mathcal{P}_t. \tag{5.2}$$

$D_t(P_t^c, Z_t)$ is the output level that the firm would have produced and sold under competitive conditions. Therefore, had pricing been competitive, the output shortfall under monopoly, as a percentage of the potentially competitive output, is

$$\ell_t = \frac{D_t\left(P_t^c, Z_t\right) - D_t(P_t, Z_t)}{D_t\left(P_t^c, Z_t\right)}. \tag{5.3}$$

Equation (5.3) can be interpreted as the fraction of a year's worth of competitive-level output not produced at date t and delayed for later time because the monopoly price is too high. The ratio in (5.3) defines the delay in the rate of diffusion as a relative measure, analogous to the relative measure of Comin and Hobijn (2010) but defined in (5.3) in relation to the *potential* level of competitive output.

As an alternative to delay, one can also define the *speed* of diffusion relative to the potential level under competition as

$$sp_t^c = \frac{D_t(P_t, Z_t)}{D_t\left(P_t^c, Z_t\right)}, \text{ which is in } [0, 1]. \tag{5.4}$$

so that if the speed is 0.76, then the delay is measured as 0.26 years' worth of equivalent *competitive* output.

Returning to (5.1), the demand elasticity defines the markup $\theta_t/(\theta_t - 1)$ and profit margin of a monopolist. In the next section, demand elasticities are estimated empirically. Therefore, for the rest of this section, I assume that *the demand elasticity for the firm's product is known.*

As explained in chapter 1, to assess (5.3) quantitatively, one has two options. The first uses a log-linear approximation, while the second is to assume that it takes a well-recognized and commonly used form. It was proved in chapter 1 that for the case of a log-linear approximation, the speed and delay are simple and independent of θ_t:

$$\frac{D_t\left(P_t^c, Z_t\right) - D_t(P_t, Z_t)}{D_t\left(P_t^c, Z_t\right)} = 0.5. \tag{5.5}$$

Equation (5.5) implies that the speed of diffusion $D_t(P_t, Z_t)/D_t(P_t^c, Z_t) = 0.5$ of the potential competitive output.

For the special case of a demand function $D_t(P_t, Z_t) = G_t P_t^{-\theta_t} Z_t^{\psi}$, the delay in diffusion is

$$\ell_t = \frac{D_t\left(P_t^c, Z_t\right) - D_t(P_t, Z_t)}{D_t\left(P_t^c, Z_t\right)} = 1 - \left(\frac{\theta_t}{\theta_t - 1}\right)^{-\theta_t}. \tag{5.6}$$

5.2.2　Market Demand Versus Firm Demand

The typical case of market power that one encounters does not involve permanent monopoly power. Indeed, firms have fluctuating market power, with a market share that varies over time. To adapt (5.6) to a firm with fluctuating market power, one distinguishes between the market demand function and the firm's demand function. The reasoning behind (5.1)–(5.4) continues to be applicable to the firm, with a firm demand elasticity of θ_t and markup of $\mathcal{P}_t$, which may be different from the market demand elasticity. In the estimates made in the rest of this chapter, I will employ the widely used market demand function with constant demand elasticity χ_t defined by

$$D_t(P_t, Z_t) = H_t P_t^{-\chi_t} Z_t^{\psi}. \tag{5.7}$$

In this case, the delay in diffusion is then

$$\ell_t = \frac{H_t\left(P_t^c\right)^{-\chi_t} Z_t^\psi - H_t P_t^{-\chi_t} Z_t^\psi}{H_t\left(P_t^c\right)^{-\chi_t} Z_t^\psi} = 1 - \left(\frac{P_t}{P_t^c}\right)^{-\chi_t} \tag{5.8a}$$

and the speed of diffusion is

$$s_t^p = \frac{H_t P_t^{-\chi_t} Z_t^\psi}{H_t\left(P_t^c\right)^{-\chi_t} Z_t^\psi} = \left(\frac{P_t}{P_t^c}\right)^{-\chi_t}. \tag{5.8b}$$

If we estimate the markup P_t/P_t^c of the leading firm, this markup can be used to compute the industry's rates of diffusion in (5.8a) and (5.8b) because it is plausible to assume the leading firm sets the price and markup for the industry. Using the notation of θ_t and markup $\mathcal{P}_t$ deduced from the leading firm, the two measures become

$$\ell_t = 1 - \left(\frac{\theta_t}{\theta_t - 1}\right)^{-\chi_t}, \tag{5.9a}$$

and the speed of diffusion is

$$S_t^p = \left(\frac{\theta_t}{\theta_t - 1}\right)^{-\chi_t}. \tag{5.9b}$$

In applying these measures of diffusion to General Electric, the value of χ_t is about 2.3 and is a constant. Table 5.1 shows the implied delay and speed of diffusion for different firm markups.

TABLE 5.1 Delay and speed with $\chi = 2.3$

θ_t	Delay	Speed
100	0.023	0.977
40	0.057	0.943
30	0.075	0.925
20	0.111	0.889
10	0.215	0.785
5	0.401	0.599
3	0.606	0.394
2	0.797	0.203

5.3   The Slow Diffusion of Electricity from 1888 to 1929

5.3.1   A Brief History of Electricity Diffusion and the Question of Timing

The basic scientific principles of producing electricity were discovered by Faraday in 1832; however, during the nineteenth century, extensive scientific and engineering research was needed to achieve successful commercial application. This research culminated in several major inventions in the late 1800s. In 1879, Charles Brush, the American pioneer of exterior arc-lighting, installed the first arc-lighting system to replace gas street illumination. In 1882, Thomas Edison invented high-resistance incandescent lamps and subsequently launched the modern electric utility system by opening the direct current (DC) Pearl Street Station in New York. In 1887, Frank Sprague developed improved motors and brakes for streetcars, and in 1888 he constructed the first successful large electric street railway system in Richmond, Virginia. In 1886, George Westinghouse developed the first alternating current (AC) incandescent lighting system and promoted AC, while during the period of 1887–1888, Nikola Tesla invented the AC induction motor. This last stage was crucial because the transmission of direct current over distances longer than one mile is inefficient due to heavy energy losses and the need for thick electric wires. To enhance safety and limit energy loss, customers have to be very close to DC generating stations. In contrast, AC power can be transmitted long distances at high voltage through much smaller wires by means of transformers that reduce the voltage to the level needed by customers. Thus, AC generating stations are large, more efficient, and situated at more distant locations from consumers.

These important innovations in the final stage of electricity development are summarized here in order to reflect on the term "innovation diffusion," which presumes some level of clarity on the start and end dates of this process. The year 1832 is clearly not the start date of this account because much scientific and engineering development was needed to advance the technology to its level in that year. Some take 1882, when Edison's Pearl Street lighting station was inaugurated, as the start date of the commercial use of electricity, but this may be too early because without the development of the AC motor, widespread commercial use was not feasible. Ignoring such factors can lead to questionable choices of boundary points. For example, Comin and Hobijn (2010) take 1882 as the date of invention and, applying their method of assessing the delay in the process of "adopting" an invention, they conclude that electricity was "adopted" in the United States in 1901, which is thus the end date of the process in their view.

My empirical study begins with the formation of GE. However, regardless of where in the decade 1882–1892 one places the invention date of *commercial* electricity, the question is why (as table 5.2 shows) in 1910 only 15 percent of all

TABLE 5.2 The slow diffustion of electricity

Year	Percent of all dwellings with electric services	Percent of urban and rural nonfarm dwellings with electric service	Percent of manufacturing primary power capacity electrified	Electric utility real output (index 1929 = 100)
1899	—	—	4.4	2.00
1900	3.1	—	—	2.49
1904	—	—	10.2	4.40
1907	8.0	—	—	7.50
1909	—	—	22.6	9.70
1910	15.0	—	—	10.70
1912	15.9	—	—	13.0
1914	—	—	35.2	15.20
1915	—	—	—	16.60
1917	—	—	—	21.10
1919	24.3	—	—	24.50
1920	—	—	51.6	36.00
1921	34.7	47.4	—	39.30
1923	40.0	—	—	41.2
1925	53.2	69.4	68.3	63.50
1927	63.1	—	73.8	81.70
1929	67.9	84.2	77.4	100.00

Source: Columns 2–3: Historical Statistics of the US (1971), table S 109–111. Column 4: Du Boff (1979), table 15. Column 5: Kendrick (1961), table H–VI; data for 1900 and 1910 interpolated geometrically.

dwellings and only 23 percent of primary power capacity used in manufacturing had been electrified. This span of eighteen to twenty-eight years (relative to 1882–1892) was certainly long enough for customers to have learned about the new invention and for rational businesspeople to have recognized that electricity was the future of manufacturing. The period of eighteen to twenty-eight years was also long enough to have modified buildings, management techniques, and factory layouts so that electricity could be used by a larger proportion of potential users. This leads to my main question: Why was the growth rate of electricity use so low?

My question thus addresses *the rate* at which electricity diffused in the United States, which is distinct from the question of how long it took for electricity to be "adopted." Determining the end date of this process is not straighforward. The Comin and Hobijn (2010) estimate of 1901 as the "completion" date of electricity diffusion appears far too early from my point of view. Note that electricity is a GPT, a very broad invention with a wide range of applications. Important changes took place between 1882 and 1910, and these make selecting an end date of the diffusion process rather difficult. To clarify this point, I briefly review the stages of electricity diffusion.

In its early days, there were three key markets for electricity: illumination, public transportation, and manufacturing. Over time, electricity applications had an impact on all sectors of the economy. I thus confine my analysis to these three first-stage markets. In the cases of illumination and transportation, the existing technologies were far inferior to those made possible by electricity. Therefore, demand for electricity in these two markets had the lowest elasticity, and they saw the fastest conversion to electricity, even in the face of high prices. For lighting, in the early nineteenth century, dwellings were lit by candles, whale oil, and wood, with kerosene lamps later becoming more popular. Gas was commonly used for street illumination, and as safety concerns were alleviated, it became a central source of illumination in dwellings. In the market for public transportation within cities, the alternative technology was mostly horse wagons, although stationary steam engines that pull cables throughout the city was also feasible, as was the case in San Francisco and other cities.

On the other hand, the third market—manufacturing—had both large adjustment frictions and ample substitute technologies.[1] At the time, manufacturing used either steam or hydro engines to generate mechanical motion. Late in the nineteenth century, mechanical power was transmitted to the machines in manufacturing plants by a central mechanical link to a powering source that drove it. Typically, a single prime mover, such as a water wheel or steam engine, provided the power to turn, with pulleys, leather belts, and line shafts that transmitted motion to machines at work. Consequently, the conversion of a plant from steam or water to electricity required a change in both the *source of energy* used and the *organization of production* in the plant.

Compared to the electrification process of urban lighting and transportation, that of manufacturing was more complex because steam technology continued to improve and the organizational-managerial problems involved required time to be resolved. Therefore, the net gain from conversion to electricity varied across industries and depended more heavily upon the cost of conversion in comparison with the cost of steam power generation. Indeed, some U.S. manufacturers continued to use steam power even up to 1939. It is thus not surprising that in the early stages, diffusion of electricity in illumination and transportation was more rapid than in manufacturing. For obvious reasons, rural electrification was by far the slowest to grow and was a distinct beneficiary of the major public investments in power-generating capacity in the United States during the Great

---

[1] Devine (1983) details the mechanical problems that manufacturing faced in the conversion to electricity and the different stages at which manufacturing converted to the use of electricity as a result. This research is an excellent reference.

Depression years. The percentage of farms with electric service in 1929 was 9.2 percent, but it rose to 35 percent by 1941.

Under steam power, machines in factories were activated by a prime moving power source that turned a single direct drive or line shaft, often hanging from the ceiling, that extended the entire length of each floor of the factory. This line shaft turned, with pulleys and leather belts, the production machines that were lined up on the floor of the factory in rows parallel to the line shafts. Power was transmitted to the second floor of a large plant by belts running through openings in the ceiling. This entire system functioned continuously in tandem, regardless of the number of machines actually being used, and came to a grinding halt in case of a breakdown anywhere. Moving shafts and belts required continuous lubrication, and this resulted in grease-laden dust circulating everywhere, causing walls to become dirty. These were rarely cleaned. The system was also noisy and dusty, with poor ventilation and illumination. In view of these conditions, electrification of manufacturing occurred in three stages, using three designs. Each design began to be used at a distinct date, but there is some overlap in their periods of use.

In the first stage, beginning around 1883, Edison's DC electric motor was used as a replacement for the mechanism connecting the source of power and the main shaft. That is, in this stage, an *electric line shaft* simply replaced the mechanical drive, while the entire plant, with all the pulleys and belts, remained intact. Electricity was viewed only as a means of transmitting mechanical power to plants, with no change to the distribution of power within the plant. There were several advantages to electrification of this stage. Factories no longer had to be located right next to the energy source (i.e., a water or steam plant) because electricity could be produced from several sources at some distance from the factory, allowing access to cheaper energy. Early electric motors had, however, a capacity of just one horsepower, and despite the introduction by Edison General Electric Co. of the higher-capacity Sprague motor, the cost of such motors was high. Thus, the assessment at the time was that when a small amount of power was needed, the electric motor had the advantage over steam, but for larger power needs, steam was deemed cheaper (see Devine, 1983, p. 335, Bell, 1891). The main advantage of electricity was its ability to improve working conditions and ease control of production, and therefore early manufacturing firms that converted to electricity were in industries such as textile manufacturing and printing, in which steady power, speed, and ease of control were very important.

The second stage began around 1894, when the *group drive* was introduced and the narrow view of electricity gave way to the realization that electricity can alter the way that manufacturing was done. In this stage, machines were sorted into groups that tended to work together, where each group was operated like the prior system, with pulleys and belts, but now each group of machines was driven by a short line shaft turned by its own electric motor. This change raised operational efficiency; increased flexibility in arranging machines and workers on the floor; and reduced the risk of plant shutdown because, in the new design, the breakdown of a single machine did not shut down the entire plant. By then, motors could use AC, which came with greater efficiency and less fire risk. That electricity could alter the use of space in a plant and improve production management was clear to anyone; the real issue was, again, cost. The assignment of electric motors to each group meant that the plant had to buy more motors than before and that some motors would be idle while others were operating. This required heavier capital investments. On the other hand, the increased operational efficiency reduced energy loss and lowered variable costs, requiring an assessment of the net benefits of lower variable costs versus heavier capital investments. Many early users of this design located their plants near water sources of power to reduce costs, and in the case of DC transmission, this proximity to the power source cut back on power loss.

The third stage began around 1904, when manufacturing began to convert to electric unit drives, with each machine assigned an electric motor of its own, eliminating line shaft drives and the entire system of leather belts and pulleys. This resulted in a complete overhaul of production methods, design of space, energy use, and working conditions, with rising efficiency and drastic reductions in operating cost. But, again, it required heavier capital investments in a much larger number of electric motors, with the knowledge that machines would be operating on their own and that there would be times when many machines would be idle while others were fully employed. The unit drive technology was the basic manufacturing method used for the rest of the twentieth century. By 1910, the infrastructure needed for this technology was available, management techniques were adjusting to the new plant environment, and no political or legal limitations prevented firms from using this innovation. Nevertheless, as table 5.2 shows, only 23 percent of manufacturing primary power capacity was electrified.

Returning to the question of determining the end date of the diffusion process or the "adoption" date of electricity, I focus on the three markets discussed above and the stages of their development. Within GE, there were always some engineers and thinkers with deeper insight who anticipated areas where GE would expand. They developed applications in other markets such as the X-ray machine (1896), radio (1906), electric toaster (1909), and vacuum tube (1912), but GE's first president, Charles A. Coffin, did not see such applications as central to GE's business. Coffin was president of the Thomson-Houston Electric Company, founded in 1883 to market arc-lighting systems, which merged with Edison General Electric to form GE in 1892. Coffin then became the president of the merged firm, where he stayed until he shifted into the role of chair of the board from 1913 to 1922. Coffin was a hard-driven product of GE's formation and aimed for GE to attain supremacy in the production of electrical equipment for the three markets with the strongest demand at the turn of the century: illumination, public transportation, and manufacturing. However, after thirty years at the helm, Coffin retired in 1922 and was replaced by Owen Young as chair of the board and Gerard Swope as GE's president. This was a turning point in GE's history on several important levels that I discuss now and note again later.

Swope, a Massachusetts Institute of Technology (MIT) engineer, understood that opportunities for future market power lay in other industries. As table 5.2 shows, by 1925, 69.4 percent of all U.S. nonfarm dwellings and 68.3 percent of all manufacturing capacity were electrified, and by 1929, these numbers had grown to 84.2 percent and 77.4 percent, respectively. Swope was a firm believer that GE's destiny was to be the leader in applications of electricity in all parts of the economy. He described GE's dedication to "the benign circle of electric power," whereby turbines and appliances would contribute to each other's growth, and his aim was to put the GE's monogram in every home in America (see Fleck, 2009, p. 29). In the decade following World War I, GE was able to reinvent itself and become an advanced technology firm rather than just a manufacturer of electric equipment for the three markets it had dominated. Its plants accelerated production of home appliances, X-ray machines, and a rising number of advanced electric products that were either invented at GE or whose patents were purchased from the products' inventors. This required a complete reorganization of GE's production plants, with a reduction in their number, an increase of their size, and a boost to the technical skills of GE's employees. This policy turned GE into a twentieth-century technology giant that offered diverse products performing one task: electricity activating a mechanical device or a voice or moving a picture. "Diffusion of electricity" is too broad a term to describe the process that the company underwent because markets for electric appliances like radio and refrigerators are entirely different from markets for turbines and streetcars, and the diffusion of electricity in those markets is a different process with little in common with the one discussed in this chapter.

This is why I focus only on the diffusion of electricity in illumination, public transportation, and manufacturing. The end date of this process is sometime in the 1920s, when the diffusion of electricity in these three market segments was complete. The year 1922 is significant as the one when Swope took over, but it took Swope several more years to transform GE, and therefore the date may be moved up to 1929.

5.3.2 The Regime Transformation Explanation of the Slow Diffusion of Electricity

The most detailed explanation given for the slow diffusion of electricity has been the regime transformation hypothesis. It was proposed by Freeman and Perez

(1986); developed by David (1989, 1990a,b), Bresnahan and Trajtenberg (1995), and Helpman and Trajtenberg (1994); and refined by David (2000) and David and Wright (1999, 2004). This explanation focuses on GPTs that foster the creation of complementary technologies that emerge from the primary GPT and could not occur without it. Hence, the effect of a GPT cascades through the entire economy and over time changes the way we live. The central argument is then that regime transformations take a great deal of time to ripple through the economy because all of society and its institutions must change and adapt to them. Electricity is a major innovation, classified as a GPT, that changed the entire twentieth century; therefore, this argument insists, it became available only in the 1920s for general applications.

A detailed application of the theory of GPTs to electricity diffusion is carried out by David (1989, 1990a,b) and David and Wright (1999, 2004), but this research actually addresses two distinct problems. One is the problem of explaining the slow diffusion of electricity. The second, which is not of central concern here, is the association between electricity diffusion and productivity growth. The first problem is addressed by invoking the general reasoning of the theory of GPTs and adding the specific details noted earlier, namely, that (1) it takes a long time to build the infrastructure needed for the production and transmission of electricity, (2) managerial education and adaptation to new technologies requires time, and (3) institutions and legal structures change slowly.

This general reasoning leads David (1989) to compare the slow diffusions of the computer and the dynamo. It is claimed that the slow adaptation to the computer is analogous to the slow adaptation to electricity and that the productivity slowdown during the 1970s–1980s is analogous to the productivity slowdown—or at least the pause in productivity growth—in 1890–1910. David recalls Robert Solow's (1987) quip that "you can see the computer age everywhere but in the productivity statistics" and proposes that in the period 1890–1910, one could have said "we can see the dynamos everywhere but in the economic statistics" (36). Is the regime transformation argument a compelling explanation, then, of the slow diffusion of electricity?

There is no doubt that major innovations take a long time to have a full impact on society, and electricity exemplifies this fact. Its production method was invented in 1832, but it took half a century for electricity to be ready for commercial application and another seventy years to transform our homes with lights, radios, vacuum cleaners, refrigerators, washing machines, and televisions, and transform the public space with city lights and movies. It then took another forty years to transform the economy: from air conditioning, which changed the Southwest, to stadium lighting, which altered the way sport activities are enjoyed. In short, electricity changed everything in the twentieth century. However, this long view ignores the fact that from the 1890s, the use of electricity grew at very distinct stages. Each stage required its own innovations and its own products and took place in different sectors of the economy. The later stages led to developments that were far afield from the initial stage of electricity, as a technology that illuminated streets and homes, revolutionized city transportation, and replaced steam in manufacturing. Each stage had its own technological, institutional, and legal problems to solve, and the diffusion processes of the particular innovations rather than that of the entire GPT should be studied on their own.

Thus, I seek an explanation for the specific question of the slow diffusion of electricity in illumination, public transportation, and manufacturing. Taking this narrow view, I suggest that, when the unit drive was introduced in 1904, the infrastructure for the use of electricity was in place and there were no legal or political forces that opposed its use. Most of the reasons for slow diffusion offered by David (1989) were no longer operative, and the GPT perspective does not help us understand the slow diffusion of electricity in these three specific markets.

To understand why in the period 1890–1910 most firms decided that the time had not arrived for them to convert to the new electric technology, one must recognize that it was not profitable for them to do so. Put differently, electricity was too expensive. Figure 5.1 shows that the output of electricity rose over time as the price declined. Indeed, it shows that the price had to decline substantially before rapid output expansion would take place. The figure also reveals that—as will be discussed in detail later—the use of electricity accelerated even before the decade of the 1920s, which is often characterized as the turning point. The growth rate of electric output took a sharp turn upward as early as 1915–1916. These facts naturally raise the following question: Why was the price so high early on? Standard competitive reasoning would argue the price was so high because of high cost that resulted from the fact that electric technology had not developed enough to compete with steam and that, although the efficiency of electricity generation was increasing, it was slower than the rate at which the efficiency of steam power was improving.

Many studies conducted around the turn of the century compared the cost and efficiency of electricity with those of steam power (see, e.g., Devine, 1983, pp. 354–355; Bell, 1891). As noted, their main conclusion was that relative to steam, electricity was too expensive to provide the large-scale power needed to operate the large plants. The main drawback of these studies, and the reason I do not explore them here, is that *they always take the prices of electricity and of equipment to produce electricity as given instead of exploring if those prices reflected manufacturers' production cost*. Because I seek to explore the impact of monopoly pricing, I must take an alternate approach to the problem, which is my next task.

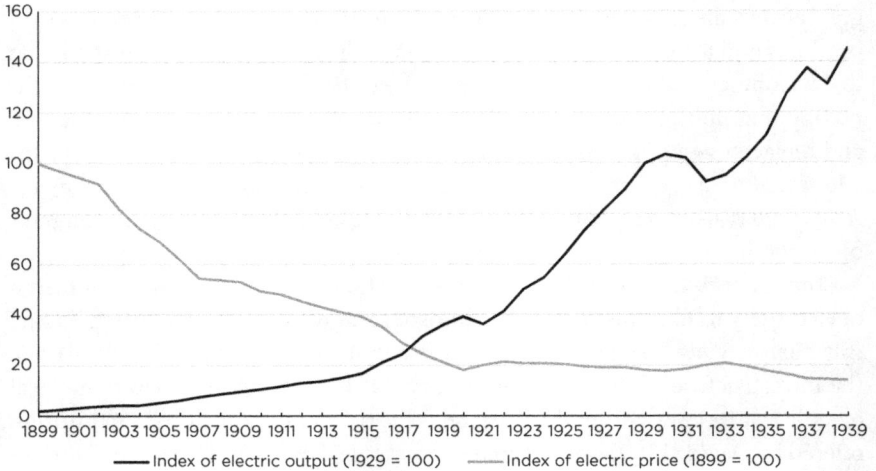

Figure 5.1   Price index of electricity (1899 = 100) and index of electric output (1929 = 100)

Sources: Output: Kendrick (1961), Table H–VI; data for 1900 and 1910 interpolated geometrically.
Price index: Bureau of the Census (1989), Table S 116. Index created by using CPI in David and Solar
(1977). Missing years interpolated.
Data provided in the online data appendix.

5.3.3   The First Gilded Age and the Rise of the Electricity Monopoly

During the 1870s, as the age of electricity was approaching, several companies were incorporated with the aim of developing their market share. In 1876,
Thomas Edison started his laboratory in Menlo Park, New Jersey, and subsequently formed several companies to market his innovations. His first lighting station on Pearl Street in New York supplied DC electricity to fifty-nine
dwellings. In 1890, he consolidated them into the Edison General Electric Company. It soon purchased the Sprague Electric Railway & Motor Company, which
owned all the major innovations related to electric streetcars. Amid bitter competition about whether to use AC or DC to distribute electric power, many entrepreneurs were entering the markets for both manufacturing lamps and electrical equipment, while others were starting municipal lighting companies in all
major cities.

J. P. Morgan was among Edison's early financial supporters. His experience
in consolidating the railroads to increase their market power led him to seek
a consolidation of the nascent electricity industry. In 1892, using his financial
muscle, he formed General Electric by merging two main fierce competitors, the
Edison General Electric Company and the Thomson-Houston Company. Over

the years, GE acquired many electric utilities and small producers of electrical supplies and equipment, and bought out innovators who aimed to compete with the firm. These acquisitions complemented the vast holdings that GE inherited from the merger, consisting of stocks and bonds of a large number of electric utilities, electric rail companies, and small electrical manufacturers. GE's investments in the electric utility industry were a major source of economic power because many of the companies partially owned by GE were also its customers.

GE's large financial holdings in the electricity industry took some years to sort out. The initial loans taken to create GE were based on the expectation of selling securities to pay down the debt. This was a serious error because the prices of these securities plummeted in the 1893–1895 depression, making the financial reports of GE for 1892 and 1893 very complex and not really representative of a manufacturing firm. For this reason, my study of GE begins in 1894.

The management team of the combined company came entirely from the Thomson-Houston Company, led by Charles A. Coffin, a shrewd and disciplined manager, credited as the founder of GE. The merger made GE the sole owner of all key patents and vital DC technologies of the new electric industry, but not the AC technology because the merger did not include Westinghouse, which controlled the AC technology by virtue of a patent agreement with Tesla. GE and Westinghouse had been engaged in the "war of the current" for some time, and although this war ended in late 1893 with the full victory of the AC current at the Chicago World's Fair, the two companies continued to engage in fierce battles, including endless patent infringement lawsuits.

In 1896, the two companies reached a full patent-sharing agreement that in effect gave the two firms a monopoly power over all U.S. electricity generation and transmission equipment. This was the birth of a new Gilded Age monopoly that fixed prices and market shares. GE was the senior partner, largely thanks to Coffin's superior managerial skills in comparison with those of George Westinghouse, but it was the two firms acting in concert that gave them such pricing power. Both Edison and Tesla turned to other ventures, and during the 1890s, a new crop of innovators became the leaders of the new AC technology at GE. In 1900, GE opened its General Electric Research Laboratory, the first industrial research facility in the United States. Its most noted contribution at the time was the 1909 invention of the tungsten filament light bulb. The laboratory was a source of many patents on electric products that consolidated GE's technological monopoly position. To control the pricing of light bulbs, GE created the National Electric Lamp Association, which was essentially a cartel consisting of most of the small producers of electric bulbs but who did not have access to the advanced technology owned by the GE-Westinghouse combination. This cartel completed the full monopoly power of GE and Westinghouse over the market for electrical supplies and equipment. This monopoly power reached its zenith in the first decade of the twentieth century (see further discussion in section 5.6) and then fluctuated over time as the reform movement slowly moved to curb businesses' market power after 1901. Given the origins of this monopoly power, my next central question is: What was the effect of this monopoly power on the diffusion rate of electricity in illumination, transportation, and manufacturing?

5.4   The Effect of General Electric's Monopoly Power on Electricity Diffusion

The setting for my measurement is the same as that in section 1.4.2 and equation (1.4) in chapter 1, with unknown parameter α_t, which may change and needs to be estimated. Under the same assumptions made in chapter 1, optimal pricing leads to the following conditions:

$$\text{Labor income} \quad W_t L_t = \frac{\theta_t - 1}{\theta_t}(1 - \alpha_t)P_t Y_t \qquad (5.10a)$$

$$\text{Capital income} \quad R_t K_t = \frac{\theta_t - 1}{\theta_t}\alpha_t P_t Y_t \qquad (5.10b)$$

$$\text{Monopoly profits } P_t Y_t - W_t L_t - R_t K_t = \frac{1}{\theta_t}P_t Y_t. \qquad (5.10c)$$

The time variability of θ_t reflects the changing market power of the firm.

The methodology that I use here follows the methods developed in chapter 4, where market power is deduced from relative shares. I use the observed factor payments, based on wage and capital rental data from GE's financial reports, to construct these relative shares. All information about the data used to estimate the GE relative shares is available in the detailed online data appendix, where I provide the actual data that I constructed for GE for the period 1894–1939.

5.4.1   GE's Monopoly Power: Historical Narrative

I start by examining GE's income distribution with a view to comparing it with the aggregate distribution in the private sector that I explored in chapter 4. Figure 5.2 presents the relative share of labor at GE from 1894 to 1939.

The sharp decline in GE's labor share during the First Gilded Age mirrors the result for the entire private sector. In figure 5.2, the low point is reached in 1901, *exactly the same year that the low point is reached in figure 4.3 of chapter 4 for the private sector as a whole.* Deduced from an entirely different data source, the current result leads to the same conclusion about the impact of the

Figure 5.2 GE's labor share, 1894–1934

reform movement of the time. The rise of labor share at GE after 1901 is more pronounced than that for the private sector as a whole, as seen in chapter 4, because GE's wages rose faster than the mean U.S. manufacturing wage in that period (see the online data appendix). Similar to the volatility in figure 4.3, GE's labor share fluctuated due to the Panic of 1907, the recession of 1910, and World War I. It peaked in the early 1930s and declined during the Great Depression.

Turning to the relative share of capital, figure 5.3 shows that the share of capital steadily *declined* throughout this period, although this trend is obscured somewhat by the effect of the Panic of 1907, when GE's sales plummeted, and by the effect of World War I. This decline contrasts with the relatively *slow rise* of the share of capital in the entire private sector during the same period, as seen in figure 4.4. A *rising* labor share and a *declining* capital share, together with conditions (5.10a) and (5.10b), imply that the ratio

$$\frac{W_t L_t}{R_t K_t} = \frac{1 - \alpha_t}{\alpha_t}$$

rose during the period. As a consequence, α_t-GE's elasticity of output with re-spect to capital-exhibited a declining *trend* from 1894 to 1939, in contrast to the *relative constancy* of the ratio $(W_t L_t)/(R_t K_t)$ for the private sector in the same time frame in figure 4.11. This suggests that conditions at GE were different from those in the private sector as a whole, and I return to this interesting question in section 5.5.

The pattern of GE's share of profits in figure 5.4 is different from that of the aggregate private sector in figure 4.9. As explained earlier, GE was not profitable in its first years of operation, but its monopoly power and profits rose rapidly

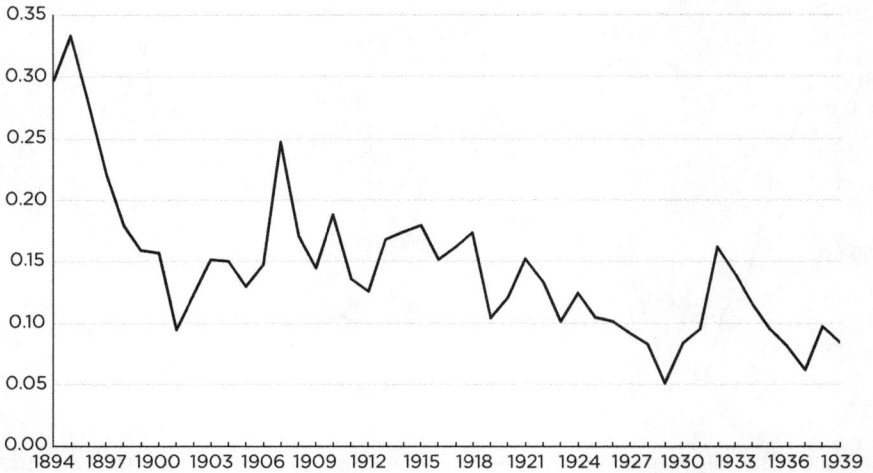

Figure 5.3 GE's capital share, 1894–1934

after 1896, when it reached its patent-sharing agreement with Westinghouse. While the mean market power in the private economy clearly declined from 1907 to 1929, as seen in figure 4.9, this was not the case for GE.

After the consolidation of monopoly power in the electricity industry in 1896, the relative share of profits in GE's income rose sharply, to the extraordinary level of 42 percent, in 1901. In the long run, the relative share of monopoly profits is driven by the forces of technology and policy, but in the short run,

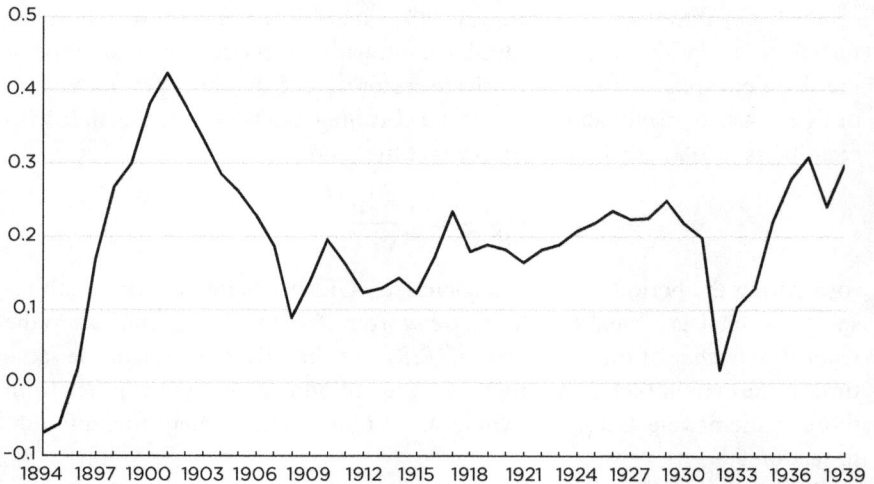

Figure 5.4 GE's profit share, 1894–1934

demand shocks alter estimated market power as well. Macroeconomic demand shocks can lower profits and investments, temporarily reducing monopoly power and the diffusion rate. Such shocks can sometimes obscure the long-run evolution of market power, but the time pattern of GE's market power, exhibited in figure 5.4, is relatively clear. As I argue in chapter 4, the cause of the decline in market power immediately after 1901 is the change in policy, but the decline in GE's monopoly power after 1901 was exacerbated by the 1907 panic and ensuing 1908 recession, which had a devastating effect on GE's revenue. In contrast with the private sector as a whole, where market power continued to fall from 1907 to 1928, GE's monopoly position recovered and strengthened during this period, as seen in figure 5.4. I return to the discussion of the factors that contributed to this time pattern shortly.

The onset of the Great Depression in 1930–1932 lowered GE's market power dramatically, but even after this initial decline, its share of profits recovered and reached 30 percent in 1939. It is, however, important to note that what matters for the rate of diffusion is the *average level* of market power, and the decisive fact is that GE's market power remained elevated throughout the whole thirty-four-year period from 1896 to 1929.

In section 5.3, I explained that the firm's rising market power after 1922 was qualitatively different from its earlier monopoly power. GE's mix of markets and products was moving away from the basic three markets (illumination, public transportation, and manufacturing) in which it had operated in the earlier phases. My focus here is mostly on the earlier phases, although GE's market power very likely had a similar effect on the diffusion of radio, television, and jet engines. Although AC was invented in 1888, it took time for Tesla and Westinghouse to start marketing AC products, and the depression of 1893–1895 sharply slowed down the diffusion process. Therefore, most of my research on the slow diffusion centers on the twenty-seven years from 1896 to about 1922 or the thirty-four years from 1896 to 1929, questioning why the use of electricity expanded so slowly during those years. I find that the diffusion of electricity was slow because, during those years, markets were subject either to powerful monopoly power that made electricity and electric products much too expensive or to major recessions that reduced the desire to invest in the new technology. This is indeed the main findings of this chapter.

Several factors contributed to the fact that the GE-Westinghouse monopoly power after 1901 did not recover its earlier level. Some patents they owned were expiring, and this opened the door to some competition, although GE was successful in innovating some alternative technologies and new products. Consequently, changes in the policy environment and demand shocks are more decisive in explaining the time series of GE's market power. I start with economic policy. The ascension of Theodore Roosevelt, in September 1901, ushered in the trust-busting Progressive movement that ushered in an active antitrust policy

and placed new limitations on corporate mergers. In addition, the policy introduced public regulations on various sectors ranging from food, by the new Food
and Drug Administration, to railroads, by the newly established Department of
Commerce. Labor union membership expanded as state and federal efforts to
crush strikes became less frequent, and collective bargaining rights gained some
protection in legislation like the Clayton Act of 1914.

Of particular importance to GE was the end of the unregulated monopoly
power of municipal electric utilities, that purchased their equipment from GE.
Municipalities' practice of granting electric utilities franchises to generate and
distribute electricity was corrupt and inefficient. This regime began to change in
1907, when New York and Wisconsin created state commissions to regulate the
capacity and prices of electric utilities. From 1907 to 1914, twenty-seven states
enacted public utility laws, and all states later followed suit. Regulations initiated
public pressure to lower the price of electricity, making it difficult for utilities to
justify accepting GE's high prices of electric equipment and supplies. Indeed,
pressure began to build to lower the high prices charged for equipment that the
utilities were purchasing from GE.

The general economic background also presented challenges to GE's
monopoly power. The Panic of 1907, in which the stock market lost 50 percent of its value, and the ensuing steep recession of 1907–1908 had a significant
financial impact. GE's revenue declined by 35 percent in 1908 alone. The period
of slow U.S. growth from 1907 to 1915, when the GNP growth rate was below
2 percent, was an era of productivity "pause" discussed by David (1989) and
David and Wright (1999, 2004). The 1907 panic was a sharp financial crisis that
resulted in major damage to the banking system, and it is well understood (e.g.,
Reinhart and Rogoff, 2009) that financial crises cause lasting damage that takes
a long time to repair.

The period of slow growth could have lasted longer in the absence of the economic boost provided by exports to the European powers embroiled in World
War I, which is one possible explanation for 1916 being the year when the
slow growth came to an end. This development also explains the timing of the
resurgence of growth and the diffusion of electricity. Most discussion of this
era appears to point to the 1920s as the time when rapid aggregate growth resumed, bolstered by rapid diffusion of electricity (i.e., see David, 1989; David
and Wright, 1999, 2004). However, this is not the conclusion that one draws
from GE's data. GE's sales rose in real terms by 36 percent from 1915 to 1917
and by 21 percent in 1916 alone. The growth continued at 10.1 percent in 1918,
6.1 percent in 1919, and 19.9 percent in 1920. The war was an important trigger
for the resumption of growth and the acceleration of the diffusion of electricity.

To combat the force of technological obsolescence, GE's research lab made
great efforts to find substitute technologies. Sometimes it succeeded, as was the

case with Edison's incandescent lamp. In 1909, GE engineers developed the brighter, longer-lived modern tungsten filament light bulb, which came to market in 1911. As GE's product line expanded to include home appliances and advanced instruments, smaller firms were more often successful in competing in such narrow market segments. However, the data also show that GE was able to find a response to this competition, and after 1914, its market power recovered and continued to rise up to 1939.

5.4.2   Measuring the Effect of Monopoly Power on the Rate of Electricity Diffusion

Given the estimated share of profits, I compute the elasticity θ_t and markup $\mathcal{P}_t$ from (5.10c); proceed to estimate for each year the measures of electricity diffusion, namely, delay in (5.9a) and speed in (5.9b); and then compute the means over the intervals from 1896 to 1922 and from 1896 to 1929. These are chosen because GE did not function as a monopoly before 1896 and because the date at which the diffusion of electricity for illumination, transportation, and manufacturing came to an end is estimated, as explained above, to be between 1922 and 1929.

To carry out this program, I need an estimate of the demand elasticity of the market for electricity generation equipment and electrical supplies. To obtain this, I return to figure 5.4, which reports the value of $1/\theta_t$ for GE. GE, Westinghouse, and the National Electric Lamp Association, acting at the time like a single, uncontested monopoly, together reached their zenith in terms of market power around 1901, when GE's share of profits reached the peak of 42 percent, and an average of 38 percent for 1900–1902, implying $\theta_t = 2.63$. With GE being a full monopolist, this estimate can then be taken as an the estimate of the elasticity of the market demand for electric supplies and equipment. This suggests that χ_t, the market demand elasticity, was close to 2.63. It is well known that the elasticity of demand for electricity was larger than 1 late in the nineteenth century and declined as the use of electricity expanded around the world (see Fouquet, 2014; Fouquet and Pearson, 2012). However, this does not mean that the demand elasticity for electric supplies and electricity generation equipment necessarily declined during the relatively short period at hand. Given the uncertainty about this demand elasticity, I assume it is a constant but compute the results for the three values of $\chi = 3.0, 2.63, 2$, covering the entire interval between 2 and 3.

The assumption that χ_t is constant implies that all fluctuations in the estimated markup P_t/P_t^c are due to fluctuations in the effective market power. This conclusion enables me to use (5.8a) to estimate the delay in diffusion and (5.8b) to estimate the speed of diffusion.

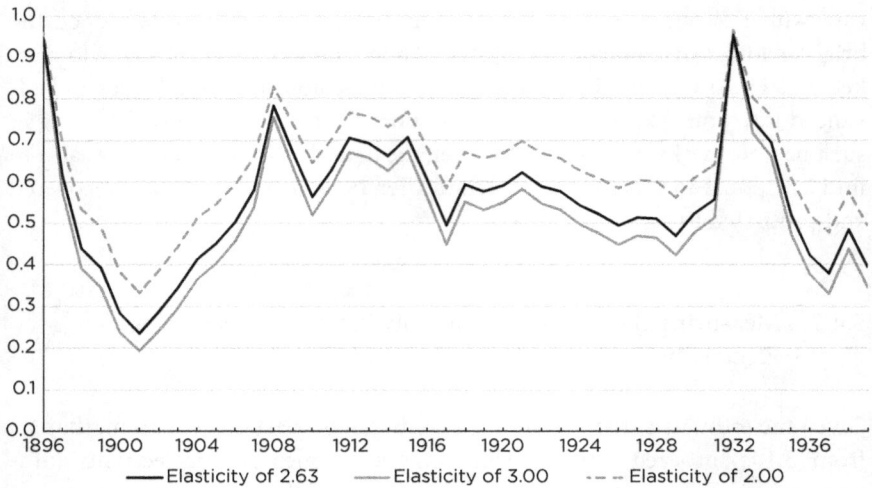

Figure 5.5 Speed of electricity diffusion

In figure 5.5, I report the computed speed of electricity diffusion for the three values. I stress that the term "speed" is used here relative to the estimated GE markup. As explained earlier, such a measure is affected by short-term macroeconomic shocks. This means that the speed of diffusion depends on variations in true monopoly power but also upon short-term demand shocks. Taking averages over the periods at hand is useful for minimizing the effects of these short-term factors.

Figure 5.5 shows that only a small error is caused by wrong selection of the reference elasticity, and the qualitative results are the same for all values around $\chi = 2.63$. The slowest speed was realized during the period 1897–1907, when GE's market power was at its peak. After 1901 and leading to World War I, GE's monopoly power declined and the speed of diffusion increased. This was reversed after the war when GE's market power rose and the speed of diffusion declined, continuing into the late 1920s. This is paradoxical because table 5.1 shows that U.S. electrification sped up after the war and was complete by 1929. This expansion was propelled by the lower price of electricity, but the marginal cost declined as well. Consequently, it remains true that, although electrification was expedited after the war, the rate of diffusion was low relative to what was possible without the restraining market power of the leading electric companies.

Expressing the results in terms of delay, the top panel of table 5.3 presents the mean delay as a fraction of the feasible *competitive* output. It shows that for an elasticity of about 3, the mean delay is about 0.5, which is the same as the results obtained by means of a log-linear approximation.

TABLE 5.3 Mean delay of electricity diffusion

Measure of diffusion	Reference elasticity = 2.0	Reference elasticity = 2.63	Reference elasticity = 3.0
Mean delay at competitive output			
1896–1922	0.366	0.445	0.486
1923–1929	0.394	0.482	0.527
Mean delay at monopoly output			
1896–1922	0.677	1.002	1.230
1923–1929	0.653	0.937	1.126

One can express the delay as a fraction of monopoly output by defining this delay as

$$\ell_t^{MON} = \frac{D_t\left(P_t^c, Z_t\right) - D_t\left(P_t^c, Z_t\right)}{D_t(P_t, Z_t)} = \left(\frac{\theta_t - 1}{\theta_t}\right)^{-\chi_t} - 1.$$

The mean delay in units of monopoly output is presented in the lower panel of table 5.3. It is interpreted as the output level lost due to monopoly power, measured in terms of the annual monopoly output level. Note again the conclusion that, although this measure of mean delay is more sensitive to the market elasticity, the average delay over the three reference elasticities in the bottom panel is 0.94, which is again close to the result that one obtains from the log-linear approximation.

Table 5.3 also shows that the mean delays are essentially the same for the two time spans. I have noted that the rising monopoly power in the 1920s did not occur in the context of the same market mix as that in previous periods because GE was changing as a result of its expanded sale of electric tools and appliances. It is rather surprising then that the two measures of diffusion are the same for the two time spans, ending in 1922 or in 1929.

The main conclusion of this chapter, seen in table 5.3, is that, during both 1896–1922 and 1896–1929, the mean annual delay in diffusion of electricity for illumination, transportation, and manufacturing was about 0.45 years' worth of potential competitive output or one year's worth of equivalent monopoly output and that, on average, the diffusion of electricity progressed at an annual speed of about 55 percent of the potential reference competitive output. These conclusions are deduced from the assumption of a constant elasticity demand function. If one postulates a general demand function and uses a log-linear approxima- tion, the conclusion is that the mean delay was one year's worth of monopoly

TABLE 5.4 Effect of market power on electricity diffusion

Actual diffusion under monopoly	Years needed under competitive pricing	Added years of diffusion
1896–1922: 27 years, speed 0.555	14.85	12.15
1896–1929: 34 years, speed 0.547	18.60	15.40

output and that the speed was equal to 0.50, numbers that are close to those reported in table 5.3.

I now translate the results in table 5.3 into estimates of the added number of years that it took for the diffusion of electricity in the United States to be completed, with this diffusion to apply to illumination, transportation, and manufacturing only. Recall that the method of Comin and Hobijn (2010) sets 1882 as the invention date of electricity and concludes that electricity was adopted by the United States in 1901. In contrast, my measures can be applied to any time interval; the relevant intervals for the effect of monopoly power are the twenty-seven years from 1896 to 1922 or the thirty-four years from 1896 to 1922. The question is then, how many of these twenty-seven or thirty-four years that it took electricity to diffuse in the United States are attributable to GE's monopoly power? That is, how many fewer years would it have taken for the electrification of the United States to be completed under the reference competitive pricing in the absence of monopoly power? Table 5.4 provides the answer: had production been set at the competitive level, the twenty-seven years would have been shortened to 14.85 years, and the thirty-four years would have been shortened to 18.60 years. Monopoly pricing and output levels thus added 12.15 years out of the twenty-seven year and 15.40 years out of the thirty-four year diffusion process.

5.4.3   A Qualification

The existence of technological monopoly arises from the desire of society to reward innovators for their efforts. Therefore, society protects innovators' intellectual property rights by granting them, for a period, monopoly power over the products of their innovations. Thus, it is argued, the absence of monopoly power would result in lower rates of innovation. Such effect could lead the counterfactual competitive world to be less desirable than I have assumed in the estimates above if the harm from a slower rate of innovation outweighs the benefit from faster diffusion of those innovations. The implication is that one must first specify an optimal level of monopoly power to be awarded to innovators and then measure the rate of diffusion of electricity relative to that optimal level. This is clearly a valid argument, and I address the question of the best policy in chapter 9.

Here I note two points, on which I further elaborate in chapter 9. First, it is not true that, to maintain a high level of innovation, one must adopt a policy that permits the formation of a fully developed monopoly power, much less a policy that allows that power to consolidate and endure for an entire century. Second, my aim has been to show the order of magnitude of the damage caused by monopoly power and the profound paradox that it entails. Public policy grants an innovator a monopoly over a new product and allows his or her firm to charge as high a price as is profit maximizing for the firm to charge. However, the more society needs the new product, the longer it will have to wait to benefit from it because the optimal strategy for the monopolist is to place an exorbitant price on the highly demanded product. Such a high price renders inaccessible the exact product from which policy aims for us to benefit. In the case of vital medicines, this delay often becomes a question of life or death, and in the aggregate case of all products, it is the cause of income inequality and of many other socially harmful consequences.

The analysis presented here offers a quantitative measure of a factor often used to explain the very rapid growth rates of the Asian Tigers in the 1990s and China since the 1990s. In many important cases, proprietary advanced Western technologies were either copied and adopted or reverse-engineered in ways that would have been contested as infringements of intellectual property rights in the West. That is, these economies were able to extract and rapidly adopt advanced Western technologies at no cost. The evidence presented in this chapter shows that if advanced technologies were to become freely available for adoption by any firm, the rate of diffusion of these technologies would be much faster, about twice as fast, as the diffusion rates in the West. In addition, competition lowers the prices of goods produced with those technologies, enabling the process to accelerate the aggregate economic growth rate.

5.5   Estimating α: The Changing Direction of GE

In the historical narrative provided in section 5.4.1, I noted that α_t exhibited a declining trend from 1894 to 1929 and that this is an interesting case of a changing production structure. Figure 5.6 presents the estimated value of α_t deduced from the equilibrium conditions (5.10a) and (5.10b). The estimates confirm the historical narrative that highlighted the transformation of GE from a nineteenth-century manufacturer of industrial equipment to one of the leading

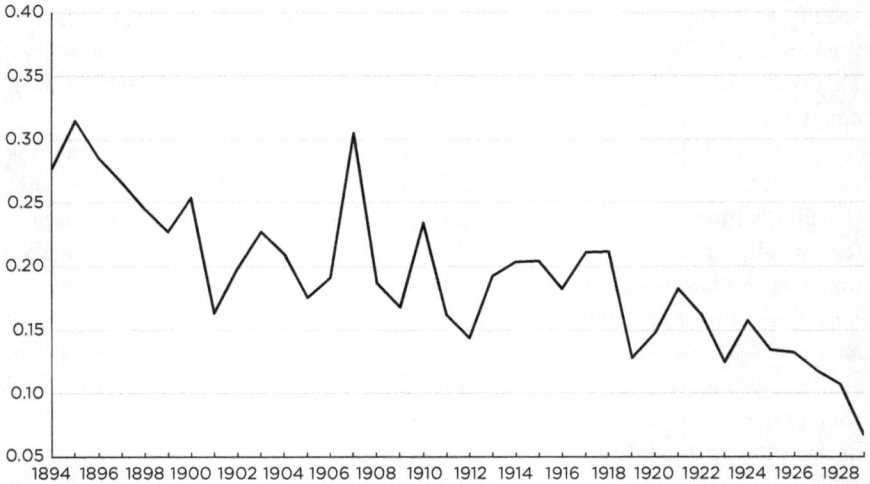

Figure 5.6　GE's elasticity of output with respect to capital, 1894–1929

high-tech companies of the twentieth century. Figure 5.6 suggests that the GE of 1894 and the GE of 1929 were different companies: The elasticity of output with respect to labor was higher in 1929 than in 1894, and the role of the labor input was rising within the company, particularly after World War I. Equations (5.10a) and (5.10b) explain that *an increase in the α parameter is the result of labor income rising faster than capital income*. To explain this, one needs to go back to the history of GE.

Two factors were at work after the start of World War I. First, after slow growth up to 1915, GE's sales took off, partly due to military demand but mostly due to increasing demand for electricity. As I have already noted, sales rose in real terms by 36 percent from 1915 to 1917. Second, Swope's transition to the GE presidency in 1922 marked the end of the first stage of GE's growth. After the war, and mostly under Swope's leadership, GE shifted to implement a progressive relationship with its employees, in whom it saw its future. In 1916, GE's board awarded employees with at least five years of service a bonus of 5 percent. Beyond the 1912 pension plan, GE adopted several programs to benefit employees at different times after 1920:

- A stock purchase plan offering stock to workers at a discount.
- Home purchase or homebuilding assistance, in which GE guaranteed a second mortgage.
- Life insurance financed by GE with an option for added insurance paid by employees.

- An apprentice program during the Great Depression to train young future employees and support their technical education. In addition, the company recruited qualified young future employees, who received support for advanced education and then returned to work for GE.

Above all, mean U.S. wages rose rapidly in the 1920s, but GE wages rose faster. I have noted earlier that according to GE's annual reports, GE's mean wage in 1919 was equal to the mean U.S. manufacturing wage. In 1923, it was 8.9 percent higher, and the gap had grown to 19.3 percent by 1927, to 31.0 percent by 1935 and to 40.4 percent by 1939, showing that GE *continued to raise its workers' skill level and wages during the Great Depression.* According to Swope's biographer, Swope viewed workers as partners in a great mission (see Loth, 1958, chap. 9), and he placed his concern for workers ahead of that for stockholders (see Fleck, 2009, p. 23). He is described as mingling with workers and treating unions with respect, viewing them as a fact of business life (see Loth, 1958, p. 169). GE employees became the envy of U.S. manufacturing workers for their working conditions and for the opportunities that GE offered them, and the employees were equally known for their loyalty and dedication to the company.

While labor input at GE was rising with sales, the input of capital was not because GE was deploying capital with great care. Fixed assets employed by GE were valued at $70.9 million in 1921 and were engaged in producing sales of $221.0 million, but the stock of assets declined to $51.7 million in 1929, at which time it was engaged in generating sales of $415.3 million. In all years from 1894 to 1939, GE did not have a single year in which it recorded losses, and it continued to pay dividends through the Great Depression.

In sum, the rise in GE's wage income that was faster than in its capital income is the technical reason for the rise in α, but this technical reason obscures the more profound change that took place in the skill level of GE's employees, in its product mix, and in the central role that technology played in advancing GE's productivity and market power. It is best to think of GE as being transformed, under the leadership of Swope, into a high-tech firm that sought to create and own major technological innovations. Instead of manufacturing equipment for public utilities and streetcars, GE was set to be the future producer of radio, television networks, magnetic resonance imaging (MRI) scanners, and jet engines. It employed the best electrical engineers one could have.

If GE's products in the twentieth century used electricity to activate mechanical devices, voice or moving pictures, its decline in the twenty-first century reflects the falling growth rates of such products. In the digital age, products use electricity to *transmit information* rather than to *activate mechanical devices.* The digital age requires different specializations and engineering skills that were not available at GE, and up to this time, the company has not been able to adapt fast enough to these changes.

5.6   GE's Market Power and Antitrust Policy

In seeking a better policy that could have been applied to the GE-Westinghouse monopoly, I have already noted that current antitrust policy fails to solve the problem of technological monopoly power. I address this question in chapters 8–9. Here, I explore the empirical evidence as to whether GE's lasting market power actually stemmed directly from new innovations made by GE. This evidence provides an invaluable backdrop to the more general conceptual evaluation of the trade-off between innovation and market power in chapter 7. To that end I now explore in more detail the antitrust aspects of the National Electric Lamp Association mentioned in section 5.3.

GE was created by First Gilded Age financiers who merged the leading producers of electric supplies in order to restrain competition. At the time of the merger, GE's market power derived entirely from the ideas of leading innovators of the era such as Thomas Edison, Frank Sprague, Elihu Thomson, Nikola Tesla, and many others. The problem of assessing GE's record is that, after its creation, GE's market power was not based only on new and improved GE innovations. Instead, throughout the twentieth century, its business model was also based on efforts to maintain market power by expanding its control over advanced technology by any possible means, legal or not. Beginning with the GE and Westinghouse patent-sharing agreement in 1896, which was declared legal in 1926 by the Supreme Court, GE found all possible loopholes in antitrust laws. That patent-sharing agreement led to the creation of a cartel in the sale of incandescent lamps.

Initially, GE and Westinghouse fixed their respective market shares at the ratio of 5:3. This cartel was later expanded to include smaller producers. The problem at the time was that the key patent for Edison's carbon filament incandescent bulb expired in 1894, leaving the market with multiple lamp technologies used by different competing manufacturers. This did not threaten GE's market power because it had patent protection on virtually all the equipment used in the production of its lamps, and breaking all of the patents was difficult. In addition, GE purchased many competing technologies and worked on a superior replacement to the Edison lamp, leading to the 1909 invention of the tungsten filament lamp. Even before developing this technical superiority, GE sought to establish its full control of the incandescent lamp market. It was the small producers' fear of GE's technological superiority that motivated them to cooperate with GE in forming, in 1901, the National Electric Lamp Association, 75 percent owned by GE and financed by GE (see Reich, 1992 and Hammond, 1941, chap. 33). It gave GE complete control over prices of incandescent lamps.

Small firms could compete with GE and Westinghouse in manufacturing lamps because production required skilled workers to blow the glass bulb sleeves and place *by hand* the mounts and bases on the lamps. Consequently, the larger firms had no scale advantage in production. On the other hand, small producers did not have the resources to cover the fixed cost of navigating the rapidly changing conditions of research, marketing, engineering and financing in the lamp market. The National Electric Lamp Association was GE's cooperative solution. In the cartel, each firm operated its own plant, but the National Electric Lamp Association pooled the cost of research, engineering, and marketing, which were carried out in the common facilities. GE provided the capital needed to set up the joint facilities, and it was GE's technology that was made available to the cartel. Naturally, GE fixed the pricing of lamps and directly allocated market shares. The National Electric Lamp Association became fully active in 1904, but GE did not manage it; its ownership position was kept secret.

In 1911, the Justice Department brought suit against GE for violating many provisions of the Sherman Antitrust Act. Initially, GE planned to dispute the allegations, but it later changed its mind and agreed to all facts alleged in the suit. However, it claimed that it was well within its rights as a patent monopolist to fix prices and market shares. This argument proved powerful, and ultimately the Justice Department backed down and agreed to an out-of-court settlement. The resulting consent decree covered many issues, but the central one of interest to GE was the prohibition on controlling the pricing of *other firms*, as distinct from controlling *its own price* (see Reich, 1992; Rogers, 1982; and Hammond, 1941, chap. 38). To satisfy the conditions of the consent decree, GE dissolved the cartel by merging it into GE and adopting a pricing policy based on an agency relation with local dealers, who became GE agents under contract to sell GE lamps. It thus managed to preserve the same monopolistic pricing policy that the Justice Department had tried to prevent.

In 1926, both GE's pricing practices and the GE-Westinghouse patent-sharing agreement came under further examination by a Justice Department suit, which ended in an appeal to the Supreme Court. The court's decision (see Reich, 1992) was a total victory for GE and Westinghouse because the court agreed that patent rights grant complete monopoly power, which permits fixing prices with the methods used by GE and setting market shares as agreed with Westinghouse. This court decision is important because there is no obvious economic reason to accept the proposition that ownership of a technology must come with the freedom to set any prices and choose any marketing strategy. This court ruling appears frequently in arguments aiming to restrict drug companies' pricing when they own the technology to produce the drugs. I return to this issue in chapter 9.

In 1925, the international Phoebus cartel was formed in Switzerland by a consortium of manufacturers that included General Electric. It controlled the manufacturing and pricing of incandescent light bulbs. The cartel agreement called for cooperation over thirty years, up to 1955, but it was suspended in 1939 due to the war. This cartel was a landmark in the expansion of anticompetitive efforts to a global scale.

For the rest of the twentieth century, electric manufacturers never stopped trying to fix prices and market shares. They also engaged in major research efforts to widen the scope of their products and to improve their quality. To understand the nature of that effort, it is instructive to examine the research efforts of the GE lab, one of the most successful industrial research laboratories in U.S. business history.

To examine GE's research record, I studied a list of eleven products that are often cited as the most important products developed and marketed by GE. The question is how many of them were inventions of GE, and how many were invented by others and then either GE purchased their patents or they were developed by GE after the initial patent expired. Table 7.1 in chapter 7 reports this information for these eleven leading products. The table shows that not a single one was invented at GE. They were all initially invented by somebody else and later taken up by GE, improved substantially, and marketed as a GE product. Indeed, after being invented, most of these products went through multiple stages of development before they reached a point where mass marketing by GE was feasible.

The invention of some of these products would not have been possible without the development of fundamental scientific knowledge. Such development requires risky and time-consuming basic research, which is rarely undertaken by private business. However, in most cases, there was also a secondary problem that arose even after the scientific problem was solved and a prototype existed. This problem was the *cost of production and effectiveness of design*. This is the stage at which GE excelled. For example, a practical X-ray machine was initially designed by Elihu Thomson, but GE was able to reduce its size and complexity to the point that it could be used on the battlefields of World War I. Table 7.1 thus points to GE's systematic ability to take existing prototypes developed by other inventors and improve them to the point where consumers found them desirable and they could be mass-produced at reasonable cost.

CHAPTER 6

MARKET POWER AND ASSET PRICES, 1950–2019

Monopoly wealth is the capitalized value of perceived future profits owned by stockholders, thus establishing a direct relation between profits due to market power and an asset's price.[1] This relation is stochastic and is often obscured by inaccurate market forecasts of future profits and by the inherent excess volatility of stock prices. But in the long run, changes in market power change profits, and therefore they also alter wealth distribution in society. Due to the central role of wealth inequality, it is important to study the effect of rising or falling market power on asset prices and on the way financial markets work. Such knowledge is needed for a better understanding of the forces that shape the distribution of wealth. To narrow down this problem, note that in chapter 4, I developed measures of aggregate market power deduced from aggregate data. To answer more detailed questions about changes in monopoly wealth of individual firms, in this chapter I explore data on individual firms and focus on four specific questions:

1. How is the rising market power since the 1980s reflected in asset prices and in measured monopoly wealth?
2. What is the difference between the growth rate of wealth and the growth rate of capital employed, and how does it affect changes in the aggregate capital/output ratio?

---

[1] Wharton Research Data Services (WRDS) was used in preparing this chapter. This service and the data available thereon constitute valuable intellectual property and trade secrets of WRDS and/or its third-party suppliers.

3. What effect does rising monopoly wealth have on corporate leverage?
4. How is rising monopoly wealth distributed among different firms and different sectors?

In exploring these questions, keep in mind that information technology (IT) is the dominant general-purpose technology (GPT) of this age, and the innovation wave in the last forty years constitutes the IT revolution. Therefore, the rise of market power since the 1980s is the result of this strong wave of IT innovations combined with a very passive public policy that made no effort to contain the rising technological market power and whose basic premise has been not to restrain free markets and free technological competition.

Before proceeding, I note that any analysis based on stock prices encounters two difficulties. One arises from the volatility of asset prices, and the second results from the inaccuracy of corporate financial data compared with accurate replacement values of assets and liabilities based on market values. My goal is to measure the monopoly power effects of IT and its impact on financial markets. Therefore *only general trends and relative magnitudes matter*: conclusions are drawn only when they are based on significant trends and magnitudes.

6.1   The Evolution of Monopoly Wealth, 1950–2019

6.1.1   Conceptual Issues, Metehodology, and Related Literature

To compute any measure of aggregate wealth, one may start by asking, Who owns that wealth? In this context, one usually thinks of a political entity, like a nation, as a unit of measurement. This is how the Federal Reserve and the U.S. Bureau of Economic Analysis (BEA) define aggregate U.S. wealth in table B.1 of "Z.1 Financial Accounts of the United States" (in short, Z.1), which reports net wealth of U.S. residents. This is not my approach. My unit of measurement is the firm, and I ask two questions: how much capital does it employ and how much wealth does it create for its owners, *regardless of who they are and where they live*? Because I assess the market value of wealth the firm creates, my firm needs to have securities that trade on public exchanges with market prices. Such a firm employs capital, which consists of assets valued in the firm's financial reports. The wealth created by the firm, shared by stockholders and bondholders,[2] is then deduced from the market value of the firm's securities.

---

[2]To that end, I adopt the convention, common in the finance literature, that considers the firm a joint enterprise of stockholders and bondholders. The rules of ownership stipulate that bondholders are promised a specific return, and stockholders receive all residual profits and take all residual risk. Assets of the firm and profits of stockholders constitute the collateral of the bondholders.

Given the above criteria, I decided to use the Wharton Research Data Services (WRDS) Compustat data files for 1950–2019 that provide standard financial reports on all firms with securities trading on public exchanges. The number of firms reporting and the coverage of files change from year to year for various reasons: not all firms report; some firms provide incomplete information; new firms go public; and old firms disappear due to mergers, failure, or other reasons. These problems are more pronounced in the earlier years of 1950–1970, when the number of reporting firms is relatively smaller. After 1970, the sample sizes exceed 3,000 firms; they contain all significant U.S. corporations, and the aggregates are reliable. An online data appendix provides detailed information about the files used. I mention here that I study only U.S.-based firms for which equity values are either available or could be constructed. Because the Compustat universe focuses on corporate business, it may appear that it covers the combined sectors of "nonfinancial corporate business" and "financial corporate business" in the Z.1 report. This is not the case because the Z.1 reports cover all corporations, *including private corporate firms with securities that do not trade publicly*, and therefore their values are imputed by Z.1 staff. Nevertheless, because my key arguments are based on orders of magnitude of the phenomena at hand, comparison with aggregates of the Z.1 reports show that *aggregates* of firms with traded securities in the Compustat samples are very representative of the entire corporate private sector.

The complex accounting of *financial intermediaries* and the multiple participants in risk bearing of such firms raise deep and well-known conceptual issues. Therefore, sorting through myriad financial assets and liabilities to construct "capital employed" in the bank's production function is a task beyond the aim of this study. I thus avoid the Compustat individual balance sheets of financial intermediaries and study mostly nonfinancial firms, which excludes from most of my samples all firms with SIC codes 6000–6499 (i.e., wider than just banks). For the set of financial firms in Compustat for which market value can be constructed, I used only data for three aggregates of such firms: market value, net worth, and intangible assets. This procedure makes it impossible to study detailed data on individual financial firms. Whenever possible, I report results for combining nonfinancial Compustat aggregates with these financial aggregates. When estimated asset values and capital are needed, results are reported only for Compustat samples of nonfinancial firms. I will show, however, that my key results are virtually the same for the two sectors.

An important fact needs to be mentioned to help clarify the results presented in this chapter. All Compustat asset values are stated in *historical* terms and need to be adjusted to current prices. I do it by using table B.103 of Z.1 where current and historical asset values are provided for different asset categories, and the ratio between them for 1950–2019 is used to adjust my Compustat asset values from historical to current values.

Because I use accounting data, I first present some accounting identities that explain my methodology and discuss adjustments I make in the financial reports to approximate monopoly wealth. I then present in table 6.1 several examples of these magnitudes for individual firms.

Start with standard accounting terms of total assets, intangible assets, total liabilities, and market value, which is the market values of common stock at the date of the annual report plus value of preferred stock. Net worth = total assets − total liabilities then leads to the definition of

$$\text{Excess Market Value} = \text{Market Value of Equity (V)} - \text{Net Worth.} \quad (6.1)$$

Absent any other factor, excess market value = monopoly wealth. The fact is, however, that monopoly wealth is not necessarily equal to (6.1) because intangible assets must be separated. It follows from the discussion in chapter 3 that

$$K = \text{Capital} = \text{Real Tangible Assets} = \text{Total Assets} - \text{Intangible Assets.} \quad (6.2)$$

The definition of monopoly wealth is then

$$\text{MW} = \text{Monopoly Wealth} = \text{Excess Market Value} + \text{Intangible Assets.} \quad (6.3)$$

Total wealth created by the firm is the sum of the wealth of stockholders and bondholders:

$$\text{TW} = \text{Total Wealth} = \text{Market Value of Equity (V)} + \text{Liabilities;} \quad (6.4a)$$

hence, by (6.4a),

$$\text{Total Wealth} - \text{Total Assets} = \text{Excess Market Value} \quad (6.4b)$$

and combining (6.2), (6.3), and (6.4b), I have

$$\text{Monopoly Wealth (MW)} = \text{Total Wealth (TW)} - \text{Capital Employed (K).} \quad (6.5)$$

As explained in chapter 3, the value of intangible assets is monopoly wealth *already on the balance sheet* of firms. In a fully flexible Walrasian competitive economy, *monopoly wealth = zero* holds at all dates or, in a stochastic setting, monopoly wealth fluctuates around zero. The fact that the market value of a firm can be different from replacement value is well known. It is the basis of Tobin's q (Brainard and Tobin, 1968; Tobin, 1969), which is meant to measure *adjustment* potential of a firm in a competitive economy toward the market value of the cost of its replacement. In practical applications, such cost includes intangible assets because intangible assets would be a fixed cost of creating an identical replacement firm. Because any Tobin's q different from 1 is seen as a temporary deviation from replacement value, economic theory would suggest that competitive markets should force Tobin's q back to 1 in the long run.

There are two key differences between Tobin's q computations and estimation of monopoly wealth. First, my starting point is that the economy is not competitive and monopoly wealth is created by market power. Therefore, in equilibrium there is a difference between market value and replacement cost, and I show in chapter 7 that there is no adjustment mechanism to eliminate it. Second, to compute monopoly wealth, one compares market value with net worth at market value, excluding intangible assets *which are part of the firm's monopoly wealth*. It is possible that the value of intangibles on the books of a firm are exactly equal to its monopoly wealth; in that case the firm's market value is exactly equal to its replacement cost (including intangibles), as defined by the Tobin's q computation, leading to the false inference that the market is in a long-term competitive equilibrium.

Although Tobin's q is an inappropriate tool for the study of economies with market power, a large body of research uses the Tobin's q for the study of problems related to economic concentration, which mostly reflect the existence of market power. These studies show q fluctuates and explains concentration of economic activity, but such conclusions are often derived in the context of a competitive economy (e.g., Salinger, 1984; Wright, 2004; Gonzalez and Trivin, 2019; Gutiérrez and Philippon, 2016; Peters and Taylor, 2017). I note particularly Wright's (2004) important observation that the historical average of Tobin's q over 1900–2002 is less than 1 but, in its fluctuations, *it rose in 1999 to the highest value in the twentieth century of about 1.8*. Other research shows increased concentration without using Tobin's q (e.g., Bessen, 2016, 2020; Azar et al., 2022, 2018; Grullon et al., 2019), and some of them explain that increased market power of firms has *caused* the rising concentration.

The above empirical results support the core idea of this chapter by providing vital empirical evidence for growing economic concentration and rising market power. Naturally, my perspective is different. When firms have market power, fluctuations of Tobin's q do not reflect adjustment of a competitive economy to shocks and the three measures of (1) rising Tobin's q, (2) increased market concentration, and (3) rising pricing power *are all endogenous outcomes* of the impact of expanding technology that causes increased market power and the passive public policy to restrain it since the 1980s.

6.1.2 Monopoly Wealth in 2019

Table 6.1 explains my approach[3] and demonstrates the association of IT with monopoly wealth. It contains four groups of firms. Those in the first are in decline or slow growing, resulting in negative monopoly wealth. One may view negative monopoly wealth as reflecting too high a value of capital, but the measure is market dependent, and price changes can eliminate such values. The first group, defined by $S = (MW)/(TW) \leq 0$, then constitutes 18.5 percent of my universe of 3,811 nonfinancial firms in 2019. The second group, defined by $0. \leq S \leq 0.30$, consists of relatively low tech firms selling standard goods or services with close substitutes and only small market advantage. It constitutes 17 percent of the universe in 2019. The third group, which constitutes 33.5 percent of the firms, is defined by $0.30 \leq S \leq 0.70$. Firms in this group have a solid technological base and major market advantage. The fourth group, defined by $S \geq 0.7$, constitutes 31.1 percent of the 2019 firms and reflects the advanced U.S. sector transformed by IT where most innovations take place. To interpret these facts correctly, recall that IT is a GPT; therefore, its reach is not restricted to traditional sectors such as semiconductors and computers but applies to all firms in *diverse economic sectors* that have an advanced technological base transformed by the IT revolution. Technologically advanced firms have monopoly wealth that, in many cases, exceeds 70 percent of total wealth created.

When considering the aggregates, I find that in 2019, monopoly wealth was 51 percent of all wealth created and 78 percent of total market value of nonfinancial firms. If I add the aggregates of *financial* firms, the ratio of monopoly wealth to total market value is 75 percent. This implies that trading stocks on public exchanges in 2019 entails mostly the trading of monopoly wealth. Today, 71 percent of capital invested is financed by bondholders, while stockholders mostly own and trade monopoly wealth, and in all likelihood this percentage will continue to rise. As one can see from table 6.1, for some U.S. corporations, the proportion of capital financed by bondholders already exceeds 100 percent. I will later discuss the implications of these developments.

Examination of table 6.1 confirms my argument in chapter 1 that many firms have legal market power derived from such sources as reputation and brand names, asymmetry of information, network externalities, and other specialized

---

[3] In examining table 6.1, recall that, according to the data adjustment procedure explained in the text and in the online data appendix, the values of tangible and intangible assets reported in table 6.1 are their historical values adjusted to market prices by using factors deduced from table B.103 of the Z.1 report. This increases the value of capital employed and reduces monopoly wealth. For rapidly growing high-tech firms, most assets are recently acquired, so this procedure causes a downward bias in their estimated monopoly wealth. For example, the book value of Facebook Inc.'s assets was only $133.376 billion, and most were acquired in recent years, yet table 6.1 records them at $161.81 billion.

TABLE 6.1 Selected statistics for some U.S. firms, fiscal year 2019*

Sample firm by four groups	Total assets at current prices	Intangible assets at current prices	Total debt	Market value (V)	Capital employed (K)	Monopoly wealth (MW)	Total wealth (TW)	$\frac{MW}{TW}$	$\frac{MW}{V}$
US Steel	12,499	174	7,515	1,940	12,324	−2,869	9,455	−0.30	−1.48
Marathon Oil	26,210	106	8,092	10,810	26,105	−7,203	18,902	−0.38	−0.67
General Motors	246,961	5,930	182,080	51,240	241,032	−7,712	233,320	−0.03	−0.15
Chevron Corp	308,275	4,959	92,220	226,820	303,316	15,724	319,040	0.05	0.07
Berkshire Hathaway	895,590	126,142	389,166	552,079	769,449	171,797	941,245	0.18	0.31
General Electric Co.	290,156	41,541	235,748	97,527	248,615	84,660	333,275	0.25	0.87
Norfolk Southern Corp.	48,107	0	22,739	50,067	48,107	24,699	72,806	0.34	0.49
Caterpillar Inc.	88,850	8,623	63,824	81,236	80,227	64,833	145,060	0.45	0.80
Southwest Airlines	29,586	1,407	16,063	28,019	28,180	15,903	44,082	0.36	0.57
Dow Chemical	68,013	13,950	46,430	40,582	54,063	32,949	87,012	0.38	0.81
Alphabet (Google)	311,899	25,114	74,467	921,138	286,785	708,820	995,605	0.71	0.77
Microsoft	329,174	55,306	184,226	1,023,856	273,868	934,214	1,208,082	0.77	0.91
Honeywell Internat.	63,347	21,441	39,966	125,865	41,906	123,925	165,831	0.75	0.98
3M Corp.	51,508	22,025	34,533	101,474	29,483	106,525	136,007	0.78	1.05
PepsiCo, Inc.	94,617	35,049	63,679	190,108	59,569	194,218	253,787	0.77	1.02
Amazon.com, Inc.	275,486	20,892	163,188	920,224	254,594	828,818	1,083,412	0.77	0.90
Amgen, Inc.	66,851	37,906	50,034	142,569	28,944	163,659	192,603	0.85	1.15
Facebook	161,810	21,788	32,322	585,373	140,022	477,673	617,695	0.77	0.82
Nonfinancial aggregate (N = 3,811)								0.51	0.78
Including financials (N = 4,589)								N/A	0.75

*Millions of 2019 dollars.
Source: WRDS Compustat files for 2019.

sources discussed in chapter 1. For example, PepsiCo Inc. owns many brands with an extensive following, and the firm has a good reputation among consumers. 3M has a strong technological base, its proprietary products are recognized around the world. Facebook's market power is the result of strong network externalities and exclusive control over a vast amount of private information of its members.

The intangibles in table 6.1 contain added examples of the monopoly wealth of acquired firms appearing as intangibles on the balance sheet of the acquiring firm, as presented in table 0.3b. This is particularly noticeable in the case of Facebook. This firm was started in 2003 as a social website at Harvard University and was incorporated in 2004. As an ongoing firm, it began with an initial investment of less than $50 million but raised $16 billion in its initial public offering in 2012. During 2012–2014, it acquired Instagram, Whatsapp, Pryte, and LiveRail—all with negligible capital on their balance sheet—for about $20 billion, accounting for most of its intangibles in 2019. By May 2019, its monopoly wealth reached $481 billion because it was growing fast and, together with Alphabet, had no effective competitors in online advertising. Competitors like LinkedIn can establish, at best, a subnetwork with a narrow focus. Technologically speaking, Facebook controls a world public utility with strong externalities.

Facebook shows why intangibles *are associated with rapid acquisitions*. In table 6.1 Amgen, Celgene, PepsiCo, Alphabet, Honeywell, General Electric, and Berkshire Hathaway also own a large fraction of intangibles due to active acquisitions. Apple, Amazon, Chevron, and Southwest Airlines do not have such history and own a small fraction of intangibles. Also, (6.4a) and (6.5) imply that if $(MW)/V > 1$, debt exceeds capital. It holds true for many firms and can occur when an acquired firm constitutes a liquid asset that stands on its own and may be used as a collateral for bondholders to finance such acquisition. In such a case, bondholders may own more than a firm's capital.

6.1.3   Monopoly Wealth, 1950–2019

1. *The general tendency.* Although Compustat files are not a panel, aggregate ratios computed for the universe of firms are reliable and consistent over time. I draw in figure 6.1 two curves for the period from 1950 to 2019 that describe the evolution of (monopoly wealth)/(market value). One is for the Compustat nonfinancial firms, and a second combines the financial and nonfinancial firms. These two are practically the same, and one may conclude that for the purpose of this study most results for nonfinancial firms are representative of the U.S. corporate sector.

Figure 6.1 shows that the large amount of 2019 monopoly wealth in table 6.1 is the culmination of growth that began in the 1970s–1980s. In the mid-1950s,

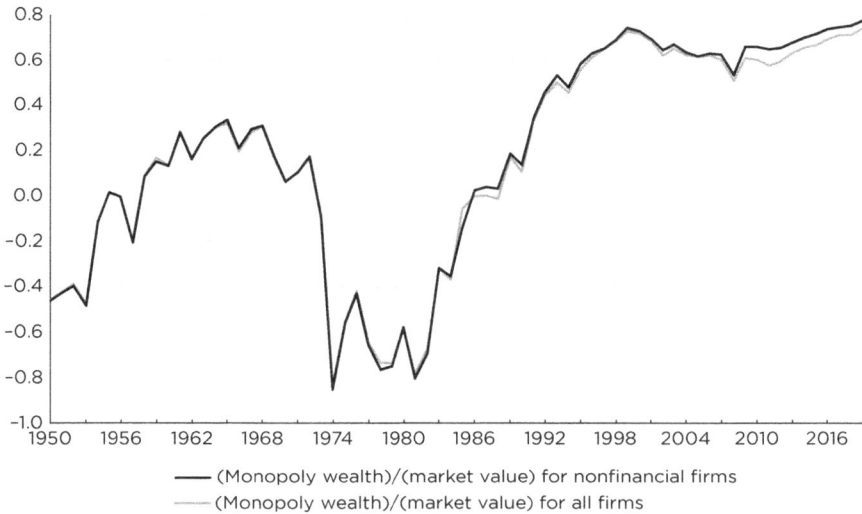

- (Monopoly wealth)/(market value) for nonfinancial firms
- (Monopoly wealth)/(market value) for all firms

Figure 6.1   Evolution of monopoly wealth, 1950–2019

there was no aggregate monopoly wealth[4] up to about 1960, after which significant monopoly wealth developed as a result of the hardware innovation phase of the IT revolution in the 1960s. This monopoly wealth did not last. Most discussions of the early 1970s focus on productivity slowdown and stagflation, but figure 6.1 shows the effect on corporate profits and private wealth was catastrophic: total monopoly wealth fell from $234 billion and 31 percent of total market value in 1968 to −$526 billion in 1974.

Conditions changed, and a new era began around 1978–1981 that has continued until 2019. This is the span of time that corresponds exactly to the second software phase of the IT revolution. Figure 6.1 shows that monopoly wealth stopped falling in 1974 and fluctuated until 1981 when it began to rise. This timing matches the dawn of the software innovation phase of the IT revolution, and two events mark it: Apple 1 was released in 1976, and IBM's PC was released in 1981. The figure also shows that actual long-term recovery of monopoly wealth began in the early 1980s, when the new software innovation phase of IT went into high gear. IBM adopted Microsoft's disk-operating system (DOS) as the PC operating system in 1981, and the military communication network (ARPANET) adopted in 1983 the protocol Transmission Control Protocol/Internet Protocol (TCP/IP) which expedited development of what we call today the internet.

---

[4] Keep in mind my earlier observation that, prior to 1970, the Compustat population is relatively small and the computed ratio of monopoly wealth to market value is less representative of the entire population of firms. In fact, Compustat discourages use of its data for periods prior to 1962.

If monopoly wealth is the discounted value of the market's perceived future profits, then the market's anticipation in the late 1970s and early 1980s was very gloomy. In the grip of the 1970s oil shocks, productivity slowdown, and stagflation, the market did not anticipate the dramatic rise of profits that was to change U.S. economy and society fundamentally in the next forty years. A possible bias toward undervaluation is consistent with Wright's (2004) observation that the historical average of Tobin's q is less than 1. I explore this market underestimation by comparing it later to the actual flow of profits. This underestimation may be easier to understand when one considers the component of public policy and the central role of the changed policy of the 1980s. Even with the benefit of hindsight, there is very little to support the view that the market should have forecasted such a change. More generally, because market power is unobserved and changes very slowly with little evidence about its empirical regularity, it is entirely reasonable to assume it cannot be forecasted with any accuracy. If, in addition, one adds unexpected changes in policy, it lends much stronger support to the view that for a substantial period before and after the early 1980s, the market could not have anticipated the growth of corporate profits after the 1980s. This makes the data on negative monopoly wealth just a reflection of market sentiment with limited economic significance. Beyond this observation, there is little else that can be deduced from the massive negative monopoly wealth up to 1985.

The rise of monopoly wealth accelerated during the 1990s, and this timing corresponds to the fact that in 1993, Marc Andreesen developed Mosaic, the first web browser, which changed its name in 1994 to Netscape Navigator. It led to a battle over dominance of search engines, which resulted in the temporary dominance of Microsoft's Internet Explorer, released in August 1995. Other milestones that accompany the rise of monopoly wealth are the following;

- Amazon was founded in 1994.
- Expedia was founded in 1996.
- Netflix and Priceline.com were founded in 1997.
- Google was founded in 1998, and its algorithm came to dominate internet search.
- Many other innovations sharply accelerated usage of the internet and inaugurated the sharp rise of capital spending and economic expansion in 1995–1999. It led to the dot-com boom.
- Facebook was founded in 2004.
- Uber was founded in 2009.

The IT revolution not only transformed many older firms; it also spawned a large number of new firms. Most of the firms with the largest monopoly wealth in 2019 did not even exist before 1974.

TABLE 6.2 Size and composition of monopoly wealth*

Year	Nonfinancials excess market value	Nonfinancials intangible assets	Nonfinancials monopoly wealth	Financial sector monopoly wealth	Total monopoly wealth
1985	−736	180	−557	300	−256
1990	132	514	646	−82	564
1995	4,142	840	4,982	705	5,687
2000	11,499	2,325	13,823	2,564	16,387
2005	7,027	2,840	9,867	2,361	12,228
2010	6,283	3,773	10,056	929	10,985
2015	10,401	5,149	15,550	1,693	17,243
2019	15,623	6,415	22,039	3,065	25,104

*Billions of 2019 dollars.

This argument does not end with the technology that generated the rising market power. Economic policy since 1981 played an equally important role in enabling the changes recorded in figure 6.1. Two events mark the change in policy: first, the Economic Recovery Act of 1981, which cut the top personal income tax rate from 70 percent to 50 percent and the lowest rate from 14 percent to 11 percent, and second, the Tax Reform Act of 1986, which lowered the top income tax rate from 50 percent to 28 percent and raised the lowest rate from 11 percent to 15 percent. As explained in chapters 1 and 4, the change eliminated the policy of constraining market power and of using the tax law as a tool to attain an egalitarian income and wealth distribution.

Monopoly wealth rose from the low in 1974 to a temporary peak of $11.39 trillion in current prices and 72 percent of total market value in 2000. During 2000–2019, monopoly wealth and total wealth continued to rise, but the ratio of (monopoly wealth)/(market value) remained in the 70 percent to 80 percent range except for 2008–2012. The temporary high level in 1999–2000 resulted from the excessive valuations of the dot-com boom, and the decline in 2008–2012 was due to the Great Recession. Monopoly wealth reached 75 percent of the stock market value in 2019, and it is hard to find any evidence that the process of rising monopoly wealth has reached a peak.

2. *The real size of monopoly wealth, 1985–2019.* How large is monopoly wealth and what is its composition? I present in table 6.2 real values for selected years in *billions of 2019 prices* (using gross national product [GNP] deflator). The table shows that *between 1985 and 2019, real monopoly wealth increased by $25.36 trillion* with heavily concentrated ownership accounting for the sharp rise in personal wealth inequality.

The steep rise of monopoly wealth over such a relatively short period is an important indicator of the change in the social fabric between 1985 and 2019. The fact that monopoly wealth has grown to a point where 75 percent of the value of stocks traded on public exchanges is monopoly wealth rather than capital suggests that stock trading is mostly a mechanism for allocating resources across different concentrations of market power rather than the traditional view of it as a mechanism for allocating capital across firms with different social needs.

6.2   Growth Rates of Capital and Wealth: Capital/Output Ratio Versus Wealth/Output Ratio

The rapid growth of monopoly wealth suggests that it is important to understand the change in composition of wealth. Because wealth = capital + monopoly wealth, I explore the time paths and growth rates of these two components. Figure 6.2 presents the two ratios of capital/wealth and of (monopoly wealth)/(wealth) for nonfinancial firms. It shows that from 1950 to 1980, the components fluctuated in a wide but constant band, not exhibiting a clear trend. This changed around 1980.

From 1980 to 2019, the two components exhibited opposite trends. The fraction of capital in total wealth decreased from 1.29 to 0.49, and the fraction of monopoly wealth rose from −0.29 to 0.51, reflecting the fact that capital invested

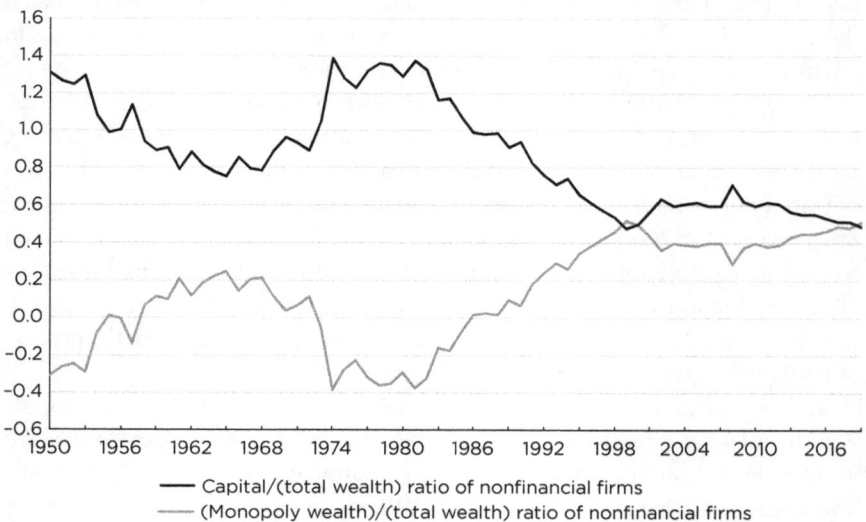

——— Capital/(total wealth) ratio of nonfinancial firms
——— (Monopoly wealth)/(total wealth) ratio of nonfinancial firms

Figure 6.2 Evolution of the components of wealth, 1950–2019

grew much slower than total wealth. In the following tabulation, I compare these two growth rates by using the GNP deflator to restate both nonfinancial values in millions of 2019 dollars:

	1980 value	2019 value	Mean growth rate, 1980–2019
Wealth of nonfinancial firms	6,729,665	42,976,933	4.87 percent
Capital of nonfinancial firms	8,685,083	20,938,335	2.28 percent.

From 1980 to 2019, total wealth created by nonfinancial firms grew annually by 2.59 percentage points faster than capital employed by these firms. There are two implications of these figures that I explore: first, for the dynamics of the capital/output ratio, which I discuss next, and second, for corporate financing of capital, which I discuss in the following section.

In chapter 1, I briefly discussed the dynamics of the capital/output ratio, where the case was made for a clear distinction between capital and wealth. As noted there, some authors estimate wealth using standard methods based on stock market prices of firms and then identify wealth with capital employed by firms. For example, Piketty and Zucman (2014) use such a method, from which they deduce the main result of their research, which correctly shows that the *wealth/output ratio* has risen since 1980. The problem is that they identify the growth of their *wealth/output ratio* with the growth of the capital/output ratio defined by the production relation (1.2a) in chapter 1. They then claim to have shown, as a new result, that this measure of the capital/output ratio has been rising. This last claim motivated the title of their work, "Capital Is Back," and this is the conclusion that I question.

To clarify the issue, I estimate the capital/output ratio, using BEA data for capital, defined as the real value of fixed assets (BEA, table 1.2), and for output, the real value of gross domestic product (GDP) (BEA, table 1.1.6). Figure 6.3 presents the capital/output ratio, from 1945 to 2018 for the aggregate U.S. economy. The capital/output ratio has not risen; it has, in fact, fallen significantly. My theory, expressed in proposition 2.3, predicts that it would fall when market power rises, and figure 6.3 shows that most of the decline occurred during the period of rising market power since 1981.

In contrast with a declining capital/output ratio in figure 6.3, I reproduce in figure 6.4 the wealth/output ratio estimated by Piketty and Zucman (2014) from 1870 to 2010, and note the rise of the ratio from 1980 to 2010 which they view as an increase of the capital/output ratio. It is also well-documented that the combined share of capital and profits has risen at the same time (Piketty and Zucman, 2014, p. 1302). These two conclusions cannot occur with a constant returns to scale production function; therefore Piketty and Zucman (2014) deduce that it must reflect increasing returns to scale, a conclusion that is typically negated by studies of the aggregate production function. The error of such

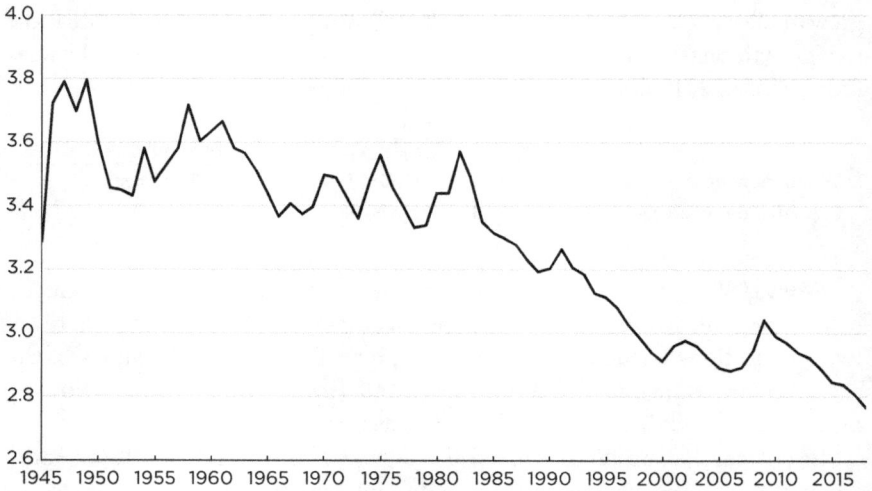

Figure 6.3 Capital/output ratios for the United States, 1947–2018

Sources: BEA tables 1.2 and 1.1.6.

reasoning flows from the fact that the wealth/output ratio is not equal to the capital/output ratio in (1.2a), where capital excludes monopoly wealth, and from the mistaken claim that the capital/output ratio has risen since the 1980s. The same error regarding long-run trends of the capital/output ratio are made by Piketty (2014) when his estimates of the capital stock are deduced from stock market prices.

An examination of figure 6.4 also reveals that the wealth/output ratio rose from 1870 to late 1890s, *reflecting the rising monopoly wealth during the First Gilded Age*. The ratio rose sharply during the Great Depression because output contracted and capital sat idle, and similarly it fell sharply during World War II because output boomed and capital was used heavily, but these fluctuations are not too informative about the overall trend. Leaving aside these two extremes, the wealth/output ratio declined from the early 1900s to the 1970s, mirroring the reform agenda during the eighty years of a more egalitarian policy. My conclusion is that the decline of the capital/output ratio combined with the rise of the wealth/output ratio since the 1980s reflects the fact that market power, monopoly wealth, and the Gilded Age are back, placing the United States today in a Second Gilded Age.

Finally, how could the growth rate of wealth exceed the growth rate of capital for such a long time? Analysis of the model in chapter 2 implies that from the 1980s to 2019, the economy was not in steady state because in such a state these two magnitudes change at the same rate. The rapid growth of wealth is then

Figure 6.4   Wealth/output ratios for the United States, 1870–2010

Sources: Piketty and Zucman (2014), table US 1, data appendix.

the direct result of the rise in market power: it shifted income from labor and capital to profits, enabling profits to rise at a rate much higher than normal. Profits are then capitalized at an accelerated rate, causing stock prices to rise at a rate above trend. In addition, the analysis in section 2.8 about the sharp effect of changing policy regimes explains why the dramatic rise began in the 1980s, after the change in policy. As noted there, the capital/output ratio in 1980 was too high for the new policy and needed a long time to decline to its new steady state, to adjust to the rising market power that lowered the demand for capital and labor. It led to a decline in investment, a fall in the share of capital and labor, and a rise in profits at a rate that is abnormally high for a long time, measured in decades.

6.3   The Dynamics of Debt-Financed Capital Employed

I turn now to the question of corporate finance. Although much of the difference between the growth of wealth and the growth of capital of nonfinancial firms is explained by the rise of monopoly wealth, total wealth includes a fraction owned by debt holders, and wealth created by nonfinancial firms also satisfies the equality wealth = market value + debt. This implies that a rise of monopoly wealth may alter the way firms finance the amount of capital invested.

Figure 6.5 plots the debt/capital ratio of nonfinancial firms from 1950 to 2019. It shows a sustained rise in corporate financing of capital needs with

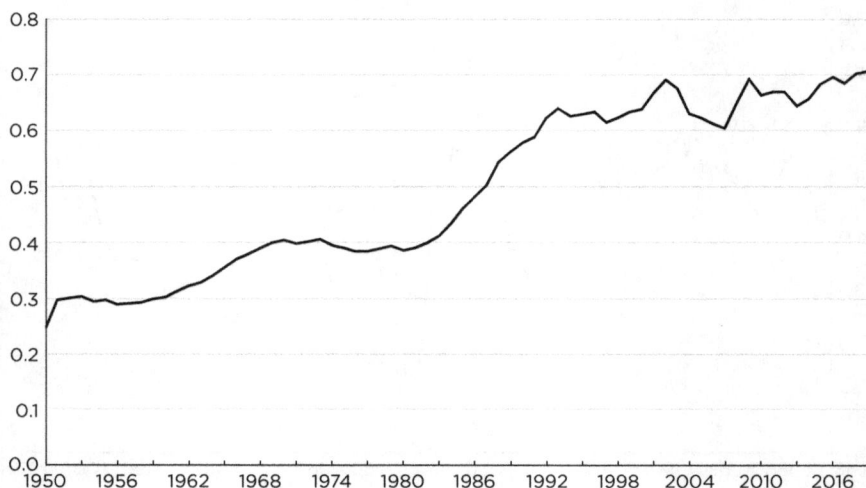

Figure 6.5 Rising debt/capital ratio, 1950–2019

debt, raising the proportion of capital financed by debt from 25 percent in 1950 to 71 percent in 2019. A large number of advanced technology firms exhibit debt/capital > 1. These percentages do not address the more general question of leverage, which is typically measured with different ratios, such as debt/assets or debt/(market value). The figure does show that lenders, who usually seek specific assets as collateral, are showing a willingness to accept monopoly wealth as liquid collateral for financing investments.

These changes suggest that there is a trend toward the financial structure of the nonfinancial corporate sector being approximated with a debt/capital ratio of 1, where bondholders finance the capital stock and receive a stipulated return, while stockholders own and trade monopoly wealth, bearing all profit risks. Such division is possible if monopoly wealth is liquid enough to provide bondholders with added safety against default. It also suggests that the current trend reflects a change in the nature of risk associated with stock market investments. Such risk is becoming mostly about innovations, technological competition, changes in productivity, and public policy to contain market power.

6.4   Comparing Monopoly Wealth with Profit Share of Income: A Plausibility Test

The estimates of monopoly wealth in section 6.1 are very large, but are they plausible? In chapter 4, I present estimates of the share of profits deduced from income flows, whereas in this chapter, results about market power are presented using stocks of monopoly wealth. Are these consistent? They are clearly inconsistent if the stock market does not forecast accurately the change in profits brought about by changing market power, which is the source of profits. Although the Dow Jones stock index reached a low point in July 1982, the negative values of monopoly wealth up to 1985 indicate that the full significance of the changed environment took a few years to be incorporated into investors' expectations and asset prices. For this reason, the question of plausibility is applicable only after 1985 or even later, as better expectations were being formed.

To set up a simple plausibility test for the estimated monopoly wealth of the nonfinancial corporate sector, I start by noting that both ordinary capital and monopoly wealth can be traded on open markets. Capital is traded mostly in debt markets and some in stock markets, and monopoly wealth is traded mostly in stock markets. Denote by R the rate of return on capital and by $(R + \rho)$ the return on monopoly wealth. As explained in chapter 4, capital investment is less risky than monopoly wealth, which is assigned the risk premium ρ for the risk of pricing, strategic competition, innovations, marketing, and public policy. Denote by K capital employed, Y output, MW monopoly wealth, TW total wealth, γ_w the fraction of monopoly wealth out of total wealth, S_L labor share, and S_{TX} the share of taxes in corporate value added. There are three identities from which one can deduce the share of profits implied by the size of MW:

$$RK + (R + \rho)MW = \left(1 - S_L - S_{TX}\right) Y \tag{6.6a}$$

$$MW = \gamma_w TW \tag{6.6b}$$

$$TW = K + MW. \tag{6.6c}$$

It follows that

$$\frac{(R + \rho)MW}{Y} = \gamma_w \left(1 - S_L - S_{TX}\right) + \rho \left(1 - \gamma_w\right) \frac{MW}{Y}. \tag{6.7}$$

Except for the premium ρ, each of the terms on the right is known either from actual data or from the estimated value of total wealth and monopoly wealth. The question comes down to the premium. Because there are no data from which to deduce a precise value for this parameter, a plausible estimate of this premium would place it in the range of 4 percent to 6 percent. Figure 6.6 reports the result.

In the early years of the IT revolution, the market did not forecast correctly the magnitude of future profits, resulting in negative monopoly wealth and a divergence of the share implied by monopoly wealth from the share of profits estimated directly in chapter 4. As the rate of profitability rose, markets began

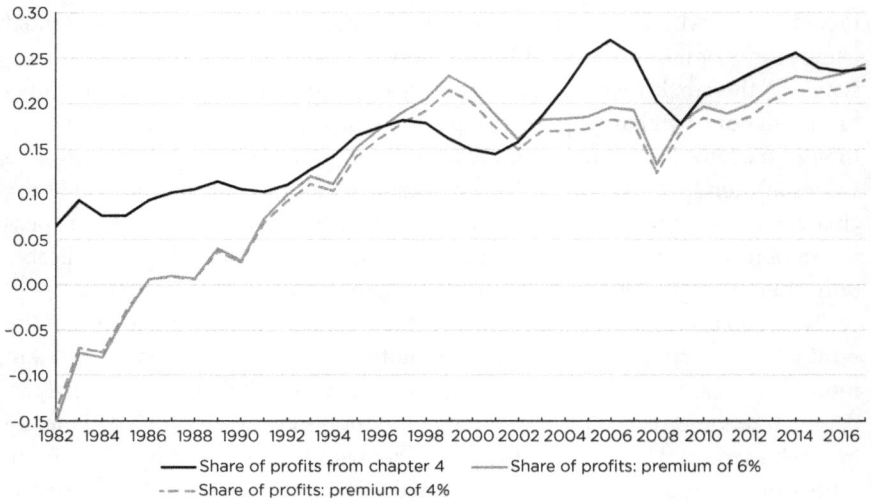

Figure 6.6 Estimated profit share versus share implied by monopoly wealth

to recognize the significance of the changed environment, asset prices adjusted, and consequently the two estimates become close after about 1992. This means that at least the positive values of estimated monopoly wealth after 1992 are consistent with the estimated shares of profits in chapter 4. In this narrow sense, the estimated values of monopoly wealth are plausible.

6.5   Most Monopoly Wealth Is Created by Technology

The theory outlined in chapter 1 predicts that most monopoly wealth originates from the creation of proprietary technology. It then proposes that, in recent years, a great deal of such wealth was derived from innovations associated with the IT revolution, which is the source of market power since the 1970s. But because IT is a GPT, it has an impact on all firms as the process of innovations enabled by IT proliferates throughout the economy. Case studies of individual firms can certainly establish the source of their excess returns and monopoly wealth, but in studying a broad population of firms like Compustat, it is difficult to construct a clear econometric definition to identify those firms whose technologies have been transformed by IT. The only alternative is to seek indirect, and therefore imprecise, evidence that enables an approximate assessment, and that is what I do now.

Emphasis on the effect of IT will later draw our attention to younger firms created by the IT revolution after the 1970s. However, it is important to keep in mind that most of America's surviving legacy firms have remained influential because they have reinvented themselves by transforming into the digital age in diverse sectors of the economy. A few examples can illustrate: IBM in computer services, AT&T in communication, DuPont in chemicals and biology, Procter and Gamble in consumer products, Honeywell in heat regulation technology, Johnson and Johnson in health technology and drugs. Even old industrial firms like General Motors and Ford appear to be reinventing themselves these days, moving into the forefront of electric vehicle and autonomous driving technologies. In addition, there is a group of firms with significant monopoly wealth created, in part, by their long reputation for quality and by consumers' loyalty to them, factors cited in chapter 1 as creators of some market power of firms such as Coca-Cola, Gillette, and General Mills. This monopoly wealth from brand loyalty fluctuates in value but exhibits long-term durability.

Seeking to identify the source of rising market power, De Loecker et al. (2020) use the same Compustat data I use in this chapter to estimate firm-level markups from 1950 to 2016. Noting that the average markup rose sharply from 1980 to 2016, they decompose this increase and claim that it is driven mainly by the growing size (relative to the economy) of existing firms with high markup. They find that rising markups of the same firms over time play a small role in the overall rise, as does firm entry. Cumulatively over the whole period, they find that the rising relative size of high-markup firms accounts for more than 80 percent of the rise of 0.35 average markup. This same conclusion is deduced by Autor et al. (2020), who use the same data decomposition method to argue that the fall in the labor share has been driven by the rise in the relative size of firms with low labor shares.

To assess these conclusions, it helps to clarify the terminology used. To that end, suppose we measure some variable X_t (i.e., markup, labor share, or monopoly wealth) that is an aggregate of firm-specific values X_{it}, and the aggregation weights are the firm's proportion of total sales:

$$X_t = \sum_{i=1}^{N} s_{it} X_{it}, \text{ where } s_{it} = \frac{S_{it}}{S_t}.$$

De Loecker et al. (2020) and Autor et al. (2020) use a decomposition identity developed by Haltiwanger (1997) and Foster et al. (2001), who study whether productivity gains take place from the increased relative size of high productivity establishments or from increased productivity in establishments of a given size. Using Haltiwanger's notation, I call the firms that are present in the sample in year $t-1$ and year t continuers. The role of increased size of firms with high value of the measured variable X_{it}, versus increased X_{it} given the relative size of firms, can only be studied for these firms. Firms that exit or enter the market in a given year give rise to an additional entry and exit term. There is also a cross term, the interaction between changes in X_{it} and changes in market share, but this is second order. The change in X_t is then decomposed with the following identity:

$$X_t - X_{t-1} = \sum_{i \in continuers} s_{i,t-1} \left(X_{it} - X_{i,t-1} \right) + \sum_{i \in continuers} X_{i,t-1} \left(s_{it} - s_{i,t-1} \right)$$

$$+ \sum_{i \in continuers} \left(X_{it} - X_{i,t-1} \right) \left(s_{it} - s_{i,t-1} \right)$$

$$+ \left[\sum_{i \in enterers} s_{it}X_{it} - \sum_{i \in exiters} s_{i,t-1}X_{i,t-1} \right].$$

(6.8)

The four terms measure the following four effects, as components of the change in X from $t - 1$ to t:

$$\sum_{i \in continuers} s_{i,t-1} \left(X_{it} - X_{i,t-1} \right)$$ — change of X_{it} *within firms*, given their

relative size;

$$\sum_{i \in continuers} X_{i,t-1} \left(s_{it} - s_{i,t-1} \right)$$ — change in *firms' relative sizes*, given their X_{it};

$$\sum_{i \in continuers} \left(X_{it} - X_{i,t-1} \right) \left(s_{it} - s_{i,t-1} \right)$$ — interaction of changes in X_{it} and

relative size;

$$\sum_{i \in enterers} s_{it}X_{it} - \sum_{i \in exiters} s_{i,t-1}X_{i,t-1}$$ — change due to exit and entry of new firms.

I turn now to the specific problem at hand, which is clarifying the source of rising markup, falling labor share, and rising monopoly wealth. These evolve over long periods of time but exhibit a high degree of persistence. De Loecker et al. (2020) and Autor et al. (2020) claim that the cause of the change is mostly the rising share of output in the hands of a small number of superstar firms with an initially high degree of market power but due relatively little to the contribution of the organic rise of market power within firms or to the entry of new firms with a high degree of market power that was not there before. In questioning the economic meaning of this finding, I now argue that the methodology of cumulating the annual decomposition of the sources of change paints a false picture of the true economic source of changing monopoly wealth, markup, or labor share, although their finding is a correct mechanical result of cumulating the annual decomposition of the changes.

Keeping in mind that the phenomena at hand exhibit high persistence, the results of a mechanical decomposition depend crucially upon the time unit used to measure the change because the method is biased against measuring the long-lasting effects of major changes. Consider the example of firms like Amazon, Apple, Microsoft, or Facebook. They appear in the Compustat data first when they go public and their effect on total monopoly wealth or markup, as new entries, is counted only once when they appear first. Although they represent the new technology of IT, in all years after going public, their increased monopoly wealth or markup is not distinguished from the rise of monopoly wealth or markup at old firms like McDonald's, Coca-Cola, or Procter and Gamble. To identify the impact of major events with lasting effect, one must carry out the decomposition for different time units.

Because this is my evaluation of the conclusions of De Loecker et al. (2020) and Autor et al. (2020), I now explore the decomposition of markup, not monopoly wealth. In table 6.3, I carry out this decomposition and, in measuring the change, I document the cumulative sources of the rise of 0.35 in the average markup reported by De Loecker et al. (2020) for different time horizons.[5] These time horizons are defined as follows: the annual horizon corresponds to that reported by De Loecker et al. (2020); the ten-year horizon uses the years 1980, 1990, 2010 and 2016; the eighteen-year horizon uses the years 1980, 1998 and 2016; and the 1980–2016 horizon uses the entire time interval from 1980 to 2016. The sample includes 3,515 Compustat firms in 1980 and 4,621 firms in 2016, but only 540 firms existed in both 1980 and 2016.[6] The firms that were present in the sample for the entire time period represented 42 percent of sales in 1980 and 33 percent of sales in 2016 but, as I will show, had almost no effect on the dynamics of markups. The new firms are at the center of the rise in markups, and virtually all of it is because those firms formed after 1980, which include all older firms that reinvented themselves and were merged or combined into those newly created.

De Loecker et al. (2020) and Autor et al. (2020) base their economic story on the fact that, when cumulating changes over one year at a time, 28/35 of the change in markup (or, in a similar analysis, a large fraction of labor share) can be attributed to changes in firms' relative size, which means it results from increased size of existing firms with high markup. But the story changes completely as we stretch the time horizon. In comparing 1980 to 2016, a proportion of 30/35 results from entry of new firms with high markup, the vast majority of

---

[5]The estimated average markup of 1.21 in 1980 and 1.56 in 1916 by De Loecker et al. (2020) is disputed by Hall (2018) and many others. But the problem is not to evaluate the level of markup, but only the decomposition used to identify the sources of the 0.35 change in average markup. Answering this question does not require acceptance of the markup level estimated by De Loecker et al.

[6]Although De Loecker et al. (2020) used fiscal years for identifying the annual data, they included in 2016 only firms that reported by December 2016. This is an error because it omits firms whose fiscal year is 2016 but report after December 2016. I included in 2016 all firms reporting for the 2016 fiscal year, which reduces aggregate markup from 1.61 to 1.56 in 2016 and leaves all the other years unaffected.

TABLE 6.3 Cumulative decomposition of markup with different time units*

Component	One year	10 years	18 years	2016 versus 1980
Firm size reallocation	0.278	0.175	0.074	0.019
Within firm rise	0.044	0.071	0.088	0.039
Cross effect	−0.034	−0.031	−0.016	−0.006
Effect of entry and exit	0.061	0.134	0.203	0.297

*Components add up to a total change of 0.35.

which are the products of the IT revolution. The table thus shows that as high-technology firms that charged higher markups were born or created between 1980 and 2016, their high markup explains about 85 percent of the changed markup. In addition, 4/35 of the change resulted from increased market power of existing firms. I will later explain that this increase is because IT is a GPT that has transformed other sectors of the economy. This 4/35 is then also attributed to the effect of IT, enabling older firms to reinvent themselves and adapt to the digital age. Only 2/35 can be attributed to the rise in relative size of firms with high markup at the start. This 2/35 should also be interpreted with care. It includes old American legacy firms that have benefitted from strong consumer loyalty and who have adapted to the digital age in addition to the effect of mergers, as I will shortly explain.

This comparison of 1980 with 2016 obscures the rise in markups due to increased relative size of high-markup firms that were born during the age of IT. Firms like Apple, Google, and Amazon began as leaders of the IT revolution with high markups, and then grew in size over the past twenty years, raising the average markup. In annual accounting, this is classified as "changes in firms' relative size." That interpretation would be made by Autor et al. (2020), who aim to show that the rise of markup was due to the superstar firms passively expanding at the expense of their small, inefficient rivals. According to this account, these weak rivals have defaulted because globalization caused increased market "toughness" which directed their customers to migrate to big firms that expanded in size relative to the economy. This effect of rising firm size is seen even in the intermediate time units of ten or eighteen years in table 6.3.

The problem is that neither the effect of rising firms' relative size deduced from firms created after 1980 nor the 2/35 fraction of average markup explained by rising firm size from 1980 to 2016 supports the economic interpretation offered by Autor et al. (2020). This passive interpretation of the expanding leviathans is contradicted by very simple statistics that accompany the decomposition. However, before studying the statistics, I need to explain a second fault of the decomposition method, which is an error in identifying the cause of change. Consider the effect of an acquisition or a merger of two firms in year t. In that year, the data show a one time exit-and-entry effect of the disappearance of one firm, while the acquiring firm is considered a survivor from $t - 1$ to t. This means that all increased size of the acquiring firms due to mergers or acquisitions are recorded as the effect of rising firm size in that year. The economic interpretation is then that the effect of rising firm size can reflect two opposed phenomena. It can either reflect the default of weak inefficient firms whose customers migrate voluntarily to the leviathans, or it may reflect the fact that the leviathans simply devoured the rivals. What statistics do we have about that?

In 1998, the Compustat population of publicly traded firms swelled to 7,429 firms, implying that this population rose by 3,914 firms from 1980 to 1998. The number then declined by 2,808 firms from 1998 to 2016, when the population stood at 4,621. Publicly traded firms default only rarely; to preserve value they are acquired or merged before they run into financial difficulties. This means that from 1998 to 2016, the big firms acquired most of the 2,808 publicly traded firms that disappeared from the Compustat population. This is not an exaggerated picture because I demonstrate in chapter 9 that just the five firms of Microsoft, Facebook, Salesforce, Google, and Amazon acquired 721 firms (public and private) between 1987 and 2020. In this span of years, Microsoft acquired 237 firms and Google acquired 236 firms. The acquired firms were not just rivals whose customers migrated voluntarily to the big acquiring firms. The flood of acquisitions reflects the quest for expanded technological market power, and the acquired customers migrate to the acquiring firm not because they passively seek the more efficient firm but because the acquiring firm owns the technology these customers need to use.

In sum, the evidence points to IT and the technologies it spawned as the sources of rising markups or monopoly wealth. These changes took place either in the form of new or newly combined firms that adapted to the digital age or by the older legacy firms that adapted to the new age. An extensive study of the pattern of all acquisitions since the 1980s is beyond the scope of this research and cannot be pursued here. Instead of focusing on acquisitions, we can gain more insight into the effect of IT on the growth of monopoly wealth by using the available Compustat data to study the dynamic changes of the age composition of firms with monopoly wealth.

The age of a firm is defined by the date when it was founded. Therefore, in cases of merger, name change, or both, the question of identification requires extra care because the Compustat data is not constructed as a panel but as a sequence of independent files. It was thus necessary to ensure the correct identity of each firm in my files. For that, I relied on the data files of Loughran and Ritter (2004) but electronically searched for the founding dates of firms not covered by their study. The most important effort was to identify firms that appeared to be young, as defined by their first date on Compustat files, but that

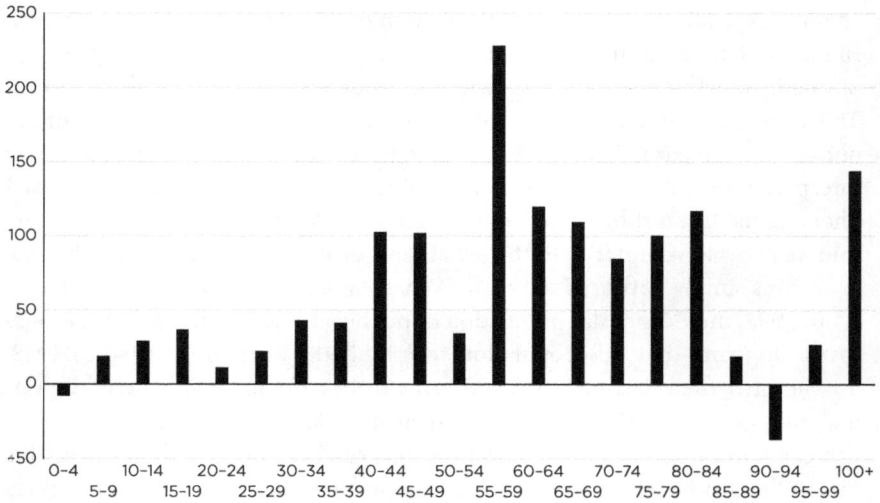

Figure 6.7a Monopoly wealth by firm age, 1968

were, in fact, old firms involved in a merger or name change within the last half century.

Nominal monopoly wealth was converted into real monopoly wealth in 2019 prices by using the GDP deflator, and figures 6.7a to 6.7e trace the changes in the age distribution of real monopoly wealth since 1968. In 1968, monopoly wealth was distributed in diverse sectors of the economy. In figure 6.7a, the leading technology firms of the 1960s like General Electric and IBM exhibit some monopoly wealth and are between the ages of forty to seventy. Postwar technology firms under the age of twenty-four, mostly in electronics, computers and semiconductor industries (e.g., Texas Instruments, Litton Industries, Intel, Applied Materials) also exhibit some monopoly wealth.

The productivity slowdown of the 1970s, together with the associated decline in asset prices, eliminated all monopoly wealth. It turned negative and remained negative up to the mid-1980s. Figure 6.7b shows these effects. Even the legacy firms with strong consumer loyalty were not spared.

As an approximation, I define Apple's foundation in 1974 as the start of the IT revolution and, as time progresses, the maximal age of firms created by that revolution rises. To identify these firms, note that in 1980 most firms less than seven years old were products of that revolution. In 1990 they were less than seventeen years old, and in 2019 they were less than forty-six years old. Figure 6.7c, for 1990, reveals the direction of the dynamic process underway. Apart from a scattering of positive or negative monopoly wealth, sustained positive wealth is found in two groups: the legacy firms and the young firms who were less than seventeen years old. I have already noted the reputational effect

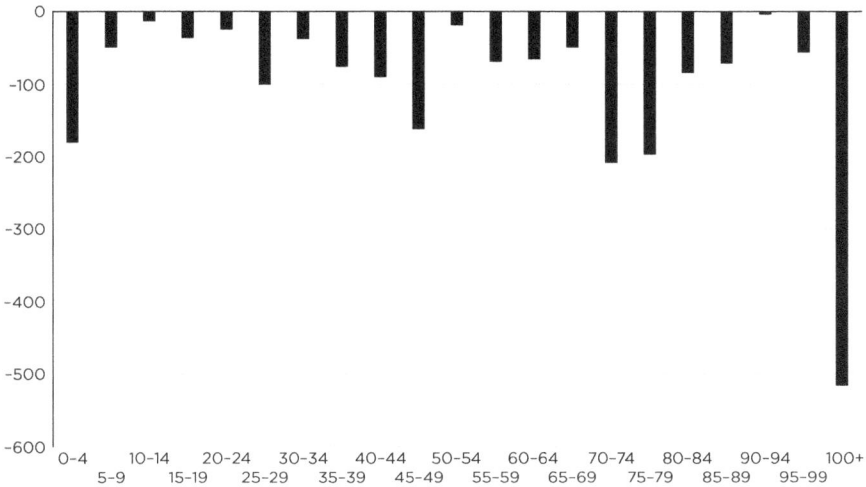

Figure 6.7b   Monopoly wealth by firm age, 1980

and the technological adaptation of most legacy firms. But here we also see the emergence of firms exhibiting monopoly wealth that was created in electronics and semiconductor technology industries founded after 1950, who were then in the twenty-to-forty age group, or in the younger technology firms founded after 1974.

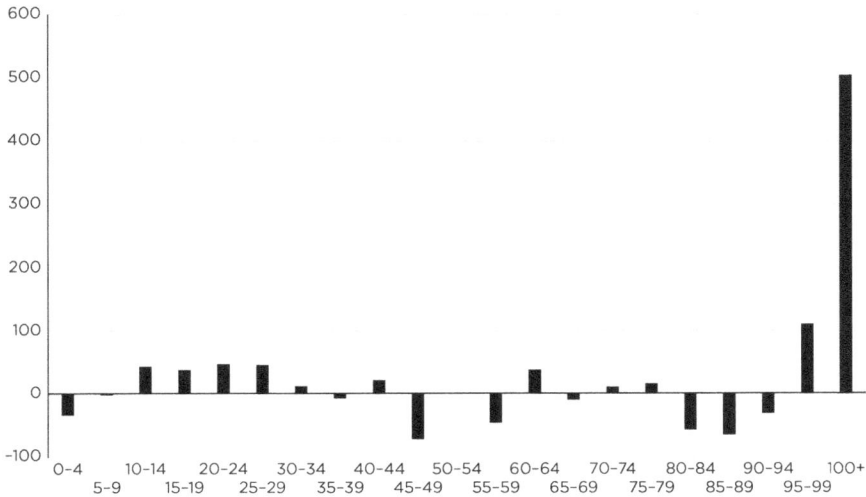

Figure 6.7c   Monopoly wealth by firm age, 1990

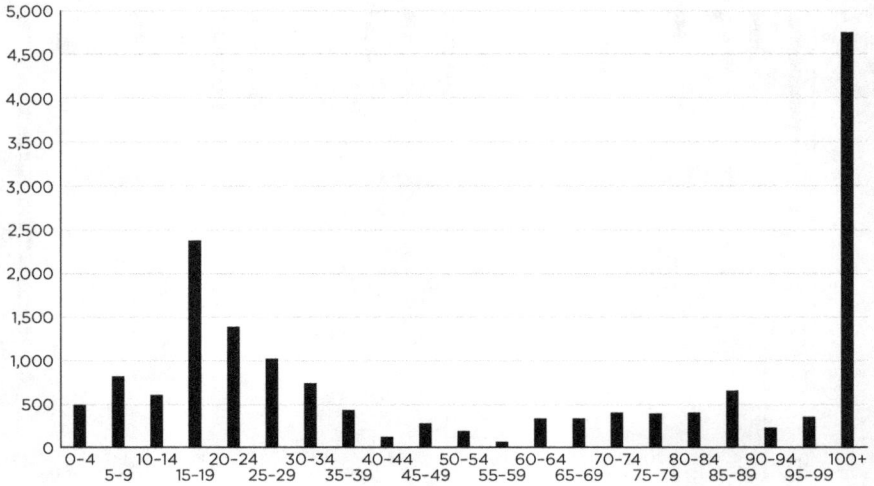

Figure 6.7d Monopoly wealth by firm age, 2000

The clearer story is then revealed in figure 6.7d for 2000. The legacy firms continue to expand. However, in 2000, the 1950s technology firms belong to the age groups of thirty to forty-nine. Together with the young technology firms that were created by the IT revolution, they had most of the monopoly wealth created. However, the firms with the largest concentration of monopoly wealth were in the zero to twenty-four age group, and these were the leading firms of the IT revolution.

Figure 6.7e completes the picture. Three groups possess most monopoly wealth in 2019: first, firms founded after 1973 that are highly technological and are aged less than forty-seven in 2019; second, high-technology firms founded after 1950 and noted earlier, such as Intel, Texas Instruments, and Applied Materials, who belong to age groups fifty to sixty-nine; and third, the legacy firms that have been transformed and adapted to functioning in the digital age.

A partial summary is provided in table 6.4. Firms founded after 1973, the vast majority of them founded on IT innovations, created 48.2 percent of total monopoly wealth in 2019. Their share was only 5.8 percent in 1990. The 2019 share of the firms founded between 1950 and 1973 is 15.5 percent of total monopoly wealth, which, combined with those founded after 1973, is 63.8 percent of monopoly wealth.

The third group is a result of IT being a GPT and creating monopoly wealth by the application of IT in other sectors. It results from the adaptation of the legacy firms to IT and reinventing themselves. This is the source of monopoly wealth in banking, financial services, pharmaceuticals, communication, social

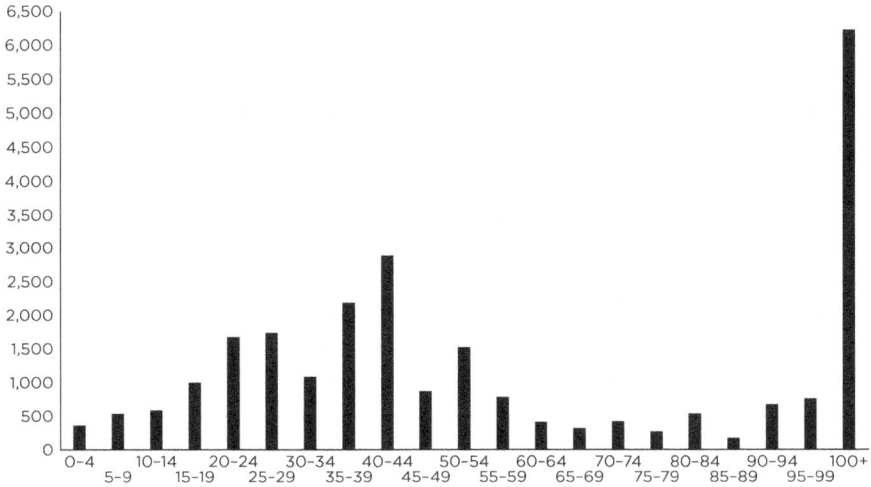

Figure 6.7e Monopoly wealth by firm age, 2019

TABLE 6.4 **Share of monopoly wealth of firms founded after 1973**

Year	Percentage share
1990	5.8
1995	26.4
2005	34.8
2015	43.3
2019	48.2

media, advertising, the defense industry, and online retailing. It is not possible to compute an exact measure of total monopoly wealth created by the IT revolution, but this partial analysis shows the proportion is very high, as predicted by the theory in chapter 1.

CHAPTER 7

R&D AND TECHNOLOGICAL COMPETITION

Technological competition is a central component of the theory advanced in this book, and this chapter explores its unique characteristics. It is carried out by simulating the equilibrium of an economy, modeled as a single industry operating under technological competition among a large number of firms, and studying its endogenously emerging industrial structure. This requires the development of several preliminary ideas that are ultimately integrated in section 7.5. These include an evaluation of the role of government in driving innovations, the difference between basic research and corporate research and development (R&D), and a detailed exploration of the principle of success breeds success, which is at the foundation of technological competition.

7.1 Dual Motives and Dual Compensation for Scientific Progress and Innovations

Michael Faraday discovered electromagnetic induction, the principle underlying the electric generator and transformer, in 1831. But it took several generations of basic research before Nicola Tesla could invent, in 1887, the alternating current (AC) motor that enabled efficient transmission and distribution of electricity. Radiation and radioactivity were discovered in the late nineteenth century, but developing nuclear power was delayed until Enrico Fermi could achieve, in 1942, the first controlled nuclear chain reaction. One may wonder whether a profit-motivated private firm would have begun, in 1831, an R&D project that aimed to produce electricity or to develop, in 1900, commercial applications of nuclear power?

The obvious answer is that no private firm would have done so. This highlights the fact that, although many inventions result from trial and error, preceding the discovery of the scientific principles that underlie them, most major innovations since the Industrial Revolution were made possible by a prior discovery of the science underlying them. Such basic scientific research is very risky; it takes a long time, sometimes generations; and it has been driven by humankind's curiosity and sometimes by desire for honor or power, but always by the deep dedication of the most brilliant minds to scientific discovery. On the other hand, capitalism is able to mobilize technology to increase profits because new technology enables a more efficient production of existing products, or it makes it possible to introduce new and more desirable versions of products that satisfy human needs. These changes enable a firm to increase profits because innovations give it an advantage over competitors. Such advantage is the source of market power that renders the enterprise more profitable.

The preceding examples highlight the distinction between scientific progress motivated by the desire for pure scientific discovery and technological innovations motivated by profits. This distinction implies that technology affects the economy through two different processes, driven by two different motives of participants who are compensated in two different manners. Nevertheless, the process of scientific discovery is the basic source that ultimately propels all profit-motivated innovations that are indispensable for economic progress. This distinction also suggests that, to have an impact on the translation of technological progress into economic growth, policy must consist of two distinct components with two different objectives and tools.

What are the origins of this duality? I discussed the question in chapter 1, where I explain that the second channel, innovation made on a broad scale for profit, arose only in the modern age, after the seventeenth century. Innovations have been made throughout human history. Imperial China, for example, had a rich record of inventions. I noted in chapter 1 Needham's (1965, p. 17) argument that there is no evidence that economic rewards were the drivers of innovations. A similar picture emerges from studying any civilization before the modern age. I also noted in chapter 1 that in China, as well as in the West, the prevailing doctrine, up to the modern age, was that knowledge passed from ancestors *was all the knowledge that humans could have*. Innovations were just rediscoveries of known facts that have been forgotten. New ideas about humanity's ability to control nature were developed during the Age of Enlightenment. Mokyr (2018) argues that the emerging worldview, that there was a cumulative process of innovation and technological progress that could be expected, was the spark that ignited the Industrial Revolution.

Driven by these developments, after the seventeenth century, modern capitalism mobilized innovations and technology for competitive advantage and excess returns. This was welcomed by governments seeking to encourage innovations that create economic value in an economy with private ownership of technology. To do so, they established a method of compensating innovators. A number of countries in early modern Europe created legal frameworks to protect and reward those who innovated for profit. England led the way, introducing patents and other forms of intellectual property rights in the Statute of Monopolies of 1624. The merits of this system are still debated to this day (see Johns, 2009). Given that substantial and perhaps most scientific knowledge was developed without financial rewards, the deeper questions remain: is financial compensation needed for innovations, and if so, which innovations are actually incentivized by financial compensation?

The evolution of science and technology since the seventeenth century has also demonstrated that technological development is a crucial component of economic growth. This fact has raised the question of how best to design public policy to promote economic growth driven by technological innovations. But to do that, we need to better understand how innovations emerge from human effort and the impact of technological competition on this process. This chapter explores these questions by examining the role of the public and private sectors in technological progress and the characteristics of R&D competition, a subject that will bring into focus the question of firm heterogeneity and its implication for public policy.

7.2   The Central Role of Government in Driving Innovations and Economic Growth

Perhaps the greatest fallacy in American public life is the distorted notion that government is incompetent, unable to make rational decisions, and only prevents the private sector from realizing its full potential in solving humanity's problems. When it comes to innovations and the organization of research to develop new technologies, the truth is exactly the opposite.

7.2.1   An Adequacy Principle for Basic Research

A very influential literature in the 1990s studied the unique role of R&D investment and showed how it differed from capital investment. In the Romer (1990) model and the following literature on endogenous growth (for example, Grossman and Helpman, 1991; Aghion and Howitt, 1992, 1996, 2008; and Aghion et al., 2014), R&D is the source of rising productivity, making R&D central to economic growth. For example, in Romer (1990), output is defined by a production function like

$$Y(t) = F(K(t), A(t)L_y(t)), \tag{7.1a}$$

where A measures productivity, identified as a stock of scientific discoveries, and L_y is the input of labor in production. The research sector employs designers or scientists who conduct research and generates, in continuous time, economic productivity in accordance with

$$\dot{A}(t) = \delta L_R(t)A(t), \tag{7.1b}$$

where L_R is the number of specialized workers employed in the research sector. The model then implies that society can increase the growth rate of output by increasing R&D employment of designers and scientists in research. The assumption of proportionality of $\delta L_R(t)$ with $A(t)$ creates an R&D scale effect of rising growth rate as the population of scientists grows, which is not plausible and is rejected by the data (Jones, 1995b). Several refinements of this assumption were proposed (e.g., Jones, 1995a,b; Kortum, 1997; and Segerstrom, 1998), all designed to moderate the effect of R&D on productivity. These newer models imply that long-run productivity growth would be zero without population growth, and the asymptotic growth rate of economic aggregates is *proportional* to the growth rate of population.

One of my objections to the endogenous growth model is its failure to recognize the importance of the duality I have noted. If basic scientific discoveries and business inventions are two distinct processes, then a theory that combines them into a single simple mechanism in which economic growth is generated by firms employing researchers is missing something fundamental to the nature of scientific progress. To set the stage for my alternative approach, I start by questioning the role of corporate R&D, as distinct from scientific progress, in long-run economic growth.

A simple logarithmic plot of income per capita against time, for the last 150 years shows the best fit of such a plot is a straight line,[1] implying that, in the long run, the growth of labor productivity is a geometric progression. Much has changed and fluctuated during the past 150 years, but scientific knowledge—the basis for productivity growth—has steadily accumulated, and this should not be too surprising. Scientific work progresses at its own cumulative pace, where new ideas at each stage are explored, discussed, published, and evaluated from all

---

[1]See Jones (1995b), figure 1, for an example of such a figure that covers the period since 1880.

angles by a community of researchers with common interests. Progress is made on the foundations of previous commonly known results. Evidence to support the advance of science may come from scientific experiments or from business experience and, to that extent, business experience can contribute to the advancement of knowledge. Scientific effort may carry the imprint of a leading creative scholar who makes seminal contributions to that effort, but it is almost always advanced, at its own pace, by the contributions of many members of a broad scientific community.

In essence, scientific research advances through the exploration of new ideas by a community of scholars who carry out their studies in the format of *open science*. That is, when research is completed, all results are published and made publicly available for general study, evaluation, and discussion. The progress of basic scientific knowledge is then determined by the rate at which new ideas emerge and are explored, and virtually nothing will change this dynamic. This growth rate is crucial for determining the rate of economic progress as well. Business-oriented research is indispensable for translating into practical applications discoveries made by basic science, and such translation can cause economic growth to proceed, for some time, at a faster or slower pace than the progress of scientific knowledge, but in the long run it is the rate of scientific progress that is the long-term speed limit on the rate of economic growth.

I noted in chapter 1 that in Imperial China, most research and innovative work was done in public imperial workshops. We also know that past human creative innovations in such areas as engineering projects, architecture, naval navigation, and even music and art were financed mostly by public sources such as municipalities, sovereigns, or the church. In more recent recorded history, when more is known about how research work has been done, we know that basic research has been conducted by scholars who carry out their work within academic, religious, or other nonprofit institutions. In these environments, they combine research with teaching or with other activities advanced by those institutions. Modern basic research requires more financial support than ever before because it uses laboratories with expensive equipment, from particle accelerators to telescopes. With few exceptions, the main source for financing basic research is public funds. The natural question is, Can government expenditures on basic research increase the rate of economic growth as proposed by the endogenous growth theory?

My earlier discussion shows that, on the one hand, scientific ideas grow at an exogenous pace and *no public funding of basic research can accelerate them*. On the other hand, in the modern age of technology, basic research requires a complex infrastructure of universities, research institutes, and supporting facilities. This nonprofit system needs to finance its regular operations to enable scholars to function, communicate, and collaborate. If such infrastructure falls short or is lacking, it can affect the pace at which science can progress. The implication is that there exists a *potential* rate of scientific progress, and public expenditures on basic research determine the degree to which that potential materializes. Public investments in scientific research cannot push the growth rate beyond potential level, but a shortfall in public funding can prevent that potential from materializing. Ample evidence has been presented in the literature showing that public funding for basic research in the United States has been running, for the last thirty years, below the level required for the United States to attain that potential (e.g., Jones and Williams, 2000).

These considerations lead to an *adequacy principle* as a guide to optimal public investments on basic research. It says the government and nonprofit institutions that aim for society to reach its potential should spend on basic research just the adequate amount needed to realize the potential growth rate at which scientific knowledge can advance. Any spending below that level reduces the growth rate of an economy, but any spending beyond that point does not contribute to the growth of scientific knowledge. It is obvious that this cutoff point is hard to determine, but the knowledge that such a point exists is important for determining the budget for basic research. The quest for this cutoff point may explain why funding of basic research is evaluated primarily by a peer review process that aims to determine if a proposed project merits support from a purely scientific perspective. Regardless of society's level of support for basic research, such research is funded outside the private sector, and therefore the growth rate of scientific knowledge must be taken by the firms as an exogenous factor.

The implication for economic growth is direct. The growth of scientific knowledge sets an upper limit on the *potential* productivity growth rate of an economy, and that rate is exogenous to the private sector. Society can realize this upper limit with adequate support for basic research.[2] Therefore, it is best to think of the production of basic research as taking place outside the economic model. Although technical change is a central component of the dynamics of economic development, the growth rate of an economy is determined by society and public policy but not by the private sector.

The realized growth rate, which I denote g, plays a central role in my analysis in this book. It is then essential that government funds basic research to realize a high level of g, and this is an additional reflection of the fact that the vitality of a profit-motivated, advanced capitalist economy hinges on public policy and on collective actions.

---

[2] In an ideal world, basic research would be done and shared by all scholars around the world. In reality, only the advanced economies have invested in the infrastructure needed for basic research. This fact leads to different economies spending different amounts on basic research. However, because basic research is done with open science, many countries inevitably free-ride the basic research supported by the larger and richer economies. I ignore this problem in the development below because the discussion will focus on one economy only.

7.2.2   Government as a Primary Driver of Innovations

It is common to argue that the main difference between the motives and organization of general scientific research and those of corporate R&D flows from the need of private firms to appropriate the results of their R&D in order to cover their costs, while publicly supported research creates knowledge that is made available to all. Indeed, a private firm that engages in basic research and attempts to keep the results confidential will fail to do so because many people work on the same set of issues, and ideas are difficult to keep secret (Nordhaus, 2004). But it is a fact that scientists working in the private sector have the same human curiosity as all other scientists, and the evidence shows that important discoveries, such as the transistor at Bell Labs, computer technology at IBM, or advanced chemistry at DuPont, contributed to basic research. Cummings (2002) documents the significant number of Nobel Prizes in science that were awarded to scientists who had done their research in the private sector. The problem is that even if one recognizes the contribution made by the private sector to basic research, primary incentives distinguish the private from the public sector. Beyond the basic incentive I noted earlier, I focus on three crucial differences between public and private research that make private R&D ill-suited for the conduct of basic research: (1) the nature of risk and private willingness to take such risk, (2) the organization of research, and (3) the unique interests of the public sector. These are the major reasons why basic research is supported by the government or by private nonprofit sources.

Private firms do not engage in basic research because it is too risky, it is too expensive, and it takes too long to reach a stage of commercial applications. Private firms sometimes avoid projects that are highly applied, not considered basic research, because they require investments that are too big or too broad for a single firm to undertake (e.g., Block and Keller, 2015; Braun and MacDonald, 1978; Mazzucato, 2015; and Wright, 2020). The private sector is sometimes reluctant to undertake large joint projects because they require coordination among the participating firms, which is too complex, too risky, and above the skill level of any one firm (see Winter and Nelson, 1982; Gross and Sampat, 2020).

The second problem arises from the organization of research. Basic research is carried out by a *cooperative* community of scholars who regularly communicate with each other and collaborate on some projects. All conduct their work in an environment of open science, where at their publication stage, research results are circulated, shared, and discussed. Individual scholars or teams of researchers certainly compete and keep secret their work in progress, but the outcome of their effort is shared and built upon by all. The success of this organizational structure over the centuries suggests that *the competitive firm is not an efficient organization for conducting basic research.* This cooperative, open science model is sometimes used to solve problems that are not even classified as basic research (e.g., large-scale military projects) and where a solution emerges from cooperation achieved by government acting as a coordinator of the participating private firms.

Third, and this goes beyond basic research, government policy aims to maximize social welfare by often seeking innovations that cannot be profitable for a private firm. In the last half century these have been mostly centered on national security, space technology, public health, and climate policy. Problems in such fields may have some basic research components, such as nuclear power, hard disk storage, space explorations, or renewable power generation. Technologies the government is concerned with are often designed to solve specific public needs but, in many cases, have extensive indirect commercial applications. Under these conditions a private firm is likely to have no incentive to undertake the basic developmental activity, but if the government makes the initial R&D investments, there are then large spillovers to the private sector in terms of commercial applications.

To illustrate how these factors affect policy, consider the U.S. government's role since World War II in promoting innovations. The war necessitated a vast expansion of research by all sides to the conflict, with results that ultimately revolutionized all aspects of life. The war also expedited development of prewar inventions such as the tank, airplane, penicillin (invented in 1928), and nylon (invented in 1935), which were vastly improved during the war. Indeed, it is difficult to identify a product whose postwar version did not benefit from technology developed during the war (see Gross and Sampat, 2020). The impact of innovations on the conduct of the war motivated the celebrated 1945 report of Vannevar Bush to President Roosevelt (see Bush, 1945). Based on the experience of the war, the report proposed that the federal government create a unified agency to support basic research for civilian and military needs because, as explained above, the private sector is not likely to do it on its own. No such agency was ever created.

Apart from the National Science Foundation (NSF) and the National Institutes of Health (NIH), federal support for research in the postwar era was financed mostly out of the military budget and subject to military control. However, relative to the pre–World War II era, the level of support was vast in scale, the organization for directing it was bold and innovative, and its impact was much greater than expected.[3] Many of these programs favored both military projects as well as institutions and research universities on the West Coast, and, in doing so, these government investments in research are credited by most scholars for laying the foundations for Silicon Valley.

---

[3] For more recent contributions that contain extensive references to writings since 1945 see Block (2008, 2015), Block and Keller (2015), Braun and MacDonald (1978), Fuchs (2010), Lécuyer (2006), Mazzucato (2015), Wright (2020), Gross and Sampat (2020), and Moretti et al. (2019).

Reviewing the growth of early electronics in Silicon Valley, Wright (2020) explains that, although the transistor was invented in 1947 at Bell Labs, because of the demand of the military for electronics, 85 percent of semiconductor research was financed by the military. He notes that some of the earliest demand for computers came from the aerospace and missile companies in Southern California, which provided the market for the growing computer electronics industry in the North. The onset of the Cold War, and later the Korean War, increased demand for devices that use semiconductors. Consequently, the early pioneers of Silicon Valley concentrated mostly on semiconductors, financed mostly by military contracts, making government funding the force behind major developments in semiconductor technology.

A change in direction came when, in response to Soviet launch of Sputnik, the government created, in 1958, the Advanced Research Project Agency (ARPA), whose mission was to prevent technological surprises to the U.S. military. From the start, the agency was dedicated to promoting collaboration of the best in industry, government, and academia in order to conceive, design, and execute research projects that build future technologies and advance the frontier of knowledge to benefit society at large, not only the military. The name and nominal mission changed over time from ARPA to DARPA in 1972, back to ARPA in 1993, only to revert back to DARPA in 1996, but the core of its operational methods remained essentially intact (see Fuchs, 2010). The agency not only financed research, it also made standard entrepreneurial decisions about identifying sets of promising technologies, coordinating among projects engaged in research of these technologies, eliminating projects that were not making good progress, and even offering loans to private firms to develop promising technologies when private venture capital considered them too risky. Military project managers went further by initiating promising projects and funding new university departments in computer science in order to support their research effort. The agency has been credited by scholars for spurring the development of major innovations such as the internet, the personal computer, the laser, and Microsoft Windows. Its model of operation has been replicated by ARPA-E in the Department of Energy, the Small Business Innovation Research Program (SBIR), and the National Nanotechnology Initiative (NNI).

Funding for basic research has come, since World War II, mostly from public sources. The origins of the NIH can be traced back to late nineteenth century, but it received its current name with increased funding only in 1948, while the NSF was established by Congress in 1950. During the war, the military played a constructive role even in financing basic science, supporting academic research through the Office of Naval Research (ONR). After the war, the ONR kept intact its wartime partnerships with academic scientists and academic departments. It supported projects at 200 institutions by adopting a very broad conception of the mission of defense-related research.

It should then be recognized that the federal government's participation in advancing basic research and applications has been a central component of U.S. innovative activity since World War II. Analyzing the government's research role since World War II, Gross and Sampat (2020) show that government research funding created new clusters of research that shaped the postwar geography of high-tech industries. Lazonick (2013) argues the government played a central innovative role going back to the nineteenth century, when it supported agricultural research and the construction of the railroads. Mazzucato (2015) offers an extensive survey showing that during the twentieth century the government paved the way for manufacturing and high-technology industries. To illustrate how broad an impact government research programs have had on business technology, Mazzucato (2015) demonstrates that the origin of *every single key component* of Apple's iPhone is an innovation financed by the U.S. government!

In summary, the evidence for the unique capacity of the government to promote innovation and the historical efficacy of its efforts leads to the clear conclusion that government must play a crucial role in promoting, directing, and financing research in any market economy. This conclusion contradicts the ideological view that government decisions, not being subject to market forces, are irrational. This ideological view promotes the fallacy that private enterprise is the only creator of economic growth, when the truth is that without public action to direct, support, and finance research, the private sector undersupplies basic research, leading to a lower rate of economic growth.

7.2.3   What Is the Role of Corporate R&D?

Innovations result in profits if they generate market power. Therefore, a profit-maximizing firm spends R&D resources only on projects that create new market power or on those that promote and consolidate existing market power. Mergers and acquisitions also aim to increase market power. Some attain it via the well-understood route of increased market share. But in the age of technology, most acquisitions increase market power through technological complementarities. A firm acquires a technology that increases its technological reach and thereby increases its market power in the same way an innovation creates a technological advantage. That is, from the perspective of expanding the technological prowess of a firm, R&D and technological mergers and acquisitions lead to the same outcome. For this reason, the term "firm R&D" in this chapter always describes the commonly used meaning of this term together with the firm's mergers and acquisitions that aim to expand its technological base.

Technological competition does not necessarily direct corporate R&D to enhance social productivity. Increased productivity or reduction of social costs occur as indirect results of the motive to create proprietary knowledge used to increase market power and increase profits. Sometimes, the creation of proprietary knowledge can actually reduce social productivity. The development of Oxycontin led to opioid addiction. Technology firms profit from users' increased involvement with their products, but evidence shows that these have caused a rise in what some researchers characterize as "addiction" to services like video games, smartphones, and social media (e.g., Price, 2018; Allcott et al., 2020), which reduces productivity.[4] Because acquisition of proprietary knowledge and direct R&D expenditures are equivalent activities from the firm's perspective, empirical evidence shows (see sections 1.1–1.2) that purchasing technology and acquiring potential competitors who own potentially valuable technologies are often used as tools to deter entry. R&D is used to finance patent strategies to increase the life of a primary patent, and the purchase of competing innovations is sometimes done to suppress them. These are not productivity-enhancing R&D strategies; they are designed to enhance and strengthen the firm's market power with socially questionable consequences.

What is the empirical evidence about corporate R&D? A major proportion of products offered to markets by corporate business were not invented by the business firm that market them. Some were invented by individual inventors or by scientific research financed by public sources. Consider the examples of several major innovations. Charles Babbage, an English mechanical engineer, is credited for originating in 1833 the concept of a programmable computer. The basic concepts of digital computing are due to academic research, such as Turing's (1937) and Shannon's (1938) work. If we take the Universal Automatic Computer (UNIVAC) 1101 or IBM 701, introduced in 1950 and 1953, respectively, as the first commercial digital computers, then all research leading to the digital computer up to the late 1940s was made within academic or governmental institutions. The disk-operating system (DOS), the basic operating system of Microsoft, was not developed by Microsoft. It was developed in 1980 by Tim Peterson, who modified an earlier version developed by another small developer, Gary Kildall. Microsoft purchased the program for $50,000 and used it as the operating system of the IBM PC.

To learn what firms do engage in, consider General Electric (GE), a firm with one of the most distinguished technological records in U.S. history. To examine GE's research record, I compiled a list of products universally cited as the most important products to come out of the GE research laboratory in Schenectady, New York. The question I ask is, How many of them were originally invented by GE? Table 7.1 reports the answer for GE's eleven leading products. It shows

---

[4]The term "addiction" is used in such studies to define a compulsive and irrational behavior as distinct from a rationally chosen leisure activity.

TABLE 7.1   Who invented the leading products of the
GE Schenectady Laboratory?

Product	The initial inventor	Date of initial invention
AC induction motor	Nikola Tesla	1887
Incandescent lamp	Thomas Edison	1879
Radio	Guglielmo Marconi	1894
Electric locomotive	Robert Davidson	1837
X-ray machine	Wilhelm C. Roentgen	1895
Electric fan	Schuyler S. Wheeler	1887
Electric toaster	Alan MacMasters	1893
Refrigerator	Fred W. Wolf	1913
Jet engine	Frank Whittle	1928
Digital clock	Josef Pallweber	1883
Magnetic resonance imaging (MRI)	Paul C. Lauterbur	1971

that *all products were invented by somebody else* and later taken up by GE, improved and marketed as GE products. Indeed, careful study of the history of these products shows that each one of them has actually gone through multiple stages of development by others before reaching a point where mass marketing by GE was undertaken. GE's central contribution has been to the D component of R&D but a relatively small contribution to the R component.

On the other hand, basic research does not create new consumer products or services. Private business R&D plays an indispensable role in translating new scientific ideas into products and processes that increase productivity and enhance living standards. Private innovative activity and basic research are both indispensable for economic progress, and they are complements, not substitutes. The problem is to clarify how public policy and private incentives can work together to promote economic welfare.

The last two points lead to an important observation that motivates some of the ideas developed later. The results of basic scientific research that lead to public recognition, such as Nobel Prizes, are often celebrated as national achievements, shared by all. On the other hand, corporate R&D creates new products and increases social productivity, but it also leads to the creation of large firms with negative social side effects. Such corporate accomplishments are celebrated only by some, not by all. This reflects the fact that R&D develops proprietary technologies that lead to the creation of market power and the use of strategies, discussed in chapter 1, that impede the growth of other firms. Current research often highlights the positive spillover effects of proprietary technologies on other firms, but the negative impediment effects are ignored.

7.2.4   Process and Product Innovations

Much research that studies innovations begins with the Arrow (1962) example of a firm that innovates to increase its own productivity or to lower its own cost.[5] This class of innovations was later called process innovations, as distinct from product innovations, that entail the invention of a new or improved product, sold by monopolists that own these new technologies.

Process innovations refers to innovations in production methods rather than in the character of the firm's products. However, the term raises some subtle issues about who owns the innovation and who uses it. Because I am interested in the motive of the firm to innovate, in the context of this chapter, the term "process innovation" is used to refer to an improvement in productivity that *applies only to the firm's own process of production and not marketed to other firms.* Such process innovation may be made by the firm that uses the innovation, or it can be thought of as being purchased in a market where innovators and start-ups sell their innovations and that exists outside the model. Either way, in the context of the model here, process innovations are not tradeable.

Analogous to process innovations, the literature on product innovations is extensive. It is the cornerstone of Romer's (1990) model of a firm's R&D investments to increase productivity by increasing product variety and is at the foundations of the frequently used infinite product models of monopolistic competition equilibrium (e.g., Ethier, 1982; Grossman and Helpman, 1991; Aghion and Howitt, 1992, 2008; Aghion et al., 2001; Howitt, 1999), where a firm can always innovate a new product. But what does such product innovation mean? I explained in chapter 2 that technological competition should be interpreted to require head-on confrontation of alternative technologies, and the freedom to just add one more product is far too easy resolution of such a conflict. In fact, as I have noted before, the assumption of an infinite number of firms in such models is justified by Triffin (1940), who developed it, as a model of a unimpeded competitive equilibrium when firms have a small differential advantage, like fixed cost or location, and the entry of a new firm with a new product is a simple device of free competition. The use of this device to describe the difficult entry problem of an innovator trying to displace a strong incumbent adversary that has market power and ample strategies to impede such entry is not persuasive.

A product innovation by a firm is interpreted, in this chapter, as the act of upgrading an existing product by increasing its quality. On the other hand, process innovation leads to a direct increase in productivity or reduction in production cost. In the model of technological competition developed later, a finite number of symmetric firms produce differentiated alternative products used to

---

[5] For an excellent survey, assessment, and references of this large literature, see Tirole (1988, chapter 10). For a more formal treatment, see Shy (1995, chapter 9).

satisfy consumption. However, over time, some are unsuccessful in using R&D to upgrade their productivity.

7.3   Adapting the Growth Model of Chapter 2 to Incorporate R&D

7.3.1   Some Preliminaries

To study the effect of corporate R&D, I adapt the model developed in chapter 2 in several ways. The first modification is to the market structure. Technological competition and firm R&D result in firm heterogeneity. Therefore, I do not assume, as in chapter 2, that all M firms are the same and take P_t as given. Now I suppose that M may be small or large, but each firm takes into account the effect it has on P_t. This means the firm estimates its pricing effect on the relative price P_{jt}/P_t because this ratio has a first-order effect on its demand function. But if the noncompetitive firm considers its effect on the price P_t of the consumption aggregate, P_t must be a quantity with a realistic meaning. This was not the case in chapter 2, where an abstract unit of account was used. To make it relevant requires the introduction of an explicit numéraire, and with this in mind, I assume the economy consists of two sectors. First is a competitive sector where many small firms employ factor inputs (K_t^b, L_t^b) to produce a basic homogeneous commodity whose output is denoted by Y_t^b. This commodity is used for consumption C_t^b or investment, and it is the numéraire with price equal to 1. Second is an imperfectly competitive technological sector, in which M firms produce M intermediate goods that are then aggregated to create a consumption good whose quantity is denoted C_t and its price is P_t. One may think of the second consumption good as technological consumption because it is produced by the M intermediate products of firms with market power based on their proprietary advanced technology. This sectoral division will be shown to make the firm's estimate of the effect of its price on P_t a function of the estimated effect of its price *on its relative market share*.

As in chapter 2, the optimization of the representative household in (2.12a) is routine

$$\text{Max}_{(C^b, C, I, L)} \sum_{\tau=0}^{\infty} \beta^\tau \left[B\left(\log C_\tau^b \right) + \log C_\tau - \frac{\mathcal{H}}{1+\eta} L_\tau^{1+\eta} \right], \qquad (7.2a)$$

subject to the budget constraint

$$C_t^b + P_t C_t + K_{t+1} = W_t L_t + K_t(R_t + (1-\delta)) + \Pi_t, \qquad R_t = r_t + \delta. \qquad (7.2b)$$

Turning to the production side, I examine, as noted, two types of innovations. *Process innovations* are those that improve firm productivity. Process innovation consists of either doing R&D or purchasing technologies developed by the R&D of others. Such activity is performed subject to three conditions:

1. The state of scientific knowledge is exogenous, and it is one component of firm productivity.
2. A firm's productivity, relative to the productivity level of other firms, is made possible by cumulative successful R&D expenditures.
3. Corporate R&D cannot alter the asymptotic growth rate of the firm's productivity, only the level of its productivity relative to the trend of aggregate productivity.

To translate these conditions, recall that intermediate goods firms were assumed in chapter 2 to have production functions of the form

$$Y_{jt} = \psi_{jt}\zeta_t(K_{jt})^\alpha(A_tL_{jt})^{(1-\alpha)}.$$ (7.3)

The expression $\zeta_t A_t^{(1-\alpha)}$ is the component of productivity derived from the publicly available state of scientific knowledge advanced by the community of researchers. This component is *common to all firms*. The variable ψ_{jt} is a firm-specific cumulative productivity, reflecting the firm's ownership of proprietary technology not shared by other firms and built with R&D or mergers and acquisitions (M&A). An increased ψ_{jt} increases the productivity level of capital and labor in producing intermediate good j, and the multiplicative form of (7.3) shows that corporate R&D and basic scientific knowledge are complements. Successful corporate effort raises the *level* of the growth path of the firm but has no impact on the firm's asymptotic growth rate because ψ_{jt} is bounded, with a finite steady state.

To specify the initial[6] dynamics of ψ_{jt}, I need a measure of total accumulated R&D stock that reflects knowledge that is in actual use. I thus define the stock of cumulative R&D spending by

$$RD_{jt}^\Psi = \left(1 - \delta_j^\Psi\right)RD_{j,t-1}^\Psi + D_{jt}^\Psi$$ (7.4a)

where D_{jt}^ψ is the amount spent on process innovations at date t. A simplistic approach would reject the depreciation/obsolescence of the stock RD^Ψ on the ground that knowledge is not forgotten and old knowledge is the basis of new knowledge. This is true of general scientific knowledge, where basic scientific principles build on earlier developed ideas. But in the business world, privately owned knowledge can fall out of use, enter the public domain, or reveal itself not to be particularly profitable. The issue at hand is not whether knowledge is forgotten but whether it is useful for giving a firm an advantage over other

---

[6]I will later introduce a crucial random element to reflect the success or failure of the R&D effort, in addition to public policy effects that will aim to alter this dynamic process.

firms. Because private R&D develops applications of general scientific knowledge, with the passage of time, old designs and techniques are not used in later developments. Engineering designs from the nineteenth century are not in use today, and the depreciation in (7.4a) is a substitute for a detailed vintage model in which technology is embodied in specific designs. I therefore follow the standard practice among accountants and economists who study R&D and think about a high rate of depreciation for R&D, in fact higher than real capital assets.

The firm's own productivity ψ_{jt} is then defined by its stock of knowledge *relative to the trend at which knowledge grows*, in the simple form

$$\psi_{jt} = \left(\frac{RD_{jt}^{\Psi}}{A_t} \right)^{\natural}.$$ (7.4b)

The value $\natural = 0.12$ is deduced as an average from the different research examples that report estimates of the effect of R&D on productivity (see Hall et al., 2010, table 2a). Equation (7.4b) is analogous to Segerstrom's (1998) measure defined relative to the R&D "difficulty." It is different from the endogenous growth literature, where it is assumed that the rate of productivity growth is proportional to the level of accumulated privately owned knowledge.[7] Because I assume, for simplicity, that the growth factor of A is at a constant geometric rate g, the steady state of the firm's own relative productivity level is

$$\psi_j^{\star} = \left(\frac{d_j^{\Psi\star}}{g + \delta_j^{\Psi} - 1} \right)^{\natural},$$

where $d_j^{\Psi\star}$ is the steady-state value of D_{jt}^{Ψ}/A_t. This level is determined by the R&D choice of the firms. When comparing two economies with the same growth factor g, if their R&D investments are different, the one that invests more in R&D will have a higher standard of living but not a higher long-run growth rate.

---

[7]Ideas developed in this chapter deviate from assumptions made in the endogenous growth theory (e.g., Romer, 1990; Grossman and Helpman, 1991) or those made in the the the parallel Schumpeterian theory (see Aghion and Howitt, 1992; Aghion et al., 2001; Howitt, 1999). These contributions usually do not distinguish between basic research and corporate research and therefore do not retain an exogenous component for technological progress. As noted earlier, most insist on defining research input by the number of scientists engaged in research rather than by the cost of research, and therefore conclude the dominant component of growth is the growth rate of population. Apart from this important distinction, the debate between these scholars and their critics also centers on empirical questions related to differences of growth rates among countries. If R&D can cause such differences, then we should be able to see it in the data because there are large differences in the long-run R&D investments among countries (see Mankiw et al., 1992; Barro and Sala-I-Martin, 1992; Evans, 1996; Howitt, 2000). The data do not support the implication of the effect of population growth rate.

The values of Ψ_{jt} vary across firms. In the real economy, the distributions of firm size and productivity are skewed, with a few firms being very large and very profitable relative to other firms. So far, the model outlined is one of deterministic R&D investment, and without any uncertainty, all firms would be symmetric. It is clear that the structure of uncertainty in R&D is intimately related to the question of firm heterogeneity. In section 7.5, I introduce stochastic R&D investment, and those shocks are then compounded by a process where firms that are more successful in their R&D gain an advantage in the acquisition of new R&D. This can generate realistic amounts of dispersion and skewness in firm productivity.

Turning to improvements in the quality and efficacy of existing products, recall that in chapter 2, equation (2.2) defined the production of the final consumption good from intermediate goods with the constant elasticity of substitution (CES) function

$$C_t + I_t = Y_t = \left[\sum_{i=1}^{M} \vartheta_{it}(Y_{it})^{\frac{\chi-1}{\chi}} \right]^{\frac{\chi}{\chi-1}}, \quad P_t(C_t + I_t) = \sum_{j=1}^{M} P_{jt} Y_{jt} \qquad (7.5)$$

with $\chi > 1$. In chapter 2, this parameter in the demand function was denoted θ, but here I denote it χ for reasons that will shortly become clear. The variable ϑ_{jt} measures the quality and efficacy of intermediate good j as a component in consumption. Now I examine the implications of firms being able to alter it strategically. Firm j can increase the quality of product j by increasing ϑ_{jt}, which increases the weight of intermediate good j in final consumption. To see the effect of such action, recall that, as in (2.6), the implied demand function is

$$Y_{jt} = \left(\frac{P_{jt}}{\vartheta_{jt} P_t} \right)^{-\chi} Y_t \qquad (7.6a)$$

where the price P_t is defined by

$$P_t = \left[\sum_{i=1}^{M} \vartheta_{it} \left(\frac{P_{it}}{\vartheta_{it}} \right)^{1-\chi} \right]^{\frac{1}{1-\chi}}. \qquad (7.7)$$

Now consider the new market structure, where the firm takes into account its effect on the aggregate price in computing its optimal price P_{jt}. By (7.6a) and (7.7), the demand function of firm j becomes

$$Y_{jt} = \left(\frac{P_{jt}}{\vartheta_{jt}} \right)^{-\chi} \left[\sum_{i=1}^{M} \vartheta_{it} \left(\frac{P_{it}}{\vartheta_{it}} \right)^{1-\chi} \right]^{\frac{\chi}{1-\chi}} Y_t. \qquad (7.6b)$$

A change in firm j's product quality ϑ_{jt} has then two effects: one is a direct effect on the weight of the jth intermediate good in producing consumption, measured in (7.5), and a second effect is on the equilibrium price P_t in (7.7).

To define the dynamic process that governs ϑ_{jt}, I define the cumulative R&D spending on innovations in product quality by

$$RD^{\vartheta}_{j,t} = \left(1 - \delta_j{}^{\vartheta}\right)RD^{\vartheta}_{j,t-1} + D_t{}^{\vartheta} \tag{7.8a}$$

where $D_t{}^{\vartheta}$ is the amount spent on product quality R&D in date t. As to the transition of ϑ_{jt}, it is defined by

$$\vartheta_{j,t+1} = \frac{RD^{\vartheta}_{jt}}{A_t} \tag{7.8b}$$

with a steady-state

$$\vartheta_j^{\star} = \frac{d_j{}^{\vartheta\star}}{g + \delta_j - 1}. \tag{7.9}$$

It is important to interpret (7.8b) correctly. Because I describe the economy with a finite number of goods, a primitive hut and a modern house are both dwellings. But the switch from the hut to the modern heated house requires developments in basic research and therefore is being accounted for by the growth of shared scientific knowledge expressed by A_t. Therefore, any R&D effort to improve quality is defined relative to improvements already embodied in A_t. In that case, ϑ_{jt} measures the quality of housing produced by firm j, *relative to the general technology used for housing at date t, determined by the level A_t.* Different economies may enjoy products with different ϑ_{jt}, and this could mean that whatever the technology of housing, some economies attain more advanced housing technology that consumers like, while others attain a less desirable housing technology. As noted, the model enables a comparison of two different economies with equal basic knowledge embodied in A_t but with different quality levels of individual products, where their quality level is defined relative to the prevailing level of scientific knowledge.

Before proceeding to a general equilibrium analysis of R&D competition where leading firms can impede the growth of smaller firms, I examine the effective difference between R&D investment in quality innovations and R&D investment in process innovations.

7.3.2   The Different Effects on Aggregate Productivity of Process and Product Quality Innovations

I can now address a simple question. From the point of view of aggregate productivity, what is the difference between product quality innovation and process innovation?

The answer to this question is related to empirical results on the effect of R&D on productivity (e.g., Scherer, 1980; Griliches, 1987, 1994). A key finding in this literature is that the price indexes used for measuring inputs and output have a pivotal effect on computed productivity of a firm or industry. Consequently, if care is not taken to measure inputs and outputs by the correct price indexes, measured productivity is wrong and changes in measured "real output" contain an error. Even if we control correctly for the measures of true quantities of inputs, an incorrect price index leads to an incorrect measure of productivity.

Given the demand function (7.6b), firm j's demand elasticity θ_{jt} is now defined by

$$\frac{\partial Y_{jt}}{\partial P_{jt}} = -\chi \frac{Y_{jt}}{P_{jt}} \left(1 - \frac{P_{jt}^{1-\chi} \vartheta_{jt}^{\chi}}{P_t^{1-\chi}} \right) \Rightarrow \theta_{jt} = \chi \left(1 - \left(\frac{P_{jt}}{P_t} \right)^{1-\chi} \vartheta_{jt}^{\chi} \right). \quad (7.10)$$

To see what (7.10) implies, note that the market share of firm j, among technology firms, is defined by

$$\frac{P_{jt} Y_{jt}}{\sum_{i=1}^{M} P_{it} Y_{it}} = \frac{P_{jt}^{1-\chi} \vartheta_{jt}^{\chi} P_t^{\chi}}{\sum_{i=1}^{M} P_{it}^{1-\chi} \vartheta_{it}^{\chi} P_t^{\chi}} = \left(\frac{P_{jt}}{P_t} \right)^{1-\chi} \vartheta_{jt}^{\chi} = sh_{jt}. \quad (7.11)$$

Therefore, the elasticity of demand for firm j's product is a function of the firm's market share

$$\theta_{jt} = \chi(1 - sh_{jt}), \quad (7.12)$$

which shows that now the elasticity of demand falls with the market share of the firm, a condition required by Autor et al. (2020). The model is applicable when $\theta_{jt} > 1$, and for this to be satisfied, it is required that $\chi > (1 - sh_{jt})^{-1}$ for all j. In this setup, the firm aims to raise its market share so that with lower demand elasticity it can charge a higher markup. Higher market share reflects the firm's increased market power. The profit function of firm j in units of the basic consumption good B is

$$P_{j\tau} Y_{j\tau} - W_\tau L_{j\tau} - R_\tau K_{j\tau} - \left(D_{j\tau}^{\Psi} + D_{j\tau}^{\vartheta} \right)$$

and the optimization of the firm with respect to its capital and labor inputs is defined as in equation (2.7a). This leads to the first-order conditions

$$W_t = P_{jt} \frac{(\theta_{jt} - 1)}{\theta_{jt}} (1 - \alpha) \psi_{jt} \zeta_t A_t^{1-\alpha} K_{jt}^{\alpha} L_{jt}^{-\alpha} \quad (7.13a)$$

and

$$R_t = P_{jt} \frac{(\theta_{jt} - 1)}{\theta_{jt}} \alpha \psi_{jt} \zeta_t A_t^{1-\alpha} K_{jt}^{\alpha-1} L_{jt}^{1-\alpha}. \quad (7.13b)$$

Now an equilibrium is typically asymmetric because θ_{jt} varies across firms. The effects of R&D on a firm's market share, market power, and aggregate productivity can then be deduced from the following proposition. The proposition itself is derived just from the firms' optimized price and factor levels, and holds for any level of R&D and other resources.

Proposition 7.1. *In an equilibrium:*

1. *Price and productivity satisfy* $P_{jt}\psi_{jt}\dfrac{\chi\left(1-\left(\frac{P_{jt}}{P_t}\right)^{1-\chi}\vartheta_{jt}^{\chi}\right)-1}{\chi\left(1-\left(\frac{P_{jt}}{P_t}\right)^{1-\chi}\vartheta_{jt}^{\chi}\right)} = \varphi_t$ *for all j.*

2. *R&D that raises either a firm's own productivity ψ_{jt} or the quality of its product ϑ_{jt} results in increased market share sh_{jt}, increased market power $\mathcal{P}_j$, and increased aggregate productivity.*

Proof.   1. As in proposition 2.1, the proof is the result of the capital/labor ratio being the same for all firms.

2. For given resource inputs, an increased ψ_{jt} leads to an increased output of intermediate good j and increased ϑ_{jt} leads to an increased consumption level. Therefore, both result in increased productivity.

Using the definition of sh_{jt} in (7.11) and result (1), I compute the derivative

$$\frac{\partial sh_{jt}}{\partial \psi_{jt}} = \frac{1}{\psi}\frac{\chi(1-sh_{jt})-1}{\chi} > 0. \tag{7.14a}$$

On the other hand, using (7.11), I show that increased product quality has the same impact on market share because

$$\frac{\partial(sh_j)}{\partial \vartheta_{jt}} = \frac{\chi}{\vartheta_{jt}}sh_{jt}(1-sh_{jt}) > 0. \tag{7.14b}$$

It follows that increased quality raises the firm market share. By (7.12), a higher value of sh_{jt} leads to a lower value of θ_{jt}, and this means increased market power $\mathcal{P}_{jt}$.

□

I showed in chapter 2 that φ_t is a component of aggregate productivity, and it follows from proposition 7.1 that if firm j uses R&D to raise ψ_{jt}, the first-order effect of such a change is a decline in the firm's relative price and an increase in its market share. But I also show that if the firm's R&D effort is directed toward increasing the quality ϑ_{jt} of its own product, it will also result in a decline in the firm's relative price and an increase in its market share and consequently in productivity. This shows that firms maximize profits by selecting an optimal path of productivity and product quality $(\psi_{jt},\vartheta_{jt})$, both of which ultimately have similar effects on measured productivity φ_t as seen in statement (1) of proposition (7.1).

Proposition (7.1) then reveals that competitive pressure spurs innovations that generate increased productivity and product quality, and their measured effect on aggregate productivity is highly dependent on equilibrium prices, as seen in condition (1) of the proposition. A firm has the incentive to innovate, without which it loses market share, but in a symmetric equilibrium without uncertainty all firms invest equally in R&D and no firm gains market share. But even if no firm gains market share, the aggregate effect is increased productivity of all firms. The effect of process innovations on productivity is virtually the same as increased quality of inputs, and there is little reason to study them together.

In the rest of this chapter, I thus study the general equilibrium implication of ideas developed so far. To do so, I assume that R&D takes only the form of process innovations. I will then assume for the rest of the chapter that

$$\vartheta_{jt} = 1 \text{ for all } t$$

and the initial conditions of all the firms are the same. All firms start with the same technology. Although firms start off being symmetric, the introduction of uncertainty changes all this because uncertainty causes random diversity that arises from luck in their R&D effort. Such diversity is sharply magnified by a process that I define in the next section. The two main questions are then simple: starting from symmetric foundations, how much heterogeneity occurs due to pure luck? And how should public policy respond to such a mechanism? The stochastic component of the model I use later to answer these questions utilizes ideas from a literature on a process called *success breed success*. I review these ideas first.

7.4   R&D and the Principle of Success Breeds Success

Models of R&D and endogenous growth typically include the act of innovation as a draw, in each period, of a random variable from a specified probability distribution. Because there is free entry to R&D and M&A, it is assumed that every firm has the same probability distribution. When many draws of such a random variable are taken over time, the law of large numbers and the central limit theorem are at work: the mean outcome for each firm converges to the expected value of the random variable under the specified distribution and the limit distribution of outcomes across firms tends to be symmetric.

Consequently, scholars who study firm heterogeneity[8] and its implications for antitrust policy typically model asymmetric equilibria by imposing

---

[8]See my discussion in chapter 1 and chapter 4 about the applicability of antitrust laws against those firms that are more productive. See also Autor et al. (2020) and Van Reenen (2018) and the summary of the issue in chapter 8.

different random initial conditions. This ignores the very important process by which firms come to differ in productivity. After all, a corporation is a humanmade institution and, given the same technological knowledge, there are no inherent differences among firms to provide a cause for heterogeneity at birth.

Yet it is obvious there are big differences in technological levels and in degrees of market power among firms, *and that distribution is very skewed*. A small number of very large firms dominate both the technology and the market in each industry, and other firms lag behind them significantly. The family of models I study in this section proposes that such heterogeneity is often a matter of pure luck. But it is a very special kind of luck, not in the outcome of any one result of R&D, but rather it is due to the cumulative effect of those random events. It is related to a large literature in statistics that has branched into other fields like biology and sociology and is about the process of *success breeds success* which originates in the theory of Pólya urn models.

The basic idea of success-breeds-success models is that early success creates an initial *random advantage* for which competitors find it hard to make up and only with declining probabilities. It is motivated by the existence of many phenomena where success results from a random discovery of a good idea, and a good idea leads to other good ideas. That is, coming up with a good idea increases the probability of coming up, in the next random draw, with a good idea, whereas coming up with a bad idea is likely to lead nowhere. More precisely, having a record of good ideas increases the probability of coming up with a good idea, and a record of bad ideas increases the probability of going nowhere. This is not a question of high serial correlation because the issue at hand is one of changing probability of success, depending upon the sequencing of past results. Price (1976) used the alternate terminology of "cumulative advantage processes," which has been widely adopted and is now used in many disciplines. Such processes have been used to explain the existence of skewed distributions such as Bradford's Law, Lotka's Law, or the Pareto and Zipf distributions. I present here three variants in order to explain why a cumulative advantage process is a natural mechanism to describe technological competition. It leads to very different outcomes from regular atomistic competition. As I explained, the advantage gained by the winners is due to the nature of uncertainty, which is exactly the advantage gained from a successful innovation. But firms that benefit from this random cumulative advantage can then, *in addition*, use the strategies outlined in chapter 1 to impede the growth of their competitors, consolidate their position, and expand their market power. These two advantages complement each other and amplify the creation of market power, and the new, purely random mechanism is an additional force that reinforces my argument in chapter 1 on the durability of market power.

7.4.1   Pólya Urn Process

Urn processes are simple counting mechanisms that permit the use of combinatorial methods to deduce probability distributions of success or failure. The Pólya urn process is a celebrated model with a success-breeds-success feature. It should actually be called the Pólya-Eggenberger urn process because it was first published by Eggenberger and Pólya (1923). Consider an urn with W_0 initial white balls and B_0 initial black balls, $N_0 = W_0 + B_0$, and at each date one ball is drawn from the urn. If a white ball is drawn, it is recorded as *a success*, the white ball is returned to the urn, and an additional white ball is placed in the urn. Similarly, the draw of a black ball is recorded as *a failure*; the ball is returned to the urn and a black ball is added to the urn. Let W_n denote the number of white balls after n draws and B_n the number of black balls after n draws. Because a ball is added at each time, the number of balls $N_n = N_0 + n$. The process is said to be *balanced* if the number of balls in the urn is independent of the sequence of draws, and it is clear that the Pólya urn process is balanced.

A Pólya urn scheme penalizes failed draws by the fact that each failed draw increases the probability of future failure. Indeed, the many generalizations of the Pólya urn process considered in the literature focus on alternative number of added white or black balls after a success or failure. Some generalizations also involve adding some number of black balls after a draw of a white ball and a different number of white balls after a draw of a black ball, in which case the model would describe a process of success breeds failure.

Let X_n be the outcome of the nth draw, which can be either w or b. What is the probability of a white ball on draw $n+1$, given that k white balls have already been drawn up to draw n? Some reflection leads to the conclusion that

$$\text{Prob}[X_{n+1} = w \mid W_n - W_0 = k] = \frac{W_0 + k}{N_0 + n} = \frac{W_n}{N_n}. \qquad (7.15)$$

If an urn is particularly lucky and has a long run of n successive white balls at the start, the probability of a white ball on draw $n + 1$ grows to

$$\text{Prob}[X_{n+1} = w \mid X_1 = X_2 = \ldots X_n = w] = \frac{W_0 + n}{N_0 + n}. \qquad (7.16)$$

Such a successive draw of white balls, *at the start*, endows that urn with a permanent advantage of success in which the probability of white balls rises to a point where it will take a *greater* miracle to bring the odds of success back to the average. The initial lucky success breeds a future *permanent* success! In subsequent research, Pólya (1930) interpreted this phenomenon as model of contagion, and over the years many other interpretations and applications in various disciplines were developed.[9]

To complete the description of the model, I state now standard results about the probability distribution of the random variable $W_n = k$ and about its limit distribution. To do that, I introduce the following notation, for any sequence of integers:

$$Z_0^{[k]} = Z_0(Z_0 + 1)(Z_0 + 2) \dots (Z_0 + k - 1)$$

$$\binom{n}{k} = \frac{n!}{k!(n-k)!}.$$

Then we have the following well-known results:

$$\text{Prob}[W_n = k] = \binom{n}{k} \frac{W_0^{[k]} B_0^{[n-k]}}{N_0^{[n]}} \tag{7.17a}$$

$$E[W_n] = \frac{W_0}{N_0} n + W_0 \tag{7.17b}$$

$$\text{Var}[W_n] = \frac{W_0 B_0 n (N_0 + n)}{N_0^2 (N_0 + 1)} \tag{7.17c}$$

$$\text{Prob}\left[\frac{W_n}{n} = x\right] \Rightarrow \text{Beta}(W_0, B_0) = \frac{\Gamma(N_0)}{\Gamma(W_0)\Gamma(B_0)} x^{W_0 - 1}(1 - x)^{B_0 - 1} \tag{7.17d}$$

where (7.17d) is the limit distribution, and $\Gamma(\cdot)$ is the gamma function. For proofs, see Mahmoud (2008), theorems 3.1 and 3.2, and Johnson and Kotz (1977), sections 4.2 and 6.2.

These results explain that the initial cumulative advantage of the few will be preserved permanently. The beta distribution has different possible shapes depending upon the two parameters. However, for studying consequences of economic R&D, the relevant case is one with a small initial probability of success, where W_0/N_0 is small, so the limit distribution is right-skewed. Figure 7.1 presents three examples of the limit density for $W_0 = 1$ and $B_0 = 10, 20$, and 30.

The urn model is a drastically simplified description of the process of technological competition. Each urn represents a firm, and the proportion of white balls represents the degree of productivity level as a result of R&D. A draw

---

[9] Johnson and Kotz (1977) and Mahmoud (2008) are standard texts on the subject; they study many applications and provide detailed references. Merton (1968) introduced the ideas in sociology, while Allison and Stewart (1974) offer some evidence in that field. DiPrete and Eirich (2006) is an excellent survey. Price (1976) introduced the terminology of "cumulative advantage" while Egghe and Rousseau (1995) is an example of application in informetrics and bibliometrics.

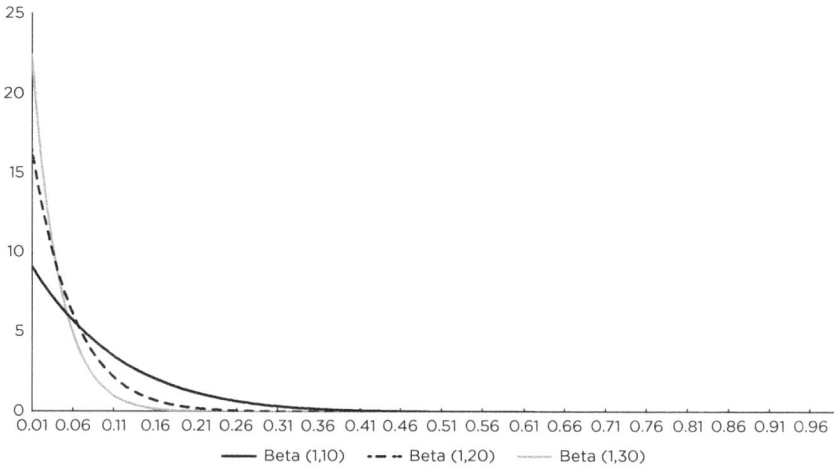

Figure 7.1 Three beta probability density functions

from the urn is an attempt by the firm to progress forward in its lines of research or acquisition of technology. Cumulative successful attempts open the
door to new avenues of research by suggesting new ideas of how to proceed,
and a failure closes doors on a line of research because a failure reflects not only
the failure of a particular act but the failure of a whole line of thinking. This
may be too harsh an assumption, and I will later consider a model where no
black ball is placed in the urn upon failure. This approach proposes to think of
a "failure" in terms of a specific act that fails to fit the needs of the firm but
without wider implications. The perspective of the urn model offers further
support to a combined view of R&D with M&A. Some acquisitions are spec-
tacularly successful, but many others fail by not fitting into an intended firm's
technology.

The urn model is then a simple and powerful probability model not only of
technological competition but also of the accumulation of market power. In reality, a firm with a small technological advantage enjoys more profits and a more
rapid growth rate, and grows larger in size, but such a firm also employs additional business strategies that exploit the probability structure it faces. The urn
model clearly does not address all these economic and financial considerations.
By focusing on the nature of technological uncertainty, the urn model can be
a powerful supplement to an economic model that gives economic meaning to
the terms "success" and "failure."

To understand the implications of the urn model for inequality, I now examine the case of a large number of initial firms, represented by a large number of
urns. *All urns start at identically the same conditions*, representing the fact that

TABLE 7.2   Limit distribution of 100 firms' productivity

Initial probability	Mean productivity	Percent of firms with limit productivity at least 300 percent above the mean	Percent of bankrupt firms with productivity less than 100 percent above the mean
$W_0 = 1, B_0 = 10$	0.0909	1.09	86.6
$W_0 = 1, B_0 = 20$	0.0476	1.46	86.5
$W_0 = 1, B_0 = 30$	0.0323	1.59	86.5

all potential firms begin with equal access to the available inputs into research effort. Suppose the urns have the initial probabilities used in figure 7.1. Limit productivity is the fraction of white balls of the firm in the limit. In this process, it is not the case that there is "survival of the fittest" and that the only firm that survives is the one with the highest productivity. In real markets, firms can end up with different productivity, different market shares, different market power, and different profitability. This is the conclusion of a large literature on firm heterogeneity, and I have referred to it before as heterogeneity argument. To accommodate this view, I assume that in the model, market shares are distributed in accordance with limit productivity. Suppose that firms with a technological advantage of, say, 300 percent above the mean productivity end up dominating the industry, and all firms with limit productivity less than 100 percent above the mean default and are eliminated. The question is then, if we start with 100 potential firms, how many firms will end up with productivity above 300 percent of the mean and how many firms will default because their limit productivity will be less than 100 percent above the mean? Table 7.2 provides the answer.[10] The table shows that only one or two firms will survive with productivity of 300 percent above the mean. On the other side, 86.5 percent will default because they could not pass the 100 percent mark above the limit mean productivity. Although I am not proposing these numbers as applicable to any particular sector of the economy, what is compelling is the simplicity of the model and its power to demonstrate the impact of uncertainty as a force that determines economic heterogeneity.

---

[10]The main point is that models that incorporate success breeds success lead to a great deal of skewness, and that skewness increases the less likely success is. A model with more skewness has more mass in the tails and, in terms of measures of concentration, such models exhibit higher Herfindahl-Hirschman indexes (HHIs). The introduction of bankruptcy changes that a bit. As long as bankrupt firms are small, greater skewness implies a higher HHI index as well.

7.4.2 A Modified Pólya Urn Process Without a Penalty on Failure

Price (1976) and others have argued that, in the applications to bibliometrics, which is the study of the pattern of innovative publications of researchers, a weak publication has no effect and should be treated as a nonevent, not as a failure. Based on this, Price (1976) proposed to modify the Pólya urn process by eliminating the addition of a black ball when a black ball is drawn. The mathematical implication of this assumption is drastic because the urn process becomes unbalanced; N_n, the total number of balls in the urn after n draws, is stochastic and depends upon the sequence of draws. On the other hand, the limit distribution becomes trivial because only white balls can be added, and over time the number of balls in the urn can grow only by the addition of white balls. Therefore, the fraction of white balls in the urn converges to 1 with probability 1.

This reasoning suggests that the modified urn model is a useful tool to study only phenomena over a finite number of dates. To understand technological change over longer horizons, it's possible to think about the modified urn model occuring repeatedly. At some point, as the probability distribution converges, something triggers a renewal, sending the process back to its starting point. This restarts the process, and an entirely new generation of firms becomes involved. In the context of bibliometrics, this assumption reflects the finite life of a scholar. In the context of technological innovations, this may be viewed as a formal process by which a new general-purpose technology (GPT) sparks a new wave of innovation. Big changes resulting from innovations such as electricity or the computer and internet, amount to a restart of the innovation process. They trigger a renewed process of technological competition among potential new firms and the existing large firms can adapt and thrive, but they have only limited advantage. Because such waves of innovations occur perhaps every three or four generations, I will conduct the analysis under the assumption that the modified urn process lasts only fifty years.

Although the probability of the event $\{W_n = k\}$ does not have a simple closed-form representation, the conditional probability of a white or black ball in the $n + 1$ draw given $\{W_n = k\}$ is very simple:

$$\text{Prob}[X_{n+1} = w \mid W_n] = \frac{W_n}{W_n + B_0}. \tag{7.18}$$

The simplicity of this expression shows we can identify a set of states by the number of white balls in the urn so that in state S_k, there are $W_k = k + W_0$ white balls in the urn. When in state S_k, a transition from S_k can occur only into two possible states: either remain in the state S_k or move up to the state S_{k+1}.

These two transition probabilities are:

$$\text{Prob}[S_{k+1} \mid S_k] = \frac{B_0}{W_k + B_0}, \quad \text{Prob}[S_{k+1} \mid S_k] = \frac{W_k}{W_k + B_0}. \quad (7.19)$$

Therefore, the urn model is a Markov chain, with transition probability over the infinite number of states $\{S_0, S_1, S_2, S_3, \ldots\}$ that identify the number of white balls in the urn. From this construction, it should be clear that, although starting with state S_0 one can reach state S_k via many different permutations of draws with different probabilities; one can average such patterns by computing the n-step transition probabilities and the associated Chapman-Kolmogorov equations. More specifically, if one is interested in the distribution after fifty periods, then there are only fifty-one possible states that can be reached—the initial number of white balls plus a maximum addition of fifty balls. This means that we need to compute only the fifty-one transition probabilities from S_0 to $\{S_0, S_1, S_2, S_3, \ldots S_{50}\}$, making it a tractable problem.

I computed the limit fifty-step probabilities for three initial distributions of $(W_0 = 1, B_0 = 10)$, $(W_0 = 1, B_0 = 20)$, and $(W_0 = 1, B_0 = 30)$, and figure 7.2 exhibits the probability distribution of the number of white balls in the urn after fifty periods. Note that, as with the beta distribution, the phenomenon of skewness arises only for low initial probability of success. High initial probability of success offers enough opportunities for competitors to experience a run of good luck that can compensate for the cumulative disadvantage of early failure, resulting in more symmetric distribution. In the case of the modified urn problem, *given enough time*, every urn has an opportunity for recovery because the

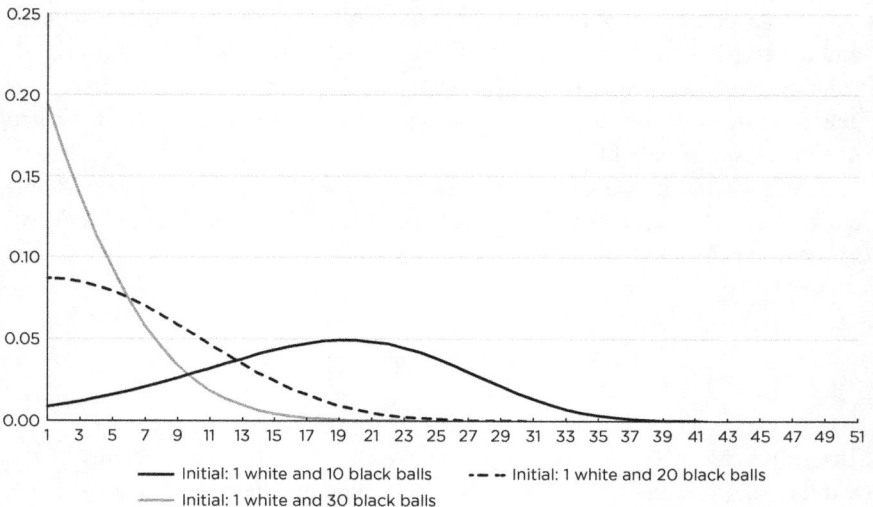

Figure 7.2   Probability of white balls for fifty draws

TABLE 7.3 Limit distribution after fifty years

Initial probability	Mean number of white balls	Firms with limit productivity at least 300 percent higher than the mean	Bankrupt firms with productivity lower than 100 percent above the mean
$W_0 = 1, B_0 = 10$	18.04	0	99.7
$W_0 = 1, B_0 = 20$	7.51	0.01	91.9
$W_0 = 1, B_0 = 30$	4.42	0.30	87.9

number of white balls is rising and the probability of success is rising with them. Therefore, in the case of the modified urn process, there is tension between the length of time the process is operative and the initial probability of success.

Consider now the case of a large number of initial firms that start under exactly equal conditions represented by the modified urn. Figure 7.2 shows that the technological horizon of fifty years is long enough for almost everybody to recover from the impact of an initial failure probability of 10/11. Putting it a different way, with initial success probability of 1/11, the distribution of productivity across firms, measured by the fraction of white balls in the urn, is skewed for horizon of thirty years but becomes essentially symmetric after fifty years. However, with initial success probabilities of 1/21 or 1/31, figure 7.2 shows the results are very skewed.

The expected success and failure rates after fifty years are summarized in table 7.3. If we start with a large number of potential technological competitors, with initial success probability of 1/11, the two boundaries are meaningless. Four times above the mean is not feasible because $72.16 > 51$, which is the maximal number of white balls in fifty draws, and for this symmetric distribution, twice the mean is so high that only 0.3 percent will not default. However, starting with success probabilities of 1/21 or 1/31 results in very skewed distributions. With an initial probability of 1/21, 91.9 percent of the firms default because they do not exceed twice the mean productivity, and only 0.01 percent end up above 300 percent of the mean. The skewness is slightly different with initial success probability of 1/31: 87.9 percent default and 0.3 percent benefit from the cumulative advantage earned by being very lucky at the very start.

7.4.3 Other Cumulative Advantage Processes

The first two examples are of the urn model, but many other processes feature the success-breeds-success or cumulative advantage phenomenon. DiPrete and

Eirich (2006) review many examples of cumulative advantage processes in the social and natural sciences, and I mention one that is a simple version of the Yule process. Conside the comparison of N firms, starting from the same initial value $Y_0 = 1$, under a mechanism that generates random growth shocks γ_{it} for $i = 1, 2, \ldots N$ that are independent and identically distributed (i.i.d.) over time and uniformly distributed on $[0, 1]$. The resulting growth rate is

$$\frac{dY_{it}}{dt} = \gamma_{it} Y_{it} \tag{7.20}$$

or its difference equation version

$$Y_{it} - Y_{i,t-1} = \gamma_{it} Y_{i,t-1}.$$

In either case, a lucky firm that draws at the start a sequence of large γ_{it} has a permanent advantage. Cumulative advantage stresses only the dependence of success on the current state; it does not stipulate how decisive the advantage is and therefore does not require unboundedness. For example, an adaptation of the process in (7.20) produces logistic growth and implies a cumulative advantage described by the bounded growth process

$$\frac{dY_{it}}{dt} = \gamma_{it} Y_{it} \left(1 - \frac{Y_{it}}{Y^\star}\right).$$

Statistical models of cumulative advantage do not reflect the full complexity of strategic interaction among firms. They highlight only the long-term impact of small differences in the probabilities of success and failure early in a firm's existence. In real economic life, once an advantage of any one firm is established, other factors come into play because firms take actions to press their advantage or, equally important, impede the development of other, weaker firms, as discussed in chapter 1. The models discussed so far do not contain any action that the firms themselves can take to consolidate their own advantage and impede the progress of others. This will be the main topic of section 7.5.

7.4.4   Some Implications of Cumulative Advantage to Technological Competition

Cumulative advantage bolsters the argument laid out in chapter 1 that technological competition is fundamentally different from standard competition. If technological competition is characterized by a higher degree of cumulative advantage, and I argue that it is, then technological competition creates insurmountable barriers to entry even if formally no such barriers exist. The technological leader will have better technology and be able to acquire new technology more easily, so the catch-up or entry cost will exceed the potential profits of either laggards or potential entrants.

The cumulative advantage reasoning has several important economic implications. The first addresses the fact that endogenous growth models typically assume free entry into R&D and innovations, leading to the claim that technological competition restrains excess profit margins in the same way regular atomistic competition restrains excess profits in a competitive equilibrium. The results of this chapter show that, this is a flawed analogy. As noted in chapter 1, free entry in technological competition requires superior innovations, which may not be feasible. Therefore, R&D investments cannot guarantee a zero profit condition. Here, the reasoning of cumulative advantage shows that, even without the strategies of chapter 1, cumulative advantage on its own erects such barriers to entry that raise the cost of entry to a level that makes entry unprofitable. The combined effect of innovations and cumulative advantage strengthens the position of market leaders to a point where the focus of policy should shift to the question of how to restrain the ability of the leaders to impede the progress of competitors in the ways discussed in chapter 1. Note the contrast between the ability of leaders to impede the progress of other firms and the extensive literature emphasizing technological spillovers that are beneficial to others.

Second, the reasoning of cumulative advantage, which explains persistence of success because of pure luck and not because of any inherent superior traits, can go a long way toward explaining the literature on the heterogeneity in investing, entrepreneurial, or managerial skill that purports to show some individual investors, entrepreneurs, and managers are consistently more capable than others. Some of the biggest differences in individual performances result from long-term relations of these individuals with corporate entities in which they are either officers or investors, and their financial success is derived from the success of the corporations with which they happened to be linked. If the success of the firm is a reflection of random cumulative advantage, so is the success of individuals linked to them. This argument then questions the interpretation of recent evidence of persistent diversity of realized individual investment returns (see Bach et al., 2020; Fagereng et al., 2020; Smith et al., 2019). These authors interpret the data as revealing persistent diversity in the intrinsic ability of investors. Presumed diversity of individual investment ability is also at the center of the literature on the Pareto distribution (see Gabaix, 2009; Gabaix et al., 2016; Benhabib et al., 2011; Benhabib et al., 2017; Jones and Kim, 2018). If there are cumulative advantage effects, there can be persistent advantages even when there are no differences in underlying skill. In addition, there may be cumulative advantages in the performance of individuals on their own. Those who are successful early on may gain a reputation, access to capital or the supply of high-quality talent, and so on, that lead to more successes in the future. It would appear to be the result of skill differences but would in fact be a product of a cumulative advantage process.

This is not to discount the role of skill differences, which are important, because there are differences in ability among people. Unfortunately, the studies cited do not offer a compelling decomposition of the sources of realized returns with which to isolate the effect of intrinsic ability from that of cumulative advantage.

Third, the model of cumulative advantage offers an accurate dynamic explanation for the formation of the superstar firm. In Autor et al. (2020) such a firm is simply an outcome of a single random productivity assignment that occurs at time 0, where the superstar firm is defined to be the one that is randomly awarded the highest productivity. Because this selection is made once and for all, no policy can change it. In this case, antitrust policy would only punish the successful for being successful. But this explanation fades once the problem is framed in the dynamic context of cumulative advantage because it offers a channel for policy to affect the distribution of productivity and increase social welfare. This is demonstrated in the next section.

7.5   Technological Competition and the Microsoft Policy to Control the Superstar Firm

I turn now to integrate the various parts developed up to now by formulating a dynamic process of technological competition and study its implications. To explore such competition, I use the method of numerical simulations, which requires further simplification. I use the modified model of chapter 2, as outlined in section 7.3, but under added assumptions, some of which are discussed in the next section. Here I interpret the model as assuming that the economy under study has only two industries and produces only two final commodities. A competitive industry produces the basic commodity, and a single technological industry produces C_t. The M firms are then interpreted as producing substitute proprietary intermediate goods used to produce C_t. These firms are technological competitors using R&D to advance their own productivity and impede the growth of their competitors.

The basic commodity is used only to handle the pricing problem; therefore the model actually formulates an economy with a single industry in general equilibrium. This enables the analysis to focus on the resulting industrial structure. It is therefore important that M is large, reflecting the fact that competition is open to all. The M firms have the same production functions as in (7.3), and under the assumption of $\vartheta_{jt} = 1$, have a symmetric contribution to consumption in (7.5). At the starting point of the process, the firms are then fully symmetric and have equal probability in successfully using R&D to develop their proprietary technologies, increase their productivity, and expand their market power. The outcome of their competition is an endogenously determined industrial structure. The two central questions are then simple: What is the outcome of that competition, and should it be of concern to public policy?

7.5.1   Cumulative Advantage and Impeding Competitors: A Dynamic Theory of the Superstar Firm

The relationship between R&D stock and firm productivity (7.4b) means that a firm's productivity is monotonically increasing in its cumulative stock of successful R&D in use. Therefore, heterogeneity in productivity is expressed by the variability in this stock across firms. Recall that increases in the R&D stock as defined here can be achieved by conducting research, by the acquisition of firms that own a desired technology, or by direct patent purchases. All of these actions are included in the concept of investment in R&D. The dynamic evolution of each firm's R&D stock represents its technological capacity relative to other firms and is determined by the rates of successful investments and depreciation. I introduce the mechanism of success breeds success, or cumulative advantage, by assuming that a firm with a larger relative R&D stock has an increased probability of further successful increases of its stock. The relative R&D stock acts like the percentage of white balls in the Pólya urn.

I assume that for any amount D_{jt} invested in R&D, the resulting increase in R&D stock can take two values: if the firm is successful, the R&D stock increases by the higher amount hD_{jt}, while if it fails, the R&D stock is unchanged. To explain the stipulated probability of success, recall that in chapter 1, I explored how leading firms employ strategies that reduce the productivity of other firms and thereby impede the growth of competitors. To model this dynamic, I assume that the probability of future success depends on the *fraction* of the firm's successful R&D stock out of total industry R&D stock. It then means that the firm that just maintains the absolute level of its R&D stock suffers a decline in its probability of future success because of the advance of the successful firms. The rapid growth of a successful firm's R&D stock impedes the future success probability of all other firms just because they are unable to keep up with the leader. To that end, I reformulate (7.4a) by defining the random growth of the firm's stock of R&D as follows:

$$RD_{j,t+1} = (1 - \delta)RD_{jt} + \xi_{j,t+1}D_{jt}, \text{Prob}[\xi_{j,t+1} = h] = \Lambda\ell_{jt},$$
$$\text{Prob}[\xi_{j,t+1} = 0] = (1 - \Lambda\ell_{jt}) \quad \text{i.i.d.} \ ^{11} \tag{7.21a}$$

---

[11] Note that the simpler notation RD_{jt} identifies, in this section, the same object named RD_{jt}^{Ψ} in the previous one. All innovations are assumed to be productivity-enhancing process innovations, so the notation of Ψ is not needed.

where ℓ_{jt} is a function of the past accumulated R&D stock

$$RD_t = \sum_{j=1}^{M} RD_{jt}, \quad \ell_{jt} = pr + \frac{RD_{jt}}{RD_t}. \tag{7.21b}$$

A larger value for h means that successful investments have a larger impact, and the constant Λ is an adjustment factor for the probabilities. The shock ξ_{jt} in (7.21a) has a cumulative advantage property: failure results in no addition to the stock RD_{jt} of firm j's privately owned technological knowledge, while success results in boosting the stock by a factor h of current investment. The cumulative advantage arises from the dependence of the probability on accumulation of past successes, expressed by the existing proportion of the R&D stock owned by the firm.

Consider now the economy described in section 7.3 with $M = 25$ firms used as a platform for studying technological competition. Because the firms are initially symmetric and play a symmetric role in consumption, the parameter χ regulates how competitive the industry is, or how differentiated the goods are. Because differentiated goods generally have different prices, technological competition among them will entail differences in both productivity and price. A firm that is successful in using R&D to raise productivity will dominate the technology, but if the goods are sufficiently differentiated (χ is small), low productivity firms that do not dominate technologically may cut their output, raise prices, and maintain substantial market share in terms of revenue. On the other hand, if the goods are undifferentiated (χ is large), the prices charged by the large firms are disciplined by their smaller competitors, and public policy is marginally useful for effectively reducing the markups. For example, if $\chi = 14$ and the industry consists of a duopoly, each with market share of 40 percent, and a small competitive fringe, then by (7.12), the leading firms have $\theta_{jt} = 8.4$ and charge a markup of 12 percent, which is only mildly a cause for aggressive public action. This implies that, to be a useful description of technological competition, the goods cannot be too differentiated; therefore, I have chosen the substitution parameter to be larger than 6. To make the policy problem relevant, I simulate the model for χ values not in excess of 10. The elasticity of substitution is also important when it comes to discussing the meaning of the term "survival." I will define "survival" in terms of the success of a firm in using R&D to advance its productivity, but one must keep in mind that, for small values of χ, firms that lag far behind in terms of productivity can still survive by having a non-negligible share of sales revenue because they can raise prices.

To complete the assumption of symmetry, the twenty-five firms are assumed to start with the same R&D stock at date $t = 0$. This stock equals the steady-state value, defined by the expected value of R&D investments. In this case, the normalized transition function (7.21a) takes the following value

$$rd^\star = \frac{1}{g}\left[(1-\delta)rd^\star + \left(\frac{\Lambda}{25}h\right)d^\star\right], \quad d_{jt} = \frac{D_{jt}}{A_t}, \quad rd_{jt} = \frac{RD_{jt}}{A_t},$$
$$rd_t = \sum_{j=1}^{M}\frac{RD_{jt}}{A_t}. \tag{7.22}$$

A random draw is taken every quarter. I simulate this economy for up to 200 years and examine the distribution of the firms' productivity after five, ten, fifteen, fifty, and sometimes after 200 years. To accomplish this, the model will be simplified because an equilibrium with twenty-five firms, each making its own, separate, intertemporal decision is too high-dimensional to solve with existing solution methods for dynamic economic models. However, the essential effects of the success-breeds-success process on the size distribution is retained. To that end, I make the following assumptions:

1. There is no real capital in the economy, thus no intertemporal capital decision is made by the households, who do not save. Therefore, they select optimal consumption and labor supply given their disposable income. All savings are done by firms in the form of R&D investment.

2. Production functions of the basic commodity and of the intermediate products are linear in labor, and the exogenous shock is set at $\zeta_t = 1$. Therefore, $Y_{jt} = \psi_{jt}A_tL_{jt}$, $Y_t^b = A_tL_t^b$.

3. Each intermediate producer is assumed to invest a fraction of its gross profits in R&D to enhance productivity, where the fraction rises with the probability of success:

$$d_{jt} = (s_0 + s_1\ell_{jt})(P_{jt}y_{jt} - w_tL_{jt}). \tag{7.23a}$$

Because the households receive wages and profits as income used to finance consumption, reinvesting the firms' profits in R&D deprives households of potential consumption. It is thus important to find out how the households evaluate the different investment strategies. That is, although firms make the investment decisions, we can find the households' desired investment choices simply by assessing the welfare consequences of different parameters of the postulated investment function.

A detailed statement of this economy's equilibrium conditions and the parameters used is provided in the mathematical appendix to this chapter. The code for the simulations is available in the Online Appendix.

The full symmetry in the composition of consumption and in the production functions of the intermediate goods imply that differences among the firms over time depend entirely upon their R&D stocks. Differences in R&D stocks are the only cause of heterogeneity in productivity, market share, prices, and profits.

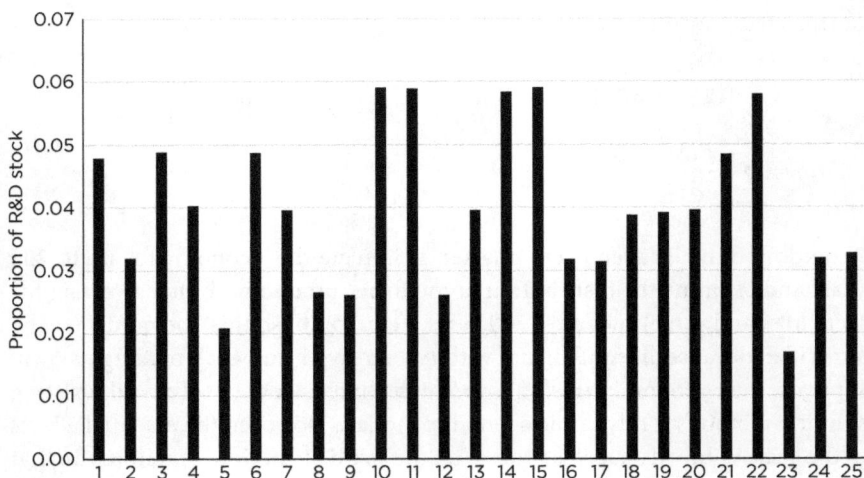

Figure 7.3a   Distribution after five years

But, then, the model at hand is a useful guide to the role of heterogeneity only if the firms are motivated to invest in R&D. This is most likely to occur during periods of high innovation rates and rapid technological developments. Because it is not possible to deduce the fully optimal investment strategies of the firms, the firms are assumed to invest heavily in R&D. This is not an unusual assumption because most technology firms do not pay any dividends and invest most profits due to market power in research or acquisitions. In the model, those investments correspond to D_{jt}, and if successful, they add to the R&D stock. Therefore, given the high rate of depreciation, which is assumed to be 15 percent (see Hall, 2005 for more on depreciation rates of R&D), one must view the relevant values of s_0 to be between 0.25 and 1.00 and s_1 from 0 to 0.50.

To explore the simulation results, I start by assessing the case of $s_0 = 0.25$ and $s_1 = 0.50$. Figure 7.3a shows that, starting from the steady state where all firms are identically the same, after five years, some heterogeneity in productivity begins to show, with small random advantage of some firms.

Figures 7.3b and 7.3c reveal that by the tenth year, only four firms remain in contention and that the decisive change takes place between year ten and year fifteen. By the fifteenth year, firm 14 acquires 70 percent of the productivity stock and takes a lead, which will be permanent. In year 50, it is virtually a monopolist. A superstar monopolist is thus randomly born. I will define "survival" as a firm having a share of at least 10 percent of the total R&D stock, so, in this case, three firms survive after ten years, and only one firm survives after fifteen years.

Is it a general conclusion that firm 14 will emerge as the sole winner? No, it is not. To understand why, note that the probability of success defined in (7.21a)

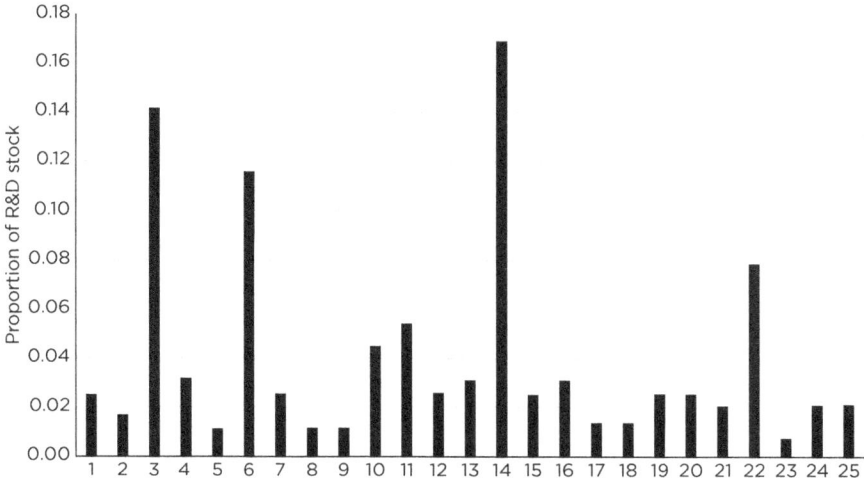

Figure 7.3b   Distribution after ten years

implies that the stochastic growth process of the R&D stocks has multiple limits. The mechanism of success breeding success leads to outcomes that are history dependent, with strong externalities caused by the interdependence in the probabilities of success. This means that the random process involved does not have a unique long-term outcome. In contrast, for any given vector of R&D stocks $rd_t = (rd_{1t}, \ldots, rd_{Mt})$, the short-term, static, equilibrium value of variables such as consumption or output, outlined in the mathematical appendix, are unique,

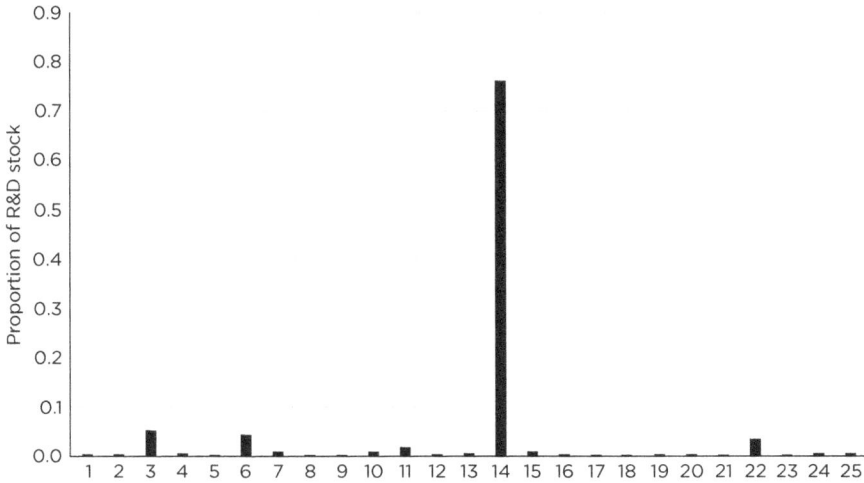

Figure 7.3c   Distribution after fifteen years

showing that all the complexity arises from the dynamic properties of the R&D sequences. There are four facts that characterize this complexity:

1. In the absence of regulations, technological competition results in the emergence of a small number of superstar dominant firms.
2. For different realized sequences $\xi_{jt}, t = 1, \ldots, 200$, *different firms emerge as dominant firms*: the identity of the superstar firms are products of pure luck. I demonstrate this effect later on in Table 7.6.
3. Heterogeneity in ultimate R&D stocks results in heterogeneity in ultimate prices charged by the surviving firms.
4. For a given realized sequence $\xi_{jt}, t = 1 \ldots 200$, it is possible for one firm to dominate the R&D stock while the product market is a duopoly, especially in the case of small values of χ. For example, the leading firm may have 99 percent of the R&D stock and 60 percent of sales and be highly profitable, while the second place firm may have 0.5 percent of the R&D stock, 30 percent of the sales, higher prices, and very low profits (because of its low productivity). These firms both survive because the lagging firm with low productivity is able to cover its cost by raising the price of the differentiated product it sells.

To somewhat offset the effect of prices on survival in terms of market shares, in table 7.4 I define survival in R&D as a firm having at least a 10 percent share of total R&D stock after 200 years, but survival in sales is defined as exceeding only an 8 percent share because, as explained, this share has a component of price effect. The reported frequency distribution of firms' survival is computed for a random sample of 100 sequences of ξ_t. Each cell in table 7.4 reports two numbers: the top number is *survival rate in R&D* and the bottom number is the *survival rate in sales*.

The main result seen in table 7.4 is that, for most realizations, unregulated technological competition results in the emergence of one or two superstar firms. For small values of χ, at most three firms emerge as dominant. Second, for larger values of the elasticity χ, fewer firms survive. When χ is larger, consumers can substitute more easily the products of the competing firms, and the resulting markup of the dominant firms is smaller. Consequently, the advantage of productivity is more decisive and causes fewer firms to survive. Higher χ values also lead to an increased variance of the distribution of outcomes. The distribution of productivity is more unequal than the distribution of market shares; it is noted in the fact that the firms with a large share of the R&D stock have a somewhat smaller share of total sales, while the firms with very small R&D stocks and very low productivities have a sales share that exceeds their share of the R&D stock.

A third conclusion is about the impact of the investment function. The effect of s_0 is different from the effect of s_1. In general, for a given s_0, increased s_1 results

TABLE 7.4 Proportion of surviving firms after 200 years*

Survivors (no. of firms) →	χ = 6			χ = 8				χ = 10			
	1	2	3	1	2	3	4	1	2	3	4
$s_0 = 0.25, s_1 = 0.50$	68	30	2	80	20	0	0	100	0	0	0
	59	39	2	4	60	33	3	0	88	12	0
$s_0 = 0.50, s_1 = 0.00$	1	75	24	27	72	1	0	62	38	0	0
	0	76	24	0	88	12	0	0	100	0	0
$s_0 = 0.50, s_1 = 0.25$	24	65	11	56	44	0	0	81	19	0	0
	19	69	12	2	76	18	4	0	93	7	0
$s_0 = 0.50, s_1 = 0.50$	44	54	2	68	32	0	0	86	14	0	0
	32	66	2	3	65	28	4	0	95	4	1
$s_0 = 0.75, s_1 = 0.00$	1	75	24	27	72	1	0	62	38	0	0
	0	76	24	0	88	12	0	0	98	2	0
$s_0 = 0.75, s_1 = 0.25$	13	75	12	49	51	0	0	75	25	0	0
	10	77	13	1	82	14	3	0	95	5	0
$s_0 = 1.00, s_1 = 0.00$	1	75	24	27	72	1	0	62	38	0	0
	1	75	24	0	89	11	0	0	97	3	0

*The top percentage is for survival measured by share of total R&D stock, and the bottom percentage is for survival measured by share of total sales.

in fewer firms surviving, while for a given s_1, increased s_0 results in a larger number of firms surviving. The reason for this pattern is that larger s_1 enables the more successful firm to invest more, amplifying the effect of their success, while larger s_0 helps lagging firms by giving them a better chance to succeed in the future.

Finally, the impediment caused by the leader, which is built into the process itself, may be viewed as a general proxy for the specific strategies used by firms in the real world and discussed in chapter 1. These strategies may have far greater impact than the level of impediment allowed here. It is then entirely possible that in reality, the actual winner of technological competition, under some circumstances, may not be the most productive. Because these other strategies are not explicitly permitted in the present model, any firm with long-term dominance in R&D is, by the model's construction, the most productive.

This last conclusion is not accidental. One of the reasons for developing my model of the superstar firm was to test the oft-repeated argument that applying antitrust to a leading firm is punishing the most productive for being the most productive (e.g., Posner, 2014; Autor et al., 2020). Similar heterogeneity arguments are also used often in the industrial organization literature to minimize the importance of growing market power since the 1980s (e.g., Van Reenen, 2018). The dominant firm in figure 7.3c is the most productive! The questions that must now be addressed are simple: Is there a superior policy to control the superstar firms that emerge from an unregulated market environment? Is this dominance socially desirable?

7.5.2   Controlling the Superstar Firm with a Microsoft Policy

I will now demonstrate that the answer to the above questions is clear: the productivity dominance of the superstar firm is not socially desirable, and there is a welfare-improving policy to control the power of such firms. To understand this policy, I begin with a real-world example that motivates it, the government's antitrust action against Microsoft.

In the 1990s, as the internet was developing, Netscape was the leading web browser, but Microsoft, the leading software firm, developed a competitor, Internet Explorer. This competition changed in 1995 when, recognizing the importance of the internet, Bill Gates declared war on Netscape (see Gates, 1995). He aimed to break Netscape's market position by bundling Microsoft's free Internet Explorer browser with Windows and by pressuring other companies to use it instead of Netscape. Netscape sought government help against Microsoft's anticompetitive behavior.

The problem was that current antitrust laws were (and are) not designed to address problems created by technological market power, and much of the government's legal case was a search for a theory to justify public action. Microsoft created impediments to the development of competing firms in a variety of ways, but the legality of most of them was in question, while some may not have violated the Sherman Antitrust law because they were within the scope of Microsoft's proprietary technology. However, the fact remains that Microsoft actually tried to control access to the web itself by investing in broadband deployment and by acquiring online commerce firms with the hope of charging fees for internet transactions made with Microsoft technology.

Finally, in 1998, the government filed suit against Microsoft. This was too late for Netscape, which had lost its market share, but the lawsuit had substantial long-term consequences. The court found that Microsoft had committed antitrust violations and ordered the firm to be broken up into two firms, one that produces software and one that produces operating systems. The case was appealed, and the ruling was vacated by the appeals court, at which point the Bush Justice Department settled the case. In the settlement, Microsoft agreed to increase transparency, making it easier for competitors to develop software applications for their operating system. To avoid future government actions against it, Microsoft adopted a softer strategy toward competitors. This less aggressive stance lowered Microsoft's potential productivity gains. Without the lawsuit, it would have likely been more aggressive in research, acquisitions, entering new markets, and otherwise impeding the growth of its competitors. This softer strategy gave other firms, including Google, Apple, and Amazon, the opportunity and breathing space to develop their own internet-related products and services. In some areas, Microsoft actually fell behind (e.g., cloud services) and needed to alter its organizational structure, leadership, and strategy to catch up. The growth pattern of these younger competitors would have been different had they faced the aggressive impediments to their growth that Microsoft could have created. In the same way that Microsoft had previously benefited from the government suit against IBM, these other firms benefited from a policy to contain Microsoft.

There are other examples of legal suits against technological leaders that served the public interest by removing the impediments that leading firms create. These antitrust actions open up opportunities for competitors to develop their own innovations rather than being acquired or crushed by the superstar leader. The innovations of these competitors increase their productivity and enable them to compete in market segments that would have been closed to them without public action.

I propose a framework for public action that I call a Microsoft Policy modeled after the Microsoft case. The unique feature of a Microsoft Policy is that it is directed only against the leading firms, those considered the most productive. As I have noted, the leading conservative argument against antitrust policy is based on the claim that technological competition mirrors regular competition, and if we allow competition to work normally, others will find their way to the top. The model simulations studied above show that this does not happen in un-regulated technological competition, which is why a different policy framework is necessary. I will define the policy so that it will target the firms that are the most successful in terms of productivity. Such targeting reduces their ability to increase productivity by acquisitions and research, but it also reduces their abil-ity to impede the productivity growth of other firms. The policy has therefore two effects: it restrains the productivity growth of the leaders and increases the productivity growth rate of the firms that lag behind. This means that the pol-icy creates a trade-off that calls for lower productivity of the leader in exchange for higher productivity of all other less productive firms. The question is then simple: Is such a policy welfare-improving?

I formulate the policy by imposing a legal restriction that if firms' R&D stock exceeds a specified level, they can no longer invest in R&D or engage in tech-nological mergers and acquisitions that aim to purchase technology. This im-plies the following investment function, where GOV is the threshold specified in the policy:

$$\text{For all } j \quad \frac{rd_{jt}}{rd_t} \leq GOV.$$

This is then translated into the following investment function:

$$d_{jt} = \begin{cases} (s_0 + s_1\ell_{jt})(P_{jt}y_{jt} - w_tL_{jt}) & \text{if } (rd_{jt})/(rd_t) < GOV \\ 0 & \text{if } (rd_{jt})/(rd_t) \geq GOV \end{cases}. \qquad (7.23b)$$

I maintain the same parameters of the investment function, $s_0 = 0.25$ and $s_1 = 0.50$. To illustrate the effect of the policy, I first simulate the economy under the policy choice of $GOV = 0.20$ that allows every firm to grow its R&D share to a maximum of 20 percent. Figures 7.4a and 7.4b show the effect of the policy. After fifteen years, the number of leading firms is four, compared to one in 7.3c.

But it is the long-run behavior in figure 7.4c that reveals the power of the policy to increase social dynamism and offer better opportunities to all firms. In particular, firm 16 was lagging behind after fifteen years, but it was able to recover and grow so that after fifty years, the market was divided among five competing firms.

It is clear that the policy choice is crucial. I next use the same investment parameters but choose a less restrictive policy. Figures 7.5a and 7.5b show the results of the policies of $GOV = 0.4$ and $GOV = 0.6$, respectively. They show that a less active policy leads to a greater long-run concentration of firms. With $GOV = 0.4$, the industry will ultimately consist of three firms, and under the policy of $GOV = 0.6$, it will consist of only two firms.

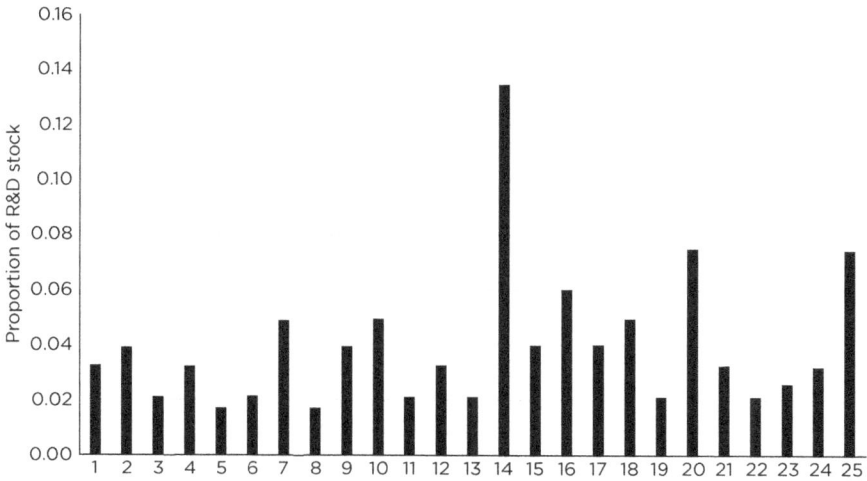

Figure 7.4a Distribution after five years under policy of $GOV = 0.2$

It should be clear from the discussion of the no-policy case reported in table 7.4 that the long-run industrial concentration under any policy depends upon the underlying elasticity of substitution between the products of the firms and upon the investment function. The simulations reveal a simple and natural conclusion: for every specific public objective of long-run concentration, policy must be more aggressive (i.e., set a smaller value of GOV) if the investment

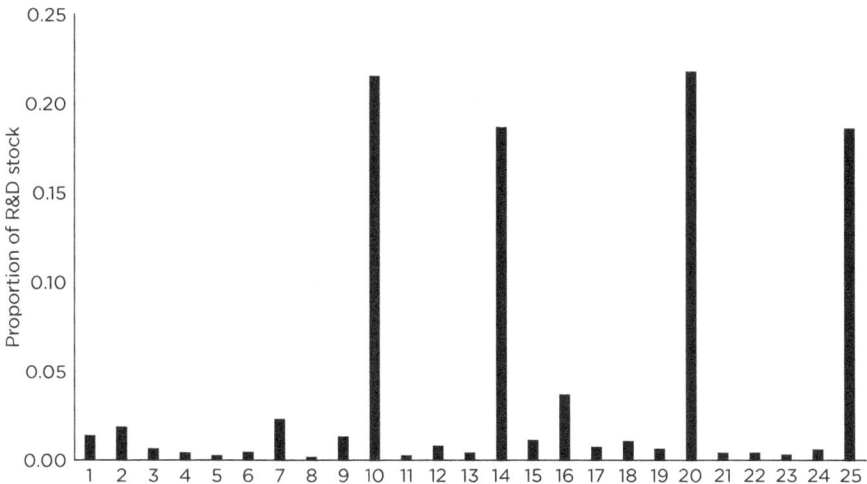

Figure 7.4b Distribution after fifteen years under policy of $GOV = 0.2$

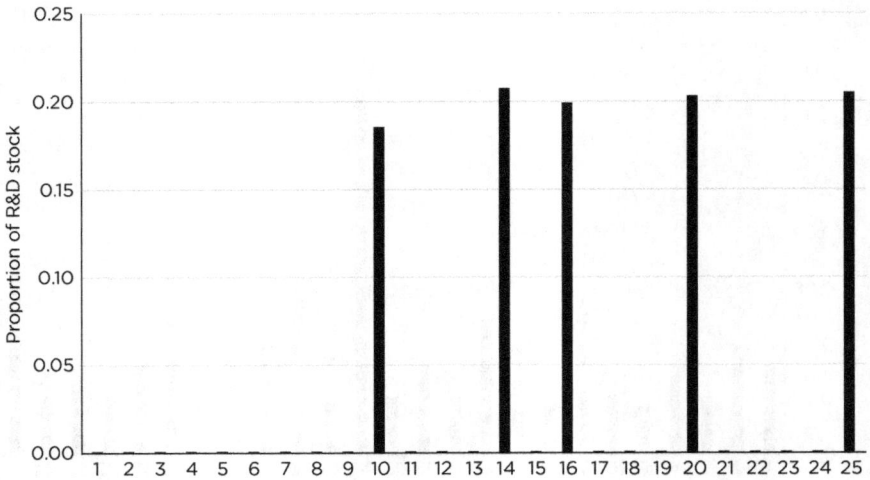

Figure 7.4c   Distribution after fifty years under policy of $GOV = 0.2$

function of the private sector is more aggressive. Similarly, policy must be more aggressive to achieve a target level of competition if χ is higher because, for larger values of χ, fewer firms survive under the no-policy condition.

While in the real world welfare is typically measured with gross national product (GNP) real GNP is still an imperfect measure. In the context of the model, welfare can be measured directly by using the utility function of the

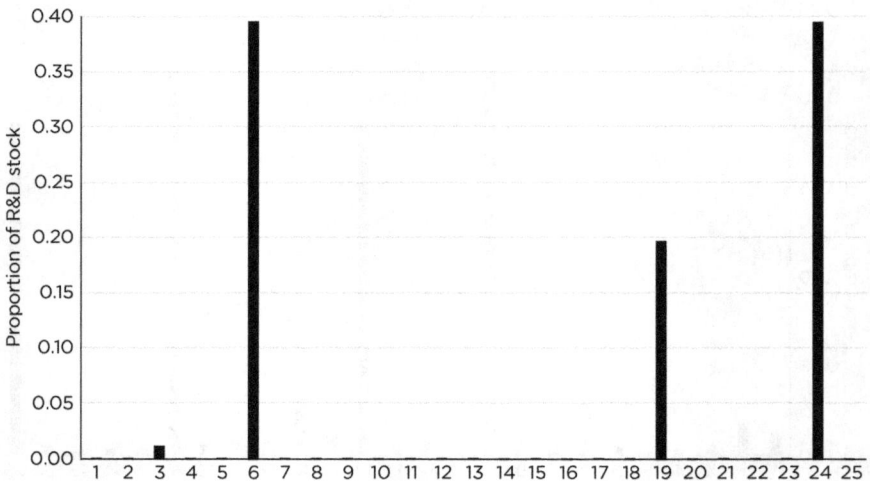

Figure 7.5a   Distribution after fifty years under policy of $GOV = 0.4$

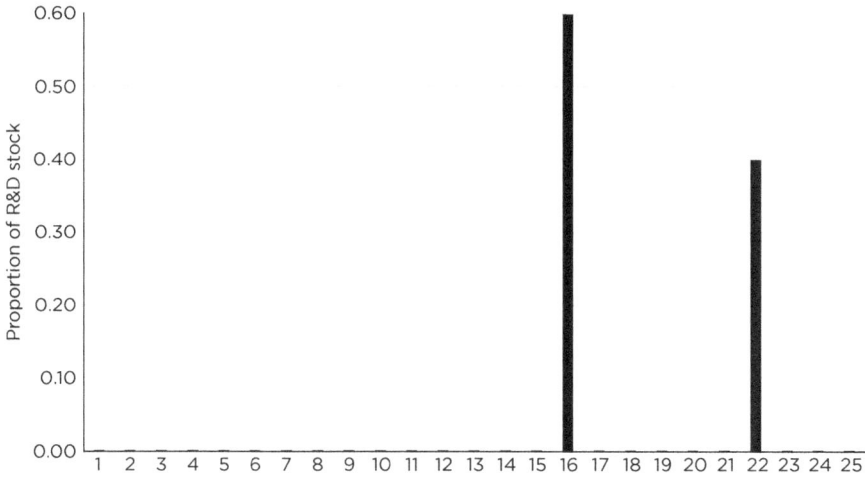

Figure 7.5b   Distribution after fifty years under policy of $GOV = 0.6$

households. This takes into account both the disutility of work and the positive gain from consumption. As noted earlier, this gives us the opportunity to discover not only the optimal public policy for a given fixed investment function of the private sector but also the households' preference among investment functions. Tables 7.5a and 7.5b present the terminal utility level for each of seven investment functions and eight policies. The policy that maximizes welfare for a given investment function is in bold. The differences between the two tables demonstrate that the effect of different random sequences ξ can be significant, stressing the pure luck effect of the winner. The term "optimum" applies here for a given random sequence. These simulations have been computed for fifty years.

The tables confirm the earlier general observation: the best policy is more aggressive if the investment policies are more aggressive. Comparison of the last rows of table 7.5a with table 7.5b shows that the random sequence ξ has the most significant effects when policy is inactive. Also, we have seen that with a strong policy like $GOV = 0.2$, it is almost certain that five firms will survive. With no policy, however, as shown in table 7.4, sometimes one firm survives and sometimes two firms survive, entirely due to randomness. Indeed, ξ^1, in table 7.5a, is one of those random sequences in which one firm survives. Therefore, the no-policy case, featuring a single dominant monopolist, is substantially worse for households than the case of $GOV = 0.7$. The variable ξ^2, on the other hand, is a random sequence that leads to two surviving firms, and therefore neither of their shares of the R&D stock exceed 0.6, and the $GOV = 0.6$, $GOV = 0.7$, and no-policy cases are all the same. This underscores that without active policy, consumers may experience different market structures entirely because of random chance.

TABLE 7.5a Terminal welfare levels of alternative policies and investment functions, $\chi = 8, \xi = \xi^1$

	Investment								
Policy GOV	0.25 0.00	0.25 0.25	0.25 0.50	0.50 0.00	0.50 0.25	0.50 0.50	0.75 0.00	0.75 0.25	1.00 0.00
0.1	−3.24418	−3.2266	−3.22862	−3.18281	−3.18864	−3.16005	−3.15629	−3.15193	−3.14369
0.2	−3.15015	−3.1397	−3.13046	−3.09405	−3.06762	−3.10807	−3.06656	−3.06253	−3.0509
0.3	−3.1624	−3.14865	−3.14757	−3.0919	−3.07293	−3.07539	**−3.04102**	**−3.03909**	**−3.01019**
0.4	−3.09341	**−3.07507**	**−3.06533**	**−3.06236**	**−3.03448**	**−3.03387**	−3.06467	−3.06878	−3.07998
0.5	**−3.08244**	−3.10281	−3.09379	−3.08518	−3.07489	−3.08019	−3.10389	−3.06227	−3.13477
0.6	−3.10094	−3.08253	−3.08415	−3.08654	−3.09119	−3.10297	−3.10387	−3.11779	−3.13473
0.7	−3.09991	−3.08445	−3.09276	−3.08589	−3.09146	−3.1054	−3.1044	−3.11868	−3.13475
No policy	−3.16739	−3.30228	−3.3993	−3.16465	−3.33591	−3.42942	−3.19355	−3.38259	−3.23397

TABLE 7.5b Terminal welfare levels of alternative policies and investment functions, $\chi = 8$, $\xi = \xi^2$

Policy GOV	Investment								
	0.25	0.25	0.25	0.50	0.50	0.50	0.75	0.75	1.00
	0.00	0.25	0.50	0.00	0.25	0.50	0.00	0.25	0.00
0.1	-3.26565	-3.25177	-3.29215	-3.19414	-3.19627	-3.18696	-3.17432	-3.18267	-3.16135
0.2	-3.17065	-3.1533	-3.13217	-3.11256	-3.0922	-3.08933	-3.08972	**-3.05697**	**-3.0471**
0.3	-3.14986	-3.14534	-3.23518	-3.1015	-3.17	-3.14154	-3.08385	-3.17	-3.08783
0.4	-3.0982	-3.09816	-3.09796	**-3.0704**	**-3.08321**	**-3.0861**	**-3.07086**	-3.08929	-3.08595
0.5	-3.14336	-3.10194	-3.09522	-3.09626	-3.08468	-3.10144	-3.08284	-3.07896	-3.0828
0.6	**-3.09503**	**-3.08116**	**-3.08331**	-3.08229	-3.08949	-3.10186	-3.10187	-3.11655	-3.13357
0.7	**-3.09503**	**-3.08116**	-3.08923	-3.08229	-3.08949	-3.10186	-3.10187	-3.11655	-3.13357
No Policy	**-3.09503**	**-3.08116**	-3.09108	-3.08229	-3.08949	-3.10186	-3.10187	-3.11655	-3.13357

The two tables together show that the outcome of no policy is almost always inferior to the outcome under some active policy. When the rate of investment in R&D is low, the difference among firms declines, and the value of any active policy declines. When the rate of investment is high, the disparities between the firms can grow large, and policy is particularly valuable in reducing these disparities.

A more complete picture emerges from computing the discounted present value of utility sequences of consumption and labor inputs for each random sequence. Using the HTCondor software (Thain et al., 2005) and the computational resources and assistance of the University of Wisconsin at Madison's Center For High Throughput Computing (CHTC), I compute 100 random sequences of $\xi_{jt}, t = 1, 2, \ldots, 200$ for each of seven investment functions, eight policies, and three values of χ. I then examine the present discounted utility of consumers over the whole period, using a discount rate of 5 percent per year. A random sample of 200-year sequences results in a distribution of outcomes which, again, depend upon the investment function, the public policy employed, and the specified elasticity χ. The model delegates all investment decisions to the firms and all policy decisions to the government. Therefore, to find out what is optimal for the households, I seek the maximum discounted utility over both the parameters of the investment function as well as the parameter values defining public policy, including the case of no policy. Because I examine present discounted utility, I take into account the intertemporal trade-offs of the households and determine the industrial structure that maximizes their utility. Table 7.6 reports the frequency distribution of the optimal mixture of private investment and public policy generated by the simulations for three values of the elasticity χ. *In all cases the application of some public policy is superior to the case of no policy.*

Table 7.6 shows that aggressive investment strategies by the firms are consistently preferred by the consumers, as is aggressive public policy to prevent the emergence of the superstar firms. The policy of $GOV < 0.5$ is optimal in 66 percent of the cases and $GOV < 0.4$ in 49 percent of the cases. A typical distribution of market shares that results from the application of public policy is seen in figure 7.6. It is a sample of the optimal distribution, in the case of $\chi = 8$, that results from an application of the optimal investment strategy of $s_0 = 0.75$, $s_1 = 0.25$, and the optimal policy of $GOV = 0.3$. It shows that the monopoly or duopoly that arises from unregulated technological competition should be replaced by an active policy that establishes a superior industrial structure of five large firms, each with a market share of less than 26 percent, and a few small firms that survive on the competitive fringe.

For a more complete picture of the effect of policy, table 7.7 reports the number of firms that survive under the optimal policy for the three levels of χ. For $\chi < 10$, most cases result in an optimal number of firms between three and five,

TABLE 7.6   Distribution of optimal investment and policy for 100 ξ sequences*

Policies	$\chi = 6$		$\chi = 8$				$\chi = 10$	
	0.2	0.3	0.2	0.3	0.4	0.5	0.4	0.5
$s_0 = 0.25, s_1 = 0.50$	0	0	0	0	0	0	0	0
$s_0 = 0.50, s_1 = 0.00$	0	0	0	0	0	0	0	0
$s_0 = 0.50, s_1 = 0.25$	0	0	0	0	0	0	0	0
$s_0 = 0.50, s_1 = 0.50$	3	2	0	0	0	3	0	3
$s_0 = 0.75, s_1 = 0.00$	35	1	0	2	15	14	0	1
$s_0 = 0.75, s_1 = 0.25$	58	1	0	5	9	11	3	20
$s_0 = 1.00, s_1 = 0.00$	0	0	11	30	0	0	23	50

*Percent distribution, over investment parameters and policies, of cases with maximal present value of discounted utility.

with a competitive fringe of smaller firms. In all cases, the share of any firm in total revenue is lower than its share in the R&D stock. For $\chi = 10$, in a significant proportion of cases, two firms are optimal, but in that case the urgency for active public action is not great because the markup achieved with two or three firms is already in the acceptable range of public objective, which is the optimal balance between productivity and firm diversity.

This is perhaps the clearest rejection of the heterogeneity argument. Yes, the proposed policy punishes the most successful for being successful because, in being successful, they use their market power to impede the development of a healthy economy with more firms, more competition, increased number of

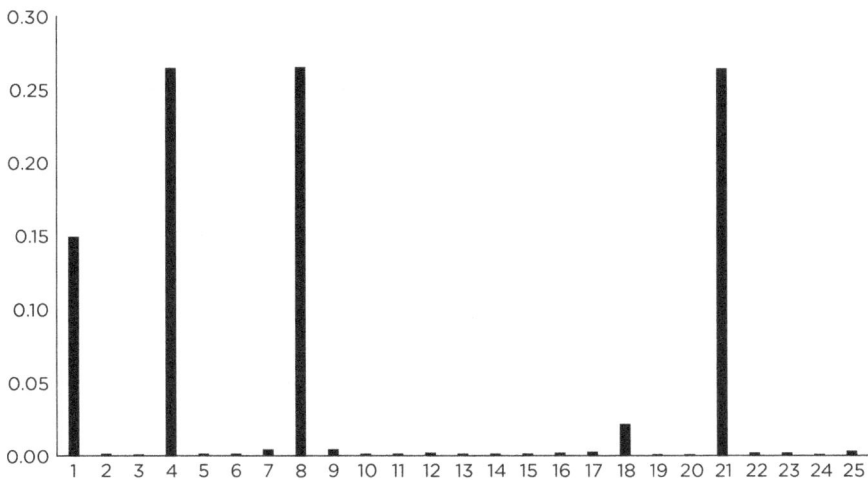

Figure 7.6   Market share under optimal investments and policy after fifty years

TABLE 7.7 Distribution of Optimal Number of Surviving Firms, for 100 ξ sequences*

| Number of Firms | $\chi = 6$ | | $\chi = 8$ | | | | $\chi = 10$ | |
| | | | Policies | | | | | |
	0.2	0.3	0.2	0.3	0.4	0.5	0.4	0.5
2	0	0	0	0	0	28	0	73
3	0	0	0	15	24	0	26	1
4	0	4	0	22	0	0	0	0
5	96	0	11	0	0	3	0	0

*Percent distribution, over investment parameters and policies, of cases with maximal present value of discounted utility.

products available and higher productivity. Society at large is then better off. The policy proposed here, to establish a bound on the technological market power that any firm should be allowed to have, is at the heart of the policy analysis of chapter 9.

Mathematical Appendix to Chapter 7

The optimization of the representative household is

$$\text{Max}_{(C^b, C, I, L)} \sum_{\tau=0}^{\infty} \beta^\tau \left[\log C_\tau^b + \Xi \log C_\tau - \frac{\mathcal{H}}{1+\eta} L_\tau^{1+\eta} \right],$$

subject to the budget constraint

$$C_t^b + P_t C_t = W_t L_t + \Pi_t.$$

All equilibrium conditions are normalized through division by $A_t = g^t$.

Aggregate Conditions

Definition of consumption: $c_t = \left[\sum_{j=1}^{M} y_{jt}^{\frac{\chi-1}{\chi}} \right]^{\frac{\chi}{\chi-1}}$, $P_t c_t = \sum_{j=1}^{M} P_{jt} y_{jt}$

Production of basic commodity: $y_t^b = L_t^b$

Market clearance of basic commodity: $y_t^b = c_t^b + d_t$

Aggregate investment in research and development (R&D): $d_t = \sum_{j=1}^{M} d_{jt}$

Household budget constraint: $y_t^c = c_t^b + P_t c_t$

Disposable income: $y_t^c = w_t L_t + \pi_t, \quad \pi_t = \sum_{j=1}^{M} (P_{jt} y_{jt} - w_t L_{jt} - d_{jt})$

Basic commodity optimal consumption: $c_t^b = \dfrac{B}{B+1} y_t^c$

Optimal technological consumption: $\quad P_t c_t = \dfrac{1}{B+1} y_t^c$

Optimal labor supply: $\mathcal{H} c_t^b L_t^{\eta} = B w_t$

Equilibrium price of consumption good: $P_t = \left[\sum_{j=1}^{M} (P_{jt})^{1-\chi} \right]^{\frac{1}{1-\chi}}$

Labor market clearing condition: $L_t^b + \sum_{j=1}^{M} L_{jt} = L_t$

Individual Firm Conditions $j = 1, \dots M$

Demand function for commodity j: $\quad y_{jt} = \left(\dfrac{P_{jt}}{P_t} \right)^{-\chi} c_t$

Demand elasticity of j: $\quad \theta_{jt} = \chi \left(1 - \left(\dfrac{P_{jt}}{P_t} \right)^{1-\chi} \right)$

Output of commodity of j: $\quad y_{jt} = \psi_{jt} L_{jt}$

Impact of R&D on productivity: $\quad \psi_{jt} = (r d_{jt})^{0.12}$

Optimal demand for labor:

$$w_t = P_{jt} \dfrac{(\theta_{jt} - 1)}{\theta_{jt}} \psi_{jt}, \quad w_t = 1 \quad \Rightarrow \quad P_{jt} \psi_{jt} \dfrac{\theta_{jt} - 1}{\theta_{jt}} = 1$$

Transition function of R&D stock of j:

$$rd_{j,t+1} = (1 - \delta)rd_{jt} + \xi_{j,t+1}d_{jt}, \text{Prob}[\xi_{j,t+1} = h] = \Lambda \ell_{jt},$$
$$\text{Prob}[\xi_{j,t+1} = 0] = (1 - \Lambda \ell_{jt}) \text{ i.i.d.,}$$

where $\ell_{jt} = pr + \dfrac{rd_{jt}}{rd_t}$

Policy function: for all j: $\dfrac{rd_{jt}}{rd_t} \leq GOV$

Investment function under the effect of policy:

$$d_{jt} = \left\{ \begin{array}{ll} (s_0 + s_1 \ell_{jt}) \left(P_{jt} y_{jt} - w_t L_{jt} \right) & \text{if } (rd_{jt})/(rd_t) < GOV \\ 0 & \text{if } (rd_{jt})/(rd_t) \geq GOV \end{array} \right\}$$

Parameter Values Beyond the Basic Selected in Chapter 2

- $\chi = 8$
- $\natural = 0.12$
- $\delta = 0.15$, but computations were conducted for quarters where quarterly $\delta = 0.0398154$
- $g = 1.014$, but the quarterly rate was set at 1.0034817
- $\eta = 2$
- $\mathcal{H} = 28.5$
- $h = 1.2$
- $\Lambda = 4$
- $pr = 0.01$
- Experiments were conducted with the investment parameters. The variable s_0 was varied from 0.25 to 1.00 and s_1 from 0 to 0.50.
- The policy parameter was varied from 0.1 to 0.7.

CHAPTER 8

ON POLICY REFORM

T his chapter is the first part of my discussion of a new policy agenda designed to reverse the negative impact of rising market power. Earlier chapters described the historical circumstances that led to the present policy regime and studied the consequences of the current policy. Now I move to advocating a new policy agenda. Here, in chapter 8, I address the broader social, constitutional, and ideological problems that will be encountered in implementing a new policy agenda. This provides a general motivation for the proposals developed in chapters 9–10.

8.1 The Two Gilded Ages

Considering the last 140 years of American economic history, the two Gilded Ages appear surprisingly similar in many respects, although they take place at drastically different stages of American development. The nineteenth-century American economy was primarily agricultural, with relatively small farms and a rapidly rising manufacturing sector in the Northeast, consisting of small and medium-sized firms, without any major concentration of economic power. Economic policy during that era was laissez-faire. By the end of the century, this democratic society, with a relatively decentralized, competitive economy, turned into a plutocracy, where vast economic power, income, and wealth were concentrated in the hands of a few robber barons.

The ideology underlying laissez-faire policy is based on the premise of individual freedom and for individuals to take full responsibility for all their economic actions and have the rights to all the benefits from what they produce. With private enterprise engaged in satisfying all needs, little is required from collective action apart from security and protection of property rights. All other community activities are to be undertaken by charities and nongovernmental institutions. Some of these ideas are also principles included in the U.S. Constitution, leading some to adopt the legal opinion that the U.S. Constitution is a natural legal document for the foundation of a capitalist economy. If a court adopts this legal view, then any issues left ambiguous in the Constitution can be resolved with a presumption in favor of the free competitive market and against government intervention. This perspective is useful for understanding the legal foundations of the Sherman Antitrust Act of 1890 that viewed free competition as the natural order. It is also a good guide for thinking about the long battles between the Supreme Court and the reform-minded administrations since 1901.

In contrast to the nineteenth century, in the 1980s the American economy was the leading industrial power with the highest standard of living in the world. Yet two facts caused their economic and political environments to be similar. First, both experienced the inventions of major general-purpose technologies (GPTs) that resulted in a wave of innovations. The dominant GPTs in the First Gilded Age were electricity and the combustion engine, and the leading GPT since the 1980s has been information technology (IT). Second, policymakers at both times adopted the laissez-faire economic policy. As explained in chapters 1 and 4, these two features led to the same consequences of rising inequality; declining economic vitality; negative effects on output, consumption, and investment; and weaker foundations of democratic institutions.

The massive policy shift introduced by the administration in 2021 appears to be analogous to the policy change in 1901. If this is the case, it may usher in the end of the Second Gilded Age, in which case the policy reform proposed in chapters 9–10 may be timely. Before moving on, I want to briefly stop to consider the role economic theory often plays in justifying laissez-faire policy.

It is commonly claimed that economic theory proves that a laissez-faire policy guides the economy to full efficiency, and any deviation from it leaves some people worse off. The subject of this book is the failure of a market economy to improve economic efficiency by restraining the rise of market power. But this is not the only area where unregulated markets fail to deliver efficient outcomes. I will just mention the need for aggregate stabilization policy, investments in basic research and social infrastructure, and the problem of climate change as added examples of vast social need. These issues are in addition to a vast literature about market inefficiency that results from increasing returns to scale, interaction among economic activities, network effects, and asymmetry of information. All these imply that an equilibrium of the real economy under laissez-faire policy fails to deliver an efficient, Pareto-optimal allocation. To improve economic performance, the economy needs active government policy to address these collective problems. But because some distributional problems that arise in the age of technology are permanent, I argue later that any new policy must declare, as its central aim, the creation of *permanent* institutions to restrain technological market power and preserve the integrity of the middle class.

8.2   The Search for Pareto-Optimal Innovation Policy

8.2.1   Without Compensation, Free Trade and Free Innovation Policies Are Not Pareto Optimal

Perhaps the most basic idea we teach in economics courses is that opening to free trade is an efficient, Pareto-optimal policy because specialization of trading partners benefits all participants in trade. But this simple statement is false. Opening a country to free trade almost always results in some parties losing and others gaining, and the losers are often displaced workers. The same problem arises with any public policy that benefits some groups and harms others. In many cases, the actual practice is to offer compensation to those harmed. When government builds a road, it compensates landowners whose property is used in the construction. When an oil company is granted the rights for a pipeline, it assumes a legal obligation to compensate all harmed by damage it causes.

When a policy is put in place with little or no compensation given to the losers, some economists remain unconcerned about the distributional impact. They invoke the Kaldor-Hicks efficiency criterion that requires the policy to be beneficial enough that the winners could, in theory, afford to compensate the losers and leave everyone better off. It is often coupled with the mistaken assumption that the losing parties can find alternative employment elsewhere and receive the same compensation as before. This is too weak a criterion, and many such changes leave society as a whole worse off. A change in trade policy results in some industries being eliminated. In the age of technology, where workers develop industry-specific skills, the elimination of an industry results in decline of the demand for some technical skills and therefore in the devaluation of a lifetime of accumulated human capital. The problem is more acute if the displaced workers are old, when retraining is difficult and requires heavy investments, and the new employment is located elsewhere. Moving to the newly thriving location may require a family to relocate to a place without family or friends, something workers have been less able or willing to do in recent years (see Molloy et al., 2017). In short, restarting a professional career late in life is difficult, expensive, and often painful. When such a policy takes effect on a large scale, it becomes a catastrophe for a large number of workers.

The problem of compensation is of greater importance when applied to policy about innovation. It is an efficient public policy to pay compensation to workers whose jobs were eliminated. Such policy can be financed by taxing the products of innovations that displace workers or the purchase of machines used for such displacement (Costinot and Werning, 2018). Tax revenue can help correct the negative effects of today's laissez-faire policies that have enabled a rising concentration of wealth, accompanied by the despair of millions of workers who see the future foreclosed. Most in big tech reject such a principle, which runs counter to their current ideology of unrestrained capitalism (see Thiel, 2014). Firms, according to this view, have the natural right to engage in innovations and the right to gain monopoly power over them, without government taxing or regulating them to compensate those harmed. On the other hand, some corporate leaders have recently expressed openness to policies that hold corporations responsible for the effects of their actions on society. Some have even argued that, in the long run, capitalism would be made better off by such changes (see Henderson, 2020; Henderson et al., 2020). For a very long time, the policy of free innovations with no compensation amounted to a policy of allowing innovators to accumulate vast wealth at the expense of the middle class and the unskilled workers of America. The economic and political consequences have become unacceptable to many.

In contemplating a new policy, it is clear that precise compensation that takes into account both the cost and benefits each individual worker receives from innovations is not practical. Instead, as a compensation policy, the government needs to improve the standard of living of those at the bottom of the income distribution. This can be accomplished through cash transfers and through creating good-quality jobs that offer dislocated workers feasible new opportunities.

The advancement in robotics and artificial intelligence raises the question of whether they will displace labor and thereby cut the supply of good-quality jobs. Is there some trade-off between (1) technologies that result in higher productive efficiency but replace labor and eliminate jobs, and (2) technologies that result in slightly lower productive efficiency but create good-quality jobs with higher wages by cooperation between machine and humans? How could policy alter the incentives of innovators to create technologies that complement labor and increase labor productivity rather than displace labor and disrupt people's lives?

The wrong lesson to take from the run-up in inequality since the 1980s is that we should leave in place the policies that allow the unchecked growth of market power but increase taxes and transfers to produce a more egalitarian distribution of income and wealth. The standard argument of those who propose this approach is that laissez-faire policy is good at increasing economic output, and the government should intervene only through taxes and transfers. The analogy made is that deregulation increases the size of the economic "pie," while taxes and transfers allow society to choose how to divide that pie. This is questionable logic. Given the degree of current market power, the level of taxation and redistribution needed to restore economic efficiency must be massive because it must remove all profits resulting from market power. In fact, I show in chapter 10 that a corporate profit tax cannot be sufficient to cover the cost of subsidies that need to be paid to labor and capital inputs in order to restore efficient factor allocation. The cost of removing all factor price distortions caused by market power with simple transfers is prohibitive.

In short, taxes and transfers are important components of a policy response to income inequality, but they are only a component. Instead, antitrust regulations that directly intervene in markets to make them more competitive are necessary to attain growth and reduce inequality.

8.2.2 Capitalism and Democracy in the Age of Technology: Why Democracies Fail

The political experience since the 1980s shows that one of the most significant problems caused by the existing laissez-faire policy is the decrease in social cohesion and the rising threat to democracy. It would thus be useful to review some of the literature on the question.

A vast literature on the modernization hypothesis emerged following Lipset's (1959) argument that as society gets wealthier, its members increase their demand for democracy. Empirical studies have also considered whether the causation could run in the other direction. Among many other contributions, Acemoglu et al. (2005) provide a forceful argument that the inclusive institutions of democracy allow wide participation of citizens, enforce the rule of law, and protect property rights, all of which incentivize investment and economic growth. However, the economic rise of nondemocratic China; the rapid growth rates of authoritarian states around the world; and the decline in the stature of democratic institutions globally, including in the United States, has gradually shifted the consensus to the view that democracy may not promote higher growth. This growing consensus was challenged by Acemoglu et al. (2019) with empirical analysis based on the theory developed in Acemoglu and Robinson (2001) and fleshed out in Acemoglu and Robinson (2006, 2012).

Some of the Acemoglu and Robinson (2006, 2012) ideas are developed with the aid of a mathematical game-theoretic model where the rich and poor negotiate. The rich can impose heavy taxation, but the poor can revolt, and an equilibrium for a stable solution with credible taxation under democratic institutions. Their book, *Why Nations Fail*, combines the results of the model with the theory of Acemoglu et al. (2005), together with extensive empirical and historical analysis, to make the case that undemocratic societies develop extractive institutions that cause poor economic performance. Accordingly, nations fail when they permit the functioning of extractive institutions that enable the elite to extract income and wealth from the rest of the citizenry. Extractive institutions lead to long-run failure because they remove the incentives of citizens to participate, invest, build, and innovate.

Although, as noted earlier, the American political tradition seems to presume that free society and free markets must go together, capitalism has no clear constitution. Private property, functioning markets, and optimization by buyers and sellers can exist in other societies such as Nazi Germany, South American dictatorships, or China today. That is, a capitalist market economy in a technological age may function in either democratic or nondemocratic societies.

For such unregulated capitalist market societies, the Acemoglu and Robinson theory misses the most fundamental dynamic force that determines its destiny: the evolution of market power due to the impact of technology. Their study of the institutions that promote stability and growth lead them to claim that the standard unregulated capitalist institutions of a free-market economy that respect private property and permit free optimization by buyers and sellers are not extractive and therefore promote stability and growth. Indeed, the authors could cite the emergence of these institutions of free markets in China as explaining China's rise to its present level of economic development. Acemoglu and Robinson's conclusions are deduced mostly from historical analysis. They reject the role of exogenous factors, such as geography or religion, and insist that random configuration of historical events have a persistent effect on social and economic developments. Thus, pluralistic and inclusive institutions that may emerge accidentally are persistent, bring about increased liberty and economic growth, and therefore reinforce democracy. They then conclude that democracy is stable and persistent because its pluralistic institutions are persistent. Unique configuration of historical events in the West lead Acemoglu and Robinson to suggest that Western democracies under free capitalist market economies have been able to maintain efficient stable economic systems. My analysis contradicts this conclusion.

I have demonstrated that under any form of government, in the age of technology, free capitalism with unchecked market power leads to rising inequality, declining power of labor and average citizens, and in growing political power of the rich. Consequently, in a democracy, the rich can shift society to an equilibrium favorable to them simply by putting together a winning coalition that establishes a free, laissez-faire economic policy. Capitalism then does the rest by enhancing their wealth and preserving their power at the expense of the rest of society. My conclusion is that, in the age of technology, democracy under unregulated free-market capitalism is an unstable economic system; it results in the decline of social cohesion and in a political progression toward plutocracy.

For a capitalist market economy, a policy to contain market power is a necessary condition for both democracy and economic growth to succeed.

8.3   Some Impediments to, and the Challenges of, Policy Reform

A policy regime to contain market power should not aim to destroy all market power because, without any market power, the incentive to innovate would be substantially lessened. Therefore, under any efficient policy, some market power gained by innovators remains a permanent feature of capitalism in a technological age. But any market power of business, combined with the financial power of the wealthy, lays the groundwork for a cycle in which the wealthy use their political power to gain concessions to further increase their market power, making them richer and more powerful, thus demanding additional concessions. Therefore, if market power is to be regulated rather than eliminated, democracy must limit the ability of the rich to exercise political power, and the regulatory regime must resist political pressure to permit increased market power.

I next examine the two primary impediments that are encountered by any policy reform to restrain market power, the legal challenge and the political challenge. I will then discuss the merits, or lack thereof, of the argument of heterogeneity that has emerged to oppose policy reform.

8.3.1   The Constitutional Problem

The U.S. Constitution created a political balance of power designed to give the fledgling republic a better chance to survive and sustain a vital democracy. It sought to prevent any branch of government from having too much power, prevent the majority from oppressing the minority, and protect the individual from the tyranny of the state. This constitutional arrangement did not create any mechanism for the poor to protect themselves from exploitation by the rich or for the rich to protect themselves from the expropriation of their wealth by the poor. Virtually all other constitutional structures in history created some economic balance of power where the rich and poor could work together to preserve social order. For example, although there was no formal constitution in the Roman Republic, only an uncodified set of principles established by precedent, there were three centers of power that balanced one another: the executive magistrates of consuls and praetors controlling the administration and warfare; the Senate, composed of rich patricians with the power over revenue, expenses, and the choice of leaders; and the Assembly, consisting of ordinary Roman citizens that appointed, as executive magistrates, a number of tribunes with varying powers who could protect citizens against actions by the consuls or praetors. At the height of their power, tribunes could grant clemency, veto legislation, block actions of the other branches, and initiate plebiscites in the assembly. In the British system, the aristocracy is represented in the House of Lords and ordinary citizens in the House of Commons.

The constitutional scholar Ganesh Sitaraman (2017) explains that the framers expected the United States to remain an egalitarian society and thus designed a constitution that did not address conflicts between rich and poor. It was an egalitarian society at birth (excepting the original sin of slavery and the exclusion of women) and remained so for a long time because of the prevalence of small-scale farming and the abundance of land available to any hard-working person. Sitaraman makes a persuasive case that, lacking a mechanism for economic balance of power, democratic institutions in the United States rely for their stability on a strong middle class with the incentive to find compromises and prevent the extremes from taking over or prevailing in the pursuit of narrow interests. Because rising inequality has caused a drastic decline of the middle class, he asserts that democracy is in peril.

Without a constitutionally based economic balance of power, the Supreme Court has become key to economic policy; any law with major economic implications ultimately requires the consent of the Court. From the 1890s until 1937, the Court essentially acted as though laissez-faire economics was an implicit part of the U.S. Constitution, and as if *The Wealth of Nations* was their point of reference. On the grounds that it violated the Fourteenth Amendment, the Court struck down a New York state law that requires a bakery's hours of employment to be fewer than ten hours a day and sixty hours a week (*Lochner v. New York*, 1905). The Fourteenth Amendment was interpreted to enshrine a right to make contracts free from government interference. The *Lochner* era that followed saw the Court strike down many of the Progressive movement's regulations in diverse economic areas. The Court used broad interpretations of the Tenth and Fourteenth Amendments to strike down minimum-wage and maximum-hours laws, child labor prohibitions, and a variety of pro-union laws. This legal battle continued into the 1930s and was the cause of the clash between the Roosevelt administrations and the Court. The *Lochner* era ended with the case of *West Coast Hotel Co. v. Parrish* (1937), when minimum-wage legislation enacted by the state of Washington was upheld by the Supreme Court. But this was not the last change of economic doctrine adopted by the Supreme Court.

While the *Lochner* (1905) decision reflects the laissez-faire doctrine of the First Gilded Age, the decision in *Citizens United v. Federal Election Commission* (2010) reflects the laissez-faire doctrine of the Second Gilded Age. *Lochner* was based on the Court's interpretation of the Fourteenth Amendment, whereas the battle in the Second Gilded Age has focused on the free speech provisions of the First Amendment.

Any economics student would make the elementary inference, from the heavy spending of business on advertising, that advertising is profitable because it succeeds in altering consumer demand in favor of the advertiser. The same student would also assume from the vast spending by political candidates on elections, and the great efforts they make to raise money, that money has a great impact on politics. This conclusion is in contrast with many studies that fail to find evidence that financial support has an effect on election results. Regardless of whether one can demonstrate the effectiveness of money in altering election results, political candidates actively search for financial support. Political candidates prefer to win elections without using financial support of rich contributors, but all candidates expend their own time and effort to raise funds, and some have gone so far in search of funds that they become ethically compromised or even violate the law. Campaign contributions must have a strong impact on the voting patterns of elected representatives; otherwise there would be no lobbying. For examples of the ways in which the rich use their wealth to influence the vote in Congress, see Krugman (2019) and Philippon (2019).

The strong desire of the rich to influence election outcomes, the extensive lobbying by corporations, and the fact that all candidates spend much of their time raising money, support the universal view that money has a corrupting effect on the democratic process. Yet the Supreme Court decided a corporation has the same right to free speech as any voter and can spend as much as it wants to promote a candidate who would then be beholden to that corporation. In doing so, the Court ignored the fact that corporations do not have the right to vote and that a large corporation has vastly more money than any typical voter. The danger that corporations use that money to promote their market power by political means was entirely disregarded.

The corrupting influence of money on politics is well documented in many studies (see, for example, Kalla and Broockman, 2016) and attempts to regulate campaign finance have a long history. The Court clearly made its decision after examining the many years of research, debate, and past legislation. It chose to adopt an economic doctrine that is contradicted by scientific reasoning and ignores the available evidence. One possible explanation is the Court's belief in competition among corporations: if one corporation supports a candidate, a second corporation can support the opponent. This is similar to the reason conservative economists oppose antitrust policy, an issue I discuss in the next section.

The conclusion of my short review is that, like reformers in the early twentieth century who battled the Supreme Court for over thirty years before *Lochner* was reversed, those seeking policy reforms to contain market power may be hindered by an ideologically conservative Court for a long time. This has only become more true in recent years because the Court has shifted to the right with the replacements of Justices Kennedy and Ginsburg. This Court is heading back toward the legal doctrine of the *Lochner* era.

8.3.2   Ideological and Social Barriers

The next impediment to policy reform is the politically influential conservative ideology that holds that the rich deserve their gains and antitrust policy should not be enacted to combat corporate market power. The stated aim of the Sherman Antitrust Act of 1890 and the two laws enacted to strengthen it, the Clayton Act of 1914 and the Robinson-Patman Act of 1936, was to suppress all restraints on trade in order to maintain free competition. The Supreme Court considered these acts a "charter of freedom"[1] designed to protect free enterprise. Despite their sweeping intent, in practice these acts were interpreted as requiring the elimination of market power gained by a list of illegal, mostly collusive activities defined by the law as restraining trade.

Conservative thinkers have consistently opposed even this limited antitrust regime. They argue that it restrains the natural functioning of markets in which the most successful may attain market power through the superiority of their products, services, or business practices. Even serious scholars like Milton Friedman and Richard Posner, who recognized that the Sherman Antitrust Act is used to eliminate corrupt, collusive, and even violent acts, ultimately opposed the antitrust regime (Friedman, 1999; Posner, 2014; Bork, 1978). For example, Posner (2014) articulates the standard argument that antitrust policy punishes the most successful for being successful and that any market power is temporary, even if attained by collusive behavior. In this telling, market power is not of concern to society because it will be erased by competition initiated by those with superior business practices and abilities.

The idea that competitive forces break down existing market power is both theoretically deficient and contradicted by the evidence. The Posner (2014) view is more of a wish than a fully developed theory because, as I show in chapters 1 and 7, technological competition is different from normal competition. Its most important characteristic is that it has only one or few winners who automatically gain market power that can be consolidated and maintained for a very long time. The empirical evidence confirms these conclusions, and the literature on superstar firms reflects exactly the prediction of my theory.

The conservative view on wealth inequality, that being wealthy is the result of the superior ability of the rich and the successful, has a long tradition. This belief took a particular form during the First Gilded Age. Reflecting upon his wealth, Andrew Carnegie wrote in 1889 a book entitled *The Gospel of Wealth*, offering advice on how to succeed in business. He explained his own success by appealing to Herbert Spencer's social Darwinism and the work of the eugenicist Francis Galton. These theories applied natural selection to human intelligence and behavior. What determines the winners, Carnegie wrote, is the survival of the fittest, and Carnegie's superior qualities are what made him rich. Eugenics

---

[1]See *Appalachian Coals, Inc. v. United States* (1933).

was a popular doctrine in the First Gilded Age in part because it provided the wealthy a theory to explain that they were innately superior to, and therefore more deserving than, others who were not as rich.

Although explicit eugenics is a discredited doctrine, similar appeals are made today to the random nature of genetic endowments that create heterogeneity in ability among individuals. Heterogeneity in ability and in the quality of human capital may explain differences in individual skills. But that does not imply that the top 1 percent have superior abilities that justify their vast income and wealth.

In the last fifty years, the opposition to an egalitarian policy and the substantial political pressure to lower taxes has been driven mostly by the rich. They justified their demands in exactly the same way as earlier generations, arguing they deserve their hard-earned income and wealth. Such a sense of entitlement fueled the growth of the tax avoidance industry (see Saez and Zucman, 2019b). Today, these ideas are used by the rich to justify their tax evasion and their hiding of wealth abroad in tax shelters (see Johns and Slemrod, 2010; Zucman, 2013).

Individual genetic diversity is certainly a reason for policymakers to be cautious in distorting the incentives of talented individuals to work and innovate. But unlike individuals, corporations have no innate characteristics. Those who are opposed to antitrust policy and seek to exempt corporations with vast market power on the basis of their superior productivity surely do not base it on any genetic foundation. Corporations are organizations that deploy business strategies, and these can be copied or imitated, although such imitations are difficult. At the basis of any difficult-to-imitate corporate practice is some technological advantage, scale, reputation, private information, business culture, or other proprietary factors giving rise to market power. Antitrust regulators can scrutinize this market power and weigh its negative economic effects against the benefits created by the firm. Instead, the current practice is simply to exempt technological firms from all antitrust scrutiny.

The more general question of firm heterogeneity was briefly discussed in chapter 4, in reference to the literature on the topic (see, for example, Van Reenen, 2018; Autor et al., 2020). Similar to the Posner (2014) argument against the antitrust regime, that literature views rising technological market power as a reflection of the superior productivity of today's large firms, calling them superstar firms, and arguing they should not be a public policy concern because they have the most productive technologies. I next summarize the reasons that this valorization of some firms as deserving exemption from antitrust law is misguided.

8.3.3   Why Reject the Heterogeneity Argument?

The heterogeneity argument exempts the superstar firms from intent to build their market power and insists that technological competition, in the long run, restores regular competition. In the short run, the superior productivity of the top firms benefits society so much that society should accept any negative consequences of their temporary market power. There are several reasons why this argument should be rejected:

1. *Market power has destructive impact regardless of the productivity of powerful firms.* Firms with market power have destructive social impact, as documented extensively in this book. This fact by itself implies that public policy should weigh the cost of market power against the benefits of economic efficiency. Because market power is often gained by buying or squashing other smaller competitors, the cost accounting must also take into account the history of impediments to innovation and economic growth created by leading firms on the way to acquiring their market power.

2. *Firms with market power may not be the most productive.* Firms with market power exhibit high profitability without necessarily being the most productive because they often set standards for the industry (see David, 1985). Because they have market power and are able to charge high prices, it appears that they are producing a great deal of value using relatively few inputs. Empirical studies measuring productivity typically observe only total sales revenues, and these are distorted by the firm's noncompetitive pricing. Those that do observe firms' quantities, as in Foster et al.'s (2008) study of U.S. manufacturing firms producing homogeneous goods or Forlani et al.'s (2016) study of Belgian manufacturing firms, find the quantity-based measure of productivity diverges significantly from the revenue-based one resulting from the effect of markups.

3. *Market power is durable.* In the often-cited example of a cartel, the standard argument why it will not persist is based on static "prisoner's dilemma" models. But this argument is rejected by models of repeated games, where a cartel's stability is supported by dynamic punishment strategies of other members. These dynamic effects are particularly important in technological competition, where an incumbent with technological market power has the option of financing research and innovation to suppress a potential competitor. Therefore, most innovators who are potential entrants find it more profitable to sell their technology to an incumbent technological monopolist rather than sustain the cost of a struggle with a well-financed adversary. These buyouts benefit both the incumbents and their competitors, much like cartelization. Therefore, it takes a very long time, and perhaps the coming of a revolutionary GPT, for technological market power to fade away. Finally, even if a superior competitor emerges to replace the old one, this is merely the substitution of one market power for another.

4. *Technological competition results in a small number of lucky leaders.* The success-breeds-success process explored in chapter 7 shows that innovation via technological competition advantages those firms lucky enough to find early success. This process results in very few firms rising to the top with superior productivity,

while most competitors run out of steam, defaulting, being bought out, or surviving at the margin with lower productivity. In that model, the superstar firms reaching the very top are not inherently superior because their success is mostly a result of pure luck combined with the creation of impediments to the success of those behind.

5. *Restraining excessive market power at the top boosts the productivity of all and results in superior social outcome.* The analysis of chapter 7 also shows that by curtailing the power of those lucky firms at the top, public policy restrains their ability to impede the productivity growth of firms at the lower levels. Furthermore, it reduces the ability of top firms to acquire newly developed technologies to further consolidate their market power. This improves the productivity of all other firms in the economy. An active policy to curtail the power of the superstar firms results in an equilibrium with a less skewed distribution of firm productivity, a larger number of higher productivity firms at the top, and welfare-enhancing allocation of resources.

In short, the existence of any market power should be a public policy concern. The alleged superior productivity of corporations with vast market power should not exempt them from the scrutiny of public policy. Such market power has drastic economic and political consequences. Public policy must recognize the incentives of individuals to innovate and ensure that they benefit from their efforts. But it must also prevent them from using the initial market power gained by those innovations as the foundation of a long-lasting and excessive power that harms society.

8.3.4   The Challenging Random Poverty Trap

Because much of economic activity is subject to uncertainty, random factors are fundamental to the distribution of income and wealth. Even if a hypothetical society begins with equally able individuals, over time, idiosyncratic random factors will cause individual wealth to be unequally distributed. If we start with an equal society, all risk-averse individuals favor a tax on the lucky that is redistributed to the unlucky, which acts as an insurance policy that provides a valuable risk-sharing mechanism. This shows that, even if the underlying conditions were fully egalitarian, income distribution problems emerge, and their solution requires not a temporary but a permanent policy to be put in place.

Inequality caused by idiosyncratic shocks is amplified by the persistence of income inequality. The wealthy tend to have descendants who are better educated and have better opportunities that allow them to be wealthy many years down the road. The poor have descendants who are less educated, suffer from poor nutrition, and have fewer opportunities to exit the state of poverty. The well-known implication is that the stability of a society depends upon social mobility between the middle class and the wealthy on one hand, and between the middle class and the poor on the other. The decline of social mobility has recently received some well-deserved attention from the economics profession (Chetty et al., 2014). With regard to poverty, two rates matter: the rate at which people fall on hard times, and the rate at which poor people work their way out of poverty and back into the middle class. If the recovery rate is high enough relative to the rate at which people fall into poverty, the class of people in poverty can remain small. Two factors act to lower mobility without any difference in innate ability: random shocks to the entire economy, and the finiteness of life of each member.

When faced with a shock to the economy, such as a recession or a pandemic, the ability of members to weather the shock economically depends upon their financial strength. The rich have resources to sustain the effect of aggregate shocks, while the poor are hit relatively harder and become poorer as a result. Aggregate shocks are then an important force reducing social mobility and contributing to inequality.

Life being finite implies the poverty of parents is translated into poverty of their children. As noted earlier, in poverty, children receive inadequate nutrition, inferior medical treatment, and poor education. These children begin their life in a worse position than their peers of similar ability who are born into better economic circumstances. This process creates a poverty trap even in a society that begins with a fully egalitarian distribution of ability. This poverty trap creates differences resulting from disparities in childhood education and health, where none were innate.

That random factors produce a permanently poor class is well-known. This is relevant here because of its policy implications, given the objective of countering the rapid decline of the middle class since the 1980s. The implication is that a successful policy designed to stabilize the distribution of income and wealth must contain a permanent and strong mechanism to attain a high rate of mobility from poverty into the middle class. The key term here is "permanent"—the forces that push members of society into poverty and keep them there are not going away. As such, the institution that is needed to counter those forces must be a permanent one and not subject to annual budgetary politics. In chapter 10, I discuss my proposal for such an institution.

8.4   Five Policy Objectives

The policy problem in an economy with technology-based market power is to minimize that power while preserving most incentives to innovate. Because this entails having an antitrust policy that preserves some degree of market power, a policy reform should have multiple components. I thus briefly describe the five basic objectives of the reforms outlined in chapters 9–10:

1. *Contain the expansion of market power created by innovations.* This objective is the heart of a new policy regime. It can be accomplished by expanding the Sherman Antitrust regime to control the level of technology-based market power and by reforming patent law. Regulations of market power should aim to counteract the business strategies listed in section 1.4, which are used to expand and entrench market power. Some advocate the elimination of all legal protection of intellectual property rights to achieve this goal.[2] Although eliminating such legal protection would restrain market power, I have repeatedly argued that patent law is not the primary cause of most market power and that patent laws have important advantages to society. My approach is that, in the absence of a better alternative, it is best to improve the existing law.

2. *Redistribute monopoly profits and boost employment of capital and labor.* It is standard practice in the theory of optimal taxation to treat the corporate tax as a tax on capital, leading to the well-known conclusion that corporate profits should not be taxed (see, for example, Judd, 1985; Chamley, 1986). I propose that corporate income tax be imposed only on monopoly profits, which are a result of market power and should certainly be taxed. However, such a tax reduces the incentive to innovate. In chapter 9, I study this incentive and conclude the tax should not exceed 50 percent. I outline a procedure for the Internal Revenue Service (IRS) to compute such profits. The revenue from such a tax may be spent on efforts to finance programs to assist those displaced by technology and boost demand for capital investments and for labor employment in order to correct the inefficiency caused by the existence of market power.

3. *Restrict the link between market power and political power.* Policy has a crucial impact on market power, but policy is formulated by political leaders. If they are beholden to financial interests, a socially desirable policy will never be enforced or even enacted. This suggests that *Citizens United* has to be overturned. The political system is trapped in a cycle where money and corporate power influence elections, and the only force to counter it is a well-informed public that actively advocates for democracy.

4. *Expand public investments in research and technology.* In chapter 7, I argue that the vitality of economic growth depends, to a large extent, on the progress of basic research and the vitality of basic institutions of science and culture. Therefore, there is an urgent need to expand public investments in basic research and education.

---

[2] For history of the question, see Johns (2009), and for recent discussion, see Boldrin and Levine (2013).

5. *Rebuild the middle class and build a permanent mechanism to overcome the poverty trap.* I have argued repeatedly that the restoration of the American middle class is a vital policy goal. To achieve it, substantial improvements in the levels of health and education of the poorer 50 percent of Americans are necessary. Indeed, the most important mechanisms for increasing upward mobility from the bottom 50 percent of the income distribution are improvements in the health and education of the children of the poorer Americans. In my view, the best way to do it is to apply some of the famous principles of Franklin Roosevelt's Second Bill of Rights to the children of the families in the bottom 50 percent of the income distribution. My proposal in chapter 10 addresses this need with the creation of a national fund for equity and democracy.

CHAPTER 9

POLICY TO RESTRAIN THE EXPANSION OF MARKET POWER

The present antitrust policy seeks to remove all restraint of trade and, in so doing, preserve free enterprise. But the Sherman Antitrust regime exempts technological market power, which is interpreted to be "innocent monopoly," that is monopoly achieved solely by merit. There are two legal manifestations of this exemption. First, in *U.S. v. General Electric Co.* (1926), the Supreme Court held that antitrust laws do not apply to patented innovations. As long as they stay within the scope of their patents, firms may engage in otherwise illegal activities, like price fixing of the products of their patented innovations. Second, in the 1920s, antitrust laws were interpreted to prohibit only those ways of acquiring market power deemed "unfair." Innovation was always held to belong to a class of activities that are "fair" and thus permitted (see Feldman, 2008, citing *U.S. v. Am. Can Co.*, 1921 and *U.S. v. U.S. Steel Corp.*, 1920). This exemption of innovations was further entrenched in the 1980s when the Chicago School of antitrust took hold. The courts avoided enforcing antitrust laws whenever possible, fearing that doing so would hamper innovation or reduce output of the most productive firms. In view of the growth of technological market power exhibited in chapter 4, this exemption is a contradiction within the policy. The growth of corporate market power among innovative firms and the economic, social, and political consequences of the vast power they wield indicates that an expansion of the Sherman Antitrust regime is needed. The task of such expansion is to add, to the current objective of removing restraints of trade, an explicit objective of containing technological market power and restoring an optimal balance of power in society.

An expansion of the Sherman Antitrust regime must balance rewarding innovation and preventing market power from expanding beyond a stipulated level. However, changes in the antitrust regime typically take a long time to work their way through the economy. It is easy to propose breaking up technological monopolies or oligopolies. It is, however, far from clear how to break up Apple's iPhone business or Google's search and advertising business without causing serious harm to economic efficiency. It is therefore important to distinguish between policy actions that take a long time to change the course of the economy and those that have immediate effect. Changes in the antitrust regime are, by and large, made as long-run policies, and these are considered in the present chapter. Some policies with more immediate effects are also considered in this chapter, including the prospect of breaking up vertically integrated technological conglomerates into separate firms. However, the short-run policies I primarily advocate to alleviate the burden of market power are taxation and redistribution policies, which are studied in chapter 10.

9.1   Contain Expansion of Market Power: A Radically New Principle of Antitrust Policy

The objective of patent law is to determine the optimal degree of monopoly power to compensate innovators for their contribution to society. The grant of monopoly power from patent law should be an optimal choice along a number of dimensions. The U.S. legal system sets many parameters for patents, and, while not always explicit, they are policy choices and could be modified by legislation. Those parameters include coverage, duration, compensation for infringement, and many other specific restrictions. I discuss reforms of patent law in section 9.2, but I do not advocate abandoning it altogether because, by incentivizing innovation, patent law offers sufficient advantages to society to be worth preserving. I presume that, subject to the reforms I propose in section 9.2, the level of market power created by patent law will be sufficiently low and of short enough duration to be compatible with otherwise long-run competitive markets in a free enterprise economy. I also take it as given that the degree of market power granted by patent law is primarily a political decision, an issue I discuss later in section 9.2. Given these facts, my central proposal for the expansion of the Sherman Antitrust regime is the following broad principle:

> Expand the Sherman Antitrust regime to include the objective of restraining an entity's technological market power down to the level granted by patent law, and by other competitive advantages such as trade secrets, that arise naturally from innovation in free markets.

This principle means that when an economic entity, usually a corporation, attains a degree of market power granted by a patent or sustained by trade secrets, or by other initial advantages spelled out in chapter 1, public policy must prevent its build-up and extension over time above and beyond that legally granted degree. Adoption of such policy will prohibit certain activities, detailed in chapter 1 and considered to constitute monopolization, by which the entity expands its technological market power. If such activities are prevented, technological market power will slowly decay. Patents expire, trade secrets become common knowledge, and competitors will not be prevented from entering the market.

This expansion of the antitrust regime implies that the Federal Trade Commission (FTC) would benefit from ongoing assessment of the technological market power of firms, measured in three ways. The first is a qualitative assessment of the substitutability of the products produced by the different technologies in the markets under consideration. The second measure is the estimated markup of the firm, based either on its detailed cost data or on the share of profits out of its value added (as in chapter 4). The third is the firm's estimated monopoly wealth as a proportion of the total wealth created by the firm, as is estimated in chapter 6. Regulators would also be helped by an evaluation of the record of innovations owned by a firm to determine if its market power exceeds the level that would have been obtained through the technologies it actually innovated. If its privately owned technology is entirely innovated by the firm itself (as distinct from having been acquired) and it does not take any actions to erect additional barriers to entry, its market power is then protected by patent laws. In the rest of this section, I develop the rules that follow from the above general principle.

9.1.1   Mergers, Acquisitions, and Technology Purchasing

Technological acquisitions are the most important weapon in the expansion of market power. An entity increases its market power above the level granted by patent law not by innovating but by adding the market power of other innovators to its arsenal. That is, when one firm becomes the owner of two competing but complementary technologies, aggregate market power rises above the level that prevails when the two technologies are owned by two competing firms. As explained in chapter 1, given the presence of an established firm with market power, potential competitors have the option of either entering into battle with a powerful incumbent or selling their firm or technology to the incumbent. Those who are reluctant to sell find that the incumbent will price below cost, pressure suppliers, leverage its position in adjacent markets, advertise, and otherwise use its position to destroy their market as much as it is able to. The volume of acquisitions is an approximate measure of the speed at which innovations by others

TABLE 9.1 The number of acquisitions of a sample of firms

Firm	Time period	Number of acquisitions
Microsoft	1987–2020	237
Facebook	2005–2020	87
Salesforce	2006–2020	59
Google	2001–2020	236
Amazon	1998–2020	102

Source: Wikipedia acquisition page of each of the firm in the table.

contribute to the amplification of an existing firm's market power without any innovation by the acquiring firm. Table 9.1 suggests that the scale involved is very large.

The size of these acquisitions, of course, also matters. But this torrent of merger and acquisition (M&A) activity offers a direct measure of the annual volume of acquisitions, which is pivotal to the rapid growth of these firms. In some sectors, like pharmaceutical, most research and development (R&D) investments and innovations are made on the level of smaller firms that carry out their work as joint ventures with the larger firms and are subsequently acquired if the projects are successful. That is, a substantial part of the work of innovation is done not by the firms with market power but by smaller firms, where much of the innovative talent is found. In addition to purchasing firms, companies also acquire ownership of technology through direct purchases of patents and other intellectual property rights.

Examination of all acquisitions reveals that not infrequently the acquired technology does not make it to market. Some of these acquisitions are still considered a success for the acquiring firm because they allow the firm to suppress the technology and prevent it from being obtained by others. The majority of technology acquisitions do succeed and contribute substantially to the growth and market power of the acquiring firms. Also, incumbent firms often correctly anticipate future developments in their markets, and they are thus able to acquire valuable assets at low prices. For example, Facebook paid for Instagram (in 2012), and WhatsApp (in 2014) about $20 billion, and these were estimated in 2020 to be worth, within Facebook, over ten times that price.

Given the importance of mergers and acquisitions as tools for expanding technological market power, the proposed policy is that any technological merger or acquisition should be subject to public scrutiny. Indeed, the presumption of the policy must be that any technological acquisition aims to expand market power, and the firm proposing the acquisition has the burden of proof that it will not expand it beyond the legal limit. Once a firm is declared to possess market power that exceeds the legally allowable level, no defense of the efficiency of an acquisition should be accepted. Technological efficiency is an acceptable motivation of a firm desiring an acquisition, but such acquisition should not be a tool for strengthening market power or preventing other firms from gaining such improved efficiency. Blocking acquisitions raises two questions. First, what criteria should be considered, relative to the goal of preventing the expansion of market power, by the regulator in deciding whether to approve a merger or an acquisition? Second, if a merger or acquisition is approved by the regulator, how should the acquired technology be treated when its ownership is transferred to the buyer?

(A) Criterion for approval or rejection of a merger or acquisition. In considering a merger or acquisition, the regulator needs to assess the combined impact of increased market share of products together with increased technological market power. The existing framework of the Sherman Antitrust Act focuses on market share, but my argument is that the dynamics of technology and technological market power are equally vital and need their own place in merger review. The existing framework focuses on humanmade, collusive barriers to entry. Technology-based market power is about the control of a technology that generates a collection of products whose production and use are linked to that technology. This link enables a firm that owns the technology to establish an indirect monopoly over a market segment. Therefore, control over technology gives the firm an advantage over competitors and allows it to restrict the choice of consumers or suppliers, thereby giving its products some advantage. Technological domination may not provide an immediate advantage but may lead to future outcomes that the current antitrust regime aims to avoid. For example, if a firm has a technological edge, it may expand into adjacent markets and grow in size over time. To integrate the current antitrust regime with the goal of restricting technological market power, the proposed unified policy criterion is then:

> Prevent a firm from restraining trade in its market and, in addition, prevent its technological market power from exceeding a threshold maximal level beyond which its dominance limits competition and suppresses competitors' ability to innovate and grow their own market share. Such a maximal level varies across economic sectors. Past this maximal level, mergers and acquisitions should be disallowed.

This criterion may appear insufficiently operational, but it becomes relatively simple in most cases when considering the real circumstances of each industry. I consider three examples.

Amazon's market share of 2018 gross online commerce was 49 percent. Moreover, more than 50 percent of Amazon's total sales are derived from third-party vendors. Thus, apart from its domination of online retail trade, the company is also an aggressive monopsonist that uses multiple tactics to dominate its suppliers. In 2018, there were other firms active in online retail, such as eBay (6.6 percent share), Apple (3.9 percent share), and Walmart (3.7 percent share). One might conclude from this that the online retail market is contestable and requires no public scrutiny. But after surviving the 1999–2000 dot-com setback, by about 2005 Amazon became a technologically dominant firm with a high degree of market power. On this basis, under my proposed policy, none of its eighty-five acquisitions since 2005 would have been approved by regulators. This would have given competitors a better chance to develop their own internet technologies more rapidly, and the market would be less concentrated today.

In 2020, the duopoly of Facebook and Google dominated the online advertising business, with Google taking a 37.2 percent share and Facebook a share of 19.6 percent. Advertising is the main source of income for these firms. Both have owned the dominant technologies in this online market from inception. As a result, none of the eighty-seven acquisitions made by Facebook or the 236 made by Google would have been approved under the criterion stated above. Furthermore, Facebook's technology and its business model have resulted in extremely abusive practices. These facts lead me to the view that Facebook should be turned by regulators into a public utility.

In 2019, Apple sold 13.5 percent of all the smartphones sold in the world, but its share of total revenue was 51 percent because the iPhone sold for an average price of $800. Its nearest competitor, Samsung Electronics, sold 15.7 percent of all units, with an average selling price of $254. If one restricts attention to the top-quality segment of the market, Apple's phone offers the dominant technology, with Samsung being a lagging second. Here again, technological superiority gave Apple its unchallenged position as a technological monopolist long before its market share became so high. Very little technological competition exists today in that market. Apple's technological superiority took some time to develop, but using the criterion formulated earlier, none of the eighty-nine acquisitions it made since about 2010 would have been approved. Any firm could conceivably enter the market for top-quality phones; Google and Microsoft have tried. So the market is, in theory, contestable. However, Apple uses its technological dominance to stay ahead. It also innovates specific technologies that lock users into its platform, like iMessage, which is designed to work only between iPhones and iCloud and is practically inaccessible from a Windows computer.

As to exemption of small firms, as in the Sherman Antitrust regime, restrictions on technological mergers and acquisitions should not apply to small firms with both limited market power and small market share. For that reason, all rules proposed here would restrict acquisitions of technology only by firms above some minimal size. Firm size may be defined either by sales or capital invested and should be chosen by the regulator. It appears prudent to set this threshold to be at most $1 billion but at least $500 million of revenue of the entire firm under consideration, including all subsidiaries. This level of revenue[1] may not be appropriate to some industries, and this choice is left to the discretion of regulators.

The subtle but crucial question is, How do we define the maximal level of market power? Because I have linked it to the level set by patent law, for firms above the threshold size in revenue, one possibility is to start by assuming the level of market power prior to the merger or acquisition was in accordance with patent law. Therefore, the maximal level becomes the level that prevailed before the merger or acquisition. Two examples will clarify the point. If the acquiring firm demonstrates that the technology of the acquired firm is unrelated and does not complement its own technology, then the change in ownership does not change the level of market power. The second example considers firm A with sales of $600 million planning to acquire firm B with sales of $500 million and with two technologies that are complementary. Because its revenue will be $1.1 billion, it will exceed the size limit, and because the combination of the two technologies will raise market power, the merger should be rejected.

In sum, the policy criterion I propose is intentionally flexible so that it may be applied differently under different circumstances, while its intent remains clear. It is to be expected that the threshold for technological dominance would complement the current antitrust regime's aim to eliminate restraint of trade. The technological dominance standard will require careful attention to the specific properties of each technology. Arguments for exemption from antitrust will reappear, such as the claim that there is adequate technological competition if the market is defined broadly enough. Over time, experience would allow the identification of more specific conditions for the law's applicability, and it can be updated, just as the Clayton Act of 1914 and the Robinson-Patman Act of 1936 strengthened the 1890 Sherman Antitrust Act.

What would have been the consequences of this policy if it had been in effect in the past thirty years or so? The vast majority of the 721 acquisitions reported in table 9.1 would not have been approved by regulators, and the consequences would have been profound:

1. The largest and most valuable U.S. corporations would have been smaller than they are today, with substantially less market power.
2. In particular, the scope of these firms would have been narrower; acquisitions enabled them to expand into a large number of market segments.
3. Large firms would have been compelled to do more R&D internally to protect their market power and market value.

---

[1] The 2013 census reveals 732 firms with revenue exceeding $1 billion and 1,069 firms with revenue between $500 million and $1 billion. Therefore, the size of the population subject to regulation of market power would have been less than 1,801 firms in 2013.

4. More intensive technological competition would have emerged from the smaller firms that were suppressed, and this would have resulted in more innovations and more new firms that do not exist today.

5. Independent innovators would have either engaged in more entrepreneurial efforts to market their own innovations or would have been acquired by smaller firms that were more invested in developing these technologies and in marketing the products they created.

6. More firms would be operating overall. Some new firms would have been formed and survived, and many of the acquired firms would remain and be functioning today. This would have attenuated or reversed the trend of a declining number of firms since 1997.

(B) Restrictions imposed on the acquiring firm if an acquisition is approved. Another way to prevent technological firms from entrenching their market power, aside from blocking acquisitions, is to place restrictions on the merged firm. In antitrust law, these are called conduct remedies. What remedies can regulators use to prevent technological firms from suppressing competition when a merger or acquisition is approved? I have noted that combining two complementary innovations into one firm increases that firm's market power. With that in mind, consider a firm that has market power arising from a technology protected by a patent or trade secret. That firm may attempt to own a second patent that complements and amplifies the applicability of the first technology. This would allow the entity to increase its market power above the level arising from the first technology. The firm could acquire this second patent in one of two ways:

1. The firm itself may be filing for a patent on the second innovation. In this case, the patent is what I define, in section 9.2, as a secondary patent. In section 9.2.2A, I argue that if the application is justified and the patent granted, it should be only for a duration of half the life granted to a primary patent today.

2. The firm may acquire the second patent by a merger with another firm, by an acquisition of that firm, or by direct purchase of the patent in the market. In all cases, I propose that the remaining duration of the patent should be cut by half when ownership is transferred. In case of a merger or acquisition, all patents involved must be compared to determine which is secondary and whose life span is reduced by half. This decision can be affected by requiring, as a condition of consent to the merger, that the firm not enforce the terms of that patent for the excluded period.

In the first case, the patent is granted in much the same way as today, but the duration of a secondary patent is set at half that of primary patents. In the second case, any technology acquired that complements existing technology is treated as secondary technology. Consequently, if regulators approve the acquisition, the duration of all acquired patents that complement the first technology owned by the firm would be halved. Apart from the desire to prevent rising market power, the above provisions are motivated by a desire to encourage entrepreneurship and discourage trading in patents. The explanation for this is provided in section 9.2 concerning the reform of patent law.

A complete exemption from my proposed rules regarding technological acquisitions should be granted where a firm that seeks to acquire a second firm or its assets is willing to cancel all patents owned by the second firm and make publicly available all that firm's trade secrets. In that case, the merger or acquisition should be assessed entirely on the basis of the traditional Sherman Antitrust Act objective of preventing the restraint of trade.

Finally, being a basic change in policy, this proposed expansion of the antitrust regime will work itself slowly through the economy. It will take a long time before the desired results emerge because these regulations merely prevent companies from expanding their market power and deepening their economic moat. They won't immediately alter the balance of power in today's markets. In contrast, some other proposals in this chapter, as well as the taxation and redistribution plans laid out in chapter 10, are designed to have a more immediate impact.

9.1.2   Break Up Vertically Integrated Technological Conglomerates

Many large technology firms use profits from their initial innovations to expand into unrelated market segments. For example, financial reports submitted by Amazon to the Securities and Exchange Commission (SEC) reveal that its business consists of the following segments:

- An online retail business;
- A retail business performed through physical stores;
- AmazonBasics, which manufactures a variety of nondurable consumer goods;
- Amazon Web Services, the most extensive cloud-computing platform;
- Amazon Studios, which produces television shows and films;
- Amazon Advertising, which offers digital advertising services;
- Amazon Care, which offers virtual health clinics and in-home follow-up visits; and
- PillPack, an at-home, prescription drug delivery service.

Amazon is rapidly expanding into a growing number of unrelated businesses. These businesses promote one another, as Amazon increases its market power in these added markets. The firm uses its online retail data to target its manufacturing investments, offers discounts to its Prime retail customers at its Whole Foods grocery stores, and distributes Amazon Studios' productions through its Prime video-streaming service. These vertically tied products do not increase efficiency: Amazon would be equally able to sell these products on its platform if they belonged to other firms. But Amazon's dominance in the online retail space allows it to gain market share for its products in other markets.

Alphabet, Google's parent company, is an even more diverse conglomerate offering over fifty products and services. Of its revenue, 56 percent comes from advertising on its search engine, which accounts for more than 70 percent of all online searches. Its other businesses cover diverse areas such as autonomous driving, mobile phones, email, internet service provision, video, life sciences, online document creation, and cloud computing. In this case, it is even harder to identify the connection among the parts except, perhaps, the company's official desire "to organize the world's information and make it universally accessible and useful."

As a third example, Facebook Inc. offers three distinct services that have operated independently of each other: the Facebook social network and linked Messenger app that enables people to communicate with each other directly; Instagram, the photo-sharing network; and WhatsApp, the mobile messaging app. Fearing that regulators might seek to break up the firm into its component services, Facebook recently linked the Messenger app with Instagram. This is part of a broader strategy to link the three services into one network. This is not a technological improvement but a defense against regulators who should recognize that this integration could be made by the users and take place outside firm boundaries; it is not necessary for the three services to have the same owner for them to be linked.

As large firms, supported by an army of lobbyists, expand their market power and political power, it is natural to question whether the diversity of a conglomerate is socially useful. As in prior eras, conglomeration enables managers of profitable firms to retain profits and widen their economic and political reach by expanding into a growing number of unrelated fields. Executive pay and prestige increase with firm size. It is thus in the interest of executives to reinvest profits and expand into adjacent markets as opposed to paying dividends to shareholders. And again, as in prior eras, in the long run it is likely to result in a wave of corporate breakups. In the meantime, their excessive economic and political power is damaging, and it is important to consider breaking up at least some now rather than later.

To achieve the objective of containing market power, regulators should prioritize breaking up large firms into components that can function independently and equally efficiently. But then regulators will have to identify the natural boundaries for breaking up a firm while maintaining the efficiency of its independent components. Entities without significant market power may be spun off separately. Execution of such a program is clearly a complex process, and a reformed antitrust policy should set standards to identify vertical conglomerates that must be broken up. The burden must be on the conglomerates to demonstrate that, if broken up, the resulting firms would be unable to collaborate across the new boundaries and produce the same products with equal efficiency. Regulators also need the staff and funding to study these firms carefully and identify the natural boundaries.

9.1.3   Platforms' Market Power and Technological Compatibility

The largest firms in the digital economy act as platforms, or intermediaries, connecting third-party sellers to consumers. The basic question involved here is whether the public has any right to object to the conduct of platform operators. For example, once someone purchases an iPhone, what are the limits to their ownership of that phone? If a developer comes up with a new app, can that developer freely contract with the owners of the phone to sell them the app at a given price? Or does Apple Inc. have the right, because they created the phone, to require the developer to pay it 30 percent of the revenue stream resulting from the sale of that app? The simple analogy to this example is the purchase of a new General Motors (GM) car. Does GM have the right to restrict a company from selling new tires for the car or to demand a fee for every new tire purchased for use on GM cars? The obvious answer is that GM has no such rights and that the seller of the iPhone is the same as the seller of the car. The Apple Store uses market power in the phone industry to extract large rents on software. The company should be found in violation of antitrust laws, both under existing prohibitions on tying and bundling, and under a new provision I propose called "abuse of superior bargaining power," detailed in section 9.1.5.

The added charges of the Apple Store are an example of the power of the digital platforms. The problem of powerful platforms that earn excess monopoly profits is more general. It arises in what are known as two-sided markets,[2] such as those for video game consoles, online marketplaces, and credit cards. These markets are typically organized around platforms that allow buyers of services provided on the platform (for example, users of video games or of smartphones) to trade with providers of the services (for example, game and app developers). The theory of two-sided markets calls for equilibria with complex pricing structures that depend upon the externalities involved in the exchange. To

---

[2]See Caillaud and Jullien (2003), Rochet and Tirole (2003), Parker and Van Alstyne (2005), Armstrong (2006), and Jullien and Sand-Zantman (2021) for discussions of the economics of two-sided markets.

understand these, consider a video game. The gaming console provides the hardware platform on which game developers trade with gamers who use the games developed for that console. A developer earns higher profits if more gamers purchase their game, and gamers prefer to own the gaming console for which more games are developed. An optimal strategy for the platform owner may be to pay developers to create games for its platform so that consumers are attracted by a rich ecosystem of games while charging a very high price for the consumers to buy the console. Alternatively, it might be optimal to sell the console to consumers at a very low price and charge high fees to developers. Developers are then attracted by the large number of gamers who use the platform, despite the fees. And that is just the static case. It might be dynamically optimal to subsidize developers who use the platform and consumers who purchase the platform if, once they use it, there are high costs to switching. The equilibrium pricing depends upon these network externalities. In many two-sided markets, such as Google's search platform and Facebook's social network, the advertisers pay everything, and the general public of searchers and communicators pay nothing.

The existence of a two-sided market is not, on its own, of concern to antitrust policy because it does not imply that a platform owner necessarily stifles competition (see Auer and Petit, 2015). But such a firm is in a uniquely powerful position to stifle competition by virtue of owning the platform. Examination of the literature reveals that the commonly made but mistaken assumption is that platform owners are competitive firms. However, the fact is that proprietary technology, network externalities, and increasing returns to scale of platforms enable them to expand their market power. Using such power, owners of platforms routinely extract rents from participants. Therefore, the owners of the platform are targets of the expanded antitrust policy, just like other regular firms with market power. The Apple App Store extracts monopoly profits from developers, and Google and Facebook extract monopoly profits from advertisers.

Just like other firms with market power, platform owners should also be subject to antitrust scrutiny when they refuse to achieve greater compatibility among platforms and often create compulsory linkages to products or services on their other platforms. Platform compatibility is not a new topic. Progressive-era reformers recognized that to promote innovation in the uses of electricity, it was necessary to prevent suppliers of electricity from charging excessive prices, ensure every innovator in electric appliances could access the grid on an equal footing, and standardize the types of electricity supplied (see Wyman, 1904). These reformers created public utility law, which ensured that electricity was accessible. The law did so by regulating prices and standardizing electricity supply. It also prevented electric companies from expanding into adjacent industries where they would have the incentive to give preference to their related products. The most obvious parallel today to the electric utilities is internet service providers. Owners of dominant platforms can and do use their power to restrict access and drive out third-party innovators with monopoly pricing. I thus also propose in section 9.1.5 a new provision of antitrust law, with the title "abuse of superior bargaining position," that would create a cause of action for small firms exploited by large platform owners.

Compatible standards and interoperability can promote competition. As with a uniform system of telephone numbers, the public gains obvious benefits from the technical compatibility of platforms. If standards are compatible across platforms, an application has broader functionality (see, for example, Economides, 1989). For this reason, a policy to enforce greater compatibility is beneficial to users. Unfortunately, the Supreme Court, with its questionable wisdom and proclivity for inventing new economic doctrines, recently dealt a severe blow to attaining compatibility and bolstered the formation and maintenance of market power on digital platforms (see Khan, 2018).

In the case of *Ohio v. American Express Co.* (2018), the Supreme Court made an important decision about two-sided markets. It dealt a blow to regulators who want to enforce the present antitrust regime against owners of two-sided platforms who use anticompetitive practices to differentiate themselves from equivalent competing platforms. The court's decision will serve to bolster their market power unrestrained by antitrust concerns.

The American Express (AmEx) card is a platform that enables merchants and cardholders to trade, but other cards offer the same service. The fees AmEx charges merchants are higher than those of other cards. In its contracts with merchants, AmEx forbids them from so much as mentioning to cardholders that other cards impose lower transaction fees, let alone offering consumers lower prices if they use those other cards. These restrictions on the free flow of information and price competition have allowed AmEx to maintain the higher fees. These higher fees are obviously passed on to all customers, including those using the AmEx card, in the form of higher prices. The anti-steering provisions of the contracts signed by the merchants are clearly monopolistic provisions designed to restrain trade on the platform by preventing competition and compatibility with equivalent platforms.

After a lengthy trial, the District Court of the Eastern District of New York ruled that these anti-steering provisions are illegal. The court correctly found that these are monopolistic provisions that curtail the entry of low-fee competitors whose offers are ineffective because merchants are barred from signaling to customers that the alternatives are cheaper. The absence of price competition lets major credit card networks charge merchants exorbitant transaction fees. These fees, well in excess of the cost of processing the transactions, are estimated at over $80 billion each year—the cost to consumers increases by this amount.

The American Express Company gives AmEx members some rewards in the form of gift cards and lower flight costs, thus sharing with card members the gains from this monopolistic practice. Nevertheless, the district court found these perks only partially offset the higher prices they pay. The remainder of the rents were profits available for the shareholders of American Express Company. Consumers who do not use any credit card end up paying higher prices for the products sold without getting any relief from American Express Company.

The Court of Appeals for the Second Circuit reversed the district court's decision. The reasoning offered by the court reveals its ignorance of elementary economics. The court invented the doctrine that, because American Express serves both merchants and cardholders, to demonstrate a monopolistic behavior, the government must show harm is caused to both sides! It is insufficient to show that the merchants and customers were worse off; it is necessary to show that cardholders are also worse off. The court concluded that because the cardholders receive some perks, the government failed to show that they are ultimately worse off. The court is correct in noting that AmEx cardholders are better off with some perks because they share in the monopoly profits. But the court's idea that an obvious monopolistic practice by a firm must not benefit anyone else to be considered monopolistic has no precedence in law and no logical foundation in economics. It is nothing but total ignorance of elementary economic reasoning.

What about all other consumers who do not use a credit card and end up paying higher prices? To see the more basic point, note that if AmEx cardholders' total financial gains exceed the fees paid to AmEx by merchants, American Express Company will lose money. Clearly, this is not the case because the firm is very profitable. Moreover, the gain or loss of cardholders is irrelevant. In demonstrating the applicability of antitrust laws, it should be entirely sufficient to show that the owner of the platform exercises market power that results in someone gaining monopolistic profits. The allocation of these profits has never been a consideration of antitrust policy. The ruling implies that, in order to demonstrate that the Apple App Store is a monopolistic scheme, it is not sufficient to show that Apple Inc. is using its market power to extract 30 percent of the income of the app developers. The ruling requires the government to show that no one else shares the profits with Apple Inc.

On June 25, 2018, in a 5–4 decision, the Supreme Court affirmed the appeals court's ruling that the steering provisions do not violate antitrust laws. The "wisdom" of this decision applies to virtually any product or service traded online because most such trade takes place in two-sided markets. The decision offers a safe harbor to every monopolistic practice on digital platforms.

9.1.4   Outlaw the Issuance of Multiple Classes of Voting Shares

A large proportion of high-technology firms issue shares with different voting rights, mostly designed to enable the founders to continue to exert control even after other investors own much more common equity than is owned by the founders. For example, Facebook and Alphabet created two classes of shares: regular shares and shares with super voting rights.[3] Shares with super voting rights are typically not traded but are instead closely held by the founders, giving a small number of shareholders effective control of the firm. In any important vote, the number of votes available to the shares with the super voting rights is sufficient to overcome any combination of the regular shares. The majority of Facebook voting shares are controlled by one person, and Alphabet's voting shares are controlled by its two founders.

The voting structure just described arises from a quest for power and reflects an authoritarian managerial style that characterizes some high-tech founders. It leads to arbitrary corporate governance that disregards the impact of the corporation on some stakeholders. It leads managers to divert resources of the corporation to private ends, like increasing their salaries and acquiring firms at inflated prices (see Bebchuk et al. [2000] and Masulis et al. [2009] for theory and empirical evidence, respectively). It also weakens the corporation by depriving it of the benefits of self-examination and the internal balance of power gained from managerial accountability.

9.1.5 Abuse of Superior Bargaining Position

A growing number of firms have devised aggressive business practices that have puzzled regulators. Sometimes, as in the case of predatory pricing by Amazon (see Khan, 2016), these practices are in clear violation of present antitrust laws. But other practices are new and employ the market power of these firms to extract profits by pressuring consumers and suppliers. These constitute abuse of market power. At the same time, following the example of the European Union (EU), legislation has been developed in several countries to address the problem of what is termed "abuse of a dominant market position." This development has been controversial and placed the United States and the EU on a collision course with regard to antitrust policy.

The EU's antitrust policy originates in Article 82 of the European Community Treaty, which establishes the principle that the abuse of a dominant market position is prohibited. This has been interpreted to cover two phenomena, one of which is familiar to a U.S. audience, and a second that is quite alien. First, it is considered abuse of dominance to erect barriers to entry and to free

---

[3] Typically there are tradeable shares that have a single vote and nontraded shares that have multiple votes, with a majority of votes being held by the nontraded shares. There are firms with even more complex structures for voting shares such as Alphabet, which has three; Class C has no voting rights at all.

competition that enable the emergence of firms with a dominant market position. They call this exclusionary abuse. This prohibition is similar to section 2 of the Sherman Antitrust Act, which prohibits monopolization, although it is enforced with more vigor in the EU. Second, the European Court of Justice interpreted the abuse of dominance principle to also prohibit "exploitative abuses." Exploitative conduct includes, among other things, a dominant firm "imposing unfair purchase or selling prices." This has been interpreted to prohibit not only unfairly low predatory prices but also those prices considered unfairly too high. The regulator is then empowered to determine when a market price is unfair. The principle of prohibiting excessively high prices has been recognized as ground for an independent cause of action by the EU, and at the national level by the United Kingdom, Austria, France, Germany, Italy, Japan, Korea, and the Slovak Republic. The overall EU antitrust policy has been controversial, leading to active public discussion.[4]

U.S. opposition to the policy approach of the EU is summarized in three points contained in The OECD Competition Committee (2011): (1) restricted price-setting diminishes incentives to compete and innovate; (2) neither the courts nor antitrust agencies know the correct price; and (3) price setting by government results in inefficient resource allocation, false market signals, and rationing. This was the received wisdom among antitrust enforcers worldwide in the 1980s, when Robert Bork and the Chicago School had a firm grasp on the antitrust discourse.

The European and American regimes take similar, lenient views of barriers to entry erected by technological innovation. But where firms erect barriers to entry via collusion or anticompetitive conduct, these two regimes diverge. The American perspective is that, regardless of the conduct of incumbent firms, potential entrants will typically find a way to enter the market and this, or the threat of entry, will discipline the prices of the incumbent firms. The European approach instead assumes that there is the potential for substantial market power to emerge from barriers to entry created by collusion and anticompetitive behavior. The European remedy, price regulation, originates from a long tradition of questioning the ability of an unregulated market to result in a competitive price and the belief that firms ensconced in a market with high barriers to entry ought to charge a "fair" or "just" price (Gal, 2013). The American perspective is somewhat unrealistic because substantial market power has been maintained because of brand names, reputation, and other permanent advantages that have

---

[4] The OECD Competition Committee (2011) and Lianos and Geradin (2013) offer an overview of the issues, and Gal (2013) provides a comprehensive assessment of the historical and ethical reasons for the EU policy. Katsoulacos and Jenny (2018) present an exposition of the opposition to EU policy and indirectly support for the U.S. policy. Shiraishi (2017) offers a detailed assessment of the Japanese position.

been present throughout the twentieth century in both the United States and Europe. The Europeans want to address these special circumstances with some limit on pricing, while the United States addresses them with regulations and hope that competition will remove them.

The much more significant problem arises with respect to technological market power gained by innovations, which is supported by law in both the United States and Europe. Because of this legal reality, the difference between the European and the American practices is, in fact, minimal: technological market power supported by patent law enables firms to charge excessive prices in both places. Even equipped with the European Court of Justice's interpretation, all the European regulator can do is be slightly more aggressive than U.S. regulators in pursuing what they consider exploitative violations of some high-tech firms. This more aggressive stance can address the more egregious use of market power but does not alter the essential nature of the problem. It all clearly reveals the internal contradiction between patent law and antitrust law, and unless this conflict is resolved, no coherent policy is possible.

The need to eradicate unfair negotiating tactics by those with superior economic power is entirely separate from the question of price regulation, although they are both policy problems that apply to firms with technological market power. The abuse can arise at any firm in a superior bargaining position relative to its customers, suppliers, or other smaller and weaker firms it encounters in the normal course of business. It may be useful to examine what other countries have done to address these issues.

Japan has taken the far-reaching step of introducing an explicit policy to prohibit the "abuse of a superior bargaining position" in the economy. The policy prohibits a variety of actions by large firms with market power in their negotiations with smaller firms (see ICN, 2008, for an international perspective). The Japanese law prohibits the unjust use of a superior bargaining position over a counterparty—a consumer or another smaller firm—during the course of normal business. Acts considered abusive include refusing to receive goods in transactions agreed upon, delaying payment, arbitrarily reducing the amount agreed upon, or otherwise changing trade terms in a manner disadvantageous to the counterparty. A separate but similar subcontract law applies to small and medium-sized firms and to digital platforms that extract superfluous private information from consumers or use that private information in unnecessary or unsafe ways. Accordingly, the law specifies acts by owners of platforms considered unlawful, including (1) acquiring the private information of customers without full disclosure of the reason for seeking it, (2) selling this private information without explicit consent, and (3) acquiring the information without taking precautions for its safe management.

What is unique about Japanese law is that it only requires that firms have superior bargaining power in the particular relationship being examined. This is not the case in European law and is absent from proposals to adopt a similar standard in the United States. In Japan, firms do not have to be dominant in the overall market for the prohibitions to apply. If, for example, a small cell phone carrier were to sell the location data of its users, supported by the fine print of its terms and conditions, that would be abusive practice because the cell phone provider has more bargaining power than its local customers. It does not matter whether the firm is dominant or a small player in the national cell phone market. For this and other reasons, the Japanese law encountered some opposition and has been applied in only a few cases.

I suggest adopting a standard similar to that adopted by Japan but apply it only when the abuse of superior negotiating power is systemic, reflecting a business culture. It should take the form of an additional antitrust-related cause of action available to firms and individuals who encounter instances of such abuse. I give three examples of systemic abuses of bargaining power that should be prohibited by law:

1. *Threats issued by stronger firms.* I have noted the frequent use of threats by larger technology firms against smaller and weaker firms with complementary technology that the larger and stronger firm wanted to acquire. Facebook has been known to adopt a "copy, acquire, and kill" strategy when rivals emerge, and to acquire Instagram, it threatened to develop a competing technology.

2. *Amazon and its suppliers.* Khan (2016) documents Amazon's practices in its manufacturing business. Independent suppliers may come up with a new product that requires market testing and marketing development, which is undertaken by the suppliers. Amazon monitors their sales on its platform, and if the supplier is successful and its sales expand rapidly, Amazon enters the market by manufacturing a copy of the product and pricing it to undercut the original supplier. The law should be specific in protecting the weaker supplier.[5] It should require the stronger party to inform the supplier of its intent to enter the market with its own product and prohibit that stronger party from doing so for three years after giving such notice.

3. *Disadvantageous clauses in the labor contracts of low-wage workers.* In section 9.3.1B, I explain that low-wage workers are forced to sign contracts with clauses that harm their ability to search freely for better jobs and that restrict their access to employment benefits. Such clauses reflect the stronger bargaining position of the employers and this practice should be made illegal.

A general consensus exists among all who study digital markets that the big technology firms use abusive methods that harm consumers, suppliers, and

---

[5] Amazon is facing a new antitrust investigation into its practices on its online marketplace. See   www.businessinsider.com/amazon-antitrust-probe-ftc-new-york-california-online-marketplace-2020-8.

small competitors. Some of these actions may be prohibited by existing antitrust legislation and are being tested in court. Many other abusive methods call for new legislation because they fit the category of exploitative actions not covered by existing legislation.

9.2   Reform Patent Laws

Patent law has many defects, and outright opposition to such law has existed ever since its first enactment[6] and has persisted to the present day. Recently, Boldrin and Levine (2013) made a case for the elimination of patent law, claiming there is no empirical evidence that the law increases innovation and productivity. Moser (2012) studies countries that had patent protection in the nineteenth century and suggests these were no more innovative than those without such laws. Opposition to intellectual property rights legislation also emerged recently in the legal literature, with some proposing to replace it with open science or "intellectual production without intellectual property" (see, for example, Kapczynski, 2016). This proposal is supported by two lines of thought. The first is a commons-based approach that draws on the examples of open-source software and Wikipedia. The approach is based on the belief that the production of information can be motivated by a desire for social improvement and indirect appropriation through cooperation. The second, the norms-based approach, argues that norms can provide an alternative to intellectual property law. Examples given include magicians, stand-up comedians, and French chefs who successfully innovate and rely on informal norms against copying, enforced by sanctions to the reputation of violators. Moser (2013) and other authors, in a growing literature that I review below, argue that patents are used to suppress innovation.

Although the abolition of patent laws would contribute to restraining market power, these laws do serve some very useful purposes. First, patent law compensates innovators and, in this narrow sense, it is accomplishing what it is designed to do. Second, patents disclose publicly all technical information about new products, which makes valuable information available to users and all other innovators. Third, a patent enforces order in the market and reduces uncertainty about final products. Without it, consumers would be confronted by a confusing array of product imitations of varying and unknown quality. Based on these considerations, my approach is that, in the absence of a better alternative to promote innovation, patent law is a compromise that is here to stay; it is better to improve the existing law than abolish it. Here I concentrate only on the specific aspects of patent law that impinge upon the consolidation and growth of technological market power.

---

[6]For a detailed history of the question, see Johns (2009).

TABLE 9.2 **Patents owned by top American corporations in 2019**

Corporation	Active patents owned
IBM Corporation	61,760
Microsoft Corporation	35,813
Intel Corporation	34,259
Google, Inc.	26,472
Qualcomm, Inc.	24,997
General Electric	22,578
Broadcom, Inc	19,688
Apple, Inc	18,617

Source: Market Research IAM.

9.2.1 Patents As Tools to Suppress Innovations

I present in table 9.2 the total number of active U.S. patents owned by a sample of top American corporations in 2019. The firm that owned the most U.S. patents in that year was Samsung Electronics Company, with 87,102. Table 9.2 reports only the American corporations among the top twenty patent owners.

The firms in table 9.2 produce well-known goods and services, and it's easy to imagine that their patents cover components of those products. But thousands of patents are owned by a different kind of firm, one that is not engaged in any productive activity. These patent assertion entities, also known as trolls, acquire patents and then seek to profit from patent litigation. Feldman (2008) shows that 58.7 percent of all patent litigation involves these trolls, whose only business is the ownership of patents. I discuss these trolls further in section 9.2.1B.

The number of patents issued far exceeds the number being actively used. This raises the question of why firms own so many patents. Many unused patents exist to block competitors from entering the market, while others are simply the results of dead-end research. It is the patents with anticompetitive intent that are of concern because they allow corporations to entrench their market power. There is no decisive data source one can employ to understand the motive of firms and answer this question precisely. Most of the inference has to be made from indirect sources or survey studies where inventors are asked about their motivations behind filing for patents.

(A) Blocking with patents, shelving, and killer acquisitions. "Blocking patents" refers to patents taken out not with an intent to use the patented innovation but instead only with the intent to prevent it from being obtained and used by others. For example, in the 1940s, DuPont patented over 200 substitutes for Nylon to protect its core invention, although it did not intend to produce any of them

(see Hounshell et al., 1988). The broad coverage of the DuPont patents was intended only to block their development by other firms. "Shelving a patent" refers to the purchase of a patent from a potential competitor, and then not developing the technology but instead leaving it "on the shelf." "Killer acquisitions" refer to acquisitions of firms or patents with the objective of their suppression. From an economic point of view, all three practices are the same: they are tools in a strategy to suppress innovation by potential competitors.

As noted, most of the available evidence about the intent of firms comes from surveys where they report on the status of their patents and their reasons for taking out or purchasing those patents. Cunningham et al. (2021) are, however, able to determine whether acquired prescription drugs are more or less likely to be developed because the acquired firms hold patents on specific drug molecules that can be tracked. With such knowledge, one can find out if the drugs reach market. The authors show that acquired drugs that overlap with an acquiring firms' existing patented drugs are 23.4 percent less likely to reach market. This implies that firms reduce effort and therefore reduce innovations that are related to the acquired drugs. The authors show that the acquiring firms in the study sought to avoid antitrust scrutiny, suggesting they knew their actions were anticompetitive. However, whatever the reason, the conclusion is that part of the acquired drugs were "killed" by the acquirer. In a similar vein, Haucap and Stiebale (2016) show that pharmaceutical mergers lead to reduced innovation by the merged firms.

I then turn to surveys that study the blocking and shelving patents that remain unused. Giuri et al. (2007) ask firms in a survey: "How important were the following reasons in your decision to patent this innovation: licensing this patent, cross-licensing, and blocking competitors?" They also ask if the patent is used or not used, when the term "not used" means the patent is not used in production, not licensed, and not intended to be licensed. They find that 36.1 percent of all patents are "not used" in this strict sense. Their study also shows that 18.7 percent of all European patents are not used and are patented for blocking reasons. Blocking is more common among large firms and in the chemical and pharmaceutical sectors. The authors find that 11 percent of patents are licensed and that in the case of an additional 7 percent, the firm would be willing to license the patent but has not found a buyer. Motohashi (2008) conducts a similar survey in Japan and finds that 33 percent of patents are for blocking purposes, with another 16 percent going unused for other reasons; this implies that 49 percent of all patents are not used.

Walsh et al. (2016) apply this methodology of surveying patent use to U.S. patents and find that four to seven years after being granted, 45 percent remained unused. The authors posit several possible reasons for patenting and find that 38.4 percent of the unused patents were acquired, among other reasons, to preempt other innovations, or, using their terms, for "blocking other firms" or "preventing inventing-around." This implies that, out of the total outstanding patents, about 17 percent were used for blocking innovations. However, Walsh et al. (2016) also found that only 3 percent of all outstanding patents were patented exclusively for purposes of blocking or preventing inventing-around. The other 14 percent list another motive alongside blocking.

Walsh et al. (2016) also look into the characteristics of blocking patents. They find that the patents that are rated higher on technical significance by their own inventors were more likely to be commercialized and less likely to be blocked. If inventors perceived the existence of more competitors for the technology, or if they perceived that patents were more effective in their industry, then they were more likely to list blocking as a motivation and, more generally, to have unused patents. Larger firms also engaged in more practices of blocking and nonuse.

Torrisi et al. (2016) conduct an analysis in the United States, Europe, and Japan and ask, "How important were the following reasons for patenting this invention at the time when the patent was filed?" One of the reasons given is "blocking patents (prevent others from patenting similar inventions, complements or substitutes)," and they define the reply as "blocking patents" if the response is "somewhat important" or higher on that option. This doesn't mean blocking is the only, or even the primary, motivation. The authors define "use" as the affirmative answer to the questions "Have you used this invention in a product or manufacturing process?" and "Have you licensed or sold this invention?" They then find that 36 percent of U.S. patents, 38 percent of European patents, and 46 percent of patents in Japan are unused. They also find that 24 percent of U.S. patents fall into the category of strategic or blocking patents, as do 24 percent of the patents in Europe and 36 percent of those in Japan. The authors also find that firms with many competitors are more likely to patent for blocking purposes. As was the case in the other surveys mentioned, they find that large firms are about twice as likely as small firms to engage in practices of blocking and nonuse in general.

Torrisi et al. (2016) conclude that "a more stringent inventive-step criterion in patent examination and post-grant reviews would likely increase the quality of patent applications and discourage patent filings that aim mostly at creating strategic defenses and barriers to entry" (1384). They also find that policies of more stringent inventive requirement in patent examination and post-grant reviews lead to more valuable patents. These conclusions are supported by Cornelli and Schankerman (1999) and by De Rassenfosse and Jaffe (2018). Torrisi et al.'s conclusions regarding blocking are also supported by Blind et al. (2009) and by Lemley and Shapiro (2005).

(B) Patent Trolls. I have already noted the emergence, in recent years, of patent trolls. A patent troll relies on many innovators choosing to simply pay off the patent troll to avoid litigation of patent infringement, and see their products reach market. A distinguishing feature of trolls is that, unlike regular entities, they rarely try to reach licensing deals with companies before suing. The

prevalence of patent trolls has declined in recent years, following key Supreme Court decisions that require them to pay legal costs and sue in the state in which the defendant is incorporated (see Shambaugh et al., 2017). Many of the patents these patent trolls own are overly broad; it is rare for them to own a patent that is the basis of an actual existing product. Some of their patents are comical in their breadth, such as patents covering photo contests or audio-based series.[7]

Feng and Jaravel (2020) show that patent trolls buy patents that are vague in their text and that were granted by lenient patent examiners. They explain that patents purchased by trolls are "lacking in technological merit." Frakes and Wasserman (2017) show that a shortfall in funding for the patent office has led to its being more lenient today. There are also anecdotal reports of firms being approached by patent brokers looking to buy not the patents they value but those they consider useless. In 2011, the fifth-largest owner of patents in the United States was a firm named Intellectual Ventures that engages only in patent litigation and licensing.

9.2.2   Four Reforms

A consensus has thus emerged among all who study the problem that the number of patents outstanding is far greater than is socially desirable. The evidence reveals a rising share of unused and uncited patents (see Crystal et al., 2019). Citations are a good proxy measure of the significance of a patent, pointing to the fact that a growing share of patents do not reflect advances in knowledge (see Hall et al., 2005; Posner, 2012). Equally troubling is the fact that patent law is extensively used in strategies to expand and consolidate market power. An active patent left on the shelf and never used is an indirect suppression of a line of research that could have increased productivity. Patents owned by firms that aim to litigate patent infringement against random innovators who come too close to the patent-protected technology serve no social purpose. The aim of policy must first be to promote the use of patents to protect the intellectual property rights of innovators. But the second aim should be to prevent patents from being used in strategies to expand and consolidate market power by suppressing innovation and wasting social resources on litigation. With these aims in mind, I avoid consideration of many reforms that have been proposed regarding specific technical aspects of patent law. Instead, I propose four general reforms supported by economic principles. I have noted earlier some aspects of the proposed change, but now I outline the specifics of these proposals.

---

[7]Personal Audio LLC sued a comedian and threatened smaller podcasters, claiming they had infringed their patent on audio-based series that covered a "system for disseminating media content" in serialized episodes. A countersuit resulted in the invalidation of the patent on the ground that it overlapped with an existing patent by a radio company. For more details, see https://www.eff.org/deeplinks/2018/05/eff-wins-final-victory-over-podcasting-patent.

I propose shifting away from a system in which patent examiners can either grant a patent conferring twenty years of monopoly rights or deny an application. I advocate a two-tiered system in which a patent examiner can deny a patent application or grant one of two kinds of patents: a primary or a secondary patent. I must then first more fully define the concept of a secondary patent. It is simple in the case of drugs (see Abud et al., 2015; Kapczynski et al., 2012). A primary patent covers the chemistry of a drug, while secondary patents specify the manner in which the drug is to be administered. This secondary innovation is not insignificant and can be based on experimental results that may take years to complete after the primary patent is filed. Abud et al. (2015) find, however, that secondary patents are largely manipulated to extend the life of existing patents. Rarely do they encourage innovation that would not have occurred otherwise. Moving beyond the case of prescription drugs, I then offer a more general definition of a secondary patent:

> A patent is a secondary patent if it complements, expands, or amplifies the commercial use of another valid (primary) patent, and its main effect is to extend the applicability and efficacy of the primary patent.

This definition distinguishes between an invention that relies on another patented idea and aims to complement, expand, or amplify its value, and a primary invention that is truly new. The aim of a secondary patent is often to extend the life or value of other patented inventions.[8] Application of such distinction to the use of patents requires judgment but also some technical expertise. It is thus important that the Patent and Trademark Office be provided all technical assistance needed for its expanded task. The shorter duration of secondary patents means that minor modifications would be less effective in extending the duration of expiring patents, a practice that has allowed firms to extend their monopoly power over technology far past the intent of the original patent.

(A) The duration of a secondary patent will be half the life of the primary patent. The first proposed reform is drastic but simple:

> The duration of a secondary patent should be half the duration of the primary patent. If the application for a primary patent is made necessary by a regulatory requirement, the duration of the primary patent should be extended and begin at the date when the regulatory process is completed.

---

[8] All inventions build upon the knowledge learned from other ideas or inventions, and this interdependence is how scientific knowledge grows. The question at hand is whether the new invention builds on an *active* patented invention or on general human knowledge. An application for a patent is considered secondary only if it is an extension, expansion, or wider application of an existing patented invention.

The exception to the simple rule regarding duration is motivated by the case of drugs, where the applicant must disclose to the Food and Drug Administration (FDA) the nature of the process to be used in the clinical stage. This creates a legal delay in the firm's process of bringing the drug to market; part of the reason for a secondary patent is to make up for time lost to the regulatory process. The shorter duration of secondary patents may prevent this time from being fully made up. The exception above allows the firm to seek an extension of its primary patent by having the period of protection run from the date when the regulatory process ends, whether favorably or not.

In most cases, it would be easy to distinguish between the primary and secondary patents. But borderline cases would certainly arise, and the patent office would need a process to judge whether a patent is primary or secondary. This would require a greater degree of technical analysis than in the current accept-or-reject system. The budget of the patent office must be increased sufficiently to finance a significant expansion of the scientific and technical capability of the office. This would more than pay for itself in reduced litigation costs. In addition, the office should be given the budget to form outside technical advisory boards in the different fields. These advisory boards could be called upon periodically to assess complex or borderline applications. An increase in the scientific and technical capability of the patent office would have a secondary aim, which is contained in the second proposed reform.

(B) Increase the degree of nonobviousness required to grant a patent. I have already noted the consensus that too many patents are outstanding. It is also the case that poorly funded divisions of the Patent and Trademark Office are more likely to "over-grant" patents (see Frakes and Wasserman, 2015). Low standards for patents increase litigation rates and burden the legal system with the enforcement of patents that should not have been granted. Jaffe and Lerner (2004) and Feng and Jaravel (2020) provide evidence of this waste. Hunt (2004) and Scotchmer (2004) offer economic criteria for determining optimal conditions for granting a patent application. This leads to a simple proposal:

> Because a major fraction of patents are considered useless or harmful to the innovation process, the policy aim is to improve the nonobviousness of the knowledge covered in approved patents and to reduce the number of outstanding approved patents.

(C) Return purchased and unused patents to their original owners after four years. The problem of patent trolls and their harmful effect would be only partially solved by the first two reforms proposed here. Patent blocking will continue to suppress innovations, even if some blocking patents are now categorized as secondary. I propose a simple solution that begins with the premise that society's interest is for any patented knowledge to be used to produce something

useful or else for the protection of that patent to be canceled. Therefore, the purchaser of a patent should have intent and be ready to use that patent to make a useful contribution to society. They can then purchase a patent, subject to two restrictions:

1. The remaining duration of a purchased patent is cut by half; and
2. The purchaser of a patent has *four years* to use the patent to produce something of value sold through a regular market. If they fail to do so within those years, the patent reverts, at no cost, to the original owner without further changes in the remaining duration. If the original owner no longer exists as a legal entity, the patent expires. Any subsequent sale does not restart the four-year period allowed for development; only one development period is available for all patent buyers, regardless of how many times the patent is sold.

The law should require the contract of sale for every patent sold to contain a clause detailing this legal restriction. In case of violation, the law should award the original owner the right to sue for the costless return of the patent. The courts would need to interpret the question of what constitutes "using the patent in producing something of value sold through regular markets." But the mere requirement of this use will minimize the trading or hoarding of patents for merely strategic reasons. The duration restriction in (1) is a universal restriction, consistent with section 9.1.1, that cuts by half the remaining duration of any acquired patent.

(D) Modification regarding patents gained through merger or acquisition. The acquisition of a patent may occur either through a direct sale or a merger or firm's acquisition. In the latter case, the patent may not have even been the object of the merger. In either case, the universal restriction on the duration of patents applies, but the four-year development provision does not:

> If instead the patent is acquired through a merger or an acquisition of the firm that owns it, the life of the acquired patents will be cut by half (as in section 9.1.1), but there will be no development requirement.

The exemption of mergers and acquisitions from the four-year development requirement relevant to patent sales is based on the premise that the merger or acquisition is not primarily motivated by the patent. To avoid market distortions, the law could stipulate that a transaction is exempt from a four-year development if the parties demonstrate that the merger or acquisition involves other assets and the value of the patent at hand is a small fraction of the transaction's total value.

9.3   Remove Labor Market Distortions and Restore Labor's Vitality

Expansion of the Sherman Antitrust regime, as outlined in section 9.1, can be bolstered by strengthening the bargaining position of capital and labor. But reforms of the labor market require more than just restoring the growth of wages. In the age of technology, low-skilled workers with less than a full college education, which is the state of the majority of workers, are faced with challenges that require important institutional changes. This section will therefore cover the need for reform in three dimensions of the labor market.

9.3.1   Tighten Efforts to Eradicate Monopsony in Labor Markets

In the study of corporate market power in the period 1889–2017 set out in chapter 4, I did not detect a pattern of long-run aggregate level monopsony power in the labor market. However, extensive evidence has surfaced in recent years for growing labor market monopsony power on a firm and individual market levels (see Manning, 2021, for an excellent survey). Monopsony power may have grown because of the decline of unions and the erosion of the minimum wage, which acts as a weapon against monopsony (see section 9.3.2). Modern theory stresses search and matching friction in a labor market as the central cause of monopsony power. Friction arises either as a result of workers' employment preferences or the high cost of search and matching. Consequently, research has focused on the elasticities of quits and hires with respect to wage and to minimum wage policy. These elasticities vary according to many factors, such as location, job type, and industry. The evidence for the presence of monopsony power is substantial and can be illustrated with a few examples. Benmelech et al. (2018) find wages are lower in more heavily concentrated labor markets across geographic locations. Azar et al. (2019) find the employment elasticity of the minimum wage to be more positive in cases of higher labor market concentration when examined over counties, months, and occupations. In less urbanized areas, hospitals are located far apart, and each hospital thus becomes a monopsonist in the local market for nursing labor (see Sullivan, 1989; Staiger et al., 2010; Dube et al., 2020). These studies show monopsony power in the on-demand platforms that operate online, such as Amazon Mechanical Turk (see also Dube et al., 2016), establishing the presence of monopsony power by studying the change in quit rate in response to changes in the minimum wage by some states.

   With monopsony power, a firm can pay workers lower wages than those prevailing in an equivalent competitive market with lower search and match friction. Consequently, the firm earns excess profits. Naidu et al. (2018) argue that existing antitrust laws can be used to combat such monopsony power because many tests for and analyses of labor market concentration are analogous to current antitrust measures in product markets. These measures establish criteria for defining the relevant labor market segment for which monopsony power is evaluated, together with tests for the degree of that power, and available enforcement mechanisms, all of which are analogous to those employed in relation to product markets. This is a sound program but faces difficult problems of implementation. For that purpose, I propose four remedies. The first three are: cracking down on no-poaching agreements, restricting the use of noncompete clauses, and ending the practice of treating employees as contractors. For a further discussion of these and other proposals to combat monopsony power, see Manning (2021), Krueger (2017, 2018), and Krueger and Posner (2018). The fourth remedy is simple: raise the minimum wage to $15, which will solve the monopsony problem altogether. I discuss this issue in section 9.3.2.

(A) Enforce laws to prevent no-poaching practices. Krueger and Ashenfelter (2018) find that many franchise chains prevent a franchisee from hiring workers employed by other franchisees—the no-poaching employment practice. The only reason for the practice is to restrict worker mobility and opportunities, thus suppressing wages. In addition, collusion among big employers in Silicon Valley (see Gibson, 2021) and other tight labor markets has resulted in agreements not to attract employees of other firms with offers of better working conditions (see Krueger, 2017). This latter form of collusion is expressly illegal under current antitrust laws. However, regulators need more resources to combat these practices and should impose harsher penalties on violators. Colluding franchisees and firms like Uber that set prices for independent contractors occupy a legal gray area (see Steinbaum, 2019). Firms are, of course, permitted to set uniform prices charged by their retail outlets. But the law should clarify that when nominally independent contractors or franchisees coordinate prices, it constitutes illegal price fixing (see Paul, 2019). If entities want to set a single wage as opposed to allowing wage competition, they need to organize themselves into a firm and take on all of the associated obligations of doing so.

(B) Tighten requirements of noncompete clauses for low-wage workers. In the age of technology, many firms maintain technological superiority with trade secrets instead of patents, and they share some of those secrets with some of their employees. The use of noncompete clauses in some labor agreements is thus justified for the preservation of the intellectual property rights of the firm. But because firms have the incentive to claim that every worker is privy to trade secrets, it is not clear how to determine when a noncompete employment clause is abusive. It is definitely not plausible that about 30 percent of low-wage workers need to sign noncompete clauses (Colvin and Shierholz, 2019). Such a clause

in the employment contract of a low-wage earner has the effect of reducing the mobility and the bargaining power of that worker (Starr et al., 2020). A simple law should be enacted to ban noncompete clauses in employment agreements of all workers with a low wage. As an approximation, a wage of around $28 an hour (to be reviewed from time to time and adjust for inflation and rising living standards) is a reasonable cut-off point.

(C) Outlaw false long-term contract labor. Contract labor is a status designed for short-term or independent work arrangements. It was designed to allow a bar to hire a musician for a night or a company to hire an architect to design their new headquarters. These short-term, independent employees did not need to be added to the firm's payroll and afforded the protections of traditional workers. In recent years, however, the number of contract workers has grown dramatically. In fact, many of these new contract workers are neither temporary nor independent. Instead, the contract worker status is being used to deny these workers the benefits of traditional employment: learning on the job, healthcare, unemployment insurance, and the right to organize. The magnitude of the rise of contract labor is difficult to measure accurately. Katz and Krueger (2019) study the rise of what they call "alternative work arrangements," defined as temporary help, agency workers, on-call workers, contract workers, and independent contractors or freelancers. They report the percent of U.S. workers in such work arrangements rose from 10.7 percent in 2005 to as high as 15.8 percent in late 2015. Collins et al. (2019), using data from tax records, argue that the Katz and Krueger (2019) conclusions are driven by a growth in secondary jobs that supplement, rather than replace, income from regular employment. This results from economic necessity to supplement the low income from regular employment. Whether or not there has been a large increase in full-time employment in contract jobs, there is clearly a substantial segment of the workforce that relies on contract work as their only source of income (Reich, 2020, shows that the majority of rides on app-based driving services are from full-time drivers). There is some validity to the argument that these gigs are merely voluntary contracts between workers and employers, but it is necessary to explore the limits of this reasoning.

One certainly should not prohibit and reclassify self-employed entrepreneurs who are independent contractors such as architects, photographers, or carpenters. They are paid by the client for the work done but are in control of how to do the work, at what hours, and under what conditions. In contrast, the long-run contract labor of concern to public policy relates to workers who are an integral part of the firm's labor force. They work under conditions specified by the firm and carry out tasks as instructed by their supervisors like all other employees. Katz and Krueger (2019) and Jackson et al. (2017) find that from 2005 to 2015, the rise in labor contracting was higher among low-wage than high-wage workers. They found that independent contracting rose sharply from 2005 to 2015, while entrepreneurial activity remained relatively constant, suggesting that the new independent contractors are not really small firms.

The main reason the rise of contract labor should be of concern to public policy is that it reflects the weakening power of labor. Low-wage workers take these jobs not because they like them but because they have little choice; the supply of full-time, good-quality jobs is not sufficient to meet their demand. Five reasons explain why these jobs are of poorer quality:

1. Contract workers are not protected by standard labor protection laws such as the Fair Labor Standards Act, the Family and Medical Leave Act, and the Employment Non-Discrimination Act. Consequently, their hours of work are not regulated, and their rights to union organization and against discrimination and harassment are unprotected. They are not guaranteed unpaid time off for the birth of a child, nor is their health insurance protected at that time.

2. Contract workers are not entitled to any benefits such as employer-provided health and pension benefits, sick leave, vacation time, maternity leave, or corporate insurance plans. They are not eligible for unemployment benefits and are not protected by minimum wage laws. They must pay both employer and employee payroll taxes and must keep their own accounts for possible audit by the Internal Revenue Service (IRS).

3. Lacking any legal relation with these workers, employers have no incentive to invest in their on-the-job training, and the socially desirable, increased productivity that typically results from such training is foreclosed.

4. Without benefits and training, the effective wage for contract workers remains low. Jackson et al. (2017) find the standard self-employed entrepreneur is doing very well. In the gig economy, however, average annual earnings are only $37,000. Mishel (2018) shows that taxi drivers across the United States earn on average $12.49 per hour. In contrast, an Uber driver earns on average only $10.87 an hour, but with adjustments for the benefits that such a driver must pay by himself, the actual net hourly rate is only $9.21 per hour. Parrott and Reich (2020) show this net rate is $9.73 in Seattle, and Reich (2020) demonstrates a range of $3.97 to $9.22 per hour in the major cities of California. In many states where Uber operates, the rates are below the minimum wage; had their drivers been regular employees in these states, the Uber pay would have been illegal.

5. Contract workers are not independent at all; they are subject to the same firm discipline and restrictions on their free choice as are other firm employees who earn more than they do.

The growth of contracted low-wage, long-term work is then a form of monopsony power that results in lower wages and worse working conditions. To remedy this, I propose that the federal government enact a law like California's Assembly Bill 5, which creates a presumption that a worker is an employee that can be rebutted only if a firm shows that a contractor:

1. Is free from the control and direction of the hiring firm;
2. Performs work that is outside the usual course of the hiring firm's business; and
3. Is customarily engaged in a business that offers the kind of work they are contracted to do, and they are not just engaging in it during their relationship with the hiring firm. This would categorize most low-wage independent contractors as employees and give them access to the benefits associated with that status.

Concurrently, there has been a rise in contract labor that takes the form of true subcontracting. Weil (2014) calls this the "fissured workplace." Unlike independent-contractor arrangements in which workers are not tied to an employer, these workers are supervised by their own employer but have a subcontractor status that is a legal fiction. These formal subcontractor jobs are designed to function outside the traditional employment relationship. For example, instead of hiring maintenance workers, many large firms now contract a maintenance-services firm to supply these workers. The crucial point is that the workers are now supervised by the contracted firm, not the employer. These workers are real contractors who are supervised by an external firm. But these workers are placed at a substantial disadvantage relative to other workers; they lose the benefits of attachment to firms such as rent sharing, on-the-job training, and access to internal career possibilities. Dube and Kaplan (2010) and Goldschmidt and Schmieder (2017) show that before a firm contracts out certain low-wage occupations, workers in those occupations share in the rents of firms. After subcontracting, those low-wage workers no longer receive any portion of firms' rents. Abowd et al. (2018) and Gregory (2020) show that working at a higher-wage firm leads workers to develop more skills and earn more over their lifetimes.

In many cases, labor subcontracting helps firms avoid labor regulation. For instance, a firm with over fifty employees has to provide a healthcare insurance plan to its workers. But if it can contract out some of those jobs to firms with fewer than fifty employees, it can avoid that requirement. Sometimes those subcontracting firms add an additional layer of contracting. For instance, many janitorial subcontracting companies actually operate as a network of individual janitors who are "franchises" of the larger subcontracting company, employees in all but name. This subcontracting dynamic is difficult to reverse. Song et al. (2019) offer compelling empirical evidence that successful firms desire to share rents with a narrow, core group of workers, but exclude low-wage workers. One place to start in remedying this is to ensure that every firm pays a minimum amount per labor-hour employed in unemployment insurance, health benefits, and Medicare and Social Security taxes. Economic theory might suggest that such an increase in labor cost would reduce wages one-for-one, but such theoretical predictions have not been borne out in practice (see, for example, Kopczuk et al., 2013).

The growth of contracted low-wage, long-term work is then a complex hidden form of monopsony power that results in effectively lower wages and worse working conditions. The outlawing of these labor contracts is also part of my proposal in section 9.3.3 to revitalize the labor market. This can be done by creating more high-quality jobs in a more cooperative labor market with more resources available for improved education, technical retraining, and on-the-job training. As to the conditions of other workers in the gig economy who are regularly employed but without the legal status of regular employees, one way their conditions could improve is through unionization. For example, organized Uber workers could resolve all open problems that remain unresolved following the public's affirmation of the 2020 proposition excluding Uber and Lyft drivers from the application of the California law requiring they be declared regular employees.

9.3.2   Raise the Minimum Wage to $15 and Index It to the Cost of Living

There is a broad consensus among scholars who study the labor market that raising the minimum wage is a simple policy change with large benefits to low-skilled workers. The federal minimum wage was last raised in July 2009, when it was set at $7.25 per hour. Just to keep pace with inflation, it should have reached $12 per hour in 2022. If we start in 1968 and index the minimum wage to inflation and growth in labor productivity, it should have been set at $18.67 in 2020. I join those who propose raising the federal minimum wage to $15 per hour, which would boost the income of 42.4 percent of American workers who make less than $15 per hour. It would likely also raise the incomes of 10 million more workers who make slightly more than $15 per hour (CBO, 2019). It would also help close gender and racial gaps in income; minimum wage workers are disproportionately black and female (Derenoncourt and Montialoux, 2021; Reich, 2019). The rise in the quality of life of these Americans will contribute to restoring a measure of equity to the distribution of income in the United States. Increasing the minimum wage is also very popular and will have a political impact, providing a positive signal to a large number of angry Americans who have lost faith in the ability of democratic institutions to respond to their needs.

As to the economic effects of raising the minimum wage, the literature exploring this question is large and does not need to be reviewed in detail. There is a clear consensus among researchers that, notwithstanding the political opposition and business warnings of lost jobs, there is no evidence that an increase in the minimum wage would lead to loss of jobs (for a sample of recent studies see Allegretto and Reich, 2018; Godøy and Reich, 2021; Reich, 2019; Azar et al., 2019; Berger et al., 2019; Cengiz et al., 2019; Derenoncourt and Montialoux, 2021; and Cooper et al., 2020). There is mild disagreement on how to explain why a rise in the minimum wage to $15 should not be expected to reduce job availability. The reason I find compelling proposes that raising the minimum wage alters monopsony power at low wages.

I have already noted the evidence for the presence of monopsony power in many labor markets. In such markets, each firm faces an upward-sloping labor supply curve rather than a constant exogenous wage, which leads firms to choose labor employment by selecting an optimal wage they would pay. The wage set by each firm is then lower relative to the wage that would prevail if the market had been more competitive.

A minimum wage prevents a firm with monopsony power from fully exercising it. Without a minimum wage, firms might find it optimal to hire few workers at very low wages. So while the minimum wage could cause some firms to exit or engage in automation, thus eliminating some low-skilled jobs, for many low-skilled jobs, firms' optimal response to a higher minimum wage is to increase employment. The minimum wage then has the consequence of destroying monopsonies in low-skilled labor markets! But these changes occur only if the minimum wage binds. If the real minimum wage declines, as it has since 2009, then it binds for fewer and fewer firms, and more firms will reduce employment and pay the lower monopsony wage. Raising the minimum wage to $15 per hour and indexing it to future inflation will curtail monopsony power over low-skilled workers, leading employment in those markets to rise.

Raising the minimum wage has then two opposite effects. When employers have monopsony power, there would be an increase in employment resulting from the change in firm optimization. However, some very low skilled jobs will be eliminated, and in some competitive market segments, the rise in the minimum wage would also lower employment. The fact that estimates of the employment effects of raising the minimum wage cluster around zero suggest that these two effects cancel each other.

9.3.3   Improve Labor Market Cooperation and Mobilize Unions to Solve Labor's Problems

The deterioration in the labor market is a complex problem whose solution has many dimensions that include altering the balance of power in the labor market and making further improvements in education and retraining. Here I address the balance of power in the labor market. Before proceeding, I make a short comment on the European experience in tackling similar problems.

In Northern Europe, strong unions retrain workers and assist in relocating unemployed workers. Together with the practice of national-level collective bargaining that sets industry-wide minimum wages, these practices have contributed substantially to social cohesion, high cooperation in the labor market, and low unemployment rates. Moene and Wallerstein (1995) report that these features of the policy were essential to the stability and economic prosperity of the countries that were then members of the European Free Trade Association (Austria, Finland, Norway, Sweden, and Switzerland), which, from 1978 to 1992, had an average unemployment rate of 2.95 percent. More generally, in several countries (for example, Germany and Denmark), strong unions have played a constructive role in fostering cooperation in the labor market. Some unions are engaged in training workers, helping match them with jobs, and providing social services to members. Some unions encourage job sharing to reduce unemployment and, in some cases, accepted lower wages to enhance export competitiveness.

This comment does not intend to suggest that the European model is suitable for the United States. Rather, it is to acknowledge that the United States faces difficult labor market problems that require innovative thinking about a broad set of problems. As discussed repeatedly in this book, a majority of U.S. workers hold unskilled jobs and are particularly vulnerable to the impact of changing technology and market power. Since the 1970s, the existing institutions of the labor market have failed to solve the problems of this majority of workers, and their conditions have only deteriorated (see Case and Deaton, 2020; Krueger, 2017; and Pfeffer, 2018). The problems are far more than slow growth of wages and extend to an urgent need for drastic improvements in workers' health, morale, family stability, drug addiction, and job training. The no-compensation policy has left these workers alienated from the institutions of democracy, and their anger and frustration have played a major part in the rise of antidemocratic populism. Many proposals have been advanced to address the problem (see Block and Sachs (2020) for more detailed ideas to improve labor power). My proposal, which aims to increase union membership and broaden the scope of union activities, is motivated more by the need to develop new cooperative institutions for addressing the social problems of workers than by the search for a better mechanism for wage setting. As explained in chapter 1, I doubt the ability of unions to improve labor share.

(A) Abolish right-to-work laws and facilitate unionization. Right-to-work laws allow workers to reap the benefits of collective bargaining at their establishment without paying the cost of union membership. Supporters of right-to-work laws argue that they preserve individual freedom of choice, but this is just a case of the free-rider problem. Paying the fair share of any public good is a standard problem in public finance, and principles of free choice can legitimately be invoked

at the stage when a union is formed. Once formed, it becomes a collective good, and, as is the case with any public good, free choice has to be curtailed to prevent free riding. As long as collective bargaining is permitted by law and the union is lawfully and democratically formed, the right-to-work laws only degrade the ability of the union to function properly.

The right-to-work laws were enacted under the 1947 Taft-Hartley Act, as part of legislation that repealed the closed-shop provisions of the Wagner Act of 1935. Supporters of right-to-work laws argue they are needed as a weapon against corrupt union leaders who used union funds for private ends. It is thus legitimate to require that facilitation of unionization be accompanied by strict legal control over the financial decisions of unions. Union finances should be regularly audited to ensure all funds are properly used for the specified needs of workers. This is particularly important because I propose that the revitalized unions play a more active role in addressing the needs of workers. Half a century of efforts to weaken unions in the United States resulted in the decline of union membership from 33.2 percent of the labor force in 1956 to only 10.5 percent in 2018. To reverse this trend and allow unions to play a more significant role in solving labor problems, it is necessary that laws be enacted to make forming unions easier. Congress can do this by expanding unionization rights to agricultural, personal service, and public sector workers, as well as to those incorrectly classified as independent contractors. It can also streamline the union election process, remove Taft-Hartley limits on worker strikes, and increase penalties on businesses for labor rights violations. Union bargaining offers one more solution to the difficult problem of monopsony wage setting and could also contribute to improving worker morale.

(B) Enable more risk sharing and have unions shoulder a share of the effort. Unions want to negotiate wage agreements, and the European experience suggests that such negotiations should take place at the broadest possible national level to be an effective tool of wage equity. Dube (2019) shows that in many European countries, union membership is low. However, most workers are covered by collective bargaining agreements at the sectoral level. France is the extreme case, where 8 percent of workers are union members, but those unions set the terms of employment for 95 percent of workers.

In the age of technology, with job losses and stagnant wages of low-skilled workers, revitalized unions could play an important role by working with management and government to solve problems faced by workers. The following objectives are shared by both workers and employers because meeting them would benefit workers and increase labor productivity:

- Retrain workers so that they acquire in-demand skills;
- Enable higher labor mobility to take good-quality jobs elsewhere in the United States;

- Provide counseling to workers' families who are in distress;
- Ensure the availability of health insurance;
- Promote risk-sharing arrangements to insure retirement savings and pension plans;
- Fight drug addiction;
- Encourage the development of apprenticeships and on-the-job training of young workers; and
- Work with government and employers to provide unemployment insurance, including job sharing and change of working hours instead of unemployment. Rothstein (1992) shows that in countries where unions provide unemployment insurance, there are much higher rates of unionization.

Employers, unions, and governments need to work together to establish cooperative arrangements for the creation of good-quality jobs and thus a healthier and more productive labor force. Using the terminology of Case and Deaton (2020), such new institutions should end the despair in the labor market.

9.4   The Years 1901 and 2021: Has a New Era of Reform Begun?

Demands for reform in the United States intensified in the years leading up to the 2020 election, and the resurgence of progressive forces in the United States has signaled, for some time, that the resistance to the forty years of laissez-faire policy has increased in intensity. Opposition to reform on the right has intensified as well, but such opposition has deteriorated in quality. It lost its fundamental support for free markets and opposition to government redistribution legislation, and has taken the form of an aggressive, authoritarian populist movement. As a result, Joe Biden's ascension to the presidency in 2021 may have led to a major change in public policy. It has also been associated with the introduction in Congress of a large number of bills for antitrust reform, changes in labor markets, and increased regulations of high-technology firms. This flow of proposed legislation is similar to the large number of bills proposed to Congress in the years leading to 1901, which went nowhere until Theodore Roosevelt became president. Like 1901, Joe Biden's presidency may alter the political landscape by introducing three drastic changes in the direction of economic policy. The first is a significant act of redistribution. The American Rescue Plan Act of 2021 offered cash transfers for recovery from the COVID-19 epidemic. The second consists of the massive investment in physical infrastructure in the bipartisan infrastructure bill, as well as proposals to spend trillions more on green technology, families, and care. These bills, if enacted, will upgrade American infrastructure and the social safety net on a scale not seen since the Great Depression.

The third change, perhaps more symbolic than practical, is the July 9, 2021, Executive Order on Promoting Competition in the American Economy. It is a massive order consisting of seventy-two separate actions that cover diverse issues aiming to promote competition. These include active antitrust measures, reform of the labor market, public actions to create good-quality jobs, and raising wages. Being an executive order, it relies on existing laws and existing tax rates. After the president signed the order, the White House explained it by saying that "today President Biden is taking decisive action to reduce the trend of corporate consolidation, increase competition, and deliver concrete benefits to America's consumers, workers, farmers, and small businesses" (White House, 2021). In addition, the White House made a special effort to place the action in its historical context by saying:

> When past presidents faced similar threats from growing corporate power, they took bold action. In the early 1900s, Teddy Roosevelt's Administration broke up the trusts controlling the economy—Standard Oil, J.P. Morgan's railroads, and others—giving the little guy a fighting chance. In the late 1930s, FDR's administration supercharged antitrust enforcement, increasing more than eightfold the number of cases brought in just two years—enforcement actions that saved consumers billions in today's dollars and helped unleash decades of sustained, inclusive economic growth.

President Biden clearly sees the actions he has been taking as a sharp turn in public policy. However, as explained in this chapter, and as will be further explained in chapter 10, a real change in policy requires a drastic change in laws that govern the regulation of corporate market power and necessitates raising taxes on individuals and corporations substantially higher than they are today. Significant parts of such legal action will encounter resistance of the Supreme Court in the same way the Court resisted reforms after 1901, leading to a legal battle that lasted until 1937. In addition, the initial attempt at reform may fail, leading to higher inequality and deeper social division.

If the Biden presidency has indeed ushered in the beginning of a new era with stronger antitrust activity, increased regulation of business, higher wages, and a more egalitarian American society, what important economic trends will accompany the changes as the level of market power declines? It is important to keep in mind the changes we can expect because such understanding can serve as a useful guide for policymakers. The list of changes can be deduced from the conclusions of chapter 2 about the effects of a drastic and unexpected change in policy regime:

- A higher rate of capital investment that will result in a long-term rise of the capital/output ratio;

- The rapid rise of asset prices since the 1980s will come to an end;
- A lower rate of rising asset prices will result in a long-term decline of the wealth/output ratio (I have stressed at several points in this book the fact that, in response to changes in market power, the capital/output and wealth/output ratios change in opposite directions);
- Higher short- and long-term interest rates than in 2021;
- Decreased share of profits in corporate income;
- Higher wages, higher labor share, and higher share of capital income;
- Permanently higher levels of output, consumption, and investment; and
- A long, transitory phase of about twenty to thirty years that results from the abrupt change in policy, during which the economy will experience higher than normal growth rates of gross national product (GNP), consumption, and investment.

CHAPTER 10

TAXATION, PUBLIC INVESTMENTS, AND REDISTRIBUTION

In chapter 9, I outlined proposed reforms that would, in the long run, lower the duration of monopoly power gained from innovations while maintaining the incentives to innovate. Some of those reforms would take many years to make meaningful reductions in the level of market power in the economy. On the other hand, taxation, public investments, and redistribution policies are important for having an impact on the economy immediately. Consequently, the explicit aim of these policies is to restrain market power expeditiously and attain a more equitable distribution of income and wealth. But one must keep in mind that the tax and investment policies used to transition to a more equitable distribution may not be the policies needed to maintain it. It is then important to distinguish between permanent and transitory components of the policy.

Even if the degree of market power is reduced to a more sustainable level, inheritances, dispersion in skills, variations of labor productivity, and random business fluctuations will ensure that inequality of pretax income and wealth will persist. Progressive income taxation is therefore required to maintain an acceptable level of inequality (see Atkinson et al., 2011; Piketty, 2014). Progressive income taxes are also an essential source of revenue to finance the extensive public investment needed to maintain that modest degree of inequality. But because the question of personal income taxation has been extensively studied by economists, my discussion of this topic is limited to a few comments. The questions of corporate income taxation, public investments, and redistribution require far more careful examination.

10.1   Personal Income Tax

Some early work in optimal tax theory argued for tax schedules that should be, at least in part, regressive. Mirrlees (1971) decomposed income into two parts: ability or productivity, which is inelastically supplied, and hours worked or effort, which is elastically supplied. While the government would like to tax only the returns to ability, it cannot distinguish between the two. Furthermore, taxes on high earners disproportionately discourage the efforts of the most able taxpayers. But this conclusion depends upon an assumed but unknown distribution of ability, particularly at the very top. Some studies following Mirrlees (1971), such as Tuomala (1990), assume log-normal distributions of ability. This implies that declining marginal tax rates at the top of the income distribution are optimal. This conclusion, that regressive taxation is optimal, conflicts with the common desire for progressivity in the tax code.

Diamond (1998), Saez (2001), and Diamond and Saez (2011) empirically study progressive taxation and find strong support for it. Their approach bypasses the formal Mirrlees (1971) model and directly utilizes the elasticities of effort and income with respect to the tax. This approach relies on the observed distribution of income, which is well approximated by the Pareto distribution, particularly at the very top. This method permits a compelling demonstration that the top marginal rates (for incomes above $400,000 per year) should be higher than 50 percent and most likely around 70 percent. The current effective top marginal rate, including the Medicare, sales, and state income tax, varies across states, but is on average around 46 percent. Increasing this rate to 70 percent would raise federal revenue by the significant amount of about 1.5 percent of gross domestic product (GDP).

10.2   Corporate Income Tax and the Incentive to Innovate

10.2.1   Should the Corporate Tax Rate Be Equal to Zero?

The corporate income tax has traditionally been viewed as a tax on savings. This led many economists, concerned with the effects of reduced savings on long-run growth, to argue that the corporate income tax rate should be zero (Judd, 1985; Chamley, 1986). Opposing views are based on two considerations. One view (e.g., see, Saez and Zucman, 2019b) follows from a desire for progressivity of personal income taxation. It is based on the fact that many wealthy individuals pay little income tax but have vast holdings of corporate common stock that pay small or no dividends. The increase in their wealth is driven by the unrealized capital gains created by the rising values of their corporate holdings. Consequently, a corporate income tax is, in fact, a tax on the undistributed income of the very wealthy and thus an indirect method of restoring progressivity to the tax code. A second view, offered by Diamond and Banks (2010), Saez (2013), and Straub and Werning (2020), questions the assumptions underlying the zero corporate tax theorem. These assumptions include a perfectly competitive capital market, correct forecasting of future incomes, infinitely lived agents, a requirement that tax schedules be linear, and an implausibly low elasticity of intertemporal substitution. Extensive recent research casts some doubt on the accuracy of these assumptions. And, if these do not hold, their zero-taxation implication may be questioned. This question is not central to the problems addressed in this book; therefore, it is best to leave its resolution for future research.

All sides of the debates over capital taxation have failed to consider the fact that, in an economy with market power, the rate of return on capital is suppressed by corporate monopoly power. Under monopoly, the return to capital is too low, capital is underutilized, and a policy to restore efficiency would call for the *subsidization* of capital rather than its taxation. This fact is a pivotal component of my argument about the appropriate taxation of corporate income.

My analysis of the corporate income tax is based on the important distinction between capital income and monopoly profits. Reported corporate income is a mixture of the return on the component of the firm's capital stock that it owns (as opposed to the capital it rents) and monopoly profits. I showed in chapter 6 that most capital employed by the U.S. corporate sector today is financed by debt. It thus follows from standard corporate financial analysis that most capital can be treated as owned by the debt holders and rented to the firm. Consequently, most of U.S. corporate profits today are the result of market power, which originates from corporations' ownership of proprietary technology and innovations. My proposal applies only to monopoly profits.

The implication of this distinction is that reported corporate profits should be divided into these two components, and my proposal is to apply a different tax rate to each component. Taxes on these components can be assessed separately without much difficulty. Profits tax will fall on revenue minus costs of materials, labor, and capital. Capital costs equal depreciation plus interest on debt plus imputed interest on capital owned by the firm. The tax on capital income falls on imputed income of the portion of capital owned by the firm.

In the case of a zero tax on capital income, the tax authorities can simplify the procedure of computing taxable profits by allowing the firms to write off all capital purchases. This creates a more complex problem, namely, how to transition, during a period when past investments have not been written off, to a fully written-off capital stock. The following procedure deals with that problem of transition. First, assignment is made of the ratio of total value of capital not written off and debt used to finance capital; call this ratio $\aleph$. This proportion will decline to 0 as capital is written off. Then, in the initial phase the tax will fall on revenue minus costs of material, labor, depreciation, $\aleph \times$ (debt service), and total value of investment. When all capital is written off, taxable profits are computed using standard accounting methods, including the deduction of the cost of investment, but not deducting any cost of debt service. Some debt may remain on the books after all capital is written off. I do not propose that its cost be deduced from profits.

The tax rate on the income of capital owned by the firm should be set based upon consideration of trading off the cost of reduced capital accumulation with the benefits of reduced inequality. The tax rate on monopoly profits resulting from market power needs to be examined further. It depends upon the incentive to innovate, not on the incentive to save or work, and this opens up a new and little-studied question.

10.2.2   Tax on Innovations: Two Alternative Approaches

Innovation is very risky but is also the source of the greatest wealth. Because so much of corporate profits derive from innovations and proprietary technology, one would expect that taxing profits would have a negative incentive effect on innovations. Yet there are factors that mitigate this disincentive effect. I focus here on two major mitigating factors. The first is related to the great variations in the financial outcome of innovations and suggests that a marginal tax will have no effect if an innovator cannot imagine the financial outcome of their discovery. The second mitigating factor arises from the fact that innovation has several other effects: personal satisfaction, social recognition, and a sense of accomplishment. These factors mean that innovations respond to taxation less than a formal analysis would suggest.

For a tax to have an incentive effect on innovation, the innovator must consider expected profits when making their innovation decision. That is, for a marginal tax rate on income or wealth above some threshold level to have a negative impact on the effort of an innovator, it must be that, at the time of making that effort, they place a positive probability on the realization of income or wealth exceeding that threshold. No reliable data exists on the expectations of innovators, but there is anecdotal evidence regarding the great innovators of our time. The innovative journeys of individuals like Bill Gates, Steve Jobs, Larry Page, Sergey Brin, Mark Zuckerberg, Jeff Bezos, and many others started from modest beginnings. The wealth they actually created is far beyond anything they could have imagined. But then, a tax on income that is not expected has little effect on one's decision. To state this conclusion more concretely, suppose that at the time of their decisions, a progressive income tax had been imposed on annual income that exceeds, say, $100 million; it would have had little effect on their initial decisions to innovate. The same is true for a tax on corporate profits: none of these individuals initially saw themselves as being in the process of founding massive corporations. However, given their actual success and their accumulated wealth, the imposition of such a tax could have an impact on the subsequent innovations created by their firms. But then, there are two factors to consider in assessing this effect.

In chapters 1 and 7, I trace the evolution of market power. I explain that following a major primary innovation, subsequent related innovations are motivated not only by a desire to increase profits but also by a strategy to consolidate and defend market position. A firm in this position is compelled to innovate because of technological competition and the potential loss if it does not.[1] Therefore, the imposition of a modest tax is not likely to reduce the innovator's effort lower than it would have been in the absence of both the tax and the desire to defend existing market power. That is, the tax's negative effect on the incentive to innovate is partly neutralized by the positive efficiency effect, creating an incentive to innovate in order to defend an existing market position. The final effect depends, of course, upon the specifics of the tax and its effect on potential rivals, on how successful the firm is, and on what value the firm stands to lose if it does not defend its position. There can be marginal firms with a low level of productivity that the tax may force into default and in this case the tax will have a negative effect on innovation. However, the big successful technology firms stand to lose a great deal if they fail to innovate or acquire new innovations, and therefore a modest corporate tax is not likely to have a major negative effect on innovations because of their need to protect their market power. This effect is even stronger if the innovator's personal wealth is heavily concentrated in the firm whose market power is derived from the innovator's technology.

This discussion shows that a tax will have a negative incentive to innovate on two categories of innovators. First, beginning individual innovators and newly formed firms are likely to reduce their innovative efforts if faced with a higher corporate tax rate. The second category comprises individuals or firms who innovate in diverse areas and do not have major ownership stakes in prior innovations that need to be defended in technological races.

I turn now to a second factor mitigating the negative effect of an income or wealth tax on the incentives to innovate: the nonpecuniary benefits of innovation. This factor affects my choice of method for determining the desired corporate tax rate. During most of the twentieth century, innovators faced very high personal and corporate income tax rates. Despite this, the rate of innovations during the golden age of 1945–1973 remained very high. Why was this rate so high when marginal tax rates were also high? Although one might expect taxation to have significant effects on innovations, there are forces that subdue this negative incentive effect. The first is the emotional aspect that leads well-focused

---

[1] This is known as the efficiency effect of the strategy of an incumbent monopolist (see Tirole, 1988, chapter 8).

individuals to be attracted to activities that give them the highest satisfaction. Creative people are attracted to the process of innovation because this is what they like to do! The second subduing factor follows from the fact that innovative people are also highly competitive in the search for excellence. As Frank (2008) shows, people who care about having the highest salary do not mind paying taxes as long as their competitors pay the same rates. Innovators also get satisfaction from being recognized for their achievements in venues outside the market. Financial reward may be only one among many factors having an impact on their incentives, alongside accepted views of what is "fair" compensation for their work and social norms that determine societal status and recognition for one's achievements.

These two factors lead to different approaches of taxing corporate profits. To study the question further and to derive exact magnitudes for the corporate tax rates, I then employ two approaches. The first is based on the negotiation theory of Aumann and Kurz (1977). The second follows the approach of the optimal taxation literature and is based on the formulation by Diamond (1998), Saez (2001), and Diamond and Saez (2011).

In Aumann and Kurz (1977), the focus is not on the optimal tax that maximizes the social welfare function of an abstract planner. Instead, we study the tax rate that emerges from the negotiations and competition of diverse individuals and interest groups (coalitions) in a majority-vote democracy. This begins with a set of rules for a political process in which coalitions compete. When a coalition achieves a majority, it gets the power to set economic policy and tax rates that could be as high as the majority wishes. Many potential coalitions may constitute a majority, and each recognizes the danger of taking too extreme actions. Such actions would prompt an alternative majority to form and overturn the current majority coalition, forcing many members of the coalition in power to become part of the minority.

The outcome of such a game depends upon two things: a constitution and the rules for selecting outcomes. A constitution specifies what private property is, what the rights are of each individual, and what strategies coalitions are allowed to employ. The rules to select an outcome specify how that choice is made. These also reflect an underlying value system accepted by all, which includes a view of fairness that requires equality of outcomes for individuals who have the same characteristics (i.e., symmetry). The final allocation each individual receives is then an income compensation for their two contributions: the resources they privately own and their vote. Although political power may be the driving force in the game, the outcome also reflects basic principles of fairness embodied in the rules. In considering any policy proposed by a coalition, the agents certainly take into account individual incentives in response to a policy or a tax. But they also take into account the limited power of each group as deduced from their collective voting and property rights. A majority cannot impose taxation that is too high because it must consider the marginal contribution of each minority coalition and the ability of its members to oppose an unfair and oppressive majority by withholding their contribution to society, which the majority needs. That is, apart from displacing the majority by using their votes, the powerless minority has the ultimate power to prevent the majority from confiscating the possessions of the minority by destroying them and by refusing to contribute their work by striking against the majority.

In the case of innovators, they do not function in a vacuum and have to fear that other groups will act against them if they come to power. Innovators rely for success on both public goods and other actors: skilled workers trained by using public funds, universities, clusters of high-tech firms, the physical and financial infrastructure of the economy, and the legal protection of intellectual property rights. The Aumann-Kurz theory gives a simple answer to the tax question: in the case of corporate risk neutrality the universal marginal tax rate should be 50 percent, but a higher tax by those who are risk averse. Since risk aversion is not observable, the practical prediction of the theory is of a 50 percemt marginal rate.

The alternative procedure is to focus on the response elasticities of innovations to income tax rates in the manner of the optimal taxation literature. Following that literature, it is important to incorporate a synthetic parameter Λ that measures society's valuation of income in the hands of innovators compared with income in the hands of the government. If $\Lambda = 0$, the policy places no value on income being in the hands of innovators and sets the tax rate to maximize government revenue, taking into account only its incentive effect on innovators. If the valuation is $\Lambda = 1$, then the policy is designed on the basis that income of innovators is equally important as income in the hands of the public. Because innovators are substantially richer than the rest of society and therefore get less utility from a dollar than most people, plausible values of Λ are close to 0. A similar argument is often made when studying income taxes on the wealthy.

The crucial elasticity needed for this analysis is the elasticity of innovation income with respect to the tax rate, particularly of innovators who work at a corporation or plan to form one to market their innovations. Although the data on this subject are not well developed, the excellent studies of Akcigit et al. (2018) and Akcigit and Stantcheva (2020) offer the best available estimates. To compute the optimal tax, I use the Saez (2001) and Diamond and Saez (2011) formulation, and for that, I introduce the following notation:

y—income from innovations;

τ—tax rate, therefore $(1 - \tau)$ is the net-of-tax rate;

ξ—the average uncompensated elasticity of y with respect to $(1 - \tau)$;

η—the income effect;

Λ—the planner's average rate of substitution between innovators' income and public income; and

a—the power parameter of the Pareto distribution.

TABLE 10.1 **Optimal corporate tax rate**

	$\xi = 0.7\ a = 1.5\ \Lambda = 0$	$\xi = 0.8\ a = 1.5\ \Lambda = 0$
$-\eta = 0.00$	48.8 percent	45.5 percent
$-\eta = 0.50$	43.5 percent	40.8 percent

Under the assumption that innovation income is Pareto distributed, Saez (2001) shows that the optimal tax rate is:

$$\tau = \frac{1 - \Lambda}{(1 - \Lambda) + \xi a - \eta(a - 1)}.$$

The Pareto parameter is estimated by Diamond and Saez (2011) to be around 1.5. That value is estimated from labor income inequality. Although it is likely that innovation income is more unequally distributed, there is no data on the distribution of innovation income. Akcigit and Stantcheva (2020) report that the elasticity of patenting with respect to income taxation is 0.6–0.7, while for patent citations, it is 0.8–0.9. This means that a 10 percent increase in income taxes would reduce patenting by 6% to 7%. I will use those impacts as a proxy for innovation income and examine the tax rate for the middle values of 0.7–0.8. The income effect of leisure is questionable. For general effort, estimates range from 0 to 1, but Saez (2001) takes it to be close to 0.25. This may not be a reasonable view of innovators who, like other creative people, may not value leisure as much, making the income effect negligible. I thus consider values of $(-\eta)$ in the range of 0 to 0.50 but regard the zero effect as the more likely. As to the innovator-government substitution parameter Λ, Saez (2001) sets it between 0 and 0.25, while Diamond and Saez (2011) assume the government maximizes revenue from top income earners and set this parameter equal to zero. That is the approach I take to the issue, which is consistent with the Aumann and Kurz (1977) theory. Table 10.1 presents the implied range of optimal tax rates on corporate monopoly profits.

Note that for $\eta = 0$, the two theories I used to estimate the corporate tax lead to similar results.

10.2.3 Implementation: Should We Tax Profits and Subsidize Capital and Labor?

The corporate tax in section 10.2.2 is imposed on monopoly profits, not on corporate profits as defined in standard accounting. This fact leads then to the question of how the government should use the tax revenue? One policy could place the revenue in general funds to finance public investments or other public needs. An alternative is to pay labor and capital a time-varying-per-unit subsidy, aiming to remove the distortions in the allocation of capital and labor resulting from the monopoly power of firms. Suppose that, to remove the distortion, the government decides to set $\Lambda = 0$ and extract the maximal revenue from the tax. By how much can such a policy reverse the monopoly factor price distortion? Is such a policy desirable?

In the appendix to this chapter, I show that if the profit tax rate is v_t, the subsidy rate (per dollar spent on labor and capital) required to remedy the entire distortion is $s_t = (1 - v_t)/\theta_t$, where θ_t is the price elasticity of demand, reflecting the degree of competition in the economy. Suppose then that we use the tax to cover the entire subsidy, and therefore the distortion is removed. With a 50 percent tax and a pretax profit share of 25 percent (meaning the markup is 1.33 and $\theta_t = 4$), the subsidy rate required to fully remove the distortion would be 12.5 percent. This would be 12.5 percent of the sum of labor and capital incomes, which would then be equal to GDP. This is a very expensive proposition. If such a subsidy program were implemented, revenues from the corporate profit tax would fall to 0 because corporations would increase output to maximize their subsidy instead of suppressing their output. Thus, if the tax rate is 50 percent, the subsidy rate is 12.5 percent, costs are 12.5 percent of GDP, and revenues are 0. This is a contradiction, proving that with a 50 percent tax, there is no revenue to pay for the subsidy. More generally, I show in the appendix that the revenue from the corporate profits tax will *never* be enough to pay for the full, distortion-eliminating subsidy.

Given that paying the cost of the entire distortion is impossible, what is the maximal fraction of the distortion that can be eliminated if the subsidy is funded by the corporate tax revenue? I show in the appendix that if the subsidy is financed by a 50 percent corporate tax rate, the maximum fraction of the full subsidy rate is $1/\theta_t$. If $\theta_t = 4$, this is 1/4 of the optimal subsidy, which is a 3.1 percent subsidy rate. Equation (A10.5) in the appendix shows that a 3.1 percent subsidy lowers the markup from 1.33 to 1.2 and raises the combined share of labor and capital from 75 percent to 80 percent. In this example, the distortion is 0.25 (1-0.75) that matters, and the 0.05 improvement (from 0.75 to 0.80) obtained using the tax and a subsidy is actually a 20 percent reduction in the distortion. But even this appears to be too small a gain.

The conclusion that I draw from this analysis is that using tax on corporate profits to finance a subsidy that aims to remove the monopoly factor price distortions is inferior to a direct antitrust policy to contain market power. I instead advocate for the revenue from corporate profit tax to be used to finance investments that promote long-term efficiency and growth, and for active antitrust policy to remove some of the distortion in factor prices.

10.2.4   Corporate Tax Avoidance

The last issue to be addressed is that firms may use deceitful accounting strategies to lower their taxes, such as transfer pricing and other strategies of locating assets and obligations to shift profits to low-tax countries. Firms also move their corporate domicile to low-tax countries to avoid taxes (called tax inversion). The use of these and similar strategies was a key reason given for lowering corporate income tax in the Tax Cuts and Jobs Act of 2017. It is true that if no remedial action is taken, higher corporate income tax rates increase the incentive of firms to escape the tax by moving corporate profits to a low-tax location. But this is possible only because the United States has accepted accounting practices that define profits by the territorial allocation of assets on the books of the firms. Lowering the corporate tax rate was not the right solution. The problem is an accounting problem, and an accounting device must be used to solve it.

The simplest solution uses a method called sales factor apportionment, which is used by many U.S. states to assess their corporate taxes (Clausing, 2016). Sales factor apportionment in the global context calculates a firm's profits for tax purposes as its global profits multiplied by the proportion of its sales in a given country (see Zucman, 2018). This means that the corporate income tax base can be defined by allocating its consolidated world profits in proportion to the location of its sales, disregarding all transfer pricing and location of assets or liabilities. If a firm sells 27 percent of its products in the United States, the U.S. government should define its U.S.-taxable profits to be 27 percent of its global profits. The Internal Revenue Service (IRS) already has all the information needed for such allocation because firms are required to provide information about their income, broken down by location. This would render irrelevant the location where profits were earned and remove the incentives to shift the location of assets and liabilities. This simple solution is a natural recognition of the arcane nature of the accounting practices of multinational corporations. The idea is not new; it was advocated by Avi-Yonah et al. (2008) and Eichner and Runkel (2008), but it is enjoying a resurgence in popularity.

A more structural solution is available (see Saez and Zucman, 2019b; Clausing et al., 2020). It calls for an agreement among the advanced countries on the minimum corporate tax rate to be collected. They have a strong incentive to reach such an agreement because all stand to benefit, and it would prevent tax revenue from escaping to the various tax havens around the world. All multinational firms would then be required to provide all tax authorities with detailed reports on their country-by-country operations. Each country can then impose the agreed-upon tax rate on the income reported by the corporations without having to alter the existing tax law. In addition, each home country (the country where the firm is domiciled) must impose on corporations domiciled there the agreed-upon minimum tax on the firm's world income, giving a tax credit for all taxes paid to foreign governments. If a lower tax is imposed by some of the other countries, the home country will, in effect, impose the agreed-upon tax on the income not taxed by those lower-tax jurisdictions. The United States will then, for example, impose on its own corporations the taxes that Bermuda does not charge them. This method of taxation renders irrelevant the shift of profits to offshore locations because those profits are now taxed by the home country at the same agreed-upon tax rate. Such a preliminary agreement, to set a tax of at least 15 percent, was reached in June 2021 by the G7 nations.

To see an example, suppose that Apple uses transfer pricing to shift to Ireland $1 billion of profits, which are taxed in Ireland at the rate of 5 percent, while the agreed-upon minimum corporate tax is 25 percent. When Apple provides the IRS its income report, its Ireland income will be taxed at 25 percent, but Apple will receive credit for the 5 percent tax actually paid in Ireland. The United States will tax Apple's Irish income at the outstanding 20 percent. If Apple has income in Australia and it pays a 25 percent income tax on that reported income, the United States will not tax that income again.

With such reforms in place, an increase of the corporate profit tax would not be undermined by firms changing their domicile or by transfer pricing. As long as a firm reports its income honestly, then under these taxation methods, there is much lower incentive to shift income or assets to an offshore location.

10.2.5   Illustration of Tax Liability on Global Corporate Income

In table 10.2, column 3, I estimate, for a sample of representative firms, their global monopoly profits as a result of market power. In making these estimates, I assume, for simplicity, a 4 percent capital cost (excluding depreciation). Data used in the computations are from the 2019 Compustat database. I also provide for each firm the U.S. and foreign reported tax payments under the actual tax rates that prevailed in 2019 and the reported U.S. accounting profits. The table shows that a tax on monopoly profits would fall mostly on two categories of firms. The first category includes the leading firms with valuable proprietary technologies derived from the information technology (IT) revolution or other highly technological industries such as pharmaceuticals. In the second are all firms that gain market power from their brands and traditional consumer preference for their brand names, such as Coca-Cola. This conclusion is consistent with the distribution of monopoly profits reported in figure 6.7e.

As explained in chapter 6, given the high leverage of U.S. corporations, their average debt/capital ratio is above 70 percent. For some advanced technology firms, it is larger than 100 percent. Consequently, for highly leveraged firms, the fraction of capital owned is close to zero, and for those firms actual reported

TABLE 10.2 Optimal corporate tax rate

Firm	Global accounting profits (in millions of dollars)	Global profits resulting from market power (in millions of dollars)	Proposed 50 percent tax on global profits (in millions of dollars)	Actual U.S. tax (in millions of dollars)	Foreign tax (in millions of dollars)	U.S. accounting profits (in millions of dollars)
Apple Inc.	65,737	60,989	30,495	6,384	3,962	21,437
Microsoft Corp.	43,688	40,102	20,051	4,718	5,531	15,799
Johnson and Johnson	17,328	17,887	8,943	−535	2,744	3,543
Coca-Cola Co.	10,786	10,794	5,397	508	1,479	3,249
American Express	8,429	7,614	3,807	1,108	437	7,262
Salesforce Inc.	983	886	443	0	117	839
General Electric	1,149	634	317	146	2,008	506
American Electric Power	1,907	−1,226	0	−7	−55	1,907
Chevron Corp.	5,536	−2,908	0	−73	4,577	−5,483
Dow Chemical	−1,247	−1,552	0	−287	960	−1,196

Source: Compustat files for 2019.

corporate profits are close to total monopoly profits. The market value of such firms is mostly monopoly wealth.

These are multinational firms, as evidenced by the great discrepancy between global accounting profits and U.S. accounting profits. Regardless of the tax rate that would ultimately be agreed upon by the G7 or by a longer list of nations, the United States can always follow the method of sales factor apportionment and impose its own 45 percent tax on monopoly profits. Like all decisions about taxation, it all depends upon the overall goals of public policy.

10.3   Wealth Taxation: Transitory Wealth Redistribution Policy

10.3.1   Why Oppose a Permanent and Broad Wealth Tax?

Wealth taxation has attracted a great deal of attention in recent years because of the very high degree of wealth inequality in the Second Gilded Age. The idea of imposing a wealth tax reached the political arena in the 2020 Democratic primary because it offers a direct and rapid route to income and wealth redistribution. It is, however, important to recognize what is actually being taxed by a wealth tax.

I showed in chapter 6 that from the 1980s to 2019, total monopoly wealth rose from about zero in 1986 to $25.1 trillion in 2019, as deduced from the market value of the securities of the corporate sector traded on public exchanges. In 2019, the level of monopoly wealth reached 75 percent of the total stock market value. The other 25 percent is the proportion of the value of capital owned by the firms, out of their total market value. A wealth tax must then be broken, according to ideas developed in this book, into two components: a tax on capital (which is a tax on savings) and a tax on monopoly wealth (which is a tax on wealth created by market power). As explained in section 10.2.1, a tax on capital or on its income has undesirable effects because it disincentivizes savings and capital accumulation, reducing output in the long run. This becomes an even more severe problem in an economy with market power, where the return on capital is already too low and the real question becomes whether to subsidize instead of taxing that capital income (see section 10.2.3). As to the second component of a wealth tax, monopoly wealth is just the capitalization of future expected monopoly profits. In the presence of a tax on monopoly profits, a wealth tax then acts as a second tax on these profits. If a corporate profits tax is set at anything close to 50 percent and antitrust policy is applied to technological market power, then, over time, total monopoly wealth will decline. Consequently, over time, wealth taxation will gradually become a tax on savings, with the negative implications noted above.

Broad wealth taxation has other undesirable features. Such a tax is imposed on illiquid assets. Some such assets—for example, real estate or privately held corporations—do not trade regularly on open markets and do not have posted prices. Others, such as jewelry, art, and other collectibles, have unique values that can be appraised, but they are traded mostly on very thin markets. A wealth tax that requires cash payment for wealth stored in illiquid assets creates a hardship of its own.

The preceding discussion implies that broad wealth taxation should not be a permanent tool of a policy that aims to lower long-run wealth inequality. This brings me back to the distinction made in the introduction of this chapter, between permanent and transitory taxation. In my view, a tax on monopoly wealth should not be used as a permanent policy instrument. Many countries that tried to create a permanent wealth taxation encountered these issues and ended up abolishing these taxes. However, if carefully crafted, a wealth tax can be a very effective tool for a transitory policy.

These considerations do not prevent the use of specialized wealth taxation on specific assets with well-defined prices, designed to achieve a limited goal, such as the local financing of education with real estate taxes. Short-term wealth taxation was used by many countries for emergency needs, like wars. Wealth taxation can be an effective tool to shift quickly from the current extremely high level of wealth inequality to a permanently more egalitarian distribution. But after such transition, the egalitarian distribution can be effectively maintained by a combination of personal income tax, a tax on corporate profits, and an active antitrust policy to restrain the expansion of technological market power.

The temporary, one-time nature of such a wealth tax also serves to mitigate the harm of taxing savings. Economists have long known that the most efficient tax is a one-time expropriation of private capital, called a capital levy (see Keynes, 1940; see also Eichengreen, 1989, on Japan's 1947 implementation of this levy). Models of capital taxation like Chamley (1986) have to rule out the immediate, one-time capital tax. Otherwise, the government could simply confiscate all private capital and share its proceeds equally with no efficiency costs.

Of course, despite its theoretical appeal, such an action would be damaging in practice. Private capital markets are vital to ensuring the efficient allocation of resources. The uncertainty created by the prospect that the government might again seize private capital would reduce incentives to save in the same way as a capital gains tax would. I propose a wealth tax that would raise less than 10 percent of private wealth; countries in Northern Europe have well-functioning capital markets with much higher degrees of state ownership. The tax that I propose must be explained by the short-term need to change the wealth distribution and seed a national fund (a proposal I explain in section 10.4). After the temporary tax is implemented, this fund would have an endowment that distributes its earnings to the bottom 50 percent of the income distribution while keeping its principal intact. Once the fund is capitalized, no one will expect a return to the circumstances that justified the wealth tax in the first place, so there will be no fear of a future wealth tax. This temporary policy has the benefit of taxing today's capital stock, which has no behavioral response to the tax, without the damaging aspect of taxing future savings.

10.3.2 Child Tax Credit, Minimum Income Guarantee, or Programs of Direct Investments ln Children

Given the high level of present-day inequality and the very high proportion of children living in poverty, a consensus has emerged that there is an urgent need for programs to reduce children's poverty and hasten the transition to a more egalitarian income distribution by increasing mobility of households from the bottom 50 percent of the income distribution back into the middle class. There is, however, no consensus on the method to accomplish this goal.

One of the more drastic actions taken by the American Rescue Plan of 2021 was to include a one-year program of child tax credit of $250 per month for each child aged six to seventeen, and $300 per month for children of lower ages. The credit can be claimed only by single tax filers who earn less than $112,500 a year and joint filers earning up to $150,000 a year. Although such a plan will reduce poverty immediately, it has substantial disadvantages. First, it was approved only for one year, and its future is subject to annual budgetary review. Second, because the funds are paid to the families, part of these funds will be spent for the benefit of adults, not the children, and the true net benefits received by the children are yet to be determined. Third, the credit creates an extremely high artificial income tax rate that distorts incentives at income of $112,500 for individuals and $150,000 for joint filers. Fourth, a substantial number of families will not receive benefits because they did not file for income tax in the past and the IRS does not have a bank account or an address for them. To prevent fraud, management problems will result in a substantial number of families never receiving benefits.

An alternative approach that has been discussed for a very long time is a minimum income guarantee, which is a tax credit that is not restricted to children. Massive experiments to study the impact of such plans were conducted in the 1970s using large samples of low-income families in New Jersey, Denver, and Seattle. Although new experiments have been initiated in recent years, a great deal is already known about their efficacy. These are clearly direct redistribution plans that aim to attain a more egalitarian distribution of after-tax income. Their advantage is that they act rapidly to redistribute income and reduce poverty. However, they suffer from the same defects I have listed for the child tax credit. In addition, such plans create artificial negative incentive effects at low income that depend on the size of the income guaranteed, and they discourage transition from unemployment to work. These effects are caused by the progressivity in the actual support received, assigning lower support for families with higher income. But as income from other sources increases, the amount paid by the government decreases, creating a tax incentive in the program.

I noted in chapter 1 that one of the reasons for the decline in the New Deal egalitarian policy after the 1970s was the sharp fall in public support for direct cash redistribution programs. But the most decisive argument against them is that they do not address the main goal of all long-term egalitarian policies, which is to help individuals improve their skill and motivation to earn, on their own, income above poverty level and perhaps join the middle class. I will later explain in more detail that the most effective government programs to achieve that goal are public investments in the health and education of the children of low-income families. Such direct investments pay very high returns by increasing the children's human capital and skill to such a high level that they have the best chance of leaving the bottom 50 percent of the income distribution and joining the middle class. Attempts to attain the same results with adults have not been nearly as successful. In short, children of families in the bottom 50 percent of the income distribution constitute the most wasted human resources in our society, and direct investments in them are the most beneficial. The solution I propose is the creation of a permanent national institution for promoting the health and education of these children. This is the next topic.

10.4   National Fund for Equity and Democracy

10.4.1   Justification and Goals for the Fund

I have already discussed in detail the negative effect of the declining middle class on the integrity of democratic institutions. It is also clear that technological innovations in general, and artificial intelligence (AI) in particular, will continue to produce a flow of workers out of the middle class; therefore a solution requires a permanent institution dedicated to a permanent reversal of that flow. I propose it takes the form of a National Fund for Equity and Democracy.

Living in or close to poverty, children of those at the bottom of the income distribution receive a poor education, poor nutrition, and poor health services. In addition, they are exposed to pollutants like lead and airborne particulates that hamper cognitive development. These factors entrench the culture of poverty, leading to permanent class divisions. To address this problem, these children are the main beneficiaries of my proposed fund.

Recent research provides strong empirical evidence that supports the goals of the proposed fund. Hendren and Sprung-Keyser (2020) construct a measure to evaluate the net benefits of public investments. They demonstrate that historically, direct public investments in the health and education of low-income children yield, by their measure, the highest values possible. They show that many of these programs have, in fact, paid for themselves because governments have recouped the cost of their initial investment through additional taxes paid and reduced transfers. Those programs that did not fully pay for themselves still raised the direct recipients' lifetime income and welfare, which is very beneficial, at very little cost to the government. Benefits tend to be larger the younger the recipient. Programs targeted at young children and teens have very large returns, those targeted at young adults have mixed results, and those targeted at older adults have small social returns.

I emphasize the need to create a permanent institution that will help maintain a stable middle class. Being permanent means that the institution is free from changing budgetary conditions or short-term policy choices of the specific administration in power or the specific configuration of members of Congress at any particular session. It must be able to engage in long-run planning with a predictable level of resources at its disposal. This is why I am proposing the creation of an administrative body that will ultimately own a significant amount of national wealth to carry out its annual program on a large scale. By forming this permanent institution, the decline of the middle class will be reversed, despite the forces of technological change acting to hasten that decline. As Sitaraman (2017) argues, a strong middle class is vital to the functioning of American democracy, and the creation of a permanent institution dedicated to the goal of maintaining the vitality of the middle class is an important policy choice.

10.4.2   Structure and Operation of the Fund

I propose the fund functions as an independent agency of the federal government, similar to the Federal Reserve. Some may prefer a name like "agency for child poverty," but this may not reflect well the need for the total independence of the fund and its permanency, as an institution.[2] The agency would be run by a director and a board, nominated by the president and confirmed by the Senate for a term of six years. To create more distance from current policy, the law should stipulate these officers can be removed only for cause. The board and the fund must operate in a fully transparent manner, with books open to public

---

[2] This is to distinguish it from the Administration for Children and Families, which is a division of the Department of Health and Human Services created to allocate to states and other territories funds approved by Congress and designed to finance programs for children and families.

inspection, regular audits, and periodic public hearings at the appropriate congressional committees.

Board appointees should be made up of members from two groups. The first would consist of experts in three fields—economics, education, and medicine—because knowledge in these fields is needed for making the fund's investment decisions. The second group would include experienced members of the business community. Members of this group would help in evaluating management practices of the fund's grantees and broaden the fund's financial sources. The fund should aim to be a home for the bequests or donations from wealthy Americans who wish to express their thanks to the country that has enabled them to succeed. The hope is that the fund would be successful and enjoy strong public support as a national institution that provides opportunities for all. Similar permanent funds in Alaska and Norway are very popular there.

The fund would be dedicated to assisting the children of families with income in the bottom 50 percent of the income distribution. Depending upon future growth rates and population trends, this will cover approximately 30 to 35 million children. As explained later, the fund would start operating upon its creation. It would take one year to appoint its officers, recruit its professional employees, and open its field offices. Expenditures at the level of $250 billion per year, above normal public spending on health and education, would begin in its second year of operation, but it would reach its full development at the end of the fifth year.

The aim of the fully operational fund is to improve the quality of education, nutrition, and health of children of families in the bottom 50 percent of the income distribution in the following ways:

- Improve education, from preschool to community colleges, by supporting facilities, increasing teachers' salaries, attracting better teachers, and providing basic in-school medical services. Medical services should include regular vaccination.
- Create nutrition programs in all schools, from preschool through high school, and teach children how to improve and maintain a high level of nutrition.
- For children below school age, provide support for good-quality day care with nutrition programs.
- Provide food stamps to enable families to purchase high-quality food for children and teach children the need for good nutrition and how to attain it.
- Ensure the availability of medical insurance to all children, from birth through high school, by complementing the available subsidies of all federal and state programs with the fund paying the added, uncovered cost of the children's medical insurance.
- Improve children's medical facilities in poor communities, including subsidized construction of private clinics and/or children's hospitals that serve the community.

- Provide scholarships for all low-income students who wish and are able to attend college and/or technical school for free.
- Support low-income families in moving to high-opportunity neighborhoods.

Benefits fall into two categories. The first includes individual benefits, like medical insurance, food stamps, or college scholarships. These are provided to children who qualify based on the specific family income. Because such income changes, these benefits may also change. To avoid creating a negative incentive to increase their income, once qualified, a child's benefits would be provided for four years, independent of family income, allowing a slow adjustment to the different level of family income. It is thus important that state and federal tax agencies share their data with the staff of the fund to handle the process of qualification by income.

The second category of benefits is those provided to the community, like investments in day care facilities, schools, or community medical facilities. Because the aim is to reach low-income families, the problem of choosing schools raises the more general question of how to choose the geographic unit that qualifies for support. My preference is to use the school district as the basic geographic unit. Any school district with a median family income less than a specified threshold would qualify. Once qualified, all children in that school district would enjoy the community benefits, but only families with income below the threshold would qualify for individual benefits. Gordon and Ruffini (2018) show that a school breakfast program that was delivered using this community-benefit approach improved child welfare compared with an individual-benefit approach. They hypothesized this effect could be driven by the reduced stigma of accessing the benefits or by bad design of the individual program that results in low-income students not receiving access to benefits. This supports my general aim, stressed in chapter 1, of designing programs with as universal participation as possible.

I include the cost of moving low-income families to high-opportunity neighborhoods. Recent research (for example, Chetty et al., 2018; Chyn, 2018; Chetty and Hendren, 2018) demonstrates the effect of moving children to "higher opportunity" (usually more prosperous) neighborhoods. Chyn (2018) studies an episode in which Chicago demolished a public housing building. The former residents were given vouchers and moved into a variety of different neighborhoods in the city. Some children moved to wealthier neighborhoods, interacted with wealthier peers, went to better schools, and saw better role models, and this resulted in their earning more later in life. The same is true of the lottery in Chetty et al. (2018). Bergman et al. (2019) conducted an experiment that spent $2,660 per family helping recipients of Section 8 housing vouchers move to wealthier neighborhoods. The federal vouchers cover the cost of rent. The experiment's funding was spent on the challenges of finding apartments, educating residents on which areas are high opportunity, communicating with landlords, and sometimes lending capital for rental deposits. The experiment increased the share of families that used their voucher to move to a high-opportunity neighborhood from 15 percent to 53 percent. They estimate that, per child that moves, the lifetime increase in income is $214,000. I thus suggest that the fund consider creating a program that is analogous to the Bergman et al. (2019) experiment. Any family that qualifies on the basis of the criteria specified and then moves to a different school district would continue to receive the stipulated individual benefits.

10.4.3   Financing of the Fund

The overarching goal of the fund is to own 10 percent of the market value of domestic corporations and to thus transfer 10 percent of corporate wealth from the top to the bottom of the wealth distribution. The fund would then be an institution that holds in trust 10 percent of the market value of domestic corporations for the benefit of the children of households in the bottom of the income distribution. These investments should earn the private rate of return on behalf of the children. The wealth would then be dedicated to increasing the upward mobility of individuals in the bottom 50 percent of the income distribution. The identity of those who fall on hard times and find themselves at the bottom changes over time. However, this 50 percent, although it has a fluctuating membership, would continue to own 10 percent of corporate wealth, dedicated to helping their children have a better future.

To gain a sense of the magnitude of the fund, I note that the total market value of domestic corporations was $45.4 trillion in March 2020. Suppose this value rises to $50 trillion in 2025, and the fund owns $5 trillion in real terms. If we think of these $5 trillion as assets belonging to the bottom 50 percent, whose total net worth is currently only $2 trillion, my plan would increase the wealth of that bottom 50 percent from $2 trillion to $7 trillion. The plan calls for the fund to ultimately spend 5 percent of its assets annually, with an annual budget of $250 billion. The budget would be larger if the fund receives either more tax support or additional private donations. The fund's spending is *above and beyond the regular state and federal spending on education, nutrition, and health.* The regular spending has been insufficient to improve poor school districts or the quality of life of children of families with income in the bottom 50 percent. These districts and families have not been able to attain the level of health and education necessary to lift their children into a more promising future.

The question is, How should the fund acquire 10 percent of the market value of domestic corporations? The plan consists of two parts. The first is a tax on new financing, which would gradually build the wealth of the fund over time. This would fall mostly on high-technology firms that grow rapidly and need additional capital. These firms are precisely those most likely to displace workers. Their tax payment would indirectly compensate those displaced by their innovations. The second is a short-run and rapid buildup of the assets of the fund using a five-year wealth tax. This would allow it to start operations immediately and provide support within one year of its establishment. Below, I detail how each of these taxes would be structured.

The first tax, which would fall, for the most part, on rapidly growing firms, would tax capital raised by the corporation. A firm that issues any equity security would be required to pay a tax of 10 percent in the form of the security itself, not cash payment. This applies to all securities issued (common stocks, preferred stock, etc.) by all corporations, private or public. The tax would be imposed on all security issues, including those used as compensation of officers, employees, or board members. Every security issued to the fund, and then owned by the fund, would have the following features:

- It will have no voting rights but participate in all dividend payments.
- If sold to a private party, it would be converted to the same security as those issued to the public.
- It is protected from dilution until converted by the fund through sale to a private party.

From the perspective of young, newly formed firms, the tax would apply just when the value of their security is relatively low.

The tax on the issue of private debt is the same as equity, but is moderated by the maturity of the debt issued. I propose the following scale:

- For debt with maturity of less than one year, the tax is 0.
- For debt with maturity of thirty-one years or more, the tax is 10 percent.
- For debt with maturity of one to thirty-one years, the tax is set by a linear scale with increments of 0.333 percent for each year to maturity.

These taxes apply only to corporations with equity capital of at least $25 million, thus exempting small private businesses.

The fund would be required to hold each security for twenty years or to maturity, whichever is shorter. At that time, it must sell them on the open market, if a market exists. For securities that do not trade on public markets, such as equity or debt of private corporations, the fund would either auction them or negotiate with private parties to convert these assets to cash. However, in the case of inadequate funding from existing investments, with a two-thirds majority, the board can decide to sell some securities ahead of schedule. After twenty

TABLE 10.3   Data for tax computations: Five-year transitory tax plan

Wealth group (in millions of dollars)	Marginal tax	Effective marginal tax	Year	Number of households (in millions)	Total wealth (in billions of dollars)
$10–$100	3.5%	2.56%	1	1.136	24,337
			2	1.253	26,115
			3	1.390	28,191
			4	1.519	30,258
			5	1.694	32,707
$100+	5.5%	4.02%	1	0.0386	12,513
			2	0.0416	12,881
			3	0.0441	13,193
			4	0.0464	13,489
			5	0.0502	13,915

years, assets must be invested in an index fund that tracks the entire market. The exact details of the index fund are left to the fund's discretion.

The second tax aims to build the fund rapidly by using a five-year wealth tax that would allow the fund to start operation in the same year the tax is imposed. In table 10.3, I compute the potential revenue raised from this temporary wealth tax. The computations are made using the Saez and Zucman (2019b) methodology from their website Taxjusticenow.org.[3] The wealth distribution data comes from two alternative sources. One source is the Survey of Consumer Finances (SCF) for 2019, reported by the Federal Reserve in 2020. It deliberately excludes households that appear on the Forbes 400 list of the wealthiest individuals to protect their privacy. Therefore, as is standard, the data file is supplemented with the public wealth estimates from the Forbes 400 list. The second source, Saez and Zucman (2016), capitalizes the flows of income from tax data to estimate the household wealth distribution. The specific file I use for 2019 employs the Saez and Zucman (2019a) methodology of using, for wealth of less than $2.1 billion, an average of the SCF estimates and the wealth estimates of the Distributional National Accounts developed by Piketty et al. (2018). My plan exempts from taxation all household wealth below $10 million, which drastically reduces the

---

[3] The website uses a wealth distribution computed by averaging the estimates from the wealth distribution of the Survey of Consumer Finances (SCF) together with the Forbes 400 and the tax implied by the wealth reported in Piketty et al. (2018), Distributional National Accounts. The top and bottom parts of table 10.3 report these two computations separately instead of averaging them together.

number of households subject to tax. The tax schedule consists of two marginal tax rates:

- A 3.5 percent tax on wealth from $10 million to $100 million.
- A 5.5 percent tax on wealth above $100 million.

However, the legal form of the significant part of the wealth that is taxed is that of unrealized capital gains. Many wealthy individuals never realize these gains, an option that offers opportunities to avoid the tax. These opportunities include contributing the assets to a tax-free foundation run by that same individual or bequeathing the assets to heirs who are exempt from taxation because of the stepped-up basis loophole. To pay the tax with cash, they may need to sell the securities and first pay capital gains tax. Assuming a federal capital gains tax of 20 percent and average state taxes of around 7 percent, owners of these stocks may then have to pay a 27 percent capital gains tax. They would then be taxed again by a wealth tax computed on the value before capital gains tax.

To avoid this double taxation, my plan calls for allowing individuals to pay the tax with the assets they own, valued at the time the tax report is filed. Being allowed to pay the wealth tax with untaxed assets, they would receive an effective discount on their tax obligation, which accomplishes two other goals. First, it reduces the probability of tax evasion because it enables individuals to pay at a lower effective tax rate. Second, in effect it brings forward future capital gains tax revenue that, had the securities stayed in private hands, would have been paid gradually, or even never paid, because of avoidance with available methods. It is thus a particularly desirable side effect of capitalizing a national fund. The discount is seen in the difference between the plan's marginal tax rate and the effective marginal rate paid. The computations are done in reference to 2019 data and 2019 dollars, assuming a 2 percent inflation rate, 5 percent real return, and 0.9 percent population growth, as in Saez and Zucman (2019a).

The actual amount raised by the tax depends upon the rate of tax evasion, which can have a significant effect on the amount raised. To evaluate this problem, note that my wealth taxes are imposed for only five years, and the government that decides to enforce it has the means to do so because, thanks to the $10 million exemption, most assets involved are legally registered and thus take forms that can be uncovered by a determined administration. Therefore, my assumed baseline evasion rate is 16 percent, which is what Saez and Zucman (2019a) use in analyzing a tax rate of 2 percent. On the other hand, a burgeoning literature[4] studies the elasticity of reported wealth with respect to wealth

---

[4]In addition to those noted in the text, see Brülhart et al. (2019), De Simone et al. (2020), Duran-Cabré et al. (2019), Jakobsen et al. (2020), Johannesen et al. (2020), Johannesen and Zucman (2014), Londoño-Vélez and Ávila-Mahecha (2021), Seim (2017), and Zoutman (2018).

TABLE 10.4   Tax revenue after evasion

Year	Evasion rate of 16 percent	Evasion rates: 18.7 percent and 24.4 percent
1	814 Billion of $	740 Billion of $
2	856 Billion of $	782 Billion of $
3	901 Billion of $	826 Billion of $
4	949 Billion of $	873 Billion of $
5	1,000 Billion of $	924 Billion of $

taxation. I follow Saez and Zucman (2019a) in averaging the evasion rates implied by the diverse elasticities reported, resulting in alternative evasion rates of 18.7 percent in response to a 3.5 percent tax and 24.4 percent in response to a tax of 5.5 percent.

Table 10.4 summarizes the total tax revenue after evasion at the two alternative rates. As I noted, my computations are based on the 16 percent evasion rate. The tax evasion statistics in the literature are deduced from data on permanent rather than transitory wealth taxation, and from countries where the governments responsible for their implementation did not make significant efforts to enforce them. Small effort and expenditure on enforcement can go a long way in reducing evasion, as Johannesen et al. (2020) show in the case of the Reports of Foreign Bank and Financial Accounts (FBAR) regulation, Johannesen and Zucman (2014) show for tax information exchange agreements, and De Simone et al. (2020) show for the Foreign Accounts Tax Compliance Act (FATCA). Enforcement is more a matter of political will, and a reform-minded government that adopted the tax I am proposing would take significant steps to enforce it.

The fund's assets would be invested in a market-indexed fund, which is assumed to earn 5 percent per year. If year 1 is used for organization, and actual spending of $250 billion commences in the second year, then excluding tax on new issues, the fund's assets would reach the value of $4,087 billion at the end of year 5, when the temporary wealth tax comes to an end. This amount would allow the fund to spend $250 billion per year for the transition to a steady-state level. Together with the taxation of new issues, this amount would enable the fund to own, over the long run, 10 percent of existing corporate stock values.

10.5   The Urgent Need for Public Investment in Basic Research

Figure 10.1 shows that, in keeping with the laissez-faire policy since the 1980s, the federal government has gradually withdrawn support for research and

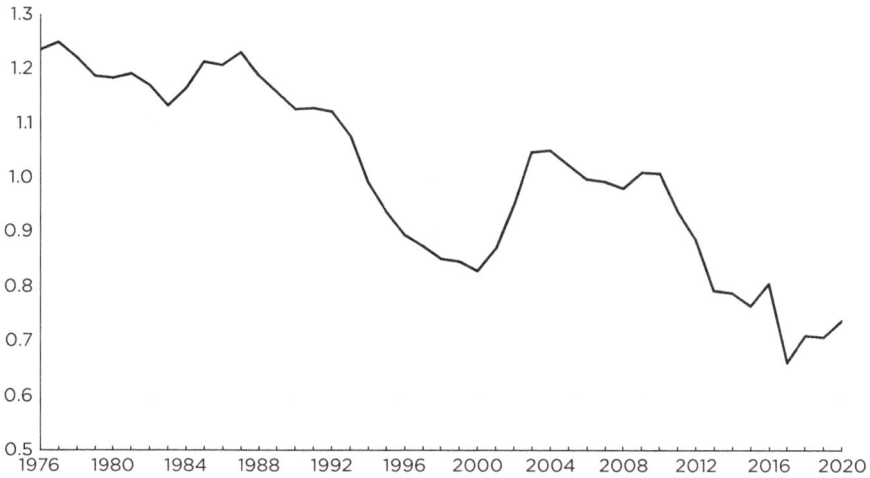

Figure 10.1   Federal R&D as a percent of GDP

Source: Historical trends in federal R&D, American Association for the Advancement of Science

development (R&D). Because the federal government is the main supporter of basic research, the overall funding of basic research has declined. More specifically, National Science Foundation (NSF) data show the federal government provided 70 percent of the total amount spent on basic research throughout the 1960s and 1970s. That share has now declined to well below 40 percent. Most of the decline in this share resulted from actual decline in federal spending on basic research. However, some of this decline is the result of a significant rise, since 2012, in corporate funding of R&D that reflects the rising investments of the pharmaceutical and biotech industries on activities classified by the NSF as basic research. Unlike other items classified as basic research, the results of pharmaceutical research are appropriated by the industry in the form of patents on drugs.

The justification for this drastic cut in federal support for basic research has been the assertion that the private sector will conduct the level of research that is optimal for economic growth. But as explained in chapter 7, the growth rate of the economy is the outcome of two complementary forces. The first, social investments in basic research, is the "R" component, which determines the feasible growth rate of the economy. Second, private R&D, which focuses more on the "D" component, can allow that growth rate to be realized through commercial application of basic research. I have noted that there are instances, like the transistor at Bell Labs and DuPont chemistry research, of corporate-financed R&D that was proper basic research, some of which was awarded Nobel Prizes (see Cummings, 2002). But the vast majority of private R&D is skewed heavily toward the "D" component and focuses on translating basic research results into commercial applications. But once the feasible rate is reached, private R&D cannot increase the economy's growth rate. That can be attained only by higher investments in basic research, designed to attain the maximal feasible growth rate of the economy. It is then not surprising that empirical research on the question shows that the rate of return on federal R&D spending is very high (see, for example, Jones and Williams, 2000).

It is thus essential that federal support for basic research be restored to the level of the 1960s, when the federal government supported 70 percent of basic research. In the absence of federal funding, universities and private foundations have increased their contribution to basic research, but that contribution falls far short of what is needed. The U.S. growth rate would improve if the federal government raises its support of R&D to 1.3 percent to 1.5 percent of GDP.

10.6   Public Investments and the Need to Innovate Good-Quality Jobs

One of this book's main themes is the central role of public policy in directing the market to a socially desirable allocation of resources. Here I focus on a challenging and important problem unique to our time: ensuring that a good-quality job is available to every unskilled worker. This includes upgrading the educational and technical level of unskilled workers, and recognizing the negative externalities of many innovations on the availability of such jobs.

I note that, since the Industrial Revolution, most machines, particularly those that operate along assembly lines, have replaced elementary and repetitive operations that required mostly physical energy and dexterity but required few other human qualities. As the service economy emerged, demand rapidly increased for other human attributes. However, most unskilled work continues to involve only elementary tasks that do not employ other human attributes such as rational judgment, compassion, and artistic or culinary taste. As workers become more educated, more of their human characteristics can be employed to perform more complex tasks. This is where the greatest potential is found for future cooperation between humans and machines. A properly designed machine can permit better trained, formerly unskilled workers to make better use of their human qualities. To borrow an analogy from Leamer et al. (2000), the ideal innovation, like a forklift, reduces the importance of physical strength and allows workers to use their cognitive abilities instead. The outcome of this process is that it upgrades the quality of existing tasks.

These considerations also imply that a very efficient innovation that replaces workers may not be as socially desirable as one that is less efficient but involves cooperation with labor, enhances worker productivity, and increases the demand for labor. Given these externalities, policy needs to increase the private sector's incentives to develop technologies that work together with low-skilled workers and increase the demand for such workers rather than technologies that replace them.

10.6.1   Policy to Promote Innovations of Good-Quality Jobs

Given that most workers do not have a college degree, imagine that to raise the wages of workers in the bottom 50 percent of the income distribution, a massive effort is initiated to increase the level of education and technical skills of all workers classified as "unskilled" or "low skilled." This could be done slowly over a long time by providing sufficient funds for these workers to study or train at state colleges, community colleges, or technical schools or to enroll in other job-training programs. Although I support such an educational effort, in the absence of change in the demand for labor, such effort is not likely to succeed (see Morgan and Steinbaum, 2018). There must exist higher-quality, better-paying jobs that would be available for those workers. One recognizes that someone who is currently a secretary is not likely to become a physicist, and an assembly-line worker is not likely to become an architect. The economy must then create new high-quality jobs that can utilize the improvement in the education level and technical skill of those workers.

In using the term "good jobs," I refer to jobs that provide permanent employment, safe working conditions, opportunities for learning and advancing on the job, and a high enough wage to support a middle-class standard of living with some vacation time and savings. Earning income that offers middle-class living standards entails a wage rate above $28 per hour.[5] The question is, How can technological innovations, together with improved education and skill level, lead to the creation of those jobs? The answer is that it requires a different kind of innovation than those brought to market in the last half century. In addition, a policy needs to be crafted that encourages innovations that promote partnership of workers with machines and enhances the productivity of the unskilled rather than replaces them.

I use the term "machine" broadly, to identify a technological product created by IT innovations to enhance productivity. Products that match this description include programmed industrial equipment, robots, computers with specialized software, video devices, and so on. But why is this a policy challenge? Innovation

---

[5] This wage rate is computed by assuming that the middle class begins in 2020 at an annual income of $48,000 and that the number of hours worked in a year is 1811. I then adjusted this computed rate for the price change from 2020 prices to expected prices in 2022.

policy has been based on the idea that any innovation is welcomed if it is profitable. As a result, businesses engage in innovations that are profitable by lowering the costs of labor or capital, but since the Industrial Revolution, most innovations displace workers, particularly low-skilled workers. Substantial research has emerged about the problem, particularly about the effect of robots and AI.[6] Although workers displaced by machines have also benefited from their creation, average benefits pale in comparison to the loss of a middle-aged worker replaced by a machine. Such a loss entails major cost of human capital, reduced health, and decline of life expectancy, as I have documented before. The fact is that the unskilled bear most of the costs of being displaced by machines, while the benefits are enjoyed by others.

Robots bring this issue to the fore. On net, they may be detrimental to social welfare because they actually cause a decline in the wages and living standards of workers, and this situation is likely to get worse. The policy problem results from the fact that it has been easier, and perhaps cheaper, to innovate labor-displacing innovations, and this is supported by the existing no-compensation policy. As Acemoglu et al. (2020) argue, government has also incentivized such innovations with a tax system built on the premise that labor should be taxed and capital should be exempt. Today, innovations earn profits, and the costs of labor displacement and community destruction caused by some innovations are ignored. This leads to a private cost of innovations being much lower than their social cost, effectively subsidizing AI's displacement of labor. This displacement is attracting a rapidly rising volume of research.[7]

10.6.2   Three Policy Proposals

One approach to solving the problem is to compensate displaced workers by using public investments. The proposal often made is to offer retraining, cash transfers, or a subsidy for the employment of displaced and unemployed workers. These have all been done by the Trade Adjustment Assistance program and have proven grossly inadequate (see Autor, 2014). Because of low and declining worker mobility, the problem has acquired a regional dimenson: poorer regions in the middle of the country have seen greater displacement and have become centers of economic decline, with large fraction of unemployed and immobile workers. Consequently, this approach has been drastically modified by a more

---

[6]For some recent work, with particular emphasis on the effect of robots, see Acemoglu and Restrepo (2018a,b, 2019, 2020), Peretto and Seater (2013), Brynjolfsson and McAfee (2014), Zeira (1998), and Zuleta (2008).

[7]For a sample of recent papers, see Acemoglu and Restrepo (2018a,b, 2019, 2020), Austin et al. (2018), Autor et al. (2019), Miller-Adams et al. (2019), and Rodrik and Sabel (2020).

general approach that initiates direct public investments dedicated to promoting activities that increase the supply of high-quality jobs in these regions. Such a regional policy is the basis of proposals made by Austin et al. (2018) and by Rodrik and Sabel (2020). They propose that, in order to create good-quality jobs for displaced workers, policy should aim to attract private investments that will support the regions' increased participation in the growth of modern industries, such as alternative energy, electric vehicles and autonomous driving, pharmaceuticals, biotechnology, or even cloud computing in areas with low energy cost. To that end, government policy should make the heavy capital investment in local infrastructure and in human capital needed for improving the skill level of workers who live in these regions. If done on a large enough scale, such public programs could ameliorate the conditions of workers.

The problem with this solution is that it requires taxpayers to pay for negative externalities of innovations and globalization initiated by the private sector. Nevertheless, these proposals should be applauded. Such an investment program is also an important component of President Biden's two massive infrastructure bills that are likely to change the American economy.

A second policy option is to alter the future direction of innovation by minimizing the negative externalities of machines. This is a much more difficult undertaking, but it is worthwhile. One direct way to do this is to tax machines that displace workers and subsidize machines that enhance cooperation between humans and machines. Aghion et al. (2016) show that taxes change relative prices and shape what R&D firms do, creating inventions that would not otherwise have existed. It is easy to apply this principle to robots that only displace workers. It is not so easy to apply it to technologies that have mixed effects: these may displace some workers but cooperate with others. For example, the PC has displaced many workers, such as secretaries, but has enhanced the cooperation between humans and machines in performing countless professional tasks. This points out the fact that the tax rates must differentiate among IT products depending upon their negative effect on employment. But this also points out the problem with the proposed tax system: virtually all contemporary IT products contain some element of labor displacement, and it will be very difficult to maintain a complex tax system with such great diversity of tax rates. For this reason, I do not regard the tax proposals as realistic.

However, the reasoning for taxing labor-displacing innovations is the same as the reasoning that leads to a subsidy for labor-enhancing innovations. Therefore, I propose a simpler program that would offer a subsidy for any labor-enhancing innovations, combined with my proposal in section 10.2 to raise the corporate income tax to 50 percent. The policy's aim is to encourage innovations that complement labor employment, increase labor productivity, and increase the demand for labor. This is accomplished by a major exemption from corporate taxation of all profits from innovations that satisfy the conditions specified by the policy and qualify for the exemption. The burden of proof that the innovation is qualified for the subsidy is to fall on the firm that applies for the exemption from taxation. Applications need to be examined by professionals who understand the nature of the technology.

A third direction in which policy may advance is in assessing the risk introduced by IT innovations, and particularly by AI. The legal assignment of risk has a strong effect on incentives for innovation. Consider an industry where high labor cost creates an incentive to develop a machine to reduce cost but where it could be catastrophic if the work is performed incorrectly. Examples include hospitals or legal offices. Decisions made by humans may lead to bad outcomes. But unless gross negligence on the part of employers is demonstrated, they are not held liable for these human decisions. For example, hospitals can be held liable for doctors' decisions only if members of hospital management were grossly negligent. Suppose a robot is invented to reduce cost. It can be introduced under two alternative legal systems. The first views a robot as a qualified decision maker, like a human employee, and exempts the employer from any liability for decisions made by the robot. The employer may carry insurance for an error by the robot, but that insurance would be inexpensive. The second legal system recognizes the fact that robots can make catastrophic decisions and therefore holds the employer liable for gross negligence of any robot's decisions, allowing injured parties to sue for triple damages if the robot makes an incorrect decision. Insurance for errors by the robot becomes extremely expensive.

The riskiness of robots is a very serious problem. Developers of AI are constantly warning about the risks that AI presents and stress the need to regulate or restrict the development of AI applications.[8] Once we get beyond automating elementary tasks along the assembly line and begin to automate high-stakes decisions such as automobile driving, medical treatment, and genetic modifications, we open the door to catastrophic consequences. Because AI is now rapidly developing, it is hard to assess how it may be applied in the future. It is clear, however, that corporate incentives surrounding its development can be altered drastically by laws that regulate the consequences of AI.

Exempting employers from liability for the robot's actions increases the profitability of robots that replace humans. But strong employer liability for the robot's actions not only reduces their profitability but also creates a strong incentive to innovate different robots. It becomes relatively more profitable to innovate a robot that rapidly assembles all information and cooperates with humans who need to assess the information. However, all decision making is left to highly qualified humans who can synthesize all the information presented. Such robots increase the productivity of workers. But they also require these

---

[8]For a survey of the various long-term risks of AI, including that it could contribute to totalitarianism, conflict, and catastrophic accidents, see Dafoe (2018).

workers to be suitably trained to work with robots and be able to assess the information and options made available. In medical applications, AI diagnostic tools would increase the productivity of doctors and nurses; the same number of workers could handle a larger number of patients, lowering cost and raising output without increasing the risk faced by, let's say, a hospital. Lower medical costs can increase demand for medical services and can therefore increase demand for doctors and nurses.

Mathematical Appendix to Chapter 10

The question is, What is the fraction of the subsidy which is needed to restore efficiency that can be financed by corporate tax on profits? To answer this question, note that the combination of tax v_t and subsidy s_t implies that the profits of the firm after tax and subsidy are defined by

$$\Pi_{jt}^{at} = (1 - v_t)\Pi_{jt} + s_t(P_t W_t N_{jt} + P_t R_t K_{jt})$$
$$= (1 - v_t)P_t Y_{jt} - (1 - v_t - s_t)(P_t W_t N_{jt} + P_t R_t K_{jt}). \tag{A10.1}$$

Maximization of after-tax profits results in the following static optimization conditions:

$$W_t = \frac{(1 - v_t)}{(1 - v_t - s_t)}\left(\frac{\theta_t - 1}{\theta_t}\right)\frac{P_{jt}}{P_t}(1 - \alpha)\psi_{jt}A_t^{1-\alpha}K_{jt}^\alpha N_{jt}^{-\alpha} \tag{A10.2a}$$

$$R_t = \frac{(1 - v_t)}{(1 - v_t - s_t)}\left(\frac{\theta_t - 1}{\theta_t}\right)\frac{P_{jt}}{P_t}\alpha\psi_{jt}A_t^{1-\alpha}K_{jt}^{\alpha-1}N_{jt}^{1-\alpha}. \tag{A10.2b}$$

To eliminate the monopoly factor price distortion fully, the subsidy must be set so that

$$\frac{(1 - v_t)}{(1 - v_t - s_t)}\left(\frac{\theta_t - 1}{\theta_t}\right) = 1,$$

which requires the subsidy to be

$$s_t = \frac{1 - v_t}{\theta_t}. \tag{A10.3}$$

No matter what tax system is in place, the corporate tax will not be sufficient to eliminate entirely the monopoly factor price distortion. To see why, note that there is distortion at the outset, and the subsidy that eliminates it must be positive. But if the subsidy is sufficiently large to remove the distortions, then the monopoly power is neutralized; in which case, there would not be any profits. Thus, the total corporate tax is zero, and therefore the balanced budget condition would imply a zero subsidy. This is a contradiction. The question then becomes, What is the maximal fraction of the optimal subsidy that can be financed by an optimal corporate tax rate? That is, the feasible subsidy is defined by

$$S_t^F = \kappa_t \frac{1 - \nu_t}{\theta_t}, \qquad\qquad (A10.3a)$$

and the problem is to characterize the maximal value that κ_t can take.

To accomplish this, note that the maximal subsidy possible, given the tax, is defined by the zero net taxation balanced budget condition of

$$-\nu_t \left(\frac{P_{jt} Y_{jt} - P_t W_t N_{jt} - P_t R_t K_{jt}}{P_{jt} Y_{jt}} \right) + s_t^F \left(\frac{P_t W_t N_{jt} + P_t R_t K_{jt}}{P_{jt} Y_{jt}} \right) = 0.$$

Proposition 10.1: Assume a corporate tax of 50%. The largest feasible fraction of the subsidy is

$$\kappa_t = \frac{1}{\theta_t}.$$

Proof. Equations (A10.2a) and (A10.2b) imply that

$$\frac{P_{jt} Y_{jt} - P_t W_t N_{jt} - P_t R_t K_{jt}}{P_{jt} Y_{jt}} = 1 - \left(\frac{1 - \nu_t}{1 - \nu_t - s_t} \right) \frac{\theta_t - 1}{\theta_t}.$$

Therefore, the balanced budget condition requires

$$-\nu \left[1 - \left(\frac{1 - \nu_t}{1 - \nu_t - s_t^F} \right) \frac{\theta_t - 1}{\theta_t} \right] + s_t^F \left[\left(\frac{1 - \nu_t}{1 - \nu_t - s_t^F} \right) \frac{\theta_t - 1}{\theta_t} \right] = 0.$$

Inserting (A10.3a) and simplifying leads to

$$1 - \frac{\theta_t - 1}{\theta_t - \kappa_t} = \left(\frac{1 - \nu_t}{\nu_t} \right) \kappa_t \frac{\theta_t - 1}{\theta_t - \kappa_t}. \qquad\qquad (A10.4)$$

Because, by assumption, $\nu = 0.50$, (A10.4) implies

$$\kappa_t = \frac{1}{\theta_t}.$$

$\square$

A numerical example may clarify the improvement in efficiency resulting from the combined tax and subsidy. Suppose that $\theta_t = 3$ with a markup of 1.5 and a price distortion before the tax and subsidy of $(\theta_t - 1)/\theta_t = 0.67$. After the tax of 0.50 and maximal subsidy, the resulting distortion is:

$$\left[\left(\frac{1 - v}{1 - v - \left(\frac{1}{\theta_t}\right)\frac{1-v}{\theta_t}}\right)\frac{\theta_t - 1}{\theta_t}\right] = \frac{\theta_t}{\theta_t + 1}. \qquad (A10.5)$$

For $\theta_t = 3$, the distortion is 0.75, which is a slight improvement.

CONCLUDING REMARKS

In the 1980s the Reagan administration ushered in a new era of economic policy and social values. It rejected the egalitarian ideal of the reform movement and the New Deal that prevailed in most of the twentieth century. Instead, the Reagan era placed individual incentives and needs at its center, viewing government as an inefficient decision maker and as the source of all economic and social problems. Declaring freedom as the goal, the Reagan reforms championed individual responsibility, encouraged activity motivated by private gain and labeled collective values un-American. Elimination of business regulations and lowering of individual and corporate tax rates were cheered even by many economists who viewed them as a policy to promote economic efficiency, investments, and economic growth.

Forty years later, we know the consequence of that policy. It resulted in drastic economic inequality, a slower rate of investment, and many other negative consequences documented in this book. In this era of technological innovations and laissez-faire economic policy, America (and some other countries) has thus entered a Second Gilded Age. It has resulted in deep social divisions, the origin of which is the contrast between rising power of the wealthy and the highly educated elite, together with the falling or stagnant incomes of the massive number of the less educated Americans. Most of these are workers whose well-paying jobs were replaced either by machines or by lower-cost foreign jobs. These American workers were mostly left to fend for themselves because, after all, individual responsibility is absolute, and society does not owe them compensation for their misfortune. We have thus created a society in which a small number of people can accumulate unimaginable wealth at the expense of a large number of poor people who do not benefit from the vast gains of technology. In a democratic society, which has promised social justice and fair division of the fruits of progress, this unfair outcome has been perceived as a betrayal of the poor by the prevailing order and by the elite that has managed it. The most consequential component of this sense of betrayal is the loss of trust in democratic institutions by the less educated, who bear the brunt of the rising inequality.

The central theoretical principle developed in this book explains why the Reagan laissez-faire policy of unregulated free markets failed. That principle says that in an era of technological progress, a free-market capitalist economy perpetually creates new technological market power and, if unregulated, such power will consolidate and expand. This market power will not be eliminated by technological competition because technological competition results in one or only a few winners, whereas regular price competition results in many surviving firms. Rising technological market power causes rising inequality and depresses the shares of labor and capital in income. It also slows down investment and lowers the level of output and consumption. It is difficult to estimate the degree to which economic inequality will rise in an unregulated free-market economy, but my estimates suggest that it will cause a decline of labor and capital shares to a degree that is incompatible with democracy.

The lesson I draw from my historical study is that America has experienced in this Second Gilded Age the same social dynamics as in the First Gilded Age, when the forces of technology and policy resulted in the same outcome. Economic conditions at the end of the 19th century energized the reform movement to mobilize the institutions of democracy that ultimately led to the emergence of the generally egalitarian society of the twentieth century. Having come full circle, we are now faced with the same problems that we faced at the start of the twentieth century. Policy was focused after 1901 on eliminating the market power of trusts and other entities created by human collusion. Today we understand better the vital impact of technology on market power, and we therefore need to expand the set of public actions that can control the rise of such power in the age of technology.

Economists have studied the effect of private property and free markets on various categories of inequality among individuals, firms, or factors. Indeed, the standard free-market, competitive equilibrium model establishes a clear explanation of inequality that is compatible with economic efficiency. In contrast, the cumulative effect of technology on market power creates a different set of problems because it causes vast economic distortions, leads to economic inefficiency, and has other deep political and social consequences. Perhaps the most obvious among these is that an unregulated economy undergoing technological change cannot be a competitive economy because technological market power is durable, and technological competition does not eliminate it. Technological change in an unregulated free market economy is in conflict with perfect competition. The conflict is already clear when one considers what I would call the patent paradox. We promote innovations to improve our lives; therefore our policy supports innovators by allowing a monopoly price to be charged for an innovated product. But the more we need the product, the longer we wait to benefit from it because the initial price could be so high as to render inaccessible the exact product whose use by the public was the reason for the policy to begin with. In the case of vital medicines, this delay may become a question of life or death, and in the aggregate of all products, it is the cause of many socially harmful consequences.

The conflict noted leads to an entirely new approach to antitrust policy that this book introduces. It implies that a good policy to regulate market power must be a modification of, or an addition to, the current antitrust regime because the stated aim of the Sherman Antitrust Act of 1890 and the two laws enacted to strengthen it, the Clayton Act of 1914 and the Robinson-Patman Act of 1936, is to eradicate all restraints on trade in order to maintain the natural order of free competition. My new perspective shows that to promote innovations and allow innovators to benefit from their creativity, policy must be crafted as a compromise between two conflicting goals of promoting innovations and preventing excessive inefficiency. Or it can be framed as a compromise between equality and creative innovations. The compromise is needed because creative innovations generate rising market power that give rise to widening inequality, and suppression of such market power requires a reduction in the reward to innovations. Each society must take a stand on this trade-off that presents itself repeatedly in tax and regulatory policy that determines the reward for innovations. All policy proposals made in this book are derived from one simple principle: the aim of policy should be to establish regulations and administrative procedures to ensure that market power gained by an innovation is dissipated at the rate determined by patent law. Or policy must prevent market power from expanding beyond that level chosen by society as the appropriate level of such power needed to attain an optimal rate of innovations.

There are many economic and political forces that would oppose a policy reform. History shows that the Supreme Court will most likely be the last bastion of resistance to progress. As I have noted at various points, some of the Court's decisions demonstrate surprising ignorance of elementary economic principles. Reflecting common opinions of jurisprudence experts, many Court decisions are based on the implied but mistaken assumption that a free and unregulated market economy is inherent and deeply rooted in the U.S. Constitution. It is thus unconstitutional to introduce policies that aim to regulate the outcomes of a free-market economy.

In this book, I undertake the task of describing technological market power as an important force that economists and policymakers should consider because it shapes market structure, resource allocation, and inequality. Furthermore, the fact that technology is the ultimate cause of market power has other implications that have not been explored in this book and that should be investigated. In addition, several issues have been analyzed with insufficient data and some questions are only briefly addressed. Consequently, much research is left to be done on important issues raised here. I hope these will offer fertile grounds for young researchers and encourage them to look into those questions when seeking new ideas for their own advanced research.

BIBLIOGRAPHY

Abowd, J. M., K. L. McKinney, and N. L. Zhao. (2018). "Earnings Inequality and Mobility Trends in the United States: Nationally Representative Estimates from Longitudinally Linked Employer-Employee Data." *Journal of Labor Economics*, 36, S183–S300.

Abud, M. J., B. Hall, and C. Helmers. (2015). "An Empirical Analysis of Primary and Secondary Pharmaceutical Patents in Chile." *PLoS One*, 10, e0124257.

Acemoglu, D., U. Akcigit, H. Alp, N. Bloom, and W. Kerr. (2018). "Innovation, Reallocation, and Growth." *American Economic Review*, 108, 3450–3491.

Acemoglu, D., and D. Autor. (2011). "Skills, Tasks and Technologies: Implications for Employment and Earnings." In *Handbook of Labor Economics*, ed. by D. Card and O. Ashenfelter. Amsterdam: North-Holland, vol. 4, 1043–1171.

Acemoglu, D., S. Johnson, and J. A. Robinson. (2005). "Institutions as a Fundamental Cause of Long-Run Growth." In *Handbook of Economic Growth*, ed. by P. Aghion and S. N. Durlauf. Amsterdam: North-Holland, vol. 1, 386–472.

Acemoglu, D., A. Manera, and P. Restrepo. (2020). "Does the US Tax Code Favor Automation?" NBER Working Paper 27052, National Bureau of Economic Research.

Acemoglu, D., S. Naidu, P. Restrepo, and J. A. Robinson. (2019). "Democracy Does Cause Growth." *Journal of Political Economy*, 127, 47–100.

Acemoglu, D., and P. Restrepo. (2018a). "Modeling Automation." *AEA Papers and Proceedings*, 108, 48–53.

——. (2018b). "The Race Between Man and Machine: Implications of Technology for Growth, Factor Shares, and Employment." *American Economic Review*, 108, 1488–1542.

——. (2019). "Automation and New Tasks: How Technology Displaces and Reinstates Labor." *Journal of Economic Perspectives*, 33, 3–30.

——. (2020). "Robots and Jobs: Evidence from US Labor Markets." *Journal of Political Economy*, 128, 2188–2244.

Acemoglu, D., and J. A. Robinson. (2001). "A Theory of Political Transitions." *American Economic Review*, 91, 938–963.

——. (2006). *Economic Origins of Dictatorship and Democracy.* Cambridge: Cambridge University Press.

——. (2012). *Why Nations Fail: The Origins of Power, Prosperity, and Poverty.* New York: Crown Business.

Advanced Micro Devices (AMD) v. Intel. (2007). 496 F. Supp. 2d, 404, (D. Del.).

Aghion, P., U. Akcigit, and P. Howitt. (2014). "What Do We Learn from Schumpeterian Growth Theory?" In *Handbook of Economic Growth,* ed. by P. Aghion and S. N. Durlauf. Amsterdam: North-Holland, vol. 2, 515–563.

Aghion, P., A. Dechezleprêtre, D. Hémous, R. Martin, and J. Van Reenen. (2016). "Carbon Taxes, Path Dependency, and Directed Technical Change: Evidence from the Auto Industry." *Journal of Political Economy,* 124, 1–51.

Aghion, P., C. Harris, P. Howitt, and J. Vickers. (2001). "Competition, Imitation and Growth with Step-by-Step Innovation." *The Review of Economic Studies,* 68, 467–492.

Aghion, P., and P. Howitt. (1992). "A Model of Growth Through Creative Destruction." *Econometrica,* 60, 323–351.

——. (1996). "Research and Development in the Growth Process." *Journal of Economic Growth,* 1, 49–73.

——. (2008). *The Economics of Growth.* Cambridge, MA: MIT Press.

Akcigit, U., J. Grigsby, T. Nicholas, and S. Stantcheva. (2018). "Taxation and Innovation in the 20th Century." NBER Working Paper 24982, National Bureau of Economic Research.

Akcigit, U., and S. Stantcheva. (2020). "Taxation and Innovation: What Do We Know?" NBER Working Paper 27109, National Bureau of Economic Research.

Akerlof, G. A. (1982). "Labor Contracts as Partial Gift Exchange." *The Quarterly Journal of Economics,* 97, 543–569.

Allcott, H., L. Braghieri, S. Eichmeyer, and M. Gentzkow. (2020). "The Welfare Effects of Social Media." *American Economic Review,* 110, 629–76.

Allegretto, S., and M. Reich. (2018). "Are Local Minimum Wages Absorbed by Price Increases? Estimates from Internet-Based Restaurant Menus." *Industrial and Labor Relations Review,* 71, 35–63.

Allison, P. D., and J. A. Stewart. (1974). "Productivity Differences Among Scientists: Evidence for Accumulative Advantage." *American Sociological Review,* 39, 596–606.

Alm, R., and W. M. Cox. (1996). "The Economy at Light Speed: Technology and Growth in the Information Age and Beyond." *Annual Report of the Federal Reserve Bank of Dallas,* 2–17.

Andrews, D., C. Criscuolo, and P. N. Gal. (2016). "The Best Versus the Rest: The Global Productivity Slowdown, Divergence Across Firms and the Role of Public Policy." OECD Productivity Working Paper 5, OECD Publishing.

Appalachian Coals, Inc. v. United States. (1933). 288 U.S. 344.

Armstrong, M. (2006). "Competition in Two-Sided Markets." *RAND Journal of Economics,* 37, 668–691.

Arrow, K. (1962). "Economic Welfare and the Allocation of Resources for Invention." In *The Rate and Direction of Inventive Activity: Economic and Social Factors,* ed. by R. Nelson. Princeton, NJ: Princeton University Press, 609–626.

Arrow, K., and M. Kurz. (1970). *Public Investment, the Rate of Return, and Optimal Fiscal Policy.* Baltimore: Johns Hopkins University Press.

Arthur, W. B. (1989). "Competing Technologies, Increasing Returns, and Lock-In by Historical Events." *The Economic Journal,* 99, 116–131.

Atkinson, A. B., T. Piketty, and E. Saez. (2011). "Top Incomes in the Long Run of History." *Journal of Economic Literature,* 49, 3–71.

Auer, D., and N. Petit. (2015). "Two-Sided Markets and the Challenge of Turning Economic Theory into Antitrust Policy." *The Antitrust Bulletin,* 60, 426–461.

Aumann, R. J., and M. Kurz. (1977). "Power and Taxes." *Econometrica*, 45, 1137–1161.

Austin, B., E. Glaeser, and L. Summers. (2018). "Jobs for the Heartland: Place-Based Policies in 21st-Century America." *Brookings Papers on Economic Activity*, 151–255.

Autor, D. (2014). "Skills, Education, and the Rise of Earnings Inequality Among the 'Other 99 Percent.'" *Science*, 344, 843–851.

Autor, D., D. Dorn, L. F. Katz, C. Patterson, and J. Van Reenen. (2020). "The Fall of the Labor Share and the Rise of Superstar Firms." *The Quarterly Journal of Economics*, 135, 645–709.

Autor, D., L. F. Katz, and A. B. Krueger. (1998). "Computing Inequality: Have Computers Changed the Labor Market?" *The Quarterly Journal of Economics*, 113, 1169–1213.

Autor, D., F. Levy, and R. J. Murnane. (2003). "The Skill Content of Recent Technological Change: An Empirical Exploration." *The Quarterly Journal of Economics*, 118, 1279–1333.

Autor, D., A. Li, and M. Notowidigdo. (2019). "Preparing for the Work of the Future: A Research Agenda." Report, J-PAL: North America.

Autor, D., and D. Dorn. (2013). "The Growth of Low-Skill Service Jobs and the Polarization of the US Labor Market." *American Economic Review*, 103, 1553–97.

Avi-Yonah, R. S., K. A. Clausing, and M. C. Durst. (2008). "Allocating Business Profits for Tax Purposes: A Proposal to Adopt a Formulary Profit Split." *Florida Tax Review*, 9, 497–554.

Azar, J., E. Huet-Vaughn, I. Marinescu, B. Taska, and T. Von Wachter. (2019). "Minimum Wage Employment Effects and Labor Market Concentration." NBER Working Paper 26101, National Bureau of Economic Research.

Azar, J., S. Raina, and M. Schmalz. (2022). "Ultimate Ownership and Bank Competition." *Financial Management*, 51, 227–269.

Azar, J., M. C. Schmalz, and I. Tecu. (2018). "Anticompetitive Effects of Common Ownership." *The Journal of Finance*, 73, 1513–1565.

Bach, L., L. E. Calvet, and P. Sodini. (2020). "Rich Pickings? Risk, Return, and Skill in Household Wealth." *American Economic Review*, 110, 2703–47.

Bain, J. S. (1956). *Barriers to New Competition*. Cambridge, MA: Harvard University Press.

Baker, R. B., C. Frydman, and E. Hilt. (2018). "Political Discretion and Antitrust Policy: Evidence from the Assassination of President McKinley." NBER Working Paper 25237, National Bureau of Economic Research.

Banerjee, A. V. (1992). "A Simple Model of Herd Behavior." *The Quarterly Journal of Economics*, 107, 797–817.

Barkai, S. (2020). "Declining Labor and Capital Shares." *The Journal of Finance*, 75, 2421–2463.

Barkai, S., and S. G. Benzell. (2018). "70 Years of US Corporate Profits." New Working Paper Series 22, Stigler Center for the Study of the Economy and the State.

Barro, R. J., and X. Sala-I-Martin. (1992). "Convergence." *Journal of Political Economy*, 100, 223–251.

Barsky, R. B., and J. B. De Long. (1991). "Forecasting Pre-World War I Inflation: The Fisher Effect and the Gold Standard." *The Quarterly Journal of Economics*, 106, 815–836.

Basu, S., J. G. Fernald, and M. S. Kimball. (2006). "Are Technology Improvements Contractionary?" *American Economic Review*, 96, 1418–1448.

Bebchuk, L. A., R. Kraakman, and G. Triantis. (2000). "Stock Pyramids, Cross-Ownership, and Dual Class Equity." In *Concentrated Corporate Ownership*, ed. by R. K. Morck. Chicago: University of Chicago Press, 295–318.

Becker, G. S. (1964). *Human Capital: A Theoretical and Empirical Analysis, with Special Reference to Education*. Chicago: University of Chicago Press.

Bell, L. (1891). "Electricity as the Rival of Steam." *Electrical World*, 17, 212–227.

Benhabib, J., A. Bisin, and M. Luo. (2017). "Earnings Inequality and Other Determinants of Wealth Inequality." *American Economic Review*, 107, 593–97.

Benhabib, J., A. Bisin, and S. Zhu. (2011). "The Distribution of Wealth and Fiscal Policy in Economies with Finitely Lived Agents." *Econometrica*, 79, 123–157.

Benmelech, E., N. K. Bergman, and H. Kim. (2018). "Strong Employers and Weak Employees: How Does Employer Concentration Affect Wages?" NBER working paper W24307.

Bergeaud, A., G. Cette, and R. Lecat. (2016). "Productivity Trends in Advanced Countries Between 1890 and 2012." *Review of Income and Wealth*, 62, 420–444.

Berger, D. W., K. F. Herkenhoff, and S. Mongey. (2019). "Labor Market Power." NBER Working Paper 25719, National Bureau of Economic Research.

Bergman, P., R. Chetty, S. DeLuca, N. Hendren, L. F. Katz, and C. Palmer. (2019). "Creating Moves to Opportunity: Experimental Evidence on Barriers to Neighborhood Choice." NBER Working Paper 26164, National Bureau of Economic Research.

Bessen, J. (2020). "Industry Concentration and Information Technology." *The Journal of Law and Economics*, 63, 531–555.

Bessen, J. E. (2016). "Accounting for Rising Corporate Profits: Intangibles or Regulatory Rents?" Law and Economics Research Paper 16-18, Boston University School of Law.

Bewley, T. F. (1999). *Why Wages Don't Fall During a Recession*. Cambridge, MA: Harvard University Press.

Binder, C. C. (2016). "Estimation of Historical Inflation Expectations." *Explorations in Economic History*, 61, 1–31.

Blind, K., K. Cremers, and E. Mueller. (2009). "The Influence of Strategic Patenting on Companies' Patent Portfolios." *Research Policy*, 38, 428–436.

Block, F. (2008). "Swimming Against the Current: The Rise of a Hidden Developmental State in the United States." *Politics & Society*, 36, 169–206.

———. (2015). "Innovation and the Invisible Hand of Government." In *State of Innovation: The U.S. Government's Role in Technology Development*, ed. by F. L. Block and M. R. Keller. New York: Routledge, 9–34.

Block, F., and M. R. Keller. (2015). *State of Innovation: The U.S. Government's Role in Technology Development*. New York: Routledge.

Block, S., and B. Sachs. (2020). "Clean Slate for Worker Power: Building a Just Economy and Democracy." Labor and Worklife Program, Harvard Law School.

Boldrin, M., and D. K. Levine. (2013). "The Case Against Patents." *Journal of Economic Perspectives*, 27, 3–22.

Bork, R. (1978). *The Antitrust Paradox*. New York: The Free Press.

Bottomley, S. (2019). "The Returns to Invention During the British Industrial Revolution." *The Economic History Review*, 72, 510–530.

Brainard, W. C., and J. Tobin. (1968). "Pitfalls in Financial Model Building." *American Economic Review*, 58, 99–122.

Brakman, S., and B. J. Heijdra. (2001). *The Monopolistic Competition Revolution in Retrospect*. Cambridge: Cambridge University Press.

Braun, E., and S. MacDonald. (1978). *Revolution in Miniature: The History and Impact of Semiconductor Electronics*. Cambridge: Cambridge University Press.

Bresnahan, T. F., and D. M. Raff. (1991). "Intra-Industry Heterogeneity and the Great Depression: The American Motor Vehicles Industry, 1929–1935." *The Journal of Economic History*, 51, 317–331.

Bresnahan, T. F., and M. Trajtenberg. (1995). "General Purpose Technologies 'Engines of Growth'?" *Journal of Econometrics*, 65, 83–108.

Bridgman, B. (2018). "Is Labor's Loss Capital's Gain? Gross Versus Net Labor Shares." *Macroeconomic Dynamics*, 22, 2070–2087.

Brinkley, A. (1996). *The End of Reform: New Deal Liberalism in Recession and War*. New York: Vintage.

Brülhart, M., J. Gruber, M. Krapf, and K. Schmidheiny. (2019). "Behavioral Responses to Wealth Taxes: Evidence from Switzerland." CESifo Working Paper 7908.

Brynjolfsson, E., and A. McAfee. (2014). *The Second Machine Age: Work, Progress, and Prosperity in a Time of Brilliant Technologies*. New York: Norton.

Bureau of the Census. (1989). *Bicentennial Edition: Historical Statistics of the United States, Colonial Times to 1970*. Washington, DC: U.S. Government Printing Office.

Bush, V. (1945). "Science: The Endless Frontier." Report to the President by Director of the Office of Scientific Research and Development. Washington, DC: U.S. Government Printing Office.

Caillaud, B., and B. Jullien. (2003). "Chicken & Egg: Competition Among Intermediation Service Providers." *RAND Journal of Economics*, 34, 309–328.

Card, D., and J. E. DiNardo. (2002). "Skill-Biased Technological Change and Rising Wage Inequality: Some Problems and Puzzles." *Journal of Labor Economics*, 20, 733–783.

Case, A., and A. Deaton. (2020). *Deaths of Despair and the Future of Capitalism*. Princeton, NJ: Princeton University Press.

CBO. (2019). *The Effects on Employment and Family Income of Increasing the Federal Minimum Wage*. Washington, DC: Congressional Budget Office.

Cengiz, D., A. Dube, A. Lindner, and B. Zipperer. (2019). "The Effect of Minimum Wages on Low-Wage Jobs." *The Quarterly Journal of Economics*, 134, 1405–1454.

Cette, G., J. Lopez, and J. Mairesse. (2016). "Market Regulations, Prices, and Productivity." *American Economic Review*, 106, 104–08.

Chamley, C. (1986). "Optimal Taxation of Capital Income in General Equilibrium with Infinite Lives." *Econometrica*, 54, 607–622.

Chari, V. V., and H. Hopenhayn. (1991). "Vintage Human Capital, Growth, and the Diffusion of New Technology." *Journal of Political Economy*, 99, 1142–1165.

Chatterjee, S., and R. Cooper. (1993). "Entry and Exit, Product Variety and the Business Cycle." NBER Working Paper 4562, National Bureau of Economic Research.

Chen, C., and O. L. Mangasarian. (1996). "A Class of Smoothing Functions for Nonlinear and Mixed Complementarity Problems." *Computational Optimization and Applications*, 5, 97–138.

Chetty, R., J. N. Friedman, N. Hendren, M. R. Jones, and S. R. Porter. (2018). "The Opportunity Atlas: Mapping the Childhood Roots of Social Mobility." NBER Working Paper 25147, National Bureau of Economic Research.

Chetty, R., and N. Hendren. (2018). "The Impacts of Neighborhoods on Intergenerational Mobility I: Childhood Exposure Effects." *The Quarterly Journal of Economics*, 133, 1107–1162.

Chetty, R., N. Hendren, P. Kline, and E. Saez. (2014). "Where Is the Land of Opportunity? The Geography of Intergenerational Mobility in the United States." *The Quarterly Journal of Economics*, 129, 1553–1623.

Christensen, C. M. (1997). *The Innovator's Dilemma: When New Technologies Cause Great Firms to Fail*. Cambridge, MA: Harvard Business Review Press.

Chyn, E. (2018). "Moved to Opportunity: The Long-Run Effects of Public Housing Demolition on Children." *American Economic Review*, 108, 3028–56.

Citizens United v. Federal Election Commission. (2010). *558 U.S. 310*.

Clausing, K. A. (2016). "The U.S. State Experience Under Formulary Apportionment: Are There Lessons for International Reform?" *National Tax Journal*, 69, 353–385.

Clausing, K. A., E. Saez, and G. Zucman. (2020). "Ending Corporate Tax Avoidance and Tax Competition: A Plan to Collect the Tax Deficit of Multinationals." Law-Econ Research Paper 20-12, UCLA School of Law.

Cobb, C. W., and P. H. Douglas. (1928). "A Theory of Production." *American Economic Review*, 18, 139–165.

Coleman, J. S., E. Katz, and H. Menzel. (1966). *Medical Innovation: A Diffusion Study.* Indianapolis, IN: Bobbs-Merrill.

Collins, B., A. Garin, E. Jackson, D. Koustas, and M. Payne. (2019). "Is Gig Work Replacing Traditional Employment? Evidence from Two Decades of Tax Returns." Working Paper, IRS SOI Joint Statistical Research Program.

Colvin, A., and H. Shierholz. (2019). "Noncompete Agreements." Economic Policy Institute Report 179414.

Comin, D., and B. Hobijn. (2010). "An Exploration of Technology Diffusion." *American Economic Review*, 100, 2031–59.

Comin, D., and M. Mestieri. (2014). "Technology Diffusion: Measurement, Causes, and Consequences." In *Handbook of Economic Growth*, ed. by P. Aghion and S. N. Durlauf. Amsterdam: North-Holland, vol. 2, 565–622.

——. (2018). "If Technology Has Arrived Everywhere, Why Has Income Diverged?" *American Economic Journal: Macroeconomics*, 10, 137–78.

Cooper, D., M. J. Luengo-Prado, and J. A. Parker. (2020). "The Local Aggregate Effects of Minimum Wage Increases." *Journal of Money, Credit and Banking*, 52, 5–35.

Cornelli, F., and M. Schankerman. (1999). "Patent Renewals and R&D Incentives." *RAND Journal of Economics*, 30, 197–213.

Costinot, A., and I. Werning. (2018). "Robots, Trade, and Luddism: A Sufficient Statistic Approach to Optimal Technology Regulation." NBER Working Paper 25103, National Bureau of Economic Research.

Crabbe, L. (1989). "The International Gold Standard and US Monetary Policy from World War I to the New Deal." *Federal Reserve Bulletin*, 75, 423–440.

Crystal, M., N. Gandal, R. Shilony, and M. Shur-Ofry. (2019). "Out of Sight: A Study of Uncited Patents." CEPR Discussion Paper 13982, Center for Economic Policy and Research.

Cummings, K. (2002). "Nobel Science Prizes in Industry: The Promise and the Challenge of Science in the 'Real World.'" Unpublished paper, Vanderbilt University.

Cunningham, C., F. Ederer, and S. Ma. (2021). "Killer Acquisitions." *Journal of Political Economy*, 129, 649–702.

Dafoe, A. (2018). "AI Governance: A Research Agenda." Report, Centre for the Governance of AI, Future of Humanity Institute, University of Oxford.

David, P. A. (1985). "Clio and the Economics of QWERTY." *American Economic Review*, 75, 332–337.

——. (1989). "Computer and Dynamo: The Modern Productivity Paradox in a Not-Too Distant Mirror." The Warwick Economics Research Paper Series (TWERPS) 339, University of Warwick, Department of Economics.

——. (1990a). "The Dynamo and the Computer: An Historical Perspective on the Modern Productivity Paradox." *American Economic Review*, 80, 355–361.

——. (1990b). "General Purpose Engines, Investment, and Productivity Growth from the Dynamo Revolution to the Computer Revolution." In *Technology and Investment: Crucial Issues for the 1990s*, ed. by E. Deiaco, E. Hornell, and G. Vickery. London: Pinter, 141–154.

——. (2000). "Understanding Digital Technology's Evolution and the Path of Measured Productivity Growth: Present and Future in the Mirror of the Past." In *Understanding the Digital Economy: Data, Tools and Research*, ed. by E. Brynjolfsson and B. Kahin. Cambridge, MA: MIT Press, 49–95.

David, P. A., and P. Solar. (1977). "A Bicentenary Contribution to the History of the Cost of Living in America." *Research in Economic History*, 2, 1–80.

David, P. A., and G. Wright. (1999). "Early Twentieth Century Productivity Growth Dynamics: An Inquiry into the Economic History of 'Our Ignorance.'" Discussion Paper in Economic and Social History 33, University of Oxford.

———. (2004). "General Purpose Technologies and Productivity Surges: Historical Reflections on the Future of the ICT Revolution." In *The Economic Future in Historical Perspective*, ed. by P. A. David and M. Thomas. Oxford: Oxford University Press.

Davies, S. (1979). *The Diffusion of Process Innovations*. Cambridge: Cambridge University Press.

De Loecker, J., J. Eeckhout, and G. Unger. (2020). "The Rise of Market Power and the Macroeconomic Implications." *The Quarterly Journal of Economics*, 135, 561–644.

De Loecker, J., P. K. Goldberg, A. K. Khandelwal, and N. Pavcnik. (2016). "Prices, Markups, and Trade Reform." *Econometrica*, 84, 445–510.

De Rassenfosse, G., and A. B. Jaffe. (2018). "Are Patent Fees Effective at Weeding out Low-Quality Patents?" *Journal of Economics & Management Strategy*, 27, 134–148.

Derenoncourt, E., and C. Montialoux. (2021). "Minimum Wages and Racial Inequality." *The Quarterly Journal of Economics*, 136, 169–228.

De Simone, L., R. Lester, and K. Markle. (2020). "Transparency and Tax Evasion: Evidence from the Foreign Account Tax Compliance Act (FATCA)." *Journal of Accounting Research*, 58, 105–153.

Devine, W. D. (1983). "From Shafts to Wires: Historical Perspective on Electrification." *The Journal of Economic History*, 43, 347–372.

Diamond, P. A. (1965). "National Debt in a Neoclassical Growth Model." *American Economic Review*, 55, 1126–1150.

———. (1998). "Optimal Income Taxation: An Example with a U-Shaped Pattern of Optimal Marginal Tax Rates." *American Economic Review*, 88, 83–95.

Diamond, P. A., and J. Banks. (2010). "The Base for Direct Taxation." In *Dimensions of Tax Design: The Mirrlees Review*, ed. by J. A. Mirrlees, S. Adam, T. J. Besley, R. Blundell, S. Bond, R. Chote, M. Gammie, P. Johnson, G. D. Myles, and J. M. Poterba. Oxford: Oxford University Press, 548–648.

Diamond, P. A., and E. Saez. (2011). "The Case for a Progressive Tax: From Basic Research to Policy Recommendations." *Journal of Economic Perspectives*, 25, 165–90.

DiPrete, T. A., and G. M. Eirich. (2006). "Cumulative Advantage as a Mechanism for Inequality: A Review of Theoretical and Empirical Developments." *Annual Review of Sociology*, 32, 271–297.

Dixit, A. K., and J. E. Stiglitz. (1977). "Monopolistic Competition and Optimum Product Diversity." *American Economic Review*, 67, 297–308.

Dube, A. (2019). "Using Wage Boards to Raise Pay." Policy Brief 4, Economists for Inclusive Prosperity.

Dube, A., J. Jacobs, S. Naidu, and S. Suri. (2020). "Monopsony in Online Labor Markets." *American Economic Review: Insights*, 2, 33–46.

Dube, A., and E. Kaplan. (2010). "Does Outsourcing Reduce Wages in the Low-Wage Service Occupations? Evidence from Janitors and Guards." *Industrial and Labor Relations Review*, 63, 287–306.

Dube, A., T. W. Lester, and M. Reich. (2016). "Minimum Wage Shocks, Employment Flows, and Labor Market Frictions." *Journal of Labor Economics*, 34, 663–704.

Du Boff, R. B. (1979). *Electric Power in American Manufacturing, 1889–1958*. New York: Arno Press.

Duran-Cabré, J. M., A. Esteller-Moré, and M. Mas-Montserrat. (2019). "Behavioural Responses to the (Re)Introduction of Wealth Taxes: Evidence from Spain." Working papers 2019/04, Institut d'Economia de Barcelona (IEB).

Economides, N. (1989). "Desirability of Compatibility in the Absence of Network Externalities." *American Economic Review*, 79, 1165–1181.

Égert, B. (2016). "Regulation, Institutions, and Productivity: New Macroeconomic Evidence from OECD Countries." *American Economic Review*, 106, 109–13.

Eggenberger, F., and G. Pólya. (1923). "Über die Statistik verketteter Vorgänge." *ZAMM— Journal of Applied Mathematics and Mechanics/Zeitschrift für Angewandte Mathematik und Mechanik*, 3, 279–289.

Eggertsson, G. B., J. A. Robbins, and E. G. Wold. (2018). "Kaldor and Piketty's Facts: The Rise of Monopoly Power in the United States." NBER Working Paper 24287, National Bureau of Economic Research.

Egghe, L., and R. Rousseau. (1995). "Generalized Success-Breeds-Success Principle Leading to Time-Dependent Informetric Distributions." *Journal of the American Society for Information Science*, 46, 426–445.

Eichengreen, B. (1989). "The Capital Levy in Theory and Practice." NBER Working Paper 3096, National Bureau of Economic Research.

Eichner, T., and M. Runkel. (2008). "Why the European Union Should Adopt Formula Apportionment with a Sales Factor." *Scandinavian Journal of Economics*, 110, 567–589.

Eisfeldt, A. L., and D. Papanikolaou. (2013). "Organization Capital and the Cross-Section of Expected Returns." *The Journal of Finance*, 68, 1365–1406.

Elsby, M. W., B. Hobijn, and A. Şahin. (2013). "The Decline of the US Labor Share." *Brookings Papers on Economic Activity*, Fall 2013, 1–63.

Ethier, W. J. (1982). "National and International Returns to Scale in the Modern Theory of International Trade." *American Economic Review*, 72, 389–405.

Evans, P. (1996). "Using Cross-Country Variances to Evaluate Growth Theories." *Journal of Economic Dynamics and Control*, 20, 1027–1049.

Fagereng, A., L. Guiso, D. Malacrino, and L. Pistaferri. (2020). "Heterogeneity and Persistence in Returns to Wealth." *Econometrica*, 88, 115–170.

Farhi, E., and F. Gourio. (2018, Fall). "Accounting for Macro-Finance Trends: Market Power, Intangibles, and Risk Premia." *Brookings Papers on Economic Activity*, 147–250.

Feldman, R. (2008). "Patent and Antitrust: Differing Shades of Meaning." *Virginia Journal of Law and Technology*, 13, 1–20.

Feng, J., and X. Jaravel. (2020). "Crafting Intellectual Property Rights: Implications for Patent Assertion Entities, Litigation, and Innovation." *American Economic Journal: Applied Economics*, 12, 140–181.

Field, A. J. (2006). "Technological Change and US Productivity Growth in the Interwar Years." *The Journal of Economic History*, 66, 203–236.

Fisher, I. (1930). *Theory of Interest: As Determined by Impatience to Spend Income and Opportunity to Invest It*. Clifton, NY: Macmillan.

Fleck, D. L. (2009). *The Building and Development of the American Electrical Manufacturing Industry and Its Top Two Companies—General Electric & Westinghouse*. No. 388 in Relatórios COPPEAD. Rio de Janeiro: UFRJ COPPEAD.

Forlani, E., R. Martin, G. Mion, and M. Muûls. (2016). "Unraveling Firms: Demand, Productivity and Markups Heterogeneity." CEPR Discussion Paper 11058, Center for Economic Policy and Research.

Foster, L., J. Haltiwanger, and C. J. Krizan. (2001). "Aggregate Productivity Growth: Lessons from Microeconomic Evidence." In *New Developments in Productivity Analysis*, ed. by C. R. Hulten, E. R. Dean, and M. J. Harper. Chicago: University of Chicago Press, 303–372.

Foster, L., J. Haltiwanger, and C. Syverson. (2008). "Reallocation, Firm Turnover, and Efficiency: Selection on Productivity or Profitability?" *American Economic Review*, 98, 394–425.

Fouquet, R. (2014). "Long-Run Demand for Energy Services: Income and Price Elasticities over Two Hundred Years." *Review of Environmental Economics and Policy*, 8, 186–207.

Fouquet, R., and P. J. Pearson. (2012). "The Long Run Demand for Lighting: Elasticities and Rebound Effects in Different Phases of Economic Development." *Economics of Energy & Environmental Policy*, 1, 83–100.

Frakes, M. D., and M. F. Wasserman. (2015). "Does the US Patent and Trademark Office Grant Too Many Bad Patents: Evidence from a Quasi-Experiment." *Stanford Law Review*, 67, 613–676.

——. (2017). "Is the Time Allocated to Review Patent Applications Inducing Examiners to Grant Invalid Patents? Evidence from Microlevel Application Data." *The Review of Economics and Statistics*, 99, 550–563.

Frank, R. H. (2008). "Should Public Policy Respond to Positional Externalities?" *Journal of Public Economics*, 92, 1777–1786.

Freeman, C., and C. Perez. (1986). "The Diffusion of Technical Innovations and Changes of Techno-economic Paradigm." Presentation, The Conference on Innovation Diffusion, Venice.

Frey, C. B. (2019). *The Technology Trap*. Princeton, NJ: Princeton University Press.

Friedman, M. (1962). *Capitalism and Freedom*. Chicago: University of Chicago Press.

——. (1970). "The Social Responsibility of Business Is to Increase Its Profits." *New York Times Magazine*, SM17, September 13.

——. (1999). "The Business Community's Suicidal Impulse." *Cato Policy Report*, 21, 6–7.

Friedman, M., and A. J. Schwartz. (1963). *A Monetary History of the United States, 1867–1960*. Princeton, NJ: Princeton University Press.

Fuchs, E. R. H. (2010). "Rethinking the Role of the State in Technology Development: DARPA and the Case for Embedded Network Governance." *Research Policy*, 39, 1133–1147.

Gabaix, X. (2009). "Power Laws in Economics and Finance." *Annual Review of Economics*, 1, 255–294.

Gabaix, X., J.-M. Lasry, P.-L. Lions, and B. Moll. (2016). "The Dynamics of Inequality." *Econometrica*, 84, 2071–2111.

Gal, M. S. (2013). "Abuse of Dominance—Exploitative Abuses." In *Handbook on European Competition Law*, ed. by I. Lianos and D. Geradin. Cheltenham: Edward Elgar Publishing, 385–422.

Garcia-Macia, D., C.-T. Hsieh, and P. J. Klenow. (2019). "How Destructive Is Innovation?" *Econometrica*, 87, 1507–1541.

Gates, B. (1995). "The Internet Tidal Wave." Internal memorandum, Microsoft Corporation.

Geroski, P. A. (2000). "Models of Technology Diffusion." *Research Policy*, 29, 603–625.

Gibson, M. (2021). "Policy Brief: Employer Market Power in Silicon Valley." IZA Policy Paper 182, Institute of Labor Economics (IZA).

Gilbert, R. J., and D. M. Newbery. (1982). "Preemptive Patenting and the Persistence of Monopoly." *American Economic Review*, 72, 514–526.

Giuri, P., M. Mariani, S. Brusoni, G. Crespi, D. Francoz, A. Gambardella, W. Garcia-Fontes, A. Geuna, R. Gonzales, D. Harhoff, K. Hoisl, C. Le Bas, A. Luzzi, L. Magazzini, L. Nesta, Ö. Nomaler, N. Palomeras, P. Patel, M. Romanelli, and B. Verspagen. (2007). "Inventors and Invention Processes in Europe: Results from the PatVal-EU Survey." *Research Policy*, 36, 1107–1127.

Godøy, A., and M. Reich. (2021). "Are Minimum Wage Effects Greater in Low-Wage Areas?" *Industrial Relations: A Journal of Economy and Society*, 60, 36–83.

Goldin, C., and L. F. Katz. (1998). "The Origins of Technology-Skill Complementarity." *The Quarterly Journal of Economics*, 113, 693–732.

———. (2010). *The Race Between Education and Technology*. Cambridge, MA: Harvard University Press.

Goldschmidt, D., and J. F. Schmieder. (2017). "The Rise of Domestic Outsourcing and the Evolution of the German Wage Structure." *The Quarterly Journal of Economics*, 132, 1165–1217.

Goldsmith, R. W. (1955). *A Study of Saving in the United States*, vol. 2. Princeton, NJ: Princeton University Press.

Gollin, D. (2002). "Getting Income Shares Right." *Journal of Political Economy*, 110, 458–474.

Gonzalez, I., and P. Trivin. (2019). "The Global Rise of Asset Prices and the Decline of the Labor Share." SSRN Working Paper 2964329, Social Science Research Network.

Gordon, N. E., and K. J. Ruffini. (2018). "School Nutrition and Student Discipline: Effects of Schoolwide Free Meals." NBER Working Paper 24986, National Bureau of Economic Research.

Gordon, R. J. (1990). *The Measurement of Durable Goods Prices*, NBER Books. Chicago: University of Chicago Press.

———. (2017). *The Rise and Fall of American Growth*. Princeton, NJ: Princeton University Press.

Gort, M., and S. Klepper. (1982). "Time Paths in the Diffusion of Product Innovations." *The Economic Journal*, 92, 630–653.

Greenwood, J., and B. Jovanovic. (1999). "The Information-Technology Revolution and the Stock Market." *American Economic Review*, 89, 116–122.

Gregory, V. (2020). "Firms as Learning Environments: Implications for Earnings Dynamics and Job Search." Working Paper 2020-036B, Federal Reserve Bank of St. Louis.

Greif, A. (2006). *Institutions and the Path to the Modern Economy: Lessons from Medieval Trade*. Cambridge: Cambridge University Press.

Griliches, Z. (1957). "Hybrid Corn: An Exploration in the Economics of Technological Change." *Econometrica*, 25, 501–522.

———. (1969). "Capital-Skill Complementarity." *The Review of Economics and Statistics*, 51, 465–468.

———. (1987). "R&D and Productivity: Measurement Issues and Econometric Results." *Science*, 237, 31–35.

———. (1994). "Productivity, R&D, and the Data Constraint." *American Economic Review*, 84, 1–23.

Gross, D. P., and B. N. Sampat. (2020). "Inventing the Endless Frontier: The Effects of the World War II Research Effort on Post-war Innovation." NBER Working Paper 27375, National Bureau of Economic Research.

Grossman, G. M., and E. Helpman. (1991). *Innovation and Growth in the Global Economy*. Cambridge, MA: MIT Press.

Grossman, S. J., and J. E. Stiglitz. (1980). "On the Impossibility of Informationally Efficient Markets." *American Economic Review*, 70, 393–408.

Grullon, G., Y. Larkin, and R. Michaely. (2019). "Are US Industries Becoming More Concentrated?" *Review of Finance*, 23, 697–743.

Gutiérrez, G., and T. Philippon. (2016). "Investment-less Growth: An Empirical Investigation." NBER Working Paper 22897, National Bureau of Economic Research.

———. (2017a). "Comments on 'The Rise of Market Power and the Macroeconomic Implications by De Loecker and Eeckhout.'" Working Paper, New York University.

———. (2017b). "Declining Competition and Investment in the US." NBER Working Paper 23583, National Bureau of Economic Research.

———. (2018). "How EU Markets Became More Competitive Than US Markets: A Study of Institutional Drift." CEPR Discussion Paper 12983, Center for Economic Policy and Research.

——. (2019). "The Failure of Free Entry." NBER Working Paper 26001, National Bureau of Economic Research.

Hall, B. H. (2005). "Measuring the Returns to R&D: The Depreciation Problem." In *Contributions in Memory of Zvi Griliches*, ed. by J. Mairesse and M. Trajtenberg. Cambridge: Annales d'Economie et de Statistique, vol. 79–80, 341–381.

Hall, B. H., A. Jaffe, and M. Trajtenberg. (2005). "Market Value and Patent Citations." *RAND Journal of Economics*, 36, 16–38.

Hall, B. H., J. Mairesse, and P. Mohnen. (2010). "Measuring the Returns to R&D." In *Handbook of the Economics of Innovation*, ed. by B. Hall and N. Rosenberg. Amsterdam: North-Holland, vol. 2, 1033–1082.

Hall, R. E. (1988). "The Relation Between Price and Marginal Cost in U.S. Industry." *Journal of Political Economy*, 96, 921–947.

——. (2001). "The Stock Market and Capital Accumulation." *American Economic Review*, 91, 1185–1202.

——. (2018). "Using Empirical Marginal Cost to Measure Market Power in the US Economy." NBER Working Paper 25251, National Bureau of Economic Research.

Hall, R. E., and D. W. Jorgenson. (1967). "Tax Policy and Investment Behavior." *American Economic Review*, 57, 391–414.

Haltiwanger, J. C. (1997). "Measuring and Analyzing Aggregate Fluctuations: The Importance of Building from Microeconomic Evidence." *Federal Reserve Bank of St. Louis Review*, 79, 55–78.

Hammond, J. W. (1941). *Men and Volts; The Story of General Electric*. Philadelphia: J. B. Lippincott.

Hansen, L. P., J. C. Heaton, and N. Li. (2009). "Intangible Risk." In *Measuring Capital in the New Economy*, ed. by C. Corrado, J. Haltiwanger, and D. Sichel. Chicago: University of Chicago Press, 111–152.

Haskel, J., and S. Westlake. (2017). *Capitalism Without Capital: The Rise of the Intangible Economy*. Princeton, NJ: Princeton University Press.

Haucap, J., and J. Stiebale. (2016). "How Mergers Affect Innovation: Theory and Evidence from the Pharmaceutical Industry." DICE Discussion Paper 218, Düsseldorf Institute for Competition Economics.

Helpman, E., and M. Trajtenberg. (1994). "A Time to Sow and a Time to Reap: Growth Based on General Purpose Technologies." NBER Working Paper 4854, National Bureau of Economic Research.

Henderson, R., D. B.-A. J. Lapore, and V. Vijayaraghavan. (2020). "The Business Case for Saving Democracy." *Harvard Business Review*, March 10.

Henderson, R. M. (2020). *Reimagining Capitalism in a World on Fire*. New York: Public Affairs.

Hendren, N., and B. Sprung-Keyser. (2020). "A Unified Welfare Analysis of Government Policies." *The Quarterly Journal of Economics*, 135, 1209–1318.

Hessels, J. H. (1911). "Johann Fust." In *Encyclopedia Britannica, Volume 11*. Cambridge: Cambridge University Press, 11th ed.

Hornstein, A. (1993). "Monopolistic Competition, Increasing Returns to Scale, and the Importance of Productivity Shocks." *Journal of Monetary Economics*, 31, 299–316.

Hounshell, D. A., J. K. Smith, and J. V. Smith. (1988). *Science and Corporate Strategy: Du Pont R and D, 1902–1980*. Cambridge: Cambridge University Press.

Howitt, P. (1999). "Steady Endogenous Growth with Population and R. & D. Inputs Growing." *Journal of Political Economy*, 107, 715–730.

——. (2000). "Endogenous Growth and Cross-Country Income Differences." *American Economic Review*, 90, 829–846.

Hulten, C. R., and X. Hao. (2008). "What Is a Company Really Worth? Intangible Capital and The 'Market to Book Value' Puzzle." NBER Working Paper 14548, National Bureau of Economic Research.

Hunt, R. M. (2004). "Patentability, Industry Structure, and Innovation." *The Journal of Industrial Economics*, 52, 401–425.

Hunter, H. M. (1982). "The Role of Business Liquidity During the Great Depression and Afterwards: Differences Between Large and Small Firms." *The Journal of Economic History*, 42, 883–902.

ICN. (2008). "Report on Abuse of Superior Bargaining Position." In *ICN Special Program for Kyoto Annual Conference*. Kyoto: International Competitive Network Seventh Annual Conference.

Iliffe, R. (1995). "'Is He Lilke Other Men?' The Meaning of the Principia Mathematica, and the Author as Idol." In *Culture and Society in the Stuart Restoration: Literature, Drama, History*, ed. by G. MacLean. Cambridge: Cambridge University Press, 159–176.

Jackson, E., A. Looney, and S. Ramnath. (2017). "The Rise of Alternative Work Arrangements: Evidence and Implications for Tax Filing and Benefit Coverage." Working Paper 114, Office of Tax Analysis.

Jaffe, A. B., and J. Lerner. (2004). "Patent Prescription: A Radical Cure for the Ailing U.S. Patent System." *IEEE Spectrum*, 41, 38–43.

Jäger, K. (2017). "EU KLEMS Growth and Productivity Accounts 2017 Release, Statistical Module." Data Release Description, The Conference Board.

Jakobsen, K., K. Jakobsen, H. Kleven, and G. Zucman. (2020). "Wealth Taxation and Wealth Accumulation: Theory and Evidence from Denmark." *The Quarterly Journal of Economics*, 135, 329–388.

Johannesen, N., P. Langetieg, D. Reck, M. Risch, and J. Slemrod. (2020). "Taxing Hidden Wealth: The Consequences of US Enforcement Initiatives on Evasive Foreign Accounts." *American Economic Journal: Economic Policy*, 12, 312–46.

Johannesen, N., and G. Zucman. (2014). "The End of Bank Secrecy? An Evaluation of the G20 Tax Haven Crackdown." *American Economic Journal: Economic Policy*, 6, 65–91.

Johns, A. (2009). *Piracy: The Intellectual Property Wars from Gutenberg to Gates*. Chicago: University of Chicago Press.

Johns, A., and J. Slemrod. (2010). "The Distribution of Income Tax Noncompliance." *National Tax Journal*, 63, 397–418.

Johnson, N. L., and S. Kotz. (1977). *Urn Models and Their Application—An Approach to Modern Discrete Probability Theory*. New York: John Wiley.

Jones, C. I. (1995a). "R&D-Based Models of Economic Growth." *Journal of Political Economy*, 103, 759–784.

——. (1995b). "Time Series Tests of Endogenous Growth Models." *The Quarterly Journal of Economics*, 110, 495–525.

Jones, C. I., and J. Kim. (2018). "A Schumpeterian Model of Top Income Inequality." *Journal of Political Economy*, 126, 1785–1826.

Jones, C. I., and J. C. Williams. (2000). "Too Much of a Good Thing? The Economics of Investment in R&D." *Journal of Economic Growth*, 5, 65–85.

Jorgenson, D. W., M. S. Ho, and J. D. Samuels. (2019). "Educational Attainment and the Revival of US Economic Growth." In *Education, Skills, and Technical Change: Implications for Future U.S. GDP Growth*, ed. by C. R. Hulten and V. A. Ramey. Chicago: University of Chicago Press, 23–60.

Judd, K. L. (1985). "Redistributive Taxation in a Simple Perfect Foresight Model." *Journal of Public Economics*, 28, 59–83.

Jullien, B., and W. Sand-Zantman. (2021). "The Economics of Platforms: A Theory Guide for Competition Policy." *Information Economics and Policy*, 54.

Kaldor, N. (1961). "Capital Accumulation and Economic Growth." In *The Theory of Capital*, ed. by D. C. Hague. New York: Springer, 177–222.

Kalla, J. L., and D. E. Broockman. (2016). "Congressional Officials Grant Access to Individuals Because They Have Contributed to Campaigns: A Randomized Field Experiment." *American Journal of Political Science*, 60, 545–558.

Kapczynski, A. (2016). "Order Without Intellectual Property Law: Open Science in Influenza." *Cornell Law Review*, 102, 1539–1648.

Kapczynski, A., C. Park, and B. Sampat. (2012). "Polymorphs and Prodrugs and Salts (Oh My!): An Empirical Analysis of 'Secondary' Pharmaceutical Patents." *PLoS One*, 7, e49470.

Karabarbounis, L., and B. Neiman. (2014). "The Global Decline of the Labor Share." *The Quarterly Journal of Economics*, 129, 61–103.

——. (2019). "Accounting for Factorless Income." *NBER Macroeconomics Annual*, 33, 167–228.

Katsoulacos, Y., and F. Jenny. (2018). *Excessive Pricing and Competition Law Enforcement*. New York: Springer.

Katz, L. F., and A. B. Krueger. (2019). "The Rise and Nature of Alternative Work Arrangements in the United States, 1995–2015." *Industrial and Labor Relations Review*, 72, 382–416.

Kendrick, J. W. (1961). *Productivity Trends in the United States*. Princeton, NJ: Princeton University Press.

Keynes, J. M. (1936). *The General Theory of Employment, Interest, and Money*. New York: Harcourt, Brace.

——. (1939). "Relative Movements of Real Wages and Output." *The Economic Journal*, 49, 34–51.

——. (1940). *How to Pay for the War, a Radical Plan for the Chancellor of the Exchequer*. London: Macmillan.

Khan, L. M. (2016). "Amazon's Antitrust Paradox." *Yale Law Review*, 126, 710–805.

——. (2018). "The Supreme Court Just Quietly Gutted Antitrust Law." *The Big Idea, Vox*, July 3.

King, R. G., and S. T. Rebelo. (1999). "Resuscitating Real Business Cycles." In *Handbook of Macroeconomics*, ed. by J. B. Taylor and M. Woodford. Amsterdam: North-Holland, vol. 1, 927–1007.

Klette, T. J., and S. Kortum. (2004). "Innovating Firms and Aggregate Innovation." *Journal of Political Economy*, 112, 986–1018.

Kline, P., N. Petkova, H. Williams, and O. Zidar. (2019). "Who Profits from Patents? Rent-Sharing at Innovative Firms." *The Quarterly Journal of Economics*, 134, 1343–1404.

Koh, D., R. Santaeulàlia-Llopis, and Y. Zheng. (2020). "Labor Share Decline and Intellectual Property Products Capital." *Econometrica*, 88, 2609–2628.

Kopczuk, W., J. Marion, E. Muehlegger, and J. Slemrod. (2013). "Do the Laws of Tax Incidence Hold? Point of Collection and the Pass-Through of State Diesel Taxes." NBER Working Paper 19410, National Bureau of Economic Research.

Kortum, S. S. (1997). "Research, Patenting, and Technological Change." *Econometrica*, 65, 1389–1419.

Koyck, L. M. (1954). *Distributed Lags and Investment Analysis*. Amsterdam: North-Holland.

Krueger, A. B. (2017). "The Rigged Labor Market." *Milken Institute Review*, 19, 34–45.

——. (2018). "Reflections on Dwindling Worker Bargaining Power and Monetary Policy." In *Changing Market Structures and Implications for Monetary Policy*. Kansas City: Federal Reserve Bank of Kansas City, Jackson Hole Economic Policy Symposium, 267–282.

Krueger, A. B., and O. Ashenfelter. (2018). "Theory and Evidence on Employer Collusion in the Franchise Sector." NBER Working Paper 24831, National Bureau of Economic Research.

Krueger, A. B., and E. A. Posner. (2018). "A Proposal for Protecting Low-Income Workers from Monopsony and Collusion." Hamilton Project Policy Proposal 2018-05, Brookings Institution.

Krugman, P. (2019). "Notes on Excessive Wealth Disorder: How Not to Repeat the Mistakes of 2011." *New York Times*, June 22.

Krusell, P., L. E. Ohanian, J.-V. Ríos-Rull, and G. L. Violante. (2000). "Capital-Skill Complementarity and Inequality: A Macroeconomic Analysis." *Econometrica*, 68, 1029–1053.

Kurz, M. (2016). "On the Formation of Capital and Wealth." Working Paper, Stanford University.

——. (2017). "The New Monopolists." *Project Syndicate*, September 22.

——. (2018a). "The Darker Side of Information Technology." *Milken Institute Review*, 20, 26–39.

——. (2018b). "Who Cares About Big Tech's Displaced Workers." *Project Syndicate*, April 20.

Kuznets, S. (1955). "Economic Growth and Income Inequality." *American Economic Review*, 45, 1–28.

Kuznets, S., L. Epstein, and E. Jenks. (1946). *National Product Since 1869*. New York: National Bureau of Economic Research.

Lampe, R., and P. Moser. (2016). "Patent Pools, Competition, and Innovation—Evidence from 20 US Industries Under the New Deal." *The Journal of Law, Economics, and Organization*, 32, 1–36.

Lawrence, R. Z. (2015). "Recent Declines in Labor's Share in US Income: A Preliminary Neoclassical Account." NBER Working Paper 21296, National Bureau of Economic Research.

Lazonick, W. (2013). "Strategies for Promoting US Competitiveness in World Markets." Working Paper, theAIRnet.

Leamer, E. E., L. Mishel, and T. N. Srinivasan. (2000). "Foreigners and Robots: Assistants of Some, Competitors of Others." In *Social Dimensions of US Trade Policies*, ed. by A. V. Deardorff and R. M. Stern. Ann Arbor: University of Michigan Press, Studies in International Economics, 19–64.

Lécuyer, C. (2006). *Making Silicon Valley: Innovation and the Growth of High Tech, 1930–1970*. Cambridge, MA: MIT Press.

Lemley, M. A., and C. Shapiro. (2005). "Probabilistic Patents." *Journal of Economic Perspectives*, 19, 75–98.

Lentz, R., and D. T. Mortensen. (2008). "An Empirical Model of Growth Through Product Innovation." *Econometrica*, 76, 1317–1373.

Lev, B. (2001). *Intangibles: Management, Measurement, and Reporting*. Washington, DC: Brookings Institution Press.

Lev, B., and S. Radhakrishnan. (2009). "The Valuation of Organization Capital." In *Measuring Capital in the New Economy*, ed. by C. Corrado, J. Haltiwanger, and D. Sichel. Chicago: University of Chicago Press, 73–110.

Levin, S. G., S. L. Levin, and J. B. Meisel. (1987). "A Dynamic Analysis of the Adoption of a New Technology: The Case of Optical Scanners." *The Review of Economics and Statistics*, 69, 12–17.

Levy, F., and R. J. Murnane. (2004). *The New Division of Labor: How Computers Are Creating the Next Job Market*. Princeton, NJ: Princeton University Press.

Lianos, I., and D. Geradin. (2013). *Handbook on European Competition Law: Enforcement and Procedure*. Cheltenham: Edward Elgar Publishing.

Lin, J. Y. (1995). "The Needham Puzzle: Why the Industrial Revolution Did Not Originate in China." *Economic Development and Cultural Change*, 43, 269–292.

Lipset, S. M. (1959). "Some Social Requisites of Democracy: Economic Development and Political Legitimacy." *American Political Science Review*, 53, 69–105.

Liu, Y., and C. Liu. (2007). "Diagnosing the Cause of Scientific Standstill, Unravelling the Needham Puzzle." *China Economist*, 5, 83–96.

Lochner v. New York. (1905). 198 U.S. 45.

Londoño-Vélez, J., and J. Ávila-Mahecha. (2021). "Enforcing Wealth Taxes in the Developing World: Quasi-Experimental Evidence from Colombia." *American Economic Review: Insights*, 3, 131–48.

Loth, D. (1958). *Swope of GE: The Story of Gerard Swope and General Electric in American Business*. New York: Simon and Schuster.

Loughran, T., and J. Ritter. (2004). "Why Has IPO Underpricing Changed over Time?" *Financial Management*, 33, 5–37.

Luhby, T. (2015). "Middle Class No Longer Dominates in the U.S." *CNN*, December 9.

Mahmoud, H. (2008). *Pólya Urn Models*. Boca Raton, FL: CRC Press.

Mankiw, N. G., and D. Romer. (1991). *New Keynesian Economics, Volume 2: Coordination Failures and Real Rigidities*. Cambridge, MA: MIT Press.

Mankiw, N. G., D. Romer, and D. N. Weil. (1992). "A Contribution to the Empirics of Economic Growth." *The Quarterly Journal of Economics*, 107, 407–437.

Manning, A. (2021). "Monopsony in Labor Markets: A Review." *Industrial and Labor Relations Review*, 74, 3–26.

Mansfield, E. (1961). "Technical Change and the Rate of Imitation." *Econometrica*, 29, 741–766.

——. (1963). "The Speed of Response of Firms to New Techniques." *The Quarterly Journal of Economics*, 77, 290–311.

Markham, J. W. (1962). "Inventive Activity: Government Controls and the Legal Environment." In *The Rate and Direction of Inventive Activity: Economic and Social Factors*, ed. by R. Nelson. Princeton, NJ: Princeton University Press, 609–626.

Masulis, R. W., C. Wang, and F. Xie. (2009). "Agency Problems at Dual-Class Companies." *The Journal of Finance*, 64, 1697–1727.

Mazzucato, M. (2015). *The Entrepreneurial State*. New York: Public Affairs.

McGrattan, E. R. (2020). "Intangible Capital and Measured Productivity." *Review of Economic Dynamics*, 37, S147–S166.

McGrattan, E. R., and E. C. Prescott. (2005). "Taxes, Regulations, and the Value of US and UK Corporations." *The Review of Economic Studies*, 72, 767–796.

Mehra, R., and E. C. Prescott. (1985). "The Equity Premium: A Puzzle." *Journal of Monetary Economics*, 15, 145–161.

Melitz, M. J. (2003). "The Impact of Trade on Intra-Industry Reallocations and Aggregate Industry Productivity." *Econometrica*, 71, 1695–1725.

Merton, R. K. (1968). "The Matthew Effect in Science: The Reward and Communication Systems of Science Are Considered." *Science*, 159, 56–63.

Mian, A. R., L. Straub, and A. Sufi. (2021). "What Explains the Decline in R*? Rising Income Inequality Versus Demographic Shifts." Working Paper 2021-104, University of Chicago, Becker Friedman Institute for Economics.

Miller-Adams, M., B. J. Hershbein, T. J. Bartik, B. Timmeney, A. Meyers, and L. Adams. (2019). "Building Shared Prosperity: How Communities Can Create Good Jobs for All." Report, W.E. Upjohn Institute for Employment Research.

Mincer, J. (1958). "Investment in Human Capital and Personal Income Distribution." *Journal of Political Economy*, 66, 281–302.

Mirrlees, J. A. (1971). "An Exploration in the Theory of Optimum Income Taxation." *The Review of Economic Studies*, 38, 175–208.

Mishel, L. (2018). "Uber and the Labor Market." Report 145552, Economic Policy Institute.

Moene, K. O., and M. Wallerstein. (1995). "How Social Democracy Worked: Labor-Market Institutions." *Politics & Society*, 23, 185–211.

Mokyr, J. (2018). *A Culture of Growth : The Origins of the Modern Economy*. Princeton, NJ: Princeton University Press.

Molloy, R., C. L. Smith, and A. Wozniak. (2017). "Job Changing and the Decline in Long-Distance Migration in the United States." *Demography*, 54, 631–653.

Moretti, E., C. Steinwender, and J. Van Reenen. (2019). "The Intellectual Spoils of War? Defense R&D, Productivity and International Spillovers." NBER Working Paper 26483, National Bureau of Economic Research.

Morgan, J. M., and M. Steinbaum. (2018). "The Student Debt Crisis, Labor Market Credentialization, and Racial Inequality: How the Current Student Debt Debate Gets the Economics Wrong." Report, Roosevelt Institute.

Moser, P. (2012). "Innovation Without Patents: Evidence from World's Fairs." *The Journal of Law and Economics*, 55, 43–74.

——. (2013). "Patents and Innovation: Evidence from Economic History." *Journal of Economic Perspectives*, 27, 23–44.

Motohashi, K. (2008). "Licensing or Not Licensing? An Empirical Analysis of the Strategic Use of Patents by Japanese Firms." *Research Policy*, 37, 1548–1555.

Moylan, C. E. (2008). "Employee Stock Options and the National Economic Accounts." *Survey of Current Business*, 88, 7–13.

Naidu, S., E. A. Posner, and G. Weyl. (2018). "Antitrust Remedies for Labor Market Power." *Harvard Law Review*, 132, 536–601.

Nash, G. D. (1990). *World War II and the West: Reshaping the Economy*. Lincoln: University of Nebraska Press.

Needham, J. (1965). *Science and Civilisation in China Volume 4: Physics and Physical Technology, Part II: Mechanical Engineering*. Cambridge: Cambridge University Press.

Nordhaus, W. D. (2004). "Schumpeterian Profits in the American Economy: Theory and Measurement." NBER Working Paper 10433, National Bureau of Economic Research.

Oberfield, E., and D. Raval. (2021). "Micro Data and Macro Technology." *Econometrica*, 89, 703–732.

The OECD Competition Committee. (2011). "Excessive Prices." Competition Policy Roundtables Report DAF/COMP(2011)18, Organisation for Economic Co-operation and Development.

Ohio v. American Express Co. (2018). 585 U.S. _____.

Palley, T. I. (2019). "The Fallacy of the Natural Rate of Interest and Zero Lower Bound Economics: Why Negative Interest Rates May Not Remedy Keynesian Unemployment." *Review of Keynesian Economics*, 7, 151–170.

Parker, G. G., and M. W. Van Alstyne. (2005). "Two-Sided Network Effects: A Theory of Information Product Design." *Management Science*, 51, 1494–1504.

Parrott, J., and M. Reich. (2020). "A Minimum Compensation Standard for Seattle TNC Drivers." Report for the City of Seattle, Center on Wage and Employment Dynamics.

Paul, S. (2019). "Fissuring and the Firm Exemption." *Law & Contemporary Problems*, 82, 65–87.

Peretto, P. F., and J. J. Seater. (2013). "Factor-Eliminating Technical Change." *Journal of Monetary Economics*, 60, 459–473.

Perez, S. J., and M. V. Siegler. (2003). "Inflationary Expectations and the Fisher Effect Prior to World War I." *Journal of Money, Credit and Banking*, 35, 947–965.

Peters, R. H., and L. A. Taylor. (2017). "Intangible Capital and the Investment-q Relation." *Journal of Financial Economics*, 123, 251–272.

Pfeffer, J. (2018). *Dying for a Paycheck: How Modern Management Harms Employee Health and Company Performance—and What We Can Do About It*. New York: Harper Collins.

Philippon, T. (2019). *The Great Reversal: How America Gave Up on Free Markets*. Cambridge, MA: Harvard University Press.

Piketty, T. (2014). *Capital in the Twenty-First Century*. Cambridge, MA: Harvard University Press.

Piketty, T., and E. Saez. (2003). "Income Inequality in the United States, 1913–1998." *The Quarterly Journal of Economics*, 118, 1–41.

Piketty, T., E. Saez, and S. Stantcheva. (2014). "Optimal Taxation of Top Labor Incomes: A Tale of Three Elasticities." *American Economic Journal: Economic Policy*, 6, 230–271.

Piketty, T., E. Saez, and G. Zucman. (2018). "Distributional National Accounts: Methods and Estimates for the United States." *The Quarterly Journal of Economics*, 133, 553–609.

Piketty, T., and G. Zucman. (2014). "Capital Is Back: Wealth-Income Ratios in Rich Countries 1700–2010." *The Quarterly Journal of Economics*, 129, 1255–1310.

Pólya, G. (1930). "Sur Quelques Points de la Théorie des Probabilités." *Annales De L'institut Henri Poincaré*, 1, 117–161.

Posner, R. A. (2012). "Why There Are Too Many Patents in America." *The Atlantic*.

——. (2014). *Economic Analysis of Law*. New York: Wolters Kluwer Law and Business.

Prescott, E. C., and M. Visscher. (1977). "Sequential Location Among Firms with Foresight." *Bell Journal of Economics*, 8, 378–393.

Price, C. (2018). *How to Break Up with Your Phone*. Berkeley, CA: Ten Speed Press.

Price, D. d. S. (1976). "A General Theory of Bibliometric and Other Cumulative Advantage Processes." *Journal of the American Society for Information Science*, 27, 292–306.

Qureshi, Z., J. Bell, and K. Derviş. (2019). *Productive Equity: The Twin Challenges of Reviving Productivity and Reducing Inequality*. Washington, DC: Brookings Institution Press.

Reich, L. S. (1992). "Lighting the Path to Profit: GE's Control of the Electric Lamp Industry, 1892–1941." *Business History Review*, 66, 305–334.

Reich, M. (2019). "Likely Effects of a $15 Federal Minimum Wage by 2024." Testimony Prepared for Presentation at the Hearing of the House Education and Labor Committee, Washington, DC. February 7, 2019.

——. (2020). "Pay, Passengers and Profits: Effects of Employee Status for California TNC Drivers." IRLE Working Paper 107-20, Institute for Research on Labor and Employment, University of California, Berkeley.

Reinhart, C. M., and K. S. Rogoff. (2009). *This Time Is Different*. Princeton, NJ: Princeton University Press.

Robinson, J. (1933). *The Economics of Imperfect Competition*. London: Macmillan.

Rochet, J.-C., and J. Tirole. (2003). "Platform Competition in Two-Sided Markets." *Journal of the European Economic Association*, 1, 990–1029.

Rodrik, D., and C. Sabel. (2020). "Building a Good Jobs Economy." Working Paper RWP20-001, Harvard Kennedy School Faculty Research Working Paper Series.

Rogers, R. P. (1982). "The Impact and Relevance of the 1911 General Electric Lamp Case." Working Paper 78, Federal Trade Commission.

Rognlie, M. (2015). "Deciphering the Fall and Rise in the Net Capital Share: Accumulation or Scarcity?" *Brookings Papers on Economic Activity*, Spring, 1–69.

Romer, P. M. (1990). "Endogenous Technological Change." *Journal of Political Economy*, 98, S71–S102.

Rothstein, B. (1992). "Labor-Market Institutions and Working-Class Strength." In *Structuring Politics: Historical Institutionalism in Comparative Analysis*, ed. by S. Steinmo, K. Thelen, and F. Longstreth. Cambridge: Cambridge University Press, Cambridge Studies in Comparative Politics, 33–56.

Saez, E. (2001). "Using Elasticities to Derive Optimal Income Tax Rates." *The Review of Economic Studies*, 68, 205–229.

——. (2013). "Optimal Progressive Capital Income Taxes in the Infinite Horizon Model." *Journal of Public Economics*, 97, 61–74.

Saez, E., and G. Zucman. (2016). "Wealth Inequality in the United States Since 1913: Evidence from Capitalized Income Tax Data." *The Quarterly Journal of Economics*, 131, 519–578.

——. (2019a). "Taxjusticenow.org: Tax Simulator Description." Working Paper, University of California, Berkeley.

——. (2019b). *The Triumph of Injustice: How the Rich Dodge Taxes and How to Make Them Pay*. New York: Norton.

Salinger, M. A. (1984). "Tobin's *q*, Unionization, and the Concentration-Profits Relationship." *RAND Journal of Economics*, 15, 159–170.

Scherer, F. M. (1980). *Industrial Market Structure and Economic Performance*. Boston: Houghton Mifflin Company, 2nd ed.

Schmalensee, R. (1981). "Economies of Scale and Barriers to Entry." *Journal of Political Economy*, 89, 1228–1238.

Schumpeter, J. A. (1934). *The Theory of Economic Development; An Inquiry into Profits, Capital, Credit, Interest, and the Business Cycle*, trans. by R. Opie. Cambridge, MA: Harvard University Press.

Scotchmer, S. (2004). *Innovation and Incentives*. Cambridge, MA: MIT Press.

Segerstrom, P. S. (1998). "Endogenous Growth Without Scale Effects." *American Economic Review*, 88, 1290–1310.

Seim, D. (2017). "Behavioral Responses to Wealth Taxes: Evidence from Sweden." *American Economic Journal: Economic Policy*, 9, 395–421.

Shambaugh, J., R. Nunn, and B. Portman. (2017). "Eleven Facts About Innovation and Patents." Hamilton Project Report, Brookings Institution.

Shannon, C. E. (1938). "A Symbolic Analysis of Relay and Switching Circuits." *Electrical Engineering*, 57, 713–723.

Shiraishi, T. (2017). "The Exploitative Abuse Prohibition: Activated by Modern Issues." *The Antitrust Bulletin*, 62, 737–751.

Shy, O. (1995). *Industrial Organization: Theory and Applications*. Cambridge, MA: MIT Press.

Sitaraman, G. (2017). *The Crisis of the Middle-Class Constitution: Why Economic Inequality Threatens Our Republic*. New York: Alfred A. Knopf.

Skinner, J., and D. Staiger. (2015). "Technology Diffusion and Productivity Growth in Health Care." *The Review of Economics and Statistics*, 97, 951–964.

Smith, A. (1776). *An Inquiry into the Nature and Causes of the Wealth of Nations*. London: W. Strahan and T. Cadell (repr. Random House 1937).

Smith, M., D. Yagan, O. Zidar, and E. Zwick. (2019). "Capitalists in the Twenty-First Century." *The Quarterly Journal of Economics*, 134, 1675–1745.

Solow, R. M. (1956). "A Contribution to the Theory of Economic Growth." *The Quarterly Journal of Economics*, 70, 65–94.

——. (1957). "Technical Change and the Aggregate Production Function." *The Review of Economics and Statistics*, 39, 312–320.

——. (1960). "Investment and Technical Progress." In *Mathematical Methods in the Social Sciences, 1959: Proceedings of the First Stanford Symposium*, ed. by K. Arrow, S. Karlin, and P. Suppes. Stanford, CA: Stanford University Press, no. IV in Stanford Mathematical Studies in the Social Sciences, 89–104.

——. (1979). "Another Possible Source of Wage Stickiness." *Journal of Macroeconomics*, 1, 79–82.

——. (1987). "We'd Better Watch Out." *New York Times Book Review*, 36, July 12.

Song, J., D. J. Price, F. Guvenen, N. Bloom, and T. Von Wachter. (2019). "Firming Up Inequality." *The Quarterly Journal of Economics*, 134, 1–50.

Staiger, D. O., J. Spetz, and C. S. Phibbs. (2010). "Is There Monopsony in the Labor Market? Evidence from a Natural Experiment." *Journal of Labor Economics*, 28, 211–236.

Starr, E., J. Prescott, and N. Bishara. (2020). "The Behavioral Effects of (Unenforceable) Contracts." *The Journal of Law, Economics, and Organization*, 36, 633–687.

Steinbaum, M. (2019). "Antitrust, the Gig Economy, and Labor Market Power." *Law & Contemporary Problems*, 82, 45–64.

Straub, L., and I. Werning. (2020). "Positive Long-Run Capital Taxation: Chamley–Judd Revisited." *American Economic Review*, 110, 86–119.

Sullivan, D. (1989). "Monopsony Power in the Market for Nurses." *The Journal of Law and Economics*, 32, S135–S178.

Summers, L. H., and A. Stansbury. (2019). "Whither Central Banking?" *Project Syndicate*, August 23.

Summers, M. W. (1993). *The Era of Good Stealings*. Oxford: Oxford University Press.

Swan, T. W. (1956). "Economic Growth and Capital Accumulation." *Economic Record*, 32, 334–361.

Thain, D., T. Tannenbaum, and M. Livny. (2005). "Distributed Computing in Practice: The Condor Experience." *Concurrency and Computation: Practice and Experience*, 17, 323–356.

Thiel, P. (2014). "Competition Is for Losers." *Wall Street Journal*, C1, September 13.

Tirole, J. (1988). *The Theory of Industrial Organization*. Cambridge, MA: MIT Press.

Tobin, J. (1969). "A General Equilibrium Approach to Monetary Theory." *Journal of Money, Credit and Banking*, 1, 15–29.

Torrisi, S., A. Gambardella, P. Giuri, D. Harhoff, K. Hoisl, and M. Mariani. (2016). "Used, Blocking and Sleeping Patents: Empirical Evidence from a Large-Scale Inventor Survey." *Research Policy*, 45, 1374–1385.

Traina, J. (2018). "Is Aggregate Market Power Increasing? Production Trends Using Financial Statements." New Working Paper Series 17, Stigler Center for the Study of the Economy and the State.

Triffin, R. (1940). *Monopolistic Competition and General Equilibrium Theory*. Cambridge, MA: Harvard University Press.

Tuomala, M. (1990). *Optimal Income Tax and Redistribution*. Oxford: Oxford University Press.

Turing, A. M. (1937). "On Computable Numbers, with an Application to the Entscheidungsproblem." *Proceedings of the London Mathematical Society*, s2-42, 230–265.

U.S. v. Am. Can Co. (1921). 256 U.S. 706.

U.S. v. General Electric Co. (1926). 272 U.S. 476.

U.S. v. U.S. Steel Corp. (1920). 251 U.S. 417.

Uzawa, H. (1961). "On a Two-Sector Model of Economic Growth." *The Review of Economic Studies*, 29, 40–47.

Van Reenen, J. (2018). "Increasing Differences Between Firms: Market Power and the Macro-Economy." CEP Discussion Paper 1576, Centre for Economic Performance, London School of Economics.

Walsh, J. P., Y.-N. Lee, and T. Jung. (2016). "Win, Lose or Draw? The Fate of Patented Inventions." *Research Policy*, 45, 1362–1373.

Weil, D. (2014). *The Fissured Workplace*. Cambridge, MA: Harvard University Press.

West Coast Hotel Co. v. Parrish. (1937). 300 U.S. 379.

White House. (2021). "Fact Sheet: Executive Order on Promoting Competition in the American Economy." Statements and Releases, The White House.

Winter, S. G. and R. R. Nelson. (1982). *An Evolutionary Theory of Economic Change*. Cambridge, MA: Belknap Press.

Wolff, E. N. (2017). "Household Wealth Trends in the United States, 1962 to 2016: Has Middle Class Wealth Recovered?" NBER Working Paper 24085, National Bureau of Economic Research.

Wright, G. (2020). "World War II, the Cold War, and the Knowledge Economies of the Pacific Coast." In *World War II and the West It Wrought*, ed. by M. Brilliant and D. M. Kennedy. Stanford, CA: Stanford University Press, 74–99.

Wright, S. (2004). "Measures of Stock Market Value and Returns for the US Nonfinancial Corporate Sector, 1900–2002." *Review of Income and Wealth*, 50, 561–584.

Wyman, B. (1904). "The Law of the Public Callings as a Solution of the Trust Problem." *Harvard Law Review*, 17, 156–173.

Zeira, J. (1998). "Workers, Machines, and Economic Growth." *The Quarterly Journal of Economics*, 113, 1091–1117.

Zoutman, F. T. (2018). "The Elasticity of Taxable Wealth: Evidence from the Netherlands." Working Paper, Norwegian School of Economics.

Zucman, G. (2013). *The Hidden Wealth of Nations.* Chicago: University of Chicago Press.

——. (2018). "Taxing Multinational Corporations in the 21st Century." Policy Brief 10, Economists for Inclusive Prosperity.

Zuleta, H. (2008). "Factor Saving Innovations and Factor Income Shares." *Review of Economic Dynamics*, 11, 836–851.

INDEX

Page references in *italics* refer to figures.

GPSR Authorized Representative: Easy Access System Europe, Mustamäe tee 50, 10621 Tallinn, Estonia, gpsr.requests@easproject.com